Forgotten Horrors Omnibus Edition

VOLUME ONE: 1929–1942

George E. Turner
&
Michael H. Price

Foreword by Mel Brooks

Pulp Hero Press
The Most Dangerous Books on Earth
www.PulpHeroPress.com

Although every precaution has been taken to verify the accuracy of the information contained herein, no responsibility is assumed for any errors or omissions, and no liability is assumed for damages that may result from the use of this information.

The views expressed in this book are those of the author and do not necessarily reflect the views of Pulp Hero Press.

Pulp Hero Press publishes its books in a variety of print and electronic formats. Some content that appears in one format may not appear in another.

Editor: Bob McLain
Layout: Artisanal Text
ISBN 978-1-68390-201-0
Printed in the United States of America

Pulp Hero Press | www.PulpHeroPress.com
Address queries to bob@pulpheropress.com

Contents

FORGOTTEN HORRORS OF 1932

Interstitials 73
Hell's House; Border Devils; Hell's Headquarters; Yiskor; Joseph in the Land of Egypt; Devil of the Matterhorn; Gorilla Ship; Isle of Paradise; The Jungle Killer; The Last Mile; Exposure; Klondike; Virgins of Bali; The King Murder; False Faces; The Face on the Barroom Floor; Kriss (Goona-Goona); The Unwritten Law; With Williamson Beneath the Sea

FORGOTTEN HORRORS OF 1935

Meanwhile 242

The Phantom Cowboy; Lem Hawkins' Confession; The Cactus Kid; The Lone Bandit; Hei Tiki; School for Girls; Great God Gold; The Mystery Man; Circus Shadows; The Last Wilderness; Rescue Squad; Let 'Em Have It; The Vanishing Riders; Trails of the Wild; Phantom Patrol; The Spanish Cape Mystery; Alias John Law; Legong (Dance of the Virgins)

FORGOTTEN HORRORS OF 1936

FORGOTTEN HORRORS OF 1937

FORGOTTEN HORRORS OF 1938

FORGOTTEN HORRORS OF 1941

FORGOTTEN HORRORS OF 1942

Foreword

Nobody wants their horrors to be forgotten, least of all filmmakers. I would be heartbroken to think that, in 50 years, audiences would no longer remember *Young Frankenstein*, *The Fly*, or *Dracula: Dead and Loving It*. That is one of the reasons I applaud the sterling efforts of Michael H. Price and George E. Turner in their groundbreaking book, *Forgotten Horrors*. Not only have they done an incredibly thorough job of research into the dark and dusty vaults of B-movies of the distant past, but they have written of their findings with lucidity and love.

What is it about horror entertainment that makes us want to find and savor every last rotting morsel in the pantry of our memories? When the movies of which Price & Turner write were first released, I was just a kid. I remember seeing many of them in the small independent theatres, and I was definitely a fan. Why?

Before they learn society's morality, I think, children are naturally fascinated by evil. Characters in fiction who live outside the repressive constraints of their world have more freedom to pursue their goals, however socially unacceptable. They can take what they desire and destroy what they hate without conscience—which brings us to *me* as a child.

No one understood the dizzying heights of my aspirations or the ugly depths of my hatreds. On the surface, of course, I was a little Jewish kid from Brooklyn. Only I knew that I was a Dark Deity, like the characters Bela Lugosi and Lionel Atwill played in the B-horror movies. I understood the suffering of these insane megalomaniacs and thrilled to their mad, brave pursuits of glory and revenge.

I also identified with the victims. After seeing *Frankenstein*, I was convinced that the Monster would climb the fire escape outside of my tenement window to get me. Why he would want to get me, amidst the millions who lived in New York, or why he would even be in New York in the first place, didn't enter my mind. Logic flees when Fear comes knocking.

As you can probably deduce, very few horrors have been forgotten by me. In fact, they are among my most vivid memories. Thanks to Price & Turner, you can share them with me. Perhaps our two authors have Tampered in Things That Man Should Leave Alone. But woe to those who would try to stop them. Something tells me their revenge would be too terrible to contemplate.

—Mel Brooks
Brooksfilms, Culver City

Preface to
Forgotten Horrors of 1929–1937

George E. Turner (1925-1999) had just broken into print with *The Making of King Kong*, a watershed job of film scholarship, when he pitched a collaboration in 1975: a reconstruction of the Depression Era history of Hollywood's independent studios through their motion pictures—and preferably, their *very weirdest* motion pictures. The focus would fall upon such Poverty Row studios as Mascot and Monogram, he explained; we waffled, back-and-forth, as to whether to include the better-heeled independents, such as Samuel Goldwyn and Harold Lloyd, themselves no strangers to weird menace.

With the present edition, I have reverted to George's and my original manuscript, the better to include the larger independent productions that we had removed from the first draft and then parceled into other projects. Appearing for the first time are our studies of Harold Lloyd's silent-into-talkie experiment, *Welcome Danger*, and two of Hal Roach's creepier comedies, the featurette *Oliver the Eighth* and the two-reeler "The Tin Man." (An expanded version of the "Tin Man" chapter had appeared in 2000 in *Monsters from the Vault* magazine, using a synopsis as paraphrased from James Parrott's original shooting script. The present version is based upon a refresher screening of the finished film, with story points that differ from the screenplay.)

Forgotten Horrors, we decided to call the book. As late as 1979–1980, when a first edition appeared from Great Britain's Tantivy Press and New Jersey-based A.S. Barnes & Co., the subject matter *was* popularly forgotten, with few exceptions. Yes, and 1980 also saw the emergence of a home-video market. With *Forgotten Horrors* as a misappropriated concordance, several grey-market distributors of that movies-on-tape industry began securing long-neglected prints of the films George and I had discussed. Forgotten? Yes—but not for bloody much longer.

As late as the 1970s, only the most classically attuned variety of film scholarship was deemed a respectable calling. For every *Battleship Potemkin* or *Citizen Kane* that one might find talked to death in the film-snob journals, for every *Gone with the Wind* or *The Wizard of Oz* that remained belovéd among the mass audience and its

Behind such ornate curtains as this one, many Depression-era motion pictures would give up their celluloid secrets in the glow of an immense, glass-beaded screen. The advertisements helped to keep the projectors running. Finklea Electric Co. (upper left, off-center) was owned by the family of a movie star-in-waiting, Cyd Charisse.

nostalgic reactionaries, thousands more pictures remained obscure. Even a recognized classic such as James Whale's *Bride of Frankenstein* (1935) could be dismissed with impunity as "'way above average for this kind of trash" (in Steven H. Scheuer's *TV Key Movie Reviews*) at a time when the genre lay in need of earnest regard.

The extremes of interest lay in Carlos Clarens' stuffy but fascinating *An Illustrated History of the Horror Film* (Putnam; 1967), on the one hand, and the puerile silliness (however generously illustrated) of *Famous Monsters of Filmland* magazine and its imitators. William K. Everson anchored a saner middle ground with his genre surveys, to which George and I had contributed photographs and research as an offshoot of our work on behalf of the American Film Institute.

Barnes and Tantivy promptly remaindered the 1979–1980 hardcover *Forgotten Horrors* to the Nostalgia Book Club as part of a bankruptcy scam. As far as George and I were concerned, our book was every bit as forgotten as any of the spookers we had unearthed. We asserted ownership of the copyright and began weighing new publishing prospects. As long as Big Science and Bad Medicine hold humankind in a thrall of unease, the need to know such stories as these will persist.

A slight revision saw print in 1986, from Forestville, California-based Eclipse Books. That same year, an entrepreneurial video label called Sinister Cinema introduced a *Forgotten Horrors* catalogue (without having sought our permission), with a selection of titles from our table of contents—and some titles we had omitted or (one blushes to admit) overlooked.

Which had been our point, in the first place: whip that old devil obscurity and introduce new generations to elements of the popular culture—some important, some trivial—that had slipped from view through combinations of neglect, contempt, censorship, and that peculiar recurring phenomenon of political correctitude. Yes, and where was the ebonics movement when Willie Best could have used it?

Owing to the then-buried condition of our source material and exhaustive research into long-sealed corridors of history, it had taken four years to complete the first edition of *Forgotten Horrors*—a volume that has transformed many a casual film buff into an instant authority. For a 20th-anniversary package called *Forgotten Horrors: The Definitive Edition* (1999), we gathered new information and insights and the occasional big revelation. Principal rediscoveries there had included new information on Bud Pollard's elusive *The Horror*, as tracked down through the Library of Congress and a little-known Japanese publication; the resurrection of *Chloe: Love Is Calling You*, a haunting Southern Gothic; and the recognition of such grim westerns as *God's Country and the Man*, *Lightnin' Bill Carson* (the launching of a franchise that would yield spinoffs into the 1940s), and *Branded a Coward*. George and I also reversed our original exclusions of such titles as *The Phantom Broadcast* and Tom Mix's epic serial, *The Miracle Rider*.

The present edition pursues that tack with findings that have come to hand since George Turner's death in 1999. These will become evident in due course—or sooner, if anyone should be so obsessive-compulsive as to compare contents among the editions. A popular consensus calls for the addition of 1933's *The Sin of Nora Moran*, which caps its tale of scandal and homicide with an apparition that might even be a ghost.

I should acknowledge a marginal picture from 1929, *The Phantom in the House*. This one boasts a sensational title, a director (Phil Rosen) associated with many of the *Forgotten Horrors* titles, and a pedigree from a studio that was bound to evolve into that *Forgotten Horrors* standby, Monogram Pictures. Nothing particularly weird about *The Phantom in the House*, however, beyond the atmosphere; for the sake of a heightened context, I have added the title for the present omnibus edition.

One original-edition selection, the Sicilian-American revenge movie *Amore e Morte*, receives a deeper consideration as a result of research by fellow author Gary D. Rhodes. And where George and I had tightened our original manuscript during the 1970s to exclude such larger independent productions as *The Great Gabbo*, *The Bat Whispers*, *I Cover the*

Exhibitors Screen Service provided many coming-attractions trailers for the major-league pictures and the Poverty Row titles, alike.

Waterfront, Hell Harbor, a few of Hal Roach's horror-comedy pieces, and Samuel Goldwyn's *Bulldog Drummond* and *The Unholy Garden,* I have reversed such decisions to restore the original continuity. These titles are too big for the Poverty Row distinction, but largely forgotten independents all the same.

And speaking of original continuity, here follows George Turner's and my preface to the first edition of *Forgotten Horrors.*

Preface to the First Edition

Obscurity is the overriding justification for this collection, which takes for granted that the follower of cinema will have more than a nodding acquaintance with the major studios' milestones in weird menace.

For obscurity—more so, even, than tension and dread—links the films. Only a fraction of these pictures made from 1929 through 1937 (a period popularly known as the Golden Age of the talkie horror film) will have any sort of reputation today in comparison with attention accorded the likes of 1931's *Dracula* and *Frankenstein*. We call belated notice to the present array of forgotten chillers without segregating them into such categories as western, whodunit, spooky comedy, jungle or piracy adventure, or outright horror melodrama. The criterion is a Strange Menace. H.P. Lovecraft, the brilliant writer of pulp-magazine horrors, applied such a standard to literature, holding that some of the most worthy examples of weird fiction may be found as elements of tales which have an entirely different tone overall. We would be remiss not to treat the motion pictures similarly.

Likely *The Vampire Bat* and *White Zombie* will strike a responsive chord, but many of their companions produced outside the major studios are so little known as to have escaped the notice of even the trade journals. Who remembers *Murder at Dawn, Fifteen Wives, Condemned To Live, Maniac, Drums of Jeopardy,* or *Sinister Hands*? While such sparse notice is often unjustified, it hardly defies explanation.

Their Poverty Row status (barring the occasional prosperous independent studio) contributes to the obscurity. The term is not altogether accurate in its connotation of categorically cheap production, but it distinguishes the films herein from the works of such major corporate studios as Universal, MGM, and Paramount. Most independents sought what the trade-paper *Variety* would term "the shirtsleeves audience," losing expectations of attention from the stylishly critical press.

Although the talkie horror tradition is widely supposed to have begun with *Dracula* and *Frankenstein* in 1931, these titles are in fact turning points on a road that opened in 1929 with the second all-talking feature, Warners' seriocomic *The Terror*. This and most other such pioneering talkies were built along the lines of Broadway's popular Mystery Farce tradition—such titles as *The Cat and the Canary, The Gorilla,* and *The Bat*, all of which also proved successful as silent pictures and had been reprised for sound by 1930.

Talkies in 1929 were for the most part anything but satisfactory. Arguments raged as to whether disk or optically reproduced sound-on-film would be the standard—and indeed, whether the novelty would last. Some producers were thrilled to make talking dramas

Chicago-based cartoonist Gaar Williams captures an essence of the talking-pictures revolution with a 1929 installment of his Chicago Tribune *feature,* Wotta Life! Wotta Life!

while others could hardly wait to return to the silents that they felt the public would ultimately demand. Silent-era stars were doomed by inappropriate voices, thick foreign accents, microphone fright, or the inability to memorize dialogue. Actors and technical personnel trekked into Hollywood from the New York stage, some destined to become leaders in the new medium, others unable to adapt to canned drama. Studios that could bear the cost installed sound equipment and built sound stages while insiders pondered noisily whether the perceived fad would endure. Larger studios made both silent and sound versions of most pictures, adding music, sound effects, and sprinklings of dialogue to pictures completed as silents. Many small-town and neighborhood theatres continued to show silents, but a non-talkie hadn't a chance to open in a big-city downtown house.

Because the majors were making full use of limited sound facilities, independent companies were unable to obtain sound-stage space or

*The H'wood HQ of Reliable Pictures, one of the authentic
Poverty Row studios of the 1930s.*

equipment, even if they could afford the cost. Some independents employed bootleg soundtracks to avoid a licensing fee of $500 a reel for sound-on-film. Still others doggedly kept making silent pictures for a vanishing market, and most died with the silent era.

Independents that remained during the Great Depression of the 1930s were of a few general types. The true Poverty Row outfits obtained financing, rented studio space as needed, avoided retakes and special effects, and commissioned only necessary laboratory work. They produced on shoestring budgets and fast schedules, often shooting a feature for between $8,000 and $10,000 in four to 10 days. Typical are Monogram, Mascot, Majestic, Puritan, Invincible-Chesterfield, Reliable, and Progressive. Most dealt largely in westerns for the Saturday-matinée trade. Their non-western product was designed for the also-ran lower berth of the double bills that most urban theatres would schedule.

A second category of independent production has but a few exponents. A related group comprising Tiffany, Sono Art, Educational, and World Wide had its own studio and produced some pictures comparable with those of the majors. Monogram and Mascot later established their own studios.

Yet another class, including such producers as Samuel Goldwyn, Harold Lloyd, Hal Roach's short-comedy factory, Roland West, 20th Century, and Reliance, transcends the Poverty Row stereotype; prestigious pictures from such sources enjoyed substantial backing and standing release agreements with major firms. Sam Goldwyn disdained the Poverty Row sector and might well have preferred that his high-toned strata be "included out" (to borrow a famous Goldwyn malapropism) of such a discussion. We prefer to retain such finer examples of the independent sector, both for context and for vivid examples of the development of a genre.

Efforts of the truer Poverty Row companies are best appreciated by an open-minded willingness to sidestep the more fashionable fare. Few of the shows played Broadway's picture palaces; most, therefore, were not reviewed outside the trade press. The few that were reviewed for the general public were treated as a rule with unwarranted contempt. Even within the confines of the horror genre, they delivered such rewards as an all-Technicolor, all-talking feature early in 1930, *Mamba*; the screen's first depiction of Haitian magic, in *White Zombie*; the first serial with sound, *King of the Kongo*; a late example of the vanishing art of hand-coloring, in *The Death Kiss*; an ancestor of the Bob Hope style of nervous wisecracks in counterpoint with scary doings, in *The House of Mystery*; and worthy adaptations of literary classics, including *Jane Eyre*, *The Moonstone*, and *A Study in Scarlet*.

They boast brilliant acting from such bypassed favorites of the silent era as H.B. Walthall, Francis X. Bushman, Phillips Smalley, and Conway Tearle, and high-calibre performances from the stardom-bound likes of Ginger Rogers, Walter Brennan, Boris Karloff,

*Edgar Rice Burroughs' Tarzan franchise takes the
low road in high style on Poverty Row.*

George Brent, John Wayne, and Rita (Cansino) Hayworth. And they showcase many inimitable portrayals from superb players who were not stars: money could not buy better acting than that which was provided by Lionel Atwill, Reginald Owen, Sidney Blackmer, and Jean Hersholt. Here, too, are the later works of such fine silent-film directors as Fred Newmeyer and William Nigh, as well as the fledgling work of such important directors as Richard Thorpe, Edwin L. Marin, and Bruce Humberstone. The use of dependable personnel was a necessity in independent production; retakes were unaffordable.

Inventiveness flourished along Poverty Row, which is more a state of mind and economics than a physical address. Poetic fantasy pervades the melodrama of *White Zombie*. Vampire legendry is given unique twists through a suggestion of prenatal influence in *Condemned to Live* and an infusion of science fiction in *The Vampire Bat*. Standard western fare is coupled with horror in *Tombstone Canyon*. *Deluge* is one of the few pre-World War II films to address an end-of-the-world theme. Edgar Rice Burroughs, denied narrative control on big-time MGM Pictures' adaptations of his *Tarzan* properties, turned to Poverty Row to take a more aggressive hand in the spinoff franchise: hence *Tarzan the Fearless*. *Maniac* represents an attempt to transpose Edgar Allan Poe's writings into voyeuristic erotica. Much of the sophisticated stuntwork essential to all action pictures, large and small, was developed at Mascot and Monogram.

The obscurity of certain films can be traced to the depiction of ethnic groups. Such contributions cannot be ignored, passive bigotries notwithstanding. Art, high or low, must be viewed as a product of its time; no one can expect a film of 1930 to reflect attitudes of the (enlightened?) present day, and yet one of the steadfastly fashionable components of retrospective criticism is to term a picture dated. (Yes, and are not we all?)

Such a reactionary approach becomes all the more absurd when applied to matters of ethnic or cultural identity. Films of the Depression-into-wartime years often feature black actors as superstitious servants and Asian actors as practitioners of a subversive threat known in the pulp-fiction trade as the Yellow Peril. The likes of Willie Best, Clarence Muse, Richard Loo, and Jimmy Wang were striving to portray their cultures in a dominant culture mass medium whose audiences could scarcely imagine them in anything but subordinate or threatening roles. The more accomplished black actors managed, for all that, to invert and parody the stereotypes. The very appearance of a black actor was a breakthrough during the 1930s; silent films routinely had used white actors in blackface. Well along into the talkie age, the larger studios took particular pride in their makeup departments' ability to transform major Caucasian stars into what one trade publication called "Orientals made to order." The attuned viewer will read exaggerated comedy by Negroes or villainy by Asians as products of a bygone age and appreciate the beginnings of a tendency to let the varied ethnicities interpret themselves on screen.

Rewards collected by *Dracula, Frankenstein,* and Paramount's *Dr. Jekyll & Mr. Hyde* sent the studios as a class scrambling onto the bandwagon. Independently made horror films flooded the market during 1932 and 1933, most continuing in the old-fashioned traditions of Broadway and early Vitaphone-Warners, but with interesting variations. The Old Dark House comedy-thriller formula is married to scientific horror in *Murder at Dawn* and to a theme suggestive of Mr. Poe in *The Monster Walks.* The independents produced surprisingly few unadulterated horror films of the Universal Pictures sort; these are *White Zombie, The Vampire Bat,* and (a few years later) *Condemned To Live.* As the Depression wiped out most small-time producers, other short-lived but ambitious companies took their places. In 1934, the dwindling independents managed a large output, but little of the Poverty Row product proved comparable with that of the majors. A group of small companies was leveraged by a film-laboratory owner, Herbert J. Yates, into the formation of Republic Pictures, which hovered between major and minor status. The old Monogram had been pressed into the Republic venture along with Mascot, Liberty, and Majestic; shortly thereafter, a new Monogram was formed—with staying power into the 1950s.

Then 1936–1937 saw a pronounced slackening of the horror-film cycle among both the majors and the independents, brought on partially through censorship. Most of the old-school Poverty Row companies had vanished or were soon to do so. A British-European ban on horror films administered the *coup de grace.* By 1939–1940, the genre would rise from the grave for another go at it—a story for another day, or for another compartment in this very book.

—Michael H. Price
North-by-Northwest of the Divide

Forgotten Horrors of 1929

Black Waters

British & Dominion Films, Ltd. • World Wide Pictures • 1929

A significant curiosity: the first talking feature produced by an English company was made in the United States. Herbert Wilcox, commissioned by British & Dominion Films, Ltd., to make a breakthrough talkie, could not obtain equipment in the U.K. studios, and so he traveled to America to shoot *Black Waters*, a seagoing variant upon the Old Dark House formula, in association with World Wide Pictures and Western Electric Co. The brilliant American director, Marshall "Mickey" Neilan, had compromised his security with a flippant attitude toward producers and had descended into alcoholism. The cast, too, is American, with the exception of English leading man John Loder.

The film was announced as *Fog*, title of a Broadway play by the Mystery Farce master John Willard—the basis of Willard's adapted screenplay. Advertisements emphasized the craze for talking pictures: "They don't need eyes! The dialogue is that good—but the photography is great, too!"

Charlie (John Loder) and Eunice (Mary Brian) are watching a cabaret show in San Francisco when they receive an invitation to a houseboat party at midnight. They find a ghostly sailing shop moored at a deserted wharf. An old watchman, Olaf (Ben Hendricks), warns them not to board; he ascribes a weird drumming noise to "a voodoo cannibal that does Larrabee's dirty work." (Whoever Larrabee might be—patience.)

Others gather. A grim chap, Randall (Frank Reicher), seeks revenge against one Tiger Larrabee, a crazed sea captain who had seduced and abandoned Randall's wife. Chester (Hallam Cooley), a young gad-about, had been Eunice's lover. Temple (comedian Lloyd Hamilton) is a stammering valet. The Rev. Eph Kelly (James Kirkwood), a water-front grotesque, presents himself as "a poor servant of the Lord, come to save souls." Such overt sanctimony is a keep-away sign to all other characters.

The visitors board the ship and meet a mute giant, Jeelo (Noble Johnson), who appears as savage as Olaf had described him. A bound prisoner proves to be newspaper reporter Jimmy Darcy (Robert Ames), who explains that he had been tipped to watch Tiger Larrabee. A voice over the radio warns of doom. The guests find the mooring hawser cut— no prospect of escape. One by one, Chester, Randall, Temple, and Darcy disappear overboard, killed by Jeelo's blowgun or by the elusive host. At last, only Charlie, Eunice, and Kelly remain—locked in the cabin under the baleful eye of Jeelo. Kelly is revealed as the madman Larrabee, who beats Jeelo to death. "Damn you all!" the captain shouts. "I'm giving a party in hell, and you're all coming with me!" He has set a bomb.

Charlie finds an axe, smashes the door, and throws the bomb overboard. All ends romantically well for Charlie and Eunice.

True to the publicist's rave, the acting is in fact superior by comparison with that of most early talkies. The photography is exquisite, and there are distinct contributions to sound technique. One innovative use of sonic design occurs at the climax: the camera leaves the killer, unmasked, as his ranting continues over action taking place elsewhere. Another emphatic use finds Hallam Cooley's Chester being dragged to his death, crying, "Hang *on* to me, Charlie—something's got me by the *legs*! Oh, damn it, *pull*!" The scene is more terrifying than it could have been in silent technique, which would have required an intrusive dialogue card.

Such qualities aside, *Black Waters* attracted little attention on either side of the Atlantic. That failure to connect must stem from long stretches of dialogue that slow the action and weaken the suspense. Alfred Hitchcock's *Blackmail* (1930), hailed as the first talking film produced in England, eclipsed its Anglo-American predecessor.

Because of excessive drinking by Neilan and cinematographer David Kesson, responsibility for much of the directing and camerawork fell

Robert Ames and Mary Brian.

to the production manager, Byron Haskin. Leading lady Mary Brian once recalled that Neilan appeared "worn out" during the shoot.

Though ill-equipped to adapt to the talkies after 17 years' prominence in the silents, Neilan worked on into the 1930s despite gaps between assignments—registering such high points as a story credit on *Hell's Angels* (1930), a detour to the low-rent sector to write and direct that poetic voodoo-on-the-bayou picture *Chloe: Love Is Calling You*, and a more prominent directing assignment on *The Lemon Drop Kid* (1935). Neilan made his last picture, *Swing It, Professor*, in 1937, but he maintained friendships that kept him working along the sidelines until shortly before his death in 1958. Neilan's last job was an acting role—a politician in *A Face in the Crowd* (1957), a Southern Gothic variant by Elia Kazan and Budd Schulberg upon the resolutely Jewish show-business tale of *What Makes Sammy Run?*

To tighten the grasp of the new technology, Frank Reicher, a Theatre Guild actor-director, was brought aboard to play a role and assist with dialogue. The wordplay is impressive, but the interruption of action with speech produces a halt-and-go effect. Noteworthy performances belong to James Kirkwood, as the madman, and Noble Johnson as his fearsome servant-become-victim. Lloyd Hamilton, star player of a popular series of short comedies, doffed his signature checkered bill-cap in favor of a bowler hat; the portrayal is indifferently humorous, although youngsters of the day enjoyed imitating Hamilton's gimmick of whistling in order to stop stuttering.

The screenwriter, John Willard, had crafted the source-play, *Fog*, after the fashion of his much more famous *The Cat and the Canary*, the definitive 1920s-style Mystery Farce. *The Cat and the Canary* has been adapted repeatedly and imitated, mimicked, knocked off, riffed upon, and varied interminably, from conventional Old Dark House settings (1937's *Sh! The Octopus* and 1941's *The Smiling Ghost*, for example) to futuristic science fiction (as in 1958's *It! The Terror from beyond Space* and 1979's *Alien*). The narrative temptations of mayhem, committed in cramped quarters, remain irresistible—no matter how often pressed into service.

The House of Secrets

Chesterfield Motion Picture Corp. • 1929

Globetrotting Barry Wilding (Joseph Striker) inherits the Hawk's Nest, a countryside estate, in England. Barry and detective Joe Blake (Herbert Warren) encounter menacing trespassers. Margery Gordon (Marcia Manning) seems distressed by Barry's presence. Gangsters (Harry M. Southard and Richard Stevenson) threaten Barry. A Chinese, Wu Chang (Edward Roseman), stalks the grounds.

Margery demands that Barry must leave her and her father at the estate. Home Secretary Forbes (Walter Ringham) refuses to intervene. The purported father proves to be Sir Hubert Harcourt (Francis M. Verdi), a scientist who had suffered a breakdown while developing a poisonous gas for the government. The hoodlums imprison Barry, Margery, *et al.*, while seeking a treasure. Forbes arrives in time to rescue everyone. Sir Hubert regains his senses. Barry and Margery decide to share the Hawk's Nest.

Chesterfield made approximately a dozen pictures a year from 1925 until 1937, primarily on rented stages at Universal and Pathé. Lon Young was production chief, M.A. Anderson ran the cameras, and Edward Jewell was art director; such directors as Phil Rosen, Richard Thorpe, Frank Strayer, and Charles Lamont were mainstays. The exception is *The House of Secrets*, filmed in New York with a pick-up crew.

Joseph Striker and Marcia Manning.

Rental stages and equipment were makeshift. *The House of Secrets* was made only as a talkie; most other companies were releasing both silent and sound versions of each picture. Chesterfield kept making silents, otherwise, for about a year after this foray.

Director Edmund Lawrence had quit the cinema in

1920, then returned in 1928 with a string of dramatic shorts for Paramount. *The House of Secrets* became Lawrence's first talking feature and his last assignment; he died in 1931. Camera chief George Webber photographed most of Allan Dwan's pictures for Fox and many products of Paramount's Long Island studio.

Marcia Manning, a spirited ingenue, graced many Pathé comedies. Joseph Striker, a slim and athletic New Yorker, is best known for his

John the Baptist in Cecil B. DeMille's proselytizing epic (aren't they all?) *The King of Kings* (1927). The other players are stage talents who seldom made pictures.

Though a benchmark as one of the earliest sound-on-film entries from an independent company, *The House of Secrets* drew little attention. Chesterfield mounted a remake in 1936.

Bulldog Drummond

Samuel Goldwyn • Howard Productions • United Artists • 1929

Technological breakthroughs aside, *The House of Secrets* (above) wielded no influence sufficient to argue for a vindication of talking pictures at a crucial stage. No, if any one film vindicated the talkies—at a stage where the idiom teetered between acceptance and rejection—it was Samuel Goldwyn's production of *Bulldog Drummond*.

Goldwyn, a self-educated apprentice glovemaker from the Warsaw ghetto—his genuine name was Shmuel Gelbfisz, or Goldfish—had helped to establish the Lasky Photoplay Co. in 1910. He became instrumental seven years later in the merger of Lasky with Famous Players, the embryonic form of Paramount Pictures. With the Selwyn Bros., Goldfish founded Goldwyn Pictures and changed his name accordingly.

Then in 1924, Goldwyn sold his share, including a studio in Culver City and a roaring-lion trademark, to Metro Pictures and Louis B. Mayer; the result was Metro-Goldwyn-Mayer, or MGM. Goldwyn established an autonomous company in 1925 and secured a releasing agreement with United Artists (UA), as a member-owner. Though often underestimated as merely a shrewd businessman with an abrasive manner and a gift for mangling the language, Goldwyn also possessed the tasteful instincts that make for great movies. He was as much the awkwardly assimilated immigrant Jew as any other Poverty Row impresario (Hollywood is essentially a *Yiddishe* invention), but his progressive nature and forceful manner placed the independent sector on a par with the major corporate studios.

As he demanded autonomy, so did Goldwyn bestow autonomy as a means of getting results from such artisans as William Cameron Menzies, supervising art director at UA. Menzies was appalled by the new order of picturemaking: too much talk, overlong takes, static cameras, limited action, minimalistic settings and properties. When he learned that playwright Sidney Howard was handling the script for *Bulldog Drummond*, an extravagant mixture of crime, horror, and humor, Menzies suggested a collaboration to break the trend toward photographed stage plays.

Menzies prepared hundreds of sketches, then developed 61 sets, all practical for sound and suited to dynamic and radially composed camerawork. Some of the sets permitted only one shooting angle, with forced perspectives. Menzies said he sought "a suggestion of Edgar Allan Poe...a proper air of midnight horror." (The eccentric sets also point up the tale's more comedic qualities.)

Director F. Richard Jones had started with Mack Sennett's slapstick-comedy troupe before World War I. All humor aside, Jones had demonstrated broader abilities with two 1928 assignments: *The Gaucho*, a splendid romantic adventure with Douglas Fairbanks, and a part-Technicolor Zane Grey western, *The Water Hole*, a tale of madness and death. Goldwyn hired the stage director A. Leslie Pierce to assist the silents-oriented Jones with dialogue—a common practice with the early talkers.

Two weeks of rehearsal allowed for speed and comfort. The approach to acting is right for the new medium—neither of the declamatory stage, nor of the silents' pantomimic style. Cinematographers George Barnes and Gregg Toland freed the camera from its soundproofed enclosure—a necessary inconvenience in the earlier talkies— while inventing less obtrusive methods to muffle the noises. All difficulties considered, the picture still leaves an impression of effortless accomplishment.

Capt. Hugh "Bulldog" Drummond (Ronald Colman), "too rich to work, too intelligent to play," seeks adventure. A client, Phyllis Benton (Joan Bennett), is in danger. Drummond sets out on a (dark and) stormy night with a servant (Wilson Benge) and a sidekick, Algy Longworth (Claud Allister).

Phyllis' wealthy uncle, Hiram Travers (Charles Sellon), is a hostage of one Dr. Lakington (Lawrence Grant). Phyllis is kidnapped by accomplices Peterson (Montagu Love) and Irma (Lilyan Tashman). Lakington, a brooding figure in cape and monocle, threatens Drummond.

Drummond rescues Phyllis and Travers, but all are recaptured. Lakington fondles the unconscious Phyllis. Drummond vows to kill him. Phyllis wakes to free Drummond, who strangles Lakington. Peterson and Irma escape as their henchmen, impersonating police officers, spirit them away.

Ronald Colman leavens the prevailing grimness with dashing wit. The Englishman had been fairly important as a silent star, but Goldwyn worried that bigger names were being destroyed by voices ill-suited to sound—not to mention an American intolerance of British accents. Colman's voice proved just right. *Drummond* landed him an Academy Award nomination (he lost out to George Arliss), and Colman's portrayal became the standard—although he repeated the character only once, in 1934's *Bulldog Drummond Strikes Back* for Darryl F. Zanuck's independent company, soon to assume corporate dominance as 20th Century-Fox. (Other portrayers of Drummond have included Kenneth MacKenna, Ralph Richardson, John Lodge, Ray Milland, John Howard, Tom Conway, Ron Randell, Walter Pidgeon, and Richard Johnson.)

Novelist-playwright H.C. "Sapper" McNeale had established Drummond as a hard-boiled vigilante, set forth by square-jawed Carlyle Blackwell in a British film of 1922. Jack Buchanan, of the musical-comedy stage, lightened Drummond in another English film, in 1925—the same year that Sir Gerald Du Maurier adapted the play and starred gallantly. Colman's characterization is similarly breezy.

Britisher Claud Allister is a perfect idle-rich pal to Colman's Drummond. Joan Bennett is lovely but only tentatively confident. Lawrence Grant is so vile as to want killing on the spot. Lilyan Tashman plays the villainess with charm and humor. Broad-faced Montagu Love is the romantic brute Peterson, the most popular of McNeale's bad-guy characters. Love and Tashman account for a curiously perverse scene in which they make passionate love while a captive writhes in torment. Grant's Lakington, too, makes much of his lustful intentions toward Bennett, forcing Drummond to watch. When Drummond objects, Tashman's Irma says coolly, "Just an old Spanish custom." Later, when she reacts in horror to Lakington's fate, Drummond tells her: "An old Spanish custom."

Bulldog Drummond (along with *The Bat Whispers*) suggests a blueprint for Orson Welles' 1940–1941 production of *Citizen Kane*, which Gregg Toland photographed. Here are the deep-focus shots, the exaggerated foreshortening, the ceilinged sets, and the bizarre angles that would make *Kane* a visual feast. While the influence of the German Expressionist films of the 1920s is patent, the introduction of these ideas to mainstream English-speaking cinema is important. The architectural *wrong*-ness of the sets—slants and zig-zags, with improbable vanishing points and false perspectives—proves precisely

right. Colman and Goldwyn followed through in 1931 with *The Unholy Garden*, an even weirder film.

Bulldog Drummond is leagues beyond such immediate selections as *The House of Secrets* and *The Great Gabbo*. Among other films of 1929, only Rouben Mamoulian's *Applause* and Roland West's *Alibi* made comparable contributions to talking-pictures grammar. Drummond's scattered awkward moments—players hovering near concealed microphones, occasional silent-style under-cranking of the camera to speed along the action—bespeak the transitional station without compromising the dramatic impact. Thus did F. Richard Jones establish his credential for the talkies; he died before he could make another picture.

The King of the Kongo

Mascot Pictures Corp. • 1929

Serials with sound were late in coming. Chapter plays had waned. Out-of-doors recording suffered from distortion. But the fans demanded outdoor action, and sound was becoming the standard. Universal and Pathé would not free their sound-film facilities for a class of film that had fallen from popular favor.

Nat Levine's tiny Mascot Pictures—which dealt primarily in serials—proved its slogan, "Blazing the Trail," with the first sound serial: *The King of the Kongo* would sport music, sound effects, and sporadic dialogue. (Lee Zahler's old-fashioned melodies accompanied many films, on into the 1940s.) The audio platters accounted for about $5,000 of a $40,000 budget. (There also was a silent edition.)

Boris Karloff drew $75 a week for a backup role. DeMille-Pathé star Jacqueline Logan and Pathé Pictures' serial champ Walter Miller proved affordable, given Pathé's financial bind.

Director Richard Thorpe, like Karloff, was due for better opportunities. Karloff's breakthrough came in 1931 with James Whale's *Frankenstein*, at Universal. Thorpe would reach a plateau with MGM's *Night Must Fall* in 1936.

Larry Trent (Miller) tracks ivory thieves in the Congo. A

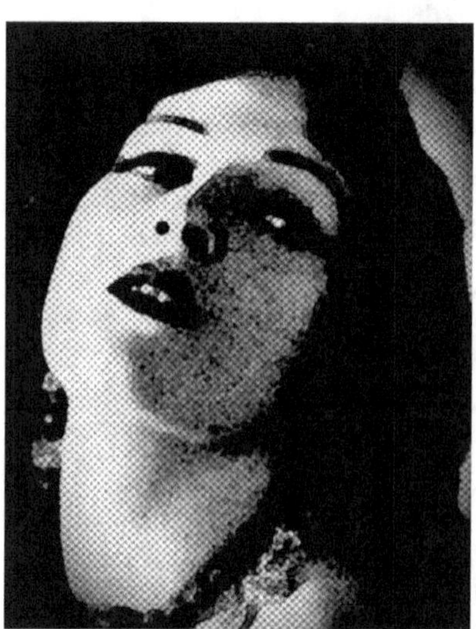

Jacqueline Logan.

gorilla guards a shunned temple. A treasure lies hidden. Diana Martin (Logan) seeks her father. Jungle racketeers hold a mysterious prisoner. The ringleader might be Scarface Macklin (Karloff). Larry reveals Macklin as Diana's father. The mob boss is an unsuspected incidental character (Larry Steers).

The jungle contains a dilapidated temple from a silent epic. Stock footage of Angkor lends depth. A dinosaur-like creature, likely lifted from a silent production, noses about a replica of the temple but does not figure in the tale.

Joe Bonomo, pre-eminent strongman of the silent screen, supplies the gorilla-suit menace. Karloff is impressive as one who appears too guilty to be the villain, but his work here has no more taken on the subtleties of his *Frankenstein*-and-after work than Thorpe's directing suggests *Night Must Fall*, his *Tarzan* pictures, the 1939 *Huckleberry Finn*, or 1952's *White Cargo*.

The Great Gabbo

James Cruze, Inc. • Sono Art-World Wide • 1929

Talkies proved an apt term, not entirely charitable, for pictures made during the plunge into audio. Top-heavy with sound over sight, the novelty was paltry compensation for the restraints imposed upon the camera. If a story lacked impact, then neither camera nor cutting room could help.

One musically charged relic, James Cruze's eerie backstage melodrama *The Great Gabbo*, bears up well in terms of story and bravura performance. The film also reveals how filmmakers sought to overcome the handicaps of sound.

The yarn withstands static photography: cinematographer Ira H. "Joe" Morgan held still only when forced to do so. Lengthy takes rely upon actorly strengths, but there is evident a willingness to test the limitations of sound. An effective touch is the use of super-imposition to herald the breakdown of Erich von Stroheim's title character with chaotic visual imagery, underscored by orchestral and ambient dissonances.

Gabbo's greater appeal lies in Stroheim's talking-picture début—a seething portrayal of gathering madness, anticipating the greater thrust of his work from here on out.

Gabbo, a self-absorbed ventriloquist, works in small-time vaude-ville with his dummy, Otto, and an assistant, Mary (Betty Compson). Gabbo can express tenderness only through Otto, and drives Mary away with his eternal *kvetching*.

Gabbo becomes a star attraction on Broadway, where he encounters Mary and her new partner, Frank (Donald Douglas). Gabbo woos Mary through Otto. When he learns that Mary and Frank have married, Gabbo snaps—in view of a capacity audience—and smashes Otto. When Mary approaches him, Gabbo seems not to recognize her. Dragging Otto, Gabbo wanders aimlessly into the street.

No longer affordable as a director on account of his stubborn extrav-agances, Stroheim contributed more to *Gabbo* than the portrayal of a haunted soul. The Stroheim-style exposition, with integrated subplot, makes patent the star's influence upon producer-director James Cruze. It has long been rumored that Stroheim ghost-directed Gabbo; there is no doubt that Stroheim took advantage of Cruze's receptiveness.

Cruze had started out as an actor. He became a director as adept at slapstick as at spectacle, fluent in sophisticated humor. Upon the completion of a Paramount contract during the late 1920s, Cruze organized a maverick company and acquired the I.E. Chadwick Studios in Los Angeles. Cruze welcomed the challenges of sound. After *Gabbo*, he delivered such strong efforts as *I Cover the Waterfront*, *David Harum*, and *Helldorado* (both from 1934), and *Sutler's Gold* (1937).

None of *Gabbo*'s weaknesses is crippling. The technology often causes the players to appear self-conscious, with muffled voices and wordy exchanges unrelieved by close-ups. The cameras were confined to a soundproofed, windowed booth, which dampened the motors but sacrificed motion. Hidden microphones (boom-miking had yet to be perfected) could capture speech only in a direct trajectory. The fear of botching synchronization with intercutting discouraged shorter takes.

Production numbers, incorporating Gershwinesque orchestral jazz (all the rage in 1929), impart motion and propel the story. One of the tunesmiths, billed as King Zany, is the great comedian Charley Chase. A pivotal song, "I'm Laughing," suggests hilarity as emotional anesthesia, but then is distorted into cruel self-contradiction as Gabbo screams, "I can laugh!" while wrecking the grand finale of his showcase production.

Ziegfeld-style spectacle merges with Expressionism in a scene strung with a huge spiderweb—a metaphor for the tangled emotions of Betty Compson. Backstage hustle-and-bustle compounds the immediacy as the performers change costumes while ridiculing Gabbo's Continental militaristic pomposity.

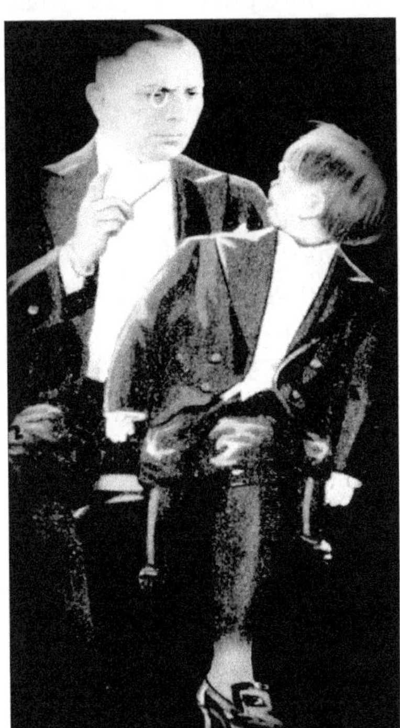

The secondary tale of a struggling show-business couple who track Gabbo's progress is a Stroheim trademark, one he had used in *Blind Husbands* (1919) and *Greed* (1925). Ben Hecht's short story, "The Rival Dummy," pictures Gabbo as a down-and-out eccentric. The film invests Gabbo with Stroheim's own superstitions, fragile self-esteem, and mock-Prussian formality. The tyrant wavers between tenderness and violence, finally lapsing into apathy. The festive Deco stage darkens, a deepening storm

"Goofy Goat," a companion-piece to Gabbo *in terms of the experimental Multicolor process.*

intensified by the blurring of music with dialogue. A huge revolving spiral is dominant—the German Expressionists' symbol for chaos.

The use of the dummy (voiced by George Grandée) anticipates Ealing Studios' acclaimed portmanteau film, *Dead of Night* (England; 1945); an *Alfred Hitchcock* tele-series episode called "The Glass Eye"; Lindsay Shonteff's U.S.-U.K. production of *The Devil Doll* (1963); and Sir Richard Attenborough's *Magic* (1978). *The Great Gabbo* is primarily a tragic study of a deteriorating mind—and all the more unnerving for that. (The routines include a nod to the famed act of Marshall Montgomery: Otto speaks while Gabbo smokes and dines.)

Joe Morgan spent the 1920s on glossy, expensive productions but by the 1930s had found himself banished to Poverty Row. Morgan spent much of the 1940s as a portrait photographer; then into the 1950s, he shot serials and *Jungle Jim* features for producer Sam Katzman's B-unit satellite of Columbia Pictures. On *Gabbo,* generalized lighting and static placements thwart Morgan's grasp of dramatic possibilities. The stage-production sequences were shot in Multicolor, a garish process that proves jarring in a film of otherwise subdued effect. The Multicolor system's proving ground was an animated cartoon, "Goofy Goat." Few prints of either have survived in Multicolor.

Stroheim dominates the cast with brusque ease. Betty Compson's bittersweet portrayal provides realistic counterweight; she was Cruze's wife during 1927–1929. Compson's strident voice scuttled her stardom in the talkies; she carried on as a backup player. (A lovely portrait of Compson in better days is a significant prop in *Invisible Ghost* [1941], where she plays a haggard intruder who drives Bela Lugosi to madness.)

Faults aside, *The Great Gabbo* delivers a fascinating story and characterizations to match. What the camera could not capture through motion is sometimes accomplished in composition. The lens has the last word: Stroheim trudges past the scene of his downfall while, above, a theatre hand removes the lapsed star's billing from the marquée.

The Phantom in the House

Trem Carr Productions • Continental Talking Pictures • 1929

We have mentioned Phil Rosen's *The Phantom in the House* as an ancestor of Monogram Pictures' signature chillers, to the finer detail of director Rosen's pivotal station in the *Forgotten Horrors* canon. The production and distribution companies were Monogram-in-embryo. The title suggests crepuscular delights that Arthur Hoerl's script neglects to deliver, but the soap-operatic story deals pleasingly in disturbing old secrets and unpunished crimes.

Peggy Milburn (Grace Valentine) seeks to enlist an investor to help her husband, Boyd Milburn (Henry B. Walthall), a struggling inventor. Peggy commits a slaying (in self-defense) when a prospective patron attempts to ravish her. Boyd Milburn takes the rap, lest his daughter, Dorothy, be left motherless. Milburn lands in prison.

Wealth accrues from Milburn's inventions. Peggy assumes a false name and claws her way to fashionable prominence. She aspires to have Dorothy (Nancy Welford) marry into the ruling class, and never mind the girl's affections for an ordinary working stiff, Paul Wallis

Ricardo Cortez.

(Ricardo Cortez). Milburn returns after 15 years; Peggy introduces her husband as merely a friend of the family.

Milburn supports Dorothy in her decision to marry for love. Peggy threatens to expose Milburn as a convict. A judge (Thomas A. Curran) who remembers the case tells Paul about Dorothy's father. A cellmate of Boyd's (Jack Curtis) kills the judge. Paul stands accused, but Dorothy learns the truth from Boyd. The killer is captured. Peggy repents and vows to begin anew with her husband and their daughter.

More atmospherically staged than tensely paced, *The Phantom in the House* reflects Rosen's photographic strengths more than it shows his emerging skills as a talking-pictures director. Herbert Kirkpatrick is the cameraman-of-record, but Rosen's command of radial composition is evident.

The source is Andrew Soutar's like-titled British novel of 1928, which in turn suggests an influence from Leonard Praskins and Ernest Pascal's stage-play *The Charlatan* (1927), in its concern with a troubled family and the torments of secrecy. *The Charlatan* also came to the screen in 1929, in both silent and part-talking editions, under director George Melford at Universal Pictures.

The Phantom in the House squanders Ricardo Cortez' dashing presence on the role of a put-upon ordinary guy. Cortez would soon enough find his niche as a mysterious rogue with a playful sense of humor.

Welcome Danger

Harold Lloyd Corp. • Paramount Pictures • 1929

Harold Lloyd, one of the great pioneering cinematic comedians, held out against sound until 1929. The about-face was reactionary in light of Lloyd's assertion in 1928 that sound was doomed—an emphatic prelude to his silent-screen development of *Welcome Danger*, a slapstick exercise grounded in scares. The relentless advance of talking pictures, however, provoked this change amidships: "We have no choice," Lloyd told the trade press. "We've got to make a sound picture."

Hesitant to start from scratch with the new picture awaiting release, Lloyd tried an experimental approach: "We've got to convert [*Welcome Danger*] into a sound picture, some way."

What changed his mind, he explained in a late-in-life interview with *Forgotten Horrors'* George E. Turner, was a combination of the tedious honing of the silent *Welcome Danger* from two hours and 45 minutes to a practical length—and his viewing of some other studio's new talkie comedy whose title Lloyd did not recall.

"They [the customers] weren't laughing at the gags, such as they were," said Lloyd. "They were laughing at the very novelty [of sound].

All the pains we take to make the visual gags work, and these rubes are laughing at the sound of ice clinking in a glass! I knew we'd be casting the pearls before the swine if we released *Welcome Danger* as a silent. Stupid sound effects had rendered our artistry passé!"

The retooling proved a chore, even with a completed picture as a springboard: a reboot is more difficult than a start-up. Lloyd hired veteran director Clyde Bruckman. (Malcolm St. Clair had directed the silent version.) Bruckman ditched half the original footage, dubbed the remainder, and shot new footage with synchronized sound. The process yielded a final cut of 115 minutes.

"The dubbing was a nightmare," said Lloyd, "because dubbing had no real precedents. We were inventing as we bumbled through." The finished film cost $980,000, including Lloyd's out-of-pocket investment of $290,000 for the addition of sound—a spectacular amount under any circumstances, more so during a deepening Depression. The picture grossed approximately $3 million to become Lloyd's greatest commercial success since *The Freshman* (1925). Lloyd's assumption proved correct: mere sound would prevail over artistry. Lloyd grew eventually to believe that the film had captured "the pace and quality of a silent...in a sound film."

An underworld figure known as the Dragon runs the dope rackets in San Francisco's Chinatown. Botanist Harold Bledsoe (Lloyd), son of a former police chief, is summoned to restore order. Harold misses his train after he pauses to pick flowers. He catches a ride with Billy Lee (Barbara Kent) and her crippled brother, Buddy Lee (Douglas Haig). (Billy is masquerading as a man, for reasons that become clear, but none too soon.) Dr. Gow (James Wang), a resistance leader who is treating Buddy, vanishes. Harold searches for Gow, with the clumsy assistance of a traffic cop, Clancy (Noah Young). Thorne (Charles Middleton), a campaigner for reform, is in fact the Dragon. Harold, disguised as a Chinese, finds himself a captive but prevails to rescue the physician. By collecting and matching fingerprints, Harold captures Thorne. Romance blossoms for Harold and Billie.

Lloyd plays Harold Bledsoe with all due boyish naïvete—the established owl-eyed image, which had become a recognizable trademark, anticipating the rounded silhouette of Mickey Mouse, even without Lloyd's name attached. Lloyd roughens the character with an ill-tempered streak. Bledsoe's early discourtesies to Barbara Kent's Billy Lee (while she passes, more or less, for a man) should earn him her disdain, but she proves a loyal romantic interest.

What distinguishes *Welcome Danger* in the present context is its immersion in exotic criminal horrors. These elements extend to Lloyd's being threatened with torture by a brutish henchman (Blue Washington)

while a captive in the depths of the underworld. Charles Middleton is ideal as the racketeer camouflaged with holier-than-thou mock-benevolence. Edgar Kennedy is his familiar impatient self as a lawman. The settings include a maze of hidden passageways, with ghostly apparitions (including the foolproof candle-on-a-turtle gag) and musical accompaniment to match. As if to indulge the novelty of sound with overemphasis, Lloyd devotes one repetitive gag to a literal and thorough blackout.

Lloyd made no bones about his resentment of sound-film technology: "It became easier to crack wise instead of inventing visual action—*gags*, as we used to call 'em," he complained. "Visual comedy requires alertness, intelligence, and timing."

The hybrid nature of *Welcome Danger* illustrates his lament: the film works most effectively during its purely visual moments. Lloyd's poetically violent slapstick is only diminished by the addition of clanging, bonking sound effects. That said, it remains that the only bad Harold Lloyd is no Harold Lloyd.

A restoration by the UCLA Film Archive includes both the talking version and an approximation of Malcolm St. Clair's silent cut, reconstructed from negative and dupe-negative elements and muted portions of the talking version.

Unmasked

Weiss Bros. • Artclass Pictures • 1929

Arthur B. Reeve's Craig Kennedy, the scientific detective, descends from Edgar Allan Poe's C. Auguste Dupin and Conan Doyle's Sherlock Holmes as a forensic sleuth of immense popular influence: all are ancestors of Chester Gould's comics feature *Dick Tracy* and its kind, and all point toward the *C.S.I.* television franchise and its ilk of times more recent. An emphasis upon procedural clue-gathering lends urgency to the chase.

Kennedy became a recurring movie character via such serials as *Exploits of Elaine* (1915) and *The Radio Detective* (1926). Edgar Lewis' *Unmasked* tones down the action of the lengthy serials—the better to concentrate upon mystery and romance in scarcely more than an hour.

During a gathering at the high-toned Brookfield Estate, Kennedy (Robert Warwick) tells of an unresolved case of poisoning: the police had suspected Mary Wayne (Susan Conroy), but Kennedy was more concerned with an East Indian mystic known as Hamid (Milton Krims). Kennedy learned that Wayne had administered the lethal draught while hypnotized by Hamid. Hamid escaped.

Back in the moment, Kennedy reveals that Hamid is among the guests, incognito. The purported Count Sebastian Domingo de Navarre is revealed as Hamid, and this time he does not escape.

The Weiss Bros.—Max, Louis, and Adolph—had branched from the lamp-manufacturing trade into the novelty of gramophones and then bought a store and a theatre in New York. An interstate chain of theatres developed, and around 1917 the Weisses began to make their own pictures. Their output grew to 14 features a year during the 1920s, with additional development of serials and short subjects.

Robert Warwick: The talking pictures' first Craig Kennedy.

For about a year, Louis Weiss also managed DeForest Phonofilm Studios for Lee DeForest, an inventor and manufacturer of sound-film stock. In 1929, Louis arranged to produce *Unmasked*—the first feature-length picture to utilize the DeForest Phonofilm process—at the New York plant where DeForest had made more than 1,000 talking shorts since 1923 as a proving ground for the proprietary technology.

Unmasked moves slowly by comparison with the frenzy of the Craig Kennedy serials, but it is not as stodgy as many other early talkies. The deadening effect of long takes and too much dialogue is lessened by the inventive construction—unusual for the time—which embraces a flashback resolved after a return to the framing story. This technique is a foreshadowing of the so-called *narratage* technique (see *The Sin of Nora Moran*) and in turn looks forward to the film noir style.

Robert Warwick makes a stern and deep-voiced Kennedy. Most of the other players are unknowns. Director Edgar Lewis, a writer and actor from Missouri, was a pioneering action director for Pathé, Fox, and Selznick. Lewis had wrapped a two-year series of westerns at Universal when he made *Unmasked*, after which he handled romantic dramas for Chesterfield. (For more about Craig Kennedy: see *The Clutching Hand*.)

The Lost Zeppelin

Tiffany-Stahl Productions • 1929

Stranded between wilderness thriller and soap opera within a science-fictional binding, *The Lost Zeppelin* is difficult to take seriously as either drama or melodrama. Its romantic triangle lacks tension: Conway Tearle and Ricardo Cortez seem too honorably loyal to one another to permit the elements of violence and treachery that are crucial to such tales. Virginia Valli—exquisite beauty aside—plays a shrill, neurotic sort who would drive away any sane man.

Expeditioner Donald Hall (Tearle) catches his wife, Miriam (Valli), on the make for his associate, Tom Armstrong (Cortez), upon the eve of a perilous journey to the South Pole. Her timing is impeccably wrong, what with morale at stake for the good of the expedition. Miriam declares her love for Armstrong. Hall takes the rebuff stoically, and he and Armstrong depart as comrades.

The dirigible reaches the frozen continent, but the zeppelin crashes. (The factual basis lies in the adventures of inventor-explorer Umberto Nobile—in particular, a 1928 crash and a complicated rescue mission.) The survivors are Hall and Armstrong and the expedition's dog. A rescue plane, ill equipped, has room for one passenger. Hall insists that Armstrong must go. Hall also sends the dog and remains alone with a week's provisions.

Armstrong returns home as a hero. Miriam reveals that her truer affections lie with her husband, after all. A dispatch announces Hall's rescue, and Miriam cables to him a declaration of her devotion.

Valli (no kin to the movies' much younger Alida Valli) was a Chicago-born stenographer who had broken into the movies in 1915 and starred in more than 30 silent pictures. Her voice proved too high-pitched for the primitive technology of the early talkers; her speech is notably grating in the present role. After two additional features, *Guilty* (1930)

The exploits of airship pioneer Umberto Nobile, pictured at right, inspired The Lost Zeppelin.

and *Night Life in Reno* (1931), Valli married the actor Charles Farrell, future mayor of Palm Springs, and retired.

Tearle and Cortez are too much the stalwart Boy Scouts in a jam to take advantage of the dramatic possibilities of a hostile setting. (While *The Lost Zeppelin* was in first-run showings, the author H.P. Lovecraft fulfilled such potential in the novella *At the Mountains of Madness*—a tale of Antarctic horrors.) Tearle registers precisely the steadfast heroic protagonism he had defined in the silents. Cortez, though established as an exotic romancer, plays the genial rival as

more the Tearle type, with outthrust chin and forthright gaze. Within two years, Cortez would become the movies' original Sam Spade, in the 1931 version of *The Maltese Falcon*.

London-born Edward Sloman had directed more than 40 features, dating from 1915, by the time he made this tentative foray into talking pictures. Sloman soon delivered such gems as *Puttin' on the Ritz* (1930), which features Irving Berlin's famous song and extravagant settings by *Bulldog Drummond*'s William Cameron Menzies, and *Gun Smoke* and *Murder by the Clock* (both from 1931). His output lessened thereafter.

The Lost Zeppelin boasts imposing visual effects, with impressive icebound miniatures and gripping depictions of the liftoff and the crash. Kenneth Peach, Sr., handled the effects camera, in collaboration with mechanical-effects specialist Jack Robson. (Peach became the unbilled second-string director of photography on the miniatures for 1933's *King Kong*.)

Failings aside, *The Lost Zeppelin* is more than a relic. It serves as a vivid, however dramatically creaky, reminder of a time when heroic adventurers risked all to seek out the last unexplored places. The prevailing cornball business retains an appeal, too, within an industry eager to seek out seemingly new emotive sensations by sorting through manipulative gimmicks of times long gone. The self-sacrificing hokum of Conway Tearle's grand gesture is replayed almost literally in 1998's *Armageddon*, in a climactic rescue sequence involving Bruce Willis and Ben Affleck. Schmaltz never lapses out of fashion, questionable taste notwithstanding.

Forgotten Horrors of 1930

The Voice from the Sky

Ben Wilson Productions • G.Y.B. Productions • 1930

In October of 1930, Universal Pictures' sound-on-film serial, *The Indians Are Coming*, opened at the Roxy Theatre on Broadway to tremendous traffic. Will Hays, president of the Motion Picture Producers & Distributors Association, acknowledged "a tremendous debt of gratitude… [*The Indians Are Coming*] brought 20 million children back to the theatre."

Universal had been beaten to the talking-serial punch, however—though to little avail. The first serial with a sound-on-film track (as opposed to the sound-on-disk system of *The King of the Kongo*) had come almost a year earlier—but it was largely ignored and seems to exist today only in a haze of memory.

The Voice from the Sky was issued without a copyright and escaped even the voracious editorial attention of the trade publications. An advertisement in *The Film Daily Yearbook* for 1930 announced availability; the release can only have been limited. Another piece touted "a story of a scientist that invented a secret formula that can destroy the world," adding: "Come and learn the secret!"

A menace known as the Man from Nowhere (John C. McCallum) can suspend all energy in the atmosphere. The madman threatens destruction unless his terms of extortion are met. Detective Jack Deering (Wally Wales) and his sweetheart, Jean Lowell (Jean Dolores), thwart the scheme.

Star player Wally Wales, hero of independent westerns, eventually became a character man under the name of Hal Taliaferro (formal name: Floyd Taliaferro Alderson). In 1974, Wales sent the following memo to historian Bill G. "Buck" Rainey: "The film was made in Hollywood—at the very beginning of sound, when no one knew how to make sound pictures. I doubt very much if it was ever released. It must have been pretty BAD! No one seemed to know what they were doing. Everyone in the early days of sound was experimenting. … [A] very bad time for all of us."

Another historian, Indiana-based Michael R. Pitts, has turned up evidence of commercial play—contrary to Wales' perception. Film archæology is a ceaseless, chronic-to-acute task.

The producer and director, Ben Wilson, enlisted scenarist Robert
Dillon and cinematographer William Nobles to handle *The Voice from
the Sky*. Wilson had played the leading man in the first American
serial, the Edison Company's *What Happened to Mary?* (1912). Wilson
and Neva Gerber, a Chicago débutante, made nine serials together,
beginning in 1917 at Universal with *The Mystery Ship*.

Together and separately, Wilson and Gerber graced many features
and short subjects but won their greatest following as a serial team,
rivaling the popularity of Walter Miller and Allene Ray at the Pathé
company. When talking pictures arrived, Miller balked at further
acting but continued to direct. *Voice*'s leading lady, Jean Dolores, is in
fact Neva Gerber, seeking a new direction. She had changed her name
for *The Lone Patrol* (1928). She retired after an additional Wilson production, *A Woman's Justice* (1930). Wilson died in 1930, Gerber in 1974.

Ingagi

Congo Productions, Ltd. • 1930

Explorers Daniel Swayne and Sir Hubert Winstead forge into Africa to seek a gorilla-worshipping tribe. They witness the abduction of a woman by an ape (played by Charles Gemora), then find a colony of gorillas and wild women. The apes attack. The expeditioners kill a 600-pound specimen. One of the women mourns her simian mate. The scientists turn back with evidence capable of altering the course of science, or at least the course of grindhouse cinema.

Although the credits acknowledge screenwriter Adam Hull Shirk (see *The House of Mystery* and *The Ape*), the presentation suggests a documentary account. The advertising campaign trumpets: "Scientific Marvel of the Age!" Such claims were typical of producer Nat Spitzer, an old-school carnival huckster. Much footage is pirated from an authentic expeditionary film of 1914–1915 by Lady Grace Mackenzie, the first white woman to lead such a safari for the purpose of ruling class vanity (about whom, more presently). Some scenes are vivid, others painfully blurred. A narrator ascribes film damage to the muggy climate.

Charlie Gemora struts his stuff with a Central Casting tribeswoman in Darkest California.

The dramatized episodes were filmed in Darkest California. A purportedly venomous reptile is a leopard tortoise bedecked with the armor of a scaly anteater. Monkeys of the tropical Americas gambol about, and an armadillo—also unique to the New World—is seen. An alligator, yet another denizen of the

Americas, nests amid eycalyptus leaves, which grow not in Africa. Tribal scenes strike a severe contrast with shots of paler black citizens in more nearly civilized attire—more cottonfield than Congo.

A preview audience recognized the supposed tribal virgin as a bit player well known at Central Casting. Her costume changes noticeably before a gorilla-suited Charles Gemora arrives to abduct her. Gemora, a stunts-and-effects master and leading portrayer of gorillas, was working in 1930 at MGM with Lon Chaney in a talking-picture remake of *The Unholy Three*. Close-ups of a genuine ape show an orangutan, native to Borneo and Sumatra. Gemora navigates upright, though stooped, instead of upon all fours, the gait of the gorilla.

Heavy promotion and heavier controversy made *Ingagi* a success. Crowds increased with each new cry of outrage. "[N]ot only the greatest

movie hoax," declared *Screenland* magazine, "but the most offensive." The American Society of Mammalologists voiced "utter disapproval" and complained of "fictitious features...mingled with genuine natural history." A query to the British Embassy turned up no such distinguished personage as Sir Hubert Winstead.

Regional censors decried the hoax and complained of a topless virgin sacrifice (terms used advisédly). Ohio's educational bureaucracy forbade showings. Several theatre circuits pulled *Ingagi* after the Better Business Bureau of New York labeled the gorilla scenes as bogus. Congo Pictures inserted an acknowledgment of dramatizations.

A federal court in New York dealt with a plagiarism suit by Byron P. Mackenzie, son of Lady Grace Mackenzie, alleging misappropriation of footage from *Heart of Africa* (aka *Lady Mackenzie's Pictures*), for which the explorer had shot 20,000 feet of film in 1914. A $150,000 judgment against Congo Pictures forbade disposal of assets. Nat Spitzer, undaunted, mounted a second national release in 1931, this time through Radio-Keith-Orpheum Distributing Corp., an affiliate of major Hollywood studio RKO-Radio Pictures. At first denied a New York license on grounds of fakery, the film was cleared in November of 1931 to run at Manhattan's Central Theatre. The eventual gross: $4 million.

Big returns on a chump-change investment, that is, and seldom such a ruckus over such brazen insignificance: Charlie Gemora had invested $5,000 in his sequence, then sold it to Spitzer for $7,000. *Ingagi* made so much money that other fast-buck *schlockmeisters* were inspired to create such Third World ersatz erotica as *Angkor, Love Life of a Gorilla*, and *Wild Women of Borneo*. The furor made *Ingagi* one of the first household words to erupt from talkie cinema: The Three Stooges dropped the occasional reference, and so did Hal Roach's Rascals troupe of child players, alias Our Gang.

Movie scholar Steve Brigati has determined that *Ingagi* was misappropriated (possibly as late as the 1960s) for purposes of racist indoctrination by the Ku Klux Klan—which seized upon the suggestion of inter-species breeding. No particular reflection upon Nat Spitzer, who was more concerned with luring a thrill-hungry audience than with advancing any crackpot social agendas.

Mamba

Color-Art • Tiffany Productions • 1930

Jean Hersholt made his mark with portrayals of maniacal ferocity. In 1930 alone, he menaced Eleanor Boardman in *Mamba*, Lupe Veléz in *Hell Harbor*, and Helen Twelvetrees in *The Cat Creeps*. Hersholt also tormented Veléz in *East Is West*, but his scenes were redone with Edward

G. Robinson upon the realization that Hersholt's Danish accent clashed with the Chinese role.

Hersholt had set forth such memorable heels as Marcus in *Greed* and Ed Munn in *Stella Dallas* (1924–1925). His villains are lustful, vulgar brutes with beady eyes and thick, wet lips—each with a distinct personality. In civilian life, Hersholt was a charitable and artistic sort, namesake of the Motion Picture Academy's Humanitarian Award.

Albert S. Rogell's groundbreaking Technicolor production of *Mamba* has Hersholt as August Bolte, a German planter in Neu Posen, East Africa. The natives call him Mamba, after the deadly snake. The year is 1914: rumors of war, fostered by the banking and manufacturing rackets, are rampant.

Disgraced Count von Linden (Josef Swickard) asks of Bolte a loan and offers his daughter, Helen (Boardman), as a wife. Bound for Africa, Bolte and Helen meet von Reiden (Ralph Forbes), a young officer. A dying native girl (Hazel Jones) accuses Bolte of rape. Von Reiden rescues Helen from a lashing and humbles Bolte. When war breaks out, Bolte flees into the jungle, where hostile tribesmen make short work of him—and then storm the plantation. Von Reiden comes to Helen's aid as British soldiers rescue the Germans.

Hersholt is irresistibly despicable. Eleanor Boardman and Ralph Forbes are mere stereotypes of romantic-heroic tradition. Strong lesser presences include Noble Johnson as a tribal leader, Will Stanton as a Cockney servant, and Josef Swickard as a shabby aristocrat.

Mamba is one of the most ambitious features ever attempted by a small studio. Costuming is elaborate, the settlement realistic. Spectacle figures in the tribal uprising—filmed on a fortress set at Universal.

Jean Hersholt, Eleanor Boardman, and Ralph Forbes.

"We kept running out of money," director Albert Rogell told us in a late-in-life interview. "Even kept identical sets of costumes. … When [the rental agents] would come and get one set, we'd bring out the other."

The use of Technicolor was a formidable undertaking; sound was problem enough. Even the majors seldom attempted a full feature in color. Technicolor was at first a two-color process, extracting hues from red and green. Fragmentary remains of *Mamba* (about 12 minutes, without sound) reveal accurate flesh tones and lush foliage.

Rogell had entered the industry in 1916. He directed extensively for Universal and First National during the 1920s and moved smoothly into the talkies and, at length, early television. His dynamic handling of *Mamba* is complemented by James C. Bradford's elaborate music, rich in *agitatos* and *mysteriosi* as well as martial themes.

Hell Harbor

Inspiration Pictures • United Artists • 1930

Inspiration Pictures dated from 1921, founded by Henry King and actor Richard Barthelmess. An initial talkie, *She Goes to War*, appeared in 1929. King chose next to prove that a talking feature could be made entirely at a remote site. The shooting of *Hell Harbor* became an ordeal befitting its title.

Construction at Rocky Point, Florida, included storm-proofed buildings, some with interior sets. A 140-ton schooner served as the hero's ship. In Key West, King advertised for bit players and extras. One role went to long-faced Rondo Hatton, a former publicist for Beecroft Studio on nearby David Island. Hatton, afflicted with a glandular disorder known as acromegaly, much later would develop a following as a horror-film star.

A gale approached while King was directing a scene with chief villain Jean Hersholt. King dispatched the RCA Photophone equipment to Tampa, hours before the storm began ripping at crucial sets. Cast and crew were back at work in two days.

Trader Joseph Horngold (Hersholt), at large in a port of criminals, intends to kill a sailor (Harry Allen) who had sold him a cache of

Gibson Gowland, left, and Jean Hersholtz.

pearls. Horngold is beaten to his prey by a shadowy but familiar figure. Vengeance, petty or otherwise, and reciprocal antagonisms are business as usual in this locale, where life is cheap and nobody could care less.

The antagonists include a family-tradition pirate, Harry Morgan (Gibson Gowland); his fiery stepdaughter, Anita (Lupe Veléz); and American trader Bob Wade (John Holland). Horngold forces Morgan to sell Anita to him as a wife. Anita proposes, instead, to sell herself to Wade. She steals Horngold's pearls, hoping to influence Wade with their value. Horngold accuses Morgan, who kills Horngold. Wade rescues Anita and arranges for her clearance of criminal charges.

The film demonstrates a communal commitment. The villainy of Gibson Gowland and Jean Hersholt overshadows even the lively Lupe Veléz. In 1924, on a dried lakebed in Death Valley, Gowland had enacted a murder scene against Hersholt in Erich von Stroheim's career-wrecking masterwork, *Greed*; the deed is repeated in *Hell Harbor* with similar intensity. The prevailing depravity—even Veléz' innocent Anita regards romance as black-market commerce—seems all the ghastlier in that such behavior makes perfect sense within a corrupt, isolated society.

The camera lingers over exquisite seascapes, pausing often to study the seamed faces of the grotesque inhabitants. Lighting seems natural, but in fact many exteriors were shot under tarps with manufactured lighting. The cinematography of John P. Fulton and Mack Stengler drew high marks: "[F]inest

Lupe Velez.

thing given to us in black-and-white," said *The Hollywood Spectator.* Fulton became a celebrated special-effects artist. Stengler spent the Depression years primarily on Poverty Row—a lasting and undeserved demotion from the heights of *Hell Harbor.*

The Bat Whispers (Twice)

Feature Productions • Artcinema Associates • United Artists • 1930

Ranking alongside Charlie Chaplin and Erich von Stroheim as an individualistic eccentric, Roland West made only a dozen features in 15 years. Three derive from the play *The Bat*, by Mary Roberts Rinehart and Avery Hopwood. West's *The Bat* dates from 1926; two talkie versions of 1930 share the title *The Bat Whispers*—but they are distinctly unalike.

A commercial filmmaker since 1915 in partnership with theatreman and mogul-to-be Joseph M. Schenck, West overcame amateurish beginnings to score with only his second picture, *Deluxe Annie*, and a stage play, *The Unknown Purple*, both in 1918. The movie version of *The Unknown Purple* came about in 1923—the tale of a vengeful scientist who masters invisibility; the prints were tinted with a purplish glow to indicate the presence of the menace.

Both *The Monster* (1925) and *The Bat* advance the stage's Mystery Farce tradition—the only West silents known to have survived. Both show the influence of the Germanic fantasy films. *The Bat* was considered lost until 1987, when a deteriorating nitrate print of all but the first reel surfaced in a private collection, entrusted first to Boise State University and then to UCLA film archivist Robert Gitt, who already had begun the restoration of both versions of *The Bat Whispers*. Reel No. 1 of *The Bat* turned up in 1988. The near-loss is astonishing for so influential a film—adapted from a theatrical hit, and second only to *The Phantom of the Opera* for nightmarish popular impact. (Ray Bradbury recorded his impressions as a first-generation viewer of *The Bat* in the autobiographical novel *Dandelion Wine*.)

The Bat, a master criminal, tracks a rival thief and a fortune in bank notes to a palatial estate, where he terrorizes the occupants. A supposed police detective proves to be the Bat. A scatterbrained housemaid captures the Bat in a bear trap. The Bat swears he will return. The simple story, complicated by intrigues among the inmates and the visitors, is

Lobby card for Roland West's 1926 version of The Bat.

related with monumental shadows and such dizzying Expressionistic flourishes as a menacing image that proves to be a moth on an automobile lamp. The Bat (whose stage disguise had been a black handkerchief) sports a fanged headpiece with bristling ears. William Cameron Menzies' masterful art direction overcomes the silent version's static camerawork, however ominous, by Arthur Edeson. Looming doorways and pools of blackness are the very definition of the Old Dark House realm. Performances are a mixed bag, with only Emily Fitzroy (as a reclusive spinster) and Louise Fazenda (as a dotty servant) as standout players. Stage singer Tullio Carminati is colorless as the false detective—particularly so, by comparison with Chester Morris' fierce portrayal in the 1930 films.

After one last silent, *The Dove* (1929), and a pacesetting talker, *Alibi* (1929; also issued as a silent), West announced *The Bat Whispers* in January of 1930 under a smokescreen title, *Love in Chicago*—going so far as to deny that he was remaking *The Bat*. (The decoy title, a commonplace among the hellbent-for-privacy studios, was calculated to discourage journalistic curiosity.) For *Alibi*, a police melodrama almost as important to talking-picture style as 1929's *Bulldog Drummond*, sharp-featured Chester Morris had joined West's company. Morris would prove crucial to the mad ferocity of *The Bat Whispers*.

Whispers' art director, Paul Roe Crawley, a protégé of Menzies, carried the master's influence over to the two talkie versions—one in conventional dimensions, the other in widescreen—with vast looming

shadows, many of them painted into the sets in order to allow cameraman Ray June greater latitude in lighting the surroundings. West justified the costly 65-millimeter Magnifilm version by explaining, "[W]e have reached the last magnitude of the old 35mm film."

Virtuoso cinematography, vast sets, and the intercutting of fantastic miniature shots make *The Bat Whispers* the most spectacular of many such comedy-thrillers of the day. The sets dominate the actors, who (in the standard 35mm version) often appear low in the frame, dwarfed by shadows. The Bat himself, in flapping cape and cowl, anticipates explicitly the comic-book character known as Batman. The film is an acknowledged influence, for that matter, upon a co-inventor of the *Batman* franchise, cartoonist Bob Kane.

Chester Morris dominates *The Bat Whispers* with a pleasingly overplayed performance. Matronly Grayce Hampton, as the reclusive Cornelia Van Gorder, lends calm assurance. Eccentric comedy is supplied by Maude Eburne—a warm-up, no doubt, for 1933's *The Vampire Bat*—and Spencer Charters and Charles Dow Clark. Secondary menaces are Gustav von Seyffertitz, Ben Bard, and Hugh Huntley. Una Merkel, as the ingénue, shows little sign of her greater ability at comedy.

The ending makes eloquent use of sound. Captured, the Bat declares, "There never was a jail built strong enough to hold the Bat. … The Bat always flies at night—and always in a straight line!" His maddened laughter gives way to an epilogue, in which the Bat descends a rope onto a stage and emerges as Chester Morris from a cloud of smoke. Morris implores the audience not to reveal the Bat's identity. Otherwise, "he's heartbroken. … He goes around for days, killing people without the slightest enjoyment for his work."

The widescreen presentation languished, doomed (like approximately a dozen other such productions from various studios) by the reluctance of most theatre owners to invest in wide-film equipment when the change to sound-film technology already had proved costly. The Motion Picture Association delivered the *coup de grace* in December of 1930, forbidding the industry to promote any further such innovations. The conventional boxy dimensions of 35mm film would remain the standard for a generation.

Roland West made one last picture, *Corsair* (1931), with Morris and Thelma Todd. The director is remembered more as a principal figure in the mysterious death of Todd in 1935 than for his contributions to cinema. West died in 1952, just as widescreen spectacle was regaining momentum among the Hollywood studios.

Borrowed Wives

Tiffany • 1930

The Old Dark House subgenre had come into its own well before James Whale's filming of J.B. Priestley's novel *Benighted* could arrive (as *The Old Dark House*) in 1932. Silent films typified by *The Cat and the Canary* and *The Gorilla* had defined the idiom, which calls for a deténte between humor and horrific business.

Frank R. Strayer had helped to effect a transition for the style into talking pictures—although Strayer's *Murder at Midnight* leans more toward a grim outlook. Strayer's *The Monster Walks* (1932) boasts a

greater leavening of comedy, to the extent of a closing punchline. Between those extremes lies Strayer's *Borrowed Wives*, a slight but worthwhile romantic farce that echoes the situation of Hal Roach's 1920 production of "Haunted Spooks" (a showcase for the nimble comedian Harold Lloyd) in a tale of matrimonial desperation in a crepuscular setting. Rex Lease is no Harold Lloyd—Lease was bound for western-movie stardom and eventual character-man dependability—but suits well the role of a hellbent-for-marriage heir at large in a setting ripe for over-reactive comedy.

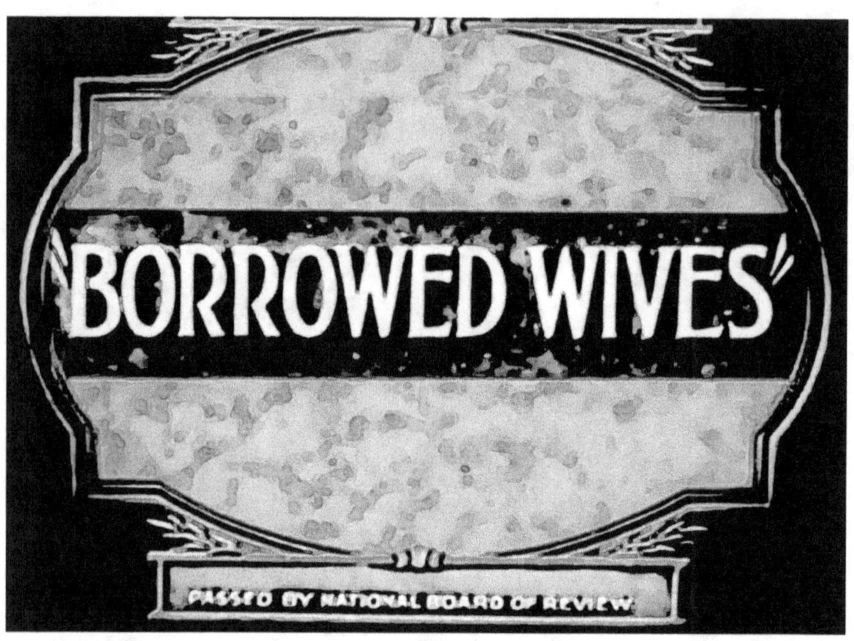

Notes genre enthusiast Mark Martucci: "*Borrowed Wives* has an Old Dark House, secret passages, a shadowy character up to no good, and just about everything required of a Forgotten Horror." Yes, and also a director, a scenarist (Scott Darling), and a studio of significance to the *Forgotten Horrors* books. Not to mention a masterful comic player, Paul Hurst, whose place in the *Forgotten Horrors* canon lies in a portrayal of hilarious indignation in one essential film, 1932's *The Thirteenth Guest*.

Hapless Peter Foley (Lease) stands to inherit $1 million, provided that he marries on a deadline. Foley intends to wed Alice Blake (Vera Reynolds) as soon as she can arrive. The forbidding home of Foley's Uncle Henry (Charles Sellon) is the destination. A delay arises. An overbearing friend (Sam Hardy), who has a stake in the inheritance, insists that his own consort, Julia (Nita Martan), must pose as Peter's wife.

A rival (Robert Randall) misinforms Alice that Peter is in fact married to Julia; she agrees to marry the interloper if his assertion should prove true. They find themselves pursued by Wild Bull Morgan (Hurst), a cop enamored of Julia. The family's lawyer (Harry Todd) turns up, hogtied. The uncle, purportedly an invalid, is exposed as a menacing scoundrel. Peter and Alice are married before the appointed hour. Not to give away too much, y'know.

Under Texas Skies

Syndicate Pictures • 1930–1931

H.P. Lovecraft wrote during the 1920s: "[M]uch of the choicest weird work [appears] in memorable fragments [of] material whose massed effect may be of a very different cast." Such horror-is-where-you-find-it appeal belongs to J.P. McGowan's *Under Texas Skies*, a tale of deception and mistaken identity in a cruel frontier. The weirdness belongs to a grimacing idiot called Dummy, played by Bob Roper with homicidal intent. (Never mind that the creep encounters only two likely victims and kills neither; the threat is sufficient.)

Roper's simian lurch suggests Boris Karloff in the following year's *Frankenstein*—coincidentally so—but foreshadows explicitly John Bleifer's lamebrained psychopath in another gem from Universal Pictures, Buck Jones' hard-charging star vehicle *The Crimson Trail* (1935).

Dummy is the enforcer for a war profiteers' gang that seeks to exploit tensions between the southwestern United States and Mexico. Horse-opera stalwarts Bill Cody and Bob Custer play undercover agents seeking to protect a rancher (Natalie Kingston). *Under Texas Skies* is essentially a conventional sagebrusher, spiced with a hint of villainy for Custer's character. Custer seems ill at ease with the sound-recording technology. Tom London seems the soul of benevolent authority until he gives himself away as a bogus cavalryman. Lane Chandler appears as another borderlands agent, musically inclined.

Forgotten Horrors of 1931

Sign of the Wolf / The Lone Trail

Webb-Douglas Productions • Syndicate Pictures • 1931

The cliffhanger factories reserved the right to pare their serialized chapter-a-week epics into features, the better to find a secondary market in theatres that might otherwise shun the serials' 10–15 week commitments.

Nat Levine of Mascot Pictures, the independent serial leader until its mid-1930s absorption by Republic Pictures, authorized the distillation of two features from a 1935 groundbreaker, *The Phantom Empire*—one, emphasizing the elements of horse opera and down-home music; the other, concentrating upon the science-fictional business. Sol Lesser's *Chandu* serial of 1934 likewise yielded two features—but these relate consecutive stories, consistent with the arc of the 214-minute episodic source. Many of Republic's serials reappeared during the 1960s as 100-minute condensations for television: *Undersea Kingdom*, for example, became the 10-reel *Sharad of Atlantis*.

Webb-Douglas Productions took an altogether different tack with *Sign of the Wolf*, a supernaturally motivated western that hinges upon three gimmicks: a dog that can sense whether a person is in need of a wag, or a mauling; a set of mystical chains, like the Philosopher's Stone of ancient alchemical legend, that can transform sand to jewels; and the indignant, lurking priest of an East Indian cult. Strange elements for an otherwise conventional shoot-'em-up, but the combination sustains interest despite conspicuous repetition over what would have been a 10-week course of viewing—a new chapter every Saturday until a bang-up finale. The directors-of-record are Forrest Sheldon and Harry S. Webb.

The prompt trimming to feature length produced *The Lone Trail*, a remarkable alteration. But for the shared production crew, ensemble cast, and consistent dramatis personae, the serial and the feature are largely unalike. But then, film cutter Frederick Bain had a great deal of final-cut material and outtakes from which to choose.

Rancher John Farnum (Harry Todd), traveling in India, purchases a puppy named King. King bears the fabled Sign of the Wolf, an

ability to read anyone's nature. Farnum also obtains the Secret of the Jewels, a set of chains capable of rendering valuable common dust. The seller had stolen these objects from a temple whose guardian, Kuva (Edmund Cobb), must retrieve them or else, no matter how long the task requires.

Years later, Farnum proposes to sell the chains to wealthy Clyde Winslow (Al Ferguson)—a decision brought on by threatening messages from Kuva, delivered via blowgun darts. Winslow, meanwhile, conspires to steal the chains with assistance from outlaw Butch Kohler (Jack Mower) and his gang. Resistance comes from Farnum's daughter, Ruth (Virginia Brown Faire); her fiancé, rancher Tom Lanning (Rex Lease); foreman Jed (Joe Bonomo); and the formidable wolf-dog, King (a splendidly trained animal named Muro).

The serial, *Sign of the Wolf*, is packed with hard riding and harried fighting, although some of the punches are less than convincing: The Pass System of photographing realistic haymakers had yet to be invented. (See the section on John Wayne's Lone Star westerns series.) Joe Bonomo, a famed strongman of the silent serials and an occasional gorilla impersonator, stands out as a fearless sidekick to career western champion Rex Lease. The plot wears thin, with seemingly endless exchanges of the enchanted chains from good guys to bad guys and back again. Edmund Cobb appears sparingly to lend an eerie grace note, although his menacing Easterner seems more interested in restoring some cosmic balance than in dispensing mayhem. The dog's ability to sense evil is largely marginalized, barring an explanation of why King is quick to attack the outlaws but gives Cobb's Prince Kuva no difficulty.

The feature version, *The Lone Trail*, de-complicates the yarn: Ranger Tom Lanning (Lease) leaves his sister under the protection of his dog, King (Muro). Upon returning, Lanning finds her slain, a victim of Butch "Tiger" Kohler (Mower). Traveling incognito with the disgraced King, Lanning catches the outlaw holding Ruth Farnum (Brown Faire) in captivity. Kohler gets the drop on Lanning, with little resistance from King. Lanning fights back and drives Kohler to the edge of a cliff. King rallies heroically to shove Kohler over the precipice. (A very similar film of 1935, Reliable Pictures' *Skull and Crown*, pits Jack Mower against another wolf-dog hero, Rin-Tin-Tin, Jr.)

Rex Lease had cracked Hollywood in 1922, rising from walk-ons and bits to second-string leading-man prominence and low-budget western-film stardom. Lease lapsed to supporting roles after the rise of Gene Autry in 1935, but he carried on as a reliable backup into the early 1960s.

Syndicate Pictures and Harry S. Webb's Wonder Pictures also delivered a phantom-at-large serial called *The Mystery Trooper* in 1931, reissued in 1935 as *Trail of the Royal Mounted* by Guaranteed Pictures.

The Phantom of the West

Mascot Pictures Corp. • 1931

Mascot's first sound-on-film serial, *The Lone Defender* (1930), had allowed the customers to hear the great canine star, Rin-Tin-Tin, snarl and bark. Mascot's next, *The Phantom of the West*, is the first talkie for Tom Tyler, who had been a top draw for FBO Pictures' line of oaters.

At liberty after FBO had sold out to become RKO-Radio Pictures—at a time when frontier films were losing ground—Tyler became one of the few to gain traction in sound. He worked for another 18 years, both as a frontiersman and a character player (notably as the title menace in 1940's *The Mummy's Hand*) until rheumatoid arthritis forced his retirement.

Tyler serves *The Phantom of the West* as rancher Jim Lester, who shelters escaped convict Francisco Cortez (Frank Lanning) until two deputies arrive to inform Jim that Cortez had killed Jim's father. Cortez overhears and escapes, leaving a note suggesting that any one of seven men in a nearby town might reveal the identity of the genuine murderer.

The settlement falls under the control of a gang called the League of the Lawless, which takes orders from a mysterious Phantom. Warning notes leave the secretive seven men in a paranoid state. Jim and Mona Cortez (Dorothy Gulliver), daughter of Cortez, seek the truth. Suspicion falls upon the sheriff (Frank S. Hagney) and Jim, among others. The Phantom kills anyone who cracks. Jim reveals a local nincompoop named Oscar (Tom Dugan) as the Phantom.

Typical of Mascot, the Phantom appears to be anybody and everybody but Tom Dugan, who handles comic relief until he turns vicious for the slam-bang finale. Dugan's stuttering act is nowhere near as good as that of Roscoe Ates, Lloyd Hamilton (*Dark Waters*), or Mel Blanc's Porky Pig. The shadow of the fiend bears no resemblance to the raspy-voiced Dugan.

Director D. Ross Lederman had known success at Warner Bros., but he was having difficulty breaking into the talking pictures. Lederman's only serial provided him with leverage into better assignments at Columbia and Warner Bros.—a prominence that lasted for another 20 years.

Producer Nat Levine's never-a-dull-moment approach prevents the talk from slowing the action. The scenery around Kernville, California, and the excellent stuntwork compensate for the prevailing crudeness of production.

King of the Wild

Mascot Pictures Corp. • 1931

Nat Levine sought with this one to cash in on MGM's African expeditionary picture of 1931, *Trader Horn*. He hired *Horn*'s star players, Harry Carey and Edwina Booth, for three serials, only to find the actors called back by MGM for retakes. Levine forged ahead with *King of the Wild*, with Richard Thorpe directing Walter Miller and Nora Lane in the leading roles. (Carey and Booth joined Mascot during 1931–1932 for a mystery-villain tale, *The Vanishing Legion*, and a wild elaboration upon James Fenimore Cooper's *The Last of the Mohicans*.)

For *King of the Wild*, Levine populated the supporting cast with bad-guy favorite Tom Santschi, Cyril McLaglen (one of Victor McLaglen's husky brothers) as an ape-man, Mischa Auer as an East Indian assassin, and Boris Karloff, just a few months away from stardom with *Frankenstein*. Karloff is effective as a North African shiek, barring a broadly conceived French-Arab accent.

Soldier of fortune Robert Grant (Miller) is framed for murder. The culprits are Dakka (Auer), animal dealer Harris (Santschi), and Sheik Mustapha (Karloff). One Mrs. LaSalle (Dorothy Christie), who has been hired to locate a diamond mine, is slain aboard a ship bearing Grant, Harris, and the apelike Bimi (McLaglen). A typhoon wrecks the steamer off Africa, freeing tigers and leopards.

Tom Armitage (Carroll Nye) knows of the diamond field but withholds its location—provoking threats from Mustapha. Grant rescues Mustapha from a leopard but is besieged by the sheik's mob. Help and complications involve Armitage's sister (Nora Lane); an agent disguised as an old woman; and a mystery man in smoked eyeglasses. Grant finds the diamond field in a volcano. Mustapha attacks. Government troops intervene. Harris, fleeing on horseback, falls from a cliff. Grant is cleared.

Cyril McLaglen as the apelike Bimi.

The serial is exciting in its over-complexity, with all the primitive charm that defines Mascot. Striking photography captures the desert outside Yuma, Arizona, and Levine's favorite location, Bronson Canyon, a quarry in Hollywood. Interiors were made at Los Angeles' Tec-Art Studios. Memorable touches include Miller's awakening aboard ship to see a bloodied hand dangling from an upper berth, and the finale, in which the ape-man carries away the corpse of his master into a symbolic sunset.

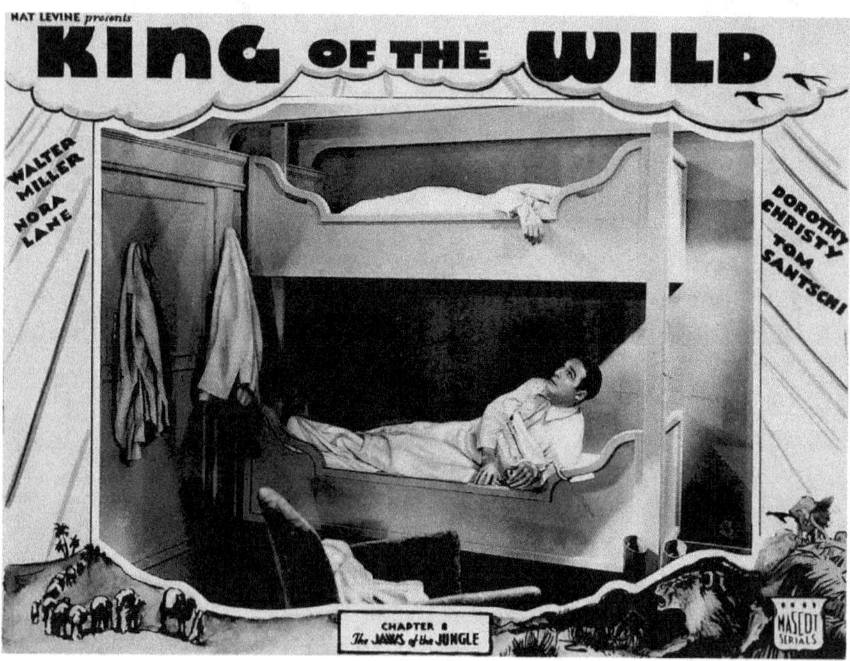

Walter Miller learns at first hand the disadvantages of being shackled to a bunk.

The Drums of Jeopardy

a.k.a. *Mark of Terror*
Tiffany Productions • 1931

In 1923, M.H. Hoffman had filmed Harold McGrath's class-war novel, *The Drums of Jeopardy*, with Wallace Beery as a vengeful Bolshevik named Boris Karlov, dispensing righteous mayhem against a family of Russia's deposed ruling class. The remake features the wonderful Warner Oland. Florence Ryerson's script differs from both book and silent film: Ryerson cannibalizes her script for Paramount's *The Return of Dr. Fu Manchu* (1930)—a star vehicle for Oland. The talking *Drums* is a melodramatic delight—as illogically exciting as a Pearl White serial. Director George B. Seitz had been a silent-screen serial master.

In Czarist Russia, scientist Boris Karlov (Oland) holds the highfalutin' Petrov family responsible for his daughter's suicide. A Petrov heirloom, a necklace known as the Drums of Jeopardy, is found in her possession. Karlov vows to return the Drums, one pendant at a time, as tokens of revenge. He becomes a ranking Bolshevik while killing off the Petrovs. Ivan Petrov (Ernest Hilliard) and nephews Nicholas and Gregor (Lloyd Hughes and Wallace MacDonald) seek the protection of American criminologist Martin Kent (Hale Hamilton). Karlov intercepts the Petrovs' ship.

Nicholas stumbles into the penthouse of Kitty Conover (June Collyer). Kitty sends her Aunt Abbie (Clara Blandick) for a doctor; Abbie entrusts the errand to a stranger—Karlov's thug, Piotr (Mischa Auer). Karlov, having strangled Ivan, poses as a doctor. Kent arrives, but Karlov escapes.

Nicholas and Gregor take shelter outside the city. Karlov commandeers an abandoned mill. Gregor—the rascal responsible for Karlov's wrathful bereavement—delivers Abbie to Karlov, who dispatches Gregor and captures Nicholas and Kitty. Kent's men lay siege. Abbie shoves Karlov to his death in a flooded cellar.

Oland specialized in Asian villains but had broadened his range with *The Jazz Singer* (1927), *Don Juan* (1926), and *The Big Gamble* (1930). After *Drums*, Oland took the lead in Fox's *Charlie Chan Carries On* (1931). Seventeen *Chan* pictures—a benevolent life sentence, given his death-in-harness—obscured Oland's history of villainy.

Drums finds in Oland a brooding if playful malevolence. June Collyer and Lloyd Hughes provide bright romantic energy. Wallace MacDonald (later a producer at Columbia) is Hughes' treacherous brother. Hale Hamilton is a stalwart detective. Mischa Auer, a young Russian, expert at eccentric roles, scores as Oland's murderous lackey. Secondary henchman Harry Semels was, like Oland, a veteran of the Pathé serials.

Hamilton and Oland establish their reciprocal antagonisms in a tense exchange of one-upsmanship—Hamilton claiming to have walked

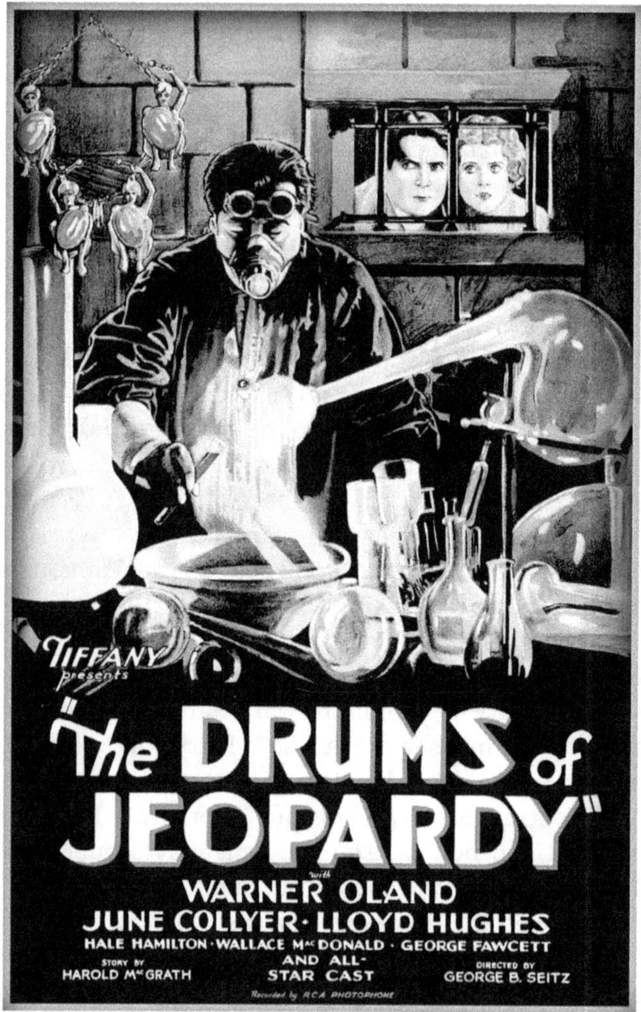

deliberately into a trap, Oland countering with sarcasm. Similarly tense exchanges between Oland and Clara Blandick serve as both comedy relief and a grim foreshadowing of the finale. (Blandick perfected that grumpy old maid presence as Tom Sawyer's overbearing Aunt Polly in two versions of Mark Twain's most famous Southern Gothic.)

The lavish texture is reminiscent of MGM's costlier productions, with imposing sets including the Petrov palace, an ocean liner, an Art Deco apartment, and an ominous mill that bears comparison with a similar property in *Frankenstein* (1931). Sounds of wind, gunfire, and thunder are artificial—faked to register on the primitive recording equipment.

George Seitz proved an able director for the talkies, with such assignments as *The Last of the Mohicans* (1935) and all but three of MGM's 16 *Hardy Family* pictures.

The Unholy Garden

Samuel Goldwyn • United Artists • 1931

"It was an interesting kind of tension we felt, working on *The Unholy Garden*," Fay Wray told us in 1989. "For all the importance that we had to each other, Ronnie Colman and Samuel Goldwyn were at odds on this particular project—not on speaking terms, for reasons that neither would explain—and Ronnie had this standing order that Mr. Goldwyn not intrude upon the set. I met with Mr. Goldwyn when I was hired, and then never heard from him again until after we had completed the principal photography."

As a team, the self-made plutocrat producer Goldwyn and the dashing matinée idol Ronald Colman had proved early on that talking pictures could become more than merely photographed stage-plays. Their demonstration was *Bulldog Drummond*, a droll high-adventure piece whose blending of words and pictures is so nearly perfect as to seem the very reason talking pictures were invented.

In silent-screen Hollywood, Goldwyn had developed a reputation as a calculating businessman of benign capitalistic instincts and fairly discriminating middlebrow tastes—an artist as keen upon nurturing artistry as upon commodifying it. He surrounded himself with creative people and inspired their finer efforts. Ronald Colman was among this select group. Moderately successful as a silent player, Coleman learned to utilize the added dimension of sound, the better to secure longevity with fickle patrons and customers in an economically unstable profession.

Bulldog Drummond had established Colman as Goldwyn's chief player. Eager—no, make that *anxious*—to build upon the bonanza, Goldwyn cast Colman in *Condemned* (1929), a grim tale of the Devil's Island penal colony; *Raffles* (1930), a comedy-melodrama about a suave crook; and *The Devil to Pay* (1930), another light melodrama. Then, Goldwyn determined he must make a Colman vehicle that would exploit the same elements that had worked so ideally in their first talker: chilling horror, comedy, romance, and artistic appeal. Goldwyn hired the eccentric but efficient team of Ben Hecht and Charles MacArthur (of the hit play, *The Front Page*) to concoct an original screenplay, *The Unholy Garden*, for the 1931 docket. A great pictorial stylist, George Fitzmaurice, was signed to direct. The Hungarian illustrator-architect-muralist Willy Pogany made the stage-influenced production designs.

As work on *Garden* commenced, Joseph M. Schenck stepped down as chief production executive at United Artists and asked Goldwyn, a part-owner of UA, to take charge. Goldwyn cranked his annual schedule accordingly from four to eight pictures, leading with *Garden*. The film was produced with Goldwyn's usual care, but the critics lambasted it so cruelly following the previews that Goldwyn withdrew the film for extensive retakes, finally releasing a modified version in October.

Fay Wray recalled: "I left for New York on a vacation, and that was when I finally had direct contact again with Mr. Goldwyn. He demanded that I must come back immediately to begin retakes. So I cut my vacation short, thanks to whatever problems Mr. Goldwyn was having.

"The opportunity to work with Ronnie Colman was a pleasure, of course, whatever the tensions may have been," added Wray. "He was a wonderfully skilled actor, and a man of genuine modesty. We became fast friends during the shooting, and we maintained that friendship over the years. A very *shielded* man, Ronnie was—didn't let out a great deal of information about himself—genial, but never garrulous. If he was outgoing to you, that meant a great deal more than it would have meant from somebody else. He was a figure of special quality."

Colman plays the fugitive Barrington Hunt. The Algerian police, believing Hunt to be bound for the desert sanctuary of Palais Royale, arrange for the notorious Mrs. Mowbry (Estelle Taylor) to set a trap. But Hunt commandeers the woman's automobile and takes her to the once-grand establishment—now in decay. The guests include the scholarly Dr. Shayne (Lawrence Grant), who had murdered three wives and uses the skull of the first as a tobacco jar; Prince Nicolai Poliakoff (Mischa Auer), a Hussar captain who had killed his sweetheart for her pearls; a Prussian Guardsman, Col. von Axt (Ulric Haupt), who swindled his government out of millions; Kid Twist (Kit Guard), a strangler; Nick-the-Goose (Henry Armetta), an international thief; and Smiley Corbin (Warren Hymer), an American hoodlum. The elderly Mme. Vollars (Lucille LaVerne) runs Palais Royale.

Aloof from the community are the aged Baron de Jonghe (Tully Marshall) and his granddaughter, Camille (Wray). The cutthroats plot against the baron, who has been promised immunity if he will return stolen securities. Hunt is greeted, meanwhile, by Smiley, a now-and-again accomplice.

When asked about the proceeds from their last job, Smiley admits, "In Tunis, y'see, I met a dame." It is decided that Hunt, as a stranger, may be able to pry the secret of the negotiables from de Jonghe. While gaining the old man's friendship, Hunt falls in love with Camille but feels unworthy of her affections. Mrs. Mowbry suspects a double-cross. Smiley seduces Mrs. Mowbry and learns that the others mean to kill Hunt and the baron, and to torture Camille. Hunt finds the stolen securities. The baron is slain. Believing Hunt the killer, Camille starts to turn Hunt over to the assassins but, swayed by love, hides him, instead.

Hunt hands to Camille the securities and orders her to hurry away: "And someday, when your eyes are shining and you meet an honest man, look at Paris for me and think of it as my wedding present." (A famous line from *Casablanca* [1942] comes to mind as a melancholy inversion: "We'll always have Paris."] Hunt and Smiley escape, dodging a hail of bullets. Smiley asks if Hunt got as much as he expected. "Much more, Smiley, and here's your share," replies Hunt, handing over the petals from a rose Camille had given to him. "I'm sorry, Smiley, but you see—I met a dame."

The consensus of history holds that *The Unholy Garden* must be the least of Colman's pictures. This simplistic dismissal takes into account some predictable elements of plotting and perhaps an overabundance of bizarre touches, but neglects to acknowledge that the production

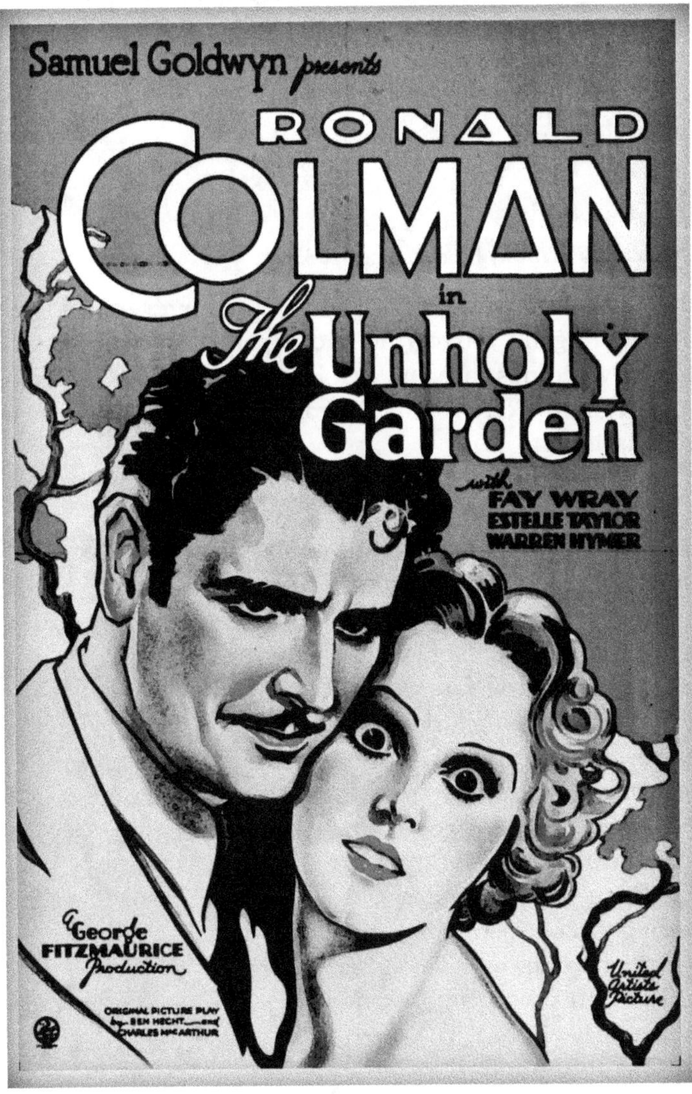

shimmers with high artistry. Not to mention that the cast in support offers up some of the most intriguing vamps and scamps, schemers and dreamers, that any devotée of melodrama could desire. *Garden* does wallow in the outré, an excess that a viewer will find either charming or offensive. The skull-as-tobacco-jar is one such example. The most effectively disturbing touch is a Christmas scene where the criminals sing carols in clashing keys and languages.

The dialogue sparkles with romance and wit. Willy Pogany's evocative settings are magnificently lighted and photographed to eerie effect. Colman's rakish sophistication is complemented beautifully by the innocence of Wray; by the crudeness of his sidekick, Warren Hymer; and by the brashness of the surprisingly vulnerable *femme fatale*, Estelle Taylor. The villains are a grand crew of seriocomic freaks and fiends under the menacing guidance of Lawrence Grant—who had provided a similarly depraved characterization as a centerpiece for *Bulldog Drummond*.

Aloha

Rogell Productions • Tiffany Productions • 1931

The fundamental horrors of estrangement and irreversible loss propel *Aloha*, Albert Rogell's harrowing and superstition-tinged remake of a 1915 gem by Thomas Ince and J.G. Hawks. Edgar G. Ulmer, just now gaining traction in Hollywood as a promising director, serves the film as Rogell's assistant.

Forbidden romance develops between a half-caste South Seas islander, Ilanu (Raquél Torres), and an American industrialist, Jimmy Bradford (Ben Lyon). Tribal custom holds that a woman who marries a white man must face some hideous fire goddess—the fate of Ilanu's mother. The tense relationship survives corporate intrigues, reversals of fortune, and family treacheries on either side of the color bar. At last the lure of tradition proves too much: Ilanu leaps to her death in a smoldering volcano—the fire goddess of ancient, or anxious, legend.

Rogell applies the same anguished intensity here with which he had distinguished *Mamba*—

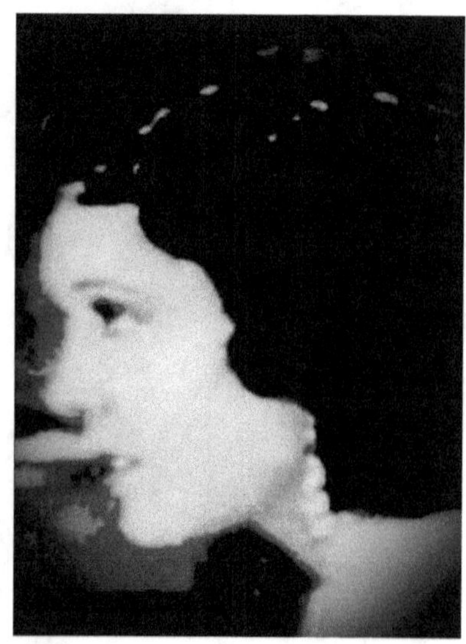

Raquel Torres

though without that picture's dominant element of villainy. Thelma Todd anchors the crucial disruptive qualities. Cast against comic type, Todd plays Ben Lyon's treacherous snob of a sister for full measure of glad-handing malice. Raquél Torres is believable as an innocent maneuvered into an awkward situation.

Otis Harlan registers well as a Harvard man whose cross-cultural marriage has left him impoverished and embittered. Dickie Moore, who also appeared briefly with Hal Roach's *Our Gang* comedies, plays the spirited child of the star-crossed couple. The seagoing settings include a famous yacht, the *Sultana*, whose owners included the robber-baron industrialists John P. Mills and E.H. Harriman.

God's Country and the Man

Trem Carr Pictures • Syndicate Pictures • 1931

So rarely are westerns of the early-talkie period shown nowadays, that each rediscovery seems fresh in its very antiquity. The truism is especially so among the Frontier Gothics—fusions of anguish with boisterous adventure. But formulas fell so solidly into place, and the talking westerns grew so plentiful, that so influential a trade journal as *The Film Daily* could dismiss the genre as "the routine blah." J.P. McCarthy's *God's Country and the Man* struck *The Film Daily* as a welcome exception. This remarkable entry prizes atmosphere over action and dispenses suspenseful deceits among protagonists and antagonists with an alarming, cold-blooded naturalism.

So much is made of the genial outlaw Stingaree Kelly—played with a vaudeville Irish brogue by George Hayes, with a broad hint of his famous "Gabby" Hayes persona of times to come—that his showy death scene rightly deprives *God's Country and the Man* of the traditional upbeat ending.

Tom Tyler is lawman Tex Malone, who is returning from a manhunt in the Texas Panhandle when pressed into a border-town assignment amidst a revolutionary uprising. He must infiltrate an outlaw settlement and bring down Livermore (Al Bridge), an untouchable gun-running racketeer. Livermore prefaces each new killing with an off-key dirge on a violin. Malone brings along Stingaree Kelly, arrested during the Panhandle assignment, for Kelly knows the territory. Malone is warned not to let his weakness for beautiful women compromise the task.

Malone flirts with Livermore's mistress, Rose (Betty Mack). Romero (Ted Adams), of the Mexican army, infiltrates the hideout but is captured. Rose reveals herself as a government agent; Livermore turns her over to the enemy faction. No sooner has Tex rescued Rose than Kelly rides up, mortally wounded, to report the slaying of Livermore.

Tom Tyler is terrific as a flawed hero. Betty Mack makes an irresistible romantic interest, bogus French accent and all. Co-scenarist Al Bridge's Livermore is a scene-stealing paranoid bully. Especially gripping is a massed confrontation with Livermore's expendable goons: as the melody of death plays, the camera pans across an array of worried faces.

The village reeks of festering corruption. A graceful mobility of cameras is unusual for the period, when each movement threatened to impose unwanted noise upon a soundtrack. Livermore's saloon, with its precipitous staircase and narrow passageways, feels more like a haunted house than a festive setting; the inmates seem perpetually on edge. A climactic gun battle is as impressive (given the time, the place, and the budget) as similar scenes in such finery as Don Siegel's *The Shootist* (1976) and Walter Hill's *Last Man Standing* (1996).

Intermezzo

Additional Titles of Interest

The following titles supply intriguing marginal context:

- *Hell Bound* (Cruze-Tiffany; 1931). Hidden passageways, mistaken identities, and a prevailing air of doom inform this gangster melodrama from *The Great Gabbo*'s James Cruze. With Leo Carillo and Lola Lane.

- *Monsters of the Deep* (Talking Picture Epics; 1931). An expedition off Baja California ends with a struggle against a 17-foot manta ray, the so-called "devil fish."

- *Hell Bent for Frisco* (Sono Art-World Wide-Thrill-O-Dramas; 1931). The gangland involvement of a banker (Edmund Burns, of 1933's *The Death Kiss*) leads to serial murder.

- *Mystery of Life: A Drama of Life as Told by Clarence Darrow* (Classic Productions & Universal Pictures; 1931). Clarence Darrow and Smith College's H.M. Parshley advance evolutionary arguments. Fancifully sculpted dinosaurs occupy a specious prehistoric setting. No creature-effects credit is given. The film arrived half a dozen years after Darrow had defended John Scopes against charges of teaching Charles Darwin's theory of evolution in defiance of Tennessee state law.

- *The Galloping Ghost* (Mascot Pictures; 1931). And what better title for a rip-snorting serial than the nickname of a celebrated athlete? And who better than Harold "Red" Grange, the Galloping Ghost himself, to tackle the title role? The gridiron adventure pivots upon gambling-racket intrigues, with a weirder essence in Theodore Lorch's portrayal of a vengeful hunchbacked brain surgeon—classic Mascot strangeness.

- *Alice in Wonderland* (Pollard Productions & Unique-Cosmos Pictures; 1931). Lewis Carroll's *Alice* tales, dating from 1865, deal as much in horror as in fantasy, what with their proto-Kafkaesque elements of disorientation, nightmarish creatures, and obsessive interest in transmogrifications and beheadings. This shoddy costume pageant is the work of Bud Pollard, who also is responsible for one of the more fascinatingly rough-edged films—1933's *The Horror*. Pollard reissued his *Alice* in 1933 to exploit popular interest in Paramount's all-star version.

- *Law of the Sea* (Monogram Pictures; 1931). Otto Brower's revenge melodrama involves a murderous rampage by schooner captain Ralph Ince. A generation later, the victims' surviving son (Rex Bell) recognizes Ince's cold-blooded laughter—a device that also figures in 1934's *West of the Divide*.

Murder at Midnight

Tiffany Productions • 1931

"It isn't murder, but an epidemic!" declares Robert Elliott in Frank R. Strayer's *Murder at Midnight*, which alternates violent death with boisterous humor.

A game of charades ends fatally. Criminologist Montrose (Hale Hamilton) takes charge. Trigger-happy host Kennedy (Kenneth Thomson) had not known the gun was loaded. A detective (Elliott) expects to find two victims—the toll reported by an anonymous caller.

Then Kennedy turns up croaked, as do two skulking servants (Alice White and Brandon Hurst). A telephone receiver proves to contain

a deadly needle. An affair becomes evident between Montrose and Mrs. Kennedy (Aileen Pringle). Montrose plots to dispose of Kennedy's meddling Aunt Julia (Clara Blandick), but the gimmick backfires and none too soon.

Comic interludes involve Clara Blandick's grouchy maiden-aunt routine and Tyrell Davis' effeminate Englishman. The opening murder is a shocker. (Screenwriter Scott Darling would retool the tale for *The Mystery of Mr. Wong* in 1939 and *The Chinese Ring* in 1947.)

Elliott and Hale Hamilton are first-rate. Alice White is a saucy maid, and Aileen Pringle is sympathetic as the conflicted wife. Brandon Hurst is the conniving but otherwise innocent butler. Strayer's light touch keeps the morbid subject matter in the service of unpredictability.

Chinatown after Dark

Action Pictures • 1931

Suspense is subordinate to frenzied pace and richness of characterization in Stuart Paton's *Chinatown after Dark*, a Yellow Peril exploitationer centered upon Carmel Myers' seductive impersonation of a Dragon Lady predator. Barbara Kent, of Harold Lloyd's *Welcome Danger*, is a spirited near-victim. Frank Mayo and Rex Lease, as adventurous brothers; Billy "Sneezer" Gilbert, as a comical detective, and

Edmund Breese, as a tragic Chinese character, help to lift the film above Action Pictures' quick-and-cheap standards.

Prince Lee Fong (Breese) had adopted the infant daughter of a fallen American comrade following an uprising in China. As the girl, Lotus (Kent), reaches womanhood, Lee Fong comprehends that she must find acceptance among her father's people. Fong, now dwelling in San Francisco, expects an inheritance via a messenger, Ralph Bonner (Mayo).

Bonner bears an ancient bejeweled dagger that has attracted thieves, including the treacherous Mme. Ying Su (Carmel Myers). Bonner and his brother, Jim (Lease), travel to meet Lee Fong. A fracas leaves Lee Fong dead and Ralph and the dagger missing. Lotus is kidnapped. Jim, framed for murder, infiltrates Ying Su's mob to buy time for a police raid that serves to rescue Lotus and Ralph. The dagger drops from a ceiling—where Ralph had thrown it during the first attack.

The Lightning Warrior

Mascot Pictures Corp. 1931

A cloaked menace, the Wolf Man, instigates Indian terrorism. Rumors persist of a lost tribe. Jimmy Carter (Frankie Darro) is orphaned in an attack. His police dog, Rin-Tin-Tin, is left at large in the confusion.

Rescues and attacks and double-crosses persist. No one can tell what citizen might be doubling as the Wolf Man. (In any Mascot serial, misleading clues abound.) The uprising proves to be the work of outlaws posing as Indians. The genuine tribesmen, indignant, emerge from hiding. Rin-Tin-Tin carries the show.

Jack L. Warner often said his favorite actor was Rin-Tin-Tin, a German Shepherd whose films of the 1920s helped to keep Warner Bros. solvent. Rinty was a war dog—rescued from a French battlefield by trainer Lee Duncan. Rinty's expressiveness remains unsurpassed. When he made *The Lightning Warrior*, the dog was 13 and growing lame; doubles helped, but Rinty still possessed the charm. He died in 1932 in the arms of a famous neighbor of Duncan's, Jean Harlow, who had become the owner of one of Rinty's first offspring.

The Lightning Warrior also showcases Frankie Darro, a champion stuntman at only age 12; Georgia Hale, casualty of a lapsed career with the advent of the talkies; and George Brent, a Broadway lead, making a screen début. Mean-looking Bob Kortman stands out among the heavies. The directors are Armand Schaefer, of Mascot's *The Galloping Ghost*, and Benjamin Kline, who worked oftener as a cameraman. The $45,000 project makes splendid use of Prudential Studio's frontier town near Kernville; a creepy tunnel in Bronson Canyon; and rented sets at Universal Pictures and Tec-Art Studio.

The Wolf Man's identity stays out of reach to the last. Producer Nat Levine enjoyed cheating on clues. The marauder is impersonated by Theodore "Ted" Lorch until a less sinister-looking individual is unmasked.

Sound is tinny, even by 1931 standards, but nonetheless heightens the sense of hovering menace. Incessant drumming (inspired, Levine said, by the jungle-telegraph percussion in 1931's *Trader Horn*) lends atmosphere. The Wolf Man's eerie outcries and the howling of the winds likewise contribute to the tension. Music figures only in the titles.

The Phantom

Action Dramas • Artclass Pictures • 1931

Alvin J. Neitz' *The Phantom*, like some distorted echo of Roland West's *The Bat Whispers*, boasts a striking similarity of angular compositions, cavernous rooms and cramped passages, and boisterous Grand Manner acting. *The Phantom* is a Mystery Farce in the tradition of *The Cat and the Canary* and the various incarnations of *The Bat*—only goofier by a landslide. Its dream-state weirdness matches *A Night of Terror* (1933) and *Sh! The Octopus* (1937) for the illusion of a rubberized reality.

The murderous Phantom taunts District Attorney Hampton (Wilfred Lucas). Brash reporter Dick Mallory (Guinn "Big Boy" Williams) interrupts a stakeout. Mallory is in love with the D.A.'s daughter, Ruth (Allene Ray), a newspaper columnist. The trail leads to the asylum of the notorious Dr. Weldon (William Gould). Accompanying Mallory and Ruth are two dimwitted servants (Bobby Dunn and Violet Knights).

An overbearing lunatic, Oscar (William Jackie), distracts Mallory with strange and disruptive behavior while Ruth is abducted to become a victim of Weldon's experiments. The servants save the day without quite comprehending the deeper urgencies. The doctor is revealed as the Phantom. All ends romantically well. Oscar gets in a creepy last word.

With two ominous old houses, loonies and skulkers enough for two or three misadventures, a memorable Scandahoovian-dialect routine by William Jackie, and Big Boy Williams' indignant reporter-hero, *The Phantom* allows nary an idle moment. The crowning touch is a top-shelf villainous presence, Sheldon Lewis, who wanders in as if from some other movie to play a mystery man of no discernible purpose other than a further touch of eerie menace.

Cowboy star-turned-sidekick Guinn Williams (the "Big Boy" monicker was bestowed by the celebrated cowboy humorist Will Rogers) fits well into the suit-and-tie role of a lovestruck newspaperman. Williams' brusque geniality and north Texas drawl should have made him a bigger name; he experienced only a tentative resurgence during the 1930s, then returned to character parts, some sympathetic and some menacing, for the long haul—right on through *The Comancheros*, in 1962.

Allene Ray makes an energetic match for Williams. She had succeeded Pearl White in 1920 as Pathé's serial queen. A squeaky voice wrecked her talkie prospects. William Gould seems a bit too normal for the mad doctor role, but he emphasizes the weirdness afoot by using a skull to demonstrate his crackpot theories. As the scared-silly maid, Violet Knights foreshadows her loopy contribution to another of Alvin J. Neitz' pictures, Ken Maynard's weird-western production of *Smoking Guns* (Universal, 1934). (Neitz also worked under the proxy names of Allan James and Alan James.) Inept chauffeur Bobby Dunn had been a player in Hal Roach's slapstick troupe. William Jackie steals the show with freakish wordplay and physical contortions—a deranged imp, at once amusing and threatening, even when administering a swift kick to Williams as a portent of greater humiliations.

A rousing jailbreak sequence—a leap from a prison wall, onto a speeding train, then onto a ladder from an airplane—appears to have come from silent-era stock footage; the same sequence is used in Chapter No. 1 of 1933's *The Whispering Shadow*.

Terror by Night

a.k.a. *The Secret Witness*

Famous Attractions • Columbia Pictures • 1931

Tense and dark-humored, designed and photographed to full Art Deco effect, Thornton Freeland's *Terror by Night* is a jewel. The source is Samuel Spewack's novel, *Murder in the Gilded Cage*. A preview drew such glowing reviews—"audience in a turmoil," said *The Hollywood Herald*—that Columbia Pictures bought the film outright for release as *The Secret Witness*.

Bert Folsom (Hooper Atchley) drives a mistress (June Clyde) to suicide, denies his wife (Rita La Roy) a divorce, and orders his bodyguard (Nat Pendleton) jailed on a false rap. Only a pet chimpanzee mourns when Folsom turns up croaked.

Lois Martin (Una Merkel) finds her lower-floor apartment invaded by a pistol-packing Casey Jones (William "Buster" Collier, Jr.), brother of the suicide. Mrs. Folsom admits to an affair with Lewis Leroy (Ralf Harolde), a friend of her husband, but they deny complicity. Another killing takes place; the ape clutches a gun. At length, Leroy admits he had triggered the weapon electronically—then kills himself with the infernal device.

The first killing seems to improve the human species. The murderer proves comparably despicable. Una Merkel courts danger in search of a solution. ZaSu Pitts is a nervous busybody, and director-turned-actor Paul Hurst is a thickheaded cop. In a fine inside joke, Pitts says she has been reading a book "about a *well*...can't quite make it out." The

book is Radcliffe Hall's *The Well of Loneliness*, a then-notorious tale of lesbianism. Buster Collier, acclaimed for King Vidor's *Street Scene*, is a tepid hero. Conviction radiates from Purnell Pratt, Ralf Harolde, athlete-actor Nat Pendleton, Australian comic Clyde Cook, and black singer-actor Clarence Muse.

The influence of *The Bat Whispers* is patent; cinematographer Robert Planck worked on both. The two films' opening shots, with the camera swooping downward along a miniature building, are very alike. Director Freeland had handled such delightful comedies as *Three Live Ghosts* and *Whoopee!* (1929–1930). On *Terror by Night*, Freeland contrasts the grim and the humorous to fine effect.

Law of the Tongs

Willis Kent Productions • Syndicate Pictures • 1931

Law of the Tongs is the most accomplished and evocative of Willis Kent's generally ragged and scandalous productions. The tong-war thriller is weirder by far than the producer's signature westerns and nowhere near as lurid as his sex-and-dope pictures disguised as social-problem dramas. Kent addressed a broad and oddly matched variety of tastes—most of them adventurous, none particularly wholesome, and all rough about the edges in terms of production values.

Law of the Tongs stands out by virtue of its better-than-fair tale of exotic menace and tangled underworld alliances. An unusual element of romantic conflict amidst treachery and murder suggests the intrigues of Warner Bros.' classier *The Hatchet Man* (1932), with the tale of a clash between ancient Asian traditions and Westernized social values. Jason Robards, a lapsed leading man in exile from Warners-First National, is excellent as a Chinese mobster who goes soft over a Caucasian dame and suffers accordingly for his perceived disloyalty to custom.

Lebanon-born Frank Lackteen provides *Law of the Tongs* with as vivid an air of menace as he had during his days as a silent-serial

Frank Lackteen (at right) menaces Phyllis Barrington and John Harron.

villain—and as a predatory figure in many talkie serials and features to come. Lackteen, very like the great mulatto actor Noble Johnson of *The Most Dangerous Game* and *King Kong*, specialized in villains of many ethnic stripes—all portrayed with scowling conviction.

Phyllis Barrington serves *Law of the Tongs* most persuasively as a street-smart innocent, stranded in a bad racket. She receives mild heroic support from John Harron, who plays an Immigration & Naturalization cop pursuing a perilous undercover assignment, only to find the disguise compromised by his interest in Barrington's

An array of Willis Kent's sleazier productions.

waiflike but resourceful character. Director Lewis D. Collins wavers between scares and sentimentality. The atmosphere radiates exotic menace—a quality emphasized and sustained by William Nobles' shadow-crossed photography.

Barrington plays Joan, a dance-hall hostess who finds herself under pressure from the seemingly destitute Doug (Harron) to quit that questionable profession. Unable to secure legitimate employment, Joan strikes up a friendship with Charlie Wong (Robards), whose secretive society traffics in slave labor by immigrants. Wong helps Joan to trace Doug to a charity haven. She is appalled to learn that Doug is an agent responsible for investigating Wong. Joan finds herself torn between sympathetic loyalties to both the crook and the lawman.

Members of Wong's tong sense Doug's mission and target him for assassination. Joan places herself in peril. Wong frees Joan but is killed by an associate (Lackteen) before Joan can summon the police.

Forgotten Horrors of 1932

The Shadow of the Eagle

Mascot Pictures Corp. • 1932

"We didn't have time to think," John Wayne told us in 1967 of his stint at low-rent Mascot Pictures. "We would put 25 reels in the can in 16 to 23 days of shooting—nights, too. They didn't hire you for acting; they wanted endurance. … [W]e didn't fool with retakes. … Your first take is your most natural and spontaneous, anyway. I loved it."

The Shadow of the Eagle, a barnstorming aviation thriller with a weird-by-nature carnival setting, marked a resurgence for Wayne, who had approached stardom at Fox Film Corp. in Raoul Walsh's widescreen western, *The Big Trail* (1930)—a premature peak, then a plunge. Agent Al Kingston brought Wayne to Mascot's Nat Levine, who was looking for a Charles Lindbergh-type leading man. Wayne signed on for three serials for a total of $2,000. Through these and a run of low-budget westerns at Warners and then Monogram Pictures, he became a star to the matinée crowd long before he attracted a mass audience.

The Shadow of the Eagle concerns a mysterious pilot's threats to an aircraft manufacturer. Aviator Gregory (Edward Hearn) accuses the company of theft. Craig McCoy (Wayne) is a stunt pilot for Gregory's

John Wayne with Little Billy Rhodes and big Ivan Linow.

carnival. A sepulchral voice, seemingly from nowhere, heralds murder. Gregory and his daughter, Jean (Dorothy Gulliver), are abducted. McCoy and a carney strongman (Ivan Linow) infiltrate a madhouse to save Gregory and Jean. A corporate chief (Walter Miller), unmasked as the menace, is killed in an escape attempt.

At 4 a.m. the day after he had signed on, Wayne traveled with Levine in a chauffeured Packard to Antelope Valley, changing into his costume and applying makeup while en route; Levine believed Wayne looked too young without cosmetic embellishments. On location by dawn, Wayne went immediately to work for an unrelieved 16 hours in primitive conditions—no trailers or tents, and sandwiches for meals.

With only one interior set, Wayne said, "We had to suggest changes of scene by changing our clothes. I got damn tired of gettin' in and out of my clothes all the time!" The experience teamed Wayne with stunt-man-actor Yakima Canutt, who became a lifelong friend and colleague.

Pioneering screenwriter Ford Beebe became a director on *Eagle*, relieved during a brief illness by B. Reeves "Breezy" Eason, who had staged the chariot race in the 1925 *Ben-Hur*. The system of alternating directors became standard serial procedure, allowing one to prepare for the next day while the other commandeered the immediate shooting. In typical Mascot fashion, the script is overcomplicated but action-packed, with first-rate stunting by Canutt, Monty Montague, and Wayne. The primitive special effects include cartoon animation for the skywriting sequences.

Interstitials

Additional Titles of Bearing

These titles serve to deepen the context:

- *Hell's House* (B.F. Ziedman Productions; 1932). In which sadistic abuses scandalize a reform school. A self-righteous do-gooder (Pat O'Brien) moonlights as a bootlegger and exploiter of youth. The film is an early star vehicle for Bette Davis, whose character interferes to provoke social reforms. The film was acknowledged by EC Comics publisher Bill Gaines as an influence upon some of the *Tales from the Crypt* yarns of the 1950s.

- *Border Devils* (Supreme-Weiss Bros. & Artclass; 1932). The ghastly Yellow Peril, a racist plot device common in Hollywood during the 1920s and 1930s, stalks the southwestern frontier. Tetsu Komai (the canine servant in 1932's *Island of Lost Souls*) plays a Chinese bandit who poisons the water table, frames Harry Carey for murder, and grabs surrounding land to smuggle explosives into Mexico.

- *Hell's Headquarters* (Action/Mayfair; 1932). Frank Mayo is a murderous safari boss stalking a trove of ivory. With Jack Mulhall and Phillips Smalley.

- *Yiskor* (Gloria Films & Judische Kunstfilm; 1932). The legend of a Jewish martyr is related with all due mayhem, suicide, debauchery, and burial alive. Pious to a fault but dour and sadistic in the extreme, the film is a talkie conversion (not a remake, but a retooling) of a 1924 Austrian silent. Amazing to discover how thoroughly steeped in torture-porn the Judæo-Christian traditions are.

- *Joseph in the Land of Egypt* (Guaranteed Pictures; 1932). And speaking of torture-porn: this Yiddish Biblical drama is as laden with supernatural terrors as with anguished piety. Jacob Greenberg infiltrates the House of Pharaoh.

- *Devil of the Matterhorn*, a.k.a. *The Devil's Rope* (Harry Revier; 1932). The title bespeaks a superstition surrounding the mortal difficulties of climbing the highest peak in the Swiss Alps. At last, the mountain assumes the aspect of a laughing Satan.

- *Gorilla Ship* (Ralph M. Like & Mayfair; 1932). The figurative gorilla here is a brutal sea captain (Ralph Ince). Wheeler Oakman provokes a mutiny that brings out the captain's more heroic nature.

- *Isle of Paradise* (Adolph Pollak; 1932). *Goona-Goona*-style travelogue sets sail for the Dutch East Indies, whose exotic diversions include a Balinese cremation ceremony.

- *The Jungle Killer* (Century Productions; 1932). Explorer Carveth Wells argues against the ruling-class custom of big-game hunting. Zulus mutilate their lips for cosmetic effect. Trigger-happy hunters are killed, here, by an elephant and, there, by a lion.

- *The Last Mile*, a.k.a. *All the World Wondered* (KBS Film & World Wide; 1932). Condemned killer Preston Foster engineers a prison-break massacre. The shattering finale finds Foster walking deliberately into a barrage.

- *Exposure* (Premiere-Tower; 1932). A maniac-killer case triggers this tale of big-city newspaper rivalries, with an indictment of the tabloids' voyeuristic scandal-mongering habits. Walter Byron is a boozy reporter, burly Nat Pendleton the maniac.

- *Klondike* (Monogram Pictures; 1932). Madness and romantic intrigues in Alaska: ill-fated Thelma Todd plays the fiancée of invalid genius Jason Robards, who conspires to murder surgeon Lyle Talbot with an electrical device.

- *Virgins of Bali* (Imperial Pictures; 1932). Strictly educational, of course. The tradepaper *Variety* called this one "a bust picture," inferring ogler appeal. A Balinese cremation ceremony lends morbid interest.

- *The King Murder* (Chesterfield; 1932). Homicide cop Conway Tearle has an awkward interest in the slaying of blackmailer Dorothy Revier. The weapon proves to be a poison-tipped phonograph needle.

- *False Faces* (KBS Film & World Wide; 1932). Crooked surgeon Lowell Sherman performs paralyzing face-lifts. Maimed patient Nance O'Neil murders the quack after his trial ends in an acquittal.

- *The Face on the Barroom Floor* (Aubrey Kennedy & Criterion Pictures; 1932). Hugh Antoine D'Arcy's narrative poem about the toll of drunkenness informs a severe melodrama of human wreckage and blood vengeance. *The Mummy*'s Bramwell Fletcher, as a derelict at large in a speakeasy, relates the grisly heart-wrencher.

- *Kriss*, a.k.a. *Goona-Goona: An Authentic Melodrama of the Isle of Bali* (André Roosevelt & Armand Denis; 1932). And yes, there is a valid reason why the culture refers to Third World expeditionary thrillers as *Goona-Goona* pictures. This is it. *Kriss* (a term for dagger) is hardly the first of its kind, but it is definitive, like 1930s *Ingagi*, in having registered a popular impression. A drug known as Goona-Goona is an erotic stimulant, administered by a tribal sorcerer. The story concerns a taboo romance and a struggle between native royalty and the laboring class.

- *The Unwritten Law* (Majestic Pictures; 1932). The backstage Hollywood thriller features Lew Cody as a scheming producer menaced by a vengeful electrician wielding a high-wattage arc-lamp. Practically everyone has a score to settle; a murder case yields any number of suspects.

- *With Williamson Beneath the Sea: Adventures among the Mysteries and Monsters of the Deep* (Principal Distributing; 1932). J. Ernest Williamson (1881–1966), pioneer of undersea photography, had launched the Submarine Film Corp. in 1915 with *Thirty Leagues under the Sea*, in which he can be seen knifing a shark. His adaptation of Jules Verne's *Twenty Thousand Leagues under the Sea* followed in 1916—then, in 1917, *The Submarine Eye*, from Williamson's original story. Additional pictures about shipwrecks, sunken treasure, and fantastic creatures led to three years' hired-gun work on MGM's *The Mysterious Island* (1929), another Verne takeoff—which wound up using none of Williamson's undersea footage.

  For *With Williamson Beneath the Sea*, the artist chose the Bahamas as a shooting region. The documentary includes bits of Williamson's earlier productions, including the first undersea color footage from 1920. An attack by a gigantic octopus climaxes the film, which Sol Lesser acquired as a Principal-Adventure title. A Library of Congress restoration dates from the 1990s.

The Monster Walks

Ralph M. Like, Ltd. • Action Pictures • 1932

The establishing scenes of Frank R. Strayer's *The Monster Walks* would do credit to some silent-screen German classic: a shrouded corpse lies in a candlelit room while lightning flashes, winds howl, and thunder rumbles. There enters the movies' most sinister housekeeper—hatchet-faced Martha Mattox, who had established the role in Universal's *The Conflict* (1921) and gave it its most celebrated exposition in *The Cat and the Canary* (1927). Elsewhere, two gaunt connivers, Sheldon Lewis and Mischa Auer, plot mayhem. The scream of a maddened ape arises. The balance among chill-inducing images can only prove too delicate to sustain.

Robert Ellis' screenplay soon betrays itself as a riff, none too inventive, upon *The Cat and the Canary*. Overfamiliarity blunts the edge. The ape proves to be a chimpanzee—a menace when angered, with formidable teeth and a vitriolic temperament, but typed even this early as a comic-relief creature in jungle pictures and juvenile comedies. Strayer,

though an able director, is hard-pressed to overcome such handicaps. There are scattered effective touches, nonetheless.

Upon arriving home from Europe, Ruth Earlton (Vera Reynolds) learns of the death of her father, a scientist. She and her fiancé, Ted Clayton (Rex Lease), hasten to the estate, whose inmates include Ruth's paralytic Uncle Robert (Lewis); the housekeeper, Mrs. Krug

(Mattox); and Mrs. Krug's strangely intense son, Hanns (Auer). The shrieks of a caged ape remind Ruth why she had left. Her father's will favors Ruth—who finds herself under attack.

Mrs. Krug turns up slain in Ruth's bed. Robert, near death, confesses to a plot that had caused Hanns—secretly his son—to strangle Mrs. Krug while intending to kill Ruth. The schemers had sought to claim the estate and place the blame upon the ape. Hanns, meanwhile, lashes the creature to a frenzy. Ted rescues Ruth as the ape makes short work of Hanns.

Mischa Auer, typecast as an eccentric menace (his specialty in droll comedy had yet to develop), offers redeeming touches. His creepy, off-key rendition of Brahms' "Lullaby" is an inside joke, in that Auer was a grandson of the great violinist Leopold Auer. Vera Reynolds, a lapsed star of Cecil B. DeMille's troupe, appears hardly so young and innocent as the script would have it. (Reynolds was the wife of screenwriter Ellis.)

Willie "Sleep 'n' Eat" Best, the black comedian, works wonders with a role that is nonetheless an indefensible stereotype. In a damnably racist excuse for a denouèmént, Best professes to perceive a family resemblance in the ape. Better prospects for Best lay ahead, including a team-comedy hitch with Bob Hope on *The Ghost Breakers* (1940). Hope often characterized Best as his favorite acting partner.

Action Pictures merged with Mayfair Pictures soon thereafter. Another murderous chimpanzee figures in Majestic Pictures' *Curtain at Eight* (1933).

Murder at Dawn

Big Four Film Corp. • 1932

Neither sequel nor follow-up, Richard Thorpe's science-fictional *Murder at Dawn* only *seems* to suggest a companionship with *Murder at Midnight* and only looks like a variant of *The Monster Walks*, what with its Old Dark House setting and Martha Mattox and Mischa Auer more or less repeating their roles.

Barry Barringer's screenplay opens with a backlash against the predatory Wall Street figures who had triggered the Great Depression—a favorite target among the Poverty Row studios—and then suggests that a bold experiment to harness solar power might lead to mass destruction. One Prof. Farrington (Frank Ball) is the scientist responsible. Wall Street insiders wants to use the invention for manipulative stock-market gain. Judge Folger (Phillips Smalley), a friend of Farrington, makes this accusation, warning the professor in the process. Meanwhile, Farrington's daughter, Doris (Josephine

BIG 4 FILM CORPORATION presents
JOSEPHINE DUNN
JACK MULHALL
MURDER AT DAWN
with
CRAUFORD KENT • MARTHA MATTOX
MARJORIE BEEBE • PHILLIPS SMALLEY
MISCHA AUER
Directed by
Richard Thorpe
Supervised by
Burton King
BIG

Dunn), and her fiancé, Danny (Jack Mulhall), approach the inventor's mountain hideaway to seek his permission to marry.

Farrington's laboratory, crammed with weird machinery, is attended by a spooky housekeeper (Mattox) and her skulking son, Henry (Auer). An intruder douses the lights. A blinding beacon cuts through the gloom. Doris finds Folger dead and Farrington vanished. The (apparent) bodies of Farrington and Henry go missing. A distinguished-looking stranger (J. Crauford Kent) arrives and takes charge. Henry holds Farrington captive; sunrise will trigger the lethal ray unless the professor reveals the formula. Henry takes a fatal fall. Danny smashes the infernal device. The stranger is exposed as a Wall Street speculator.

Studio chief John R. Freuler had started the Theatre Comique in Milwaukee in 1905 and five years later organized the American Film Co. In January of 1930, he set up Big Four Film Corp. to supply small-town theatres with westerns starring Buzz Barton and Bob Custer. *Murder at Dawn* is Big Four's only non-western—a release so successful that Freuler Film Associates was formed to produce an intended series of 18 Monarch melodramas. (See also: *The Savage Girl.*) The company disbanded in 1933, its ambitious program abandoned amidships.

Alabama newspaperman Barringer had acted in the silents opposite such stars as Mary Fuller and Dorothy Phillips. By 1917, he had become a screenwriter and carried on well into the 1930s. His curious fusion of science fiction and Mystery Farce for *Murder at Dawn* (with lowbrow comedy by Marjorie Beebe and Eddie Boland) receives an uninspired interpretation from director Thorpe. Unusual sets and shadowy photography allow for some unnerving moments; the solar-power device is the work of Kenneth Strickfaden, the engineering wizard from Santa Monica who had created the equipment seen in *Frankenstein* (1931).

Jack Mulhall and Josephine Dunn, both demoted from Warners, provide spirited portrayals. J. Crauford Kent delivers his often-repeated specialty as the unsuspected culprit (see also: *Sinister Hands,* coming right up).

Sinister Hands

Willis Kent Productions • 1932

A left-handed assailant (hence the title's double-entendre pun) uses a dagger to dispatch geezery old Richard Lang (Phillips Smalley) during a séance. Everyone present is a southpaw. Charlatan Swami Yomurda (Mischa Auer) had bamboozled the adulterous Mrs. Lang (Lillian West). Judge McLeod (J. Crauford Kent) had shared a grim confidence with Lang. The butler, ex-convict Lefty Lewis (Fletcher Norton), proposes to identify the killer but turns up slain. Detective Devlin (Jack Mulhall) exposes the judge, who acknowledges a grudge against Lang—and then swallows a draught of poison.

Willis Kent usually made cheapskate westerns. *Sinister Hands'* impressive setting is a rental space at Talisman Studios. The film makes strong use of Jack Mulhall's Irish pep and Mischa Auer's exotic air. Kent hired Auer to re-create the role of Swami Yomurda on a more menacing note in *Sucker Money.*

Director Armand Schaefer had joined the Mack Sennett comedy troupe in 1924 as a technical hand, then joined Action Pictures as an assistant. Kent engaged Schaefer in 1931. The director soon landed at Mascot but maintained ties with Kent. Schaefer later produced Gene Autry's westerns, then joined Autry in television production.

Creepy atmosphere is lacking. Comedy issues from Jimmy Burtis, as Mulhall's dim assistant. Phillips Smalley, a star-turned-director at silent-era Universal, gives a memorably nasty performance. The identity of the murderer holds no surprise: Mulhall mentions that the guilty party must be above suspicion—a sure tip-off, when Crauford Kent is in the house.

The Midnight Patrol

C.C. Burr • Monogram Pictures • 1932

The striking quality of *The Midnight Patrol*, an exercise in lurking terror, lies in a trio of willowy beauties, fast fading from prominence. Petite Betty Bronson had been chosen at the age of 17 by J.M. Barrie for the title role in Paramount's 1924 *Peter Pan*. Mary Nolan, formerly Imogene "Bubbles" Wilson of *The Ziegfeld Follies*, had starred at Universal and MGM, only to run afoul of an underworld scandal. Edwina Booth's savage beauty in MGM's African epic, *Trader Horn* (1931), had caused a sensation—but left her besieged with rumors of

an exotic disease contracted during the *Horn* safari. She was caught up, as well, in an adultery suit involving the actor Duncan Renaldo, also of the *Horn* ensemble. Booth fulfilled a contract with Mascot Pictures during 1931–1932, then sought anonymity—provoking inaccurate rumors of her death.

Only Bronson seems at ease, here, with the microphones. She plays Ellen Grey, anticipating a reunion with her sister, Joyce Greeley (Booth). Joyce is murdered upon completing a jail sentence. Reporter Johnny Martin (Regis Toomey) witnesses the killing. Ellen is unaware.

Martin thwarts an attempt to kidnap Ellen. Imprisoned murderer Dummy Black (Mischa Auer), a deaf-mute, may harbor a clue. Another woman (Nolan) pretends to be Joyce. At stake is a cache of incriminating papers. Martin and a detective (Robert Elliott) smoke out the killer.

A silent-picture aura persists. Director Christy Cabanne had been a protégé of D.W. Griffith at Biograph. Cinematographer Louis Physioc was a pioneer of special effects. The writers were veterans of comedy. More in tune with the 1930s is Regis Toomey's wisecracking manner. The Art Deco settings suggest a persistent anxiety. Comedy relief issues from slapstick ace Snub Pollard, prissy Franklin Pangborn, and Educational Pictures' resident funnyman, Ray Cooke. Mischa Auer's weird manner is distinct from his turns in *The Monster Walks*, *Murder at Dawn*, and *Sinister Hands*. Robert Elliott is in his element as a taciturn detective.

Betty Bronson, left, Mary Nolan, and Edwina Booth.

Strangers of the Evening

a.k.a. The Missing Corpse • The Hidden Corpse
Quadruple Film Corp. • Tiffany Productions • 193)

H. Bruce "Lucky" Humberstone's blackly funny *Strangers of the Evening* anticipated a trend that has lasted. Its funereal shenanigans were deemed tasteless in 1932 by many critics and would-be censors. The spirit prevailed, however, when mid-century popular tastes embraced the sardonic likes of *Arsenic and Old Lace* and *The Loved One*. And where would David Lynch, Terry Zwigoff, Peter Jackson, and Quentin Tarantino be in the new millennium without the crowd-pleasing element of morbid wit? The flighty manner of ZaSu Pitts (mistakenly billed here as Sazu) is perfect for *Strangers'* convulsive approach to maudlin matters, and perennial pipsqueak Lucien Littlefield is fittingly oblivious to the mayhem.

Frank Daniels (Littlefield) objects to the engagement of his daughter, Ruth (Miriam Seegar), and Dr. Raymond Everette (Theodor von Eltz). Everette keeps a laboratory in a mortuary—where a corpse identified as Daniels soon arrives. A ghastly apparition terrifies a novice undertaker, Tommy (Harold Waldridge). Detective Brubacher (Eugene Pallette) is flabbergasted. An amnesiac citizen reports a murder, only to be booked as a witness under the name of Richard Roe. Everette surprises mortician Chandler (Warner Richmond) in the act of disposing of bloodied clothing. Sybil (Pitts), a nervous scrubwoman who had befriended the amnesiac, becomes involved.

Exhumation finds Daniels' casket occupied by the corpse of politician Clark McNaughton—or so Chandler claims, implicating deceased crook Jack King. Everette and Tommy hijack a mob truck containing the coffin, then take the undertaker and his accomplices to Brubacher. The body in the casket is that of Jack King; the switch involves a political scandal.

Richard Roe proves to be Daniels; he had been accosted and left for dead, then taken by passersby to the mortuary where, after a snooze on a slab, he had awakened and spooked Tommy. In a happy ending against all macabre odds, Daniels accepts Everette as a worthy son-in-law and embraces Sybil.

Lucien Littlefield and ZaSu Pitts.

H. Bruce Humberstone, whose directing career begins here, had worked from age 19 as a script clerk, an assistant cameraman, an assistant director, and an actor. Having assisted 36 leading directors, he had absorbed their techniques. The critical attention paid to *Strangers of the Evening* established Humberstone as a formidable talent. His dozens of big assignments include *If I Had a Million* (1932), *I Wake Up Screaming* (1942), *Wonder Man* (1945), and *Fury at Furnace Creek* (1948).

Tiffany enlisted Arthur Edeson as camera chief—the cinematographer of *The Thief of Baghdad* (1924), *The Bat* (1926), *Frankenstein* (1931), *The Maltese Falcon* (1941), *Casablanca* (1942), and many others. Edeson's mastery of lighting and composition merges gracefully with Humberstone's pacing. Edeson characterized the genre as "perfect [for] strange camera angles and tricky lighting effects."

ZaSu Pitts flutters wide-eyed through the ordeal. Her mannerisms convulsed audiences and once prompted W.C. Fields to admonish a girl who wanted to quit school with: "Do you want to grow up to be like

ZaSu Pitts?" Erich von Stroheim had cast Pitts strikingly in tragic parts in the monumental *Greed* (1925) and *The Wedding March* (1929). The public preferred her humorous aspect.

Lucien Littlefield, put-upon but indignant, makes a splendid match for Pitts. Robust Eugene Pallette is fine as a grouchy detective, and Harold Waldridge lends amusement as a nervous apprentice undertaker.

The Blonde Captive

North Western Australian Expedition Syndicate • Imperial Distributing Corp. • Columbia Pictures • 1932

The Blonde Captive, a cruel and exploitative documentary-styled account of life in the Australian Outback, finds network news commentator Lowell Thomas relating his credulous blowhard impressions of a peculiar expedition. A physician, Paul Withington of Harvard University, and an archaeologist, Clifton Childs, seek to determine whether any remnant of the Neanderthal has survived.

The gawkers' holiday ranges the Pacific en route to Australia. The film revels in particular in Withington's vivisection of a sea turtle and a dugong (or sea cow), an oceanic mammal. Concentrating their scholarly attention upon Australian Aborigines who have been herded onto a reservation, the meddling white-supremacist eggheads at last pronounce one man to resemble a Neanderthal. Yes, anybody who lives long enough winds up looking like a monkey, to paraphrase Clarence

Williams and/or Milton Brown. The adventure peaks with the purported shock of finding a white woman living with a cave-dwelling Aboriginal husband and their blond child; it develops that the woman had survived the wreck of her original husband's pearling schooner and was taken in by the oppressed natives. She rejects the explorers' offer to take her back to civilization.

Columbia Pictures, teetering at the time along the edge of Poverty Row, acquired *The Blonde Captive* upon receiving evidence of lucrative roadshow distribution by William Pizor's Imperial brand. An assortment of versions seem to exist, given discrepancies between published descriptions from 1932 and our viewings in times more recent, during research on behalf of the American Film Institute.

Get That Girl!

Richard Talmadge Productions • Mercury Pictures • 1932

Stalkers follow Ruth Dale (Shirley Grey) to a train station. A passenger named Dick (Richard Talmadge) admires her from a distance. The menacing figures order Dick evicted from the train, the better to nab Ruth. An inheritance is at stake. Dick steals a police motorcycle and follows the hoodlums to the sanitarium of Dr. Sandro Tito (Fred Malatesta), whose crackpot experiments have left any number of women dead. Tito has ghastly plans for Ruth.

Dick is captured, then rescued by Tito's lustful wife (Geneva Mitchell) from a poison-gas barrage. The police arrive. Dick hijacks a prowl car and crashes through the gates of the sanitarium. Dick knocks Tito through a window—and into a pack of ravenous dogs.

German-born Richard Talmadge (*né* Sylvester Alphonse Metz, a.k.a Mettezetti) was raised an acrobat in his family's tradition. He leapt from circus stardom into the movies with a four-story plunge in Edwin Thanhouser's serial, *The Million-Dollar Mystery* (1914). He and his three brothers soon moved to Hollywood, where stuntmen were in demand. Dashing and boyish, Talmadge proved a quick study at filmmaking—particularly from working alongside the dashing and athletic Douglas Fairbanks—and in 1922 he combined stunting with acting in his own production of *Taking Chances*. Some 30 original silent-screen productions followed, but the talkies posed an obstacle in light of Talmadge's soft, high-pitched voice and his Germanic-Italianate accent.

He retrenched in stunt assignments while developing skills as a pace-conscious director, a talent that would serve him into the midcentury. He also produced and starred in a dozen talkies for his own family-based company, *Get That Girl!* among them. His perils here are absurd and horrific—the most unusual and obscure of all Talmadge's pictures.

An array of Richard Talmadge's stunt-driven pictures.

Old-school director (and major-studio screenwriter) George Crone and Poverty Row scenarist Charles Condon apply a cartoonish ferocity. The cast features Paramount contractée Shirley Grey as the endangered blonde innocent; dark-haired temptress Geneva Mitchell, usually associated with Columbia Pictures; and tall, dark Fred Malatesta, a veteran actor from Italy. Carl Stockdale is memorable as the chief plotter. Lloyd Ingraham, as a victim of Malatesta's experiments, retains a silent-screen style. Most of the heavies, cops, and bit players are of a more amateurish manner.

Death-defying stunts are the chief attraction, with a wild motorcycle ride, some Tarzan-style swinging from trees, a car crash through steel gates and into a building, and mob-scene fights. The grim climax, with Malatesta falling amidst the dogs, anticipates that of RKO's classic *The Most Dangerous Game*, which was released several months later. There is a major loose end: Ingraham's servant character seems intent upon helping Shirley Grey to escape, but the reasoning goes unresolved. The greater concern is with a sustained frenzy, ably captured by cinematographers Harry Jackson (later of 20th Century-Fox) and Jack Stevens, brother of the director and camera artist George Stevens. Much of the photography has a hurried look, however, and the nighttime exteriors are murky.

White Zombie

Halperin Productions • United Artists • 1932

Sporting the most resonant title of all such films of the Depression years, the Halperin Bros.' production of *White Zombie* descends from a popular craze for Afro-Caribbean superstition that had begun in 1929 with the introduction of the term *zombie* via a credulous book about Haitian *vodun*, or voodoo, William Seabrook's *The Magic Island.* The concept reached the stage via Kenneth Webb's New York production of *Zombie*, which opened in February of 1931—coinciding with another supernaturally conceived setter of trends, Universal Pictures' *Dracula*—and ran for 21 performances. In March of 1931, Webb threatened to sue filmmaking brothers Edward and Victor Hugo Halperin, who had announced a movie called *White Zombie*. The bluff failed, for the term was in the public domain of indigenous folklore.

Victor Halperin and Garnett Weston composed the script with technical advice from Marine Sgt. Faustin Wirkus, former administrator of La Gonave, an island off Haiti. (Wirkus' film, *Voodo* [*sic*], is discussed elsewhere in this collection.) With a budget of almost $65,000—bankrolled primarily by Sherman Krellberg's Amusement Securities Corp. and independent producer Phil Goldstone—the Halperins delivered *White Zombie* for a summer-of-1932 release. They had an established star, Bela Lugosi, flush with success from Universal's *Dracula* and *Murders in the Rue Morgue*, and a lapsed star of the silent pictures, Madge Bellamy, seeking a resurgence.

Director Victor Halperin and line producer Edward Halperin had come to Hollywood early in the 1920s. Victor, an alumnus of the universities of Wisconsin and Chicago, was a veteran of the stage. Edward was a graduate of Northwestern University. Their dozen silents (both independently and for First National, Inspiration-UA, and Vitagraph) had dealt primarily in big-city melodrama, typified by *Dance Magic* (1927). None of these early efforts bears any thematic resemblance to *White Zombie*, save for a core of Victorian romanticism.

The brothers analyzed successful pictures to establish structural formulas. They could not help but notice the success of *Dracula*, *Frankenstein*, and Paramount's *Dr. Jekyll and Mr. Hyde*, significant exceptions to their observation that most new pictures were overburdened with dialogue. Upon deciding to limit dialogue to 15% of a scenario, the Halperins pruned many pages from *White Zombie*—achieving a brisk smoothness in a straightforward rendering of a fairytale theme.

Lacking the major-studio connections they had enjoyed during the 1920s, on their own in a depressed economy and the tough new world of the talkies, the Halperins rented an office at RKO-Pathé Studio in Culver City and reconciled themselves to the financially constricted parameters of Poverty Row.

Speed and economy allowed for spectacular production values through proper use of settings, photography, and special effects: planning was the key. Rented shooting space at Universal provided a wealth of exotic sets. The Howard Anderson Co., an independent effects facility at Metropolitan Studio, made glass shots and optical effects. Art director Ralph Berger was a master at causing big sets to look even bigger.

Arthur Martinelli's photography is of a major-league calibre; he was intent upon leaving a favorable impression within the profession as the Depression, grinding through a third year, threatened the very industry. Credentials notwithstanding—with major-studio assignments

A Broadway opening for White Zombie.

dating from the infancy of cinema—Martinelli had become most affordable to the Poverty Row companies.

Principal photography required 11 days. A second unit filmed exteriors away from Universal. Second cameraman was J. Arthur "Jockey" Feindel, a former illustrator-designer. Assistants were Charles Bonhy and Enzo Martinelli, Arthur's nephew. Enzo told us in 1989: "I was lucky. ... [M]y only picture that year. I really needed that $30 or $40 a week.

"All the night shots were made night-for-night," Enzo continued. "My uncle always made sure to recognize the sources of the light. ... In so many shows today, they just ignore the light sources. ... [H]e always gave [the indoor sets] a little scope. ... He kept the actors well into the set, not back against the walls. The sets were nicely lighted for depth and mood."

In a picture noted for its otherwise sparse dialogue, one curious scene disposes of much narrative exposition in a five-minute take: a missionary (played by Joseph Cawthorn) explains zombiism in terms of the Hatian criminal code. The scene foreshadows Alfred Hitchcock's long takes with a mobile camera in *Rope* (1948). Victor Halperin bridged reel endings and beginnings by bringing players and objects near the lens to cause a fade-to-black effect. In this sequence, Joseph Cawthorn and leading man John Harron begin speaking over a near-black screen (Harron's back is against the lens.) The camera moves to cover the action until Harron again blocks the lens. The closing

lines come from a black screen. This dialogue has an improvisational quality, in contrast to the measured readings elsewhere.

Bound for their wedding in the mountains of Haiti, Neil Parker (Harron) and Madeline Short (Bellamy) encounter a crossroads burial—a superstition about supposed protection from ghouls. A menacing stranger appears (Lugosi, as "a man they call Murder"), followed by six ghostly shapes. The coachman (Clarence Muse) cries out, "Zombies!" and hastens his horses. The stranger snatches a scarf from Madeline.

The coach reaches the Beaumont mansion. The driver explains the nature of zombies—corpses resurrected as laborers.

Dr. Bruner (Cawthorn) arrives to conduct the wedding. Neil, a bank clerk in Port-au-Prince, has brought Madeline from America. A shipboard acquaintance, wealthy Charles Beaumont (Robert Frazer), had insisted the wedding take place at his plantation. Bruner distrusts Beaumont.

Beaumont has hired Murder Legendre to kidnap Madeline. Legendre insists that Beaumont cannot win Madeline unless she is made a zombie. Hence Bela Lugosi's famous line: "There *is* no other way!"

Madeline rejects Beaumont, who subjects her to Legendre's potion. Legendre, applying flame and the purloined scarf to a waxen effigy, brings about Madeline's apparent death. Neil's mind snaps. Legendre and Beaumont rob Madeline's grave. Neil enlists Bruner.

Beaumont objects to Madeline's revival as a soulless creature. Legendre poisons Beaumont with the zombie-making formula. Neil and Bruner approach Legendre's castle. Legendre finds Madeline stopped by a hooded figure when she is ordered to kill Neil, who rallies in time to prevent her from a suicidal leap. Legendre's zombies advance; the masked figure—Bruner—fells Legendre. The zombies topple from a ledge. Legendre rallies to threaten Neil and Bruner.

Beaumont, almost paralyzed, grapples with Legendre, and both take a fatal plunge. Madeline wakes, as if from a dream.

A dominant image is the hypnotic glow of Lugosi's eyes, as emphasized in the advertising campaign. Enzo Martinelli ascribed this quality to the simplest of special effects: Arthur Martinelli made a cardboard stencil, two eye-shapes, and shot light through it onto Lugosi's face.

Lugosi appeared aloof to the company, according to Enzo Martinelli's reflections—the actor suffered from chronic sciatica, and the pain often caused him to seem withdrawn—but invested full grand-manner intensity and a characteristically rich, sardonic delivery in a portrayal of thoroughgoing, self-possessed evil. A hawklike job of makeup, with a widow's-peak hairline and a sparse beard, completes the illusion. This aspect, and the appearance of the zombies, represent the work of *Frankenstein*'s Jack Pierce and a free-lance cosmetician, Carl Axcelle.

Lugosi later would speak bitterly of compensation of $500 for a week's work, professing astonishment at the picture's financial success. Over the years, his accounts of the figure varied. Such statements must be taken with the proverbial grain of salt: Madge Bellamy recalled being paid $5,000 for her supporting role, and of course Lugosi was the star player, at a peak of ticket-selling popular recognition.

Dr. Clarence Muse, the composer-singer-actor who portrays the coachman, once told us that Lugosi rewrote some scenes and directed some retakes, Muse's scenes among them. A different actor, stockier than Muse, appears in all but the scenes of dialogue and close-ups. The first actor had been hired because he could drive a team, but his voice was inadequate. Muse was no coachman—especially not on a winding road at night—so the performances were intercut.

Madge Bellamy, with silent-screen eyes that could express emotions beyond the reach of dialogue, found her voice ill-suited to the microphones. *White Zombie* may have balked her hopes of a comeback, although she fared well in *Charlie Chan in London* and the Buck Jones serial *Gordon of Ghost City* (both from 1934). Hardly the shy type (the role of Madeline notwithstanding), Bellamy was a superb horsewoman from Texas' hill country, known for a turbulent romantic life.

John Harron, a leading man of the silents and younger brother of D.W. Griffith's star player Robert Harron, also found the talkers an obstacle. By the middle 1930s, John had become a contract bit player at Warners. Robert Frazer proved ideal for *White Zombie*'s Byronic role of an unprincipled rogue who develops a tragically sympathetic streak. Stage veteran Joseph Cawthorn, deploying a vaudeville-Germanic accent, provides pragmatism and helpful comic relief. Tiny Dan Crimmins, another trouper from Vaudeville, appears in blackface as a helpful witch doctor. The venerable stage actor Brandon Hurst is memorable as a faithful-unto-death servant to Frazer's Beaumont.

Most impressive of the zombies—all persuasively cadaverous—is six-foot-six, 250-pound Frederick Peters. His intimidating Chauvin is of a piece with Peters' enactments of Goliath and other giant warriors in scriptural epics; he had been in the movies since 1916.

Much of the expensive look of *White Zombie* derives from Ralph Berger's set designs and Conrad Tritschler's glass paintings. Berger adapted existing sets to appear unique—a talent he would use often in such serials as Universal's *Flash Gordon* (1936). The main hall of the castle is a rearrangement of the Castle Dracula hall, augmented for long shots by glass paintings. A dizzying verandah includes the broad stairway from *Dracula* and pillars and props from 1923's *The Hunchback of Notre Dame*, among other productions. Tritschler added further architectural details, mountains, and skies, and Howard Anderson matted in the ocean. The wine cellar from *Frankenstein* and a dungeon set, which Universal was flooding for a Tom Mix starrer, *My Pal, the King*, were utilized—torrents and all—for perilous underground corridors. The exterior of the Beaumont mansion is a Spanish hacienda set, half-buried in foliage. Some interiors contain walls from *Dracula*. The sugar mill where the zombies toil is a lofty mass of girders, catwalks, and windlasses, used originally in *Uncle Tom's Cabin* (1927). Seashore scenes combine authentic coastline vistas with a glass painting of the castle. Marvelous mediæval furnishings from *Hunchback* and the monumental chairs from *The Cat and the Canary* (1927) grace the castle. A mountainous roadway is the backlot trail once traversed by Dracula's coach. Arthur Martinelli framed scenes through trees and architectural details and introduced hovering shadows.

Optical effects include the unusual (at the time) touch of superimposing main-title credits over the roadway burial. Elsewhere, a diagonally split screen shows the mesmerized girl on the balcony and her lover on the shore, both superimposed upon the glass shot of the castle.

Long silences are shattered by disturbing noises—the screeching of vultures, the scraping of a coffin as it slides into a crypt, the grinding of the mill—and occasional bursts of music from orchestrator Abe Meyer, a casualty of the obsolescence of theatre orchestras after the collapse of the silent-picture industry. He had formed Meyer Synchronizing Service to supply scores to independent talkie producers. The tribal-style drumming and chants were composed for the film by Guy Bevier Williams, a specialist in ethnic music at Universal. Also commissioned was a Spanish *jota* by Xavier Cugat, later to become famous for his fusion of big-band jazz with Latin rhythms; this work is particularly unnerving in sequences where Harron's Neil pursues the vision of his lost fiancée. Nathaniel Den's tragic spiritual, "Listen to the Lamb," yields a weird effect as hummed by alternating male and female choruses. *Agitatos* from Meyer's silent-film library compound the urgency elsewhere.

E.W. Hammons, of Educational Film Exchange and World Wide Pictures, had intended to distribute *White Zombie*. Difficulties arose from Universal's demands for overdue rental fees. Investors Krellberg and Goldstone hovered, impatient. An unexpected rescue came from product-hungry United Artists—a coup for such a small film. *White Zombie*

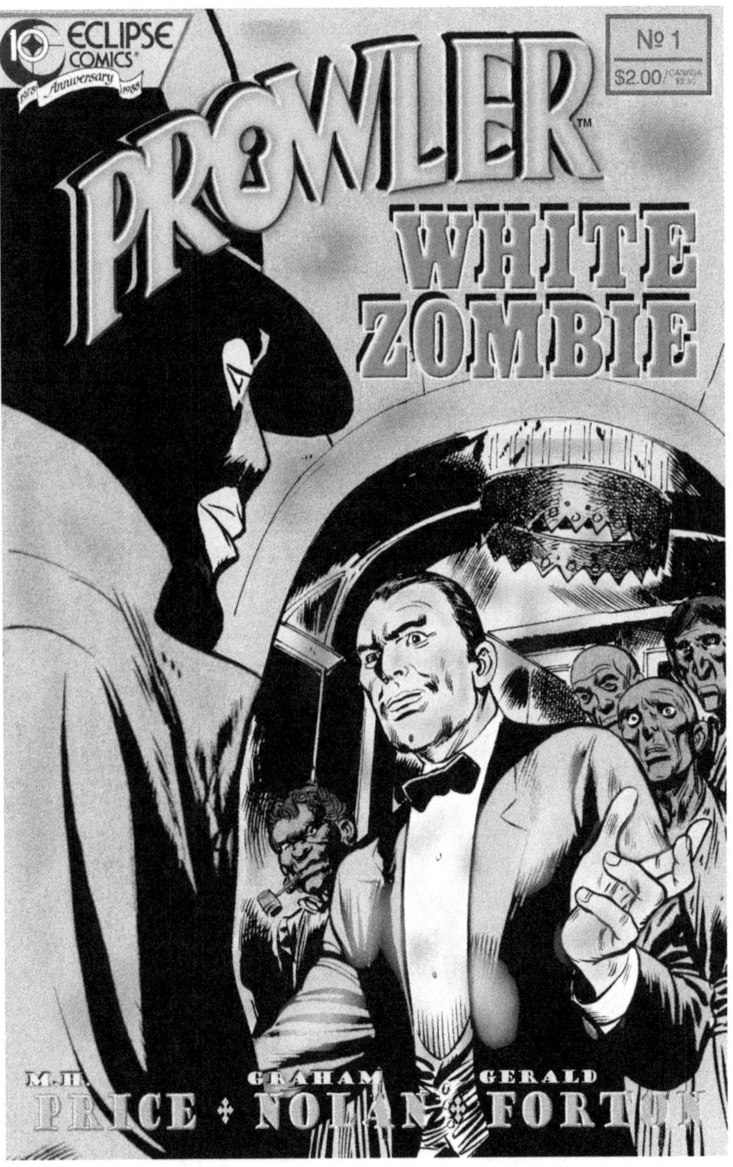

Michael H. Price's White Zombie *comic-book adaptation, from 1989.*

opened on Broadway at the Rivoli. Few movies have received so thorough a critical scourging, but the paying customers loved the picture.

We once characterized the film as "an unlikely classic," in a more technically detailed study for the camera-trade journal *American Cinematographer*, during the 1980s. Since then, *White Zombie* has attained ever greater critical and popular admiration. The belated acknowledgment is no paradox, for the critical brethren have always taken a condescending on-the-spot view of such genres as horror, crime, and westerns. The critics had been kind to *Dracula*, *Frankenstein*, and *Dr. Jekyll and Mr. Hyde*, but once a trend had taken shape the honeymoon ended.

White Zombie suffered more severely in its day because of a silent-screen style of acting. Almost a decade later, Victor Halperin would persist in encouraging in heavy-handed, pantomimic performances. Even Madge Bellamy's Cupid's-bow rouged lips represent a throwback to the 1920s.

Many elements, however, transcend such handicaps. The Halperins had mastered sound as a mood-building device, anticipating the audacious sonic dynamism of *King Kong* (1933) and *Citizen Kane* (1941). The sight-plus-sound accomplishments sustain a Gothic mood, with diabolical magnetism from Lugosi and some jarring moments of unleavened shock value. Few can forget the sight of a mill worker being crushed under the blades of a cane grinder, or the spectacle of bullets thudding into a giant's bared chest without halting the advance or drawing blood. This fairytale for grown-ups remains among the most haunting and fascinating of motion pictures.

The Thirteenth Guest

Monogram Pictures Corp. • 1932

A young blonde (Ginger Rogers, in her first star-billing role) enters an abandoned house. Finding a telephone in service, she dials Central and demands to know why the line is connected in a place that has stood vacant for 13 years. She draws from her purse an envelope that reads: "To be handed to my daughter, Marie Morgan, on her 21st birthday." Surveying the remains of a long-ago banquet, like a scene out of Dickens, the woman envisions those who had occupied 12 of 13 chairs, 13 years ago: the Morgans and their offspring, lawyer Barksdale, aunts and uncles, a bratty cousin, and a childhood sweetheart. A 13th seat had gone unoccupied. Her reverie broken, the woman turns to flee at the sound of footfalls. Outside, her driver (Harry Tenbrook) hears a scream, a gunshot, and maniacal laughter. The cabbie summons the police.

Thus begins Albert Ray's *The Thirteenth Guest*, a fine film by any standard—and a rousing chiller that delivers full measure of horror, romance, and comedy. The film established a decisive narrative voice for Monogram Pictures, which had taken shape in 1931 as a venture of such veteran independent producers as W. Ray Johnson and Trem Carr, with headquarters at Talisman Studios. M.H. Hoffman, briefly a member and the producer of this gem, preferred his own production unit at Pathé; he withdrew after *The Thirteenth Guest* to continue under the Allied brand.

The story, by *Scarface* author Armitage Trail, dictates the atmospheric treatment. The main exterior is a genuinely decrepit manor, and the Pathé interiors are properly weird. Even the comedy relief—slapstick and wordplay alike—is of a darker cast.

Private investigator Phil Winston (Lyle Talbot) arrives. Seated at the table is the body of a woman, apparently Marie Morgan. The coroner ascribes death to electrocution—but the chair is not wired. Police Capt. Ryan (J. Farrell MacDonald) explains that the head of the household had died at the table 13 years ago, "and all these folks have been waiting for their dinner ever since." The bulk of the estate was willed to the mysterious 13th guest. Ryan determines that Barksdale (Robert Klein) had ordered electricity and phone service restored. A dragnet is ordered. Ryan's patrol car goes missing.

Ryan's bumbling helper, Detective Grump (Paul Hurst), snoozes while Barksdale steals inside. A hooded figure in a hidden room presses a button to ring the telephone. Barksdale answers, only be electrocuted. Grump, roused by a hideous bellowing shriek, flees. The body of Barksdale is found—seated at the accursèd table.

Two policemen bring in Marie Morgan—alive. After someone had opened fire on her, she took cover and fled in Ryan's automobile. The dead woman's face bears surgical scars. A Dr. Sherwood (J. Crauford Kent) appears responsible. Ryan senses an inheritance scam.

Winston gathers six surviving guests. Marie's brother, Harold (James C. Eagles), and her school-days boyfriend, Thor Jensen (Eddie Phillips), seem harmless. Uncle Dick and Aunt Joan (Phillips Smalley and Ethel Wales) are patently ruthless. Spoiled Cousin Marjorie (Frances Rich) seems a nymphomaniac. Uncle John Adams (Erville Alderson) is

a rascally sort. Another uncle, Wayne Seymour (Allan Calvan), is at large. Winston warns: "As Capt. Ryan so elegantly describes it, the murderer intends to line that table with stiffs." Angered by the family's arrogance, Winston orders all jailed as material witnesses.

After Uncle Wayne turns up slain, his body pulsing with current, Winston orders the suspects freed and followed. The killer has claimed a victim while imprisoned. Grump is assigned to tail Marjorie.

Sherwood admits that Thor Jensen had ordered plastic surgery on the first victim. A message instructs Marie to visit the murder house. The masked man rings the lethal telephone, but as Marie reaches for it, the genuine phone rings. She sets down the steel receiver an instant before the fiend can close the switch. Winston is calling with a warning for Marie to get out. The hooded man captures her.

Thor admits that he and Barksdale had hired a look-alike for Marie. An unknown party had killed the proxy after Thor had frightened Marie away.

Marie surrenders the combination to a vault. The police break in as the killer is opening the safe. Marie locks him in the vault; he proves to be Uncle John Adams. The safe contains $1,000,000 in securities and a note from Marie's father: he had given his shifty in-laws time and provocation to kill one another before Marie would inherit. Winston decides not to let Marie's newfound wealth stand in the way of a courtship.

Detective Grump, meanwhile, has become intimate with Marjorie. As Ryan glares, the dumbbell cop offers an excuse: "Well, you *told* me to *tail her.*"

Ginger Rogers in one-half of a dual role.

The Thirteenth Guest proved profitable from the start. Ginger Rogers' burgeoning popularity encouraged Monogram to keep the film in circulation for years. A 1943 remake, *The Mystery of the 13th Guest*, proved lacking by comparison.

The original version benefits from urgent conviction from all concerned. The hooded killer could have stepped from the cover of one of the era's pulp-mystery magazines. The methods of killing are so graphically presented that the scenes of electrocution would not have passed the tougher censorship regulations instituted only two years later. Nor would the erotic innuendo and an angry "Damn!" muttered by Lyle Talbot—both elements lending a lifelike spontaneity.

J. Farrell MacDonald registers well as the apoplectic police captain. Paul Hurst, who alternated between comical and villainous roles, suggests a more emotional Buster Keaton as the dim-witted lawman—all the more amusing because Hurst's Detective Grump takes himself altogether seriously. His breathless description of a hair-raising wail is a peak of hilarity: "Tarzan...an' th' *devil*...an' a couple of *hyeenees*...!" Ethel Wales and Phillips Smalley are splendid as vicious socialites (a favored target of Poverty Row producers during the Depression). Erville Alderson seems so personable as to render his unmasking a surprise. Grimmer comedy works particularly well in a sequence where the high-society snootbags are jailed with an assortment of low-lifes.

Photography makes emphatic use of shifts in focus during the more confrontational scenes, and the nighttime effects are ominous. The only music is a portion of Brahms' *Academic Festival Overture* at the opening.

The Hurricane Express

Mascot Pictures Corp. • 1932

John Wayne's second Mascot serial is in every way an improvement over *The Shadow of the Eagle*. The story is *almost* logical. A clever gimmick has the mystery-man villain disguise himself as most of the principals at one time or another, making identification more difficult. This scary and disorienting touch also served an economical function, enabling players to perform double-duty. Most filming was done in the San Fernando Valley and at Bronson Canyon, evocative and formidable locations. The miniature work—involving trains and aircraft—suffers from occasional lapses in perceived realism.

Airline pilot Larry Baker (Wayne) is aloft when warned by passenger Gloria Martin (Shirley Grey), a rail-company secretary, of an imminent collision between trains—the famed *Hurricane Express* is perilously near *Old No. 57*, whose engineer has been struck down. The engineer of *No. 57* is Larry's father (J. Farrell MacDonald). Larry lands to re-route

the course, but in vain. Airline boss Walter Gray (Lloyd Whitlock) fires Larry, who vows to avenge his father's murder.

Railroad officials suspect Gray. Also under suspicion is former railroad president Stratton (Edmund Breese), who has escaped from a prison hitch into which he had been framed. Gloria is Stratton's daughter.

Larry boards the gold-laden *Hurricane* as it nears an ambush. The purported conductor—the elusive Wrecker—escapes when a biplane lowers a rope ladder. Larry prevents the derailing. Stratton hijacks the train, intending to force his clearance on the false conviction. The Wrecker's impersonations persist until the menace, felled by his own gun, proves to be a railroad lawyer (Conway Tearle), who had framed Stratton. Stratton regains control of the line and suggests a merger with Gray's company. Larry becomes chief pilot and wins Gloria's hand.

The cast, as usual, consists of seasoned professionals who lend class to the mayhem. Talents, from the boyish John Wayne to the doddering Tully Marshall, all play Jekyll-Hyde as the master criminal. Wayne performs much of his stunt work, with Eddie Parker doubling the more perilous action. Sniveling little Ernie Adams stands out as a henchman.

Directors are Armand Schaefer and the Australian J.P. McGowan, whose name is indelibly associated with railroad melodramas. In 1914, McGowan had directed the serial that started the trend, *The Hazards of Helen*, and he persisted through the likes of *The Girl and the Game*, *Whispering Smith*, *The Lost Express*, and *The Railroad Raiders* (1915–1917), and *The Train Wreckers*, *The Open Switch*, *Perils of the Rail*, *Red Signals*, and *The Lost Limited* (1925–1927). McGowan directed more than 130 productions and played roles in many of them; he died in 1952.

In addition to the railroad action, *The Hurricane Express* features abundant footage of Ford Tri-Motor aircraft.

The Phantom Express

Majestic Pictures Corp. • 1932

Railroad engineer Smoky Nolan (J. Farrell MacDonald) is forced into his first wreck of a lengthy career when a phantom headlight threatens a head-on collision. The derailing costs many lives; the cause vanishes. Smoky, dismissed for negligence, joins Bruce Harrington (William "Buster" Collier, Jr.), son of the line's president (Hobart Bosworth), to investigate: such catastrophes have placed the carrier under pressure to sell.

The apparent ghost-train proves to be a low-flying airplane rigged with locomotive lights, dispatched to scare engineers into jumping the tracks. The deadline nears for a sale. Only Smoky can make it through a storm to deliver Bruce's report. In a mad ride over crumbling bridges and landslides, Smoky pushes through in time to save the railroad. The tale bears a striking resemblance to *The Hurricane Express* (above), but a wide gulf separates the two in terms of plausibility and production values.

J. Farrell MacDonald went in rapid order from playing a railroad engineer as an early victim in *The Hurricane Express* to playing a railroad engineer as the central character of *The Phantom Express*—scarcely a stretch for the dependable character man, who dominates a strong cast in one of the more emphatic independent pictures of the Depression. *The Phantom Express* combines a hint of supernatural menace and a baffling mystery with the traditional rail thriller, a holdover from the silents.

Director Emory Johnson's original scenario accommodates a worthy ensemble cast with snappy dialogue and action sequences of a high order. A cooperative arrangement with the Southern Pacific Railroad enabled spectacle beyond the reach of most other independent production companies. Many scenes were filmed about the machine shops and the roundhouse of the S.P.'s Los Angeles headquarters, with about 125 steam locomotives on view. A wreck in the Mojave Desert used a retired locomotive, a tender, and several coaches. The train was given a three-mile start and had reached 60 miles per hour when the engineer and the fireman leaped to safety—a moment before the train struck a section of weakened track. In the convincing finished product, the train surges from the track and ploughs through the earth as the coaches pile up.

Although Johnson specialized in action pictures—including the likes of *Westbound Limited* (1923) and *The Third Alarm* (1930)—he also invests *The Phantom Express* with tense emotional currents and a brooding atmosphere. The night scenes set dramatic lighting against blackness, with unnerving storm scenes. Buster Collier and Sally Blane (sister of Loretta Young) make appealing romantic leads—she, as MacDonald's daughter; he as a likable hedonist who develops a heroic streak. MacDonald dominates the telling with a portrayal that is by turns crusty, poignant, and dauntless. Similarly commanding is Hobart Bosworth, as the railroad's beleaguered chief executive. Effective comedy relief is provided by Axel Axelson and Tom O'Brien.

Thirteen Steps

Congress Pictures Corp. • 1932

A long-lost Yellow Peril thriller that has eluded even the Catalogue of Feature Films project of the American Film Institute, John Tansey's *Thirteen Steps* appears to survive only in a dialogue-and-continuity document on file with the New York State Archive. The story concerns a Chinatown criminal known as the Scorpion, who accuses a newspaper publisher of the murder of an associate and rallies a massed campaign of vengeance—to the extent of enlisting the help of a turncoat editor. The publisher's daughter finds herself imperiled. A heroic reporter rescues the daughter and guns down the Scorpion. The cast includes Franklyn Farnum, *Tombstone Canyon*'s Sheldon Lewis, Cornelius Keefe, and Barbara Bedford, of *The Death Kiss*.

Out of Singapore

a.k.a. Gangsters of the Sea
Goldsmith Productions, Ltd. • 1932

Not only was Jack London's *The Sea Wolf* filmed repeatedly, the tale also inspired such imitations as the lively *Out of Singapore*, directed by serial daredevil Charles "Hurricane Hutch" Hutchison for producer Ken Goldsmith. Much of the charm of this elemental struggle derives from the presence of two of the movies' great villains, Noah Beery and Montagu Love.

Old Capt. Carroll (William Moran) is so strapped to find a first mate that he signs Woolf Barstow (Beery) and a scheming boatswain, Scar Murray (Love). Barstow, lusting after the captain's daughter, Mary (Miriam Seegar), plots with Murray to take control and begins to poison Carroll by degrees. The conspirators drown the second mate (Ethan Laidlaw).

Barstow registers a bogus cargo to secure an insurance settlement with a staged explosion. He hires a scrappy derelict, Steve Trent (George Walsh), as second mate. Trent's pal, Bloater (Jimmy Aubrey), signs on as cook. Carroll, upon learning of the scam, is slain. Barstow is enraged to find a romance developing between Mary and a regenerated Trent.

Barstow's wronged mistress, saloon dancer Concha (Dorothy Burgess), steals aboard to warn Mary. Having imprisoned Trent, Barstow informs Mary that she will be spared when the ship explodes with all aboard.

Barstow leaves Concha to the mercies of a drunken crew. She escapes and imprisons Barstow—but only after he has touched off a slow-burning fuse. Concha frees Mary and Trent. Trent kills Murray, then launches a lifeboat. Concha stays behind to distract the crewmen, whose frenzy covers Barstow's outcry. Concha's sensuous dance of death ends as the ship explodes.

Dorothy Burgess, as the vengeful dancer, is as intense as Beery and Love. George Walsh lacks the vocal ability to match his splendid appearance. Miriam Seegar is too old-fashioned an ingenue for the emerging talking-picture style. Both had been notables of the silent screen. Welcome comic relief is supplied by Jimmy Aubrey and Fred "Snowflake" Toones, an expressive black actor saddled with a demeaning nickname.

Goldsmith, a meticulous producer who later worked at Universal Pictures, gets a great deal out of a small budget.

The Crooked Circle

World Wide Pictures • Fox Film Corp. • 1932

Bruce Humberstone's rare gift for balancing chills with comedy to emphasize each had come across vividly in his first job of directing, *Strangers of the Evening*. His follow-through builds upon the accomplishment. *The Crooked Circle*, an elaboration upon the Mystery Farce tradition, brought prestige to World Wide, the most consistently able of the small companies. Screenwriter Ralph Spence (of the hit play-become-movie *The Gorilla*, and many script-doctor assignments) alternates gags and scares, suffused with scintillating dialogue. Weird horror becomes crime melodrama, detours into light comedy, then retrenches in mystery.

The team of James Gleason and ZaSu Pitts dates from 1929's *Oh, Yeah!* Nowhere more so than in *The Crooked Circle* do their opposing mannerisms (his exasperated indignation, her quavering dottiness) complement one another so ideally. The cast also includes Ben Lyon, of *Hell's Angels* (1930); Irene Purcell, of Paramount's rubber-reality comedy gem *Million Dollar Legs* (1932); Berton Churchill, master of pomposity; Raymond Hatton, wonderfully eccentric as a hermit; Roscoe Karns, a master of comical touches; and Munich-born Frank Reicher, from Broadway's Theatre Guild production company and school.

Cultists of the Crooked Circle threaten an organization of amateur detectives—from whose ranks wealthy Brand Osborne (Lyon) has announced his resignation, at the behest of his fiancée, Thelma Parker (Purcell). Brand's successor, a Hindu named Yoganda (C. Henry Gordon), warns of peril. The mansion of a senior member, Col. Wolters (Berton Churchill), is a forbidding place where "something always happens to somebody," as a jittery housekeeper, Nora (Pitts), puts it. Strange music, as if from nowhere, heralds disaster.

Wolters disappears. A woman screams. Osborne recognizes Thelma's voice. A nervous cop, Crimmer (Gleason), triggers a hidden doorway—which reveals the body of Wolters, a violin string about the throat. Crimmer tumbles down a chute that leads to a burial plot outside.

The introductory ritual of the title cult.

After further threats, Yoganda opens a panel that discloses the members of the Crooked Circle—Thelma among them. The Hindu proves to be a Secret Service agent; Thelma is his undercover assistant. Yoganda had placed Wolters in a trance as protection from the Circle. Crimmer is left to take credit for solving a case of whose intrigues he is ignorant.

ZaSu Pitts and James Gleason.

William Sistrom, a producer with Fox Film Corp., gathered for his first independent production a fine crew and heavy-duty resources, with the advantage of Fox distribution. The imposing sets are the work of designer Paul Roe Crawley, of 1930's *The Bat Whispers*. Photographer Robert Kurrle was one of Warners' elite ranks. Film editor Doane Harrison came aboard from Paramount Pictures. The critics and the customers alike proved enthusiastic.

Amore e Morte

Aurora Film Corp. • 1932

As lost a film as 1932's *Thirteen Steps* but more unusual in terms of subject matter, Rosario Romeo's production of *Amore e Morte* (or *Love and Death*) seems to come a bit closer within reach with the unearthing by Gary D. Rhodes of a published review. Rhodes is a filmmaker in his own right and author of such lively and essential books as *White Zombie: Anatomy of a Horror Film* and *Edgar G. Ulmer: Detour on Poverty Row*. Rhodes has supplied a copy (pictured) of that brief appraisal from the National Board of Review. The piece is consistent with co-author George E. Turner's memories of such accounts, as encountered during his youth. Turner often lamented his inability to find a print for screening during a lengthy career of aggressive and scholarly filmgoing.

The tale involves the accurséd Agro family, notorious for the indiscretions of its men. Ruggiero de Agro (Romeo), ladies' man of a farming village near Mount Etna in eastern Sicily, neglects his family to such an extent that the wife (Carmelina Romeo) must steal to survive. One of Agro's seduced-and-abandoned victims, Chiara (Clara Diana), dies after confessing her plight. Her grieving father sets out for revenge during a celebration, the *festa de raccolta*. He is about to kill Agro when a storm breaks. The family curse is fulfilled with Agro's destruction by lightning.

The resurrection of other vanished films has provided hope: The 1990s, for example, saw rediscoveries of such titles as 1912's *The Life and Death of King Richard III* and the 1925 roadshow cut of *The Lost World*—both once presumed lost.

Amore e Morte, strange and compelling by surviving accounts, is the lone production of New York-based Aurora Film Corp. Adapted from a tragedy of the *teatro dialetelle Siciliano* and enacted by American-bred Sicilians, the picture was filmed in the stony farmlands near the Watchung Mountains (a.k.a. the Blue Hills) in New Jersey. Players, costumes, and props—donkeys, farm implements, and a Sicilian *caretto* drawn by a plumed horse—came from the Teatro d'Arte, a troupe headed by Commander Giuseppe Sterni. A stone farmhouse (with vineyards, orchards, and a barn) seems an appropriate setting. The dialogue mingles Italian, Sicilian, and Italianate English, without subtitles.

The story exploits the ancestral curse for full horrific impact, establishing the villain as an unapologetic rake, bereft of compassion. The festival sequence trades upon folkloric music. The climactic storm

AMORE E MORTE (Love and Death)—*Screen story and direction by Rosario Romeo, with a cast including Rosario Romeo and Carmelina Romeo. M. Guerrera, 9 reels.* Strong Sicilian story of a father whose daughter was wronged by one of his tenants. Dramatic in the intense Italian fashion, with some pleasant interludes of peasant singing and dancing. A good deal better than most Italian films offered to American audiences. *Family audience.*

The National Board of Review weighs in on Amore e Morte.

packs a suitable ferocity, according to contemporary reports as recalled by George Turner.

Rosario Romeo and his players seem to have been known only to Italian audiences. The cameramen were prominent among the New York studios. Alfred Gandolfi had photographed the tragic expedition picture, *The Viking*. Nick Rogalli's many assignments include D.W. Griffith's last picture, *The Struggle* (1932), the tale of a drunkard's reformation. (That picture met with such hostility that United Artists withdrew it from circulation.)

Amore e Morte appears to have played well among the intended audiences. More is the loss that the film is unavailable for re-appraisal as an American ancestor of such Italianate curse-laden horrors of times more recent as Lucio Fulci's *Non si Sevizia un Paperino/Don't Torture a Duckling* (1972) and Dario Argento's *Suspiria* (1977).

Tangled Destinies

Mayfair Pictures Corp. • 1932

Frank Strayer's *Tangled Destinies* delivers a small-scale reign of terror in an ideal Old Dark House setting. Smart dialogue and unpredictable plotting serve the 13 players—veterans of stage and silent screen—with respect for their professionalism. The performances, in turn, deflect attention from the low-budget nature of the production: Sets and lighting are hardly up to major-studio standards, nor should they be.

An airliner makes a forced landing by night in a desert. A desolate house looms. Passengers and crew, nine men and four women, take refuge. A generator is put into service, only to fail. Once the power has been restored, it is discovered that a passenger has been slain. The motivation appears to be a cache of jewels. An elderly woman (Ethel Wales) remains calm while panic spreads. A purported priest (Henry Hall) argues for serenity until—but don't let's give away the game altogether.

Suspense persists, with bantering dialogue well deployed to sustain a frenzied rhythm. A clever application of suspicion, smartly deflected, makes it virtually impossible to peg the menace. Strayer directs with such ferocity as to make the confining locale essential to the momentum. The acting is uniformly persuasive, riddled with bigoted ethnic tensions (as directed at James B. Leong's character) and sparked by Syd Saylor's brash comic relief and Ethel Wales' splendid portrait of a soul at peace amidst the turmoil.

The snakebit captives of Tangled Destinies.

Hidden Valley

Monogram Pictures Corp. • 1932

No wisecracks about Hidden Valley-brand salad dressing, please: the title bespeaks raw and unseasoned menace, sufficiently flavorful upon its own merits.

Bob Steele, wiry and intense, paced and defined a weird-westerns movement with such horseback horrors as *Hidden Valley* and 1935's

Big Calibre—pictures whose seamless and audacious unions of terror and spirited adventure blur the genres to bracing effect. Steele favored peculiar elements: scarcely a month after *Hidden Valley*, he showed up in Phil Rosen's *Young Blood* as a genial outlaw framed for murder—but spared a lynching when the victim's pet monkey turns up evidence.

In *Hidden Valley*—directed by Robert North Bradbury, Steele's father—the weird-menace stakes run so high as to launch an influential western theme: the folkloric notion of a lost tribe had figured in Mascot's 1931 serial *The Lightning Warrior*, but *Hidden Valley* treats its obscure civilization as a lurking threat. The idea was pursued further in Columbia's *Unknown Valley* (1933), in which Buck Jones stumbles onto a secretive cult of religious fanatics; in Mascot's *The Phantom Empire*; and in Republic's *Riders of the Whistling Skull*.

Ranch foreman Bob Harding (Steele) accompanies an anthropological expedition in search of the treasures of an extinct tribe. A slaying and the theft of a map appear the work of Frank Gavin (Francis MacDonald), whose gang includes Jimmie Lanners (Ray Hallor), Harding's prospective brother-in-law. Harding is framed—another recurring motif with Steele and kindred frontier champions. He escapes, only to find himself roaming the desert. Overcoming a pursuer, Harding commandeers a mount. Lanners is captured as a sacrifice by descendants of the secluded tribe.

Harding's fiancée, rancher Joyce Lanners (Gertie Messenger), and a lawman (Arthur Millett) deploy a blimp. Harding, rescued, spots Jimmie Lanners' plight and parachutes into the fracas. Gavin's gang attacks. Harding and Lanners escape on horseback and are picked up by the blimp crew. The savages make short work of the remaining outlaws. Jimmie Lanners' confession clears Harding.

The most familiar strain of Gothic Western derives from the Mystery Farce tradition of Broadway and the silents-to-talkies transition, in which human villains impersonate ghosts and monsters—the better to misappropriate an inheritance. Dark mansions become coveted ranches and mines. The bigoted motif of the Yellow Peril, or Asian menace, surfaces occasionally in a frontier setting (as in *Border Phantom* and *Hair Trigger Casey*, also considered herein). A death ray is wielded by marauders in 10-gallon hats in *Ghost Patrol*.

Steele's forays into weirdness differ significantly. He was no typical cowboy star, in the first place: his contemporaries were generally tall, husky, and slow-talking. (Ken Maynard was tall, husky, and *fast*-talking.) The bantamweight, curly-haired Steele projected more romance and Byronic emotion than any other Hollywood westerner—a Hamlet of the High Plains—and he was unsurpassed at staging realistic fights, which are the essence of any horse opera worth its oats. He was an accomplished horseman, as well. As Bob Bradbury, Steele had begun a film career at age 14 in 1921, co-starring with his brother, Bill, in an actionful series of pictures produced for Pathé by their father.

In 1927, as Bob Steele, the artist became a western star for Joseph P. Kennedy's Film Booking Offices of America, an ancestor of RKO-Radio Pictures. Steele was underage, and his father signed on his behalf. Steele's popularity in this category lasted well into the 1940s, by which time he had begun moving into general-purpose character roles. (Brother Bill Bradbury became a physician.)

Count it remarkable that Steele, whose only acting experience had occurred in silent films, proved such a fine actor in the early

talkers. His expertise contrasts with the vocal clumsiness and microphone phobia that had ended the starring careers of most other silent-screen cowpunchers.

Steele also excelled as a villain in major-league productions, such as the despicable Curly in *Of Mice and Men* (1940), the cold-eyed Canino in *The Big Sleep* (1946), and the assassin in *The Enforcer* (1951). Still later, he gained a new following as a comical player on the tele-series *F Troop*.

Hidden Valley boasts production values higher than usual for the independent class, including later Steele pictures made by the likes of Supreme and Independent. The locations—far beyond the beat of most such producers—are the best California has to offer: the Alabama Hills, at the foot of Mount Whitney (at the time, the highest known mountain in the United States), and the picturesque nearby towns of Lone Pine and Independence. The same towering granite that would figure in such epics as *The Lives of a Bengal Lancer* and *Gunga Din* provides a formidable setting for a yarn about skull-worshipping Indians. Additional action was filmed 90 miles south of Lone Pine in colorful Hagen Canyon, where Universal was soon to shoot *The Mummy*; in the salt flats of Owens Valley; and in a desolate patch adjacent to Death Valley.

Director Bradbury, a handsome and muscular former actor, exerts a distinctive style on his fast-and-cheap westerns, which usually were made in a week for $25,000 each. Bradbury worked especially well with Archie Stout, one of the great scenic cinematographers, who finds here enough panoramic glories for any number of bigger films. The camera-work compares favorably with Stout's celebrated lensing of William A. Wellman's *Beau Geste* (1939) and John Ford's *Fort Apache* (1948). Stout achieves unusual compositions in the blimp-rescue sequences as silhouetted figures struggle to ascend a rope ladder.

The stuntwork ranges beyond horsemanship. Steele (or an unbilled double) plunges through a third-story window onto a roof, then leaps into a towering poplar. The fistfights, staged two years before Bradbury's collaborative invention of the Pass System of painless movie haymakers, are roughhouse encounters that can only have left the participants bruised and bleeding. A Running-W fall and a horseback dive from a cliff into a lake appear to be stock shots.

Another survivor of the silents, Francis MacDonald, is the soul of malevolence as the chief villain. A surprising presence is the belovéd George "Gabby" Hayes as a vicious henchman—a role he was bound to repeat, with variations, until his comical Old Duffer routine caught on with the matinée crowd. Petite Gertie Messenger, one of the cutest and blondest of Poverty Row's leading ladies, makes an ideally troubled romantic interest. The airship that dominates the climax is the celebrated Goodyear Blimp—less streamlined than the model of times more recent—which hovers among the crags as though it belongs there. The authentic pilot, Verner L. Smith, plays himself with adequate conviction.

The Amazon Head Hunters

a.k.a. Au Pays du Scalp
Principal Distributing Corp. • 1932

"[T]he exploits of the Marquis de Wavrin. ... Stark and grim reality..." Thus begins *The Amazon Head Hunters*, a documentary account jazzed up with music, narration, and brisk editing—with resounding scares as a cumulative effect.

Belgian explorer de Wavrin searches for a friend missing in Ecuador. De Wavrin visits the Galapagos Islands, crosses the Andes, and sees men gored while baiting the bulls in Otavalo. He befriends many tribes and witnesses a healing ritual.

De Wavrin finds the hellbent-for-decapitation Jivaro tribe pre-occupied with the beheading of rival tribesmen. A head-shrinking demonstration follows. One such trophy bears the features of the missing friend. De Wavrin departs abruptly.

De Wavrin said he had filmed the raw material over a period of four years. The ambitious Poverty Row producer Sol Lesser acquired the source film, a 1931 Belgian release called *Au Pays du Scalp* or *In the Scalp Country*, as the basis of a fourth entry in the Principal-Adventure line of featurettes. Editor Carl Himm recut the picture in five reels, about 10 minutes short of a feature-lengther. The stirring music is the work of Maurice Jaubert, who scored many French films; the orchestrations spared Lesser the expense of his usual leasing of pre-recorded music from Meyer Synchronization Service.

As cameramen go, the marquis is no James Wong Howe, but the natural scenic values convey a daunting intimacy with the murderous tribe. A lengthy build-up to the Jivaro horrors—business as usual with the tribespeople—contains many interesting and exciting moments.

Industrywide censorship was practically toothless at the time, but there was some provincial carping about the more unnerving sequences. One tongue-in-cheek review characterized the climactic discovery as "particularly gruesome" and suggested: "Nervous women and men should be advised against seeing [the film]. Such admonition will likely pack the house with the morbidly curious." The tradepaper *Variety* leered: "Nearest thing to nude of any ever shown."

The story resembles that of *Savage Gold*, which appeared some six months later. The grisly demonstrations of head-shrinking and the run-for-your-life payoff are practically identical. *Savage Gold*, however, contains more extensive dramatizations and re-enactments.

STARK AND GRIM REALITY!
SOL LESSER
presents
The AMAZON HEAD HUNTERS
A PRINCIPAL ADVENTURE FEATURE

The Midnight Warning

a.k.a. *Eyes of Mystery*
Mayfair Pictures Corp. • 1932

Spencer Gordon Bennet's history-of-filmmaking rèsumé ranges from the day of Edison to the mid-century's toll of television upon the movies. Bennet had arrived in 1912 as a stuntman and occasional actor in the Edison company's adventure pictures. He parlayed an apprenticeship to director George B. Seitz into a directing career, early in the 1920s. A specialist in serials until 1956—when he made the last American serial, *Perils of the Wilderness*—Bennett also directed (and often produced) feature-length thrillers. He told us he recalled *The Midnight Warning* more fondly than his other non-serial efforts.

The film is a beauty, all right—despite an unevenness of sound and camerawork—from its fascinating and morbid puzzle to a wealth of macabre grace-notes. Its basis in urban legendry appears to date from the Chicago World's Fair of 1893. Mayfair Pictures (successor to Action Pictures) assigned authorship to Norman Battle, but the parent tale had been written for *The New Yorker* magazine by Alexander Woolcott, who called it "The Most Maddening Story in the World." The same yarn inspired a 1947 novel by Anthony Thorne, which became a significant British film, *So Long at the Fair* (1950), starring Dirk Bogarde. By which time, the basic plot also had inspired a Rocky Lane western at Republic

Hooper Atchley and William Boyd attend to a collapsed Claudia Dell.

Pictures, *Marshal of Amarillo* (1948). The premise figured, as well, in an installment of the tele-series *Alfred Hitchcock Presents*.

Dr. Stephen Walcott (Hooper Atchley) finds the remains of someone's ear in his hotel-room fireplace at the Clarendon Arms. While discussing the discovery with investigator William Cornish (William "Stage" Boyd), Walcott is grazed by a bullet. Cornish captures Enid Van Buren (Claudia Dell) and her fiancé, Erich (John Harron), who admit they have been harassing the Clarendon in an attempt to force the owners' hand regarding a mystery: at the hotel, where she and her brother had checked in a few hours beforehand, no one professes to remember her brother; the register indicates that Enid had arrived alone.

Cornish and Walcott take up the case. Hoteliérs Gordon (Huntly Gordon), Rankin (Lloyd Whitlock), Klein (Lloyd Ingraham), and Welsh (Lon Poff) imprison Enid in a mortuary. A disembodied voice taunts her. Cornish summons the police. Cornered, the hotel bosses acknowledge a conspiracy with municipal officials: they had destroyed the body of the brother, who had died of bubonic plague, and then sought to drive Enid insane. Having shamed the plotters, Cornish declares it better that the matter remain a secret lest a panic result.

One of the finer qualities is William "Stage" Boyd's grim efficiency. The odd nickname distinguishes him from another William Boyd. The Boyd of *The Midnight Warning* (and Paramount's horrific *Murder by the Clock*) had a stronger presence on Broadway. The other Boyd was a fair-haired mainstay of Pathé-DeMille and RKO-Radio Pictures; this one became Bill Boyd for a while, to lessen the confusion. Both were well known for their boozy carousing, and each was continually being accused of the other's escapades. The death of "Stage" Boyd in 1935 settled the problem. Bill Boyd retrieved his full name, dropped the gossip-inducing misbehavior, and embarked upon a new career at Paramount as the stalwart and wholesome star player of the *Hopalong Cassidy* western series.

"Stage" Boyd dominates *The Midnight Warning* through sheer immersion in character. He takes forensic detection to an extreme by reading the lips of suspects from afar. (The tactic also figures in 1933's *The Circus Queen Murder*.) Boyd taunts the culprits by explaining to them the flaw in their scheme: the ear cartilage is "the hardest part of the body to destroy, by fire or any other means." And he exhibits the practical, resentful sense to comprehend that the conspiracy must go unexposed. Boyd wields the cudgel of intimidation with daunting authority.

More conventional scares figure in a sequence where Claudia Dell finds herself surrounded by stiffs. Groping for anchorage after a stumble, she seizes a cold foot—a nice chill, that!

Hooper Atchley plays against familiar crooked type as a Dr. Watson to Boyd. The pillar-of-society conspirators are sanctimonious to a loathsome extent. Huntly Gordon's defiant riposte to Boyd, daring him to take their plot to the authorities, crystallizes the attitude of impunity.

Dell is rightly vulnerable as the tormented ingenue, but her inexperience shows candidly in the mortuary scene: Spencer Bennet told us that Dell "didn't know how to take a stage fall. So when she had to faint in the morgue, she hit her head on the concrete floor and was knocked unconscious." The scene remains in the finished film; a retake would have been an extravagance. Dell grabs her head when she strikes the floor, then goes limp.

Bennet's ability to work fast and shave costs by editing in the camera kept him in demand along Poverty Row. This rare talent, however, often cheated Bennet of opportunities to display creative flourishes.

Strange Adventure

a.k.a. The Wayne Murder Case
Monogram Pictures Corp. • 1932

I.E. Chadwick, a leading independent producer, had established a studio during the 1920s. His silents include the 1925 version of *The Wizard of Oz*, with Larry Semon as the Scarecrow and Oliver Hardy as the Tin Woodsman. Struggling to survive in the hostile climate of the early talkies, Chadwick joined W. Ray Johnson, Trem Carr, and other independents in establishing Monogram Pictures.

An early effort is *Strange Adventure*, a striking variation upon the popular theme of the gathering of heirs at a benighted mansion to hear the reading of a will. The team-directed film (by Phil Whitman and Hampton Del Ruth) makes a splendid companion to Monogram's *The Thirteenth Guest*, another Old Dark House variation involving an ominous inheritance and serial murder.

Stately Wayne Manor—no, not *that* stately Wayne Manor—sits brooding in darkness. A police cruiser lurches to a halt and deposits two officers. The butler, Jeff (Fred "Snowflake" Toones), escorts the lawmen to meet old Silas Wayne (William V. Mong), who informs them that mayhem is afoot. The codger assembles his relatives—then pitches forward. His physician, Bailey (Jason Robards), pronounces Wayne the victim of a stabbing. The policemen place all under house arrest and summon Lt. Mitchell (Regis Toomey), a genial Irish cop.

Mitchell, assisted by a gal-reporter type known as Toodles (June Clyde), administers an interrogation. Stephen Boulter (Alan Roscoe) directs suspicion toward cousins Robert and Claude Wayne (Dwight Frye and Eddie Phillips), rivals for the affections of Silas Wayne's ward, Gloria (Nadine Doré). Mitchell sequesters Robert, but the only trace of Claude is a packed suitcase. Toodles feigns an exit, then steals back. A

hooded figure frightens her into a hiding-place—where she stumbles into Claude's body. Suspicions and counter-suspicions multiply. The masked prowler threatens Gloria. Mitchell reveals Dr. Bailey as the killer. Bailey attempts a rooftop escape, only to be electrocuted.

The scares are well deployed, as is comedy relief by two inept cops and Fred "Snowflake" Toones, the busy black actor and comedian. Regis Toomey is a study in brisk efficiency. June Clyde makes a brazen representative of the newspaper racket. William V. Mong snarls his way through the role of the hated Silas Wayne. Dwight Frye (fresh from the successes of *Dracula* and *Frankenstein*) and Alan Roscoe are suspects of a type that every mystery film should have. Lucille LaVerne (D.W. Griffith's favorite villainess) lurks grimly as the granite-faced housekeeper. Leon Shamroy's photography sets the menacing tone.

And speaking of *The Thirteenth Guest*: the mystery man's hooded costume from that gem receives a new application in *Strange Adventure*. A good prop never wears out along Old Hollywood's Poverty Row.

The Savage Girl

Freuler Film Associates • Monarch Pictures • Commonwealth Pictures • 1932

Rochelle Hudson went unseen and unbilled, though amply well heard, in many early assignments: the Bosko cartoons, Warner Bros.' minstrel-show riposte to Walt Disney's Mickey Mouse franchise, employed Hudson as a dialectical voice, feigning Negritude as Bosko's sweetheart. Her modest breakout to star billing, the title role in Harry Fraser's *The Savage Girl*, represented no less a caricature, but the assignment gave her a visibility beyond bit roles—and led to finer prospects at RKO-Radio and Fox Film Corp. Once Hudson's career had gained traction, a reissue of *The Savage Girl* capitalized upon the RKO credential with a fraudulent suggestion that Freuler-Monarch had arranged for her services with the big studio.

Scenarist Brewster Morse appropriates a concept from Edgar Rice Burroughs as blatantly as Burroughs had borrowed from Kipling, and Kipling from ancient mythology. Scientist Jim Franklin (Walter Byron) persuades Amos P. Sitch (Harry Myers) to underwrite an African expedition in search of a fabled white goddess—a cue from

1931's *Trader Horn*. Sitch, an inveterate boozer, comes along, with valet (Ted Adams) and a sports car, anomalous to the terrain. Ne'er-do-well Alec Bernouth (Adolph Milar) lusts after the purported goddess, who lives under the protection of a gorilla (Charles Gemora). Bernouth provokes a tribal uprising. Franklin faces death in a savage ritual, but Sitch routs the natives. Just as Bernouth threatens Franklin anew, the ape arrives to crush the villain. All ends romantically well for Franklin and his white savage.

Harry Myers virtually re-enacts his unforgettable drunken millionaire of Charles Chaplin's *City Lights* (1931). Walter Byron was a popular romantic lead in England. Adolph Milar, an expert at war-picture villainy, applies that same Germanic emphasis to the treacherous rival. Ted Adams, usually a heavy in westerns, is effective in a light-comedy role.

The script suggests the direct influence of Universal's gender-switch takeoff on Burroughs' *Tarzan* tales, *Lorraine of the Lions* (1925). The jungle-girl motif caught on more widely a few years later in such comic-book series as *Sheena, Queen of the Jungle*, in movie serials and matinée features, and even in major-studio star vehicles for Dorothy Lamour and Maria Montéz. Instead of a sarong, Rochelle Hudson sports a leopard-skin outfit. Director Harry Fraser, more keenly identified with westerns, gives *The Savage Girl* a straightforward melodramatic thrust. The photography is expertly handled.

Rochelle Hudson also voiced the girlfriend of Bosko,
Warner Bros.' first signature cartoon character.

The Secrets of Wu Sin

Invincible Pictures Corp. • Chesterfield Motion Pictures Corp. • 1932

The merger of Maury Cohen's Invincible Pictures in 1932 with George Batcheller's venerable Chesterfield Motion Pictures created an aggressive company that turned out a picture a month in its heyday. Most such titles were filmed on rented sets at Universal Pictures in North Hollywood; others, at RKO-Pathé in Culver City. The company made numerous mysteries, a couple of all-out horror yarns, and many romantic high-society dramas—but curiously, in a receptive marketplace for outdoor adventure, no westerns. Most of the output for 1932–1933 boasts Richard Thorpe as director.

Thorpe tackled the Yellow Peril theme, Asian villainy in bigoted them-vs.-us terms, in *Secrets of Wu Sin*, a fanciful original by Basil Dickey, author of dozens of serials (including the *Pearl White* epics) through the 1920s. The continuity is the work of Betty Burbidge, noted for western scripts. *Wu Sin* conveys precipitous momentum and a seething menace, and it showcases Thorpe's evolving command of the director's craft.

An undercover newspaperman, Jim Manning (Grant Withers), rescues a would-be suicide, Nona Gould (Lois Wilson), while investigating a slave-labor racket in Chinatown. He gives her a job but nixes her bid to help with the flesh-peddling case. Sensing suspicions among the Chinese, Manning relinquishes the assignment to reporter Eddie Morgan (Eddie Boland).

Morgan suffers a drugging while visiting a restaurant with a confederate (Jimmy Wang)

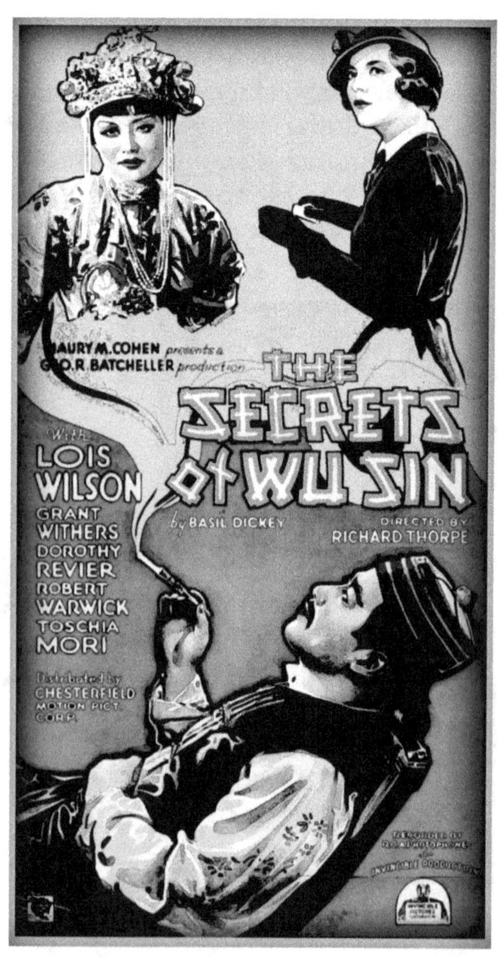

of mobster Wu Sin (Tetsu Komai). Nona, defying orders, discovers a shipment of captive immigrants. The owner of the vessel is Roger King (Robert Warwick), Manning's prospective father-in-law. King denies the accusation—and then orders Wu Sin to kill Manning. Wu Sin summons a reluctant assassin, Charlie San (Richard Loo), lover of Wu Sin's granddaughter (Toschia Mori). Manning ignores a plea from Margaret King (Dorothy Revier) that he must shield her father; she breaks the engagement. Charlie San wounds Manning but wins leniency, given his state of servitude to Wu Sin. Wu Sin commits suicide. King and Margaret leave the country. Manning and Nona marry.

Dominant among the ensemble is the Japanese Tetsu Komai. The evil Chinese, Wu Sin, strikes a sharp contrast with Komai's best-remembered role as a semi-human servant to Charles Laughton in *Island of Lost Souls* (1932). Komai remained a reliable character player into the 1960s. *Secrets of Wu Sin* also accommodates authentic Chinese actors Richard Loo, Luke Chan, and Jimmy Wang; within a decade, an outbreak of World War II melodramas would find them specializing in Japanese villains. Another Japanese, Toschia Mori, also has a Chinese part in *Wu Sin*.

The use of standing sets, enhanced by Universal's magnificent collection of authentic Asian properties, lends *Wu Sin* a substantial appearance well beyond what the budget would otherwise have permitted. The only music is a Chinese delicacy played under the credits.

The Death Kiss

KBS Productions, Inc. • World Wide Pictures • Fox Film Corp. • 1932

A seemingly spontaneous smooch from a beautiful woman proves to be a signal to hidden gunmen to open fire upon Myles Brent (Edmund Burns). The camera draws away to reveal a sound stage where a movie called *The Death Kiss* is in production. The director, Tom Avery (Edward Van Sloan) orders a retake and berates Brent for a sloppy stunt fall. The crew discovers that Brent has been shot to death.

Avery notifies studio chief Leon Grossmith (Alexander Carr), who replies with all due empathy: "*Oy!* That's gonna cost me a *fortune!*" Steiner (Bela Lugosi), the manager, summons the police.

A note implicates Marcia Lane (Adrienne Ames), Brent's former wife and the actress who had administered the kiss in the fatal scene. Screenwriter Franklyn Drew (David Manners) leaps to Marcia's defense. The .45-calibre prop-guns yield no clue: the lethal slug had come from a .38. A crowd extra (Alan Roscoe) with a grudge against Brent is caught packing an unfired .38. Grossmith and Steiner also have had scores to settle against Brent.

The murder footage is torched while the flammable nitrate film is being projected. Someone destroys the negative. Clues point toward Marcia. While prowling the darkened stage, Drew finds a .38-calibre pistol rigged to fire when a spotlight is ignited. He is clubbed down, and the gun disappears. A drunken electrician (Alan Roscoe) is found dead, arrayed to seem a suicide. Tracks outside Chalmers' bungalow match the tire-treads of Marcia's automobile.

Brent's womanizing nature had made many enemies—one, in particular, although the identity remains elusive. Drew and an impatient detective, Lt. Sheehan (John Wray), compare notes to revealing effect, only to find themselves overheard by the hidden killer. During a re-shoot in an attempt to salvage the production, the culprit douses the lights and attempts to escape through the catwalks—only to fall to his death. Director Avery's wayward wife (Mona Maris) sneers at the corpse of her husband: "He's dead, *yes*! Well, I'm *glad*!"

The phantom-killer angle raises Edwin L. Marin's *The Death Kiss* well above conventional murder-in-movieland intrigues. The greater appeal lies in a fascinating account of the moviemaking process itself, related in a manner that propels the story. This portrait of an industry extends to the very personnel: Alex Carr's Leon Grossmith is the quintessential Old World *Yiddishe* studio boss, powerful but coarsely assimilated. Grossmith's life-models occupied every front office in Hollywood at the time. A secretary, played by Harold Minjir, is a drawn-from-life Old Hollywood queen, mincing and fluttering with all the snide authority a petty sycophant can muster. Bela Lugosi's studio manager seems almost fatherly toward the personnel; *paternalistic* might be the more accurate term. Edward Van Sloan, as a noted director, is curt and cutting on the set but warm and chatty otherwise. The assistant director is a figure of tough efficiency, played by real-life former gangster Al Hill. Barbara Bedford, as a script clerk, epitomizes the attentiveness to detail crucial to any shoot. A matinée idol (Edmund Burns) is a cad whose narcissistic nature has blurred the distinction between art and life. His co-star (Adrienne Ames) seems appropriately haughty and indignant, however likable. Alan Roscoe plays a familiar industry figure, a down-and-outer who had been a valued technician. A cold-blooded publicist (Jimmy Donlan) struggles to present a nice-guy image to the press upon whose courtesies his career hangs. The grips, electricians, cameramen, and other artisans go about their tasks with wisecracking coolness.

The movie business' assumption of popular ignorance about moviemaking has yielded such insults-to-the-audience as *Won Ton Ton, the Dog That Saved Hollywood* (1976), in which a chase on a silent-movie lot takes place among rows of sound stages. *The Death Kiss* is an exception.

The investigation is conventional. John Wray, as the cop in charge, is apoplectic and stubborn, resentful of the (ultimately helpful) impositions of David Manners' screenwriter, who has a romantic stake in the case. Manners' snappy performance argues against his mild-mannered image in such Universal chillers as *Dracula*, *The Mummy*, *The Black Cat*, and *The Mystery of Edwin Drood* (1931–1935). Vince Barnett lends comedy relief as an incredibly stupid security cop; Barnett had lately scored as Paul Muni's lackey in *Scarface* (1932).

An unusual touch is the use of hand-coloring, an effect seldom employed after the silent era. Principal photography wrapped on November 17, 1932, and the producers allowed two weeks for tinting, one print at a time, by Gustav Brock. The sparse deployment of color occurs when the murder footage catches fire, and during the climax, with amber flashlight beams and red bursts of gunfire.

At 30, Edwin L. Marin received his first solo-directing assignment on *The Death Kiss*; he had been an assistant director since 1919. Marin soon graduated to the majors; his 56 features include *Bombay Mail* (1934), *A Christmas Carol* (1938), *A Gentleman after Dark* (1942), *Tall in the Saddle* (1944), *Johnny Angel* (1945), and *Fort Worth* (1951; the year of his death).

The studio had licensed Madelon St. Denis' novel, *The Death Kiss*, but the film bears no resemblance to that tale of murder in a Manhattan skyscraper. A promotional campaign depicting Bela Lugosi ogling Adrienne Ames' throat, along with the presence of three of Dracula's leading players—Lugosi, Manners, and Van Sloan—suggested further vampiric delights. The bait-and-switch tactic alienated the horror fans, but the picture delighted the critics-of-record.

The Intruder

a.k.a. Horror in the Night
Allied Pictures Corp., Ltd. • 1932

A creation of the team responsible for *The Thirteenth Guest* and *A Shriek in the Night*, Albert Ray's *The Intruder* is wilder and funnier than either, and damned near as creepy—almost an exercise in dream-logic surrealism.

Such extravagant unpredictability would place this one among the better pictures of its kind, if not for its over-obvious miniature effects and uneven camerawork. The studio photography, aboard a doomed ship, is of a high quality. Not so with the wilderness-after-dark business.

The story dispenses two murders; a jungle marauder played to the hilt by Mischa Auer; a shipwreck; skeletal remains; a drunken playboy (Arthur Houseman, best of the inebriate comics); and suspects aplenty. Monte Blue is a stalwart hero, and Lila Lee—defying the failing health that would force a premature retirement in 1937—is a spirited leading lady.

A killer strikes with a firefighting axe aboard the S.S. *Intruder*. A purported detective from San Francisco, Samson (William B. Davidson), says he had been trailing the victim, who appears to have been a thief and blackmailer. A surfeit of suspects complicates matters.

Submerged wreckage disables the ship. The passengers reach an island, where ghastly shrieks unnerve all concerned. A wild man (Auer) and his skeletal companions occupy a cave. Tough guy Cramer (Harry Cording) proves threatening, only to be slain by Samson. Samson identifies Cramer as the murderer.

Whereupon Jack Brandt (Blue), a determined passenger, rises to the occasion to identify Samson as an impostor, and Cramer as his disloyal accomplice. A French ship arrives to perform a rescue.

Upstaging all the others is Auer, who is by turns scary and hilarious. In his cave, he treats two skeletons as roommates—but sometimes lapses into a frenzy of stabbing one of them. Auer's feral act seems

A tipsy Arthur Housman puzzles Monte Blue in The Intruder.

harmless until he attacks Monte Blue. Once the survivors have been rescued, Auer among them, he places one of the skeletons in a deck chair and sits beside it. Random weirdness overrides conventional plotting, and all the better for that.

Tombstone Canyon

KBS-Tiffany Productions • World Wide Pictures • 1932

Ken Maynard's affinity for horror gave Hollywood's western sector some of its most inventive productions. So popular was the horseman, a tough and demanding taskmaster, that he had his choice of scripts, directors, and technical personnel. Maynard wrote many of his scenarios but seldom took a byline. He also composed music and shot second-unit action scenes with a private arsenal of shoulder-mounted Bell & Howell Eyemo cameras.

Maynard's more jarring pictures of the Depression years include the Universal productions of *Smoking Guns* (Halloween in a haunted house) and *King of the Arena* (mad bomber-at-large). *Tombstone Canyon*, an audacious chiller from a smaller studio, takes a cue—writ rustic—from Gaston Leroux' *The Phantom of the Opera*, filmed in 1925 at Universal.

Ken Mason (Maynard) harbors doubts about his parentage. This existential quandary renders the cowhand susceptible to treachery. A cryptic

Reissue advertisement emphasizing Burns, to the exclusion of Maynard.

message instructs Mason to seek an answer in Tombstone Canyon, a forbidding locale where a sign warns strangers to scram after sundown. Caught under fire, Ken is rescued by rancher Jenny Lee (Cecilia Parker). They hear the shriek of a phantom killer who holds the region in a thrall of fear. The ranchman who had summoned Ken turns up slain.

Ken and the local sheriff (Bob Burns) suspect the so-called Phantom. Ken goes to work for Jenny's father (Lafe McKee). Another rancher, Alf Sikes (Frank Brownlee), provokes trouble. Ken, posing as the Phantom, intimidates Sikes into a confession that goes unheard by the authorities. Sikes retaliates, slaying the sheriff and framing Ken—who captures a passel of vigilante mobsters in the depths of Tombstone Canyon. The Phantom arrives to kill Sikes' thugs but promises to free the others once he has dealt with Sikes.

The Phantom reveals himself as Sikes' brother—long presumed dead after Sikes had mutilated his face and abandoned him in the wilderness. Ken Mason rushes out of hiding. The Phantom opens fire. Sikes informs the Phantom that he has shot his own son. Sikes takes a fatal fall. His son, Clem (George Gerwing), attacks Ken but stops a bullet from the Phantom. Gunned down by Clem, the Phantom dies—imploring Ken not to think harshly of him.

When we first wrote about *Tombstone Canyon* in 1975, while preparing the American Film Institute manuscripts that would become components of *Forgotten Horrors*, the imperative was that of rediscovery. That task was accomplished upon publication of the British and American first editions of *Forgotten Horrors* during 1979–1980, and from there the coincidental but inevitable rise of the consumer-video

Ken Maynard and Cecilia Parker.

market saw to it that this stirring Gothic Western would become more familiar in the here-and-now than it had been in theatrical release or during the early years of commercial television.

With renewed familiarity, though, came controversy. Several fellow researchers have doubted that the actor playing the sheriff is Bob Burns, the famed screen-and-radio funnyman from Arkansas who gave the word *bazooka* to the language. Some have claimed that Jack Clifford is the sheriff; others insist that another guy named Bob Burns (a veteran cowboy actor) handles the role. All quibbling aside: the sheriff is the *comedian* Bob Burns (later a star at Paramount), who unaccountably goes unacknowledged in the credit titles or the original press sheet—even though he has an important role and a bewildering shocker of a death scene. Jack Clifford, a slow-talking comic-heavy who resembles Burns, plays one of *Tombstone Canyon*'s bad guys. Burns also provides an amusing sequence that plays out like one of his radio routines, involving a telephone call from his demanding wife at an inopportune moment.

Ken Maynard had settled temporarily at Tiffany, home of KBS Productions, during a period of estrangement from Universal Pictures. Maynard had a maverick streak and an explosive temperament and routinely displeased Carl Laemmle, Jr., Universal's chief of production.

Athletic horsemanship and a virile aspect, along with a contrast-laden combination of light-heartedness and grim determination, more than compensate for Maynard's limitations as an actor. His taste for the bizarre defies horse-opera stereotype to make his films the most memorable of the genre.

Maynard's Universal team, including director Alvin J. Neitz (a.k.a. Alan James), handled technical matters on *Tombstone*. Exteriors were filmed in Hagen Canyon in the Mojave Desert, whose unusual rock formations also figure in *Hidden Valley*, *The Mummy* (1932), the *Flash Gordon* cosmic gothics (1936–1940), Val Lewton's hair-raising *Apache Drums* (1951), and *Planet of the Apes* (1968).

Tombstone Canyon contains enough killings to rival the Italian westerns of two generations later, as well as chases, gunfights, and clifftop combat. The most striking feature is the grotesque Phantom, who haunts the region like some Shakespearean ghost. The role belongs to the grand old villain of the silent pictures, the Clutching Hand himself, Sheldon Lewis—who applies the same intensity he had poured into his 1920 version of *Dr. Jekyll and Mr. Hyde*. Grand-manner histrionics and a horrific makeup of his own creation make Lewis' Phantom one of the strangest characters ever to stalk the screen. One of many silent-screen luminaries who had fallen upon leaner times since the talkie surge, Lewis uses his voice most effectively, establishing a grating, mechanical timbre. He also supplies the Phantom's weird outcries and a hair-raising death-rattle.

Cecilia Parker, later a co-star of the *Hardy Family* series at MGM, is an energetic heroine. Bob Burns was better known at the time for his radio routines combining homely philosophy with an air of naïveté. As his star ascended into the 1940s, Burns remained best known for his invention of the bazooka, a crude but expressive musical instrument fashioned from a horn's mouthpiece, a whiskey funnel, a slide-whistle apparatus, and a length of gas-pipe hose; its limited range of notation sounds like a more melodic Bronx cheer, or razzberry. (Burns' coinage is a dual-purpose pun on *bazoo*, or loudmouth, and an Old World synonym for *bugle*. The military later appropriated the term for an instrument of warfare.)

Burns received solo billing on a reissue of *Tombstone Canyon*. Ken Maynard had lapsed from prominence by the mid-1930s after one altercation too many with the studio suits.

Pressbook portraits: Maynard and Burns.

Forgotten Horrors of 1933

The Horror

In Japan: Jumen (Face of Beast)
Alternate cut: John the Drunkard
(Bud Pollard Productions, Inc. • Stanley Distributing Corp. • 1933)

The diligence of cultural historians Aizu Shingo, Bill Littman, and Scott MacQueen has settled a mystery. The existence of Bud Pollard's *The Horror* had seemed in doubt until the waning 1990s, despite the persuasive evidence of a lurid advertising campaign. The trade journals seem not to have reviewed the film. Surviving associates of Pollard—a prolific hack who nonetheless was a mainstay of the Screen Directors Guild—had told George Turner they believed the film had gone uncompleted.

The missing link proves to be a pseudo-clinical featurette called *John the Drunkard* (1944). One church-and-school rental catalogue of the 1950s describes *John the Drunkard* as a condemnation of liquor but notes neither any horrific element nor Pollard's involvement. Hold that thought.

In 1996, Shingo and Littman chanced upon a contemporary review of *The Horror* in archives of a Japanese magazine, *Kinema Junpo*. The film had been released, if only noted for the critical record in Japan. Shingo and Littman forwarded the publication to MacQueen, who made an unexpected connection via the Library of Congress with *John the Drunkard*—a sanctimonious, scare-mongering condensation of *The Horror*. Go figure.

Pollard had recut *The Horror* in 1944—imposing a narration that ascribes the creepier business to *delirium tremens*, the better to appeal to the holier-than-thou crowd. A bad rascal's awakening from a nightmare in the one becomes a contrived redemption from sin and degradation in the other.

John Massey (Leslie King) steals a sacred statue from a temple in India. Guardians pursue Massey to America and invade his household. The cultists set loose a snake on Massey's wife (Nyreda Montez) and deploy a gorilla. Massey finds himself transformed into a hideous creature. He screams himself awake.

An idiomatic translation follows of the Japanese magazine's dumb-founded bluff of a review:

> ...a rare work. ... [M]ain theme is clearly the concept of fear. ... Portrays that elusive emotion well. Its rarity within its genre lies in its strange and unusual techniques.
>
> Unusual moviemaking techniques are quite noticeable, but it is beyond my comprehension how a wife sleeping with a child becomes a wife sleeping with a big snake, and how immediately the husband's face changes to that of a Mr. Hyde. The reasoning...is difficult to comprehend.

The scene in which the gorilla appears and begins fighting with the man with the beastly face is extremely thrilling. The eye that appears to float in midair is also extraordinary.

Silent-era actor Leslie King bears an uncanny resemblance to Lon Chaney, who had died in 1930. King stops short of a dramatic presence; his portrayal is an overzealous throwback—not to the intense, pantomimic style of the silents, but to the broad and over-reactive style of Victorian stage melodrama. The other players follow suit.

The trick effects and a shabby pinhead-gorilla costume bespeak an awkward self-consciousness: the artifice calls such attention to itself as to obscure the story. Even so, neither *The Horror* nor its mutilated temperance-lecture version can be dismissed as some laughable *badfilm*, to invoke a once-fashionable term. Pollard's overcooked sincerity is evident throughout—though less so in the cynically motivated *John the Drunkard*. Sanctimony is the last refuge of a scoundrel. Or one of the last refuges, at any rate.

By the time of *John the Drunkard*, Pollard had retrenched in moviemaking for black-neighborhood theatres—a long-hidden pocket of the industry—working notably with the blues-and-comedy artist Louis Jordan. History sometimes confuses the Long Island-based Pollard with the Hollywood-based Harry A. Pollard, a director of finer distinction, from whom Universal City's Pollard Lake takes its name.

Bud Pollard also had announced such titles for 1933–1934 as *Lunatic at Large*, *Dance Hall Dames*, *Metropolitan Murders*, *Framed*, and *The Green Jade*. This unrealized docket appears to have been a matter of wishful thinking on the part of the producer.

Another picture, also called *The Horror*—whether feature-lengther, or short subject, or middle-ground featurette—was made during this same general period by the stage magician Maurice Kitchen, alias Rajah Raboid, as a promotional device. That film appears to have become genuinely lost.

The Whispering Shadow

Mascot Pictures Corp. • 1933

The Whispering Shadow is the first of four serials to topline Bela Lugosi—a ticket-selling name, despite a fall from grace among the big studios—and an early instance of Mascot's use of star billing above the title. Lugosi adds an admirably sinister note, about which more presently. Further substance derives from such silent-era stars (speaking of diminished circumstances) as Henry B. Walthall, Malcolm MacGregor, George Lewis, Ethel Clayton, Roy D'Arcy, Jack Perrin, and Karl Dane.

Viva Tattersall is a delight as Lugosi's daughter; she was the wife of Sidney Toler, who would become the movies' second-best Charlie Chan (after Warner Oland, of course).

The Whispering Shadow is a mob boss whose agents assail a trucking company—a campaign of wreckage, robbery, and serial murder. The overlord can project his voice and his shadow, the better to remain unknown, even among his thugs. Disobedience means death: the Whispering Shadow wields a remotely controlled electrocution device. The crimes attract a criminologist, Raymond (Robert Warwick), and Jack Foster (MacGregor), the vengeful brother of a slain driver.

Each truck had carried a shipment bound for the wax museum of Prof. Strang (Lugosi)whose likelike figures foreshadow the movie-making and theme-park technology known as animatronics. Strang ascribes an early attack to a statue of a caveman. Foster finds himself attracted to Strang's daughter, Vera (Tattersall).

Captured for questioning, a Shadow henchman (Max Wagner) is electrocuted. Suspicion falls generally. An airborne siege results in a wild fight and a wreck atop the company's warehouse. Slayings narrow the field of suspects. The warehouse proves to conceal the Russian crown jewels. Jerome (Lafe McKee), a mysterious corporate official, is a Russian prince, incognito. Strang is a government official, feigning eerie menace. Foster exposes the Whispering Shadow as an unlikely suspect—a radio dispatcher named Sparks (Dane), whose lame-brained manner has been a ruse.

Karl Dane's casting is a curiosity—lunkheaded comic relief giving way to menace—but nonetheless in keeping with Mascot chief Nat Levine's tactic of deflecting suspicion via exaggerations and blatant audience-fooling deceit. Dane was a master pantomime artist and comedian whose thick Danish accent worked against his talking-picture prospects, notwithstanding successful talkie transitions for other dialectical comics. Dane committed suicide in 1934 after a stretch of unemployment. More curious is the portrayal of a Russian nobleman by Lafe McKee, better known as a perennial figure of fatherly author-ity in the western movies.

A location-shooting landmark is the Hollywood warehouse of Bekins Transfer & Storage Co., augmented by a miniature replica. A model autogyro appears in conjunction with the authentic warehouse. A miniature truck-crash sequence is effective, as is the depiction of the Shadow via animation.

The Vampire Bat

Majestic Pictures Corp. • 1933

Among the independent studios' many weird thrillers—the better to cash in on a vogue—few are all-out horror films. Such a rarity is Frank R. Strayer's *The Vampire Bat*, a curious marriage of superstition and science fiction, often mistaken for a product of Universal Pictures' cel-ebrated horror factory. Star player Fay Wray had recalled the picture as a Universal production, in fact, until a late-in-life rediscovery showing at Dallas' USA Film Festival reminded her that the assignment had been a Majestic Pictures project on rented Universal sets.

The benighted town is the familiar Village Frankenstein. Mad scientist Lionel Atwill holds forth in the prime real estate of James Whale's *The*

Old Dark House (1932), furnished in part from the mansion of 1927's *The Cat and the Canary*. A morgue is the wine cellar of Castle Frankenstein. A torchlit pursuit recalls Whale's 1931 *Frankenstein*, although the site is Bronson Canyon in place of Universal's manufactured cliffs. The ensemble cast includes Universal veterans Atwill, Melvyn Douglas, Dwight Frye, and Lionel Belmore. Screenwriter Edward T. Lowe had been the scenarist of Universal's *The Hunchback of Notre Dame* (1923).

The Mittel European village of Kleinschloss is in turmoil over a series of blood-draining murders. Inspector Karl Brettschneider (Douglas) perceives a human fiend; the superstitious yokels suspect a vampire. The town has been overrun with huge bats. Dr. Otto von Neimann (Atwill) treats a victim. The village idiot, Herman Glieb (Frye), displays an affection for bats—provoking suspicion.

Von Neimann promotes the vampire theory. His gloomy household and laboratory seem a right setting for such terrors. Brettschneider disagrees. The villagers drive Herman to his death in a cave and pound a stake through his heart. Von Neimann hypnotizes a helper, Emil (Robert Frazer), with orders to kill a loyal servant (Stella Adams). A crucifix, planted upon the body, implicates Herman—but word arrives that Herman is dead. Von Neimann urges Brettschneider to remain calm, then sends Emil to kill the detective.

A chapter from Michael H. Price's collaborative comic-book series, The Prowler *(1988), contains an adaptation of* The Vampire Bat.

The doctor's assistant, Ruth Bertin (Wray), overhears and confronts von Neimann, who binds her and begins boasting: "Life—created in the laboratory! ...living, growing tissue...moves, pulsates, and demands *food*! ... [W]hat are a few lives [compared with] science? ... [I have] wrested the secret of life *from life*! ... From the lives of those who have gone before, I have *created* life!" (His creation is a spongy lump.)

Brettschneider has overcome Emil and brought the slave to von Neimann's stronghold. Emil, finally aware of his role, kills the doctor and himself. Von Neimann's collapse wrecks the apparatus.

Just as Ronald Colman remains the perfect Bulldog Drummond, Warner Oland the perfect Charlie Chan, Margaret Dumont the perfect foil for Groucho Marx, and Boris Karloff the perfect Frankenstein Monster, so is Lionel Atwill the ideal mad doctor. (All due respect to Karloff's near-equal command of that image.) Atwill's smile can be more menacing than a scowl. His clipped Oxford accent substantiates the most extravagant claims of crackpot science. His enthusiasm conveys an utter belief in the wildest theories. Atwill was a handsome and personable sort who seldom wore grotesque makeups—an exception is Warners' *Mystery of the Wax Museum*, from the same period, and likewise with Fay Wray—but he projects a frightening madness with conviction.

One deft moment in *The Vampire Bat* affirms the transcendence of moral qualms: The killer balks as Atwill's telepathic control wavers. Atwill, momentarily aghast at the crime he intends, gasps and falters—then mutters, "Well, she's no better than the others."

Fay Wray, too, is perfection in the face of peril. Although her abilities embraced a greater dramatic range, the studios knew that red-blooded male moviegoers would give their eyeteeth to protect Wray from the menaces of *The Most Dangerous Game* and *Doctor X* (both from

1932), *King Kong* and *Mystery of the Wax Museum* (1933), and *Below the Sea* (1936). Beyond beauty, Wray projects a natural innocence in bold contrast with madmen and monsters. Her sessions with Atwill are testaments to the ideal matching of their artistic contrasts.

Melvyn Douglas, clever and resourceful, is a relief from the mild leading men of many horror yarns. Dwight Frye, Universal's signature nervous lunatic, has a meaty role as a halfwit with a fatal affinity for bats. George E. Stone stands out briefly as a frightened townsman. Robert Frazer is a sympathetic menace. William V. Mong is a sniveling alderman. Lionel Belmore is again (as in *Frankenstein*) the ideal His Honor the Mayor. Maude Eburne, dumpy but animated, provides comic relief as Wray's hypochondriac aunt—who delivers a closing gag: the aunt mixes some of Atwill's chemicals as an intended remedy and, having swallowed the concoction, learns the components add up to Epsom salts. The mild vulgarism would not have passed muster the following year, when the Roman Catholic Church's Legion of Decency took a censorious and parasitic stranglehold upon the Motion Picture Association.

Frank Strayer's tight direction makes amends for the misfire of *The Monster Walks*. The high-calibre photography is the work of MGM's Ira Morgan. The melodramatic opening music, from Abe Meyer's versatile library of prefabricated cues, comprises two widely used *mysteriosi* by Charles Dunworth: "Stealthy Footsteps" and "The Ghost Walks."

Interlude

Further Titles of Interest

These titles enhance the context for 1933:

- *Eat 'Em Alive* (Harold Austin-Real Life Pictures; 1933). This wildlife documentary from the American West indicts man as deadliest of the desert's inhabitants. For the climax, a bull terrier rescues a child from a rattlesnake. The film often was paired with *Virgins of Bali*.

- *Jungle Bride* (Monogram Pictures; 1933). This murder yarn (with musical interludes) finds castaways Anita Page, Charles Starrett, and Eddie Stevens at large along an African beach. Interpersonal antagonisms overshadow the threats of marauding wildlife.

- *Matto-Grosso* (Principal Distributing Corp.; 1933). This expeditionary companion piece to *The Amazon Head Hunters* in Sol Lesser's Principal-Adventure series is distinguished by the elaborate rituals heralding a hunt for jaguars in Brazil.

- *A Jungle Gigolo* (Prosperity Pictures & Principal; 1933). Likewise a companion to *Matto-Grosso* and *Head Hunters* as part of Sol Lesser's ambitious Principal-Adventure line. The tongue-in-cheek piece feigns a straightforward account of "nerve-shattering perils and ghostly nightmares" but often resorts to broad comedy of a type more commonly associated with MGM's *Pete Smith Specialties* series. A Sumatran (assigned the demeaning name of Clarence) experiences exaggerated misadventures as a wandering laborer, a gun bearer on a crocodile hunt, and the rescuer of a village from a rogue elephant. Meanwhile, another entry in

The emergence of the Legion of Decency as a force to the detriment of the motion-picture industry.

the Principal-Adventure line, Faustin Wirkus' surprisingly good vanity picture *Voodo* (*sic*), appears elsewhere in the present array as a centerpiece.

- *What Price Decency?* (Equitable Pictures & Majestic Pictures; 1933). The jungle melodrama features Dorothy Burgess as the abused wife of trader Alan Hale. She finally turns the tables, blinding Hale with a whiplashing. The local natives kill the lout as a matter of honorable principle.

- *The Shadow Laughs* (Trojan Pictures; 1933). In which a skulking killer's foredoomed accomplice lifts $100,000 from a bank vault in this conventional, derivative exercise from director Arthur Hoerl. Rose Hobart is a menaced secretary, and Walter Fenner is a banker of criminal inclinations.

- *Found Alive (On the Delta of the Rio Grande)* (Ideal-Excelsior; 1933). This tale of an estranged family, directed by pioneering stunt artist Charles "Hurricane Hutch" Hutchinson, takes place in a menacing jungle setting in Mexico, with generously deployed stock footage depicting wild-animal battles. Barbara Bedford and Robert Frazer head the cast.

- *Sing Sinner Sing* (Majestic Pictures; 74 Minutes; August 17, 1933). The basis is a true-crime case of 1932: Tobacco heir Zachary Smith Reynolds was shot to death—likely a suicide—and his wife and a family friend were charged with murder. Donald Dillaway plays the Reynolds surrogate as a loathsome menace whose demise might represent an improvement to the species. The screenwriter is Edward T. Lowe, of *The Vampire Bat*—whose attitude of oppressive gloom carries over.

- *Mr. Broadway* (Broadway-Hollywood & Malcomar Productions, Ltd., with Arthur Greenblatt, Inc.; 1933). Ed Sullivan, show-business gossip columnist and self-important nincompoop, conducts a tour of his proprietary turf in a rivalrous riposte to Walter Winchell (who delivered *two* such narcissistic films in 1933). Sullivan's music-and-comedy excursion takes a jarring detour into murder and suicide. The film is of interest primarily for its inclusion of surviving footage (approximately 20 minutes) from Edgar G. Ulmer's first English-language picture, *The Warning Shadow*, a.k.a. *Love's Interlude*, filmed in 1932 by Peerless Productions at Metropolitan Studios in Fort Lee, New Jersey. Ulmer directed *The Warning Shadow* from his collaborative screenplay. As deployed without permission in *Mr. Broadway*, the sequence finds Ulmer's signature interest in erotic obsessions and ghastly consequences already in place, two years before he would deliver similarly lust-driven *The Black Cat* at Universal.

In a late-in-life interview with George Turner, Ulmer recalled *The Warning Shadow* as a completed but unissued project: "It seems the studio couldn't pay the laboratory fees," he said, "and my property—my original scenario, my directing—became fodder for Ed Sullivan's vanity hackery. I was paid nothing.

"The studios shared a laboratory, you see," added Ulmer, "and it was common knowledge in the trade that Peerless had a picture unpaid for, in the can, already announced. Sullivan wanted a *real* story to go in the middle of his little travelogue. And when he learned this one of mine was languishing, he and Johnnie Walker [producer-director of *Mr. Broadway*] determined that the laboratory controlled the picture. ... They bought the footage out from under us, for the sake of committing butchery. Sullivan forced it into one of those *Moonlight and Pretzels* things—something to illustrate what a great raconteur he fancied himself. Of course, the story that Sullivan pretends to tell is not his own story—it's mine!" (*Moonlight and Pretzels* is a Universal musical comedy from 1933, directed by Karl Freund.)

This is the yarn that counteracts (briefly) the frivolous tone of *Mr. Broadway*: Actress Josephine Dunn asks Ed Sullivan how he gets all that material for his wonderful newspaper column. Sullivan replies, with fraudulent modesty, that everyone has a story to tell. He manages a clumsy transition, declaring that Dunn's necklace reminds him of a tale. Hence a flashback to a killing—committed for possession of a necklace by a naïve youngster (Tom Moore) at the urging of a prostitute (Dita Parlo). The boy kills himself upon finding her faithless. Back in the moment, Sullivan explains that he has not published the story lest he violate a confidence. *Mr. Broadway* gives but scant acknowledgment of Ulmer's unintended contribution to Ed Sullivan's brilliant career.

Voodo

Principal Distributing Corp. • 1933

Faustin Wirkus, a white man and former colonial administrator of the Island of La Gonave, 30 miles off Haiti, returns to study the superstitions of the black inhabitants. Wirkus witnesses ceremonies of *vodun*, or voodoo, involving the sacrifice of goats and chickens to ancient African deities. At length, he stumbles onto a ritual in which a young woman is to be slaughtered. He rescues the girl and escapes the wrath of the cult.

Sol Lesser, soon to begin applying his larger moviemaking ambitions to a lasting control of E.R. Burroughs' *Tarzan* franchise, made do for the time being with the vanity-driven expeditionary films of various dilettante filmmaker-explorers. (See *The Amazon Head Hunters*, in addition to *Matto-Grosso* and *A Jungle Gigolo*.) Such small-investment acquisitions, taken together, formed an illusion of bold productivity for Lesser's Principal-Adventure series and dispensed a wealth of thrills (however condescending toward the Third World) in the process. Faustin Wirkus' production of *Voodo* is a self-aggrandizing combination of documentary realism and utter phoniness.

History has treated Wirkus with favor. He spent 1925–1928 as governor of 10,000 denizens of La Gonave, a long-neglected island not far from Port-au-Prince, where tribal superstitions held sway over farmers

and fishermen just as in centuries past. A Marine Corps sergeant turned lieutenant in the Haitian gendarmerie, Wirkus ended generations of graft and parasitic taxation to become "the first honest official [the natives] had known," as his collaborator and biographer, Henry Wysham Lanier, put it. Added Lanier: "He left their wives and daughters alone. White though he was, he treated a poor Haitian like a human being. ... [He] fought for them with the authorities [and] had an ardent interest in their carefully hidden religion—not because he wished to raid and suppress, but apparently because he wished to know." The tribespeople honored Wirkus with the title of King Faustin I.

Early in the 1930s, Wirkus returned to film this remarkable study of voodoo practices. During the winter of 1933–1934, *Harper's Monthly* magazine published a fascinating excerpt from Wirkus' memoirs under the title "The Black Pope of Voodoo." The movie is no less engaging, even though its wild ending was staged to impart a sensationalism that had proved lacking in reality. Even with the dramatization, the film is involving and respectfully factual, more anthropology than Third World theology. It is rare to see a civilized interloper who refrains from forcing his own society's crackpot religious superstitions upon tribes that already have their own fanatical beliefs—a practice that results as often as not in the quaint tradition of the missionary stew banquet.

Wirkus' camerawork is surprisingly vivid, and his narration is straightforward and unemotional. A throbbing musical score intensifies the mood of otherworldly frenzy. At four reels, the film is conspicuously briefer than the other Principal-Adventure featurettes; this condition made for difficulties in booking.

Sucker Money

Willis Kent Productions • Progressive Pictures • 1933

The Continuing Misadventures of Swami Yomurda, Part No. 2: the character, one of Mischa Auer's more lively and sinister portrayals, had originated in Willis Kent's production of *Sinister Hands*. *Sucker Money* makes a more emphatic use of the Hindu charlatan, establishing him as a figure in need of killing. Not to give away too much, y'know.

Sucker Money is not so much a sequel as it is a variation upon a theme. Also returning from *Sinister Hands*, though in different roles, are Phyllis Barrington and Fletcher Norton.

Yomurda's exaggerated wickedness owes largely to the influence of co-director Dorothy Reid, a relentless and ham-fisted social reformer and celebrity widow of the silent-screen idol Wallace Reid. Reid's death, the result of a secretive drug habit, had been one of Old Hollywood's more notorious scandals. Mrs. Reid spent a decade on an

anti-narcotics crusade, as both actress and writer. She tackled *Sucker Money* as a means of exposing another plague: the spiritualism racket that had become a fashionable indulgence among wealthy chasers of trends. As broke-and-busted as America-at-large was during the Depression, the aloof monied class still demanded its costly frivolities. (Such circumstances persist in this bold new millennium. 'Twas ever thus, as Oliver Hardy and/or George E. Turner would have it.)

Reporter Jimmy Reeves (Earl McCarthy) accepts an assignment to get the goods on crooked psychics. He takes a job with Swami Yomurda as an impersonator of departed souls. An investment scam goes awry. After a kidnapping plot collapses, Yomurda begins a killing rampage among his own circle of crooks—finally to be gunned down by the police.

The subject had been treated more expertly in such films as Tod Browning's *The Mystic* (1925). *Sucker Money* suffers from clumsy writing and inept direction. The bright spots include Auer,

Mischa Auer

thoroughly in his element—he had yet to stake out the broader and more crowd-pleasing territory of comedy—and Mae Busch, exercising her forté as a tough dame, and Ralph Lewis, as a small-town banker who appears ripe for a fleecing.

The Three Musketeers

Mascot Pictures Corp. • 1933

The last and best of John Wayne's Mascot serials is everything an enthusiast could want, with all due apologies to Alexandre Dumas. Spectacle figures in a fast-moving tale of the French Foreign Legion, with horsemen thundering across the dunes (near Yuma, Arizona) and shouting, "Death to the unbelievers!" These are the same extras found in scores of westerns—a condition betrayed by their drawling voices. Scenic values include settings left behind by silent-era producers, and (elsewhere) craggy Bronson Canyon. A fort where Wayne is held captive is the notorious Yuma Jail.

The mysterious El Shaitan conscripts a young member of the Foreign Legion, Armand Corday (Creighton Chaney, soon to become Lon, Jr.). A siege upon a legion detachment horrifies Corday. American Tom Wayne (John Wayne) routs the Arabs. Wayne meets surviving legionnaires Clancy (Jack Mulhall), Renard (Raymond Hatton), and Schmidt (Francis X. Bushman, Jr.). Tom's fiancée, Elaine (Ruth Hall), is Corday's sister.

El Shaitan frames Wayne for trafficking in contraband. When Corday clears Wayne, the villain kills Corday and implicates Wayne. Revealed as a harmless-looking merchant (Edward Piel), the brigand chieftain is gunned down by the Musketeers.

Wayne's fellow heroic protagonists are the effervescent Jack Mulhall, Raymond Hatton (sporting an unlikely French accent), and Francis X. Bushman, Jr., a genial giant who lends comical touches. Lon Chaney, Jr.—billed as Creighton—plays a conflicted soul whose torments foreshadow the portrayals that would become his stock-in-trade in *The Wolf Man* (1941) and many other put-upon roles. (Another son

of silent-screen parentage, Noah Beery, Jr., also appears.) Ruth Hall, filmmaker Lee Garmes' athletic wife, supplies the romantic interest and a trouble-magnet distraction.

Producer Nat Levine's insistence upon keeping the bad guy's identity a secret finds El Shaitan impersonated by Yakima Canutt, Robert Frazer, and Gordon de Main—who have other roles—and by Wilfred Lucas, who does not otherwise appear. (There is little shared resemblance.) Canutt handles multiple roles and doubles Wayne in numerous feats. Armand Schaefer and Colbert Clark direct in the efficient team-helmer process. A feature-length version surfaced in 1948 as *Desert Command*, from Favorite Films.

A Shriek in the Night

Allied Pictures Corp. • 1933

M.H. "Max" Hoffman had registered as both artist and lawyer before he entered the film industry in 1910 at age 29. He was general manager of Universal, principal founder of Tiffany and Liberty, and (in 1931) founder of Allied Pictures. After a brief affiliation with Monogram, Hoffman decided to keep Allied self-contained and launched a schedule that included a series of Hoot Gibson westerns, several modern-dress versions of literary classics, and a string of mystery and action films. Allied's docket for 1932–1933 included such fine players as Reginald Denny, Myrna Loy, Lila Lee, Monte Blue, Mary Nolan, and Marian Marsh.

It was a triumph for Hoffman to reunite the stars of his hit *The Thirteenth Guest*, for Ginger Rogers and Lyle Talbot were faring well at the major studios. *A Shriek in the Night* is not a sequel but a kindred entry, using the same director (Albert Ray), scenarist (Frances Hyland), and production crew. The opening three-shot sequence seems unique: Shot No.1 shows a nighttime view of a hotel, with a gunshot and a scream coming over; No. 2, a down-shot, shows a body hurtling toward the sidewalk; No. 3 affords a closer view as the body strikes the pavement.

Slow-witted janitor Pete Peterson (Harvey Clark) identifies the stiff as a tenant. Police inspector Russell (Purnell Pratt) and his nervous assistant, Wilfred (Arthur Hoyt), catch Patricia Morgan (Rogers) prowling about; she identifies herself as the dead man's secretary. Russell finds a card depicting a coiled snake with the legend, "You Will Hear It." A hissing noise becomes associated with the case.

Newsman Ted Rand (Talbot) spots Patricia—his sweetheart, a rival reporter. Ted hijacks her story. Sacked, Patricia gains Russell's trust and turns up a second murder, with another snake card. Patricia

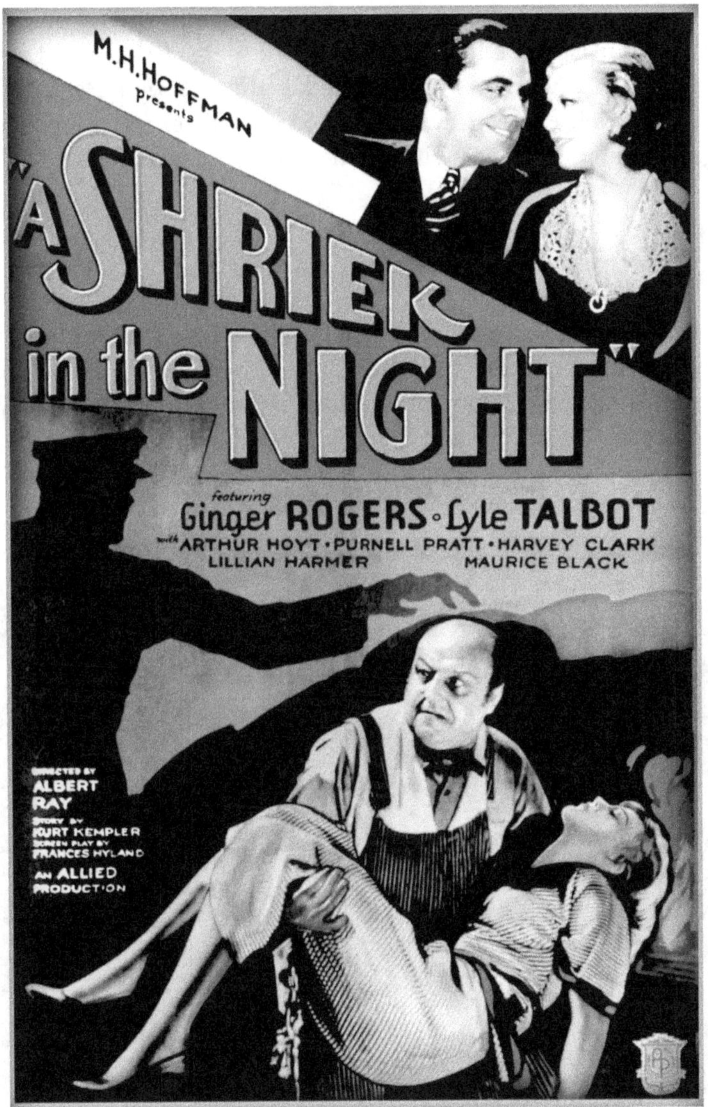

deceives Rand with a bogus story, which he calls in to *her* newspaper as if to make amends.

Underworld connections become evident. Pete seizes Patricia and attempts to roast her alive in the hotel's furnace. A rescue comes none too soon. It develops that Pete, brother of a slain gangster, has been maddened by a desire for vengeance. The serpent-like hissing had come from the release of a deadly gas.

Frances Hyland's taut screenplay alternates scares with light comedy—and with bright repartee; the mousy mannerisms (and surprising courage) of Arthur Hoyt; the antics of Lillian Harmer and

Louise Beavers as frightened servants; and the ranting of Clarence Wilson as an irascible editor. Harvey Clark seems likable and amusing until the climax, which is unexpected and ingenious. By memorable contrast, Purnell Pratt (as a hard-nosed detective) and Maurice Black (as a gangster) play things with grim straightforwardness.

A Study in Scarlet

KBS Productions • World Wide Pictures • 1933

This fantasia has little to do with Conan Doyle's novel, *A Study in Scarlet*. Reginald Owen and Warburton Gamble bear scant resemblance to the defining illustrations of Sherlock Holmes and Dr. John Watson by Frederick Dorr Steele and Sidney Paget. (Owen, the present film's Holmes, had played Dr. Watson the previous year in Fox Film Corp.'s *Sherlock Holmes*.) Discrepancies aside, the present film is a satisfying work, with capital performances.

World Wide held only titular rights. The studio paid $1,000 to Owen and the intended director, Robert Florey, to deliver a scenario involving the dwindling membership of a secret society. Some indignant know-it-alls have suggested a cribbing from Agatha Christie's *Ten Little Indians*, but Florey and Owen had scooped the overrated Dame Agatha by six years: The first filmed version of the Christie tale appeared in 1945.

Florey had left Universal in anger following his removal from *Frankenstein* (1931) and problems with management on his consolation-prize assignment, *Murders in the Rue Morgue* (1932). Upon completion of the *Scarlet* script, Florey was enticed away by Warners. Edwin L. Marin, who had excelled as a débuting director on *The Death Kiss*, replaced Florey. Marin displays a ferocious momentum, a brooding atmosphere, and offbeat characterizing touches.

Camera chief Arthur Edeson provides evocative studies of fog-shrouded Limehouse, eerie hidden rooms, and a foreboding countryside mansion. Ralph DeLacy's settings are of major-studio calibre. One intriguing sequence puts the camera subjectively in the role of a menacing figure.

Railway porters find a corpse. A cryptic advertisement lures Eileen Forrester (June Clyde) to a meeting with lawyer Thaddeus Merrydew (Alan Dinehart), who presides over the Order of the Scarlet Ring. A member has died. An earlier such casualty had been Eileen's father.

The widow (Doris Lloyd) of the rail-car victim visits detective Sherlock Holmes. Holmes seizes the opportunity to dispense with Merrydew, whose name might as well be Moriarty. As additional members die, Merrydew pretends to befriend Eileen. The purported widow (Anna May Wong) of a member seems in collusion with Merrydew. Holmes rescues Eileen from a lethal room and traps Merrydew's gang.

Far though it strays from Doyle, the complex tale is rich with details of the Holmes canon: "The game is afoot!"

Anna May Wong.

Holmes exhorts Watson. Alan Dinehart is a villain Doyle would have relished, eager to warn an innocent young woman of wickedness at large even as he plots her downfall. Holmes is properly contemptuous of Scotland Yard's Inspector Lestrade (Alan Mowbray). Notable gaffes include the placement of Holmes' address at 221-*A* Baker Street (it should be 221-*B*), and the pronunciation of Lestrade with a long *A*.

Belly Bevan's hard-drinking rural chap says of Anna May Wong's villainous character, wife of a Britisher: "You can't make English gentry out o' the 'eathen Chinee." Leila Bennett describes Wong more admiringly: "Such eyes! She walks like a cat. ... A nice bit o' goods!"

The Phantom Broadcast

Monogram Pictures Corp. • 1933

Plagiarism is so persistent within the culture that Phil Rosen's *The Phantom Broadcast* should be required viewing for any poseur tempted to misappropriate another's work. The tale of popular renown, compromised by egocentric greed and gathering madness, could just as easily take place in the present day—especially so, now that the blessing-or-curse of internet communications has made the theft of ideas and artistry as simple as the click of a mouse. (An unattributed remake from 1947, Basil Wrangell's *Heartaches*, is a similarly sobering exercise—speaking of plagiarism.)

The Phantom Broadcast is a bizarre composite riff upon *Svengali*, *The Phantom of the Opera*, *The Great Gabbo*, and *The Man Who Played God*.

Twisted psychology and ghastly secrets stand in for physical monstrousness, and the finale—where a dying hunchbacked maestro reveals his hidden artistry—is worthy of some Universal chiller of the period.

The underworld is intent upon controlling the lucrative career of singer Grant Murdock (Arnold Gray). A bounty is placed upon the life of Murdock's manager and accompanist, Norman Wilder (Ralph Forbes), a crippled artist known to a guarded few associates as the true owner of that enchanting voice. Wilder considers Murdock "a splendid dummy."

Rescued from a hit squad by bodyguard Sandy Higgins (Guinn "Big Boy" Williams), Wilder is angered to learn of Murdock's affair with gang moll Elsa Evans (Vivienne Osborne)—and more so to find Murdock planning to seduce Laura Hamilton (Gail Patrick), an aspiring singer with whom Wilder has become infatuated.

In a frenzy of jealousy, Elsa kills Murdock and leaves before the arrival of Wilder—who is contemplating murder. Upon finding the body and evidence that implicates Laura, Wilder telephones the police and reports himself responsible. Laura arrives for an appointment with Murdock. Wilder panics. While fleeing the law, Wilder is mortally wounded.

Elsa prepares to leave the country. Suddenly, the crooner's voice pours out of radios throughout the city. Wilder has reached the radio station, intent upon revealing his secret before he can die. Before a packed studio audience, the hunchback sings his heart out. Laura rushes to Wilder's side; he gives her one last bit of wise counsel, then dies in the arms of his bodyguard.

Laura and her fiancé (Paul Page) embark upon an ocean voyage. Also aboard is Elsa Evans. Neither woman knows of the other's connection with the strange crooning act. "I can't get that hunchback out of my mind," says Elsa. "I wonder who he thought he was takin' the *rap* for?"

Ralph Forbes' performance anticipates Leslie Howard's torments in the 1934 filming of Somerset Maugham's *Of Human Bondage*. The tale revels in the manipulative bitterness of the outcast genius, and yet Forbes commands sympathy. The London-born actor wears the hunchback apparatus with conviction, affecting a shuffling, apelike gait, but the performance owes more to an air of sad longing and vague derangement.

Arnold Gray plays the ungrateful mock-singer with sufficient arrogance to make his killer, however crass, seem almost heroic. Vivienne Osborne, as the low-brow *femme fatale*, blurs emphatically the narrow margin between love and hatred. Gail Patrick, a novice on loan from Paramount, radiates a dawning star quality as the naïve vocalist.

Despite such presences (usually more boisterous) as Guinn Williams, George Hayes, and Kit Guard, there is no overt comedy relief. A touch of macabre irony finds Williams attempting to warn Forbes of the mob contract in underworld lingo that the scholarly Forbes cannot comprehend. Williams is as commanding in the citified setting as he had proved himself as both leading man and sidekick in the western sector.

Rockcliffe Fellowes is a formidable mobster. Paul Page is Patrick's stalwart and trusting sweetheart; a discreet suggestion of a pre-marital domestic arrangement would have proved intolerable to the toughened censorship-and-sanctimony machinery of the following year. (Further censor bait figures in Vivienne Osborne's getting off the hook for a murder.)

Russian-born Phil Rosen, pioneering cinematographer-turned-director, is well represented in the *Forgotten Horrors* collection, with such additional gems as *Devil's Mate*, *The Sphinx*, *Picture Brides*, and *Beggars in Ermine*. In 1919, Rosen had become principal founder of the American Society of Cinematographers, the industry's oldest professional organization. A relentlessly productive director since the early 1920s, Rosen remained as innovative on Poverty Row as he had been at the silent-era majors. His command would lapse during the 1940s, with such low points as *Return of the Ape Man* and *The Chinese Cat*, but that decade also saw such memorable efforts from Rosen as Universal's *The Mystery of Marie Rogét* (1942; a semi-sequel or companion-piece to Robert Florey's *Murders in the Rue Morgue*) and an unusually good late-in-the-game entry from Monogram Pictures, *The Strange Mr. Gregory* (1946). Rosen died in 1951.

Devotees of Hollywood's geography will delight in spotting landmarks throughout *The Phantom Broadcast*. The radio studio is in the Warner Bros. Building, which housed the Warner Hollywood Theatre and the Warners' radio station. Prominent near the main entrance is the Smoke Shop—where in real life Bela Lugosi was a frequent customer. The Art Deco apartment building also is a film-capital fixture.

Broadcast's original songs are good enough that they might have provided material for Russ Columbo or Bing Crosby. The passionate lyrics are the work of George Waggner—later celebrated as a producer and director, involved with the early signature chillers of Lon Chaney, Jr. The melodists, Bernard Brown and Herbert Spencer, also worked individually—Spencer as an arranger, Brown on many Warner Bros. cartoons. The identity of the singing voice for *The Phantom Broadcast* remains a mystery.

The Flaming Signal

Wm. Berke Productions • Imperial Distributing Corp. • 1933

Action with scarcely a lag—although casting and direction leave much to be desired—propels *The Flaming Signal*, in which an intrepid pilot and his heroic German Shepherd encounter a fiendish trader and a witch doctor, with mayhem throughout.

Jim Robbins (John David Horsley) sets out for Hawaii. His dog, Flash, warns of a tail-section fire in the midst of a storm. Robbins and Flash struggle toward Tabu Island, where tensions exist between natives and interloping colonists. Von Krantz (Noah Beery) keeps the pearl-rich natives in drunken poverty. He guns down a tribal priest (Mischa Auer), triggering a rebellion. Flash lights a signal beacon, then trounces von Krantz.

As a passing ship steers for shore, Flash saves Robbins and the daughter (Marceline Day) of a meddlesome missionary (Henry B. Walthall). A sailor rescues Flash from a shark.

Curly-haired John David Horsley is astonishingly miscast; the role calls for a more virile specimen, such as a Richard Dix or a Jack Holt. Not to mention that Flash is no Rin-Tin-Tin—nowhere near as fierce as circumstances require.

Compensation abounds, however, in the professionalism of Marceline Day, Noah Beery, Henry B. Walthall as the bewildered and ineffectual missionary, and the intensity of versatile Mischa Auer. Pictorial values are of a sporadically high quality. A preview audience on December 21, 1932, in Glendale, California, had a fine old time ridiculing the film.

I Cover the Waterfront

Reliance Pictures, Inc. • United Artists • 1933

Like such other successful silent-era directors as D.W. Griffith, William Nigh, Fred Newmeyer, Marshall Neilan, and Erich von Stroheim, James Cruze found his talking-pictures career a succession of exhilarating highs and demeaning lows. The collapse of Cruze's producing company and a plunge into alcoholism blighted a decade in which his artistry veered only occasionally in a productive direction.

Cruze was hired by Reliance early in 1933 to direct its first feature, *I Cover the Waterfront*. Reliance was a venture of Edward Small and Harry Goetz, with backing from United Artists' Joseph M. Schenck—a scrappy independent, though above Poverty Row status. *Waterfront*,

from a memoir by tough-guy reporter Max Miller of the San Diego *Sun*, mingles fact with fiction in a lurid and virile mixture of near-documentary realism and chilling melodrama.

Julie Kirk (Claudette Colbert) cannot fathom why her father, Eli Kirk (Ernest Torrence), is troubled. The Coast Guard is closing in on Kirk's Chinese-smuggling operations. Reporter Joseph Miller (Ben Lyon) has vowed to expose the seafaring crook. A harbor bum (Harry Beresford) dredges up the corpse of a Chinese, bound in a chain from Kirk's fishing smack. Julie traces her father to a waterfront dive, and Miller helps her bring him home. Julie and Miller meet the next day.

Miller and federal agents board Kirk's boat. Miller slashes open a shark—and finds a Chinese. Eli, wounded in a struggle, escapes. Miller trails Kirk to a stranded barge. The smuggler is about to do away with Miller when Julie arrives. Sensing his daughter's affection for the snoop, Eli helps her take Miller to a speedboat—and then collapses in death.

In addition to its United Artists Studios work, the production involved locations at San Pedro and in the Pacific off San Pedro, San Diego, and Monterey. A harpooning expedition brought in several 20-foot sharks for scenes in which immigrants are hidden in carcasses. Snorkels enabled the Chinese extras to bear the rancid and suffocating confinement.

Authenticity radiates from such seagoing landmarks as the U.S.S. *Constitution*, the Pacific Fleet, and the *Carma*, a dilapidated yacht on which a famous explorer, Captain Walter Wanderwell, had been murdered in 1932. The company was at work on the United Artists lot when an earthquake threw Ben Lyon out of the bed in which he was emoting; the 'quake killed the power.

Claudette Colbert and Lyon do fine work as a waterfront waif and her determined suitor. Colbert has a discreet nude-swimming scene. The real star is Ernest Torrence, a former concert pianist and operatic baritone from Edinburgh, who had become famous via his portrayal of the degenerate Luke Hatburn in *Tol'able David* (1921). Six-foot-four, lantern-jawed, and muscular, Torrence renders Eli Kirk fearsome and vulgar and yet imparts poignancy. Kirk's bumbling fondness for his daughter, his loyalty to murderous colleagues, and even his drunken flailings-about are curiously affecting. Few actors have accomplished such a feat; Boris Karloff in the *Frankenstein* films comes to mind, as do Brian Donlevy in the 1939 *Beau Geste* and James Cagney in 1931's *The Public Enemy*. Torrence died shortly after the completion of *I Cover the Waterfront*. Other notables are Harry Beresford as a harbor scavenger and Hobart Cavanaugh as a happily inebriated journalist.

Camera chief Ray June overcomes Cruze's usual reluctance to vary the shooting angles; an air of somber eeriness suffuses the picture.

The Sphinx

Monogram Pictures Corp. • 1933

A janitor named Balcigalupi (Luis Alberni) testifies that Jerome Breen (Lionel Atwill), an investor and philanthropist on trial for murder, had spoken to him at the scene of the crime scene. And yet, Breen is deaf and mute. Newspaperman Jack Burton (Theodore Newton) believes Breen is not only guilty, but also responsible for other such crimes.

Jerry Crane (Sheila Terry), Burton's sweetheart and fellow journalist, is assigned to write about Breen's charitable endeavors. A Breen associate (Paul Fix) promises Burton a scoop—only to turn up murdered. The victim's mother (Lillian Leighton) identifies Breen as the killer and avers that he is no dummy. Breen has an alibi. A detective turns up slain, having noticed that Breen is overly protective of his piano. When Jerry touches the instrument, a certain note triggers

a wall panel. Breen stalks out from a hidden room. Jerry turns to face *another* Breen. Burton and the police arrive none too soon. Breen's twin had been the deaf-mute. The slayings of financiers had enabled Breen to maintain the pose as a philanthropist. With a haughty chuckle, Breen commits suicide via a poison-bearing ring.

Lionel Atwill is more terrifying without makeup than most others could be under putty. Scarcely anyone else could pack such grim meaning into simple dialogue, or convey such disdain for common decency, as when Atwill sniffs at an accusation of murder. The confrontation by two Atwills delivers a jolt without overt violence. The use of purported philanthropy as a cover for crimes conveys well the attitude of the Poverty Row studios toward the ruling class.

Atwill receives adequate support from Sheila Terry and Theodore Newton, both on loan from Warners. Luis Alberni, best known for his fawning support of John Barrymore in *Svengali* (1931), is superb in a drunken scene. Lucien Prival is an oily confidant to Atwill. Paul Hurst, as a wisecracking cop, administers the closing gag, much as he had done in *The Thirteenth Guest*. (Hurst's punch-line, involving the wired musical instrument, goes: "And you-all *laughed* when I sat down at the piano!" The saying is a riff on a well-known advertising slogan.)

Albert DeMond's unusual yarn inspires atmospheric work from director Phil Rosen and cinematographer Gil Warrenton. In a turnabout from his phantasmagorical work on *The Cat and the Canary* and *The Man Who Laughs* at the close of the silent era, Warrenton captures *The Sphinx* without bizarre visual effects; even the split-screen shot, where Atwill-times-two confronts Terry, is staged with casual naturalism.

Monogram remade *The Sphinx* a decade later as *Phantom Killer*—a title often mistakenly associated with Bela Lugosi—with the Atwill role passing to John Hamilton, the Perry White-in-waiting of *The Adventures of Superman*. The comical janitor of the remake is Mantan Moreland. A comic-book adaptation of *The Sphinx*, by Graham Nolan and Michael H. Price, appears in a companion volume, *Forgotten Horrors Comics & Stories* (2011).

Tomorrow at Seven

Jefferson Pictures • RKO-Radio Pictures • 1933

The dynamic Chester Morris heads a high-grade cast in *Tomorrow at Seven*, a slick chiller from a company organized by Joseph Schnitzer and Samuel Zierler, with a crew from the now-foundering World Wide Pictures. Suspenseful, baffling, and well balanced with comical touches, the script is vintage Ralph Spence (see *The Crooked Circle*). Director Ray Enright came aboard on loan from Warners, where he

made more than 50 features between 1927 and 1941. RKO-Radio found the picture worth acquiring for a top-of-the-line promotional campaign, including a monumental 24-sheet billboard.

In Chicago, writer Neil Broderick (Morris) is investigating a perplexing case of murder. His romantic interest, Martha Winters (Vivienne Osborne), proves to be the daughter of an assistant to a businessman named Drake (Henry Stephenson)—who has spent a fortune in an attempt to track the elusive killer. Drake receives a cryptic warning: "Tomorrow at seven."

An airborne investigation ends in a lethal attack upon Martha's father (Grant Mitchell). A forced landing points to a foreboding mansion in a swampbound region. An ominous figure, Simons (Charles Middleton), turns up crucial information that goes missing. The elusive fiend poses new threats, and Martha is dragged into the swamp by Simons—an associate of Neil, a Secret Service agent. Exposed as the killer following a struggle, Drake is done in by his own weapon.

The identity of the killer is kept tantalizingly out of reach, with each next logical suspect becoming the next victim. The varied settings, from a mansion to an airliner to a dismal swamp in Louisiana, are right for the mood of adventure gone awry.

The unjustly forgotten Vivienne Osborne made a fine nemesis for Edward G. Robinson in *Two Seconds* (1932) and a daunting murderess in *Supernatural* (1933). Osborne fares nicely as the menaced ingenue. Charles Middleton is as intimidating as ever. Henry Stephenson lends his customary dignity. Grant Mitchell seems convincingly terrified. Frank McHugh and Allen Jenkins lend comedy relief as irascible detectives.

Strange People

Chesterfield Motion Picture Corp. • 1933

Landmark sets (rented) at Universal Studios lend Richard Thorpe's *Strange People* an imposing presence. One senses Thorpe's impatience to graduate to the major leagues, where such scene-dock finery could be taken for granted. Solid use is made of the terrifying crooked stairs and forbidding nooks of the best foreboding mansion of all—the one designed by Charles D. Hall for James Whale's *The Old Dark House* (1932). On view from Whale's *Frankenstein* (1931) are graveyard props and the claustrophobia-inducing cellar. Wind, rain, menacing shadows, and unnerving noises add to the grotesque charm. Though hardly one of the finer such yarns, Jack Townley's script abounds with surprising scares and narrative twists.

Guests approach a countryside mansion during a lashing storm. Nearby, two men exhume a corpse, then hide it in a barn. The visitors— prominently, tradespeople summoned as if to work—include a plumber, a radio technician, an insurance salesman, a barber, two elderly women, an automobile salesman named Jimmy Allen (John Darrow), and his fiancée, Helen Mason (Gloria Shea). Crandall (J. Frank Glendon), a sinister butler, admits 12 arrivals and locks the door. The gathering adds up to a jury that had convicted a young man of murder. Unnerved by the recognition, the guests prepare to leave. The lights are doused.

Crandall turns up slain. The purported owner, J.E. Burton (Hale Hamilton), arrives and summons the police. Suspicion falls upon Helen, who recognizes the butler; she admits he had been her husband.

Burton explains that the scenario is a charade, enacted with Helen and his law partner, Crandall, to show the re-assembled jurors that their verdict was wrongful. The house belongs to John Davis (Wilfred Lucas), supposéd victim of the condemned man. The schemers seek to persuade the jurors to save an innocent. Crandall has in fact been murdered.

Two men announce themselves as detectives and seize Edwards (Michael S. Visaroff), the eccentric caretaker, who had fled into a maze of hidden passages. A prowler lurks in the barn, where a search reveals a body—identified as Davis. The prowler announces himself as Burke (Stanley G. Blystone), an associate of Burton, and denounces the purported investigators as poseurs; one (Frank H. LaRue) is captured, the

other found slain. Genuine detectives appear. The surviving bogus cop declares that he and his defunct partner had been robbed and framed into prison by Davis—who had faked his death in order to evade the law and dispose of his enemies. A chase leads to a struggle between Davis and Edwards over a cache of money. Their capture closes the case.

Well-placed supporting talents compensate for the mere adequacy of star players John Darrow and petite Gloria Shea. Noteworthy are smooth-as-silk Hale Hamilton, Scrooge-like Wilfred Lucas, big-and-ugly Jack Pennick, scowling Michael Visaroff, and Walter Brennan, well before his breakout to prominence as a big-studio character man. Comedy relief falls to Brennan, Jerry Mandy, Lew Kelley, Mary Foy, and Jane Keckley.

Corruption

Wm. Berke Productions • Imperial Distributing Corp. • 1933

A tale of political chicanery with the added intensity of Mischa Auer as a murderous scientist, C. Edwards Roberts' *Corruption* is one of the more unusual efforts of veteran independent producer William Berke, a determined struggler who held his impoverished ground as doggédly as any territorial major-studio mogul. Director Roberts' original screenplay deploys intriguing characters, wisecracks and underworld jargon, and a novel method of murder. Although direction falls short, strong casting compensates. Preston Foster, as a novice politico determined to unseat a corrupt regime, had begun scoring at the larger studios, and Broadway actress Evalyn Knapp had registered well at Warners.

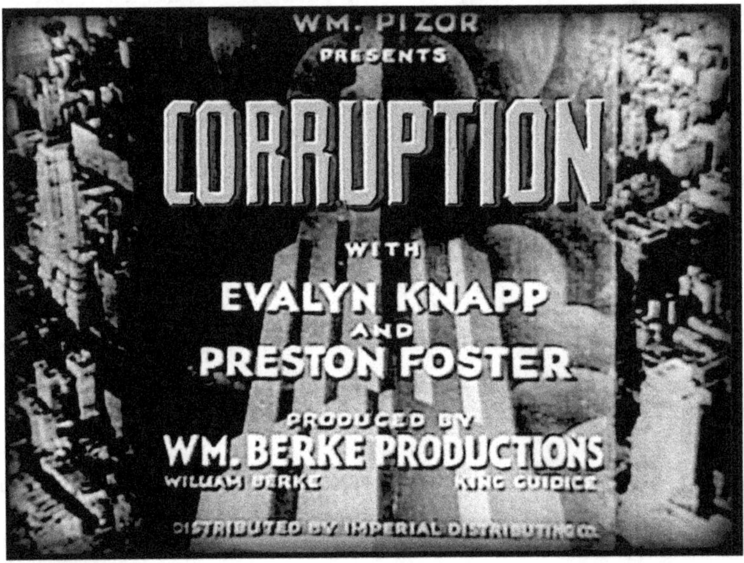

Lawyer Tim Butler (Foster), installed as mayor by a crooked City Hall gang, promises a cleanup—starting with the machine that had placed him in office. The kingmakers wreck Butler's courtship of the daughter (Natalie Moorhead) of one of the mobsters (Tully Marshall). Regan (Warner Richmond), first among scoundrels, plots further treachery. Framed for misconduct, Butler resumes his law practice with Ellen Manning (Knapp) as his secretary. Butler is promised an appointment as state's attorney if he can clear himself, but now he finds himself accused in the slaying of Regan. At length, a crazed scientist (Auer) reveals himself as the author of a campaign to eradicate human vermin—and croaks the crooked district attorney (Huntly Gordon) while delivering the confession.

The politicians, as menacing as they are menaced, are a fine lot of rascals and rotters: Huntly Gordon, Lane Chandler, Jason Robards, Fred Kohler, Jr., Nick Thompson, and Kit Guard. Natalie Moorhead and Gwen Lee fare well in the *femme fatale* department. Charles Delaney adds comedy as a brash reporter. Sidney Bracy shines in a sympathetic role. Mischa Auer, of course, steals the show.

Savage Gold

Capt. Harold Auten • 1933

The resemblance to *The Amazon Head Hunters* is likely coincidental. Cmdr. George M. Dyott, an adventure-seeking engineer and author of *Savage Gold*, had made a dozen expeditions into uncharted regions of South America by the time this account was assembled. Dyott's honors from the Royal Geographic Society counterbalanced his status as *persona non grata* in Brazil—whose jungles Dyott had searched during 1928 for the vanished Col. P.H. Fawcett. Dyott's report that Fawcett was murdered by headhunters had so outraged the Brazilian government that he found it expedient to shoot this account in Ecuador. (The film plays out like a documentary but acknowledges its fictional touches involving a search for gold, with tribal interference. A German prospector provides the fictional equivalent of Col. Fawcett.)

Dyott, at large in a mountainous region, informs the prospector that the Jivaro tribe has struck gold up the Amazon. Later, Dyott receives a message for help and assembles a rescue party. Native bearers fear to proceed.

Though welcoming at first, a chieftain turns surly when asked about the prospector. A medicine man plies his gruesome trade of shrinking human heads. One searcher finds the German beheaded— and then kills the shaman. The explorers sink the tribe's canoes and escape downriver.

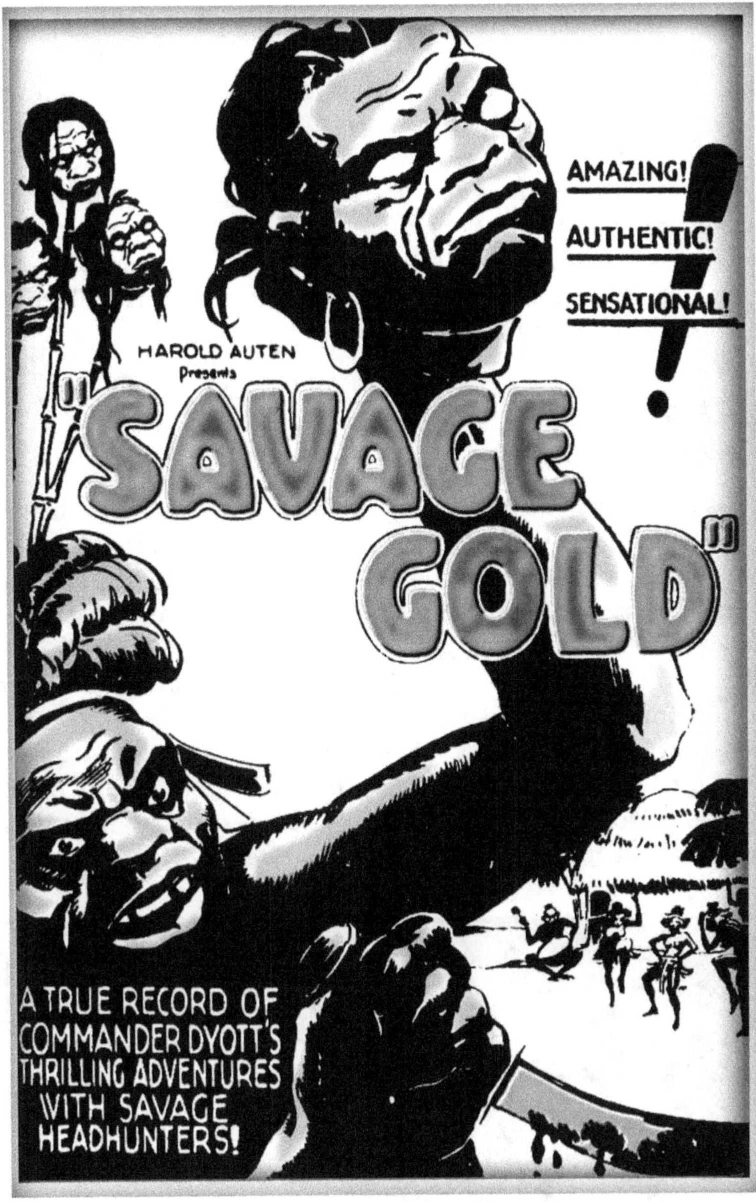

Savage Gold echoes the celebrated natural-drama filmmaking style pioneered by Merian C. Cooper and Ernest B. Schoedsack—whose *Grass* and *Chang* (1925–1927) are real-world expeditionary ancestors of 1933's made-in-Hollywood *King Kong*. Dyott enhances the sense of authenticity with a thrilling yarn that has the ring of truth if not necessarily wool-dyed fact. An acceptance of the tribal folkways (ghastly though they be) renders the film less condescending than many other such exploitationers. Exceptional photography captures the conjoined beauty and horror of the jungle. The critics responded enthusiastically.

Jivaros devour roasted caterpillars, make liquor in a communal spitting-and-chewing ritual, indulge in orgies, drag women by the hair, and kill jaguars with blowguns. A kingsnake swallows a rattlesnake. The centerpiece shocker is the ceremonial mutilation of a head—removal of the skull, curing of the flesh, shrinkage by hot gravel and sand, and the intricate moulding of the features. The interest never lags, propelled by dramatic scoring if sometimes balked by an over-enthusiastic narration.

The Avenger

Monogram Pictures Corp. • 1933

This one adds airborne firepower to a *Count of Monte Cristo* theme—a campaign of righteous ruthlessness. Scripters Tristram Tupper and Brown Holmes follow John Goodwin's source-novel closely. The picture enhanced the reputation of third-time director Edwin L. Marin, who made an additional Monogram, *The Sweetheart of Sigma Chi* (1933), and then moved along to the major-league studios. *The Avenger* also benefits from glossy photography by Warners' Sid Hickox.

Assistant D.A. Norman Craig (Ralph Forbes) is about to expose James Gordon (Arthur Vinton) as a criminal overlord. The mob frames Craig into prison. Cleared by a deathbed confession from a gangster, Craig finds that his sweetheart, Ruth Knowles (Adrienne Ames), has

Adrienne Ames and Claude Gillingwater.

married Gordon. Assuming a clandestine identity as the Avenger, Craig terrorizes his enemies—diminishing the mob while driving Gordon to suicide. Craig proves to have hidden away the other crooks as hostages.

Ralph Forbes, an English sophisticate who had played the surviving brother in Herbert Brenon's *Beau Geste* (1926), renders convincing the grim campaign. Stage veteran Arthur Vinton is right as the principal villain. Standouts in support are J. Carrol Naish, Berton Churchill, Murray Kinnell, Claude Gillingwater, James "Jimmy" Donlan, Paul Fix, and Boothe Howard. Texas-born Adrienne Ames, the Hollywood-royalty murder suspect of *The Death Kiss*, is a fascinating *femme fatale*.

Tarzan the Fearless

Principal Distributing Corp. • 1933

Tarzan, overlord of the jungle, was a born-to-play role for Clarence "Buster" Crabbe, but the circumstances were an embarrassment: "*Tarzan the Fearless* didn't have a chance against the ones Johnny Weissmuller made at MGM," Crabbe told us in 1971, summoning all the amusement of hindsight from a safe distance. "*They* had beautiful production values and a lot of great animal scenes made in Africa for *Trader Horn. We* shot most of ours on the backlot in six weeks, and we had only a few animals—a chimp, an old elephant, and a lion which, fortunately, didn't have a tooth in his head!"

Source-author Edgar Rice Burroughs had agreed in 1929 with Walter Shumway and Jack Nelson to make *Tarzan the Fearless*. Burroughs demanded a $10,000 advance and the right to cast his son-in-law, James Pierce, as the jungle man. The producers proved incapable and relinquished the contract to Sol Lesser, best known at the time for the Principal-Adventure line of documentary-styled jungle thrillers.

In 1932, while MGM was making the successful *Tarzan the Ape Man*, Lesser struck a new deal with Burroughs and paid Pierce $5,000 *not* to play Tarzan. (The veteran of the gridiron had made *Tarzan and the Golden Lion* in 1926.) Lesser wanted a younger, leaner Tarzan—whom he found in Crabbe, the freestyle swimming champion of the 1932 Olympic Games and star of Paramount's *King of the Jungle*, an excellent take-off on Burroughs.

Shot in precisely the six weeks that Crabbe remembered—at Chatsworth and Lake Sherwood, with interiors and the deep-perspective jungle set at RKO-Pathé—*Fearless* proved profitable, nowithstanding cheapskate production values and sloppy continuity. Lesser released the epic as a conventional 12-chapter serial, one episode a week, and in a new form created for the occasion: the feature-serial version comprised a 71-minute feature, edited from

Chapter Nos. 1–4, followed by eight weekly two-reel episodes (otherwise, Chapter Nos. 5–12). The surviving version is a chaotic, hour-long butchery, compressed from the original 200 minutes for television syndication during the 1950s.

An archaeologist, Dr. Brooks (E. Allyn Warren), searches Africa for a lost Aryan civilization that worships an imaginary deity known as Zar of the Emerald Fingers. Captured by the zealots, Brooks finds himself rescued by Tarzan, a white man who had been raised by apes. Brooks, seeking to contact his daughter, Mary (Jacqueline Wells), entrusts the search to Tarzan.

Mary and her fiancé, Bob Hall (Edward Woods), seek her father. Their guides, Jeff Herbert and Nick Moran (Philo McCullough and Mathew Betz), prove to be criminals, intent upon finding the Emeralds of Zar. Jeff lusts after Mary—and proposes to collect a bounty on Tarzan. Tarzan rescues Mary from a crocodile. (The sequence is no match for the crocodile-attack sequence in MGM's *Tarzan and His Mate*; nor should one expect otherwise.) Dr. Brooks is recaptured. Mary is abducted to a slave camp. Hall follows a map to the forbidden Caves of Zar. Moran is killed by a lion while he attempts to do away with Hall and Herbert, who are lured into a trap by Eltar (Mischa Auer), Priest of Zar. The explorers land in prison with Brooks.

Tarzan rescues Mary and makes love to her, then frees the captives. Herbert steals an emerald from the Idol of Zar. Tarzan refuses to disclose

The diminished circumstances of Tarzan the Fearless.

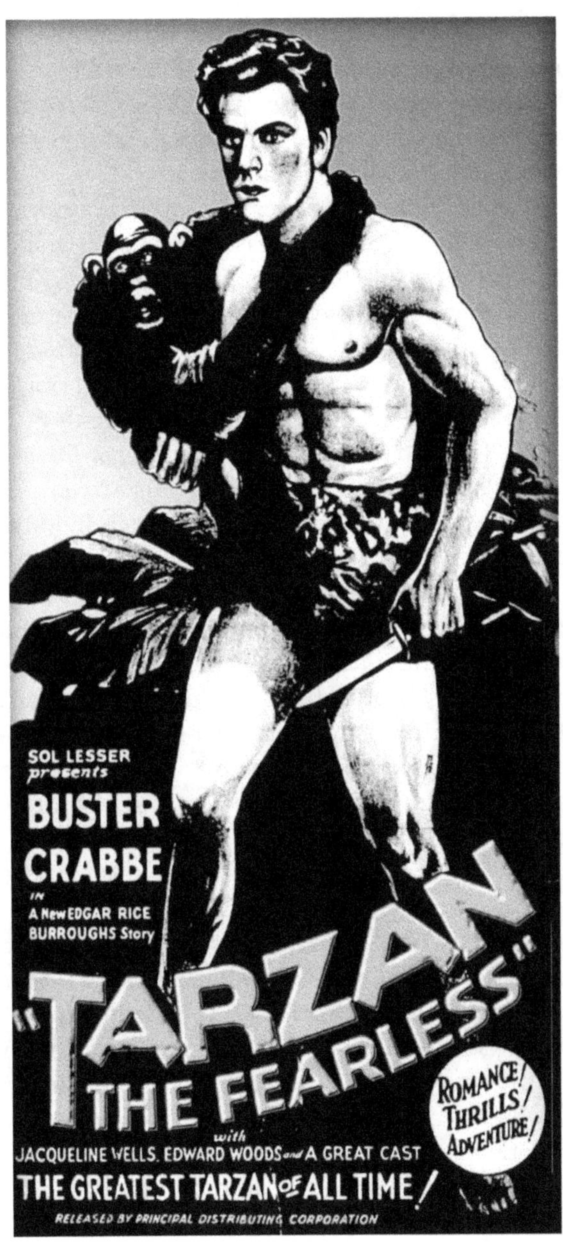

Mary's whereabouts. Returning to his cave while Herbert sneaks along behind, Tarzan kills a gorilla that has attacked Mary. Furious to learn of Mary's fondness for Tarzan, Herbert reveals that a black-sheep kinsman of the noble-born jungle man has offered a reward for proof of Tarzan's death. Mary leaves with Herbert, lest he slay Tarzan.

A cannibalistic witch doctor, allied with the Zar cult, can become a tiger at will, and never mind the non-existence of tigers in Africa. A silver bullet brings down the creature; in its place lies the hoodoo man. His tribe captures the party. Tarzan rescues Mary. A convenient eclipse enables Dr. Brooks to intimidate the savages. Tarzan recovers from an attack by Herbert. The restoration of the emerald saves the explorers. Herbert's final assault backfires, fatally so.

Of course *Tarzan the Fearless* suffers by comparison with the pacing and polish of the MGM *Tarzans*. Sol Lesser eventually would take charge of the franchise for the longer term, as a perennial at RKO-Radio—but only after MGM grew to believe it had exhausted the money-making possibilities. (A survey of the MGM *Tarzans* can be found in our collaborative book, *The Cinema of Adventure, Romance, & Terror*, published in 1989 by the American Society of Cinematographers.)

Robert F. "Bob" Hill had directed *The Adventures of Tarzan* in 1921 and spent many years as Universal Pictures' serials ace. *Fearless* bespeaks Hill's command of pictorial effects and strong individual sequences. A general choppiness mars the whole. (This observation comes from George E. Turner's repeated viewings of the authentic serial, in first run and reissues, during the 1930s and 1940s. The now-familiar television cut goes beyond choppiness.) This unevenness is surprising, inasmuch as all the writers were seasoned hands at the construction of serials.

Skillful staging distinguishes the scenes of Tarzan's rescue of Dr. Brooks; Tarzan's dramatic appearance during a storm; the rescue of Mary Brooks from a stampede; and a sequence straight out of H. Rider Haggard, where Brooks convinces the cannibals that he is responsible for an eclipse. The tree-swinging scenes, photographed by Joseph Brotherton with a gyroscope-mounted camera, prove superior to their counterparts in the MGM *Tarzans*. Many sets, properties, and costumes are remnants of a day when Cecil B. DeMille had ruled the Pathé studios.

There is a surprising wealth of erotica. (The industry-at-large looked upon the serials as diversions for children. Even after the self-righteous Catholic Legion of Decency had achieved dominance in 1934, the institutional censors seldom bothered to strip-search the cliffhangers for breaches of taste or propriety.) Tarzan stares bedazzled at Mary Brooks in her wet undergarments. Later, he carries her into his cave, with a discreet fade. The Priestess of Zar (Carlotta Monti) performs a sanctified shimmy. When a guard warns her against going unarmed to meet Tarzan, she regards her scantily clad curves and replies: "A woman is *never* unarmed."

Crabbe is not only the most handsome of Old Hollywood's Tarzans, but also the most dramatically capable. Like Johnny Weissmuller, Crabbe was muscular without being musclebound, possessed of a catlike agility. Crabbe conveys perfectly the character of one attuned to the jungle. The delicate beauty of Jacqueline Wells (previously known as Diane Duval, and later, as Julie Bishop) contrasts ideally with the bronzed hero. Mischa Auer, aided by weird lighting, is properly sinister. Eddie Woods is a stalwart secondary lead; swarthy Philo McCullough is well motivated as a crooked adventurer; Mathew Betz makes a convincingly dull-witted heavy; and Frank Lackteen, from Lebanon, seems born to the role of an Arab slaver. Carlotta Monti, who would forsake an acting career to become mistress to W.C. Fields, registers impressively as Auer's second-in-command.

Burrough's rejected son-in-law did make it onto the soundtrack: James Pierce supplies Tarzan's battle-cry, which also was heard on the *Tarzan* radio serial. A musical theme, "The Call of Tarzan," derives from the three-note jungle yodel. Silent-film *agitatos* accompany many action scenes, courtesy of Abe Meyer's vast library of pre-recorded cues.

Devil's Mate

Monogram Pictures Corp. • 1933

As convicted murderer Maloney (Kit Guard) approaches the electric chair, he decides to reveal who had ordered his crime. He drops dead before he can speak—felled by a poisoned dart.

Suspicion falls upon prison board candidate Parkhurst (Hobart Cavanaugh) and a friend, Clinton (Jason Robards). Inspector O'Brien (Preston Foster) arrests an adamant anti-smoker (Harry Holman), who carries a cigarette holder that might have served as a blowgun.

News reporter Nancy Weaver (Peggy Shannon) finds Parkhurst cooperative. She also learns from Maloney's tough sweetheart, Gwen (Barbara Barondess), that the convict had been obsessed with reaching a certain telephone number. The clue implicates Parkhurst, who has a ready explanation.

Gwen turns up poisoned. Nancy's investigation lands her in peril. O'Brien rescues Nancy after she has proved Parkhurst to be the killer.

Highly original, *Devil's Mate* is a combination of smart writing by Leonard Fields and David Silverstein, intelligent direction by Phil Rosen, splendid photography by Gil Warrenton, and thoroughgoing professionalism by a tightly wound ensemble cast. Warrenton's inventive radial compositions and ominous shadowplay recall his work in 1927 on Paul Leni's Universal classics, *The Cat and the Canary* and *The Man Who Laughs*.

The first slaying establishes a prevailing weirdness. A second murder is still more diabolical—accomplished with a tainted needle concealed in the horn of an automobile.

The identity of the killer is well hidden—with no cheating: Clues point logically to a popular favorite Milquetoast player, Hobart Cavanaugh, who manages a persuasive transition from mildness to menace. (Cava-

The execution-chamber setting in Devil's Mate.

naugh seemed an embodiment of cartoonist H.T. Webster's signature character, the Timid Soul, a.k.a. Caspar Milquetoast. Hence the term.)

Peggy Shannon's self-imposed peril is as gripping as the mystery angle. Preston Foster makes a convincing detective. Paul Fix and Barbara Barondess stand out as foredoomed low-life lovers, separated by his crime but (presumably) reunited by her death.

Phil Rosen remade the tale in 1941 at a reorganized Monogram under the similarly evocative title *I Killed That Man*—a comparably bracing picture that impressed critics with short memories as an innovative entry.

Deluge

Admiral Productions, Inc. • RKO-Radio Pictures • 1933

Tales of disaster, the myth of the cleansing flood in particular, are a cross-cultural constant, dating from antiquity. *The Sumerian Chronicles* (*ca.* 2150 B.C.) provide a narrative arc for come-lately Noah's water-logged misadventures of the Old Testament. *The Sumerian Chronicles* also describe a gravitational calamity such as the 20th-century film-maker George Pal would depict in 1951's *When Worlds Collide*. We should skip over a great deal of the rest—*Noah counting for taste*—the better to concentrate on Felix E. Feist's *Deluge* and its immediate foreshadowing in Hollywood by Michael Curtiz' big Warners project of 1929, *Noah's Ark* (silent and part-sound versions), and James Tinling's *The Flood* (1931).

S. Fowler Wright's novel, *Deluge—a Romance*, had appeared in a British edition of 1927, riffing on Noah in melodramatic science-fictional terms a year before Curtiz' film went into production. Warners-Vitaphone wanted a flood yarn but found the public domain Biblical option more affordable. Then, for *The Flood*, Columbia Pictures ordered an original scenario confined to an upheaval of the Mississippi River, with property damage running about par with mortal and emotional consequences; the debt to Wright's novel is patent though unacknowledged.

It fell to a smaller studio, Admiral Productions, to give Wright his due on a planetary scale—the very template, ill recognized, for the disaster-movie craze of the waning 20th century. Burt Kelly, Sam Bischoff, and William Saal parted ways with World Wide in 1933 and

rechristened KBS Productions as Admiral. So successful were the partners in the independent sector that all were offered positions at major studios. Their last venture together, *Deluge,* is their biggest and in many respects their best. The adaptation of Fowler Wright stands among the more exciting films of any generation; it competed formidably against special-effects pictures from the big companies. Its placement of intimate human struggles against a backdrop of nature amok is definitive of the broad subgenre.

Admiral's timing was excellent: the popularity of *King Kong*—issued in March of 1933 by RKO-Radio—had created a demand for outlandish spectacle. Admiral struck a deal in which RKO would pay half the cost on condition of a budget ceiling of $75,000. The commitment was obviously insufficient: negative cost (literally speaking, the cost of the finished negative) ran to $137,044, and the bill from Consolidated Industries for titles, optical effects, and prints brought the sum to $170,940.73—a B-picture cost for a major studio, but extravagant within Admiral's Poverty Row sector. The bosses at RKO were furious, although box-office returns justified every cent. (The B-picture designation signifies a smaller budget—not some schoolmarmish system of grading as to quality.)

An unheralded eclipse foreshadows global catastrophe. Barometers plummet. Winds rise. Seismographs register colossal shocks. Martin and Helen Webster (Sidney Blackmer and Lois Wilson) and their children flee to a quarry outside New York. Believing his family lost, Webster becomes an aimless wanderer. In New York, skyscrapers topple as the sea engulfs the Statue of Liberty and hurls ships inland.

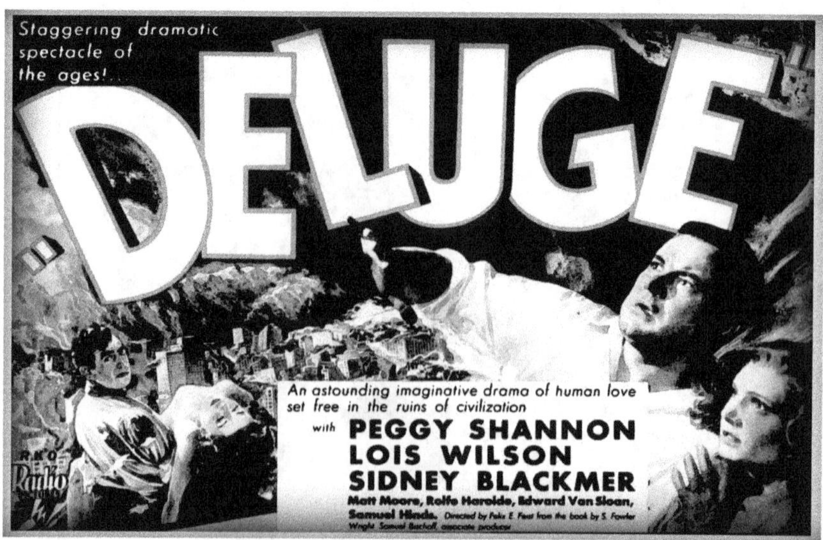

Claire Arlington (Peggy Shannon) outmaneuvers an attack by scaven-
gers Norwood and Jephson (Ralf Harolde and Fred Kohler) and swims
to where Webster has landed. Claire and Webster set up primitive
housekeeping out of necessity but soon fall in love. Claire's surviving assailant, Jephson, arrives with a marauding band. Occupants of
a nearby settlement come to the rescue.

Webster finds his wife and children. He contemplates bigamy,
although the colonists want their leader (Matt Moore) to become
Helen's mate. Claire refuses to give up Webster until she sees the children embracing their father. She swims away.

The devastation dwarfs the romantic conflict, although nightmarish struggles recapture momentum on a human scale. The end of the

thrilling wreckage sequences, however, poses greater dramatic possibilities. The censors, seeking ammunition for 1934's all-out assault upon the First Amendment, raised outcries about episodes of rape and murder in the wake of the flood, and about Peggy Shannon's seminude scenes. The Production Code Administation was deservédly toothless at the time, however, and the Legion of Decency was only just beginning to gather predatory momentum within Vatican City and its U.S. outposts.

Sidney Blackmer revels in the heroic role—a change from villainous typecasting. Lois Wilson is comparably right as the wife. Redheaded Peggy Shannon is extremely sympathetic as the other woman-by-default. The players form a triangle of inexorably shifting dimensions. (A similar predicament resurfaces, with variations, in the new century's most involving disaster tale, Robert Kirkman's collaborative graphic novel *The Walking Dead* and its adaptation for television during 2011.)

Shannon had come to Hollywood from the musical stage. Roles at Paramount, Fox, and Warners had made her a prospect for top stardom by 1933. Her career faltered during the mid-1930s, however, and she died of alcoholism in 1941.

The special effects have been misattributed to *King Kong*'s Willis O'Brien. They were supervised by Ned Herbert Mann, technical-effects director at United Artists, with cinematographer William N. "Billy" Williams and matte artist Russell Lawson. Mann had contributed to the likes of *The Thief of Baghdad* and *The Bat* and its remakes. Following *Deluge*, Mann and key crewmen helped Sir Alexander Korda's British studio with such effects-laden projects as *Things To Come* and the 1940 remake of *The Thief of Baghdad*. Lawson was a mainstay of Universal during the 1930s and 1940s. Williams, a veteran of Mack Sennett's slapstick-comedy machine, was making a gradual move during 1933 from Warner Bros. to RKO.

Mann built the model of New York, harbor included, on an indoor stage. Some buildings stood as tall as 12 feet. Huge tanks provided the tidal wave. Lawson added deeper views of the city with an undetectable matte shot. Eleven operators and eight assistants manned eight Mitchell and Bell & Howell cameras, adjusted by technician Edward Tiffany to run at 240 frames per second—10 times normal speed—with lenses of varying focal lengths.

For the earthquake, buildings were positioned upon a mobile platform made of eight automobile-chassis mechanisms, rigged with springs. The wheeled city was shoved down an undulating track, built along a desert hillside, with the eight cameras and their operators aboard. The ride shattered the plaster buildings, and the uneven track created chasms to catch the outsized miniatures. The crash caused no injuries, believe it or not.

Russ Lawson produced numerous matte shots of a desolate land-scape, with real-time elements incorporated. These atmospheric shots resemble the natural scenic imagery in Frank Wisbar's eerie *Fahrmann Maria* (Germany, 1936). There also are scenes of the collapse of the Webster homestead. Actors appear in the foreground of many large-scale shots, composited by the reliable Dunning Process as they are buried or lose their footing.

Flash shots of fleeing citizens, photographed at perhaps eight frames per second and composited into slow-motion scenes of toppling struc-tures, lend a deliberate unreality—a rare instance of Expressionism in commercial cinema. The catastrophic scenes at length would be acquired by upstart Republic Pictures as stock footage, with appear-ances in the likes of *S.O.S. Tidal Wave* (1938), *Dick Tracy vs. Crime, Incorporated* (1941), and *King of the Rocket Men* (1949). *Deluge* itself was long presumed lost. Only in times more recent has an Italian-dubbed version been found intact—fodder, with the addition of English subti-tles, for the video market.

Composers, as numerous as the cameramen, contributed to a mighty musical score. The supervisors were Val Burton and Dr. Edward Kilenyi. Englishman Burton, more widely known for his musical revues, ran the scoring departments of Tiffany and World Wide, and later wrote and produced radio dramas and movies. Hungarian-born Kilenyi, father of the like-named pianist, had been a mentor to George Gershwin, led the famed Waldorf-Astoria Orchestra, and scored many silent films. Kilenyi recruited seven colleagues from Fox Movietone to contribute to *Deluge*'s wall-to-wall accompaniment. Sonic gaps were filled with previously published compositions. The recording process—with an astonishing clarity, given the technology of the day—captures stirring performances from a 30-piece orchestra, augmented by a massive pipe organ. The score contains 104 distinct cues.

Director Felix Feist, son of an MGM executive, maintains suspense during most of the picture and musters intense emotional currents when Peggy Shannon and Lois Wilson meet as a dramatic climax builds. Dialogue is kept wisely at a minimum.

The company's hallmark of excellent photography is represented by Norbert Brodine, borrowed from MGM. The pictorial intensity is at its best in terrifying encounters with the renegades, filmed in lab-yrinthine Bronson Canyon. Don Seigel would use these same tunnels for similarly conceived chases in *Invasion of the Body Snatchers* (1956).

The Emperor Jones

Krimsky & Cochran, Inc. • United Artists • Screencraft • 1933

Brutus Jones (Paul Robeson), a figure of violence, wields false piety and vain ambition so persuasively as to seem the very embodiment of racial uplift within black society. Jones welcomes prestige, but only for so long as it leads to petty power. Jones compromises his prospects as a Pullman porter with gambling and womanizing—then murders a friend (Frank Wilson) and draws a chain-gang sentence. Jones kills a guard and escapes to Haiti.

Convincing the natives that he wields magic—"It take a silver bullet to kill Brutus Jones!"—the interloper overthrows a corrupt tribal regime and declares himself emperor. Rebellion follows. Jones flees into the trackless jungle, where visions of his crimes haunt him. A native has melted silver coins to make bullets. Jones is shot dead. A corrupt trader (Dudley Digges) delivers a contemptuous anti-eulogy.

Massachusetts-born Dudley Murphy built a film-directing career upon avant-garde and musical works, including two black-ensemble shorts of 1929, "Black and Tan" and "The St. Louis Blues," the latter boasting the only screen performance of Bessie Smith, the bravura singer known as the Empress of the Blues. It proved scarcely a stretch from empress to emperor—*Jones*, that is—and in fact Murphy had sought to adapt Eugene O'Neill's celebrated play as early as 1928. Murphy gradually developed credentials sufficient to impress novice producers John Krimsky and Gifford Cochran with the possibilities.

Paul Robeson and Fredi Washington.

An amen-corner frenzy launches Brutus Jones' brilliant career.

With O'Neill's blessing, Murphy inverted and expanded the play's stagebound monologue. The movie confines to its closing act Jones' terrified attempt at a getaway.

With a script by DuBose Heyward, co-author of the Gershwins' *Porgy and Bess*, Murphy mounted *Jones* on May 5, 1933, at Long Island's Eastern Service Studios—the former Paramount Publix Studio, abandoned since March of 1932—and wrapped the shoot late in July at a cost of $250,000 for principal photography. Murphy had intended a location trip to Haiti, but art director Herman Rosse had persuaded him that a more terrifying and technically efficient jungle could be built within the studio.

Paul Robeson, the celebrated athlete, singer, and actor, had starred in the stage version. Robeson returned from the London engagement of O'Neill's *All God's Chillun Got Wings* to give his finest screen performance. Robeson's megalomaniac Brutus Jones dominates the picture, mingling menace and pathos. He receives impressive backup from Dudley Digges, the only white player of prominence within the ensemble; and from Frank Wilson, Ruby Elzy, the beautiful Fredi Washington of Universal's *Imitation of Life* (1934), and Jackie Mabley—later known as the comedian and civil rights activist Moms Mabley.

A year after *Jones*, Robeson made known a sympathy with Soviet Communism that earned him a lasting vilification in the United States. As late as 1949, he was denounced before the House Committee on UnAmerican Activities as aspiring "to be the black Stalin among Negroes." Long a resident of France, Robeson renewed his passport in 1962 and resettled in 1963 in Philadelphia, living in seclusion until his death at 77 in 1976.

Production supervisor William C. DeMille, elder brother of the bombastic director Cecil B., has been said to have ghost-directed portions of *Jones*. Direction is fine throughout, and cinematographer Ernest Haller—one of the great pictorial stylists—conveys a naturalistic ferocity, with close attention to the characters.

Holland-bred architect, artist, and stage designer Herman Rosse displays budgetary genius in a wealth of spectacle. Rosse held an Academy Award for Universal's *The King of Jazz* (1930), and he worked on that studio's earlier signature horrors, whose visual style was widely emulated.

Mirrors fill Brutus Jones' palace—the better to convey vanity as the essence of his character. These, in turn, illustrate the ingenuity of Haller's photography: Nary a tell-tale reflection is seen of cameras or lighting fixtures. The jungle is an Impressionistic creation of lights, shadows, and simple properties. Outdoor photography involves the chain-gang sequence, filmed in a quarry, which blends unobtrusively. The music—tribal drumming, South Carolina Gullah spirituals, and jazz—is essential to the various settings. Robeson belts out three spirituals in high style.

The Wolf Dog

Mascot Pictures Corp. • 1933

After the death of the great Rin-Tin-Tin, Mascot groomed one of the dog's offspring as a replacement. Though a beautiful animal, Rinty, Jr., lacked his old man's camera savvy and required frequent doubling. These substitutions are none too subtle in *The Wolf Dog*—a generous but uneven mixture of science fiction, sentimental melodrama, and action on land and sea and in the air. The tale stretches the long arm of coincidence to an absurd extent.

Steamship boss Jim Courtney (Henry B. Walthall) is jailed on a false accusation involving the disappearance of an heir. Years later, police dog Pal (Rinty, Jr.) survives a plane crash and joins a wolf pack. Pal is found by the long-lost heir, Frank (Frankie Darro), who is intent upon escaping a cruel stepfather. Bound for Los Angeles, the boy and the dog befriend an inventor, Bob Whitlock (George J. Lewis), who plans to donate a lightning-ray device to the government. Bryan (Hale Hamilton), the very rascal who had hijacked Courtney's company, steals the ray—then deploys it for cruel purposes. After a pageant

of wild mayhem, Pal rescues Bob and sees to it that Bryan meets an appropriate demise.

Filming locations include Lake Arrowhead, a vast coastal seascape, and a precipitous stretch of Mullholland Drive above Los Angeles. The presentation is competent, given the haste of a 12-day shoot. George Lewis, often a villain, is a believable hero. Frankie Darro (older than he appears) makes a firecracker juvenile lead, and as usual Hale Hamilton conveys convincing criminal motives. H.B. Walthall makes a sympathetic victim of the conspiracy. There are numerous efficient heavies, some spectacular stunting, and chases aplenty involving boats and automobiles. Boots Mallory provides an adventurous romantic spark as Lewis' endangered sweetheart.

Jaws of Justice

Principal Pictures Corp. • 1933

Kazan the Wonder Dog was rescued from Los Angeles' Animal Control Pound by stuntman-actor Jack King. With King as his trainer and producer, Kazan became Principal Pictures' answer to Mascot Pictures' Rin-Tin-Tin, Jr. Kazan had an edge over most other police-dog stars in the ability to appear as fierce as a wolf when the occasion demanded. The general run of movie pooches seemed likelier to wag their tails while tearing into the bad guys. *Jaws of Justice*, first of three Kazan pictures, establishes an offbeat tone: the inspiration lies in Edgar Allan Poe.

Prospector Seeker Dean (Lafe McKee) has a clue to the location of a vein of gold in the Canadian wilderness. He prepares to visit government authorities to secure the rights. Boone Jackson (Robert Walker), an author who covets Dean's daughter, Judy (Ruth Sullivan), offers to drive Dean to the depot and returns with a story that Dean has instead accepted a lift from a motorist. The villagers grow anxious for Dean's return, for he had promised to share the wealth. No one suspects that Dean's body lies in a ravine.

Judy teaches Kickabout Riley (Gene Toler), a mute boy, to read and write; the lessons will prove Jackson's undoing. The boy's police dog, Kazan, has an instinctive dislike of Jackson.

A Mountie, Sgt. Kinkaid (Jack Perrin), falls in love with Judy, to Jackson's annoyance. A year passes without word from Seeker Dean,

and Kinkaid returns to investigate. Jackson opens fire upon Kazan in a fierce encounter, but the dog recovers—angrier than before.

Kickabout recognizes a cryptogram from Dean's desk as a puzzle resembling the cipher in Poe's "The Gold Bug." The boy cracks the code to reveal the location of the gold. Kazan finds the remains of Dean. Jackson flees, but the dog pursues the killer and prevents him from blowing up the mine. As Jackson attempts to escape, Kazan sends him falling to his doom while Kinkaid and Judy watch in horror.

The canine hero receives bold support from western-movie star Jack Perrin—billed here as Richard Terry, an occasional alias—as a dashing agent of the Royal Canadian Mounted Police. Robert Walker conveys a patient, lurking menace with nuances of treachery beyond the requirements of the role. Lafe McKee plays the doomed prospector for full measure of poignancy.

Spencer Gordon Bennet works the story for action, serial-style—his specialty, honed by exhaustive experience since the silent-picture days. The tale contains enough chases and fights and dirty deeds to render its lack of subtlety beside the point. On the scenic front, Lake Tahoe stands in for the wilds of Canada.

Additional starring pictures for Kazan the Wonder Dog are *Ferocious Pal* and *Outlaw's Highway*, both from 1934.

The Sin of Nora Moran

a.k.a. Voice from the Grave
Majestic Pictures Corp. • 1933

Better known today for a provocative advertising campaign than for an unusual narrative technique or a harrowing tale of sacrifice and ghostly retribution, Phil Goldstone's *The Sin of Nora Moran* marks an early use of a contrived storytelling device that the publicity department at Fox Film Corp. had termed *narratage*, an elision of *narrative* and *montage*.

This combination of nonlinear narrative with episodic flashbacks—conversational and digressive in approach, with an omniscient narrator who also is a character in the tale—had originated with the great filmmaker Preston Sturges. He applied the tactic to the screenplay for William K. Howard's *The Power and the Glory* (1933), a turbulent account of the career of a hated industrialist (Spencer Tracy).

Majestic Pictures launched *The Sin of Nora Moran* into production in June while Fox was staging previews of *The Power and the Glory* and ordering partial reshooting in anticipation of a premiere in August. The bigger film's influence was prompt and lasting: interlocked flashbacks, often narrated with sobering insight, would become crucial to the dawning film noir movement, persisting into the 21st century

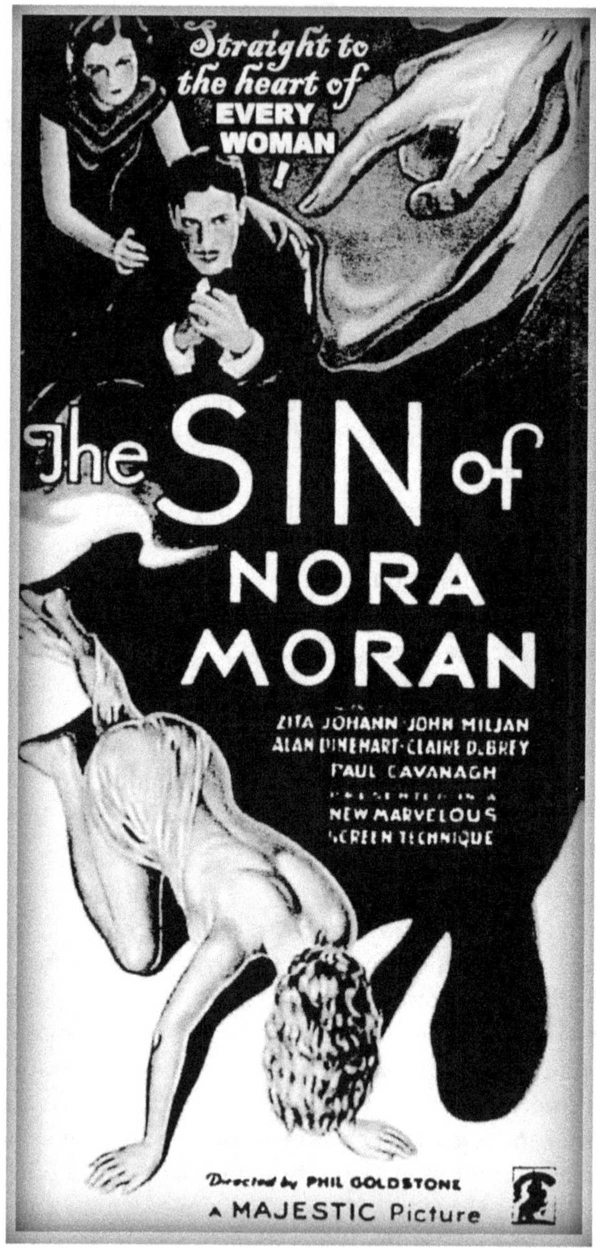

via such artists as David Lynch and Quentin Tarantino. The fatuous term *narratage* never caught on widely, however, even though Majestic Pictures hailed the approach as "a new marvelous screen technique."

Sturges explained his innovation as an attempt to re-create the spontaneity of his wife's random tales about her colorful grandfather, the cereal-company magnate C.W. Post. The effect of *narratage* also recalls ancient Greek drama, with its storytelling chorus device, and suggests a familiarity with the densely layered literary styles of Henry James and Joseph Conrad.

Majestic's mimicry in *Nora Moran* is primitive by comparison with Fox's *The Power and the Glory*, but *Moran*'s script adds the eerie twist of an existentially helpless awareness of one's eventual fate. (In one unnerving scene, a character in the present moment wears clothing from a past life.) A murder scene is rendered all the more turbulent by an effect in which the frame appears to tear itself asunder—an awareness *by* the film, *of* the film, that verges upon surrealism.

The Mummy's Zita Johann is Nora Moran, mistress of Gov. Dick Crawford (Paul Cavanagh). Her story unfolds after Edith Crawford (Claire Du Brey), the governor's widow, has found a cache of love letters. Mrs. Crawford's brother, DA John Grant (Alan Dinehart) relates the circumstances that had led to Nora Moran's execution for murder.

Cue flashback: Nora might gain a reprieve if she could explain the circumstances of the slaying. Under the influence of a drugging, she recalls her twice-orphaned upbringing, an episode of rape by a trusted employer, and her affair with Dick Crawford.

Mrs. Crawford interrupts in anger—indignant to learn that she had toiled for Crawford's campaign while he was pursuing an adulterous

Johann's other starring role of the day: A sepulchral love interest for Boris Karloff in *The Mummy*.

affair. Grant reminds his sister that she had married Crawford out of social-climbing ambition. Grant also admits that he had advanced his political imperatives through Crawford's popularity with the electorate.

Further flashback: Grant calls upon Nora. She senses fatalistically that she must admit him. Only after Grant has threatened to expose the affair does she comprehend that Crawford is married and running for high office. Nora confronts Crawford, hoping to discourage him with a false confession to other affairs. Crawford leaves in disgust. In another nonlinear shift, Nora laments to Grant that she cannot bear to re-experience the murder scene—which has yet to occur, in the first place. (Confused? You're not alone.)

Flash forward to the interim prison scene: Maddened by the forced onslaught of memory and the effects of the drug, Nora pleads that she not be allowed to fall asleep. And in the present moment, Grant reveals to Mrs. Crawford the circumstances of a homicide that Gov. Crawford could have prevented: On the night of the crime, Nora had telephoned Grant for help. She showed him the body of Paulino (John Miljan), her employer-turned-assailant of times earlier. She claimed to have killed him after he had threatened to blackmail Crawford. Grant and Nora arranged the appearance of an accident, but Nora was nonetheless arrested. She refused a lawyer.

The approach of the execution: Crawford denies a reprieve, lest anyone sense his clandestine involvement with Nora Moran. He is overwhelmed with unbidden memory: on the night of the slaying, Crawford had visited Nora's place and found Paulino there. Paulino attacked Crawford. Crawford struck him dead. Nora ordered Crawford to leave before he could be sighted.

The moment of execution: Crawford addresses Nora as though she were here in the flesh. Her spirit appears to materialize. She tells him that death holds no terror—that she will die for all the good he can accomplish as governor. He attempts on impulse to call in a confession and a pardon, but the telephone is dead. Nora's ghostly image vanishes. Obsessed with her repeated declaration, the governor composes a letter to Grant, then commits suicide.

Return to framing story: Grant asks his sister whether the tale is to end here—or to begin anew. She gives him the letters, which he destroys.

The production had begun under Howard Christy as director. He was replaced early on by Phil Goldstone—usually a producer and investor. Goldstone ordered a closed set and stationed a guard, lest the press come snooping about. The air of secrecy encouraged publicity, of course. The film reaped generous coverage in light of its *narratage* gimmick—which plays out today like business-as-usual for an audience attuned to flashbacks as a matter of routine. Assuming an attention span and an absorption in the story, that is.

Forgotten Horrors of 1934

The House of Danger

Peerless Pictures Corp. • Hoffberg Pictures • 1934

Producer Sam Efrus sometimes imparted a major-studio aspect to his inexpensive pictures, such as *On Probation*. A more typical Efrus job, *The House of Danger*, is as threadbare as threadbare comes and boasts only one player of popular recognition. Onslow Stevens brings distinction to the romantic lead, consistent with such of his Universal assignments as *Bombay Mail* and *Secret of the Blue Room*. Janet Chandler makes a passable ingenue. Englishman Desmond Roberts contributes menace.

Returning after years at sea, Ralph Nelson (James Bush) is injured when his ship explodes. Ralph sends a pal, Don Phillips (Stevens), to impersonate him at the Nelson estate. A cousin, Martin (John Andrews), is suspected of murder in the death of Ralph's father. Don tricks Martin and an accomplice (Roberts) into tipping their hand, with lethal results.

Charles Hutchison, the silent-screen hero-turned-director, sustains a bracing pace in an unremarkable melodramatic situation.

Hutchison lacks subtlety, but he fares well with straightforward action. The photography captures the mayhem efficiently. Stock scenes of a shipwreck and an automobile crash are too grainy to match up well with the new material.

In Media Res: Titles of Further Interest

The following unearthings broaden the immediate context for 1934:

- *Sixteen Fathoms Deep* (Monogram Pictures; 1934). Lon Chaney, Jr., under his formal name of Creighton, plays a sponge fisherman who runs afoul of sabotage. An undercurrent of Third World superstition ascribes the mayhem to a jinx—but commonplace human villainy is at work, instead. As James Conrad stated the case: "Man alone is quite capable of all wickedness." (Remade, after a fashion, in 1948, as *16 Fathoms Deep*, with Chaney in a different role; see *Forgotten Horrors Vol. 5: The Atom Age*.)

- *Gow* (Capt. Edward A. Salisbury & Film Exchange; 1934). This one is a recompilation of several years' worth of South Seas expeditionary footage, as superficially talkie-fied from 1928's *Gow the Head Hunter* and an interim recut of 1931. A chieftain re-enacts a raid he had led against a neighboring tribe and displays a collection of skulls, presumably harvested first-hand. The expeditionary filmmakers Merian C. Cooper and Ernest B. Schoedsack (of *King Kong*), credited as cameramen on the silent cut, go unacknowledged.

- *Playthings of Desire* (Pinnacle Productions; 1934). Gambler Jack Chapin goes gunning for playboy James Kirkwood in Florida—only to wind up devoured by alligators.

- *Curtain at Eight* (Majestic Pictures; 1934). The film suffered a tentative 1933 release and languished as both a box-office attraction and a topic of interest among the critics. It was given an emphatic formal campaign in 1934 and began to rack up the reviews. A case of serial murder involves an arrogant ham actor (Paul Cavanagh) and a homicidal chimpanzee. C. Aubrey Smith plays a genial detective who makes a questionable but satisfying moral judgment.

- *Kidnapping Gorillas*, a.k.a. *Life in the Congo* (Kinematrade; 1934). No mere knockoff of 1930's *Ingagi*, but rather a respectably informative documentary about an expedition into Africa to capture gorillas for U.S. zoological gardens. Safari footage dates from the 1920s. The picture bears no kinship to a like-titled release of 1941.

Oliver the Eighth

Hal Roach Productions • MGM Pictures • 1934

The most nearly perfect *Laurel & Hardy* comedy is this half-hour featurette—in its ambitious length, one of several foreshadowings of producer Hal Roach's 1940s series of *Streamlined Comedies* of less than an hour.

Roach's interest in horrific themes had become patent during the 1920s. Creepy settings surface in the misadventures of Roach's Rascals (a.k.a. *Our Gang*), Harold Lloyd, Thelma Todd and Patsy Kelly, and Stanley Laurel and Oliver Hardy. Standouts include "Haunted Spooks" (1920), filmed shortly after Lloyd had suffered a mangled hand in an explosive accident while shooting publicity photographs; "Moan & Groan, Inc." (1929), with its lurking lunatic (Max Davidson); and "The Tin Man", which pits Todd and Kelly against a crazed inventor (Clarence Wilson).

One smart takeoff on the Broadway-to-Hollywood Mystery Farce tradition is *The Laurel-Hardy Murder Case* (1930), a bridging piece between silents and talkies. *Murder Case* also sets forth the image of the now-spooky, now-goofy butler (played in 1930 by Frank Austin)—a presence distilled to an essence in *Oliver the Eighth*.

Both *Murder Case* and *Oliver the Eighth* err on the side of a facile resolution of mortal peril: a struggle ends in an awakening from a nightmare. Laurel hints at the finale of *Oliver the Eighth* with this line: "I was dreaming I was awake—and then I woke up and found myself asleep." (This "say what?" declaration dates from 19th-century minstrelsy; vaudevillians George Moran & Charles Mack, a.k.a. Two Black Crows, had used a variation during the 1920s.) The just-a-dream conclusion is less a cheat than a touch of darkened characterization: who would imagine that these jolly fellows could entertain such morbid fantasies? But then, Stan and Ollie also could provoke ghastly

Oliver Hardy and Mae Busch.

scrapes in waking life—witness the malicious mayhem of "Them Thar Hills" and its sequel, "Tit for Tat," from 1934–1935. And what are the movies as a class, if not a procession of somebody else's dreams?

Barbers Stan and Ollie—Stan visits a rival shop for a shave—answer a wealthy widow's appeal for a husband. Ollie ditches Stan's letter in a deceit discovered only after Ollie receives a proposal of marriage. Stan insists upon tagging along. Mrs. Fox (Mae Busch) is a black widow: wronged by one man named Oliver, she plots to murder all the Olivers she can lure.

The butler, Jitters (Jack Barty), torments the guests with bizarre card tricks and a make-believe banquet, riffing upon a routine from "Moan & Groan, Inc." The buildup to murder involves a wealth of slapstick humiliations, at Ollie's expense. The assault dissolves to a panicked awakening.

Laurel and Hardy respond beautifully to the pageant of disorientation and terror. The tale, more an elaborate sketch than a structured story, takes a cue from "Them Thar Hills" and "Tit for Tat" (also with Mae Busch) in offering supporting eccentrics who are as essential to the telling as the star players. Jack Barty and Busch, in turn, suggest the menacing combination (two years later) of Irving Pichel and Gloria Holden in *Dracula's Daughter*.

Beggars in Ermine

Monogram Pictures Corp. • 1934

The greater horror of the Great Depression lay in its having been caused by corporate greed—exerted by the same entrenched ruling class that professed to champion some nebulous common good. Big business—need we say so again?—was a favorite target for the Poverty Row producers. Monogram Pictures cranked the contempt in an unusual way with Phil Rosen's *Beggars in Ermine*. Scenarist Tristram Tupper (of *The Avenger*) may have taken a cue from H.G. Wells, whose "The Cone" (1896) pictures a steel-milling factory as a monumental implement of entrapment and murder.

Lionel Atwill, in a respite from villainy, serves *Beggars in Ermine* as John Dawson, whose steel company is threatened by a treacherous assistant, Marley (Jameson Thomas). Marley also pursues an adulterous affair with Dawson's wife, Vivian (Astrid Allyn, a.k.a. Allwyn).

Dawson resists, lest a forced merger leave the workers unemployed. A convenient purported accident costs Dawson his legs. Marley forces the takeover, then drains the Dawson estate and appropriates Dawson's family.

Dawson recovers. He and a blind friend, Marchant (Henry B. Walthall), become street vendors—and then engage other disabled merchants in a commonwealth trust, assuring prosperity for all. Dawson learns of Vivian's death and, under an assumed name,

becomes the guardian of his displaced daughter, Joyce (Betty Furness), the better to keep watch over Marley's machinations. (See also: *Vu Iz Mayn Kind?* [1937] for comparably malicious shenanigans.)

Dawson proposes to buy into the company that had driven him out. Marley, plotting to squeeze out the worker-investors, causes a stock panic. Marchant triggers a buying frenzy that saves the company. Dawson confronts Marley while angry workers gather. Marley commits suicide. Dawson regains authority, and none too soon.

The more overtly horrific films of Phil Rosen and Lionel Atwill, respectively or together, take on a greater depth of meaning for the viewer attuned to *Beggars in Ermine*, a tragedy of unusually hopeful resonance that also conveys a lurking menace. In the midst of the Depression, the film dared to suggest a healing in the resourceful gumption of not only the laboring class, but also of the legions of the outcast, homeless, and disenfranchised. Rosen emphasized the point of mobilizing marginalized citizens by hiring 150 armless, legless, and blind men as crowd extras.

Atwill serves ideally as a benevolent man of wealth who finds himself sidelined by a weasel of the sort that reinforces the predatory essence of capitalism. Jameson Thomas is suitably hateful as the snake in Atwill's garden, a role of the very type that Atwill himself plays in 1934's *The Man Who Reclaimed His Head*. Henry B. Walthall makes a persuasive partner in Atwill's wealth-sharing campaign. Further economic horrors figure in Christy Cabanne's *The World Gone Mad* (1933).

Mystery Liner

Monogram Pictures Corp. • 1934

From featured attraction at Venice's International Exhibition of Cinematographic Art in 1934 to dollar-bin DVD in the 21st century: such is the arc of William Nigh's *Mystery Liner*. Obscurity, soon or late, is the lot of innumerable films from studios small and large, but few other low-budgeters start out with such prominent recognition.

The Venice exposure had a great deal to do with the prominence of source novelist Edgar Wallace, the most prolific mystery and high-adventure author of the early 20th century. Wallace had died in 1932 in Hollywood while working at RKO-Radio Pictures on a preliminary story treatment for *King Kong*. Among many Wallace tales that had been purchased for filming was *The Ghost of John Holling*, the basis of *Mystery Liner*. The adaptation is anything but lavish, but Archie Stout's photography keeps the shipboard settings convincing and the complicated array of characters well sorted and deployed in the service of suspense. William Nigh directs with straightforward efficiency.

An inventor, Grimson (Ralph Lewis), proposes to introduce a device of staggering potential for warfare—professing an ability to control ocean liners from afar. The government schedules a test. Capt. John Holling (Noah Beery) falls ill. He is replaced by First Mate Downey (Boothe Howard), a rival of Second Officer Cliff Rogers (Cornelius Keefe). Maj. Pope (Edwin Maxwell) is among officers supervising the installation. Passengers include the outspoken Granny Plympton (Zeffie Tilbury) and a mysterious chap named von Kessling (Gustav von Seyffertitz).

Grimson is found slain; an unusual knot in a strangling rope implicates Downey. Holling has fled a hospital—whereabouts unknown. A steward (George Cleveland) claims to have sighted Holling as a ghostly apparition. Downey catches Lila (Astrid Allyn, a.k.a. Allwyn), a nurse, prowling about the captain's quarters.

The laboratory places the ship under automatic control. All lights are extinguished—the better to cast suspicion generally and enhance the suggestion of menace afoot, whether criminal or supernatural. Rogers discovers that Downey has been throttled. Pope presses an investigation. Rogers arrests von Kessling. Foreign agents scramble the controlling signal. Holling, in a startling reappearance, exposes Pope as the enemy.

Casting plays sharply against type. Noah Beery, the great villain, is excellent as the heroic and mysterious skipper. Cornelius Keefe is a romantic hero instead of his usual schemer. Even Gustav von Seyffertitz—a master of villainy, often cited as a favorite by Vincent Price—is not as malicious as he appears. George Hayes and George Cleveland play conventional character parts instead of their usual duffers. Edwin Maxwell is his familiar crooked self. Zeffie Tilbury contributes her specialty as a cantankerous sort. Astrid Allyn is in her element as the menaced heroine.

The next assignment for director Nigh at Monogram was *City Limits* (1934), a spirited crime-comedy piece with a newspaper setting.

Beyond Bengal

Harry Schenck • Showmen's Pictures, Inc. • 1934

The *magnum opus* of Harry Schenck's uneven career—most of it in silent-era short subjects—is *Beyond Bengal*, a cynical mock-documentary that revels in ritual atrocities of the Third World. Schenck stars as himself in a surreal, self-aggrandizing trek through the Malay Peninsula. He boasts of the approval of a sultan who (according to a prologue) has allowed himself to be photographed for the first time. The publicity campaign boasted of the ruler's vapid expression of hope that the film might contribute to the progress of his "only partially developed" country. (Parasitic colonial oppression is nearer the truth.)

No such Banana Republic chamber of commerce niceties apply, of course. The film, as gleefully disreputable as 1930's *Ingagi*, transcends its subgenre of "wealthy white guys' safari movies" in presenting a self-serious (and therefore absurd) commentary upon spectacles ghastly beyond belief. Natives mutilate a chimpanzee and slaughter crocodiles. One croc overtakes and (evidently) devours a screaming white man following a waterlogged chase. A constrictor scarfs down a weasel. Schenck, holding court like some overfed and oblivious Borscht Belt comedian, declares that jungle law forbids a hunter to kill "unless...to protect himself or others from harm." The footage contradicts the pompous assertion.

Schenck manipulates a tribal couple into dressing in shabby civilized attire, like the *Superman* comics' Bizarro feigning humanity in scarecrow garb, and going through the motions of a wedding, complete with music from a gramophone—hardly equipment of a sort essential to any legitimate anthropological expedition.

A purported scientist from England (played by Joan Baldwin) serves primarily as an object of endangerment, stricken with malaria. Her plight makes necessary the crossing of a crocodile-infested river. The concentration of menace suggests fakery, and yet genuine danger

seems palpable. The finale suggests the raising from the dead of a crocodile's human victim. Schenck claimed to have spent seven years compiling the footage.

Beyond Bengal? Beyond the Pale is more like it.

The Lost Jungle

Mascot Pictures Corp. • 1934

Clyde Beatty, celebrated big-cat trainer of the Hagenbeck-Wallace Circus, had proved himself a bankable movie star in 1932 with Universal's *The Big Cage*. Beatty's daredevil image overrode his limited acting ability and slight stature. His second picture, *The Lost Jungle*, grossed millions in paid admissions for Mascot Pictures, in extended release as both a serial and a feature-serial composite and, later, as a self-contained feature. The directors of all versions are Armand Schaefer and David Howard.

Setting out in a dirigible to capture animals, Beatty crash-lands on an island in the Indian Ocean—a remnant of a prehistoric land-bridge between Asia and Africa. The fanciful locale assures encounters with species of both continents, against both conventional wisdom and natural history.

A treacherous assistant, Sharkey (Warner Richmond), finds the treasure of a buried city, where a gorilla stands guard. Mutinous survivors of a seagoing expedition occupy a stockade. Beatty's pal, Larry Henderson (the overtly comical Syd Saylor), and the ship captain's daughter, Ruth Robinson (Cecilia Parker), require extravagant protection. Sharkey aligns himself with Kirby (Wheeler Oakman), leader of the mutineers. A safe getaway is a foregone conclusion for all who deserve it.

Excitement dwarfs the shabby production values—business as usual for Mascot—what with harrowing encounters with such creatures as Sammie, Hagenbeck-Wallace's sensational so-called killer lion. Most action takes place on sets consisting of bamboo camouflage over walls and cages. A lion-vs.-tiger match works up a frenzy, and a lurking gorilla (an ape-suited Charles Gemora, also of *Ingagi*) generates suspense. Repetitive action becomes tedious, and the trick-photography crash of the dirigible is poorly executed.

Warner Richmond and Wheeler Oakman top a fine ensemble of heavies. Syd Saylor—a great favorite among children, less so with the grown-up customers—generates laughs with his hyperactive Adam's apple. Mickey Rooney appears as a circus kid.

Nat Levine's feature-serial concept differs from Sol Lesser's formula for such modifications, in that *The Lost Jungle* was trimmed to a 73-minute feature, followed by 10 chapters. This initial feature comprises most of the first two chapters and 24 minutes of outtakes. A distinct feature, released a few months later, distills the entire serial to a concentration of chaos.

That second feature version allows Oakman's bad guy to reform. In the serial, however, he remains a menace to the end—last seen falling into a pit of crocodiles while the gorilla kills a fellow mutineer (Lew Meehan). In all versions, Richmond's character becomes a lion's dinner.

The House of Mystery

Monogram Pictures Corp. • 1934

In a seeming variation upon Bud Pollard's *The Horror* , the theft of valuables from a Hindu temple brings upon a wealthy household a curse, complete with rampaging gorilla: William Nigh's *The House of Mystery*, in a nutshell. The scenario belongs more rightly to colonial folklore and Rudyard Kipling, of course, than to commercial literature:

There is no stopping a notion once it has become entrenched within the communal dream-stream. The persistent question is that of whether the Third World is the white man's burden, or the white man is the Third World's burden.

John Pren (Clay Clement) has absconded with jewels and a voluptuous coochie dancer named Chanda (Joyzelle Joyner, a.k.a. Laya Joy) as the fruits of his crime. To say nothing of a paralytic condition. Pren promises various associates a share of his wealth on condition that all spend a week in his crepuscular mansion. The inmates include Pren's assistant, Ella Browning (Verna Hillie); a wisecracking salesman, Jack Armstrong (Ed Lowry); and assorted expendables. Chanda holds sway over the premises, worshipping the carcass (or *is* it?) of a gorilla.

A séance provokes murder. A false scare, the better to cause a distraction, brings on another killing. Pren is exposed as a bogus cripple. Chanda turns jealous—and summons the ape—when she overhears Pren propositioning Ella. Armstrong and the police arrive none too soon.

Smart-mouthed heroic protagonism is associated with Bob Hope, thanks to *The Cat and the Canary* (1938), among other comical chillers and crime yarns. The style, however, descends more precisely from *The House of Mystery*'s Ed Lowry—like Hope, a stage-and-radio artist; but unlike Hope, lacking in persistent momentum despite a now-arrogant, now-self-effacing attitude. *The House of Mystery* has a near-precedent in Warners' *Doctor X* (1932), with Lee Tracy as a scared but self-amused and resourceful news reporter.

Combinations of comedy and mystery were nothing new (witness the larger Mystery Farce tradition), but the addition of brash verbal humor was an innovation. A transitional piece between *The House of Mystery* and Hope's re-tailored *Cat & Canary* is RKO-Radio's *Super Sleuth* (1937), with Jack Oakie. Once Hope's outthrust chin (or nose) and air of brash defiance had gained favor, the likes of Red Skelton and Milton Berle followed suit. The defining model is Ed Lowry, who proves appealing and witty in his only feature-film appearance.

A mercurial New Yorker, Lowry had 20 years' experience as a bandleader, master of ceremonies, and occasional silent-screen actor. He was playing the Los Angeles nightclub scene when offered *The House of Mystery*. He soon returned to stage and radio. (Even such radio giants as Fred Allen, Jack Benny, and Seth Parker would bomb out in pictures.)

Director William Nigh and camera chief Archie Stout convey the right eeriness, but the gloom subdues the comedy. Verna Hillie, under contract to Paramount, is a determined leading lady. Dread radiates from Brandon Hurst, as a Hindu priest, and Dale Fuller, a fine portrayer of eccentric women, favored by Erich von Stroheim. Further menace issues from Clay Clement, George Hayes (later belovéd as

Gabby Hayes), and Mary Foy. Additional comedy is supplied by John Sheehan, George Cleveland, Irving Bacon, and Harry C. Bradley. Joyzelle Joyner, working under the temporary alias of Laya Joy, executes an eye-filling ceremonial dance.

Filming took place at General Service Studio, where Monogram held a lease. The working title echoed that of Adam Hull Shirk's source play, *The Ape*; an interim title was *Curse of Kali*. Shirk also is credited with *Ingagi*, and with Monogram's *The Ape* (1940). That Boris Karloff starrer bears no resemblance, apart from a gorilla, to *The House of Mystery*.

House's title theme, incidentally, is Henry Hadley's "Zanzibar," from Abe Meyer's stock-music library.

An early announcement under a different title. Not to be confused with 1940's The Ape, *although both have a source-author in common.*

Chloe (Love Is Calling You)

J.D. Trop • Pinnacle Productions • 1934

"By no means act normal," Marshall "Mickey" Neilan wrote during the 1920s in a flippant article. "Producers are convinced that no normal being can be a director." Furthermore, the essential qualification is "to convince producers that you are a better director than your pictures show you to be." And there are two kinds of director: "Those who make artistic pictures and those whose pictures pay."

Neilan, accomplished but erratic, was of both kinds, at one time or another: *Chloe (Love Is Calling You)*, sparsely shown in its day and long mislaid until the 1990s, represents the artistic side of Neilan. When he made this romance of the haunted bayou country, Neilan had been conspicuously absent since the surge during 1929–1930 of *Black Waters*, *The Awful Truth*, *Tanned Legs*, *The Vagabond Lover*, *Hell's Angels* (a co-writer credit), and *Sweethearts on Parade*.

Neilan's reputation as a hard-drinking playboy might have earned him a permanent berth along Poverty Row, where the off-Hollywood production of *Chloe* assurédly belongs. And yet, his confident handling of this poetic peculiarity sparked Neilan's rekindling as a talent for corporate Hollywood. In one fine touch, the director depicts the electrifying effect of a kiss upon the title character (Olive Borden) by showing her feet squirming in a run-down pair of shoes. The moment is a reminder of Neilan's heyday as a favored director of Mary Pickford. The scenario is a Neilan original.

From *Chloe*'s Aubrey Kennedy Studio (a.k.a. Kennedy City and Sun Haven Studios, in St. Petersburg, Florida), Neilan retrenched among the majors in short order to deliver *Social Register* at Columbia, the Damon Runyon wiseguy romance *The Lemon Drop Kid* at Paramount, and *This Is the Life*. Another fallow stretch followed; Neilan directed his last pictures in 1937. He worked thereafter at his convenience, as a consultant and an actor.

Chloe opens placidly upon a drifting rowboat. Only when Georgette Harvey begins calling various swampland creatures by name, does a tone of madness become manifest. Her character, Mandy, is a voodoo priestess, widow of a lynch-mob victim. Mandy has returned for vengeance, accompanied by the young woman she has raised from childhood, Chloe (Borden). A friend, Jim Strong (Philip Ober), loves Chloe in vain.

Chloe is drawn to Wade Carson (Reed Howes), a northerner summoned to investigate thefts at a turpentine distillery. Jim warns Chloe against consorting with a white man. Col. Gordon (Frank Joyner), a ruling-class planter, learns of Mandy's return and finds evidence that

Chloe may be *his* daughter, believed drowned as a child. Gordon seeks to introduce Chloe to polite society. Mandy, furious, crashes a party and berates Gordon. Chloe flees. Hill and Mose (Jess Cavin and J. Augustus Smith), distillery laborers and thieves, capture the girl for a voodoo sacrifice, led by Mandy and Mose. Jim and Hill die in a struggle.

Carson and Gordon kill Mose and rout the cultists. Mandy is turned over to the law, lest she fall prey to a new lynching. A hidden grave yields the remains of a Negro child—Mandy's true daughter. Carson embraces Chloe, now certain that she is Betty Ann Gordon.

Gus Kahn and Neil Moret's haunting song of 1927, "Chloe," is forgotten today except as gag fodder for bandleader Spike Jones and Warner Bros.' cartoon-scoring maestro, Carl Stalling. The eerie melody, with elaborate orchestration by George Henninger, provides both inspiration and leitmotif for the Neilan film. (Kahn and Moret receive no screen credit.)

The advertising art for Chloe *was re-purposed (pirated) during the 1940s for a lesser film by far.*

Production began on May 22, 1933. The reassertion of Neilan's mastery compensates for the modest staging and a prevailing amateurism among the supporting cast of (primarily) local Floridians. Chief badman Augustus "Gus" Smith is an exception—an accomplished playwright and actor, later responsible for *Drums o' Voodoo*.

High-spirited Olive Borden, a tragic figure in the larger scope of Old Hollywood, conveys Chloe's extreme youth and innocence despite her own 27 years and the collapse of her major-league career. Virginia-born and convent-schooled, Borden (*née* Sybil Tinkle) had broken into the movies a decade earlier as one of Mack Sennett's bathing beauties troupe, then became a leading lady to cowhand star Tom Mix and a favorite of Howard Hawks, John Ford, and Allan Dwan. Hers is the familiar tale of stardom done in by talking pictures, but *Chloe* finds Borden at ease with the technology; even the sub-par recording equipment captures a lilting voice and a scream that Fay Wray might have envied.

This picture occurs a year after Borden's Hollywood *résumé* ends. *Chloe* was too little seen to make a case for renewal, and by the late 1930s Borden had become a denizen of Los Angeles' Skid Row. She died in 1947 in a charity hotel.

Reed Howes, another casualty of the talkers, is in his element as Chloe's rescuer. A former model for Arrow Shirts, Howes enjoyed less than a decade of heroic stardom before his demotion to the minors and a succession of bad-guy roles. Howes' self-sacrificing rival—none too convincing at impersonating a black man—is Alabama-born Philip Ober, a stage-trained advertising executive and one-time husband of *I Love Lucy* co-star Vivian Vance. Ober dabbled in film until 1950, when he began two busy decades as an all-round character man. Frank

Olive Borden.

Marshall Neilan.

Joyner, as a benevolent southern aristocrat, scarcely conveys the emotional intensity that should come with the rediscovery of a long-vanished daughter. Georgette Harvey fares better as the conjure woman, evolving from comical befuddlement to malice. Gus Smith, looking younger than his preacherly character in *Drums o' Voodoo*, delivers a fine show of menace. Molly O'Day stands out as a socialite who is astonished to learn of her kinship to Chloe. Lesser characters perform in a now-hesitant, now-declamatory manner better suited to Little Theatre.

The musical score, conducted by Erno Rapée of Radio City Music Hall, is elaborate but repetitive. Incidental rustic music features the rambunctious Shreveport Home Wreckers, a blues-based string band.

Film editor Helene Turner later cut many of Republic Pictures' serials. During the 1940s, *Chloe* was distributed to black-neighborhood theatres by Toddy Pictures—which also used *Chloe*'s advertising art to promote a featurette called *Voodoo Devil Drums*, a.k.a. *Virgin Brides of Voodoo*.

Another taste of that 1920s article by Marshall Neilan. He asks rhetorically, "When a producer asks you the name of your best picture, what do you tell him?" The reply: "The next one I am to do for him." Aubrey Kennedy had announced that Neilan's next was to be a comeback picture for Buster Keaton called *The Fisherman*. This one was left unproduced upon Neilan's reinstatement within the major leagues of Hollywood—with bigger fish in need of frying.

The Woman Condemned

Progressive Pictures Corp. • Willis Kent Productions • 1934

Dorothy Davenport Reid worked as Mrs. Wallace Reid, the better to cash in on the notoriety of her late husband, a silent-era star done in by drug addiction. She had starred in some remarkably Expressionistic films for Thomas H. Ince, such as *Human Wreckage* and *Broken Laws* (1922–1924). Her anti-dope obsession had yielded by now to social-problem melodramas (see also: *Sucker Money*) and crime yarns.

The Woman Condemned exemplifies Mrs. Reid's involvement with Willis Kent's low-grade program. An overwrought air of the 1920s prevails. *The Film Daily* noted a climax that leaves matters inadequately explained.

Claudia Dell and Richard Hemingway, as unlikely lovers, lend little conviction. Lola Lane fares better in a dual role. Jason Robards and the unnaturally handsome Paul Ellis are fine as secondary hero and hidden villain. Mischa Auer dispenses the chills—momentarily—as a surgeon. Louise Beavers, the versatile black actress, has a small but pivotal role.

Singer Jane Merrick (Lane) has vanished. Private detective Barbara Hammond (Dell), arrested while snooping about Jane's apartment, is bailed out by reporter Jerry Beal (Hemingway), who claims to be her fiancé. A disgruntled judge (Neal Pratt) marries them on the spot.

Barbara witnesses the slaying of a woman who appears to be Jane. Found with corpse and weapon, Barbara stands accused. Beal and Jim Wallace (Robards), Jane's boss, trace a clue to a clinic where one Dr. Wagner (Auer) hovers over Jane at an operating table. They cringe as Wagner threatens to extract Jane's brain. Then Wagner relieves the tension: he is Jane's plastic surgeon. The victim was Jane's twin.

Barbara delivers a confession in the presence of a gangster known as Dapper Dan (Ellis). Dan suddenly faces an apparent ghost—Jane, of course. Dan had intended to kill Jane, who had jilted him. Barbara has played along with the law. She and Jerry make the marriage permanent.

The sting is lessened by Auer's threat-become-joke, and by the knowledge of a twin *before* the staging of the ghostly appearance. Still, Auer contributes a gripping show of sad-eyed dementia—while it lasts.

Picture Brides

Allied Pictures Corp. • 1934

Mail-order wives from New Orleans arrive in the Brazilian jungle—purchased like chattel at the behest of laborers at a diamond mine. These faded roses strike a sharp contrast with innocent Mary Lee

(Dorothy Libaire), who has come to seek employment.

One bride, Mame (Dorothy Mackaill), knows of the savagery of the boss, von Luden (Alan Hale); she swaps identification with Mary, lest the girl be harmed. Mame's assigned groom, Dave Hart (Regis Toomey), is a fugitive from a theft rap but seems an okay sort.

The women witness a display of von Luden's murderous nature. A marriage party ends with von Luden's attack upon Mary. Hart treats the brute to a beating. Von Luden rallies with the rape and murder of the local physician's mixed-race daughter (Mary Kornman). The doctor (Harvey Clark) retaliates with lethal gunfire. Hart, now under arrest, gains leniency by returning the money he had stolen. He accepts Mary as a bride—no purchase necessary.

Dorothy Mackaill.

A bigger-than-usual production for Allied, Phil Rosen's *Picture Brides* boasts RKO-studio jungle sets familiar to admirers of *The Most Dangerous Game* and *King Kong* (1932–1933). Alan Hale's monstrous von Luden—a wretched soul akin to Jean Hersholt's human beasts in *Hell Harbor* and *Mamba*—steals the show from top-billed Dorothy Mackaill, Regis Toomey, and Dorothy Libaire. Mackaill, a silent star on the wane, is quite good as a tarnished but sympathetic newcomer to Hale's private slaughterhouse.

Standouts in support are Esther Muir, Viva Tattersall, and Hal Roach Studios standby Mae Busch, as Mackaill's tough-but-decent pals; Harvey Clark (of *A Shriek in the Night*) as a vengeful, drunken doctor; Will Ahern as a witty trucker; and former *Our Gang* youngster Mary Kornman as a tragic half-native. All blend well with the oppressive setting.

Rosen directs with attention to detail and characterizing touches. Kornman milks a goat, then wakes Clark by dousing him with a bucketful. Hale is introduced as he wolfs down a meal while ogling a dancer. The naturalistic presentation is right for the dehumanizing environment.

Drums o' Voodoo

a.k.a.: Louisiana • Louisiana She Devil
Weiss Bros. • International Stageplay Pictures, Inc. • 1934

J. Augustus Smith had run away from home at 14 to join the Rabbit's Foot Minstrels, an intinerant southern troupe. He staged original plays in black communities of the South, the East, and the Midwest. Smith hit Broadway in 1933 with a guileless original melodrama called *Louisiana*, about a backwoods community torn between religious superstitions. The play drew praise from some critics, but a vicious salvo from the influential Brooks Atkinson of the *New York Times* helped to sink *Louisiana* after only eight performances.

Smith proposed a film version to Louis Weiss, the remaining active member of the Weiss Bros.' outfit (see: *Unmasked*). Targeting the market for black-neighborhood theatres, Weiss re-assembled the Broadway cast for a low-cost shoot at Long Island's Atlas Sound Studios. The result, *Drums o' Voodoo*, is more a document of the play than a cinematic reinterpretation, compromised by stagebound settings and a lack of imagination in the photography and lighting.

The adaptation is nonetheless fascinating, with intense performances and a melodious array of spirituals, blues refrains, and voodoo chants.

Illinois-born Laura Bowman, hailed as "the Negro Barrymore" (as in Ethel), is Aunt Hagar, a hoodoo priestess at odds with both crime and Bible-thumping fanaticism. She presides over a settlement in the thrall of the ancient talking drums. Elder Amos Berry (Gus Smith), a preacher and ex-convict, opposes Hagar's influence but respects her stance against corruption.

Thomas Catt (Morris McKinney), a bootlegger and pimp, seeks to conscript Berry's niece (Edna Barr) and threatens to expose Berry's past. Hagar summons lightning to blind the villain, who stumbles into a patch of quicksand and none too soon.

The role is an anomaly for Bowman, who had appeared at Buckingham Palace and London's Shaftsbury Theatre in addition to venues throughout Europe. In 1916, she had joined New York's first black dramatic company, the Lafayette Players of Harlem, and later played Broadway with the Negro Art Theatre Company.

Bowman's performance in *Drums o' Voodoo* is splendid. An expressive makeup employs shades of grey-green greasepaint. (Another black-ensemble horror film, 1940's *Son of Ingagi*, features Bowman as a renegade scientist done in by her own creation.)

Gus Smith enacts the ineffectual preacher with touching simplicity. Also noteworthy are Morris "Chick" McKinney, from the Broadway productions of *The Green Pastures* and *Porgy and Bess*, as a caricatured villain; and Lafayette Players veterans A.B. Comathiere and Lionel Monogas, blues singer Trixie Smith, and musical comedienne Edna Barr. Character names are blatant puns (Tom Catt and Elder Berry) on the one hand, and black musical allusions on the other—Aunt Hagar, as in the traditional "Aunt Hagar's Blues."

Regional censors demanded trimming. The remaining voodoo dancing is innocuous, but one bump-and-grind routine packs an erotic charge. The surviving fragmentary picture is roughly half the length of the original. In 1981, restorationist Alex Gordon mounted a reissue by Weiss Global Enterprises, descended from the Weiss Bros.' pioneering talking-picture company.

The Mystic Hour

Progressive Pictures • J.H. Hoffberg • 1934

Melville DeLay's *The Mystic Hour* received few showings via states'-rights distribution—a method of booking on a region-by-region basis, with no formal or comprehensive release. The acting is too good to have gone unseen, with two fine villains, Montagu Love and Charles Middleton, performing in the classically grand manner. The ingenue is capably set forth by blonde Lucille Powers; she had worked for most of the major studios, with particular success at MGM in King Vidor's *Billy the Kid* (1931).

A real surprise is the presence of the famed silent-era serial actor and director, Charles Hutchison—better known as "Hurricane Hutch." For undocumented reasons, Hutchison was omitted from the advertising, despite a central role. Though a dozen years older here than when he had performed breathtaking daredeviltry for Pathé, Hutchison remains enough of a rough-and-tumble stuntman to put across the purported youth of his character.

Hutchison is wealthy Bob Randall, in pursuit of a crook known as the Fox. Randall is mistaken for a prowler in the bedroom of Mary Marshall (Powers). He nabs one of the gang behind the bed. The commotion rouses Mary's guardian, Roger Thurston (Middleton), and his brother, Bradley (Eddie Phillips), who desires Mary. The Fox poisons the captured henchman.

The Fox poses as a private detective (Montagu Love). As romance blossoms for Randall and Mary, the Fox threatens Randall. Thurston is leeching off Mary's trust fund. Randall fakes his abduction, the better to smoke out the Fox and expose the crooked brothers. The scheme leads to a desperate encounter atop an oceanside cliff.

Screenwriter John F. Nattiford was a prolific author of westerns and melodramas for the independents. Melville DeLay, an assistant at the majors, became a director in earnest on Poverty Row. *The Mystic Hour* prizes action over atmosphere, but the photography is vivid.

The Tell-Tale Heart

a.k.a.: Bucket of Blood

Clifton-Hurst Productions • Fox Film Corp. • DuWorld Pictures • 1934

Edgar Allan Poe's famous story fares none too well in this British adaptation, which was made with partial underwriting from Hollywood's Fox Film Corp. Surviving prints, diminished to 49 and 55 minutes (variously) from an original length of approximately 70 minutes, display visual inventiveness, influenced by the German Expressionist films of the 1920s.

The scenic intensity is insufficient to overcome the awkward self-consciousness of the players. Novice director Brian Desmond Hurst was bound for classier assignments, including the 1951 *Scrooge*, one of the more resonant versions of Charles Dickens' "A Christmas Carol." Norman Dryden plays the youngster who finds an inspiration for murder in the diseased eye of a benefactor (John Kelt). Even at a truncated length, the picture plods. Fox Film found the result of its investment unworthy of U.S. distribution and dumped the imported version of *The Tell-Tale Heart* (under a lurid proxy title) onto an

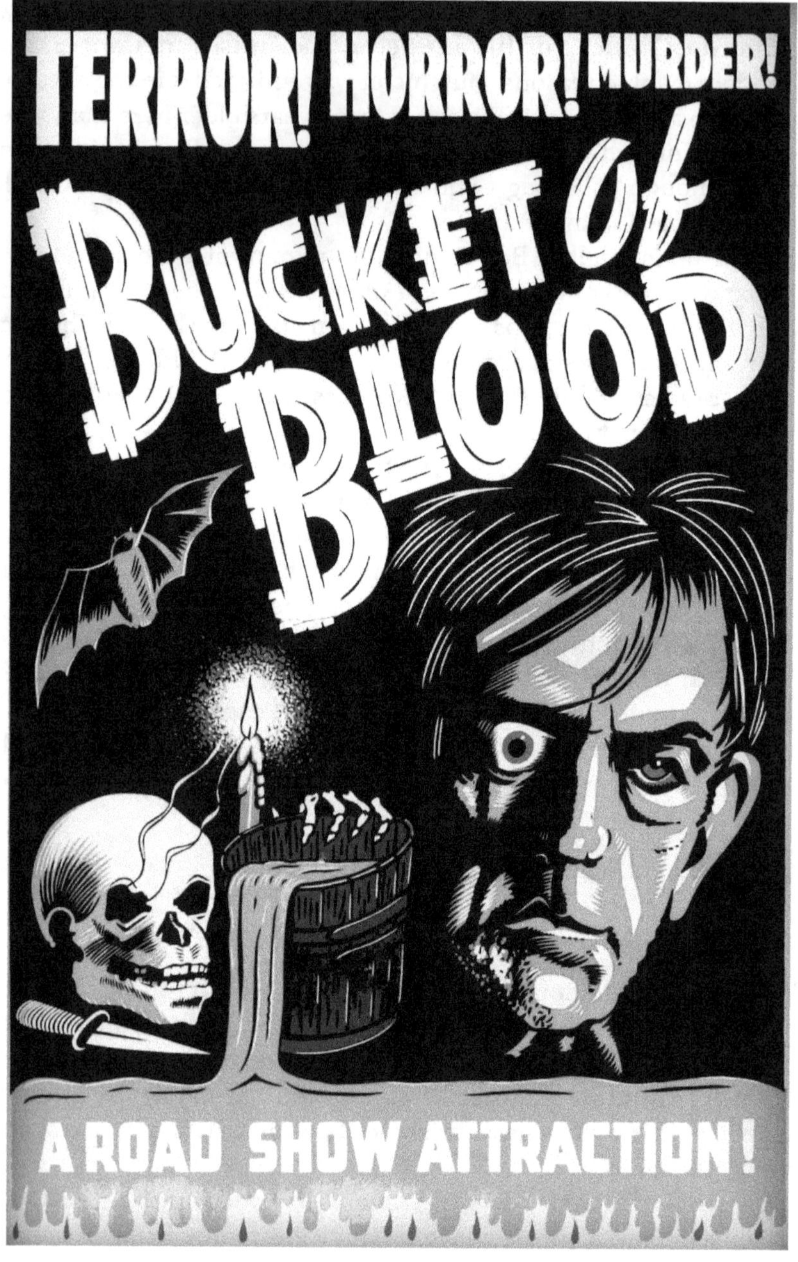

exploitation outfit, DuWorld Pictures, which in turn kept the film in profitable circulation well into the 1940s. The U.S. title, *Bucket of Blood*, often engenders confusion with Roger Corman's famous satire of the hipsters' art-and-poetry *demimonde*, *A Bucket of Blood* (1959).

The Murder in the Museum

a.k.a.: The Five Deadly Vices
Willis Kent • Progressive • Pan-Ray • 1934

Henry B. Walthall never regained the prominence he had known as D.W. Griffith's finest actor, but Walthall became a treasure to the independent studios, as well as a dependable character man at the majors. An instinctive grasp of talking-picture style gained for him an advantage that many silent-era stars lacked.

Walthall applies his customary dignity to *The Murder in the Museum*, which boasts a true-to-life carnival environment with such arresting presences as knife marksman Steve Clemente, of *The Most Dangerous Game*.

The desultory, matter-of-fact photography lacks the shadow-laden air of menace such a story requires. Melville Shyer directs for silent-picture histrionics. Comedian Donald Kerr stands out as a spieler, known in civilian terms as a barker. Leading lady Phyllis Barrington was mistakenly billed as Gertrude Messenger—another actress altogether, who does not appear.

Freak-show operator and bootlegger Carr (Lynton Brent) fears a raid, and with good reason. Reform-minded Councilman Newgate (Sam Flint), upon spotting reporter Jerry Ross (John Harron), insists that his associates proceed with a siege. Newgate falls dead as the crowd panics at the sound of gunfire. Police Commissioner Brandon (Joseph Girard) and a carny magician, Mysto (Walthall), rush to attend to the victim.

Ross and Lois Brandon (Barrington), the senior cop's daughter, fall in love—to her father's consternation. A siege on Carr's hideout ends with his slaying by a vengeful freak. Newgate's hidden killer is revealed to be Mysto, who had sought to disgrace Carr for a long-ago betrayal.

A reissue as *The Five Deadly Vices* by Pan-Ray Pictures saw the addition of poorly matched striptease footage.

Henry B. Walthall.

Fifteen Wives

Invincible-Chesterfield Pictures • 1934

Humor and horror, the sides of a coin often tossed, strike a bracing balance in Frank Strayer's *Fifteen Wives*, a tale of a blackmailing polygamist's murder and its backlash. The death of Steven Humboldt seems a matter of apoplexy until Inspector Decker Dawes (Conway Tearle) learns of the victim's 15 wives—all believing themselves widowed. Shards of glass, found in Humbolt's hotel suite, form a globe designed to break under a certain sonic frequency. The globe had contained a lethal gas.

Dawes senses a solution when a radio program about the manipulation of sound causes a globe on his desk to shatter. He finds the broadcaster (Ralf Harolde) to be married to one of Humbolt's supposed widows (Noel Francis). Another Mrs. Humboldt (Margaret Dumont) urges burial in the tradition of her spiritual cult—only to turn up murdered, having witnessed florist Jason Getty (John Wray) gloating over Humboldt's body. When confronted, Getty confesses to the poisoning, and to having placed the snooping wife's corpse in her husband's casket. Getty's wife had ditched him for Humboldt.

The script is the work of Charles S. Belden, author of Warners' *Mystery of the Wax Museum* (1933), and Frederick Stephanie, director of *Flash Gordon* (1936) and later a producer at MGM. The combination of

comical absurdities with the macabre also accommodates an unlikely romance for Conway Tearle's stalwart detective with one of the more appealing and troubled wives (Natalie Moorhead), who has marital problems of her own. The contrasts are emphasized by constant motion among the many principal players, with emphatic use of sets at Universal Studios.

An unusual touch is the presence of Margaret Dumont, celebrated foil to Groucho Marx, in the now-humorous, now-serious role of a religious fanatic with the Marxian name of Sybilla Crum. Curious, too, is the notion of having Tearle's middle-aged bachelor detective wooing a married woman—an angle that the Production Code Administration and its manipulator, the Legion of Decency, would have vetoed slightly later in 1934.

Tearle is excellent as the determined inspector. Raymond Hatton lends interest as Tearle's droll partner. John Wray is a scene stealer throughout, especially in a climactic rant.

Frontier Gothic: John Wayne and the Lone Star Westerns

Monogram Pictures Corp. • 1934-1935

Here are the films—along with his Mascot serials of 1932–1933— without which John Wayne's greater stardom might never have occurred. Wayne's decisive big-time breakthrough, John Ford's *Stagecoach* (1939), might likewise not have taken shape without the realistic stuntwork and the strides in Wayne's camera confidence that had arisen from the low-budget likes of *Randy Rides Alone*, *Blue Steel*, *The Star Packer*, and the *Lone Star Westerns* series as a class. The small films hold up on their own—the constant is a grim naturalism, with recurring weird touches—but they are more important as a proving ground for bigger developments.

After completing *The Three Musketeers* at Mascot, Wayne starred in six Warners pictures sold as the first *Lone Star Westerns* series, which producer Leon Schlesinger (better known for the seminal Warners cartoons) built around stock footage from Ken Maynard's silents for First National. Wayne took Maynard's place in the close and medium shots, and a horse named Duke—after Wayne's nickname—filled in for Maynard's famous mount, Tarzan. One such patchwork picture, *Haunted Gold*, is a gem, down to the finer point of a memorably animated title card from the *Looney Tunes* workshop. Once the stock shots had been depleted, Wayne resumed scrambling for assignments, star billing forgotten.

Monogram's Trem Carr proposed in 1933 to revive the *Lone Star* brand with eight pictures a year, offering Wayne $2,500 each. These lucrative films, made on five-day schedules for less than $10,000 each, were still in production when Monogram found itself forcibly merged (with Mascot and other studios) into Republic Pictures in 1935. Monogram made 16 *Lone Stars* between September of 1933 and April of 1935.

The producer was Paul Malvern, a former stuntman. Most were directed (and sometimes written) by Robert North "Bob" Bradbury, whose unusual pictorial sense and grim narrative voice set the prevailing tone. Continuity of style arose from stock-company casting, rugged natural scenery, and the sparkling photography of Archie Stout, who shot all the productions save two.

Location work utilized a fine town-site around Newhall, California, surrounding desert and mountain territory, the Kern River, and a deep lake at the foot of a cliff. Minimal interiors were constructed at Monogram's lone sound stage, at Metropolitan Studio. George Hayes (later known as Gabby, for his lovable-duffer roles with Bill "Hopalong Cassidy" Boyd and Roy Rogers) served most of the Monogram *Lone Stars*—sometimes as a villain, sometimes as a fatherly type, and often as a sidekick. Yakima Canutt, another stock member, usually played villains but proved adept at comedy relief and always doubled Wayne for the more perilous stunt sequences.

In a series of visits with George Turner and Michael Price dating from 1967, Wayne described his duties at Monogram: "Ride, fight, keep my hat on, and at the end of the shooting still have enough strength left to kiss the girl and ride off on my horse—of kiss my horse and ride off on the girl—whichever they wanted."

Wayne also explained that Bradbury had created the method of fighting favored throughout the industry into the present day. The multimillion-dollar action films of even the new century (homogenized digital-effects fakery aside) still owe much to a technique developed for a $10,000 horse opera.

"The way we did fights in those days was to actually hit each other on the shoulders," Wayne said. "By the end of the day, Yak [Canutt] and I were so bruised we could hardly climb onto our horses. Yak was better at pulling his punches, so he got beat up worse than I did.

"Yak was complaining so much to Bob Bradbury that Bob worked out a way to photograph fights so that we didn't have to really hit each other.

"He called it the Pass System. ... [T]he camera was placed, low and at a certain angle, so that I could swing past Yak's face and he could react as though he'd been hit. When we saw the rushes, we knew we had something.

"It worked so well that everybody started doing it that way. Sometimes when I'm working with a young stuntman, he'll start showing me how the Pass System is done—not knowing that I was the first one to do it."

Bradbury's work went unnoticed by the critics, but his contributions are fundamental. A Bradbury picture—and all were done on tight budgets and tight schedules—is as recogniz-

Robert Bradbury.

able as a film by John Ford or Alfred Hitchcock. Bradbury relished offbeat elements, and he often would add mystery, superstition, or even a garnish of science fiction.

From 1918 to 1937, Bradbury directed some 80 features, a couple of serials, and many shorts. Some feature his son, Bob, Jr.—better known as Bob Steele. One can only wonder how Bradbury's inventive genius would have fared under more generous circumstances.

A pivotal Lone Star is *Randy Rides Alone* (1934), directed by Harry Fraser from a script by Lindsley Parsons—both reporting to Bradbury, who also served as one of Monogram's associate producers. Here, Randy Bowers (Wayne) seeks evidence against an outlaw band. He prepares to enter a saloon that seems the scene of a festive occasion. His expression of happy anticipation changes abruptly to a grimace of horror as he finds the barroom strewn with corpses; the jolly music he had heard comes from an automatic player-piano, grinding away for an audience of stiffs.

Charged with murder, Bowers faces a posse that includes a grotesque hunchback, Matt the Mute (George Hayes), who communicates with cryptic scrawled notes. The barman's surviving niece, Sally Rogers (Alberta Vaughan), tells Bowers she knows the guilty parties to be Marvin Black and his gang. She helps Bowers escape.

Infiltrating Black's lair behind a waterfall, Bowers learns that Black had sought a payload, hidden somewhere within the saloon. Bowers finds the strongbox and replaces the loot with dynamite—tough luck for Black when he opens fire upon the container. Bowers establishes that Matt the Mute was the mysterious Marvin Black.

Randy Rides Alone, Lone Star No. 7, honors Bradbury's insistence upon merciless, decisive action. Bradbury had established the tone of dread in 1934's *West of the Divide*, where a killer is identified by his maniacal laughter. Grotesque mystery dominates *Randy Rides Alone*, from the eerie and gruesome opening sequence—Wayne's shocked response braces the viewer only somewhat for what the pivoting camera is about to reveal—to the ruthless destruction of the bandits' boss. Alberta Vaughan is Wayne's adventurous equal, by turns trusting and wary of his motives.

Action runs apace with the strangeness, however. Canutt's superb stunting abounds, especially in a real-time cliffside fall from a ladder—into a tree—and through the branches.

Elsewhere among the *Lone Stars*, Bob Bradbury's *The Star Packer* (1934) matches *Randy Rides Alone* for concentrated eeriness. (Another, *Blue Steel*, comes close, with an ominous dead-of-night opening sequence.) *The Star Packer* also contains a generous helping of comedy from Yakima Canutt, as an Indian sidekick. Here, Marshal John Travers (Wayne) squares off against the Shadow, whose henchmen relish murder as a function of banditry. A ghostly sniper is killing each new sheriff. Travers takes the badge and identifies the gangsters as familiar criminals: "What a nest of hornets!" He and Yak (Canutt) trace a hidden tunnel to a hollowed stump—source of the phantom attacks. The Shadow (George Hayes) proves to have been hiding in plain sight, impersonating a rancher whom he had slain.

For *The Star Packer*, Monogram indulged real spectacle in a running fight sequence that involves about 40 horsemen. The stunts, including a stagecoach rescue and a precipitous leap, are generously deployed. The film also makes extensive use of Bradbury's adaptation of the swish-pan transitional device, in which the camera sweeps over the landscape to the point of a blur. Bradbury's version picks up the characters leaving one location and then finds them arriving elsewhere at the end of the pan. This arresting whiplash tactic figures in most of Bradbury's talkies.

Jane Eyre

Monogram Pictures Corp. • 1934

Comparisons must be made against other versions, but Christy Cabanne's *Jane Eyre* stands at least as the masterwork of Poverty Row. Weighed opposite 20th Century-Fox's epic of 1943—most prominent of several *Jane Eyres*—this filming from Monogram seems as pale and timid as its heroine.

But then, Cabanne's *Jane Eyre* retains more of the source-author, Charlotte Bronte. Virginia Bruce is a prettier, less fluttery Jane than Joan Fontaine, and *Frankenstein*'s Colin Clive makes a more explicable Rochester than Orson Welles and his overplayed scowling intensity.

Robert Planck's photography seems as one with the 19th century. (The exteriors include Sherwood Forest, California.) The music is light and simple, free of bombast.

Jane Eyre, abandoned to the sanctimonious cruelties of an orphanage, grows up to become a member of the staff—but rebels at last against corrupt management to become governess to the child (Edith Fellowes) of Squire Edward Rochester. Rochester Manor stands shrouded in mystery, what with a forbidden wing that yields screams in the night, to say nothing of a general pall cast by a skulking servant, Grace Poole (Ethel Griffies).

The mystery rests with Rochester's hidden wife (Claire Du Brey). Sequestered on account of insanity, a hollow-eyed figure of disruptive menace, the wife breaks free just as Rochester and Jane are about to

marry. Having driven Jane away, Mrs. Rochester torches the house. Rochester is blinded in a futile effort to rescue the madwoman. Informed of the master's plight, Jane returns to look after Rochester.

Charlotte Bronte might even have preferred Monogram's more sensitive treatment over the magnificent but pretentious Fox version. While Clive and Bruce dominate the picture with near-perfect portrayals, there are many deft performances in support: Beryl Mercer is a kindly housekeeper. David Torrence (brother of Ernest Torrence, of *I Cover the Waterfront*) excels as the sadistic head of the orphanage. Lionel Belmore and Aileen Pringle are suitably hateful as an overbearing aristocrat and his taxing daughter. Ethel Griffies is so good as the mysterious Grace Poole that she was bound to repeat the role in the 1943 version. Jameson Thomas is a faithful solicitor. Claire Du Brey makes a brief but striking appearance as the deranged wife. Richard Quine, later a director of distinction, stands out as an over-privileged brat.

Virginia Bruce came to Monogram on loan from MGM for this comeback assignment. She had been sidelined while married to a tragic Hollywood lush, John Gilbert. After a divorce, she rejoined MGM.

An awkward visual effect mars the pivotal fire scene, which uses an obvious miniature of the manor, with disproportionately large flames. The film is nonetheless a peak in the checkered career of Christy Cabanne, whose accomplishments range from a 1915 version of *Enoch Arden*, to many pictures for D.W. Griffith and Douglas Fairbanks, to the memorable *The Last Outlaw* (1936). Cabanne also is responsible for one fine example of Universal's B-unit chillers, *The Mummy's Hand* (1940).

Jane Eyre led promptly to bigger assignments for Cabanne, who by the summer of 1934 had gone to work on *Rendezvous at Midnight* for Universal. Cabanne's anchorage along Poverty Row, however, remained a recurring constant, if not necessarily a last refuge. In his later years, though, Cabanne's underappreciated talents went to waste on increasingly cheap and unrewarding projects. One of these, 1947's *Scared to Death*, nonetheless bears rediscovering as a fascinating exercise in dreamlike absurdity, straddling a jittery barrier between avant-garde artistry and incoherence.

The interest in such literary sources must have been contagious along Poverty Row. Monogram offered Wilkie Collins' *The Moonstone* (below). Nat Levine's Mascot Pictures signed Ralph Morgan in August of 1934 for Louisa M. Alcott's *Little Men*, with a menacing reformatory setting ruled by *Forgotten Horrors* standby Gustav von Seyffertitz. By September, producer Larry Darmour and Majestic Pictures had delivered a grisly, earthy retelling of Nathaniel Hawthorne's *The Scarlet Letter*.

The Moonstone

Monogram Pictures Corp. • 1934

Reginald Barker's *The Moonstone* is a worthy condensation of Wilkie Collins' rambling cornerstone of modern detective fiction, published in 1868. The job was a departure from the norm for producer Paul Malvern and screenwriter Adele Buffington, specialists in westerns.

The necessary air of Gothic dread comes across very well, beginning with the arrival of Franklin Blake (*Dracula*'s David Manners) and his

Hindu servant (John Davidson) at gloomy Verinder Manor during a storm. Blake has come to deliver the Moonstone, a fabulous diamond stolen long ago from a temple in India—that chronic-to-acute motif of *The Horror* (1933) and *The House of Mystery* (1934), among many other such tales. Now the gem belongs to Anne Verinder (Phyllis Barry), daughter of Sir John Verinder (Herbert Bunston), a scientist.

Verinder's guests are Godfrey Ablewhite (Jameson Thomas), dealer in rare books and a third cousin to Anne, and Septimus Lucker (Gustav von Seyffertitz), a money-lender with a nefarious reputation. Also present is Dr. Ezra Jennings (Olaf Hytten), assistant to Sir John. The servants include a grim housekeeper (Elspeth Dudgeon, of 1932's *The Old Dark House*), a Cockney gardener (Fred Walton), and a maid (Evelyn Bostock) who will be revealed as a thief, acquainted with the mysterious Lucker.

Anne rejects Blake's argument to lock away the gem, which goes missing. An investigation by Scotland Yard fails to prevent an attack upon Sir John and the slaying of the maid. At last, Ablewhite is exposed as the culprit and pays for his crimes with his life.

Director Barker, a Scotsman born in 1886, had by 1914 begun handling such Thomas Ince productions as *On the Night Stage*, *The Typhoon*, *The Wrath of the Gods*, and *The Golden Claw*. He went on to deliver several of William S. Hart's severe westerns, action pictures with William Desmond for Triangle, and romantic dramas including *The Woman and the Puppet* (1920) for Samuel Goldwyn's company.

Barker met with success at Universal with *The Storm*, and he sustained the momentum at MGM, Fox, and Universal until 1930. After a four-year hiatus, Barker returned with *The Moonstone*, then delivered two additional pictures for Monogram and one for the newly organized Republic. He died in 1937.

The Moonstone boasts a predominantly British cast. David Manners and the Australian Phyllis Barry radiate romantic zest, with Manners affecting his naturally brisk and assertive manner (as in 1932's *The Death Kiss*) instead of the mild presence that he had established in *Dracula* (1931). Herbert Bunston, like Manners an alumnus of *Dracula*, is excellent as the lord of the manor, endangered but defiant. Charles Irwin enacts a Scotland Yard agent with persuasive authority.

The suspects are an unnerving lot, each seeming to harbor forbidden secrets. Robert Planck contributes an expert job of shadow-crossed cinematography. The nighttime storm effects establish an unwavering mood.

Maniac

a.k.a.: Sex Maniac
Hollywood Producers & Distributors • Esper Roadshow Attractions • Sonney
Amusements • 1934

Dwain Esper (1893–1982) was the most notorious of the fringe-dwelling roadshow exploitation impresarios—those carnival-styled hucksters who labored to undermine the self-importance of corporate Hollywood. Although Esper and his kind never sought establishment credentials, their very existence was mortifying to an industry that sought to leave behind its carny-trash prehistory and its amusement-pier nickelodeon origins and get on with the development of the cinema as a perceived art form.

In 1933, in a prelude to the excesses of *Maniac*, Esper had submitted *The Seventh Commandment*—a melodrama about venereal disease, featuring a Caesarean stillbirth—for consideration to receive a Purity Seal from the Production Code, forerunner of the Classification & Ratings Administration. The point was to tweak the nose of chief censor Joseph I. Breen, a Legion of Decency plant, who pronounced *The Seventh Commandment* "vile and disgusting." Mission accomplished, at least for Esper's prankish purposes.

Esper had no use for any Purity Seal. No hypocrite, he, Esper enjoyed a gleefully crooked reputation even among his tribe of hucksters. Colleagues and rivals often caught him selling territorial rights to a film—and then invading the same dedicated region with extra prints.

It is as well that Esper's meager talents kept him underground. Soon after *The Seventh Commandment*, Esper delivered *Maniac*, a shabby masterpiece of *psychopathia sexualis* and literary corruption. The American Film Institute does not record a submission of this sick picture to the Production Code Administration, although Esper did publish a manifesto calling for a safe-as-milk wholesomeness in cinema as a further thumb-of-the-nose to the censors—whose decisive takeover of the industry had occurred shortly before *Maniac* saw release. The film proved (surprisingly) a flop at first with the adults-only crowd.

Wild-eyed Dr. Meirschultz (Horace B. Carpenter, who had seen better days as a DeMille star) proposes to try a re-animation formula upon a corpse. His forces his assistant, Maxwell (Bill Woods), a vaudevillian wanted by the law, to impersonate the local coroner—the better to tamper with a suicide at the morgue. The dead woman comes to life, and the intruders spirit her away.

Maxwell returns empty-handed from another body-snatching mission. Meirschultz proffers a gun and demands: "Take your life— and I will give it back to you!" Maxwell kills the doctor.

A client, Mrs. Buckley (Phyllis Diller), arrives with her delusional husband (Ted Edwards), who "thinks he's the orangutan murderer in Poe's "Murders of (*sic*) the Rue Morgue." Maxwell disguises himself as Meirschultz and inoculates the madman—driving him to a frenzy. Buckley abducts the resurrected woman, tearing away her clothing. Mrs. Buckley finds the corpse of Meirschultz, for whom Maxwell proposes a re-animation. Mrs. Buckley insists that her husband be killed and restored to life as a docile slave. Matters can only get weirder.

Seeking to revive the doctor with a heart transplant, Maxwell finds that Meirschultz' cat has devoured the only available such organ. He captures the animal and gouges out an eye—and swallows it. Maxwell hides the body behind a wall of bricks. The cat crawls in with Meirschultz'

corpse. Maxwell's estranged wife (Thea Ramsey), upon learning that the fugitive is entitled to an inheritance, visits the purported Meirschultz. And so much for Maxwell's attempt to cover his tracks.

Maxwell determines to rid himself of both his wife and Mrs. Buckley: he tells each that he needs her help in subduing a dangerous patient, then gives each a hypodermic syringe and forces them into a cellar.

Police arrive to question Meirschultz. The disguised Maxwell assures the officers that the hideous noises from the cellar issue from mental patients "fighting it out." The cops rush to halt the struggle—and find Meirschultz' body behind the makeshift wall. Maxwell rants philosophically from a jail cell.

Dwain Esper and his wife, Hildagarde Stadie, officed at 6413 Willoughby Avenue in Hollywood—a home-based studio, where they raised a family in bourgeois normalcy. The couple reaped handsome profits from sleazy movies. Esper can only have relished the irony. The Espers' production of *Maniac* foreshadowed by 29 years the emergence of explicit gore as a box-office commodity with the appearance of *Blood Feast* (1963) and its companion films by David F. Friedman and Herschell Gordon Lewis.

The long heyday of Esper (and of Friedman & Lewis and their defiant kind) represented a sustained test of the First Amendment in an industry that preferred to maintain its boundaries of taste and suitability: the warty underbelly of commercial cinema was necessary to a balance, and the major studios knew better than to invade or usurp the territory of the exploitation racket.

A perverse alliance of the Roman Catholic Church's Legion of Decency and the Production Code Administration—feared by the majors and regarded with contemptuous amusement by the independents and undergrounders—began losing traction only during the waning 1960s. The so-called New Freedom that resulted made possible a refreshing frankness from the more intelligent filmmakers, such as Sam Peckinpah, John Schlesinger, and Roger Corman's larger circle of talents—but also gave rise to a chaotic state resembling nothing so much as a kindergarten classroom five minutes after the teacher has stepped away. Since the 1980s, the majors have blurred the boundaries so thoroughly, courting the family trade with institutionalized bad taste and a permissive ratings code, that Dwain Esper would be appalled. The old-school grindhouses, once preferable places for adventurous cineastes to go slumming on the bad side of town, have gone extinct. (This forced imbalance is the subject of a companion volume, *Forgotten Horrors to the Nth Degree*, by Michael H. Price and John Wooley.)

Maniac, for all its pains to offend, is withal a chaste and even entertaining picture, twisting its source material (notably, Poe's "The Black Cat," with nods to "The Murders in the Rue Morgue" and "The Tell-Tale Heart") into a marvel of nightmarish incoherence. Screams and rants abound, and yet the dialogue never indulges in profanity or vulgarisms. The nudity is gratuitous but limited. The money shot comes in the cat's-eye routine, awkwardly staged with one black cat and an entirely different one-eyed stunt-cat, with a make-believe eyeball. An offbeat humorous interlude finds a none-too-bright neighbor extolling the efficiency of his cat-furrier enterprise: "[T]he rats eat the cats, the cats eat the rats, and I get the skins!"

William Thompson's photography conveys a pervasive gloom. The settings are suitably decrepit and eerily lighted, and there are several well-conceived transitions via lap-dissolves. Esper superimposes excerpts from finer films by far—the Swedish *Witchcraft Through the Ages* (1920) and the Italian *Maciste in Hell* (1927)—to symbolize madness.

Some prints bear text inserts to suggest instructional value, mock-clinical descriptions of madness. The music underscoring these segments is Glazounov's *From the Middle Ages*, inappropriately delicate for the ratty context.

Horace Carpenter slices the ham as the doctor. Similarly overwrought performances come from Bill Woods as the impostor, Ted Edwards as the hapless madman, and J.P. Wade as a garrulous morgue attendant. The film's Phyllis Diller is not the comedienne of that name;

this one appeared only occasionally in film, with one credited performance from the silent-screen age.

Maniac, of course, was made neither to endure any tests of time, nor to appeal to anyone outside that clandestine audience that frequented the forbidden theatres that respectable citizens would not admit to visiting. Today, anyone with the price of a dollar-bin DVD can indulge. If Dwain Esper reveled in representing the seamy backstreets of cinema during his prime of artistry, then today he would be appalled to know how grotesquely domesticated his work has become.

The Return of Chandu

Principal Pictures Corp. • Fox Film Corp. • 1934

Fox Film Corp. in 1932 had adapted a radio serial, *Chandu the Magician*, into a high-design stunt film starring Edmund Lowe as the heroic sorcerer and Bela Lugosi as the evil Baron Roxor. Sol Lesser, who had a releasing agreement with Fox, leapt at the chance to produce a second *Chandu* and gave it a title suggestive of a sequel. Lesser gave Lugosi a respite from villainy, assigning him the title role.

Though hardly the type to portray Chandu's avuncular civilian self, Frank Chandler of Beverly Hills, Lugosi proved handier than Lowe with the mystical business. The tale concerns a fugitive Egyptian

Bela Lugosi in the 1932 Chandu the Magician—*a bad-guy prelude to his show of heroism in* The Return of Chandu.

princess, Nadji (Maria Alba), whose blood is sought by a cult intent upon resurrecting an ancient goddess. At stake is the restoration of the sunken continent of Lemuria. This Cult of Ubasti means business.

Nadji takes refuge in Beverly Hills with Dorothy Regent (Clara Kimball Young), widowed sister of Nadji's fiancé, Frank Chandler. Chandler—a.k.a. Chandu, Master of White Magic—finds the household invaded by the cult's priest, Vindhyan (Lucien Prival). Escaping an ambush by turning invisible, Chandu foils an attempt to poison Nadji. A treacherous butler (Frazer Acosta) is felled by a toxic dart before he can disclose the whereabouts of the Ubasti. Nadji alternates between recapture and rescue as Chandu closes in on Vindhyan. A ferocious battle ends with the priest's death in a sacrificial fire.

The cult persists with the abduction of Nadji to the ruins of Lemuria. Reaching the island after his ship has been misrouted, Chandu finds the cannibalistic Cat People on a rampage. He calls upon higher powers and releases a captive White Yogi (Josef Swickard). Prevailing over siege upon siege, Chandu rescues Nadji as the Temple of the Ubasti collapses.

The Return of Chandu was filmed at the Pathé lot and on locations north of Hollywood during the summer of 1934. It was released in two forms, as a 12-chapter serial and as a feature-serial comprising a seven-reel opener (from the first four chapters), followed by weekly deployment of the concluding chapters. The feature is self-contained, ending with the death of bad guy Lucien Prival, but sports a coda that shows the cultists still at large.

That 65-minute feature contains an unusual narrative smoothness: Lesser re-shot the cliffhangers that close each chapter to reduce their illusion of mortal peril, the better to dovetail with the start of each new development. Lesser insisted at first that theatres must book the final eight chapters to secure the feature, but later he issued the feature alone. For a subsequent sequel-like follow-through, Lesser assigned Carl Himm to edit a feature from the balance of the serial. This 67-minute condensation was released as *Chandu on the Magic Island*—less than half the length of the original 16 reels, but almost seamless in terms of continuity.

The Return of Chandu, in whatever form or forms, lacks the artistry of the Fox production, which was directed in high-style Art Deco fashion by William Cameron Menzies and Marcel Varnel. The Lesser job is a keen action piece, however, rich in supernatural business that is never explained with any forced attempts at logic. The craftsmanship of director Ray Taylor and cameraman John Hickson (from Universal's serial department) is enhanced by spectacular standing sets and stirring music. The bravura approach is leagues beyond the films of Mascot and other serial factories of the immediate period. For eye-popping stunts and breakneck action, however, *The Return of Chandu* takes a back seat to Mascot's chapter plays.

The Lemurian exteriors were filmed on the Skull Island village set from *King Kong* (1933), as built by RKO-Radio Pictures at Pathé over the ruins of sets from Cecil B. DeMille's *The King of Kings* (1927). Here it is possible to see Kong's Great Wall in broad-daylight detail. Seaport scenes were staged on sets from *Son of Kong* (1933). Temples of the Cult of Ubasti are dominated by massive idols.

Lugosi seems to relish the heroic turnabout, beaming when addressed as "Uncle Frank." He informs Chandu's displays of hypnotism and battles of will with the same dark concentration he had lavished on Count Dracula at Universal and Chandu's antagonist at Fox. Lucien Prival and Murdoch MacQuarrie are splendid villains. Josef Swickard makes the White Yogi a credible figure of an incredible nature. Maria Alba of Barcelona, complete with Castilian accent, is a worthy damsel in distress. Cyril Armbrister glowers effectively as a cultist; he had a stake in the franchise as producer of the *Chandu* program on network radio.

A real surprise is the early appearance of Gloria Holden and Beatrice Roberts—more familiar, respectively, as the star player of *Dracula's Daughter* (1936) and Queen Azura of *Flash Gordon's Trip to Mars* (1938). These severe beauties offer a lethal toast—and squeal with dismay when the poisoned goblet flies from Maria Alba's hand.

The Ghost Walks

Invincible Pictures Corp. • 1934

Scarcely a month in the making, from filming in November to release during December of 1934, Frank Strayer's *The Ghost Walks* packs all the lapsed plausibility one might expect from such haste but manages some good gags and suspenseful moments all the same. Its play-within-a-play structure, though old stuff on Broadway, is unusual for a movie of the period. Tricky lighting applies well to an Old Dark House setting at Pathé Studio, complete with sliding panels and secret passageways. The title is Broadway vernacular for payday in a show-business setting.

Broadway producer Herman Wood (Richard Carle) is traveling with playwright Prescott Ames (John Miljan). Their automobile is halted by a storm-tossed tree. At a house nearby, one Dr. Kent (Henry Kolker) offers shelter. Wood is startled by screams that Kolker attributes to a patient, Beatrice (Eve Southern)—whose murdered husband is said to appear to her as a spirit. Beatrice vanishes. Wood retreats to his room.

Ames congratulates all present for their performances. They have staged the first act of his new play, in an elaborate pitch to secure Wood's backing. But now, Beatrice is found slain.

Wood, informed of the staging, refuses to believe that he is not seeing the remainder of the play. After further strange happenings, a deranged intruder (Spencer Charters) proves responsible for the genuine perils.

John Miljan (of *The Sin of Nora Moran*) is convincing as the playwright pressed into a state of heroism, and June Collyer supplies a beautiful and convincing love interest. Henry Kolker lends dignity, and Johnny Arthur contributes his specialty as a frightened Milquetoast. Even these seasoned performers are upstaged by raspy-voiced Richard Carle as the harried producer—and Carle, in turn, is upstaged by Spencer Charters as the now-comical, now-terrifying maniac.

Mystery Mountain

Mascot Pictures Corp. • 1934

Ken Maynard, the temperamental cowboy star, had just been fired at Universal Pictures. Never mind that the bone of contention, a weird tale of frontier terrors called *Doomed to Die* that the brass found offensive, had turned out to be a moneymaker after Universal had altered the title to the generic-sounding *Smoking Guns*. Mascot Pictures' Nat Levine arranged immediately for the volatile horseman to star in one feature and two serials, *Mystery Mountain* and *The Phantom Empire*. Levine offered an unprecedented (at Mascot) $10,000 a week, certain that Maynard's popularity would justify a greater budget. The feature, *In Old Santa Fe*, turned out well, and *Mystery Mountain* became Mascot's biggest hit—a record to be surpassed only by the 1935 Tom Mix starrer, *The Miracle Rider* . *Mystery Mountain* cost $80,000—twice the budget of most Mascot serials, with Maynard's salary accounting for half.

Maynard, eager to get back in harness after a vacation in Europe, remained as difficult as he was productive—insisting upon running the show as he had done with his own unit at Universal. He persuaded Levine to rent the western town at Universal instead of a less imposing set at Mascot's lot, the Mack Sennett Studio. The clash of wills was formidable between the hard-drinking redneck horseman and the stubborn Yiddish studio boss.

Maynard thrived on such tensions. *The Film Daily* reported that he gained 10 pounds while at work on *Mystery Mountain*. Levine became anxious to rid himself of Maynard, despite the self-evident truth that Maynard's robust presence made the serial outstanding.

A weirdly prophetic note occurs at the end of the sixth chapter: Maynard is shot from the saddle by a seedy-looking bit player named Gene Autry, a Texas-bred singer seeking greener prospects in Hollywood (on advice from the humorist Will Rogers, incidentally). Autry soon

would usurp Maynard's assigned role in *The Phantom Empire*. Seldom has the descent of one star and the rise of another been so vividly crystallized in an unwittingly symbolic moment of cause-and-effect.

The Rattler, a bandit chieftain, is responsible for murderous raids upon a railroad crew. Conflict persists between a stagecoach line and a burgeoning railroad industry. Detective Ken Williams (Maynard) chases the Rattler in a stagecoach, only to topple over a cliff. The Rattler disguises himself as Williams. Williams disguises himself as the Rattler. Stagecoach heiress Jane Corwin (Verna Hillie) and newspaper reporter Breezy Baker (Syd Saylor) find that mistaken identities abound—a Mascot trademark.

Williams' horse, Tarzan, suffers a beating from the Rattler. Williams gathers the suspects before Tarzan—and the horse attacks Blayden (Edward Earle), head of the railroad. Given away as the Rattler, Blayden escapes, only to die in an explosion of his own making.

The tale, steeped in dream logic, derives from *The Hurricane Express*, to the finer detail of having the unknown villain cheat the mystery angle by disguising himself as other characters. Another standard Mascot deception finds Edmund Cobb—not otherwise in the ensemble cast—appearing in false nose, smoked eyeglasses, and moustache as the Rattler. Viewers with long memories might have noticed, at the finale, that Edward Earle, unmasked as the Rattler, had appeared *alongside the villain* in earlier episodes. Mascot was generous with the excitement but seldom played fair in the deployment of clues.

Most of the outdoor business was shot at Chatsworth and in Bronson Canyon, with the railroad camp at one end of the quarry and the Rattler's hideout at the other. Photography is often striking. Maynard and the magnificent Tarzan make a fascinating team, especially at the climax when the horse shows real emotion upon recognizing Earle as its assailant. Verna Hillie, attractive and capable in a role that might have been merely decorative, is a better actress than most other leading ladies of the serials and horse operas. Syd Saylor adds energetic comedy. The action is beautifully handled—no surprise, inasmuch as both directors, Otto Brower and B. Reeves "Breezy" Eason, were noted for their spectacular second-unit work on productions much bigger.

Sing Sing Nights

Monogram Pictures Corp. • 1934

Jameson Thomas, Hardie Albright, and George Baxter serve *Sing Sing Nights* as vengeful figures who admit to a murder that *only one of them* can have committed. All are sentenced to die. Ferdinand Gottschalk, as the inventor of a hypersensitive lie detector, determines that the victim was already dead before two of the shooters had approached. The scenario, though filtered through the cinematic intelligence of established screenwriter Marion Orth, cannot help but convey the shaggy-dog gimmickry that was the stock-in-trade of novelist Harry Stephen Keeler.

Keeler's whodunits exert the freakish fascination of a fevered dream, distinguished by a disdain for the deployment of clues, a preference for deranged inanities and rampant illogic, and the layering of contrivances that are at once remarkable and senseless.

Lewis D. Collins' filming of *Sing Sing Nights* is a faithful representation of Keeler at a comparatively saner stage of a long and often commercially successful career; the novel had appeared in 1928. Floyd Cooper (Conway Tearle) is a newspaper correspondent leading a criminal secret life. Cooper's slaying—three wounds, three weapons—leads to the arrests and confessions of Howard Trude (Albright), Robert McCaigh (Thomas), and Sergei Krenwicz (Baxter). Three convictions, for want of forensic clarification, yield three death sentences, to be carried out simultaneously.

An inventor, Varney (Gottschalk), subjects the condemned men to his machinery. Those who disclose the truth will receive pardons. Each had befriended Cooper, each had suffered ghastly losses on account of his ingratitude, and each had tracked him down with murderous intent—all at the same moment. Varney finds Krenwicz' story to be a mock-patriotic lie, calculated to hide a weapons-smuggling deal gone south. After shooting Cooper, Krenwicz had begun searching for money until Trude and McCaigh entered. The killer caused the corpse to move, puppet-like, in a threatening manner, provoking gunfire from the late arrivals.

The players approach the tale with straightforward professionalism, as if ignoring the rampant implausibilities. Director Collins' pacing often bogs down in the episodic construction, with its multiple flashbacks. Berton Churchill is credible as a politician determined to find a solution more practical than a triple execution.

Murder on the Campus

Chesterfield Motion Pictures Corp. • 1934

With a cracking good novel as a springboard—Whitman Chambers knew how to keep the reader on edge—and a sharp job of casting, *Murder on the Campus* rises to the occasion in a setting unaccustomed to such terrors. Charles Starrett is a study in tough determination as the outsider who cracks the case; it was a wise decision, not to picture the protagonist as some callow college-boy twerp.

Starrett is Bill Bartlett, a reporter researching a college-life story, who finds himself drawn to a nightclub singer, Lillian Voyne (Shirley Grey)—to the annoyance of her hoodlum boss (Maurice Black). A womanizing athlete is found murdered. Evidence accumulates against Lillian. Meanwhile, Prof. Hawley (Edward Van Sloan), a chemist and respected amateur detective, supplies Bartlett with confusing information.

Bartlett determines that Hawley is the killer, having used delayed recordings of gunfire and bursts of poison gas. Hawley attacks Bill, but the police have trailed the reporter—and arrive in time to close the case on the deranged professor.

Starrett, a former collegiate football star, had played himself (in the company of additional gridiron champions) in 1926 when a Richard Dix picture, *The Quarterback*, was shooting on location at Dartmouth. Starrett enrolled at the Academy of Dramatic Arts, joined regional and resident-stock companies, and landed on Broadway before joining Paramount Pictures' Astoria, Long Island, studio. He appeared opposite his friend Boris Karloff in *The Mask of Fu Manchu* (1932) at MGM, then alternated between secondary roles at the major studios and leads at the independents. Columbia established Starrett as a western star in 1936 with *Gallant Defender*. Starrett made more than 100 frontier pictures over 17 years, many of them as a character called the Durango Kid; he enjoyed a 10-year stretch among *Fame* magazine's roster of top moneymakers. He died in 1986.

Charles Starrett.

Starrett plays the stubborn newspaperman with outthrust chin and all due brashness. The big scene-stealers are J. Farrell MacDonald, as an impatient detective, and Edward Van Sloan as the well-concealed killer. Richard Thorpe, closing in on major-league assignments, directs with an assured sense of atmospheric menace.

The Rawhide Terror

Security Pictures Corp. • 1934

Victor Adamson, a compact and wiry New Zealander who often worked under the names of Denver Dick and Denver Dixon, devoted some 65 years to a career in independent filmmaking, prolific though financially impaired. He had begun in 1918 to produce and act in do-it-yourself, American-made westerns. Adamson introduced himself as a character named Art Mix in 1923—emphasizing the name MIX in boxcar letters alongside the name ART in smaller type in a blatant ploy to lure fans of the great Tom Mix. At length, Adamson turned the role over to George Kesterson—star of *The Rawhide Terror*—who used the name of Art Mix for the longer haul. Meanwhile, Adamson continued as a supporting actor under various other names (including Al Mix and Art James). For a while, during a dispute with Kesterson, Adamson cast Bob Roberts in the role of Art Mix.

Adamson's influence extended to a next generation of exploitation-filmmaking artistry. He inspired Sam Sherman, for example, during the 1960s to learn the moviemaking trade from the crucial vantage of distribution. With Adamson's son, the ultimately tragic filmmaker Al Adamson, Sherman delivered many Poverty Row shockers of the 1960s and 1970s, including *Dracula vs. Frankenstein*, *Blood of Ghastly Horror*, and *Five Bloody Graves*. (See our companion volume, *Forgotten Horrors to the Nth Degree*.) The generational custom persisted like folklore, handed down from the 1930s into the early 1990s—Al Adamson's last project, *Beyond This Earth!*, saw principal photography in 1993—until the dwindling tribe of exploitation producers found its province decisively overtaken by the major studios.

Sam Sherman has explained that Victor Adamson had intended *The Rawhide Terror* to be a serial called *The Pueblo Terror*—but then condensed the concept and an overabundance of footage into a short feature. This insight establishes why *The Rawhide Terror* contains many lapses of continuity and moves at such a frenzied pace. Rocky patches aside, the film is both a seminal Gothic Western and a foreshadowing of such prominent independent horrors of many years later as *The Texas Chain Saw Massacre* (1974) and its flesh-masked imitators.

White renegades, disguised as Indians, murder a man and his wife as their wagon crosses a desert. One son escapes to safety. The other boy, deranged by a blow to the head, wanders away and vanishes. Ten years later, the renegades have become respectable citizens of the town of Red Dog. Three of them have been slain by a marauder known as the Rawhide Terror—named for his grotesque mask, and because he leaves a strip of rawhide on each victim with the message: "Remember 10 years ago." Sheriff Luke (Edmund Cobb) finds the killer untraceable.

Jimmy Brent (Tommy Bupp) suffers a beating from his stepfather, Black Brent (William Barrymore), and staggers to the ranch of Tom Blake (William Desmond) and his sister, Betty (Frances Morris). Blake goes to confront Black Brent while Betty summons Sheriff Luke, her fiancé. Al Blake (George Kesterson, alias Art Mix), brother of Tom and Mary, halts a fight between Brent and Tom. Brent flees, leaving Tom wounded.

Tom goes missing. Al pursues the Rawhide Terror, who knocks him unconscious and leaves him to die in a runaway buckboard. Al escapes with Luke's help. Jimmy rescues Tom. The ex-renegade Pillars of Society die in an avalanche caused by the Terror, who also kidnaps Betty. Luke and a posse give chase. Al shoots the Terror, tracks the dying maniac to a cave, and unmasks him as Black Brent. A birthmark identifies Brent as Luke's lost brother—who has at last avenged the slaying of their parents.

Kesterson bears a slight resemblance to Tom Mix. He displays limited skill at acting, but his horsemanship is excellent and he fights like a champ. In later years, he played bad guys.

Like many such entrepreneurs, Victor Adamson found backers in small towns within range of scenic location-shooting areas of California, Utah, and Oregon. The scenery is often the best thing about an Adamson film. Such accomplished cinematographers as Bert Longenecker and Brydon Baker sometimes overcame the cheapness and the haste that characterized an Adamson shoot.

Adamson's interest in horrific elements can be traced from the 1920s. The crazed menace of *The Rawhide Terror*, with his cadaverous mask and attitude of derangement, prefigures the monstrous Leatherface of Tobe Hooper's *Chain Saw* series. Adamson's original scenario also harks forward to *Five Card Stud* (1968), in which Robert Mitchum commits serial murder in retaliation for a lynching.

Some lapses suggest *The Rawhide Terror* was made *á la mode* D.W. Griffith, without a formal script. One scene contains the shadow of a microphone. A player addresses Tommy Bupp as Tommy, rather than by his character's name, Jimmy. The brothers' names are Jim and Alec, but the grown-up Alec is known, here, as Luke, and there, as Tim. William Barrymore and Edmund Cobb are a bit long in the tooth to represent the brothers only 10 years after the prologue. Joe Weaver, who plays the doomed father, reappears with moustache and hairpiece as a civic leader.

Brutal scares are plentiful. The marauders pin the father over a campfire. George Holt makes a vicious chief renegade. Barrymore, tall and lean, conveys a chilling madness, with a pealing laugh for each new atrocity. He dresses as the renegades had appeared, shirtless, with rough vest and tattered Kiowa chaps, and his eyes stare wildly from behind the fleshly mask. He appears once as a looming shadow. The Terror kills a gila monster and says: "Demon, huh? The most poisonous animal in the desert! Your victims die a *slow* death!" His preferred tactic is to stake a victim in the desert, with a strip of wet rawhide about the neck—assuring slow strangulation as the uncured leather dries. (Barrymore also worked under the name of Boris Bullock.)

One good cliffhanger—a sequence that would have closed one chapter of the derailed serial—finds William Desmond in a pickle when approached by Tommy Bupp, who falls into a pit. Another has Kesterson hogtied in a careening wagon. Kesterson's pursuit of the buckboard is beautifully filmed, including deep-focus shots from the front of the vehicle, with Barrymore in the foreground and Kesterson in the distance.

Cobb and Desmond are particularly effective in the heroic roles. The picture includes such additional silent-era cowboy stars as Bill Patton and Victor Adamson himself—billed here as Denver Dixon.

Another Adamson production of interest is 1935's *Desert Mesa*, a.k.a. *Mormon Conquest*, an ill-documented production concerning an embattled ranch and a dual-role show of menace from Lew Meehan. Al Adamson (at about age 6) is listed among the cast of this evidently lost film, whose year of release sometimes is given as 1938.

Forgotten Horrors of 1935

The Mysterious Mr. Wong

Monogram Pictures Corp. • 1935

Harry Stephen Keeler's mysteries were hot-selling books when Monogram secured the rights to *The Twelve Coins of Confucius*. Nina Howatt's adaptation makes hash of Keeler's nuanced tale of greed and murderous ambition, although *The Mysterious Mr. Wong* combines old-fashioned melodrama and brash comedy to vigorous effect, however riddled with bigotry toward the Asian populace.

The leading players are bigger names than Monogram usually could afford in combination. Bela Lugosi had remained a popular favorite despite his waning fortunes with the major studios, and Wallace Ford and Arline Judge had built solid reputations at such larger studios as Columbia and RKO-Radio. Judge came aboard as a replacement for Dorothy Lee, the energetic blonde of RKO's *Wheeler & Woolsey* comedies. Lugosi performs with demonic relish as a murderous mandarin, although his Hungarian accent hardly matches the Asian makeup. Ford and Judge handle their wisecracking banter in typical 1930s style.

The possessor of the Coins of Confucius will rule a Chinese province—so declares a legend. In San Francisco's Chinatown, Wong (Lugosi) launches a campaign of murder in search of the tokens. Currents deeper than the usual tong-war outbreaks attract reporter Jason Barton (Ford). Barton comes accidentally into possession of a coin. He and his fiancée, Peg (Judge), seek refuge in a shop that also hides Wong's den. Barton summons help, and the police arrive to put paid to Wong's career.

William Nigh, a top director of the silent era at MGM, found Mr. Wong a comedown from his famous *Mr. Wu* (1927), starring Lon Chaney. Nigh never strayed long from Poverty Row during the remainder of his career—which curiously also included the *Mr. Wong* detective series at a reorganized Monogram. These later *Wongs*, most of them starring Boris Karloff as a genial Chinese sleuth, are unrelated to the present film except in the matter of Nigh's involvement.

The Asia-in-America setting is convincing, and the lighting implies hidden menace. Unusual for a Monogram production of the time is the use of orchestral swells and stings during the murder scenes. One such sequence packs a charge of terror as hands suddenly appear over Ford and, with a shudder, drop one of the coveted coins. As Ford and Judge flee, they must dodge a strangler's cord, a falling vase, and a barrage of daggers.

The dialogue is irremediably bigoted. To a report of a Chinatown slaying, Ford replies, "What do I care about another laundryman?" A cop, asked if he knows a Chinese named Wong, says, "I haven't run into one of 'em yet that *ain't* named Wong!" It is mentioned that "them Chinamen is jabberin' like monkeys—nothin' noiser than a Chinaman!" And as for the discovery of several murdered Chinese: "Better dead ones than live ones!"

Meanwhile: Additional Titles

These titles of further (if marginal) interest deepen the context:

- *The Phantom Cowboy* (Aywon Film Corp.; 1935). The nefarious title character motivates the mayhem in this inept film from a tiny company (*Aywon* is *A-1*, phoneticized) that made only four westerns during 1934–35. Ted Wells plays both the Phantom and heroic Bill Collins, who also pretends to be the Phantom. The better to shuffle the clues, of course.

- *Lem Hawkins' Confession*, a.k.a. *Murder in Harlem* (Micheaux Pictures Corp.; 1935). This strangler-at-large thriller sports preachy sociological overtones—and an overlong duration, as if to hammer the didacticism—business as usual for the black independent filmmaker Oscar Micheaux.

- *The Cactus Kid* (Reliable Pictures & William Steiner; 1935). In this starring picture for western champ Jack Perrin, supporting player Jayne Regan shocks a confession out of murderer Joe de la Cruz by masquerading as a ghost. Poorly staged fights show that the industry had yet to absorb Bob Bradbury's invention of the Pass System (see the *Lone Star Westerns* chapter in our 1934 section). A ghoulish element involves the burning of a corpse; the slain cowboy's harmonica outlasts the fire—all the better to yield a clue.

- *The Lone Bandit* (H&H-Empire Film & Kinematrade; 1935). Lane Chandler and Ray Gallagher are suspected by turns of being a phantom bandit, who turns out to be somebody else altogether. An installment of the *Phantom Rider* series.

- *Hei Tiki*, a.k.a. *Primitive Passions* (Principal; 1935). Sol Lesser's Principal-Adventure series of Third World exciters assumes an unusual feature-length (as opposed to featurette) running time for a romantic fantasy among tribespeople of New Zealand's Isle of Ghosts. A chieftain declares his daughter off limits to all but the God of War. Whereupon a horndog prince impersonates the God of War. Mayhem ensues.

- *School for Girls* (Liberty Pictures; 1935). In which an abusive matron (Lucille LaVerne) at a reformatory is murdered with a pistol rigged to a radio dial.

- *Great God Gold* (Monogram; 1935). Superstitious financier Sidney Blackmer is saved from the Crash of 1929 by a lucky coin toss. He fails to heed another omen and falls into bad company. Early work from director Arthur Lubin and cameraman Milton Krasner.

- *The Mystery Man* (Monogram; 1935). LeRoy Mason plays a murderous bandit known as the Eel, in conflict with Robert Armstrong as a determined reporter.

- *Circus Shadows* (Peerless; 1935). Crooked dealings on a carnival midway, with William Ruhl as a spiritualist-scam racketeer.

- *The Last Wilderness* (DuWorld Pictures; 1935). Archer Harold Hill leads a trek into Wyoming, felling a rattlesnake, a buffalo, and a mountain goat along the way. A glacier yields the remains of prehistoric insects. After a harrowing clash between bears, Hill rescues the surviving cubs—then slaughters the bear that had killed their mother.

- *Rescue Squad* (Mayfair Productions & Empire Film; 1935). An accurséd Asian effigy and a poisoning plot complicate an otherwise lighthearted romance. The star players are Ralph Forbes and Verna Hillie.

- *Let 'Em Have It* (Reliance Pictures; 1935). While *King Kong* stalwart Robert Armstrong was gracing the marquée with a heroic role in *The Mystery Man* (above), his *Kong* cohort Bruce Cabot appeared as a psychotic Public Enemy No. 1 in *Let 'Em Have It.* Cabot's face undergoes a hideous transformation via plastic surgery—a twist likely inspired by a slightly earlier episode of Chester Gould's comic strip, *Dick Tracy.* (See our companion volume, *Human Monsters*, and Michael H. Price's foreword to *The Complete Dick Tracy, Vol. No. 4,* from the Library of American Comics and IDW Publishing.)

- *The Vanishing Riders* (Spectrum Pictures & Ray Kirkwood Productions; 1935). Bill Cody and Bill Cody, Jr., star as vigilantes who rout a cattle-rustling mob by disguising themselves—and their horses—as skeletons. Laughable in the extreme, but the gimmick seems to scare the bad guys. No accounting for taste.

- *Trails of the Wild*, a.k.a. *Caryl of the Mountains* (Ambassador Pictures; 1935). Canadian Mountie Kermit Maynard tracks a murderer to a seemingly haunted region—and why else call the site Ghost Mountain?—that yields a maze of trap doors and creepy passageways. Commonplace villainy, with a welcome glaze of eeriness.

- *Phantom Patrol* (Ambassador; 1935). Harry Worth, the tormented revenge killer of 1936's *Lightnin' Bill Carson*, scores in a dual role as a notorious assassin and the author whom he imprisons and impersonates. The bad Worth is revealed when his writing is recognized as a plagiarism from Guy de Maupassant.

- *The Spanish Cape Mystery* (Liberty Pictures-M.H. Hoffman & Republic Pictures; 1935). Launcher of an Ellery Queen detective series, in which a vanished Huntly Gordon maintains a hideout on an island off Spanish Cape, California, the better to come ashore at strategic intervals to murder his kinsmen. An inheritance is at stake. Donald Cook plays Ellery Queen. See also: *The Mandarin Mystery.*

- *Alias John Law* (Supreme Pictures; 1935). Bob Steele stars as a wrongfully accused fugitive-turned-lawman who must capture killer Earl Dwire. Reciprocal antagonisms impart a lingering chill—a signature attitude of director Bob Bradbury (see also: *Lone Star Westerns*).

- *Legong: Dance of the Virgins (A Story of the South Seas)* (Bennett Pictures; 1935). This Balinese documentary encompasses a tragic romance that ends in suicide. Originally presented with some sequences in two-color Technicolor. See also: *Kliou (The Tiger).*

Life Returns

Universal Pictures • ScienArt Pictures • 1935

In May of 1934, in Berkeley, California, Dr. Robert E. Cornish announced that his team of researchers had restored life to a dog whose death Cornish had caused by clinical means. This canine Frankenstein episode, a purported breakthrough that seems to have led no further, was bolstered in turn by motion-picture footage.

True or false? No one can say, beyond Cornish's obviously self-interested account. Cornish was later denied access to the bodies of executed criminals in attempts to further his research. Apart from an additional dog-resurrection announcement, he seems to have abandoned the cause. In any event, the early declaration of success inspired an ambitious dilettante filmmaker, Dr. Eugen Frenke, to develop a heart-tugging science-fictional soap opera around the remarkable but rather dry clinical case—with Cornish's participation.

Life Returns is an inept but fascinating relic of a short-lived *cause celébre*. Though by no means a horror film, it pertains to the genre because of the very topic—to say nothing of the presence of Valerie Hobson, of 1935's *Bride of Frankenstein*, and Onslow Stevens, who would play a *Frankenstein*-styled physician-become-vampire in *House of Dracula* (1945).

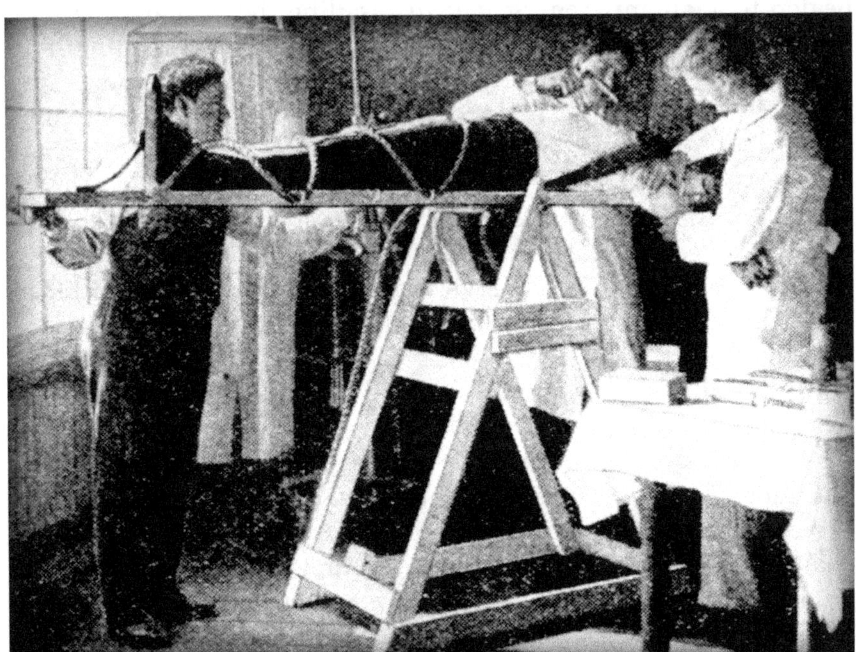

The laboratory setting of Life Returns.

The dramatic build-up is a monotonous exercise in which Cornish himself, Stevens, and Lois Wilson play medical students seeking to conquer death. Dr. Kendrick (Stevens) breaks with his friends on a maverick whim and finds himself courted by a big-time research laboratory—only to be rejected as a crackpot. Just when it seems matters can not worsen, Kendrick is confronted with the death of his wife (Hobson).

Frenke and his co-scenarists unwisely resisted the obvious temptation to have the scientist resurrect his better half. A juvenile-delinquency subplot, involving Kendrick's rebellious son (filmmaker-to-be George Breakston) and his pet dog, brings the radical theories back into play when the pooch takes a lethal gassing from the local dogcatcher (Stanley Fields). This is the melodramatic receptacle for the insertion of the Cornish laboratory footage, which leads to a hopeful ending for all concerned.

There was no hopeful ending for *Life Returns*, which Universal Pictures had bankrolled at approximately $40,000 but then pronounced unsuitable for release following previews during 1935. (This, according to one trade-publication account.)

Universal had attached Frenke in 1934 as director of an adaptation of Leo Tolstoy's *Father Sergius*. Frenke wound up handling *Life Returns*, from his original scenario, after the big studio had become apprehensive about censorship problems with *Sergius*. (Universal was already being stalked and hounded by the Legion of Decency on account of the perceived evils of *One More River* and *The Black Cat*. The Roman Catholic Legion took an anti-Semitic glee in assailing the primarily Jewish-owned studios.) But we digress: by strategically threatening legal action against Universal, Frenke managed by 1935 to remount *Life Returns* for release by ScienArt Pictures, an *ad hoc* company. The copyright notice contains no mention of Universal—but surviving prints bear the Universal ending scroll under the famous heading, "A Good Cast Is Worth Repeating." Although reviews appeared during 1935, no distribution took place until 1938, which brought a limited release.

Seldom has such fuss arisen over so insignificant a picture. Today, such a matter would be settled cheaply and efficiently with a direct-to-video edition.

Inherent flaws aside, *Life Returns* has nonetheless met unfairly with a measure of wrongheaded *kvetching*. We have witnessed some harrowing rants from the more single-minded souls among horror-movie buffs about the film's utter (and intentional) lack of shock value and overt megalomania—as though the cinema had not enough of those qualities in innumerable other pictures. Plain insipidity is the greater problem. The truer value lies in an inadvertent suggestion that all those fictional maverick doctors, from Mrs. Shelley's celebrated novel to Hollywood's Poverty Row, might have something on the ball, after all.

Obeah!

Arcturus Pictures • 1935

As forgotten a horror as ever lapsed from memory, *Obeah!* drew a rave from *The Film Daily* on February 13, 1935, and was trumpeted further with a full-page advertisement in *The Film Daily Yearbook*: "11 MONTHS—20 COUNTRIES—18,000 MILES—6,000 PEOPLE ... WITH PHILLIPS H. LORD—NBC RADIO'S 'SETH PARKER'"—and no mention of the essential topic of Third World perils.

The review sounds promising: "Punch Stuff and Authentic Nautical Atmosphere." Wrote the unsigned critic, "This is as close to being a real adventure feature of the high seas and the South Seas atmosphere as the talkies have yet produced. ... Suspense is built up beautifully. ... Sex situation between white and native girls and the star. ... With current front-page news breaks on the schooner's...wreck, it's a bear for exploitation." The reviewer judged the direction "very good" and the photography "excellent." A proxy title in England was *Mystery Ship*. The film appears to have become lost.

Phillips Lord's radio character, Seth Parker, was a pious philosopher from New England, based upon Lord's grandfather. RKO-Radio Pictures pegged the personality as a natural for the movies: The result, *Way Back Home* (1931), was a conspicuous flop that provoked a famous

Phillips Lord's Way Back Home.

headline in *Variety*: "Stix Nix Hix Pix." (Translation: "Rural markets reject rustic movies.") Lord's independent production of *Obeah!* caused even less of a stir.

Lord launches his yacht, *The Seth Parker*, in search of an explorer who has gone missing in the tropics. He finds the man alive but under an *obeah* spell on an unknown island whose inhabitants practice voodoo. (The misperception of voodoo, or *vodun*, as a predatory cultural phenomenon is business as usual for zombie-crazed Hollywood.) The explorer's daughter (Jeanne Kelly) is a prisoner. The natives prepare for a ritual sacrifice. Lord and his crew attack but fail to rescue the explorer. They escape to the schooner with the daughter and a native girl (Alice Wesslar), pursued by a curse invoked by a tribal priest. The party searches for sunken gold, indicated on the explorer's map, and a romantic triangle develops among Lord and his new passengers.

Lord's career in radio remained sturdy and progressive. Most famous of his network shows was *Gangbusters*, which he built around sensationalized re-enactments of closed-case F.B.I. files.

Obeah's director, F. Herrick Herrick, an Englishman, was the globetrotting director of RKO's *Vagabond Adventures* travelogues and producer of Universal's *Goofytone News* series, a spoof of Fox's *Movietone News* programs. Herrick also played small roles in feature films. Cinematographer Harry Smith was an operative cameraman at Universal. Leonard Weiss was an independent film editor, based in New York. Jeanne Kelly, a blonde actress who had appeared in several New York productions, became better known at Universal during the early 1940s and gained a following at RKO-Radio Pictures as Jean Brooks—wife of the director Richard Brooks. *Obeah!* marks the only film appearance of Alice Wesslar.

Queen of the Jungle

Screen Attractions • 1935

"Triumphant Wild Animal Spectacle," boasted the campaign for *Queen of the Jungle*. The film contains spectacle, indeed—but only in its extracts from Col. William M. Selig's lavish serial of 1922, *The Jungle Goddess*. The Selig production appears to survive only in what footage was misappropriated for *Queen of the Jungle*. Reed Howes, Mary Kornman, and others of the new cast are shown in the dialogue sequences and close-range shots, with most of the genuine action being silent footage featuring Elinor Field and Truman Van Dyke. The slower camera-cranking speed at which the Selig original was shot gives away the game: The pirated footage plays out at a faster clip when projected at talking-picture speed.

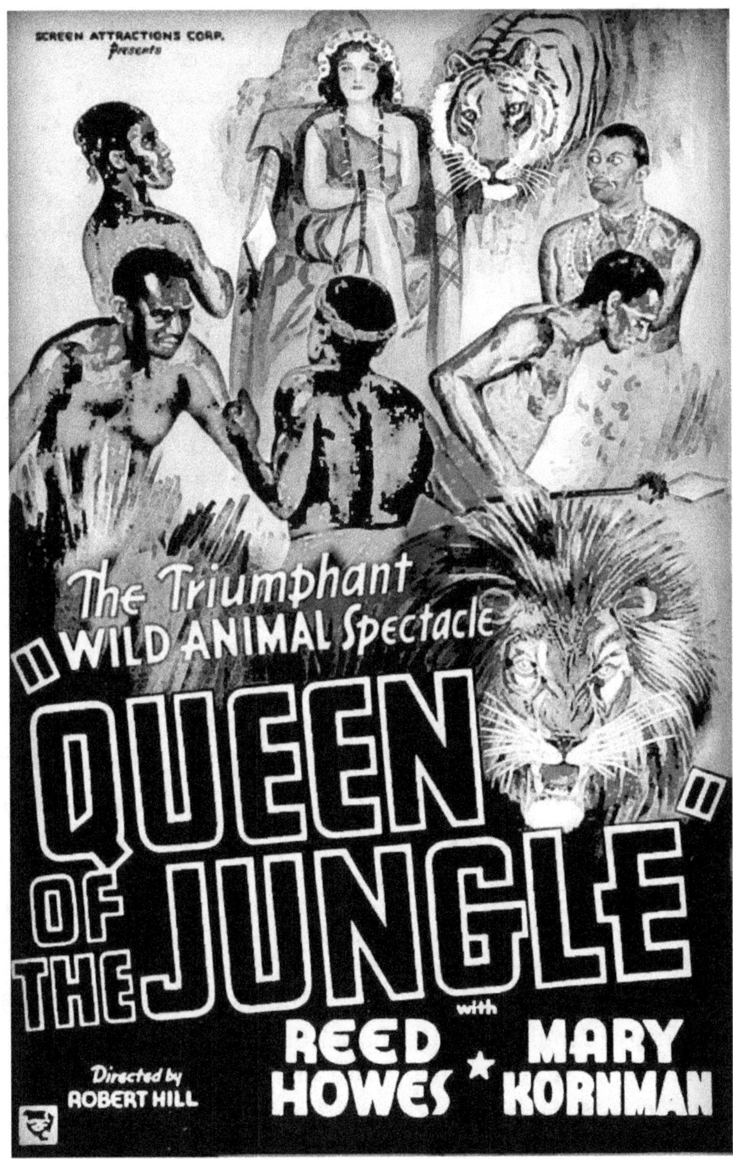

Joan Lawrence (Marilyn Spinner), child of an explorer in Africa, is carried away alone in a balloon ship. The craft is downed by a tribal archer. Joan ignites firecrackers that a playmate had given her—causing the natives to regard her as a goddess.

Years later, David Worth (Reed Howes), Joan's friend from childhood, finds traces of the balloon and mounts a safari. He is captured and brought before Joan—who has grown cruel as a ruler. An idol's radioactive eyes prove lethal to the search party. Joan spares Worth, who explains to the cultists who their perceived goddess really is.

The priest, Kali (Lafe McKee), orders that Joan be sacrificed, but she summons elephants to the rescue. The tribe retreats, and Worth is shown the source of the radiation—a mine of untapped value.

Such menaces as a gorilla and a murderous Tree Man beset Joan and Worth as they attempt to return to their people. Joan is blinded by poison and nearly dies in a waterfall. A rival tribe restores her vision.

Two reprobates (Eddie Foster and Robert Borman) come in search of the radium mine. Worth and Joan turn the tables by freeing captive animals aboard a ship. Meanwhile, Arabs have befriended Joan's distraught father (William Walsh). Further perils culminate in an attempt to sacrifice Joan. Worth charges to the rescue aboard an elephant.

The Selig serial's action, as directed by James Conway, is quite good, apart from the discrepancy between silent-speed shooting and sound-speed projection. The huge mechanical idol, a fine piece of stagecraft constructed in full scale, moves in an uncanny fashion, with radiant eyes. The partial sets used for matching up the new footage work reasonably well. Howes and Kornman look good in the leads, but the acting and Robert F. Hill's directing are uninspired. Lafe McKee, seen in scores of films as a likable duffer, fares surprisingly well as the evil priest. McKee appears in both the new footage and the silent Selig serial. *Queen of the Jungle* also was boiled to 65 minutes for a feature-length presentation.

A Shot in the Dark

Chesterfield Motion Pictures • 1935

Wittily directed and scripted, Charles Lamont's *A Shot in the Dark* benefits further from top-drawer portrayals from Edward Van Sloan, Robert Warwick, Doris Lloyd, Herbert Bunston, and John Davidson. The leads also are well cast with Charles Starrett, edging ever closer to western stardom, and Marion Shilling, an alumna of Max Reinhardt's stage productions.

The murderous use of a cattle-slaughtering tool is an unusual touch, foreshadowing by a long stretch such references in Tobe Hooper and Kim Henkel's *The Texas Chain Saw Massacre* (1974) and the Coen Bros.' *No Country for Old Men* (2008).

College student Ken Harris (Starrett) finds slain his roommate (James Bush)—a murder, made to appear a suicide. Another student (Ralph Brooks) promises information but turns up croaked. The weapon proves to be a slaughterhouse device, which had been used in a classroom demonstration. The roommate's half-brother, John Mesereux (James Bush, again), is shot to death. The killer is revealed to be a popular professor (Van Sloan)—the man who had deserted Mesereux' mother.

Chesterfield Motion Pictures had left a tenancy at Universal Pictures to assume rented space at Pathé, whose imposing sets lend a foreboding atmosphere. The killer's identity is well hidden, although suspicion might be aroused by a familiarity with Van Sloan's role as the culprit in Chesterfield's *Murder on the Campus*.

Edward Van Sloan is a grey eminence of horror films. He was born in San Francisco and had established a career in commercial art by 1907. He joined a stock company in Canada and New England and appeared on Broadway during the 1920s. This placement connected him with Bela Lugosi in the long stagebound run of *Dracula*—prelude to the 1931 film. In a stretch of Universal chillers, Van Sloan appears older than his years as the voice of reason, leading the fight against one monster after another. He also proved a capital choice to play well-hidden villains, as in *Behind the Mask* and *The Death Kiss* (both from 1932),

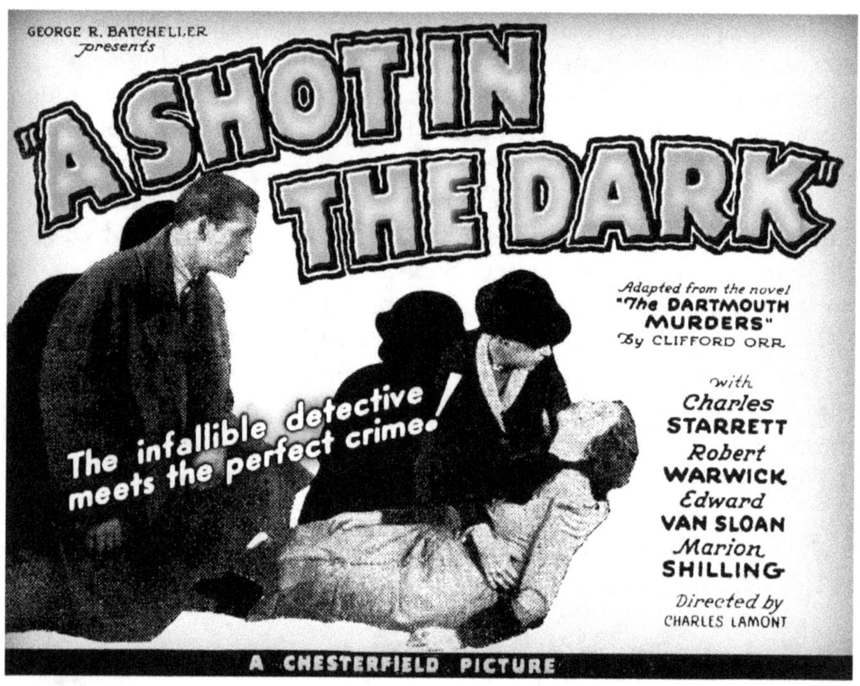

and of course these immediate Chesterfield productions. Van Sloan remained important in the horror and mystery films but was given only small, sometimes unbilled, roles in more conventional pictures. He retired in 1948 and returned to San Francisco. Widowed and in failing health, Van Sloan devoted his later years to the study of music history. He died in 1964.

The Lost City

a.k.a.: *The Lost City of the Legurian / City of Lost Men*
Regal Pictures • Super Serial Productions • 1935

A crude and overblown throwback, Harry C. Revier's *The Lost City* piles horror upon horror in a manner unseen since the silent-screen heyday of that chronically vigorous star player, Pearl White. The wild-eyed acting might be better suited to Italian opera. Credulity is stretched to the breaking point. This aggressive affront to taste and narrative sense makes for terrific entertainment, with nary a lull.

William "Stage" Boyd, as the mad monarch of a defunct kingdom, can cause cataclysms, reverse the tides, turn midgets to giants and black men to white, destroy the strongest will, and freeze electricity. Further antagonisms issue from an evil hunchback, warlike tribes, Arab slavers, a ruthless jungle queen, towering zombies, a predatory trader, and assorted beasts. Here is one of the few serials in which no repetitive padding is evident.

Inventor Bruce Gordon (Kane Richmond) assembles a safari to track the source of a global electrical storm. They reach Magnetic Mountain in Africa. The ruins of Liguria stand as a monument to a fallen race of master scientists. The madman Zolok (Boyd) professes to be "carrying on the electromagnetic traditions of my people." A reluctant partner is Dr. Manyus (Josef Swickard), a captive along with his daughter, Natcha (Claudia Dell). Zolok lures Gordon's party into a trap. Two members (William Millman and Ralph Lewis) conspire to abduct Manyus, intending to exploit his inventions. A trader (George Hayes) and a slave racketeer (Gino Corrado) covet Zolok's formula for creating giants.

Numerous perils culminate in an uprising. Zolok blasts his own stronghold. Gordon and his allies observe the destruction from a safe distance.

The technical staff includes some big-timers: camerawork by Eddie Linden, of 1933's *King Kong*, and Roland C. Price, a prolific documentarian; settings by Ralph Berger, of 1936's *Flash Gordon*; and laboratory equipment by Kenneth Strickfaden, Universal's electrical-engineering wizard. Striking effects include the transformation of a diminutive tribesman into a giant.

The use of Mack Sennett Studio—where a more purposeful tenant, Nat Levine, was establishing a sturdier corporate base for Mascot Pic-

tures—made director Revier aware of a similarly conceived rival serial at Mascot, *The Phantom Empire*. At Revier's behest, producer Sherman S. Krellberg added two production units to cut shooting time from 35 days to 21, the better to beat Mascot to the draw. (Of course, even a 35-day shoot would have been beyond Levine's wildest dreams of efficiency.)

A half-dozen glass and matte shots by effects pioneer Norman A. Dawn serve to add architectural details and massive machinery. Dawn is believed to have invented the glass-painting shooting process to enhance visual scope as early as 1907, and he developed practical variations on matte-shot technique.

Boyd's crazed scientist is tougher and more aggressive than the typical bemused fanatic. During filming of the lab-destruction

scene—Boyd's last moments in any film—the actor became roaring drunk, lending an agonized realism. Josef Swickard's scientist is reminiscent of Ernest Thesiger in *Bride of Frankenstein* (1935). George Hayes, as the renegade trader, does a late turnabout, admitting he has been "an awful rotter" as he joins the heroic contingent. The maniacal hunchback is Billy Bletcher, the little man with the big voice (and a favorite vocal villain in animated cartoons, including Disney's Ezekiel "Big Bad" Wolf).

A feature-serial version condenses the first four chapters into seven reels, followed by eight two-reel chapters. Another feature version, *City of Lost Men*, compresses the entire serial into a chaotic 74 minutes. A comic-book version surfaced during the 1940s, while the serial remained in chronic reissue.

Secrets of Chinatown

Northern Films, Ltd. & Producers Laboratories, Inc. • Syndicate Pictures • 1935

Though filmed in Canada, *Secrets of Chinatown* scarcely differs from the productions of Los Angeles' Poverty Row. Director Fred Newmeyer had seen better days as an associate of the comedian and producer Harold Lloyd. Cast members Nick Stewart, Lucile Browne, and her husband, James Flavin, were well known in Hollywood. Stuart and Browne are natural and attractive in the leads—she plays a Caucasian captive of an Asian cult—and Flavin delivers a good show of exotic villainy. The private-eye hero is overplayed as a pompous intellectual by Raymond Lawrence.

The sets are hardly up to Hollywood standards, but there are interesting exteriors in the fight scenes, including an unfamiliar cliff—distant, of course, from California's often-filmed craggier regions—from which a couple of the bad guys take a tumble.

Freelance sleuth Donegal Dawn (Lawrence), summoned to crack a crime wave in Chinatown, scoffs at the official view of tong-war reprisals. Dawn's associate, Robert Rand (Stewart) develops a crush on Zenobia (Browne), a clerk, who tells him they would be doomed if he should attempt to spirit her away from Chinatown. A knife, thrown from hiding, underscores her warning.

Rand steals into a cellar, drawn by strange music and chanting. Zenobia, entranced, officiates at a weird ceremony. The cultists capture Rand. Zenobia seems indifferent to his plight.

Dawn tracks the clandestine order to a mountainous region. A police raid serves to rescue Rand and the mesmerized Zenobia.

Producers Laboratories of New York and Kenneth Bishop's Commonwealth Productions at Willow Park, Victoria, B.C., were allied on this slight effort, which captured little attention on either side of the border. The same company teamed Browne and Stuart in a romantic comedy, *The Fighting Playboy*.

Beast of Borneo

DuWorld Pictures, Inc. • 1935

Harry Garson led an expedition in 1930 to film second-unit footage for Universal's *East of Borneo* (1931). Garson returned to the same jungles to make his own picture, *Beast of Borneo*. Similarities end with the homonymonous titles and the shared setting: The present film lacks the polish of the Universal production, which George Melford completed under controlled studio conditions. *Daily Variety* reported that *Beast of Borneo* contains outtakes from *East of Borneo*, including impressive close-up shots of a huge orangutan.

An adult ape escapes from the nets of hunter Bob Ward (John Preston), but the party captures an affectionate baby orang and names it Little Joe. Meanwhile, in London, Dr. Boris Borodoff (Eugene Sigaloff) seeks in vain to draw a human-like reaction from a brain removed from a living orangutan. Borodoff determines to search the green hell of Borneo for a male orang in an insane quest to plumb the mysteries of evolution. A colleague, Alma (Mae Stuart), accompanies him.

Borodoff finds Ward aghast at the prospect of capturing an ape for vivisection. Alma sways Ward. An orang falls captive, but hardly without a struggle. Enraged, the scientist hurls Ward's assistant (Val Durran) to his death in the clutches of the ape. The natives desert in protest.

Borodoff is about to perform an experiment when Ward bursts in. The ape breaks free and drags Ward away. Borodoff prepares to put the knife to Little Joe. Joe escapes into the jungle and finds Ward. As Borodoff gives chase, Little Joe reunites Alma and Ward. Borodoff,

wielding a gun, is crushed to death by the great ape. A rescue party approaches, late but welcome.

John Preston is a dashing hero of the square-jawed stalwart school—the same image he projects as a Canadian Mountie in *Timber Terrors* and *Courage of the North*, a matched set issued in 1935. Eugene Sigaloff had played subordinate villains at MGM. Supporting player John S. Peters was one of Erich von Stroheim's Teutonic associates. (Peters' dead-on-the-money mimicry of Stroheim graces one of the finer *Laurel & Hardy* comedies, "Double Whoopee," from 1929.) The big scene-stealer is the baby orangutan. The most imposing figure is the big orang, which appears appropriately indignant and gives forth with a rasping, blood-curdling bellow.

Big Calibre

A.W. Hackel Productions • Supreme Pictures • W. Steiner Dist. • 1935

George Turner, founding author of *Forgotten Horrors*, had remembered Robert North Bradbury's *Big Calibre* down to some finer details—a literal cliffhanger finale, in particular—during preparations for the first edition of *Forgotten Horrors*. But the title eluded him, what with its being of the generic sort (like 1935's *Smoking Guns*) that neglects to describe the story. The question could have been answered with a click or two, had the mixed blessing of the internet existed in 1975, but the process of identification required an extensive search through the federal copyright catalogues and unwieldy, dust-covered library-binding volumes of the show-business tradepapers. (The *Variety Film Review Indexes* and the *American Film Institute Catalogues* had yet to be compiled.) Such tasks can be pleasurable, in fact—a process rendered all but extinct by the shallow convenience of web-browsing mock-research.

"That's it!" said George when a contemporary review finally came to hand. "Weirdest western ever! Well, except for Ken Maynard's *Smoking Guns* or Fox's *Mystery Ranch*." (And more presently about those rip-snorting horrors on horseback.)

Bob O'Neill (Bob Steele, Old Hollywood's Hamlet of the frontier) finds that his father has been robbed and murdered by an intruder armed with an acidic gas. O'Neill finds evidence of corrosion, along with an unbroken capsule and an oddly shaped footprint. The clues lead to a chemist named Zenz (Perry Murdock), who escapes. The search drags on for a year.

At the Bowers Ranch, June Bowers (Peggy Campbell) discourages her father (Frank Ball) from paying off a mortgage held by an assayer, Gadski—a figure of aspect both goofy and ghastly. The rancher is

ambushed and left for dead. Gadski prepares to take possession of the property. June seeks a delay from Bentley (Forrest Taylor), the banker, who lusts after her.

O'Neill finds skeletal remains and a watch containing a photograph of June Bowers. He encounters a holdup in which the bandit is stunned during the getaway. O'Neill unmasks the robber as June, acting rashly in the interests of the ranch. She escapes on O'Neill's horse. O'Neill is accused in both the holdup and the disappearance of Bowers. June considers O'Neill innocent. Rusty Hicks (John Elliott), O'Neill's gold-prospecting partner, is thrown into jail in a ploy to intimidate O'Neill.

Bentley and Gadski rally a lynch mob. A capsule of poisonous gas is hurled into the cell. O'Neill and Hicks escape as the fumes dissolve the bars. O'Neill, Hicks, and June find the bonepile—the remains are those of cattle. June's father has survived to take refuge in an Indian's hut.

At a masquerade ball, Hicks overhears Gadski and Bentley plotting a burglary. The pillars of society steal into the bank, but Bentley knocks Gadski unconscious and flees with the loot. Bentley attacks June; O'Neill comes to her rescue. Gadski pursues Bentley—only to be unmasked as a disguised Zenz. Back in town, rancher Bowers identifies his assailants as Bentley and Gadski.

Zenz steals an auto-stagecoach—mechanized mass transit, in prototype. O'Neill catches the truck and struggles with Zenz. The vehicle lands, teetering, on a precipice. O'Neill frees one hand to reach his gun. Zenz produces a gas capsule, but O'Neill fires and releases the poison.

Doomed by his own weapon, Zenz falls into the canyon. O'Neill leaps to safety before the chemical can ignite the gasoline. Cleared and avenged, O'Neill finds a welcoming reception from June.

It is generally agreed that Ken Maynard's production of *Smoking Guns* (1934)—speaking of generic titles—is the strangest of early-talkie westerns, a study of madness, disease, and superstition that Maynard had intended to call *Doomed to Die*. The film's defiance of convention so angered Universal's nepotism-anointed chief of production, Carl Laemmle, Jr., that he fired Maynard. (Which is how Maynard landed at low-rent Mascot Pictures: see *Mystery Mountain*.)

Similarly monumental weirdness belongs to David Howard's *Mystery Ranch* (1932), which hangs upon Charles Middleton's portrayal of a lustful, homicidal madman. *Big Calibre* belongs in this rare class of uncompromising freakishness—a horror yarn, disguised as a frontier adventure. Bob Steele was attuned to such material, as was his father, the director Bob Bradbury. The story is the work of Perry Murdock, a lanky, curly-haired set dresser and occasional writer and actor. Murdock appears, unbilled, in the dual role of the mad chemist Zenz and the criminal assayer Gadski.

The shooting script is the work of Bradbury, who usually took a hand in his films' writing, with a preference for the bizarre and the grotesque. (Another Bradbury-Steele picture, 1935's *Western Justice*, dispatches bad guy Arthur Loft with a flaying.) A recurring theme with Bradbury is the protagonist's search for his father's killer. That the killer here is a mad scientist who wears a gruesome disguise and dispenses a corrosive chemical sets *Big Calibre* quite apart from the usual Saturday-matinée fare.

Superb pictorial sense—cameraman Bill Hyer never escaped Poverty Row, despite his fine craftsmanship—grounds the eccentricities of the script in a persuasive realism. Steele is at his energetic best, both in action and at conveying a tortured romanticism. Sidekick John Elliott and Georgia O'Dell, as an over-amorous servant, provide comic relief that sits steadily upon the bedrock of oppressiveness. Bill Quinn stands out as a drunken reveler at a barn dance, where a crime is plotted amid the gaiety. Such amusing touches enhance the horrors of a lynch mob and a madman-at-large.

Murdock's crazed villain and Forrest Taylor's calculating mask of respectability are unnerving—although Murdock's overdone, google-eyed makeup would not fool anyone in waking life. Peggy Campbell is a resourceful and attractive romantic lead, and there are memorable character portrayals from Earl Dwire, Si Jenks, and Frank Ball. Suspense crackles through the climactic chase and the precipitous ending, which provides as much spectacle as could be had from a slender budget.

Circumstantial Evidence

Chesterfield Motion Pictures Corp. • 1935

Charles Lamont, successor to Richard Thorpe as the principal work-horse at Invincible-Chesterfield, plays this topical mystery for generous impact. A heated controversy of the day centered upon the conviction on circumstantial evidence of the accused kidnapper of the infant son of aviator Charles Lindbergh. Bruno Richard Hauptmann was executed in April of 1936 without ever confessing. The provocative nature of the story—inspired by, but not based upon, the Lindbergh case—and the depravity of one character impart a remarkable intensity.

Newspaperman Jim Baldwin (Chick Chandler) is appalled to see an accused murderer (Al Bridge) condemned on circumstantial evidence. Sickened by the popular frenzy, Baldwin determines to expose such trials as uncivilized. He enlists his fiancée, courtroom sketch artist Adrienne Grey (Shirley Grey), and a fellow reporter, Spike Horton (Lee Moran). Publisher Ralph Winters (Claude King) encourages the plan.

Wealthy dilettante Fred Stevens (Arthur Vinton), a gossip columnist, feigns friendship but covets Adrienne. Stevens' suave manners disguise a morbid perversion: he keeps skeletons and mummies in his study and seeks to compromise the wives of other men. In an elaborate scheme with Baldwin, Stevens sets out to fake his death and plant evidence that seems to implicate Baldwin—purportedly to help prove Baldwin's argument. Stevens secretly intends to see Baldwin hang.

Stevens turns up genuinely dead. Baldwin faces a prompt conviction and a death sentence. Baldwin is smuggled to safety at Winters' penthouse by a bogus guard, who proves to have been hired by Winters. The police trail Baldwin. Winters is gunned down when he tries to block the officers. The publisher confesses that he had killed Stevens, who had victimized Winters' young wife (Dorothy Revier). Baldwin's campaign has succeeded, if at a personal loss.

The cast, as usual with Chesterfield, consists of seasoned professionals who are a pleasure to watch. Chick Chandler, seen oftener as a light comedian, is surprisingly good as the troubled heroic protagonist. Shirley Grey, formerly of Paramount and Universal, gives a lifelike portrayal of a working artist in an intriguing profession seldom portrayed in the movies. (Trial-court illustrators, long crucial to both newspapers and the law, have been rendered extinct in comparatively recent times by ill-advised decisions to allow cameras into the courtroom.)

Arthur Vinton is a superficially charming villain—although the character's willingness to torch his house to help prove an argument is a weakness in an otherwise (reasonably) credible picture. Dorothy Revier brings poignancy to the role of the wayward wife. Claude King is suitably dignified as a sympathetic murderer, and Robert Frazer is excellent as a flashy and ambitious district attorney.

Lamont, typical of the Chesterfield directors, graduated to the majors. He became prominent as a specialist in comedy, presiding into the 1950s over many adventures of Bud Abbott and Lou Costello, the *Francis the Talking Mule* series, and the *Ma & Pa Kettle* series.

The Tin Man, or Hal Roach's Almost-Brides of a Tinhorn Frankenstein

Hal Roach Productions • MGM Pictures Corp. • 1935

"I like to think that I was one of the first movie-biz producers to seriously explore the relationship between comedy and terror," Hal Roach told us in 1992, "[with pictures] where the scary business was a direct function of the humor, and vice versa."

One of Roach's more memorable horror-comedy pieces (see also: *Oliver the Eighth*), "The Tin Man" pits Thelma Todd & Patsy Kelly against a cranky inventor who seems to be a kindred spirit of Dr. Frankenstein. Also at large are a playfully sadistic mechanical creature and an escaped convict. Todd and Kelly make a fine team, an improvement upon Roach's original pairing of Todd with fidgety ZaSu Pitts. The Todd and Kelly shorts remained in circulation a year after Todd's

Patsy Kelly, left, and Thelma Todd.

death at age 30 in 1935. ("Murder, I call it," Roach said, perpetually rejecting a ruling of suicide.)

A former schoolteacher and model from Massachusetts, Todd had scored at Warners with *The Haunted House*, *The House of Horror*, and *Seven Footprints to Satan* (1928–1929). By 1929, Roach had drafted her into an ambitious campaign to refine, and *re-define*, slapstick with wordplay—both corny and cerebral. He sought a female counterpart to his teaming of Stan Laurel with Oliver Hardy.

"The Tin Man," prime talkie-era Roach, nods to *Frankenstein*, and to the dawning screwball school of humor, a natural progression for Roach. The now-serene, now-impulsive allure of Todd and the flustered exasperation of Kelly make for a frenzied 20 minutes, complicated by the aggressiveness of the robot. (The robot sports the thunderous voice of Billy Bletcher, the sadistic hunchback of *The Lost City* and the Big Bad Wolf of various animated cartoons from the studios of Walt Disney and Ubbe Iwerks.)

Patsy and Thelma seek shelter at a house occupied by an eccentric scientist, played by gaunt and wild-eyed Clarence Wilson—Hal Roach's most nearly Dickensian stock player. The woman-hating crank sets loose the mechanical man. (The house is to all appearances haunted, in the first place.)

The robot develops an awkward, combative crush upon Patsy. A lunkheaded fugitive (lantern-jawed Mathew Betz) sneaks in for murderous purposes, only to find himself conked cuckoo and kayoed at every turn. The robot blows a fuse and chases its master into the night. The adventure closes as the escapée begs Patsy and Thelma to drive him back to the safety of jail.

Director James Parrott, brother of Roach trouper Charley Chase, declared Todd and Kelly "an ideal team because they are direct opposites." In press materials, Patsy Kelly boasted: "There's scarcely a time that I haven't at least one black-and-blue mark...to show for my work."

An attempt to find a replacement for the deceased Todd "just didn't work," Kelly told George Turner during the 1970s, "so I went solo. ... But those wild two-reelers [with] Thelma—'specially that crazy takeoff we did on *Frankenstein*—were really the glory days, when you could be as outrageous as you pleased, tussle and scream and yell all over the place, throw out the script and make things up on the spot, and get paid just as reg'lar as if you were holdin' down a respectable job."

Wild is the word, all right, for "The Tin Man," a most inventive variation upon a theme. Among similarly conceived shorts, MGM's Technicolor "Two Hearts in Wax Time" (1935), riffs explicitly upon the Karloff-at-Universal image of the Frankenstein Monster (among other intimidating figures) in a musical fantasy involving department-store mannequins. MGM's "Third Dimensional Murder" (1940), from the *Pete Smith Metroscopix Specials* series, uses 1939's *Son of Frankenstein* as a springboard for a haunted-house pageant, garnished with three-dimensional visual trickery. "The Tin Man," conversely, appropriates Mary W. Shelley's Promethean conceit, mingling absurdity with outright menace to the extent that even Todd and Kelly seem in mortal peril.

On Probation

Hoffberg Productions • Peerless Pictures Corp. • 1935

The productions of chronically impoverished Peerless Pictures seldom rose above the off-brand class. *On Probation* is an exception—suspenseful, beautifully photographed, and boasting a spectacular climax: its symbolic fulfillment of a curse of death by a lion would become the basis of Paramount's *Night Has a Thousand Eyes*, 13 years later. Director

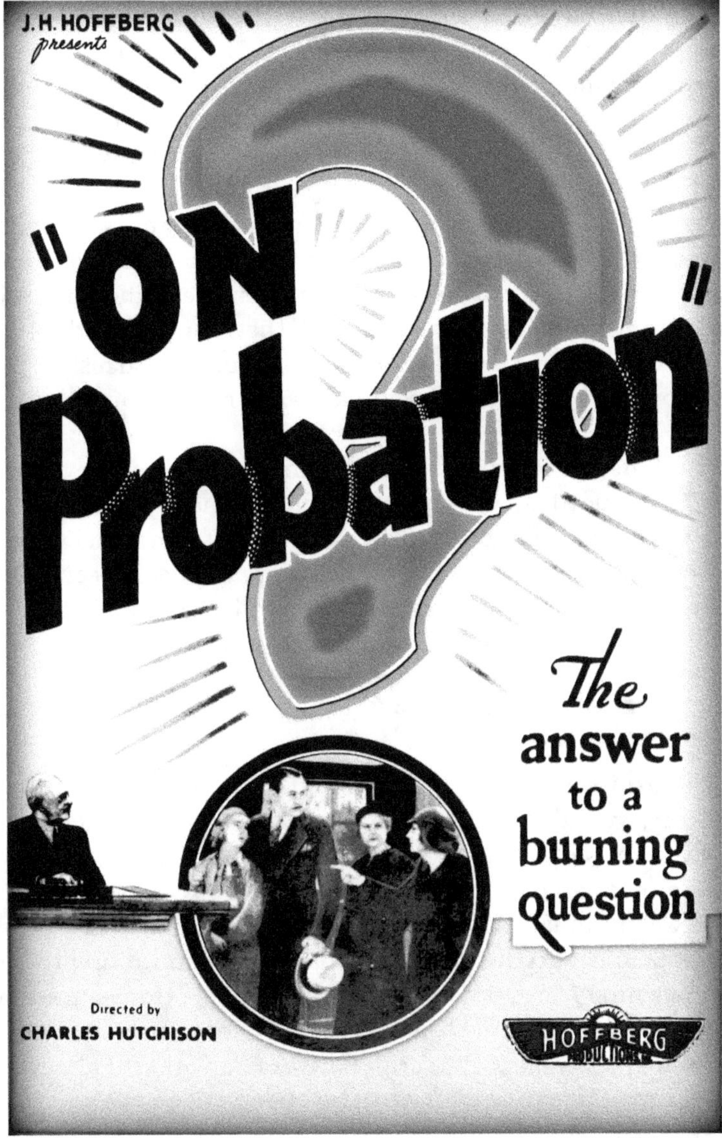

Charles Hutchison shows unaccustomed skill and finesse here. The career of the former serial daredevil was nearing an end. Hutchison takes a small role and doubles William Bakewell in an impressive rescue.

Crooked politician Al Murray (Monte Blue) becomes the guardian of a girl, Jane (Betty Jane Graham), who has been placed on probation as a pickpocket. Murray becomes the object of a curse from a hag (Margaret Fealy) who had taught the child to steal. He shrugs off the imprecation. Jane grows to womanhood (played now by Lucile Browne), and Murray grows to desire her.

Having discouraged a suitor of Jane's, Bill Coleman (Bakewell), Murray proposes marriage. She proposes to leave for Europe with Coleman. Coleman proposes to follow Jane. Upon returning, the youngsters tell Murray they are in love. Murray, now facing arrest for graft, had planned to flee the country with Jane. He threatens her. She strikes him with a statuette in the shape of a lion.

Murray's apparent death panics Coleman and Jane, who stash the body in a trunk aboard an outbound train. A rail collision causes a fire, which Coleman and Jane assume will dispose of the corpse. Upon learning from a Murray confederate (Mathew Betz) that the crook is still alive, Coleman makes a daring rescue. Murray is arrested. Merely stunned by the blow, he had feigned death in the hope of escaping the law.

Monte Blue, in one of his last leading roles, creates an almost likable blackguard—a classy rascal, his crimes notwithstanding. Lucile Browne is wholly sympathetic as the fearful, impulsive heroine. Mathew Betz, as a loyal henchman, and Margaret Fealy, seen briefly as a female Fagan, do much to make the fanciful story convincing.

One Frightened Night

Mascot Pictures Corp. • 1935

Mascot's *forté* was the serial—a breed apart from feature-length filmmaking, with distinctive narrative grammar and structural composition. Even so, Nat Levine reserved the right to produce the occasional feature, self-contained at more-or-less an hour. Mascot released 31 features between January 1927 and December 1935. When Levine leased the Mack Sennett Studio in 1935, though, he stepped up production to turn out nine features that year. One of the better such entries is Christy Cabanne's *One Frightened Night*, a Mystery Farce along the lines of *The Cat and the Canary*. The script derives from Stuart Palmer, better known for the *Hildegarde Withers* series of detective novels.

Geezery old Jasper White (Charles Grapewin) arranges for a group of conniving friends and relatives to hear a reading of his will. They stand to divide the estate, provided that White's long-lost granddaughter cannot be found. Two women are presented as the missing Doris Waverly. The first one (Evalyn Knapp) turns up poisoned. The second one, the genuine article (Mary Carlisle), is menaced by a masked intruder. Suspicion falls upon one guest after another. One of White's nephews (Regis Toomey) unmasks the killer as another guest (Lucien Littlefield).

Levine brought in Monogram Pictures executive George Yohalem to supervise. Yohalem, in turn, hired Monogram talents Cabanne and Wellyn Totman to direct and handle the scripting. Totman's script opens, in the classic manner, upon a storm-battered old house (a well-done miniature). Its clapping shutters disclose the cast-and-credits business, with photographs of the actors. The same Charles Dunworth *misterioso* theme that had opened *The Vampire Bat* is heard between peals of thunder. The photography sustains this foreboding atmosphere throughout, and the effect is heightened by bursts of venerable melodramatic music.

Charles Grapewin's eccentric codger and Wallace Ford's wisecracking vaudeville ham steal scene after scene. Upon the arrival of the false heiress, Grapewin snarls: "Ever see a bunch of hungry wolves waiting around to feast on a corpse? Looks like something ruined their dinner." Later, he admits, "I'm an old grouch. Who *wouldn't* be, with a bunch of mummies walking about?" The character types are well represented: the beautiful heiress, the stalwart hero, the crooked lawyer, the fidgety kinsman with the overbearing wife, the weasly physician, and the dumb cop with the even dumber assistant.

As with the Mascot serials, *One Frightened Night* plays fast and loose with the clues while keeping the identity of the villain a secret to the last. The tactic is to have the miscreant portrayed by anybody and everybody but the actor who comes due for an unmasking. For the masked killer in this instance, Cabanne borrowed the bandleader and actor Roger Pryor from a neighboring stage, where he was starring in *Headline Woman*. In some other scenes, stuntman Ted Mapes—about a head taller than the genuine culprit—sports the horrific mask.

The Miracle Rider

Monogram Pictures Corp. • 1935

The greatest western stars of the 1920s had been Tom Mix and William S. Hart. Hart's arena was an Old West of struggle and retribution. Mix represented fun and adventure and fancy duds. Both faded with the silent era—Hart, with a somber formal farewell on talking-picture film, and Mix, with a tentative sound-film persistence that only underscored his self-conscious incompatibility with the microphone. Mix dismissed as upstarts such talkie-attuned talents as John Wayne and Bob Steele. Mix's truer interest lay in circus life, and he was a fine horseman. He made his last feature in 1933 at Universal—just as Wayne was attaining momentum with the *Lone Star Westerns* series.

Mix was the subject of many tall tales—of which some are surprisingly true. (A war-hero image was a myth, although he *had* seen uniformed duty.) His legendary injuries, including a rebuilt jaw that made him uncomfortable around the sound-recording gizmos, were results of his roughhousing with rodeos, circuses, and the movies. Mix was no dilettante—just a showman who appreciated the value of a good yarn and a flashy presence.

Mix had made some 400 silent pictures—the highest-paid actor in cinema, for a while—and then delivered a handful of sound films. In 1935, debt-ridden on account of extravagant living, Mix accepted Nat Levine's offer of $40,000 to star in a serial, *The Miracle Rider*. Levine had made a bundle with Ken Maynard's name above the title on *Mystery Mountain*, and the producer knew that a comeback for Tom Mix would be an even bigger draw. *The Miracle*

Rider opened domestically in more than 12,000 theatres; the returns set a record at Mascot.

Rangers Capt. Tom Morgan (Mix) finds his friends, the Ravenhead Indians, under attack by a mineral-rights pirate, Zaroff (Charles Middleton). Zaroff's cohort, a mad scientist (Niles Welch), controls the formula for a powerful explosive. A futuristic aircraft seems the embodiment of a tribal curse until Morgan survives sufficient death traps to debunk the superstition. Zaroff foments a uprising among the Indians. Morgan hounds Zaroff into a fatal fall, complete with a spectacular explosion.

Mix, seamed and plagued with arthritis at 55, required stunt-doubling on much of *The Miracle Rider*—but he still comes across as *mucho hombre*, recognizable in a great deal of the action and handling a gun with style and grace. The film benefits from a mob of bad-guy players, as many hard faces as ever were gathered for one show, all dominated by Charles Middleton in his serial début. Middleton's show of callous greed resembles his insane cattle baron of *Mystery Ranch* (1932) and his famous portrayal of the Emperor Ming in three *Flash Gordon* serials.

The first Mascot epic to exceed 12 chapters, *The Miracle Rider* is at 310 minutes the longest sound serial. A documentary-styled prologue depicts the exploitation of the tribes from Colonial times to the present day. Anticipating the genre-bending conceits of *The Phantom Empire*, *The Miracle Rider* emphasizes science-fictional elements. The special effects portend great things to come for the brothers Howard and Theodore Lydecker, the inventive artisanal carpenters who soon would define the visual style of Republic Pictures' serials. Though hardly as polished as Mix's Fox silents or his Universal talkers, the film is nonetheless a good show of its class.

Mix's first serial also was his last movie. His signature circus had declined by 1940, when he was killed in an automobile crash in Arizona.

Big Boy Rides Again

Beacon Productions • First Division • 1935

Frontier Gothic: Guinn "Big Boy" Williams' star turn in Albert Herman's *Big Boy Rides Again* captures that dark manner well, arriving shortly before Hollywood's new breed of happy-cowboy musical westerns would render the genre bright and simplistic. Rancher John Duncan (Charles French) orders his estranged rodeo-riding son, Tom Duncan (Williams), to come home and take charge. Tom and a sidekick, Windy (Bud Osborne), arrive in time for the reading of John Duncan's will. The old grump had survived an attempt to poison him by his treacherous cook, Sing Fat (Louis Van Cinet, a.k.a. Vincenot)—only to be shot dead by a masked prowler.

Neighboring rancher Tap Smiley (Lafe McKee), who had proposed a merger, is angered to have gone unmentioned in the will. Smiley resents the interest of his daughter, Nancy (Connie Bergen), in Tom. An unfinished letter accompanying the will suggests a hiding place for John Duncan's fortune. The prowler returns to abduct Sing Fat and Windy; ambush Tom's foreman (Victor Potel); and lead Tom into a trap. Nancy finds an underground passageway. Tom escapes, connects clues left by his father, and finds the captives and the loot, which is snatched by the prowler. The fiend turns out to be a trusted lawyer (William

Guinn "Big Boy" Williams.

Gould). Sing Fat resumes the skulking to end the misadventure on a cryptic note.

This obscure attempt at a resurgence for Williams prizes desperation and fumbling, dumb-luck solutions over outright heroism and concerns itself with random misfortune and unambitious criminal intent, more so than any larger conspir-acies. William Gould's character seems content with a bag of money when he could be using his credential as a barrister to steal the ranch. Little official fuss is made over the murder, and no one in authority lends Big Boy a helping hand. The film makes no reference to Guinn's famous nick-name apart from the title, which only *suggests* a sequel.

Williams retains all the star quality of his silent-westerns heyday, but character parts proved more significant to his longevity. Also in 1935, Williams scored at Paramount, as a sadist in *The Glass Key* and as a maniac in *Private Worlds*. He serves *Big Boy Rides Again* as an irre-sponsible rascal who rises to the occasion, despite his being slow to decipher obvious clues. The actor's attitude of stubborn courage makes for an endearing and generous performance, free of vanity.

The story was used again, by Monogram Pictures, for 1941's *Saddle Mountain Roundup*, part of the *Range Busters* series.

The Phantom Empire

Mascot Pictures Corp. • 1935

Ken Maynard had been announced as star player of *The Phantom Empire*, a wild fantasy dreamed up by Wallace MacDonald while huffing nitrous oxide in a dentist's chair. Nat Levine reneged after experiencing difficulties with the volatile Maynard while making *Mystery Mountain* and *In Old Santa Fe*. Both those contain small roles for Gene Autry, a railroad telegrapher-turned-singer from Texas. Levine had Autry under contract at $100 a week, with lesser engagements for Autry's humorous partners, Lester "Smiley" Burnette and Frankie Marvin.

In a rare gamble, Levine switched Autry for Maynard, threw in Burnette and William Moore for comical relief, added Frankie Darro

and trick rider Betsy King Ross as daredevil youngsters—and made not only a successful serial but also a trendsetter. The $70,000 production laid for Autry the foundation of a lasting Hollywood career and popularized the blessing-or-curse of the musical-western subgenre. The film also established a vogue for science-fiction serials, with or without frontier settings.

Gene Autry's Radio Ranch, a resort that produces musical broadcasts, falls under siege by helmeted marauders, on the one hand, and on the other by Prof. Beetson (J. Frank Glendon) and his radium pirates. The so-called Thunder Riders are soldiers from the underground city of Murania. Gene, framed for a murder that Beetson had committed, flees under pursuit by both the law and a party of Thunder Riders. Believed dead after an automobile crash, Gene returns to Radio Ranch in time to stage his broadcast as usual—only to be captured by the Muranians. Gene is killed in a nuclear explosion.

Resurrected by Muranian science, Gene reunites with ranch kids Frankie and Betsy (Darro and Ross), and they escape in Beetson's airplane. Tika, Queen of Murania (Dorothy Christy), disables the craft. Gene is recaptured, but two pals (Moore and Burnette) disguise themselves as robots and sneak into Murania.

The subterranean empire is torn by rebellion. Gene rescues Tika from a disintegrating ray. She chooses to remain enthroned as Murania is destroyed in a surreal cataclysm. Gene returns home to force a confession from Beetson.

A strange film for strange times, this *Phantom Empire*. Autry rises beyond the occasion to demonstrate how he had improved as a rider and all-round screen presence in a year, helped along by stuntmasters Yakima Canutt and Yancey Lane. Autry hardly seems the type for violent action if compared with Ken Maynard or John Wayne—but then, only the players and their fans can define that elusive concept of star quality.

Exteriors for *Empire* were filmed at the Mack Sennett Lot in the San Fernando Valley and in Bronson Canyon. The Muranian throne room was set up in Los Angeles' new Griffith Park Observatory. (During the 1990s, Autry chose Griffith Park for sentimental reasons as a site for his signature Western Heritage Museum, located in view of that observatory.) The miniatures of Murania, used both in real time and in rear projection, are an improvement over the small-scale properties of the earlier Mascots. The destruction of the city was achieved by the melting of a special thickness of film emulsion. The robots are laughable; they remained so when resurrected nearly 20 years later by Columbia Pictures. Jack Coyle built the elaborate scenic and architectural models, assisted by the youthful Lydecker Bros., Howard and Theodore.

Cinematographer Bud Thackery was chosen for his insider's knowledge of miniature projection—having worked with the inventor, Willis O'Brien, on *King Kong*. The comparable scenes in *Empire*, with the actors projected into the miniature settings, are unprecedented in serials. Otto Brower and B. Reeves Eason teamed as alternating directors, one supervising a day's shooting while the other planned for the next day.

Darro and Ross upstage most of the grown-ups. Wheeler Oakman, Warner Richmond, and Frank Glendon are formidable villains. Dorothy Christy's Queen Tika recalls her portrayal of Stanley Laurel's shrew of a wife in 1933's *Sons of the Desert*. Several songs by Autry and Burnette became standards, such as the comical "Uncle Noah's Ark" (with Burnette's froglike vocal effects) and the sentimental "That Silver-Haired Daddy of Mine." The score also includes stirring chase music, a theme for Murania by Henry Hadley, and Louis J.F. Hérold's *Zampa Overture*, which had been composed more than a century earlier.

In 1940, the since-retired Mascot brand was revived for a 71-minute feature version, *Radio Ranch*, whose recutting emphasized the music and the cowboy action. An earlier condensation, *Men with Steel Faces*, shows a bias toward the science-fantasy elements. Times Films of New York issued this variant along the East Coast and in Great Britain and Continental Europe. Another condensation played in the U.K. under a cheekier title: *Couldn't Possibly Happen*.

Captured in Chinatown:
A Police Melodrama

Consolidated Pictures Corp. • Weiss Productions • Stage & Screen • 1935

Bert Sternbach, one of the more tight-fisted and less risk-prone independent producers, presented three action thrillers starring Tarzan the Police Dog. Each was given the subtitle of *A Police Melodrama*. Neither *Inside Information* nor *Million-Dollar Haul* (1934–1935) had heralded the strangeness of *Captured in Chinatown*, with its ghastly rampage of theft and murder calculated to touch off a tong war.

Tarzan manages a ferocious imitation of the mighty Rin-Tin-Tin. Some good players appear in support for *Captured in Chinatown*, notably Marion Shilling, Philo McCullough, Robert Walker, and Robert Ellis. Ellis' murderous character is a repulsive figure, indeed.

Elmer Clifton, director and co-author, will figure now and again through the course of the *Forgotten Horrors* pictures, into the post-World War II years. He had been a protégé of D.W. Griffith and, like the master, suffered from difficulties in adjusting to the different styles of acting demanded by the talking pictures. Clifton, unlike Griffith, persisted and learned—and wound up working alongside Ida Lupino, one of the more progressive new directors of the mid-century, when the actress organized her own production company.

Captured in Chinatown finds reporters Ann Parker and Bob Martin (Marion Shilling and Charles Delaney) assigned to cover the wedding of Joy Ling and Tom Wong (Bo Ling and Wing Foo). The marriage is expected to end the hatreds that have plagued their families for generations. A ceremonial necklace, given to Joy by her bridegroom, is snatched from her throat by Zamboni (Ellis), a bandit who has infiltrated the gathering in clothing resembling the ceremonial attire of the Ling family.

Zamboni kills Tom Wong when the young man rushes to help his bride. Tom's father (James B. Leong) notices the slayer's costume and declares war anew. Ann winds up in Zamboni's clutches.

At the House of Ling, Zamboni imprisons Ann, who has witnessed too much to be allowed to live. Her police-dog pal, Tarzan, tracks her, then finds Martin and brings him to the rescue. In a pitched battle, Zamboni is overcome, his plot exposed. Peace is restored between families.

Its old-fashioned histrionics aside, *Captured in Chinatown* delivers some agreeable suspense and thrills. The rented sets are effective and reasonably authentic.

Branded a Coward

Supreme Pictures Corp. • 1935

The conventional wisdom, suspect by nature, holds that the matinée western of the 1920s and 1930s is juvenile escapism by definition, and that the so-called adult western (not as in *prurient*, but as in *thoughtful and provocative*) did not appear until the arrival of such robust examples as *Shane* and *High Noon* during the 1950s. And yet in both Sam Newfield's *Branded a Coward* and his slightly later *Lightnin' Bill Carson*, one finds depths of psychological distress and hard-won redemption that can scarcely be dismissed as the stuff of most Depression-era shoot-'em-ups.

Nor can Newfield's greater body of work particularly brand him as a forward-thinking or painstaking director. In a career spanning 1919–1964, Newfield as a rule cranked out the assignments on the quick-and-cheap. He maintained such pseudonyms as Sherman Scott and Peter Stewart "to avoid an embarrassing avalanche of screen credits," as the historian Ephraim Katz once wrote. Newfield's actual name was Shmuel Neufeld, brother and frequent collaborator of the producer Sigmund Neufeld.

Newfield met the rare classier opportunity with what higher artistry the deadline and budget would permit. Some of his later films bespeak a grim *Yiddishe* intellect: *Beasts of Berlin* assailed the Third Reich in

defiance of the "America First" drivel of nationalistic isolationism. And Newfield's rubber-reality genre parody *Skipalong Rosenbloom* (1951) razzes the emerging medium of commercial television and anticipates Robert Aldrich's satirical *The Frisco Kid* (1979) by over a generation.

Branded a Coward opens very like 1934's *The Rawhide Terror*—a westward-bound family under siege, with surviving sons (one bears a prominent birthmark) who will carry the trauma into adulthood on opposing sides of the law. *Branded a Coward* forges into bolder psychological terrors. Johnny Mack Brown's ultimately heroic rodeo champion is no ordinary coward, but rather the survivor of an ordeal that has left him with both a fascination with guns and an aversion to violence. (He carries his father's heavily notched six-shooter but has counted no coups of his own.) Brown's lighthearted air lapses to unnerved paralysis—enhanced by flashback clips from the prologue—to disgust with his condition, to impulsive heroism, and back to a neurotic state.

An outlaw known as the Cat is responsible for the opening attack. Older son Billy Hume (Rex Downing) is wounded. His brother, Johnny (Mickey Rentschler), is too overcome with fear to open fire. Johnny escapes. Billy has gone missing.

Twenty years later, Johnny Hume (Brown) has become an expert rider and marksman but has a reputation for shrinking from trouble. Robbers invade a party. Hume is besieged by memories of the attack upon his family. His failure to act provokes scorn, and he departs, accompanied by a pal, Oscar (Syd Saylor). When they encounter a holdup, Hume overcomes an onslaught of crippling memory and routs the attackers. A stagecoach passenger, Ethel Carson (Billie Seward), hails him as a hero.

Residents of nearby Lawless, Arizona, offer Hume the job of marshal. He resists until he receives a warning note signed, "the Cat." Hume accepts the challenge. Ethel's father, Carson (Lloyd Ingraham), recognizes Hume as the son of a law officer who had killed Carson's brother. The Cat is a mysterious presence who has long plagued the town. "As soon as we think one Cat is done for," says one local, "there's another to take his place." Carson, seeking a showdown with Hume, is slain by a hidden member of the Cat's mob during a raid on a Wells Fargo station. Carson blames Hume, but before he can trace the killer the gang has departed.

Hume captures one outlaw, and Oscar and a posse bring in most of others. Oscar is slain while trailing a suspect. Hume corners the Cat (Brown, performing double-duty) and recognizes him by a birthmark as the lost brother—raised by the gang to inherit its leadership. A glimmer of recognition dawns upon the Cat's face, and as his last henchman intrudes, the Cat takes a bullet meant for Johnny Hume.

Hume, wounded during the affray, wakes in Ethel's care. "You got the Cat," she assures him. He mutters bitterly: "I—got—the—Cat."

The scenario mingles the psychological complications with the ticket-selling outdoor-action requirements. The lurking mob boss recalls those of the thrill-crazy Mascot serials. *Branded a Coward* raises the ante by having the badman represent a strange custom spanning generations. A runaway-stagecoach routine serves as a fine showcase for stuntman Yakima Canutt, doubling Brown. This extravagant set piece and a more elaborate replay in *Courageous Avenger* may be the earliest of several versions of Canutt's famous *Stagecoach* stunt, so called in recognition of the attention the routine aroused in John Ford's big-time western of 1939, *Stagecoach*. Another rousing stunt finds Canutt leaping from a cliff into the icy turbulence of the Kern River. Canutt also plays the original Cat.

Brown is as fit for the tough-guy business as for the more nearly cerebral material. He plays well off sidekick Syd Saylor, who lays on his kid-pleasing stammering routine more generously than usual. When asked, "Do you always stutter?" Saylor replies: "*Nuh*-no. Only when I *tuh*-talk." The genial comedian plays a larger heroic role than most horse-opera sidekicks were allowed, and his death scene comes as a bewildering jolt.

Billie Seward shows plenty of gumption—falling for Brown a bit too rapidly, but turning appropriately hostile when it appears he has killed her father. Her closing scene of forgiveness and reconciliation cuts deeper by far than the genre's customary happy ending.

Condemned To Live

Invincible-Chesterfield • 1935

One of the finer treasures of Poverty Row, Frank R. Strayer's *Condemned To Live* foreshadows by a generation the inventive, genre-enhancing approach of Great Britain's Hammer Films. The independent studios of the 1930s had little to say about vampires. *Condemned* raises the stakes—in a prologue that was censored from many prints—with the concept of prenatal influence.

Prof. Paul Kristan (Ralph Morgan) is unaware of his truer nature. Moonlight transforms him to a predatory state. His hunchbacked servant, Zan (Mischa Auer), disposes of the victims' bodies in a pit within a cave. Kristan and a searching party find the chasm.

Dr. Anders Bizét (Pedro de Cordoba), summoned to investigate, determines that Kristan's betrothed, Marguerite Mané (Maxine Doyle), loves the doctor only platonically. A villager, David (Russell Gleason), who loves Marguerite, suggests that the killer is exploiting the villagers' superstitions.

Stalking about Marguerite's house, Kristan commits another slaying. The locals, suspecting Zan, rally a mob. Kristan tells Marguerite of his blackouts and releases her from their engagement. After a struggle leaves Marguerite and Kristan unconscious, Zan lures the vigilantes away from Kristan. Bizét reveals that Kristan's mother had been attacked by a gigantic bat shortly before his birth.

Kristan and Bizét find Zan at bay in the cave. The townspeople seem moved by Kristan's confession. Kristan shows them that Zan bears the scar of vampiric enslavement. Kristan leaps to his death. Zan, stricken with grief at the loss of his master, follows suit.

The only other picture to which *Condemned To Live* bears much resemblance is Majestic's *The Vampire Bat*, which also plays variations upon the theme. *The Vampire Bat* boasts the same director, along with shared mu-

sic and prominent settings at Universal City. It moves at a headlong clip, however, where *Condemned* sustains a stately pace—to the finer detail of arch and mannered dialogue, like an ancestor of the 1980s' highbrow Merchant & Ivory films—even at a brief hour-and-change running time. The nighttime settings are lighted for evocative shadows. Suspense runs high in Ralph Morgan's climactic scenes with Maxine Doyle.

Universal Pictures provided such sets as a European street, still dressed for the just-completed *Bride of Frankenstein*; the exterior of Castle Frankenstein; and the bell tower from *The Hunchback of Notre Dame* (1923), with Ted Billings—in his costume from *Bride of Frankenstein*—ringing one of the mighty chimes. The cliffs and caves of Bronson Canyon appear part of a seascape via the cutting-in of a coastal shot and the crashing of breakers. Costumes from Universal's Dickens films, *Great Expectations* and *The Mystery of Edwin Drood* (1934–1935), are generously evident.

Morgan propels the story as a pitiable monster. Morgan is most vividly remembered as the tragic husband in MGM's *Strange Interlude*; his fame was overshadowed by that of his brother, Frank Morgan. Mischa Auer is likewise sympathetic as the slave. Pedro de Cordoba is memorable as the essential Van Helsing type. The silent-screen star Barbara Bedford is seen as the mother of a monstrous child. Doyle is a beautiful and innocent leading lady.

Main-title and end-title compositions are the work of David Brockman, former musical director at Universal. The Charles Dunworth refrain, "Stealthy Footsteps"—an often-used theme in Abe Meyer's stock-library catalogue—is heard during the establishing scenes.

Ouanga

a.k.a.: *The Love Wanga* • *Crime of Voodoo*
Real Life Dramas • Favorite Films • Paramount • J.H. Hoffberg, Inc. • 1935

Had George Terwilliger only filmed an account of the misadventures of the making of *Ouanga*—a slapdash production that sought high drama but landed at the exploitation-film grindhouses—he might have had a picture worth the trouble. *Ouanga* scarcely lives up to its potential for adventure, romance, and terror.

The story behind the story is an exercise in haywire ambition. Terwilliger—a pioneering writer-director who had worked with D.W. Griffith—had set out for the West Indies aboard the S.S. *Haiti* in 1933, intent upon filming his original screenplay (the working title was *Drums of the Night*) in an authentic setting. His company included Carl Berger, who had photographed explorer Frank Buck's *Bring 'Em Back Alive* (1933) in Africa, in addition to principal players and a technical crew. At Port-au-Prince, despite warnings of contempt for white interlopers, Terwilliger went barging into the backwoods with truckloads of equipment and a guide assigned to find a stronghold of voodoo. Friendly at first, a *papaloi*, or priest, became angry at Terwilliger's call for a ritual re-enactment. An *ouanga*, symbolic of a curse, was placed in the director's automobile. A tire was punctured. A royal palm was felled in the path. Terwilliger returned to the city to recruit dancers, drummers, and extras. The cultists, indignant, persisted with the harassment.

Terwilliger prepared to dispatch the troupe, including added Haitians, to Jamaica. The dancers vanished. The drummers and the extras landed in jail. Retrenched at Kingston, Terwilliger assembled a company and began shooting in the jungles and hills. The heat made it expedient to shoot at night under unnaturally harsh floodlighting. In developments very like the trials of location shooting for *Hell Harbor* but without such resourceful backup strategies, a flood drowned two natives, and a cyclone wrecked the sets. An American crewman fell ill and died. Insects made life miserable. Terwilliger persisted and returned to Hollywood two months later with the footage. Perhaps such hard-won results deserved better, but the picture falls short in acting, direction, photography, and writing.

Clelie Gordon (Fredi Washington), an octoroon who leads a voodoo cult, takes possession of a protective *ouanga*, lest she come to harm. Clelie, who owns a plantation, loves a neighboring planter, Adam Maynard (Philip Brandon).

Maynard introduces his fiancée, Eve Langley (Marie Paxton). Clelie learns that Eve's maid, Susie (Babe Joyce), desires Maynard's valét, Jackson (Sidney Easton). She gives Susie a passion charm and instructs her to place another object, more sinister of purpose, in Eve's purse.

During a party, a death *ouanga* falls from Eve's handbag, leaving her in a coma. Maynard learns of Clelie's curse. She begs for his love. Maynard finds Eve recovering. Then LeStrange (Sheldon Leonard), Maynard's driver and Clelie's spurned suitor, works a hoodoo of his own—dressing a corpse in clothing stolen from Clelie.

Clelie orders zombies to abduct Eve. LeStrange interferes, but Clelie wounds him—failing to notice that LeStrange has seized her life-saving *ouanga*. Susie and Jackson learn that Eve is marked for sacrifice and summon Maynard. As Clelie orders the killing, the dying LeStrange arrives to taunt her. Clelie becomes desperate to find the buried corpse and retrieve her garments. LeStrange strangles Clelie at the base of a sacramental tree. Susie works a lovemaking hoodoo upon Jackson. Eve recovers.

While dawdling with the film's cutting, Terwilliger found his story overshadowed by two similarly conceived but more impressive films—Columbia's *Black Moon*, from the novel by Clements Ripley, and the provincial independent *Chloe (Love Is Calling You)*. *Ouanga* can only have disappointed the customers, with or without comparisons. Its zombies lack special makeup or much of an undead presence, and the accomplished Fredi Washington condescends so to the less-capable talents as to appear amateurish herself.

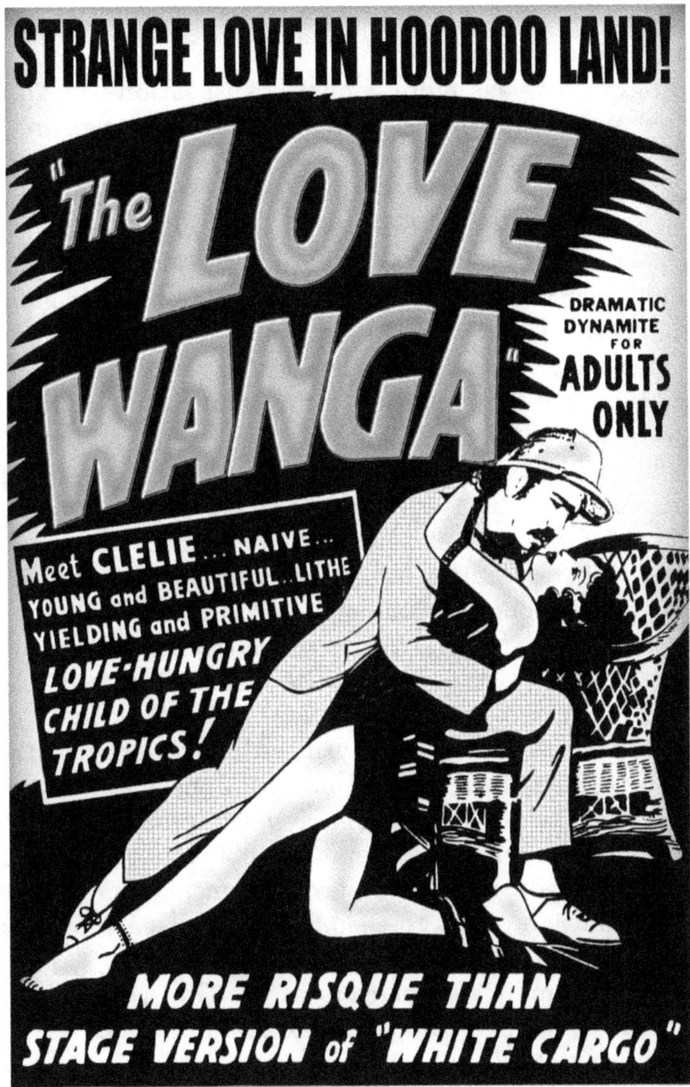

Carl Berger's photography, hampered by the garish man-made lighting, nonetheless contains some eerie compositions, notably in the final
confrontation and in a scene where the players are dwarfed by gigantic
cottonwoods. The music—light European classical and Afro-Caribbean
pulsations—is indifferently applied except during the rituals.

Smart editing helps: a process of intercutting between a dainty
soirée for the ruling class white folks and a rowdy party in the servants' quarters is a device that would work impressively more than 60
years later, in James Cameron's *Titanic* (1997)—contrasting rich-folks
shipboard accommodations with steerage. *Ouanga* also intensifies the

climactic chase via juxtaposition with a comic-relief subplot about a lovestruck servant's pursuit of her beau.

Washington displays more venom than passion—recalling her embittered overplaying opposite the great Louise Beavers in the culture-clash soap opera *Imitation of Life* (1934) more so than her scenes opposite Paul Robeson in *The Emperor Jones*. Washington's dance in *Ouanga* is a sinuous delight, however, and her voice rings with class. Sheldon Leonard, as Washington's nemesis, conveys intensity through snarls and clenched teeth. And yes, this is the same Sheldon Leonard who would become a specialist in Runyonesque gangsters—and later, a producer-director for network television. Leonard's movie career is popularly supposed to have begun with *Another Thin Man* in 1939; so much for the conventional wisdom.

Marie Paxton and assistant director Philip Brandon are dreadfully over-reactive as the upper-crust white couple, affecting silent-screen gestures and facial contortions and declamatory line readings. Brandon would fare better *behind* the cameras as a producer on foreign-location shoots, including African footage for some of the *Tarzan* pictures. Smarter portrayals by far belong to Sidney Easton and Babe Joyce, who bring wit and erotic energy to a magically enhanced courtship.

The film was registered for copyright—but never formally copyrighted—in 1935 by Real Life Dramas, for domestic U.S. release by Favorite Films. (This is not the same Favorite Films that was set up 13 years later to reissue titles from Columbia and various independents.) In a misleadingly hopeful development, Paramount Pictures bought distribution rights to *Ouanga* but released it only outside the States.

Proxy titles complicated matters as the film wavered between legitimate distribution and roadshow exploitation. Until one of these alternate-title prints, *The Love Wanga*, surfaced in an off-brand video edition during the 1980s, it was almost impossible to find anyone who had seen the film. A more authentic *Ouanga*, bearing the Real Life Dramas brand, showed up in the video catalogue of Sinister Cinema.

George Terwilliger, intent upon a salvage job, retooled his script for another project, which Arthur Leonard filmed in Jamaica in 1939 as *Pocomania*, a.k.a. *The Devil's Daughter*. More a tedious variation than a remake, *Pocomania* is an overtly comical piece, with Nina Mae McKinney and Hamtree Harrington.

Hong Kong Nights

Futter Productions • WAFilms • First Division Exchange • 1935

Producer Walter Futter (a name that W.C. Fields would have relished) had concluded that the tong-war gimmick—the Chinatown equivalent of Appalachian hillbilly feuds—was passé. Futter seized upon a tale of "smugglers' bullets and Chinese knives," to lift a line from the promotional campaign. Futter fell ill after principal photography had begun, and his friend Fenn Kimball stepped in. Filming took place at the Mack Sennett Studio and on location at Los Angeles' Chinatown and Catalina Island.

Futter may have reconsidered the irrelevance of tong wars after just such a rumpus, centered upon the movie itself, erupted on the third day of the Chinatown shoot: The On Leong Tong stormed the location in

a quest to reclaim money on behalf of a member whose wife—purchased from her father, an elderly extra in *Hong Kong Nights*—had deserted him. The matter was settled after the customary hurling of threats, knives, and rocks, and the shooting proceeded without further incident.

Customs agents Tom and Wally (Tom Keene and Warren Hymer), in pursuit of gun-running racketeers, find Trina Vidor (Wera Engels), a Viennese, in the thrall of Burris (Cornelius Keefe), a charming ex-convict. Burris decamps for a crime-infested island off Hong Kong, and Trina insists upon following him. An accomplice, Wong (Tetsu Komai), warns Burris about the investigation. Trina, after a disagreement with Burris, informs Tom of a counter-strike. Tom foils an attack by Wong, then visits Burris' waterfront office.

Wally finds a payload of weapons. Burris' attempt to bribe Tom ends in a standoff. Wong arrives with reinforcements. Tom is captured. Amid the confusion, Wong fires a shot deliberately off-target—and then explains that he is repaying Tom, who had declined to kill Wong in the shipboard attack.

Burris makes off in a yacht with the munitions, dragging Trina along for insurance. Tom stows aboard. At a seaport village, Burris accepts a chest of silver in exchange for the firepower but then speeds away with the payment *and* the bulk of the shipment. Tom is recaptured.

Wong vows revenge against Burris, who docks at a deserted atoll, hides the weapons and several barrels of oil, and imprisons Trina and Tom in a cave that will flood at high tide. Wong, arriving to reclaim the weapons, stabs Burris to death—but not before the racketeer has wounded him. Wong torches the oil drums even as he dies from Burris' gunshot. The blaze attracts a rescue ship.

Hong Kong Nights, by no standard a slick production, nonetheless achieves spectacle in the burning of a village—more than an acre of the Mack Sennett backlot. Suspense radiates from the plight of Tom Keene and Wera Engels. The romantic element is more sophisticated than in the usual independent melodrama, and tough guy Warren Hymer's lunkheaded comedy relief is always welcome.

Director E. Mason Hopper, a veteran of stagecraft, had begun in film with the Essanay company in 1911. By 1930, Hopper had handled approximately 350 pictures and written some 400 scripts, working primarily for the major studios. His specialty, prior to his demotion to the independents with the talkie era, had been romantic comedy—with such high points as *Up in Mabel's Room* and *Paris at Midnight* (both from 1926).

Tom Keene was a stage actor who, as George Duryea, had played romantic leads in early talkies before RKO-Radio changed his name for a series of westerns. Just before *Hong Kong Nights*, Keene had played the hero in King Vidor's *Our Daily Bread* (1934). After a return to westerns, Keene changed his name to Richard Powers to seek dramatic leads, but wound up instead as a character man—landing at last in Edward D. Wood, Jr.'s peculiar *Plan 9 from Outer Space*. Keene died in 1963.

Wera Engels, who replaced Molly O'Day in *Hong Kong Nights*, was a big-eyed and lush-lipped beauty from Vienna. She had appeared with Edmund Lowe in Universal's *The Great Impersonation* (1935) but failed to catch on in American films. Warren Hymer was the industry's leading portrayer of hulking muttonheads (as in 1931's *The Unholy Garden*)—so adept that film scripts often described such a character as "a Warren Hymer type." Hymer also is celebrated in Hollywood lore for having marked the termination of his contract with Columbia by urinating on the desk of studio tyrant Harry Cohn. Cornelius Keefe is in his element as a suave menace, and the Japanese Tetsu Komai repeats his specialty as a *Chinese* marauder—this time, with a self-sacrificing sympathetic streak.

Murder by Television

Cameo Productions • Imperial Distributing Corp. • 1935

We are hard-pressed to name a film of less merit than Clifford Sanforth's *Murder by Television*, whose title alone should have put it over: The concept of television was popularly regarded in 1935 as science fiction. Released briefly, shelved, and reissued two years later, *Murder by Television* never played widely until the consumer-video boom of the 1980s, when an onslaught of opportunistic grey-market vendors began using the original edition of *Forgotten Horrors* as a catalogue-building concordance.

Genre enthusiasts in 1935 would have been drawn, of course, by the presence of Bela Lugosi—but they also would have been disappointed by a dull script, static camerawork, and generally poor performances from otherwise dependable players. The film remains of interest for its peculiarities. (Also of interest: 1936's *Trapped by Television*.)

Prof. James Houghland (Charles Hill Mailes) resists corporate pressures to sell his formula for a practical television system. His sudden death during a demonstration leaves many suspects. One party had sought to bribe Arthur Perry (Lugosi), Houghland's assistant. Richard Grayson (George Meeker) had sworn to possess the technology. Dr. Scofield (Huntly Gordon) appears secretive. The plans are stolen. Perry turns up stabbed to death. The weapon is the knife of a servant, Ah Ling (Allan Jung), who had accused Perry. Perry reappears—or rather, his twin has come to investigate. He proves that Scofield had killed the professor with "the interstellar frequency that is the death ray."

Murder by Television was budgeted at $15,000 and came in under that. The studio borrowed $75,000 worth of experimental TV equipment. A fleeting high point comes when lovely June Collyer sings a ballad composed for the movie by Oliver Wallace, later acclaimed for his Disney-film scores. Hattie McDaniel, four years away from an Oscar-bait breakthrough in *Gone with the Wind* (1939), contributes a lively portrayal of boisterous humor.

Some surviving prints contain a jazz number sung by McDaniel; other prints betray vandalism by southern censors, who routinely removed showcase segments for black artists. Though saddled with a demeaning role and color-conscious gag lines, McDaniel lends pep to an otherwise dreary film.

The debits are crippling. *Murder by Television* resembles the more primitive talkies of the late 1920s, with cameras anchored and actors ill at ease with the dialogue.

The Lady in Scarlet

Chesterfield Motion Pictures Corp. • 1935

Deceptions and murderous intentions run high in Charles Lamont's *The Lady in Scarlet*, a hidden-killer melodrama sparked by an illicit drugging, a mysterious will, and John St. Polis' portrayal of a conniving lawyer. Reginald Denny is in his element as a vain but nonetheless finer specimen of the legal profession, driven by an urge to play detective. Denny's partner in the trouble-chasing game is Patricia Farr, on loan from the newly merged 20th Century-Fox—a hostile-takeover hybrid of an old-line major studio with an upstart independent company.

Albert Sayre (John T. Murray), a dealer in antiquities, resents a friendship between his wife, Julia (Dorothy Revier), and Dr. Philip Boyer (Jameson Thomas). Sayre orders his attorney, Jerome Shelby (St. Polis), to have Julia stalked and shadowed. Julia and Boyer meet at a bar, where lawyer Oliver Keith (Denny) and his secretary, Ella Carey (Farr), recognize Julia as a former actress, famed for a play called *The Lady in Scarlet*. Julia approaches Keith and confides that her husband is in trouble. Keith and Ella accompany Julia to her home, where they find Sayre murdered. Alice Sayre, the victim's daughter from a prior marriage, accuses Julia—but Alice proves to have harbored resentments over her father's threats of disinheritance. She had married her father's clerk, Arthur Pennyward (James Bush), against Sayre's objections.

Clues point to an auctioneer (Jack Adair) through whom Sayre had sold counterfeit antiques. Sayre's will and a revised version come into question, but the documents are missing, along with a fortune in negotiable bonds. A former Sayre employee, Quigley (Al Thompson), ordered by lawyer Shelby to tail Julia, threatens Dr. Boyer. Quigley is found to have been drugged with a truth serum. Keith finds Boyer slain. Assembling the suspects, Keith reveals that Sayre had been blackmailing Quigley. Pennyward is found in possession of the bonds, which Shelby proves to have planted. Shelby is revealed as the murderer—caught by Sayre in the act of thievery and seen from hiding by Sayre's cat's-paw, Quigley. Boyer had drugged Quigley in order to learn the killer's identity.

Foreboding camerawork and a witty but overcomplicated script (by Fox scribes Robert Ellis and Helen Logan) convey the menacing intrigues to fair advantage. Reginald Denny lends the lawyer-detective a streak of brooding egomania, suggesting the harsher intensity he would bring to *Midnight Phantom*. Denny's presence is leavened by Farr's bright portrayal of the assistant who may be smarter than her condescending boss. Dorothy Revier's enactment recalls her portrayal of a wayward upper-crust wife in *Circumstantial Evidence*, for the same director, Lamont, whose handling of *The Lady in Scarlet* lacks the momentum that such a story needs as a distraction from its tangled plotting.

The Crime of Dr. Crespi

Liberty Pictures Corp. • Republic Pictures Corp. • 1935

Edgar Allan Poe never wrote of any Dr. Crespi, criminal or otherwise, but *The Crime of Dr. Crespi* ascribes itself to Poe, in any event. The springboard is Poe's "The Premature Burial," that nightmare-on-paper that remains as chilling in the here-and-now as it had proved when new in the 19th century. Producer-director John H. Auer's adapted screenplay takes rewarding liberties in its concentration upon a physician (Erich von Stroheim) who seeks vengeance for a romantic disappointment. When called upon to treat Ross (John Bohn), who had married Crespi's onetime *enamorata*, the surgeon administers a drug that produces the appearance of death—but leaves the victim in possession of his senses. The drugging will not dissipate until after burial.

Physicians Arnold and Thomas (Paul Guilfoyle and Dwight Frye) develop suspicions sufficient to warrant an exhumation. They find Ross alive—a terror-sticken, ghostly figure who stalks the corridors of a hospital in his inflicted madness. Ross is led to a confrontation with Crespi, whose violent response fails to gain him any quarter. Crespi commits suicide.

Stroheim's earlier career as a great director had been destroyed by extravagances that the major studios found intolerable, but he continued to appear as an actor—directing himself, in essence, and imposing what influence he could upon his directors-of-record. Stroheim's first turn without directorial authority had been *The Great Gabbo*, but his style of directing patently affected *Gabbo*'s producer-director, James Cruze. Acting was not a task Stroheim enjoyed, for he had difficulty remembering dialogue and was frustrated at the inability to take charge.

And yet Stroheim remained nonetheless an effective actor, dominant even in supporting roles. Shortly before his return to Europe, where his genius was better appreciated, Stroheim spent just over a week in the service of the promising artist Auer, at the old Biograph Studio in the Bronx, New York. The result was *The Crime of Dr. Crespi*, a delightfully morbid reinterpretation of Poe. Auer, an immigrant from Budapest, had worked on Spanish-language films for several years.

The opening of the grave.

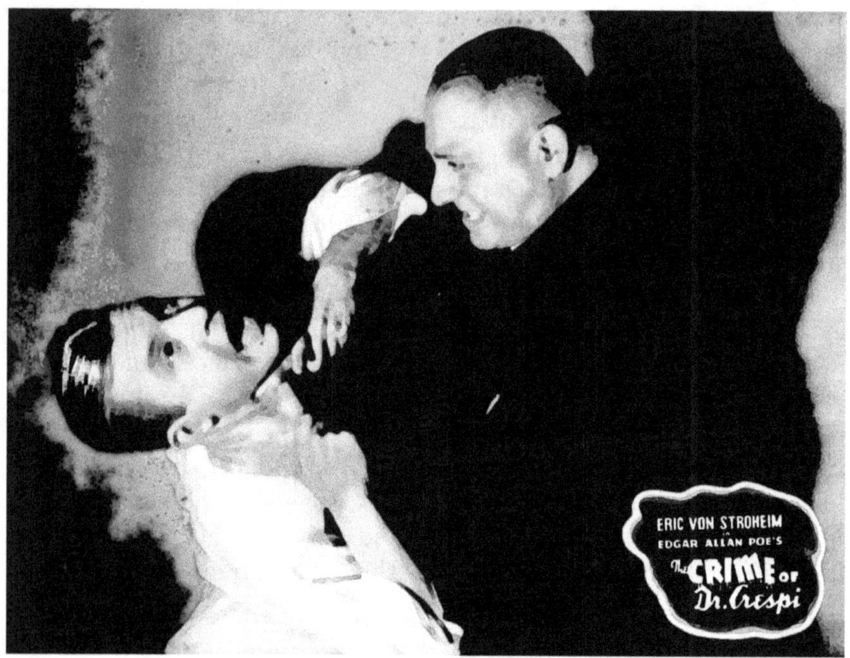

Erich von Stroheim has Dwight Frye at a disadvantage.

Crespi was completed in November of 1934, but M.H. Hoffman's Liberty Pictures proved unable to carry the film past its trade showings. When Herbert J. Yates, the principal stockholder in Biograph, formed Republic Pictures Corp. with a forced merger of studios in his debt, the combine purchased the completed output of the faltering Liberty and Majestic companies. *Crespi* saw release under the Republic brand, billed as "[the] screen's super-thriller...an epic of horror," with an assertion that the tale "starts where Frankenstein left off!"

Hardly the first or last picture to fall short of its hyperbole, *The Crime of Dr. Crespi* nonetheless is an admirably unnerving effort. Auer sustains throughout an oppressive mood of madness and macabre lust surrounding a character who lacks redeeming qualities. The horror takes a wild tangent in Crespi's victim, driven to madness by confinement in the grave. There is a minimum of comedy relief and romantic byplay.

Stroheim was advertised here—just as Universal had touted him in *Blind Husbands* (1919)—as "the man you love to hate." He seems evil made flesh as the sadistic and lecherous healer-turned-heel. When brooding in his office, wreathed in tobacco smoke as he glares balefully at a dwarf's skeleton on his desk, and when gloating over his paralyzed victim in the morgue, Stroheim comes across as the most despicable character short of Bela Lugosi's bad-juju sorcerer in *White Zombie*.

Excellent support is provided by Paul Guilfoyle, John Bohn, and Dwight Frye. Bohn appears both frightening and frightened in his revived state. Frye combines a breezy quality with the nervous mannerisms from *Dracula* and Universal's first two *Frankenstein* entries. Jeanne Kelly, in whom Frye takes a romantic interest, became much better known during the 1940s as Jean Brooks—notably in Val Lewton's RKO-Radio productions of *The Seventh Victim* and *The Leopard Man.*

Crespi's music includes only an orchestral version of Anton Rubenstein's *Kamenoi Oistrow*; a dramatic *lamento* by an unbilled composer; and Josef Pasternak's "Sometime, Somehow, Somewhere." The lights and shadows are in the right places to honor the spirit, if not the letter, of Poe.

Rip Roaring Riley

C.C. Burr Productions • Puritan Pictures Corp. • 1935

"[E]nough stuff...to get by in the less discriminating neighborhoods," commented *The Film Daily* upon the release of Elmer Clifton's *Rip Roaring Riley.* Today, the stuff of *Rip Roaring Riley* is the very thing to attract the discriminating, history-conscious enthusiast—a combination of action, suspense, romance, broad comedy, and a touch of science fiction, all in the service of a yarn that honors the traditions of two-fisted adventure while foreshadowing the Secret Agent craze of the 1960s.

A strange entry, indeed, especially when taken in context with its companion films from the newly established (in 1935) Puritan Pictures. Producer C.C. Burr made these first three Puritans—also including the thoroughly conventional *Kentucky Blue Streak* and *Skybound*—but found in *Rip Roaring Riley* a singularly outlandish quality that covers a concentrated 24 hours of action in only 57 minutes while pitching Lloyd Hughes as practically a prototype for James Bond: less ruthless, and a Yank besides, but a distinct foreshadowing.

The trailer ballyhoos Ted "Rip Roaring" Riley as "the gamest government guy [who] ever snapped a pair of handcuffs!" Riley is introduced as the most violent of participants in a saloon brawl. His greater objective is to expose one Maj. Grey, of the U.S. Army, as a subversive menace: Grey (Grant Withers) is conducting mysterious experiments. Riley stages a motorboat crash near Grey's island outpost and is welcomed (after a fashion) by Grey's henchmen (Paul Ellis, Eddie Gribbon, and Kit Guard). Riley meets his college-days professor, Baker (John Cowell), and Baker's daughter, Ann (Marion Burns). Baker, believing Grey a federal official, has invented for him the deadliest gas known to science. Riley warns the professor that Grey is up to no good.

Grey declares that no one can leave the island. Riley instigates a fight in which a servant (Joe Hikawa) topples into the huge vessel that holds the gas. Riley, Ann, and Baker barricade themselves in Grey's house. Riley contacts a Navy ship by radio. As Grey attacks, the gas spreads. All are rescued who deserve a rescue.

Elmer Clifton's direction, old-fashioned but lively, cracks right along with plenty of tension and a greater variety of camera setups than is usual in the low-budgeters. Clifton concentrates to suspenseful effect upon the ominous glass tank: a lethal leak is of course inevitable, but Clifton makes disaster seem an any-second-now proposition. The sets are spacious and angular, especially a creepy attic where the climactic scenes take place.

Marion Burns, a vivacious sort who looks good in a bathing suit, had been under contract at Fox. Later on, she married Kane Richmond—her co-star in the East Indian expeditionary picture *Devil Tiger*—and retired.

Grant Withers, onetime leading man at Warners, usually played heroic protagonists (as in *The Fighting Marines*, coming right up) but serves here as a madman plotting mass murder. Paul Ellis, who plays Withers' assistant, was a suave and sinister type from Buenos Aires who had portrayed weasels in American films since 1925 and (as Manuel Granados) wrote and starred in Spanish-language films. Plug-ugly Eddie Gribbon and Kit Guard supply both menace and thick-headed comedy.

The Fighting Marines

Mascot Pictures Corp. • 1935

A concentration of gung-ho heroic protagonism, the horrors of madness and mass destruction, and science fiction makes *The Fighting Marines* a stirring farewell to the venerable Mascot brand. Nat Levine made the serial after his studio's absorption into Republic Pictures, which released the picture as a Mascot. Levine remained in place as a Republic executive—an essential talent in the further development of the serial idiom as a breed apart from feature-filmmaking.

Marines shines with the polished swiftness that would distinguish 66 Republic chapter-plays to come. A more generous budget, a longer schedule, and improved special effects combine beautifully with Levine's mastery of the form.

Sgt. Schiller of the U.S. Marines (George J. Lewis) is a captive of crooks who want his invention, a gyro-compass. Cpl. Larry Lawrence and Sgt. Mac McGowan (Grant Withers and Adrian Morris) free him. On a test flight, Schiller's aeroplane is disabled by a ray operated by the gang of the mysterious Tiger Shark. Suspicions and perils mount in an explosive campaign of piracy. A tribe of bloodthirsty savages complicates matters. Unmasked as the least likely suspect, the Tiger Shark dies in a blast of nitroglycerine.

The collaborative script provides menace enough for a dozen melodramas— tribal sacrifice, death rays, a mad scientist, and

a spectacular assortment of heavies—and yet the film avoids the over-complexities associated with Mascot. Another SF treat is an autogyro very like that of 1933's *The Whispering Shadow*; this craft anticipates the Flying Wing (itself a prophetic device in real-world aviation) of *Dick Tracy* and *Fighting Devil Dogs* (1938). Few viewers could have guessed the identity of the Shark, whose voice is not that of the guilty native youth played by Jason Robards.

Mascot's twisted logic figures in the shooting of Adrian Morris (brother of the more prominent Chester Morris)—who charges right back into the fray. Cheating is evident between chapters: Grant Withers falls from a high window and crashes into a concrete abutment. In the next episode, he clings to the sill.

Warner Richmond, as a Shark lieutenant, is scarier and more degenerate here than in any of the other Mascots—which is saying a great deal. A disturbing sequence in a cave finds Richmond riddling the Marines with the proverbial (and literal) whole nine yards. He lapses into a grinning, glassy-eyed dementia and cannot stop shooting. Albert Finney's famous submachine-gun ballet in the Coen Bros.' *Miller's Crossing* (1990) pales by comparison. The team-directing style of B. Reeves Eason and Joseph Kane is rich with tension and headlong momentum.

Withers and Morris are believably burly and athletic. Ingenue Ann Rutherford, as the sister of the beleaguered inventor, is a Levine discovery who would graduate to the major-league studios. Frank Reicher is a classy mad scientist. A minor heavy (among a fine contingent of henchmen) is Milburn Stone—soon to become a valued character man at Universal and, later, the belovéd Doc Adams of network television's *Gunsmoke*.

Midnight Phantom / El Crimen del Media Noche

Reliable Pictures Corp. • 1935

Reginald Denny's show of suave arrogance in *The Lady in Scarlet* makes a telling prelude to his presence in B.B. Ray's *Midnight Phantom*, a pretentiously artistic treatment of an unnerving tale of pulp-fiction outlandishness. Denny's portrayal of an unstable scientist driven to madness counteracts some of the prevailing pseudo-intellectualism arising from an attempt at mannered style amid the essential freakishness. The actor's intensity grates against the tiresome writing of his character, who has a glib homily for every desperate occasion.

An opening frenzy of big-city police activity suggests the influence of such epic tenement dramas as *Street Scene* and *Symphony of*

Six Million (1931–1932). The sense of disastrous immediacy fades as style overwhelms the substance of good old cheap-thrills pulp. Arch, mock-philosophical dialogue wears thin in a picture that proclaims fiendish mayhem but delivers too little, too late. Director Bernard B. Ray plods along, causing the hour-and-change running time to drag.

Gruff Police Chief Sullivan (James A. Farley) insists his tough standards will prevail "as long as I'm alive"—a giveaway of incumbent doom. Sullivan torments subordinates, dismisses underworld threats, and denies his daughter, Diane (Claudia Dell), permission to marry plainclothesman Burke (Lloyd Hughes), half-brother of a slain crook.

Criminologist Graham (Denny), Burke's rival for Diane's affections, professes loyalty. The chief is slain. Graham accuses Burke. The lights are doused. Burke appears to have been croaked. Graham denounces Burke as "a criminal by instinct." Burke springs forward to confront Graham, who confesses. The scientist's private papers reveal a homicidal madness.

Denny makes the intense most of an overwritten scenario, conveying more in nuances of facial expression and body language—a foreshadowing of Vincent Price—than the verbose script allows.

Rock-jawed Lloyd Hughes fares well as the cop who provokes Denny, although the role is deficient in action. Claudia Dell is a headstrong romantic interest, but the harsh lighting obscures her loveliness. Barbara Bedford shines as a secretary accused of an illicit affair with the chief. Mary Foy registers an incidental chill as Bedford's overbearing mother, a mannish policewoman.

The crippling flaw lies in the literary conceit. The opening montage suggests the finer influence of Ben Hecht and Charles MacArthur's unit at Paramount, as in 1934's *Crime Without Passion*. (See our companion volume, *The Cinema of Adventure, Romance & Terror*.) Design bespeaks care, if not discerning taste, especially in Denny's Art Deco apartment.

Plain production values and passive photography betray the Poverty Row origins, which by definition should deliver more melodrama and less mock-dramatic dawdling. A climactic mad scene for Denny might have helped, but the script affords him only a weary confession.

Midnight Phantom has a strange companion piece in *El Crimen del Media Noche*, a.k.a. *El Fantasma del Media Noche*, filmed simultaneously with a Spanish-speaking cast for the international market. Jésus Topéte assisted director Ray with the dialogue. Detective Dan Burke becomes Alberto Burke. Such good Irish names as Sullivan, McCoy, and Kelly remain unchanged. Plotting and pacing are virtually identical.

Scream in the Night

a.k.a.: *Murder in Morocco*
Ray Kirkwood Productions • Astor Pictures • 1935

Ray Kirkwood ran another of the companies that dealt in quick-and-cheap westerns but made the occasional underworld picture. Kirkwood found a figure of greater potential in Lon Chaney, Jr.—still playing small parts as Creighton Chaney. The producer toplined Chaney late in 1935 in *Scream in the Night* and, in a more nearly conventional gangland yarn, *The Shadow of Silk Lennox*. *Scream* provided Chaney's first opportunity to sport an elaborate, grotesque job of makeup in the manner of his famous father. Junior serves as both protagonist and deformed villain—who looks remarkably like Chaney, Sr., in *The Road to Mandalay* (1926).

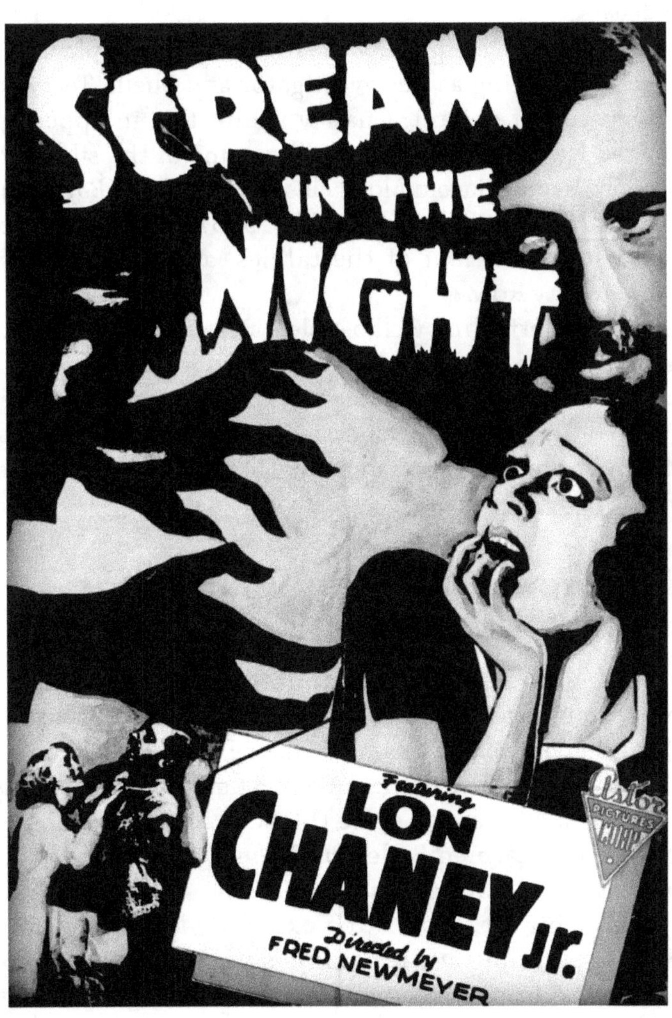

Junior preferred to design and apply his own makeups, in the manner of his father, but once situated at the larger studios he was barred from this practice by union regulations. (Surviving photographs of his rejected self-makeup for 1940's *One Million B.C.* bespeak a real talent.) Publicity for *Scream* traded upon a family tradition of character design.

In Singapore, Detective Jack Wilson (Chaney) plots the downfall of Johnny Fly (Manuél López), a homicidal thief. Wilson's friend Edith Bentley (Sheila Terry) has arrived with a wealthy uncle (John Ince), who possesses a fabulous ruby. The uncle survives an attack. Detective Wu Ting (Philson Wong, a.k.a. Philip Ahn) disguises himself and meets with Butch Curtain (Chaney), a cohort of Fly, but winds up slain.

Fly's mistress, Mora (Zarah Tazil), woos Curtain for treacherous purposes. Fly imprisons Edith. Wilson impersonates Curtain, but Mora spots the deception. Jack, rescued, frees Edith and finds a cache of stolen jewels.

The backup cast is adequate, with Richard Cramer playing against blackguard typecasting as an investigator and Sheila Terry convincingly distressed but defiant. Chaney is effective in opposing roles. Director Fred Newmeyer had been a big name in the silent era, with such triumphs as the Harold Lloyd classics *Grandma's Boy*, *Safety Last*, *Why Worry?*, and *The Freshman* (1922–1925). Newmeyer's fortunes nosedived with the ascent of the talkies, and for two decades he labored on Poverty Row.

Settings are colorful and well peopled. Bert Longenecker, a cameraman associated with outdoor adventure, provides low-key lighting and moody compositions. Such qualities went largely unseen—the film was not registered for copyright, much less systematically issued—until Astor Pictures acquired it to cash in on Chaney's ascent to horror-film stardom at Universal Pictures.

Devil Monster / El Diablo del Mar

Weiss & Landres • Theatre Classics Pictures • 1935

S. Edwin Graham's *Devil Monster* and its Spanish-language variant are as preposterous as the synopsis suggests: Robert Jackson (Barry Norton), landlubber son of a sailor (James Barton), sets out in search of a shipwrecked pal, José Francisco (Jack del Río). Jackson has fallen in love with José's financé, Louise (Blanche Mehaffy in the English-language version, Carmen Bailey *en Español*). Louise will not marry Robert until she can learn of José's fate.

Sidetracking his father's fishing expedition, Jackson prowls the South Seas—marveling at the wildlife sufficiently to transform the desperate errand into a documentary-like travelogue. He witnesses a struggle between a moray eel and an octopus and stares in horror as a shark pursues native swimmers. Finally, the wreckage of José's ship is sighted. A tribal ruler (Bill Lemuels) explains that the lone surviving crewman has become almost a son—a mighty fisherman, capable of subduing even the terrible Devil Fish. That survivor is Francisco, who proves so reluctant to leave that Robert feels compelled to Shanghai him. Francisco proves a treacherous passenger—summoning a Devil Fish, a gigantic manta ray, which he believes will wreck the ship. During the struggle, Francisco experiences a change of heart and loses an arm to the creature while rescuing Jackson. A remorseful Francisco is returned to his sweetheart and his mother. Jackson proves philosophical.

Inept and banal, bereft of dramatic structure, and wavering between attempted narrative exposition and tourist-guide digressions, the companion films run aground as soon as the expedition hits water. Barry Norton, a bilingual Argentinian *né* Alfredo Carlos Birabén, looks the part of the heroic novice sailor, and co-author Terry Grey lends comic relief as a cook. Jack del Rio, as the lost-and-found seaman, conveys disorientation and exaggerated madness. (Ramón Peréda fares better with that role in the Spanish version.) An early cut, shown as *The Sea Fiend*, appears to be a lost film.

Without the Goona-Goona padding, *Devil Monster* would be scarcely more than a short subject. Some of the underwater photography is vivid, but other segments are murky. The Devil Fish attack is incoherent in the staging and editing, and the creature is never seen at detailed close range. A simple double-exposure represents a crude attempt to place the maddened sailor in a scene with the manta. Of course, the film assumes the audience is ignorant of such creatures' tendency to steer clear of humans.

The promise of otherworldly thrills is fulfilled only in a stock-footage sequence where an octopus stalks a fish, only to find itself under attack by a moray. Tribal nudity abounds. Bill Lemuels, as the native chieftain, speaks in such a manner as to suggest he might have learned English by watching the movies of Bela Lugosi.

El Diablo del Mar was filmed simultaneously (at Mascot Studios and Argosy Studio) with variations and a native-speaker cast, under the direction of Juan Duval, an actor from Spain who also contributed to the English-language screenplay.

Shared player Barry Norton performed as a rule in English-speaking pictures but also handled leads in Spanish-language versions produced in Hollywood. (The economical dubbing process had yet to be perfected, but the majors and a few independents found the foreign market too lucrative to ignore.) In Universal's Spanish-language *Dracula* (1931), Norton assumes David Manners' role. Carlos Villarias, the captain in *Diablo*, had handled the title role in that memorable Spanish *Dracula*.

One of *Diablo*'s players, Movita Castañeda, also graces MGM's *Mutiny on the Bounty* (1935). She surfaces again in *Paradise Isle*; she once was married to Marlon Brando. The biggest Latin-market name in *Diablo* is the Castilian Ramón Peréda, a popular leading man and producer-director for many of Hollywood's *peliculas en Español*.

The screenplays are essentially alike, with a heightened emphasis upon Peréda in *El Diablo del Mar*. Manuél Paris, an actor as a rule, wrote the Spanish dialogue. Reviewing the films in New York's Spanish Harlem enclave, the *New York Times* hailed "well-made shots of deep-sea fishing and a struggle with a sea monster."

The Ghost Rider

International-Argosy-Weiss Productions • Superior Talking Pictures • 1935

Superior is a curious name for a company noted for *inferior* work. The distributor had launched badly in 1933 with a line of cheaply made films by such penny-pinching independents as Victor Adamson, Bert Sternbach, and Louis Weiss. The best from Superior is a *Range Rider* series of only two titles, starring dependable Rex Lease and juvenile player Bobby Nelson—*Cyclone of the Saddle* and *The Ghost Rider*. The latter packs a wealth of spectral mayhem and a grim revenge angle in the vein of *The Count of Monte Cristo*.

The beginning and ending sequences are unusual in terms of frontier authenticity: Jack Kirk, a real-world cowboy, sits outside a line shack and sings traditional ballads. Another distinguishing touch is the use of practical, homely ranch-hand clothing instead of the movies' usual western costumes.

Lease and Nelson are subordinate to a lapsed star, Franklyn Farnum, who is at once sympathetic and scary as a vengeful escaped convict. A stage actor from Boston, Farnum had become a convincing western protagonist in silent films and a heavy in the talkies. At length, he became a busy extra and the long-time president of the Screen Extras Guild. One of Farnum's last turns comes in Billy Wilder's *Sunset Blvd.* (1950), as a mortician for domestic pets.

Farnum serves *The Ghost Rider* as Jim Bullard, who in Arizona, 1903, trades identities with a slain fellow inmate. Bullard had killed

a member of the degenerate Raskob clan in a fight over the theft of a deed to a ranch. The Raskobs possess the deed, and Bullard seeks to reclaim the property for his children, Bobby and Linda (Nelson and Ann Carroll), who believe him dead. From a mineshaft hideout, Bullard goes prowling. Threatened by Max Raskob (Bill Patton), he kills the malicious hick and leaves an Ace of Spades—the fabled death card—as a threatening signature.

Chalky Raskob (Blackjack Ward) sets out to kill a neighbor (Lafe McKee) but winds up slain by Bullard. The Raskobs murder Bullard's friend Dad Burns (Ed Coxen), then mistake Deputy Dave Danford (Lease) for their nemesis. Bullard seizes the deed. Danford and Bobby take refuge as patriarch Rufe Raskob (Lloyd Ingraham) leads a siege. Bullard opens fire on a box of dynamite. Bull Raskob (Blackie Whiteford) attacks, but Bobby and Dave gain the advantage. The evil hillbilly topples over a cliff.

Rex Lease, stocky and athletic, makes a relentless hero. Bobby Nelson—a little kid in horse operas of 1930-1933—is by now almost as tall as Lease and cuts as dashing a figure with the horsemanship and the scrapping. Much appeal rests with such familiar faces as Lloyd Ingraham, Lafe McKee, Ed Coxen (an early star with D.W. Griffith), and Bill Desmond. (Some producers shunned the old-timers in the foolish assumption that the customers might perceive the movies as outdated.) Igraham, formerly a noted director, is fine as the clan leader.

Prominent among the inbred lot is Jerome "Blackjack" Ward, who resembles Elisha Cook, Jr., in aspect and weasly mannerisms. Ward would become notorious in 1940 for gunning down a fellow bad-guy actor, unarmed, at a hangout for movie cowboys—a deed which was ruled an act of self-defense.

Director Jack Jevne and writer John West were one person—namely, Jack Levine—who had co-scripted *I Cover the Waterfront*, among other, bigger pictures, and later worked for Hal Roach. His screenplay for *The Ghost Rider* contains nuançes unusual for a matinée western. Likewise for the photography by Art Reed and James Diamond.

Courageous Avenger

Supreme Pictures Corp. • 1935

Here we find another gem by Robert North Bradbury that is anything but run-of-the-mill. The opening sequence sets the ominous tone as an unconscious prospector is dragged away to a life of enslavement. Murder follows, along with the macabre discovery of silver bullets in the corpse. The leading lady is afflicted with a lustful stepfather, who also has ordered the slaying of her brother. Johnny Mack Brown stares in horror as a dead slave is dragged away. An aged prisoner raves: "Death is better! I'm going to set us all free!" and attempts to kill everybody in sight. Absent is the genre's customary comical sidekick— or any other leavening, for that matter, other than a more prominent element of romance than usual.

In Death Valley, Gorman (Warner Richmond) and four henchmen chain a half-dead prospector to an ore-grinding machine alongside other emaciated men. Elsewhere, Dick Stonewell (Wally West), while delivering a shipment of gold from the Davis Mine, is murdered by the Gorman mob. Enter Marshal Kirk Baxter (Brown), who is engaged to marry Stonewell's sister, Beth (Helen Ericson). Three .44-calibre silver slugs link the case to the slayings of other Davis employees. The trail ends in the desert. Baxter sends Beth away via stagecoach lest her stepfather, Carson (Ed Cassidy), a partner in the mine, persist at abusing her. Upon learning that the coach contains a payload of gold, Baxter rides in pursuit—but finds the driver dead in the wreckage. Carson had alerted Gorman via carrier pigeon.

Baxter hogties a henchman (Eddie Parker) and locates the hideout. He finds Beth imprisoned. Carson betrays Baxter's ruse, and the lawman is chained to the grinder. The gang rides out. Baxter prevents a maddened slave (Earl Dwire) from blowing up the mine, then frees the captives, kills the remaining outlaws, and sends Beth for the law. Baxter gets the drop on the bandits. Gorman breaks for freedom, but Baxter bulldogs him in a rodeo-style tackle.

The picture is stamped with Bob Bradbury's inimitable style. The director's signature swish-pan device catches Brown leaving town, then lashes ahead to arrive with him at a wrecked wagon. There is excellent scenic photography of the Alabama Hills with snow-capped Mt. Whitney in the distance, and of the edge of Death Valley at the foot of the arid Panamint crags. Cinematographer E.L. McManigal achieves maximum pictorial value. One gliding move, from a long shot of the desert to a closer view of horsemen at a dried lakebed, has the look of a crane shot—but producer A.W. Hackel could not have afforded such a rental on location. The swoop probably was shot from a camera car, inasmuch as the running chase scenes are equally flawless. (And no, it is not a zoom shot.)

Willowy Helen Ericson seems more like an eastern socialite than a desert dweller. She soon found a more congenial situation as a contract player at 20th Century-Fox. Warner Richmond, Ed Cassidy, and stuntman Eddie Parker expertly project evil. One curious scene, likely a sop to the censors, has Richmond explain to Erickson that she will not be harmed. Earl Dwire makes as much of his mad scene as he does with a brief appearance in *The Rogues' Tavern*. Wally West performs a wagon chase and a death fall without a stunt double.

The value of Johnny Mack Brown to such a picture cannot be overstated. In addition to his dramatic chops and personable nature, he also handled most of his stunts—and happened to be the most handsome of the movie cowboys. Brown performs a great deal of hard riding and engages in an unusually brutal fight with Parker. It is clearly Brown who rides a wagon tongue amidst four horses as the ground flashes past. Action ace Yakima Canutt performs the highlight of this stunt, however, when he drops to the ground and clings to the rear of the wagon, but it is Brown who then climbs aboard. Brown's genteel southern accent underscores the ferocity of the dialogue: "If you make one false move, I'll make a sieve out of you!"

Courageous Avenger inspired a remake (which neglected to acknowledge the source) during the 1950s, as an episode of the network-television series *Cimarron City*.

Forgotten Horrors of 1936

Jaws of the Jungle

a.k.a.: *Jungle Virgin*
Jay Dee Kay Productions • Continental Pictures • 1936

Authentic, expertly made expeditionary footage forms the basis of *Jaws of the Jungle*, J.D. Kendis' pageantlike tale of Third World horrors. Clever editing (by Holbrook N. Todd) makes it appear that some unknown species of gigantic vampire bat is attacking. The episode is hardly true to nature, but it is more convincing than the hijinks of 1930's *Ingagi*.

Narrator Cliff Howell introduces a Ceylonese village, where Teeto and Minta (indigenous tribespeople) declare their betrothal. A swarm of vampires swoops in. Escaping into the jungles, the villagers find only further perils. A leopard kills a woman in labor, and a python crushes a tribal elder. A rival to Teeto stirs dissent. Teeto proposes a ritual sacrifice of an old man and a child, as if to gain some cosmic

blessing. A savage fight ends in the rival's slaying by a tiger. The tribe finds a hidden valley, safe from the vampires.

The bat-attack business inspired a sequence in *Indiana Jones and the Temple of Doom* (1984). The creatures here are fruit bats—huge and scary, with a wingspread of up to five feet, but harmless to man.

Provincial censors assailed *Jaws of the Jungle* for such elements as nudity, a ceremonial mutilation, and the shoving over a cliff of a cart containing sacrificial victims—whereupon the man is devoured by a python, which the natives proceed to cut open. Hollywood's institutionalized censorship machine demanded scissoring on similar grounds. The story sustains interest with or without the supposedly objectionable elements, although writer Eddie Graneman overburdens the telling with voice-over narration.

Thunderbolt

Regal Productions • 1936

A heroic dog is the title character of Stuart Paton's crudely exhilarating study in violence and retribution. In a holdup gone haywire, two corrupt frontier lawmen kill an express office clerk, the local sheriff, and a dog belonging to the clerk's son. A miner (Kane Richmond) is accused. The miner's police dog, Thunderbolt (played by Lobo the Marvel Dog), and the clerk's son (Bobby Nelson) track a stolen cargo of gold to a barn. One of the outlaws (Frank Hagney) chokes the boy

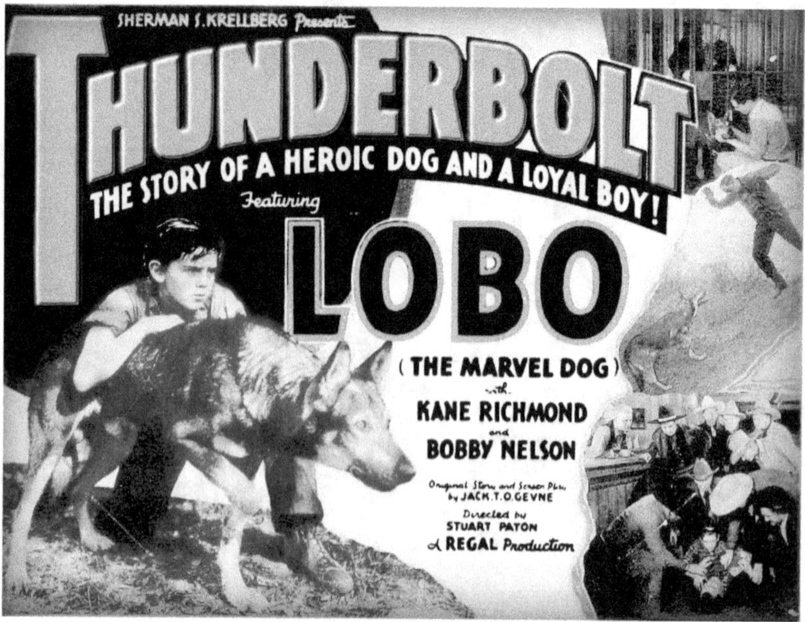

into unconsciousness. The barn catches fire. Thunderbolt rescues the youngster and leaves the killer to roast.

Variety, an influential and often condescending show-business publication, found *Thunderbolt* a reprehensible film, bemoaning its brutality for the sake of throwing a sop to the anti-violence stance of the industry's Production Code Administration and its parasitic attachment, the Legion of Decency. The Legion, a mob of blue-nosed Jesuits at war with the First Amendment, had obtained a choke-hold upon the film industry in mid-1934. A prominent early sacrifice was the scissoring of Edgar G. Ulmer's *The Black Cat*. By 1936, the censorship machine had grown so overconfident as sometimes to overlook the smaller pictures.

Hence *Variety*'s backstabbing reminder that the Code was supposed to have put a halt to such irresponsible thrill-mongering. In fact, the violence is the saving grace: the picture might otherwise just sit there looking shabby. Screenwriter Jack Jevne (*né* Jack Levine) deploys a menace as hateful as the degenerate hillbillies of *The Ghost Rider*, in conflict with the same juvenile lead, Bobby Nelson. Roland C. Price's camerawork does more passive observing than propulsive storytelling, however, and the acting is less than convincing. Lobo the Marvel Dog is no Rin-Tin-Tin, but the animal knows how to strike an intimidating pose. Sherman S. Krellberg's short-lived Regal Productions, Inc., a spin-off of Regal Distributing Corp., made only four pictures, all during 1936.

The Dark Hour

Chesterfield Motion Pictures Corp. • 1936

Here is Chesterfield in its right element, if hardly its finest moment: Charles Lamont's *The Dark Hour* draws upon a popular novel, Sinclair Gluck's *The Last Trap*. Ewart Adamson's screenplay packs a classically shadow-laden Old Dark House (a substantial rental set) with suspicious characters. Suspense is lacking, but weirdness prevails as a killer in drag stalks the inmates.

Elsa Carson (Irene Ware) enlists a detective, Jim Landis (Ray Walker), and his retired colleague, Paul Bernard (Berton Churchill), lest harm befall her eccentric uncles, Henry and Charles (William V. Mong and Hobart Bosworth). The sleuths find Elsa evasive after Henry is slain. The butler (E.E. Clive) gives a vague account of how he had found the body. Suspects include family and servants alike. The discovery among Elsa's clothing of somebody else's dress confuses matters further. Charles, who has been disguising himself as a woman, proves to have been a busy arsonist. The victims (now including the butler) may have known too much. Further complications implicate another servant. The murders turn out to have two perpetrators, each unaware of the other.

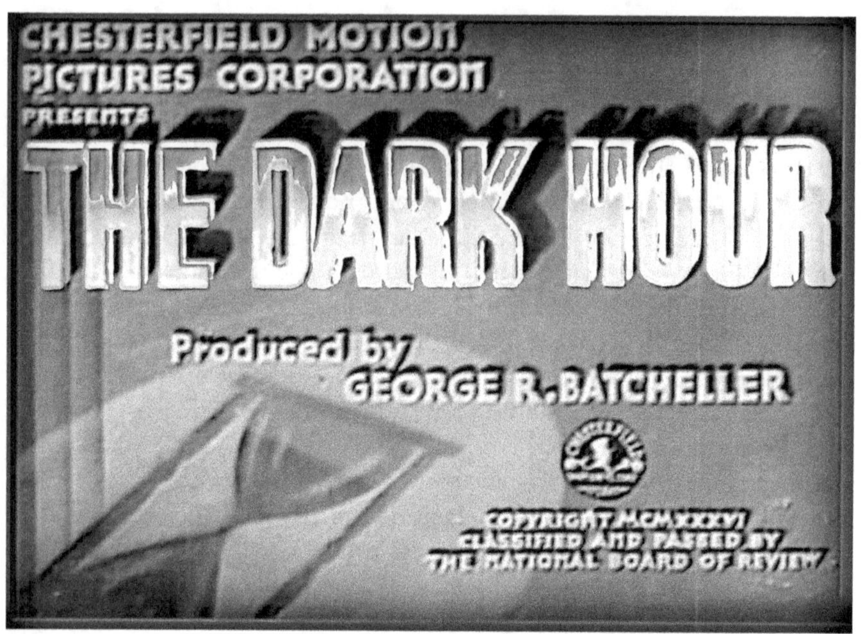

Irene Ware, also of Universal's *The Raven* (1935), is well suited to a bright and assertive role. Ray Walker reins in his customarily brash energy as a love-struck detective. Berton Churchill, as the more venerable investigator, finds a respite from pompous-crook typecasting. Hobart Bosworth and Scrooge-like William V. Mong are the eccentric brothers. Fred Kelsey offers comedy relief as a befuddled cop. Hedda Hopper, soon to find prominence as a celebrity-gossip hack in the newspaper racket, is an indignant suspect who becomes a romantic interest for Churchill.

The Lion Man

Normandy Pictures Corp. • 1936

Little known even among the *Tarzan* enthusiasts, John McCarthy's reasonably loyal adaptation of E.R. Burroughs is the final production of Normandy Pictures Corp., whose output of six titles is otherwise confined to westerns. *The Lion Man*'s Ronald Chatham (played by Charles Locher) is a desert-bound counterpart to Burroughs' jungle-dwelling Lord Greystoke. The story, adapted by Richard Gordon and John Williams, has to do with a caravan raid of which Ronald (as a child) is the lone survivor. He grows up in the care of an Arabian sage, who teaches the boy to commune with lions. The adult Ronald takes revenge on the marauding sheik (Ted Adams) who had led the massacre.

Charles Locher (*né* Loucheur) was en route to a crucial rechristening: He worked briefly as Lloyd Crane, but then as Jon Hall he would take

the lead in John Ford's *The Hurricane* (1937). The assignment established Hall as one of the more important action-adventure stars, with
such crackerjack entries as *Invisible Agent* and *Invisible Man's Revenge*
(1943–1944), *Arabian Nights* (1942), and *Last of the Redmen* (1947). Hall
became a television star during the 1950s, with *Ramar of the Jungle*.

The leading lady is the beauteous Kathleen Burke, still struggling to
no avail to shake the exotic typecasting that *Island of Lost Souls* (1932)
had imposed upon her. (She had sought that panther-woman assignment, of course, only to find the image an albatross.)

A silent-screen version is *The Lad and the Lion*, from 1917—same
year, same title, as Burroughs' original story.

The Leavenworth Case

Republic Pictures Corp. • 1936

Silas Leavenworth is an aged moneybags stock-market predator who proposes to ease his conscience with a charitable bequest. This provocation to greedy heirs distinguishes Anna Catherine Green's *The Leavenworth Case* as a building-block of modern detective fiction. (Wilkie Collins' *The Moonstone* is another such cornerstone title.)

The 1936 adaptation of Green's 1878 novel works well as a conventional Mystery Farce derivative, sparked by the gimmick of having murder dispensed by a trained monkey. The picture is more significant, however, as a benchmark pointing toward the British-European censors' ban upon horror that in 1937 would leave the genre high and

dry in Hollywood. No one picture could have provoked the embargo, of course, but Republic Pictures made some telling concessions in this instance, to the detriment of the industry-at-large.

The British Board of Censors voiced misgivings over *The Leavenworth Case* for its suggestion that an upstanding physician might be capable of murder. The English censors had objected to Universal's *Frankenstein* and Paramount's *Island of Lost Souls* during 1931–1932—both boasting fundamental contributions from respectably British talents—for those films' shared Promethean conceit, and had threatened to bar *Life Returns* in view of its claim to documentary fact. On into the late 1930s and the 1940s, even after the ban had collapsed during 1938–1939, the British censors would reserve a singular revulsion toward such truer-to-life bad-doctor melodramas as Paramount's ironically titled *The Mad Doctor* and Fox's *Shock*. All this reactionary reverence toward the healing profession, from a society whose Jack-the-Ripper was likely as not an influential physician of royal connections.

When the British censors told Republic—in advance of production—that they would not permit a picture depicting a fiendish healer, Republic foolishly cowered, back-pedaling to create a variant framing scene and finale. *The Leavenworth Case* and its alternate-reality fill-ins were shot between late November and mid-December of 1935. This remarkable indulgence could not have been allowed to become a habit: fancy a polite version of every American horror picture for the daintier sensibilities of the U.K. market!

Dr. Truman Hartwell (Donald Cook) affirms the robust health of Silas Leavenworth (Frank Sheridan). Hartwell is in love with Silas' young wife, Gloria (Erin O'Brien-Moore). Leavenworth wants to leave his estate to charity. The family is appalled. Niece Eleanor (Jean Rouverol) declares that she will thwart the plan. Silas is found dead—apparently a suicide. Henry Clavering (Gavin Gordon), Leavenworth's business partner and Eleanor's fiancé, is found to have embezzled a fortune. Gloria accuses Hartwell, who accuses Eleanor. Silas' old-maid sister, Phoebe Leavenworth (cranky Maude Eburne), proves to have been poisoning Silas by degrees while waiting to dispose of additional members of the family. Finally, the agent of murder proves to have been Hartwell's pet monkey, which had been trained to open a gas jet in Silas' chambers.

In the retooled version for the British market, Hartwell reveals that he had suspected Phoebe and trained his monkey to replace Silas' nightly meal with an uncontaminated dish—but that the damage had already been done.

Originally planned as a Monogram project, *The Leavenworth Case* suffered other frustrations en route to completion. The property lapsed to the newly organized Republic, which had absorbed Monogram. Warners loaned William Gargan for a key detective role, but at the last moment Norman Foster was installed, instead. Director Arthur Lubin had been attached, but Lewis D. Collins stepped in. For all its difficulties, *The Leavenworth Case* holds together well, with Frank Sheridan in fine curmudgeonly form as the late-to-repent speculator; Maude Eburne as a matronly menace with the good intention of killing bad people; and Warren Hymer contributing his specialty as a thick-headed investigator.

The first filming of *The Leavenworth Case*, directed by Charles Giblyn, dates from 1923.

I Conquer the Sea!

a.k.a. Sea Bandits
Halperin Pictures • Academy Pictures • Favorite Films • 1936

Edward and Victor Hugo Halperin, the methodical artists responsible for *White Zombie*, spent much of a year filming a Newfoundland whaling crew in action. Their point was to impart authenticity to this romantic-triangle tragedy called *I Conquer the Sea!* The result is unsatisfactory in dramatic terms, but the locations lend realism.

I Conquer the Sea!, with its protracted agonizing over emotional disloyalties and physical disabilities, makes for a strange companion-piece to such Halperin Bros. spookers as *Supernatural* (1933), *Revolt of the Zombies*, and of course *White Zombie*. A ghostly apparition at the conclusion of *I Conquer the Sea!* lends a slight thematic consistency: horror is where one finds it, as H.P. Lovecraft had argued.

Stanley Morner plays Tommy, a master harpoonist, who loves Rosita Gonzales (Steffi Duna), a Portugese immigrant. Rosita's brother, Pedro (Johnnie Pirrone, Jr.), cannot walk. When Tommy's brother, Leonard (Douglas Walton), a surgeon, corrects the disability, Rosita becomes enamored of Leonard. Tommy loses an arm during a whaling expedition but has no better sense than to head out with Leonard on another ill-starred voyage. The brothers find themselves stranded on an outcropping of rock. Leonard swims to summon assistance. Tommy chooses to drown. At length, his disembodied spirit drops in on his own memorial ceremony.

Apart from a copyright complaint that dragged on into the 1950s, the most interesting thing about this syrupy mess is the early starring role for Stanley Morner, as the doomed brother. The Wisconsin-born actor was handling lesser roles at MGM when the big studio loaned him out to the Halperins for the present assignment. Morner changed his performing name in 1938 to Richard Stanley, then finally settled

on Dennis Morgan—an identity that would see him through such pictures of interest as *Waterfront* and the *The Return of Dr. X* (both from 1939) and into a lasting stardom in musical comedies and action pictures. Morgan toplined the television series *21 Beacon Street* during the late 1950s.

Screenwriter Richard Carroll, meanwhile, grew to believe that *I Conquer the Sea!* owed more to his brilliance than to any artistry on the part of the Halperins. As late as 1951, Carroll was haranguing the tradepapers about a crackpot scheme to sue for distribution rights—even as he declared that all rights were contracted to revert to him, in any event. By which time, of course, *I Conquer the Sea!* and its proxy-title reissue version, *Sea Bandits*, had long since ceased to exert any bankable attraction outside the small-change provincial circuits. One can only wonder whether Carroll had actually bothered to watch the picture, which is hardly something to make an author proud.

A Face in the Fog

Victory Pictures Corp. • 1936

One of several Victory features based upon stories by Peter B. Kyne, Robert F. "Bob" Hill's *A Face in the Fog* has an unusually macabre murder plot and a pleasing ensemble cast. (The source is Kyne's "The Great Mono Miracle.") On the debit side are cheapskate production values—producer Sam Katzman's specialty—and sound reproduction approximating the primitive standards of 1929. Katzman had come to filmmaking at 13 in 1914 as a prop boy; he became a production manager and an assistant producer during the 1920s. In 1931, he produced for Screencraft, a subsidiary of Universal Pictures, and he assisted A.W. Hackel on a series of Bob Steele westerns during the middle 1930s.

Katzman launched Victory Pictures in 1936. During nearly a four-year period, he made 32 feature-lengthers and two serials at his own studio in Culver City. A New York-born Yiddish extrovert of the cigar-chomping old school, Katzman had a knack for stretching minuscule budgets over bankable products—a talent that would serve him into the 1970s. When we became acquainted with Katzman during the mid-century, he joked about his nickname of "Jungle Sam" (a reference to his *Jungle Jim* pictures, post-WWII, with Johnny Weissmuller) and told fascinating yarns about his affiliations with such exalted artists as George Zucco,

Lloyd Hughes and Judy Collyer.

Bela Lugosi, and John Carradine. Katzman wavered between unabashed disparagement and moneymaking pride in discussing his pictures.

A Face in the Fog finds a homicidal hunchback, the Fiend, attacking the cast of a show by playwright Peter Fortune (Lawrence Gray). Newspaperwoman Jean Monroe (June Collyer) hints that she can identify the Fiend. Reporter Frank Gordon (Lloyd Hughes) rescues Jean from an ambush. The victims have been poisoned by an untraceable chemical. Fortune proves to have lost a brother in a theatre fire. Fortune, caught while loading frozen pellets of poison into a gun, is slain in a police raid.

Victory retained a consistent production crew throughout—largely the same technical personnel involved with Puritan Pictures' titles, also under Katzman's ægis. Casting has a stock-company atmosphere. The likes of Lloyd Hughes, Lawrence Gray, Jack Mulhall, and Herman Brix saw duty in most of the Victory releases. Katzman discontinued the Victory line in 1937 but retained the studio base and became identified with such corporate brands as Puritan Pictures, Mercury Pictures, and Clover Productions, alias Four Leaf Productions and Four Bells Productions. Katzman continued as an independent affiliated with Monogram, later with Columbia, and eventually even with MGM. He died in 1973.

The show-business setting of *A Face in the Fog* recalls Universal's *The Last Warning* (1928), on which *Fog*'s director, Robert F. "Bob" Hill, had assisted the German master Paul Leni. Hill had become Universal's top serial director during the silent era, but his career faltered in a siege of ill health during the 1930s. The acting and direction of *A Face in the Fog* are old-fashioned, and the deficient budget limits the imaginative possibilities. There are plenty of mysterious characters, however, along with generous comic relief from Al St. John as a bumbling photographer—and a surprise ending that makes sense.

Intermission:
Additional Titles of Interest

The following titles lend perspective and kinship among titles:

- *Bridge of Sighs* (Invincible-Chesterfield; 1936). Dorothy Tree, as the sister of a man framed in a case of murder, subjects herself to the terrors of a women's prison in order to get the goods on the genuine culprit. Onslow Stevens is a love-struck district attorney. Phil Rosen, a persistent central figure in the *Forgotten Horrors* canon, directs.

- *Murder at Glen Athol*, a.k.a. *The Criminal Within* (Invincible-Chesterfield; 1936). Dapper John Miljan is a detective-turned-author who stumbles into a tangle of insanity, adultery, blackmail, bludgeonings, stabbings, and poisonings. The Legion of Decency must have been snoozing when lethal lady Iris Adrian hides incriminating papers in her cleavage and must fend off efforts to nab them. The papers, that is. The title elicits unwholesome snickering when uttered today—not unlike Warners' *The Amazing Dr. Clitterhouse*, in that regard.

- *West of Nevada* (Colony Pictures; 1936). This Rex Bell sagebrusher pivots upon a curious mingling of gold mining and taxidermy, with a mob of claim jumpers seeking to do away with a community of Indian miners.

- *The President's Mystery* (Republic Pictures; 1936). Phil Rosen directs an adaptation of Fulton Oursler's *Liberty* magazine serial—rendered inordinately famous by Oursler's claim that the yarn had been suggested by Franklin D. Roosevelt. (Oursler, alias Anthony Abbot, was a relentless name dropper.) The creepy nugget buried within is a dead-of-night scene where Henry Wilcoxson, as a lawyer covering his tracks, procures a corpse to stage a false demise.

- *She-Devil Island*, a.k.a. *Irma la Mala* (First Division-Grand National; 1936). The superficially Americanized repackaging of this Mexican production made a bundle for the chronically unstable Grand National brand. Pedro Armendáriz stars, directed by Raphaél Sevilla, in a tale of "Nature in the Raw—Wild Virgins in the Flesh!" Quote/Unquote.

- *Race Suicide*, a.k.a. *What Price Passion?* and *Victims of Passion* (Willis Kent Productions, Real Life Dramas, and DeLuxe pictures; 1937). Anti-abortion mania arises from pandering schlockmeister Willis Kent attempted sop to the Roman Catholic Church's Legion of Decency while dealing in the customary legalized voyeurism and repressive morality cop posturing. (The censors were unfavorably impressed, despite shared repressive social-political views.) The film likens its abortion racketeer to the mad doctors of conventional B-movie lineage, but Kent and his hack writers cannot resist preaching.

- *Round-Up Time in Texas* (Republic; 1937). Gene Autry and Lester "Smiley" Burnette square off against jungle perils better suited to Frank Buck or Clyde Beatty, with a diamond strike in South Africa as the provocation to mayhem. Burnette harmonizes with the Cabin Kids, an ensemble belovéd among admirers of the *Our Gang* comedies. Way off the beaten path—hence the term *offbeat*.

- *Blazing Barriers* (Monogram; 1937). Aubrey Scotto's juvenile-delinquency piece takes on disaster-movie undertones in a forest-fire climax. Hoodlums Frank "Junior" Coghlan and Edward Arnold, Jr., find a shot at redemption with the Civilian Conservation Corps. A homicidal rampage meets the quota for violent derangement.

- *Island Captives* (Falcon Film & Wm. Steiner; 1937). The western-movie device of a land-grab conspiracy, transplanted to Tahiti, places Eddie Nugent and Joan Barclay at odds with tribal temptress Carmen La Roux. Forrest Taylor accounts for the element of menace.

- *The Dead March* (Bud Pollard Productions & Imperial Productions; 1937). A year before Abel Gance remade his war-against-war epic of 1919, *J'accuse!* (*I Accuse!*), Bud Pollard delivered this found-footage tract as a *pro*-war piece. Stock scenes include the sinking of *The St. Stephan*, an Austrian ship. The fallen unknown soldiers of various nations rise from the grave to declare warmongering motivations. Pollard timed the release to coincide with the American Legion's national convention in New York. Pollard is the artist responsible for *The Horror*, that rickety supporting beam of the *Forgotten Horrors* shelf.

- *Der Dybuk*, a.k.a. *The Dybbuk* (Warzawskie Biuro Kinematograficzne Feniks & Foreign Cinema Arts; 1937-1938). Michael Waszynski's supernatural romantic fantasy, filmed in Poland with American Jewish underwriting, concerns a tragic betrothal and the consequences of tampering with generations unborn. The U.S. version retains the Yiddish dialogue, with English subtitles. A Talmudic scholar dies in a seizure of supernatural ecstasy, only to return as a demanding spirit in possession of his intended bride. One of the finer examples of the short-lived heyday of Yiddish cinema, *Der Dybuk* showcases many talents who would soon run afoul of the Nazi incursion. The film demonstrates two endangered societies: the realm of Yiddish dramatic artistry and pre-WWII Poland itself, both of which would change beyond recognition within half the span of a generation. Further discussion of the Yiddish cinema and its sporadic resurgence in America—where that rich culture would be absorbed almost entirely into a more homogenized Hebrew America—will figure in a second *Forgotten Horrors Omnibus* edition.

Darkest Africa

a.k.a.: King of Jungleland • Bat Men of Africa
Republic Pictures Corp. • 1936

The first serial to bear the Republic brand was an enormous success and the harbinger of great things for a generation to come. Planned as a Mascot sequel to *The Lost Jungle*, the film was produced under Nat Levine's supervision for the negative cost—the cumulative fee for the finished negative film, that is—of $119,343, a fortune by comparison with Mascot's budgets. Portions were shot during two weeks' location work during October and November of 1935 at W.A. "Snake" King's Jungleland, near Brownsville, Texas. A month was then spent shooting at the studio and among the rocks at Chatsworth, California.

The Texas site afforded access to a menagerie collected by King, *né* William Abraham Lieberman. (He had legally altered his name to Snake King, owing to his dealership in serpents, and signed his correspondence with "Rattling Yours.") Jungleland also provided experienced handlers, tropical scenery (augmented with boulders hauled in from Hollywood), and especially King's 12-year-old son, Manuel King. Billed as the World's Youngest Wild Animal Trainer, the chubby youngster could handle 20 lions at a time as though they were kittens. Manuel, an ideal sidekick for Clyde Beatty, plays Baru, a white boy raised in the jungle. Beatty helps Baru to rescue his sister, Valerie

(Elaine Shepherd), from a hidden city. High Priest Dagna (Lucien Prival) has enthroned the girl as a goddess. Beatty, Baru, and the boy's trained gorilla (Ray Corrigan, *né* Raymond Benard) strike out through a forbidden valley—trailed by diamond pirates Durkin and Craddock (Wheeler Oakman and Edmund Cobb). Further perils arise from Dagna's Bat Men and a tribe that worships the only tigers in Africa.

Captures, escapes, recaptures, and epic destruction follow in keeping with classic chapter-play custom. Amidst the frenzy of a rebellion, a wizard (Edward McWade) disguises himself as Valerie for a sacrificial leap, invoking a curse that triggers a volcanic eruption. Clyde and his friends head homeward.

Even more fantastically conceived than *The Phantom Empire*, *Darkest Africa* sports astounding photographic effects beyond Mascot's capabilities. The soaring Bat Men, convincing even at close range, are represented in many scenes by seven-foot figures of balsa wood, gliding along invisible wires. (The designer is Howard Lydecker.) Flocks of other such mannequins, fashioned from rubber to various scales, soar over the lost city. The finale, a spectacular upheaval, might better have been served by an over-cranked camera to suggest a greater density in the outpouring of lava.

The acting is barely adequate, but directors B. Reeves Eason and Joseph Kane seldom allow the pace to lag. The feats of Beatty and Manuel King compensate for any histrionic shortcomings. Lucien Prival, hampered by a respiratory illness, walks through a menacing role that could have been his best. Both a Bat Man leader and the heroic gorilla are played by Raymond Benard, who as Ray "Crash" Corrigan would star in Republic's next serial, *Undersea Kingdom*. Corrigan's ape-suit role alternates between amusing and frightening moves. He gave a name to each costume; this one was called Naba. Ray Turner, also a prominent villager in *King Kong*, lends a vigorously comical presence as a loyal servant to Beatty. Edward McWade is impressive as a tragic sorceror, and the villainy of Wheeler Oakman and Edmund Cobb is formidable. The animal action is augmented by footage from *The Lost Jungle*. Former Fox maestro Arthur Kay's elaborate musical scoring, augmented by stirring library cues, establishes a standard for orchestral finery that would characterize Republic over the long term. Co-director B. Reeves Eason composed the wild chant of the Tiger Men.

Portions of *Darkest Africa* can be seen in documentarian Errol Morris' *Fast, Cheap, and Out of Control* (1998), illustrating the reminiscences of a veteran trainer with the Clyde Beatty Circus. The last surviving member of the *Darkest Africa* team, Manuel King, lived on until age 92 in 2016, having spent a lifetime in the animal-handling profession.

The Rogues' Tavern

Puritan Pictures • Mercury Pictures • 1936

Sam Katzman, his signature style evident despite an uncharacteristic richness of production, delivered *The Rogues' Tavern* outside his Victory Pictures orbit, involving key Victory personnel. The producer goes unmentioned in the screen credits.

Katzman's penchant for stretching dollars—an extreme example is the chintzy Mexican folk-art puppet that he imposed upon 1957's *The Giant Claw*—also meant that he knew how to utilize found finery to grand effect. *The Rogues' Tavern* has gone unrecognized as a benchmark

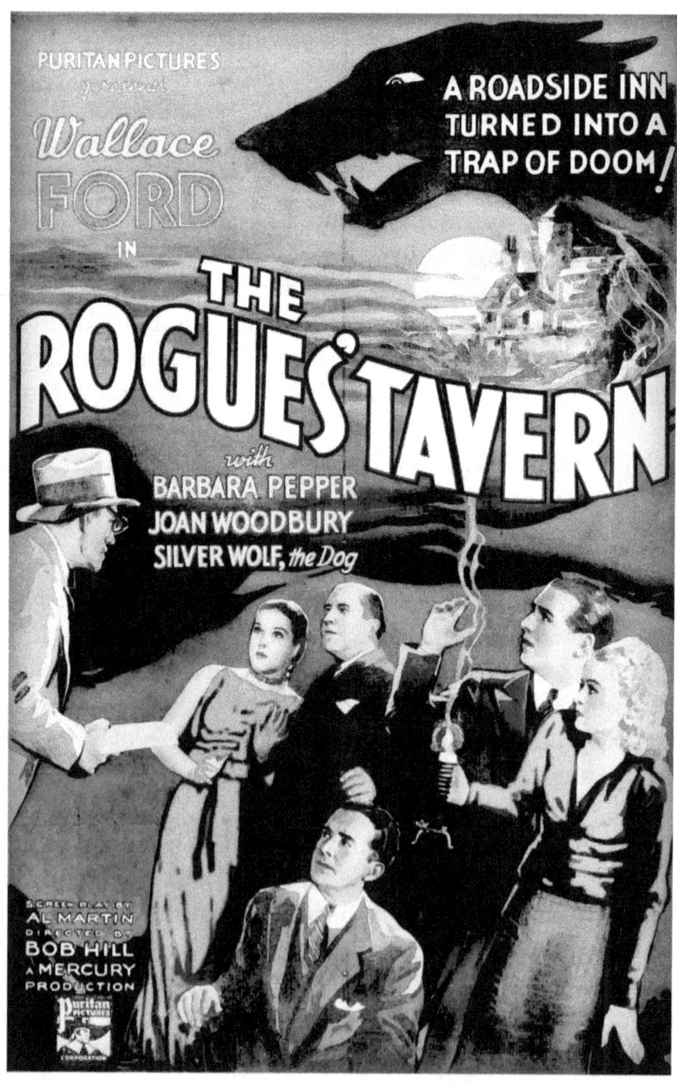

in Katzman's long career, largely because the picture looks like a million bucks. The tale itself is pure rambunctious Poverty Row, every sentence seeming to end in an exclamation point, and more power to it.

Homicidal weirdness is afoot at a rural lodge, the destination of Detective Jimmy Flavin (Wallace Ford) and his fiancée, Marjorie (Barbara Pepper). "The person that killed those two men used a set of false dog teeth!" Flavin announces upon deciphering a clue. A jewel-smuggling mob has arrived. Worse than the fabled dark and stormy night, this is "the kind of night that gives me the willies!"—as an ignoramus handyman (Vincent Dennis) declares.

The criminals have been lured by forged letters. A police dog (played by the handsome Silver Wolf, another heir presumptive to Rin-Tin-Tin) is safely in tow when another slaying occurs. Flavin finds a fanged device shaped like the head of a dog. Suspicion falls upon an intruder (Earl Dwire) who bears a grudge against the smugglers. This red herring device gives way to the matronly innkeeper (Clara Kimball Young), who harbors an even greater grudge and cares not whom she kills. Flavin pounces from hiding to rescue the dwindled party.

The most coveted scene-dock prop at RKO-Pathé Studio was a fireplace that had cost $1,000 in 1932—originally built for a Constance Bennett picture, *Lady with a Past*. After Pathé had become a leasing lot, manager G.B. Howe often played referée among independent producers who wanted to use the mantelpiece. Not only did Katzman secure the elegant property: it was a coup for such a little outfit to gain a berth at Pathé because larger producers had leased space, and the studio had barred most smaller companies by demanding minimum budgets of between $25,000 and $40,000. (An RKO budget, when that charmed fireplace was manufactured, ran into the hundreds of thousands of dollars.) The settings alone make *The Rogues' Tavern* the most sumptuous of Sam Katzman's productions, early or late.

The surprises range beyond the real estate, however: hardly the least of many revelations is the exposure (none too convincingly) of the gentle Clara Kimball Young as a serial killer. The method of murder—"false dog teeth," indeed!—may be unique in cinema. Wallace Ford and Barbara Pepper give a lively team performance patterned after William Powell and Myrna Loy in MGM's *The Thin Man* (1934). The luscious Joan Woodbury lends a sinister allure as one of the endangered criminals; her revealing attire suggests pre-Legion of Decency 1934 more so than censor-hounded 1936. Earl Dwire shines briefly as a most Karloffian mad-scientist type. The radially composed camerawork contains fluid dolly shots and lateral tracking to emphasize the grandeur of the settings.

Al Martin's unpredictable screenplay contains a wealth of wise-cracks and lowbrow comedy. Ford pronounces the suspected dog to be "very clever. … After he kills …, he cuts the telephone wires." And when Ford reveals that he is "traveling incognito," dimwitted flunky Vincent Dennis stammers: "I thought you came in a bus!"

Hair-Trigger Casey

Berke-Perrin Blue Ribbon Productions • Atlantic Pictures Corp. • 1936

Herewith, a picture to confound all who like their genres nearly compartmentalized: Harry Fraser's *Hair-Trigger Casey* merges Yellow Peril chills with frontier thrills, then cements the mixture with whodunit mystery and psychological horror. Like a charm, it works.

Late in 1935, veteran producer William Berke announced that Berke-Perrin Blue Ribbon Productions would deliver six actioners starring Jack Perrin. Tall, rock-jawed handsome, and deep of voice, Perrin was ideal for such a series. He had performed with Mack Sennett's Keystone Cops slapstick troupe before joining the Navy during World War I; played the lead in Erich von Stroheim's *Blind Husbands* in 1919; and starred in features and serials for at least 10 companies during the 1920s.

At the end of the silent era, Perrin made westerns for Universal. Typecast as a frontiersman, he wavered during the 1930s between stardom on Poverty Row and supporting assignments at the major-league studios. The Berke productions sought to restore Perrin to prominence, but they became his last starring roles: at the dawn of a new age of crooning-cowboy mania, Perrin could neither sing nor play a guitar. The Blue Ribbon pictures aside from *Casey* are *Wildcat Saunders*, *Desert Justice*, *Song of the Gun*, *Gun Grit*, and *Border Ranger*.

Perrin takes a worthy turn in *Hair-Trigger Casey* as a hardened Army officer who tackles a murder investigation and runs afoul of slave-smugglers and a tong executioner. He barks orders, rides hard, and shoots down the badmen in a manner that would become almost a thing of the past as the Hollywood western mutated into melody and romance.

Capt. Jim Casey (Perrin), summoned home to his borderlands ranch, stops in a Chinatown district. He encounters Karney (Ed Cassidy), his foreman and war buddy, who narrowly escapes death in an attack by a Chinese hatchet man, Lee Fin (Victor Wong). Casey learns of the slaying of a cowhand whose sister, Jane Elkins (Betty Mack), is Casey's sweetheart. A Chinese-smuggling slavery racket proves to be the work of the ranch's cook (Phil Dunham), another cowboy (Budd Buster)—and Karney. Karney disguises himself as a Mexican while robbing the Chinese immigrants, a practice that has earned the wrath of Lee Fin's tong. Karney gets the drop on Casey but is killed by Lee Fin.

Perrin's frequent cohort, Wally Wales, plays the protagonist's crack-shot kid brother. Betty Mack's subdued, reactive role is a far cry from her showy presence in *God's Country and the Man*.

Ed Cassidy, minus his signature moustache, is at his most despicable as a pal-turned-antagonist. Here is a role of depth, with Cassidy's Karney aware of his nature but unable to change. When Perrin's Casey rescues him in a wartime sequence, Karney says, "You should have left me in that shell hole. I'm not worth it." As death approaches, the line is repeated. Karney beats helpless Chinese prisoners, but when exposed he reveals where the captives can be found. The big death scene is a shocker, with the sound-effects department providing a ghastly *chop!* as the hatchet buries itself between Cassidy's shoulderblades.

Casting against type finds the usually comical codgers, Phil Dunham and Budd Buster, as villains; the often villainous Robert Walker as an honest border patrolman; and Victor Wong—the lovable Charlie of *King Kong* and *Son of Kong* (1933)—as the hatchet man. Fred "Snowflake" Toones, the hefty black comedian, is as genial as ever despite the script's dismissal of him as "that boy" and ill treatment by friend and foe alike. Toones manages some nice improvisations, his specialty, in which he extols the virtues of the straight razor as an emergency weapon and, later, interrupts a romantic interlude between Perrin and Mack.

Title cards (optical printing) show a gloomy Chinatown district, followed by portraits of the characters. A foggy night in the city makes a fine prelude to the outdoor action. The dialogue is rich with cowboy jargon:

Perrin refers to condensed milk as "canned cow," and Wales describes a murder scene as "darker than the inside of a cow at midnight."

Strangest of all is a flashback montage of more than three minutes, showing Casey's mental turmoil when he realizes that Karney has betrayed him. Superimposed over dissolving close-ups of Perrin's grimace of disillusionment, the sequence depicts the rescue of Karney on a French battlefield. As the montage fades, Casey is throttling Karney—only to halt when he sees Mack's horrified expression.

Jack Perrin appeared in later years in innumerable bits and extra parts, often as a policeman. His best-known such part is a foreground close-up at the finale of *Sunset Blvd.* (1950), as Gloria Swanson descends the staircase. Perrin died of a heart attack on December 17, 1967, while at work on a television episode of *Gunsmoke.*

Desert Phantom

Supreme Pictures Corp. • 1936

Johnny Mack Brown serves *Desert Phantom* as an easygoing sort with a hidden vengeful streak. A ghostly element lends the right touch of weirdness to a story that works fine otherwise as a naturalistic account of a blood feud nearing the moment of truth. A land-grabbing conspiracy is all but secondary to Brown's hatred of Ted Adams, who plays a broadly conceived Mexican gunfighter. The phantom-sniper gimmick is an elaboration upon Louis Weiss' 1932 production of *The Night Rider,* in which Harry Carey sets out after a more obviously flesh-and-blood marauder, with traces of 1934's *The Star Packer* (see our section on the *Lone Star Westerns*).

Sharpshooter Billy Donovan (Brown) is offered the job of ridding rancher Jean Haloran (Sheila Manors) of an elusive gunman. The superstitious townspeople believe that the intruder is a ghost from an abandoned gold mine. Donovan has an old grudge to settle against a local badman, Salizar (Adams). Salizar plans to kidnap Jean as his bride.

Donovan finds a tunnel connecting the mine to the ranchhouse. After Salizar abducts Jean, Donovan performs a rescue. A saloon-keeper and deputy, Jim Day (Hal Price), arrests Salizar. And yet Salizar continues to prowl—only to find himself bested in an attack on Donovan, who challenges the marauder to a duel. Salizar is gunned down. The hidden doorway opens to disclose Jim Day, who engages Donovan in a vicious slugfest. Defeated at last, Day proves to have played the phantom, in cahoots with Salizar, in the hope of driving Jean away from a hidden vein of gold.

Brown, an accomplished actor first and a western-movie person-ality second, tosses off witty banter and tackles the mystery with

a lighthearted air that makes his transformation all the more bracing. His appeal to Adams' vanity as an unbeatable gunslinger is a nice characterizing touch. The townsite has a refreshingly homely realism. Location work makes much of California's scenic Chatsworth and Susanna Pass areas. Eccentric character portrayals include Nelson McDowell as a grumpy veterinarian and Karl Hackett as Sheila Manors' gun-packing, paralyzed stepfather—whose sudden recovery renders him suspect.

Manors (a.k.a. Sheila Bromley and Sheila Manners) seems every bit the level-headed cowgirl until she launches into a peculiar speech about the psychology of paralysis. Hal Price's hidden villain is a real turn-about: he usually played benevolent lawmen. The fight between Price, heavy-set and balding, and the robust Brown—with no evidence of stunt-doubling—accounts for a harrowing finale. Throughout, *Desert Phantom* covers considerable emotional and psychological ground.

Director S. Roy Luby seems to have liked *Desert Phantom* sufficiently well to remake it at Monogram as *The Range Busters*, first in a series of 22 *Range Busters* adventures. Karl Hackett returned for the remake—this time, as the sheriff.

The House of a Thousand Candles

Republic Pictures Corp. • 1936

What had started as a vehicle for Bela Lugosi became instead a show-case for Irving Pichel. The Machiavellian spy of *The House of a Thousand Candles* would have been ideal for Lugosi, who completed several days' shooting, only to find himself sidelined by an attack of sciatica. Pichel stepped in: sepulchral of voice and voluptuous of features, Pichel etches a chilling portrait of suave, mannered evil. (Lugosi fulfilled his commitment to Republic with a splendid job in *S-O-S Coast Guard*.)

The popular view pegs Nat Levine as a maker of crude, exhilarating thrillers, given the overwhelming evidence of his fast-and-cheap Mascot

Mae Clarke visits with a Republic Pictures cohort, the ticket-sell-ing star Gene Autry, on the Thousand Candles *set.*

productions. And yet, his brief stay at Republic—a studio sufficiently well capitalized to allow Levine to concentrate upon quality—demonstrates a higher artistry. *The House of a Thousand Candles* is so slick that it might be mistaken for a lesser MGM picture. Even the cranky New York reviewers admired the film; some likened it to Alfred Hitchcock's *The 39 Steps*, a critics' darling of a few months previous.

World peace hangs upon an invisible-ink message entrusted to Tony Carleton (Phillips Holmes), who is charmed into accepting a drugged drink by Raquél (Rosita Moreno), a seductive dancer. Recovering to find the message gone, Carleton seeks out Raquél at a posh casino, the House of a Thousand Candles. Her boss, Sebastian (Pichel), is a master spy. Sebastian cannot find the message. Carol Vincent (Mae Clarke), Carleton's sweetheart, spies upon Sebastian—who kills Raquél and plots to set up Carleton as an apparent suicide. Lest Carol be harmed, Carleton agrees to show Sebastian the message. Carol tries to burn the paper, but a flame reveals the code. Sebastian, hastening to deliver the message, is killed in an automobile wreck.

House deserves every kind word, then and now, for its brisk pace, snappy dialogue, first-rate music, elaborate settings, and sparkling photography. Arthur Lubin, best known for 1943's *The Phantom of the Opera*, directs with mastery.

Phillips Holmes and Mae Clarke, notables from the larger studios, do fine work with the romantic heroism, and Fred Walton lends amusement as a light-fingered valét. The villainy is tops, from Pichel and Rosita Moreno on down to such lurking creeps as Mischa Auer, Hedwiga Reicher, Fredrik Vogeding, and Paul Ellis.

Meredith Nicholson's source-novel had been filmed in 1915 and 1919. The story takes a severe modernizing here: the presentation shows vividly (perhaps for the first time in American cinema) the influence of Hitchcock's then-recent *The Man Who Knew Too Much* and *The 39 Steps*. The nebulous maguffin (a motivating device that is never explained in detail), the terror of danger in a public place, and the arrival of help and menace from unexpected quarters—all these are Hitchcock signatures, smartly forged for this gem from upstart Republic Pictures.

Federal Agent

Winchester Pictures • Republic Pictures Corp. • 1936

Three inaugural Republics, 1935's *Burning Gold* and *Racing Luck* and *Federal Agent*, are salvage jobs from Winchester Pictures, a short-lived company set up to showcase William "Bill" Boyd. The actor had starred with Cecil B. DeMille's Pathé empire of the silent era, then stayed on as a successful talkie player after RKO-Radio had bought Pathé. Boyd found

his option dropped over a drinking problem and persistent mis-identifi-cation with another prominent carouser, William "Stage" Boyd (see *The Midnight Warning*). By 1934, Bill Boyd was scrambling for work.

The Winchesters bought time for Boyd to launch a spectacular come-back in 1935 with the *Hopalong Cassidy* series at Paramount. Some of the *Cassidys* were in release before Republic issued the Winchesters; though hardly as polished as Republic's own efforts, these titles fared well as a result of Boyd's marquée appeal and the attractive topics of oil booms, horseracing, and G-Men. Sam Newfield directed all three—a cut above his usual work, but not particularly imaginative.

Federal Agent finds a spy ring seeking a formula for a mass-destruction invention. Agent Bob Woods (Boyd) investigates the murder of a fellow operative. His agency spies upon Récard Kantos (Don Alvarado). An uneasy alliance with Helen Gray (Irene Ware), who had searched the slain agent's rooms, puts Woods in touch with crucial clues and recurring perils. After a struggle, Kantos topples into a deadly chemical bath.

The smart collaborative screenplay—lead writer Robert Ellis also delivered some of the better *Charlie Chan* scripts for Fox—is served with competence by camera chief Harry Forbes, who dealt as a rule in outdoor settings. The acid-vat dissolving of the bad guy (obscured by smoke) is underscored with unnerving sound effects. Lou Rachmil's set designs are ordinary, barring an ominous laboratory. Rachmil would become a 1940 Oscar contender for *Our Town* and, later, a producer of the *Hopalong Cassidy* pictures.

Irene Ware (of *The Dark Hour*) is a charming leading lady with a surprising interest in the investigation. Boyd is a likable hero and a snappy dresser. Don Alvarado, cast against romantic-lead type, makes a swell villain. Hatchet-faced Lenita Lane is his jealous and murderous wife.

The Lash of the Penitentes

a.k.a.: *The Penitente Murder Case* • *The Lash* • *El Asasenato de los Penitentes*
Harry Revier Productions • Stewart Productions • Telepictures Kinotrade • 1936

This film, achieved under perilous hardship, originated with legitimate documentary intentions, only to run afoul of a transformation into grindhouse fodder. A confusing array of proxy titles, further complicated by alternate versions, compounded the difficulty. Such is the shabby lot of Roland C. Price's successful attempt to film the unfilmable in a shunned region of the American Southwest. Price's failure to find a respectable outlet for his labors left *The Lash of the Penitentes* looking altogether more lurid and sensational than he had intended.

Los Hermanos Penitentes, the Order of the Penitent Brothers, is a clandestine cult of the Church of Rome, descended from the Third Order of St. Francis, a prototypical torture-pornography purveyor that espoused flagellation as a form of atonement. Such sanctimonious perversions flourished in Europe during the 13th century. The Black Death, that plague upon the land, encouraged many apostles of sado-masochistic penance. Public scourgings were encouraged by popes and crowned heads. The Spanish Conquest of the 1500s spread the poison to the New World, with an entrenched pocket in the territory that would become New Mexico.

Several thousand Penitentes still occupy the foothills of the Sangre de Cristo Mountains near Taos and Santa Fe, New Mexico. Each Good

Friday sees secretive ceremonial crucifixions, complete with log crosses and whippings. Rawhide thongs have long since replaced nails because of a high mortality rate among the masochistic local *Cristos*. Riflemen guard against infidel spies. Should a *Cristo* die, he receives a burial in secret, with tombstone and memorial homages held in abeyance for a year.

Early in 1936, journalist Carl Taylor—who had studied torture cults in the Philippines—traveled to New Mexico to investigate the Penitentes for Vincent Astor's *Today* magazine. On February 6, having submitted a sympathetic first article, Taylor was murdered by his houseboy, Modesto Trujillo, whom Taylor had pegged as an aspiring sacrificial victim.

Some months earlier, a ritual near Taos had been filmed from hiding by Roland C. Price, a pioneering cinematographer who billed himself as the Vagabond Cameraman. Undaunted by the fate of a predecessor, Charles F. Lummus—who had escaped with a bullet in the neck from such an attempt—Price captured a great deal of footage. (Price hand-cranked his camera well into the talking-picture age, even though much of his right hand was missing as a consequence of another perilous shoot.)

Price had intended a straightforward documentary account, but his footage went begging. The Roman Catholic Legion of

Decency had pronounced the topic taboo to accredited members of the Motion Picture Association. Whereupon a fellow filmmaker of shabbier bearings proposed an exploitation feature: Harry Revier, a veteran director of westerns, suggested a melodramatic framework, the better to trade upon the fresh notoriety of Carl Taylor's slaying. Revier and Price made the finished film for something over $15,000.

On February 24, 1936, Revier and Price began shooting dramatized scenes at Talisman Studios. An initial and mostly documentary cut of 43 minutes saw previews in April. A Spanish-language version was made simultaneously, with the same cast. The story concerns a writer (William Marcos) who infiltrates a Penitente cult and winds up murdered by a servant (José Rubio). Marie de Forest plays an artist's model who becomes a victim of the zealots' Klan-like tortures.

Denied the industry's Purity Seal via the conflict-of-interest interference of the Legion of Decency, Revier undertook a maverick release, represented by a sleazy advertising campaign. Later in 1936, Revier padded the running time with a vain appeal to ministers to put an end to torture within the church. Big-voiced, small-of-stature Billy Bletcher does the preaching here. This 65-minute cut (a print survives at one university archive) was distributed sporadically during 1937 by Mike J. Levinson. The still longer Spanish version, treated as a foreign art film by the Kinotrade distribution agency, contains scenes deleted from the English cuts. Despite amateurish performances and a prevailing crudeness of production, this cruel and rough-hewn film contains points of interest that compensate somewhat for its faults.

Lightnin' Bill Carson

Excelsior Pictures • Puritan Pictures Corp. • 1936

Bill Carson seems doomed to face a perilous outlook as revealed by a frontier Cassandra. And yet, Carson prevails and persists—not to give away too much—to become a long-running franchise character in grim defiance of Hollywood's emerging happy-cowboy trend. The constant element is the involvement of producer Sigmund Neufeld, in association with fellow filmmaker Sam Katzman. The Old West of Old Hollywood, as much a *Yiddishe* invention as Hollywood itself, seldom had it so good as when Sig Neufeld was dispensing the thrills. All due respect to John Ford.

The role of Bill Carson might have seemed beneath Col. Tim McCoy, a war veteran and former Indian Affairs agent who had known big-time stardom. Having painted himself into a low-budget corner, McCoy shaped Carson into a signature character. Such is the dignity of honest work.

McCoy was the most distinguished of the film cowboys on Poverty Row. He had landed at Excelsior Pictures on a fluke: Columbia had stalled at renewing his contract, and McCoy signed with Neufeld and Leslie Simmonds to tackle a series of 10 pictures. McCoy received $4,000 per picture, with each film being shot in a week, but the move kept McCoy out of the major-league studios for the balance of his career. After co-starring with Buck Jones in Monogram's *Rough Riders* series in 1942, McCoy rejoined the military (at age 51), then retired to his ranch in Wyoming. He surfaced as a television player in 1949 and graced the big screen occasionally into the 1960s. McCoy died in 1978.

Though usually better than his material along Poverty Row, McCoy found a fine showcase in *Lightnin' Bill Carson*, a foreboding meditation upon death and destiny in a cruel frontier. The film anticipates both the decisive emergence of film noir (during the 1940s, and usually associated with citified settings) and the development of the western as a cauldron of psychological torments and existential quandaries, as in *High Noon* (1952), *Johnny Guitar* (1954), and *The Big Country* (1959).

Marshal Bill Carson (McCoy) intimidates two would-be assassins. Earlier, Carson had banished the Pecos Kid (Rex Lease), a gambler whose trademark is the Black Ace, the death card of legend. A mysterious newcomer (John Merton) rides a white horse—another omen—whose shoes bear a blacksmith's mark from the hired killers' village. A fortuneteller, Dolores Costello (Lois January), warns of a lurking danger.

The mystery man, Breed Hawkins, works for a businessman, Stack Stone (Karl Hackett), who proposes to hire Carson but secretly plots his slaying. Pecos follows Hawkins, seeking to renew ties better left forgotten. Tom Rand (Harry Worth), a reclusive clerk with Stone's company, seems glad to see Pecos despite old conflicts. Carson investigates further. Hawkins kills a deputy (Edward Cobb) and frames Pecos into a lynching. Rand cracks and sets out to kill all involved.

Carson hounds Stone to acknowledge the conspiracy. Rand, wounded in a shoot-out, takes shelter with Dolores. Carson confronts Rand, who draws on the marshal. Carson guns Rand down—only to learn that Rand had chosen to brandish an empty six-shooter.

Arthur Durlam's scenario hangs upon intrigues involving rampant superstitions, estrangement, ill-motivated revenge, and ominous secrets. The traditional crisp distinctions between good and evil blur to disturbing effect, and the element of suspense overshadows violence. Rex Lease's Pecos, a Billy the Kid to McCoy's Pat Garrett, is a likable troublemaker whose lighthearted manner bespeaks doom in spades. Aces of Spades.

Though hardly the fabric of great cinema, *Lightnin' Bill Carson* is of that more important class—a picture that, without pretensions or

delusions, delivers more than expected. Thus is greatness more genuinely achieved. The film, far ahead of its time, betokens a dawning greater maturity within the genre without losing touch with its B-movie Saturday-matinée origins.

McCoy is ideal as the stern, philosophical Carson, who prefers not to use the power he controls. Lease finds his richest role—he usually handled unconflicted parts—as a dashing scoundrel who learns too late not to trust the Fates. Harry Worth, as a guardian of embittered secrets, seems a gentle loser, resigned to his lot, until he proves obsessed with a line from a certain book: "...and vengeance rode with him."

Lois January is sad loveliness personified as the reluctant seer, persuasively Latinate. Her father, lovable old Lafe McKee, struggles with a Mexican accent. John Merton revels in a clipped delivery and a withering scowl. Where Merton wears the flashy garb of a Mexican rodeo artist and rides a white horse, McCoy dresses in black and rides a black horse—a significant inversion of symbolic stereotypes.

Sam Newfield's work here, as in *Branded a Coward*, is astonishing by comparison with his usual desultory approach. He outdoes himself on *Carson*—in depth of characterization, story development, scenic values and dramatic close-ups, and sheer artistic touches. Understated acting conveys dire meaning in rich dialogue and seething, hushed tones: Poker is the Pecos Kid's metaphor for life: "Fate does all the dealing— and all the laughing." McCoy hesitates to arrest Pecos: "Maybe the Kid and I are the same, under the skin. We both like a good horse between our knees, a long trail ahead, the wind in our faces."

January's psychic, a rarity within the genre, gives the troubled Harry Worth a sendoff that anticipates the words of Maria Ouspenskaya's haunted gypsy in *The Wolf Man* (1941): "You are both the hunter and the hunted. ... You do not follow a good trail, my friend., .. *Vaya usted con Dios, amigo.*" Badman Dick Botillier combines murder with sharpshooting practice: "Right through the head—and never even moved the hat!"

Nightmarish visual devices include a spiraling effect, drawn from the German Expressionist-Surrealist style, that signals Worth's breakdown. A frenzied tracking shot follows Karl Hackett through a crowd. Suspenseful intercutting alternates Worth's killings with McCoy's campaign of psychological torments against Hackett.

The lynch-mob sequence is worthy of a Fritz Lang or a William Wellman: the stirring of hooves provides a terrified reaction to gunfire. Rex Lease's shadow crosses the hard face of Jack Rockwell, the movies' perfect frontier sheriff. The camera cuts back to ground level as Lease's cigar falls—then back to Rockwell and the shadow—then back to the descent of the death card.

Lightnin' Bill Carson runs a quarter-hour longer than the usual independent western. This length, at an industrial tax rate of $500 a reel, suggests the company realized it had something special. Many small-studio pictures were crammed onto five or six reels, and this one takes up seven. Excelsior-Puritan would not have indulged the picture without reason.

The payoff was prompt: McCoy's Bill Carson proved so popular that Sam Katzman's Victory outfit followed through with eight (lesser) sequels through 1940, making McCoy's tenure on Poverty Row more strategy than exile. Sam Newfield stayed on as director throughout. (See also: *The Fighting Renegade* series, under 1939.)

The Amazing Exploits of the Clutching Hand

a.k.a.: *The Clutching Hand*
Weiss & Mintz • Stage & Screen • 1936

Weiss & Mintz, descended from the Weiss Bros.' talkie-breakthrough company (see: *Unmasked*), resurrected heroic Craig Kennedy for *The Amazing Exploits of the Clutching Hand*. The company dissolved after *Custer's Last Stand*, *The Clutching Hand*, and *The Black Coin*. Crude, over-complicated, and old-fashioned, these serials are reckless delights, with the occasional stab at commentary and social criticism: *The Black Coin*, for example, warns against imperialist tampering with other civilizations.

The Clutching Hand is a movie buff's delight in its array of famous faces from the silent screen and the earliest talking-picture years.

There also is a star-to-be, *The Lion Man*'s Charles Locher, soon to break through to prominence as Jon Hall.

Dr. Paul Gironda (Robert Frazer), inventor of synthetic gold, vanishes—apparently nabbed by the Clutching Hand, a master criminal. Reporter Walter Jameson (Rex Lease), betrothed to Gironda's daughter (Marion Shilling), summons a consulting detective, Craig Kennedy (Jack Mulhall). Suspects and pitfalls abound. At last, Kennedy exposes Gironda as the fiend. The scientist dies by his own (clutching) hand.

The picture nods to a Pearl White serial, 1914's *The Exploits of Elaine*, in which Kennedy (Arnold Daly) tackles the definitive portrayer of the Clutching Hand, *Tombstone Canyon*'s Sheldon Lewis. Jack Mulhall serves the present film as a spirited Kennedy, with Rex Lease as a secondary heroic protagonist. Location shooting is plentiful, but the real scenic value comes in Kenneth Strickfaden's bizarre laboratory set. Stuntwork is prime Yakima Canutt, who also plays a chief accomplice. The unmasking comes as a surprise more credible than Mascot Pictures' serial denouements.

Louis Weiss' Adventure Serials, Inc., picked up where Weiss & Mintz had left off and delivered three additional serials that Columbia Pictures would acquire for 1937–1938 as a prelude to the development of an internal serial department. These are *Jungle Mystery* (condensed into a 1946 feature, *Jungle Terror*, by Favorite Films), starring the explorer Frank Buck; *The Secret of Treasure Island*, from L. Ron Hubbard's *Murder at Pirate Castle*; and *Mysterious Pilot*, starring Frank Hawkes. All are passably weird, and all bespeak a decisive infiltration of a major-league studio by Poverty Row—a model for Sam Katzman's serial-making arrangement with Columbia during the later 1940s.

The Foreign Legion angle of *The Black Coin*, incidentally, had seemed a quaint relic until the global sea change of September 11, 2001, snapped its deeper currents into focus. Like John Ford's classier *The Lost Patrol* (1934), *The Black Coin* cautions that clashing social imperatives lead to mayhem. This is how missionary meddlers wind up in the soup, and this is how mass murder passes for sacrament. Such movies revealed as much, in terms as stern as commonplace escapism for the shirtsleeves audience would allow.

Death from a Distance

Invincible-Chesterfield • 1936

Lon Young, once a stage magician known as the Great Lorenzo, is credited as production manager on most of the Invincible-Chesterfield pictures. He was the *de facto* producer, constantly on the set, determined to keep every dollar on the screen. One of Young's favorites,

Death from a Distance, inspired him to spring for one of the great special-effects artisans, Jack Cosgrove. This extra touch lends a wealth of
class when coupled with spectacularly eerie sets and properties from
Universal's just-completed *The Invisible Ray* and sites at Griffith Park
Observatory (seen also in *The Phantom Empire*). Cosgrove's polished
matte shots, simulating planetarium projection, are of the same
calibre he had applied at Universal, the Selznick Co., Walter Wanger's
studio, and other big-timers.

A lecture by the eccentric Prof. Ernst Enfield (Lee Kohlmar) is
interrupted by a fatal shooting. Brusque Detective Mallory (Russell
Hopton) offends reporter Kay Palmer (Lola Lane). Her coverage in
biased retaliation puts Mallory at a disadvantage. Many people had
motives. Kay's articles endanger Enfield. Joining Mallory as if to make
amends, she helps to trace the gunshot to the machinery of Enfield's
planetarium. Enfield's death is reported—but then, the professor reappears to spook a confession from the killer (George Marion, Sr.)—who
is done in by his own infernal device.

Director Frank Strayer makes much of the antagonisms between
Russell Hopton and Lola Lane, whose reconciliation comes by plausible

degrees. George Marion, Sr., radiates madness when cornered, and Lee Kohlmar lends comic relief to his imperiled role. Suspects include such perennial culprits as Wheeler Oakman, John Davidson, John St. Polis, and Cornelius Keefe. Suspense is secondary to mystery, but the creepy finale makes for a fine payoff.

The Mine with the Iron Door

Sol Lesser Productions • Columbia Pictures • 1936

Harold Bell Wright's popular novel *The Mine with the Iron Door* (1923), and a similarly conceived story, "It Happened Out West," remained in print for decades, enthralling millions with Wright's view of a cruel, believably romanticized frontier. Both derive from legends involving fabulous treasures, some stolen and hidden away, others waiting in the Santa Catalina Mountains of Arizona. In 1924, former theatrical exhibitor Sol Lesser produced a successful silent-screen version of *The Mine with the Iron Door*. Lesser's talkie remake was purchased by Columbia for its 1936 program and merited a reissue in 1952.

Lesser made a less foreboding, more brightly adventurous Wright-based film, *It Happened Out West*, in 1937; its acquisition by 20th Century-Fox bespeaks the ambition that distinguishes Lesser's career over the long term, alternating between big-studio executive duties and a fierce independence. The *Tarzan* franchise and the Saturday-matinée serials are but facets of Lesser's larger role within the industry.

The Mine with the Iron Door tells of a cache of mission gold, hidden for centuries. New landowner Bob Harvey (Richard Arlen) and a detective (Stanley Fields) mount a search. Marta Hill (Cecilia Parker) and her grandfather (Spencer Charters) reside on Harvey's land. A neighbor, archaeologist David Burton (Henry B. Walthall), lusts after Marta.

Burton has long since discovered the treasure. Marta's attraction to Harvey drives the professor to madness, and he takes her to the fabled site with murderous intentions. Harvey arrives in time to overpower Burton. Harvey and Marta find the iron door and, behind it, the treasure.

Ably enacted and beautifully photographed (but lacking in the spectacle suggested by the novel), *The Mine with the Iron Door* stands as a pleasing melodrama whose weird and comical elements lift it above the ordinary. Director David Howard, a seasoned hand at outdoor adventure (and formerly of Fox's foreign-language division), applies skill if not imagination. The mine setting, located at RKO-Pathé, is suitably oppressive.

Henry B. Walthall, in one of his final appearances (he died in 1936), delivers a finely shaded portrait of obsessive madness. Spencer Charters, the now-scary, now-funny maniac of *The Ghost Walks*, is a welcome sight as Cecilia Parker's crochety grandfather. Former boxer Stanley Fields, a tough-guy comedian in the Wallace Beery manner, lends amusement as a detective who sets Richard Arlen wise to the legend.

The companion film, *It Happened Out West*, is less concerned with derangement than with plain homicidal treachery. Judith Allen plays a struggling dairy operator whose crooked foreman (LeRoy Mason) seeks to force a sale before she can discover a vein of silver. An economist (career egghead Milquetoast Johnny Arthur) foresees better days for the dairy—only to wind up wounded when he stumbles onto the lode.

Undersea Kingdom

a.k.a.: *Sharad of Atlantis*
Republic Pictures Corp. • 1936

The success of *Darkest Africa* plunged Republic deeper into fantasy for its second serial, *Undersea Kingdom*, whose wild story owes as much to Alex Raymond's outer-space comic strip, *Flash Gordon*, as to any myth or literary work about the sunken continent of Atlantis. Universal Pictures was adapting *Flash Gordon* as a serial while *Undersea Kingdom* was in the planning stages; even the name of *Kingdom*'s protagonist, Crash Corrigan, has a familiar ring. Here, as in Raymond's inspired work, is an athletic hero thrown into an alien world where the swords and chariots of antiquity are pitted against robots, death rays, and rocket ships. The premise also resembles RKO-Radio's abandoned epic of 1931, *Creation*, which led to the making of *King Kong* (1933). In *Creation*, a submarine enters an undersea cave to emerge in a lost world.

Filmed in 25 days at a cost of $99,222, *Undersea Kingdom* bears favorable comparison with Universal's interplanetary gothic, *Flash Gordon*, which cost more than triple that. Ray Corrigan (*né* Ray Benard) appears

in both films—as top-billed Crash Corrigan in *Kingdom*, and in one of his signature gorilla suits in Flash's *Tournament of Death* episodes. Already established as an ape impersonator at Republic, Corrigan had the freedom to play primates at other studios on condition that he must go unbilled; he has the title role, for example, in Monogram Pictures' *The Ape*. Corrigan's sequences for *Flash Gordon* were filmed a couple of weeks before *Undersea Kingdom* went into production.

Prof. Norton's (C. Montague Shaw) invention promises to control earthquakes. He has traced a series of upheavals to the presumed site of Atlantis, and sets out in a rocket-submarine, with Crash Corrigan among the crew. Norton's schoolboy son, Billy (Lee Van Atta), stows away.

Atlantis lives on—protected by a dome, but torn by war between King Sharad (William Farnum) and power-maddened Unga Khan (Monte Blue). The earthquakes are part of Khan's plot to conquer the planet. Khan tracks the progress of the Norton expedition and captures the submarine. Norton, warped by Khan's influence, becomes a slave to a rocket-building campaign. A deadly siege seems imminent, but Crash sabotages the mechanisms, restores Norton to sanity, and calls out the U.S. Navy. The survivors of the Norton Expedition escape an instant before Khan's rocket-tower mechanism can explode.

Retaining most of the production staff of *Darkest Africa*, this entry meets the same standards in photography, trick effects, evocative settings, and extensive musical accompaniment. One epic-scale siege in Chapter No. 4 takes a cost-efficient encore in Chapter No. 10, altered slightly by darkened printing for a nighttime effect. The Mascot custom of cheating the chapter endings persists: at the end of Chapter No. 8, Corrigan is strapped to the front of an armored car that bursts through the gates of the city; the gates splinter. In the next episode, the gates open to admit the vehicle. Random inconsistencies in plotting are typical of the multiple-author serial idiom. Directors B. Reeves Eason and Joseph Kane sustain an overriding coherence.

Corrigan proved a natural for stardom in the serials and westerns, gifted with stunting skills and a breezy personality. He also ran Corriganville, the movie-location ranch near Chatsworth, California, and he persisted into the 1950s with the gorilla-suit assignments, among other monsters. Corrigan died at 72 in 1976.

Monte Blue is well cast as the mad tyrant, and William Farnum makes a convincingly beleaguered king. Lee Van Atta is plucky and natural as the juvenile hero, and distinguished C. Montague Shaw makes much of his mad scientist transformation. Lois Wilde overplays the heroine. Raymond Hatton and Lon Chaney, Jr., stand out as supporting heavies. Veteran bad-guy player John Merton (of *Lightnin' Bill Carson*) is a pleasant surprise as a secondary hero. Optical effects and the Lydecker Bros.' scale-model structures and machinery are splendid except for the necessary robots, which are too silly-looking to take seriously: picture a hot-water tank on accordion legs. These, however, represent an improvement over their counterparts in *The Phantom Empire*.

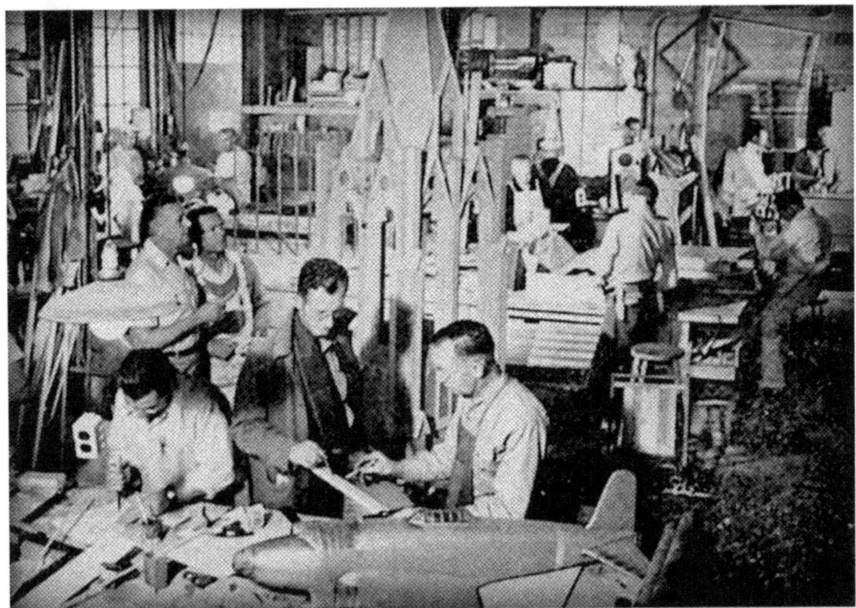

Republic Pictures' properties-and-effects workshop at the time of Undersea Kingdom.

Revolt of the Zombies

a.k.a.: Revolt of the Demons

Halperin Productions • Academy Pictures Corp. • 1936

In a long-planned attempt to repeat the success of *White Zombie*, Edward and Victor Halperin amplified a legend that the Cambodian city of Angkor Wat was built in the year 900 with a labor force of reanimated corpses. In spite of careful preparations and good ideas, *Revolt of the Zombies* proved a disappointment. Silent-era directorial methods, which had marred but hardly crippled *White Zombie*, are fatal to a picture made after four additional years' evolution of sight-and-sound technique.

Even so able an actor as Dean Jagger cannot overcome the handicap. The other players perform in an even more outmoded manner. Victor Halperin's collaborative screenplay lacks the audacious simplicity of the 1932 film, whose virtuosity in set design, photography, and cutting fails to carry over to the present film. The Asian zombies are hardly as frightening, or as individualized, as their Haitian counterparts.

Living dead men rout a German detachment in the Franco-Austrian frontier during World War I. An Asian priest, chaplain of a French regiment, prepares to burn a parchment revealing the hiding place of the zombie-raising formula. He is slain by the wily Col. Mazovia (Roy D'Arcy), who seizes the charred document. A postwar expedition searches the ruins of Angkor to destroy the secret of life-in-death. Mazovia intends to sabotage the mission but finds himself beaten to

the secret by a student of antiquities, Armand Loque (Jagger). Seduced by the power, Loque bends the searchers to his will and transforms the natives into zombies. He forces fellow expeditioner Claire Duval (Dorothy Stone) to agree to marry him, but the realization that she cannot love him drives Loque to destroy the secret and liberate the zombies—which descend upon him. An early victim (Teru Shimada) fires a bullet through Loque's heart.

Establishing shots of Angkor are intercut with studio settings comprising drops and rear projections of the ruins. Scenes representing Phnom Penh were filmed at Bernhaimer Oriental Gardens, situated on a 300-foot hilltop overlooking Hollywood. A stairway, partially washed out in times more recent, descends to the foot of the hill. This Yamashiro, or mountain palace, had been built in 1916 as a private residence—a replica of the Japanese Summer Palace at Kyoto—situated within 12 acres of spectacular gardens. The property later became an exclusive club for big shots of the movie racket. In times more recent, Yamashiro has operated as a restaurant amidst a scrupulously maintained section of the gardens.

As had occurred with *White Zombie*, the Halperin Bros. faced threats of litigation. Release of *Revolt* was delayed when Amusement Securities Corp. (headed by Sherman S. Krellberg, of *The Lost City*) complained of unfair competition from the new picture. Krellberg was promoting a re-issue of *White Zombie* on the strength of his stake as an investor. Until the dispute could be settled, *Revolt of the Zombies* was shown as *Revolt of the Demons*. Never mind the public-domain status of the term *zombie*.

The New Adventures of Tarzan

a.k.a.: *Tarzan's New Adventure* / *Tarzan and the Green Goddess*
Burroughs-Tarzan Enterprises • Dearholt-Stout & Cohen • 1936

Edgar Rice Burroughs disliked the alterations that MGM Pictures had imposed upon his *Tarzan* yarns, and so he decided to try his hand at moviemaking. Hence Burroughs-Tarzan Enterprises, a partnership with a longtime friend, the actor-turned-investor Ashton Dearholt, former representative of RKO-Radio Pictures in Guatemala.

The company approached *The New Adventures of Tarzan* with failed attempts to hire Johnny Weissmuller and/or Buster Crabbe. In October of 1934, Burroughs signed Olympic medalist Herman Brix to portray Tarzan at $75 a week. Such impressive scenes as a struggle with a lion were filmed in November at Los Angeles' Selig Zoo. In December, the Ashton Dearholt Expedition reached Guatemala with 29 members, a famous—and famously ill-tempered—chimpanzee named Jiggs, cameras, and a four-ton sound truck. A tropical storm set an ominous tone.

Danger and difficulties plagued the safari. Stinging insects ran rampant, and a sound technician suffered a bite from a poisonous snake. The problems of recording in the wild proved overwhelming. The natives' fear of Jiggs provoked labor disputes; the ape was predisposed to biting—and a chimp's bite can take off a hand or a face. The company spent four months in this green hell, shooting at Guatemala City, the Colonial Spanish capital of Antigua and the Mayan ruins at Tikal, and along the Rio Dulce.

Emotional complications completed the ordeal. Dearholt and leading lady Ula Holt fell in love. Burroughs and his wife separated. Mrs. Dearholt, nearly half the author's age, later became Mrs. Burroughs. Burroughs and Dearholt remained friends. They continued to operate Burroughs-Tarzan Enterprises as a film company until 1937.

The New Adventures of Tarzan, despite some finer moments, is crude by comparison with the MGM *Tarzans*. Distorted sound is a chronic annoyance; the company attached an awkward apology in the title cards. A few years later, the entire soundtrack of one feature version was re-recorded, but prints of the bad-sound edition remained a perennial favorite at small-town theatres.

Tarzan, lured to Guatemala by legends of a Mayan cult, joins an expedition in search of a fabled Green Goddess. Raglan, a notorious mobster, steals a crucial map. Ula Vale (Holt), who has a score to settle against Raglan, falls under Tarzan's protection. (Dearholt portrays Raglan under the make-believe name of Don Castello. Original press materials fostered a wild story about how the purported Don Castello [sometimes cited as Costello] had fallen ill upon arrival, whereupon Dearholt stepped in. Of course, Burroughs' press agents also hailed Herman Brix as a decathlon champion; Brix' specialty was the shot-put.)

Natives, angered by Raglan's cruelties, attack. Monsters from the Mayans' Dead City capture Tarzan and his loyalists. Violent complications ensue, as usual. The Green Goddess—coveted for intrinsic value and science-fictional implications—changes hands repeatedly. A storm wrecks the party's ship. The more deserving survivors are rescued.

The story lacks briskness. Edward Kull's directing is desultory, and so is the acting. The fights, however, are often more convincing than the choreographed scraps at MGM: Brix obviously takes a roughing-up. Scenic values are splendid, with hundreds of native extras. Dramatic use is made of creeping shadows. A scary sequence finds a cackling hag assailing Ula Holt, who resists with lethal results. The mortality

Herman Brix makes a suitably athletic Tarzan, but he defied typecasting over the longer term.

rate is enormous, what with machine-gunnings, skull-crackings, and falls from dizzying heights. The storm is a combination of live action, miniatures, and stock footage.

The array of versions is confusing. The first chapter in the 12-part serial, previewed during 1935, is 42 minutes long. A feature-plus-serial edition utilizes Chapter No. 1 and the first half of Chapter No. 2, then deploys further episodes in weekly installments. The first self-contained feature received a sequel in another condensation, issued in 1938 as *Tarzan and the Green Goddess*. (And no wisecracks, please, about salad dressing.)

Herman Brix moved along to a variety of roles, as if to defy jungle-man typecasting. One of his citified assignments is *Sky Racket*. In 1940, Brix began a long second career as Bruce Bennett, then became a real estate broker during the 1960s.

Kelly of the Secret Service / Blake of Scotland Yard

Victory Pictures Corp. • 1936-37

A lasting craze for government-agent thrillers had begun in earnest in 1935 with *"G" Men* and *Let 'Em Have It*, procedurals addressing crime from the vantage of federal enforcers. Sam Katzman adapted readily with one feature and one serial, adding weird-crime elements that Republic Pictures would develop further in its transformation of Dick Tracy, Chester Gould's comic-strip plainclothes cop, into an FBI operative. (See also: *Dick Tracy*.)

Katzman's productions of *Kelly of the Secret Service*, a feature-lengther, and the following year's *Blake of Scotland Yard*, a 15-chapter serial, combine such elements as espionage, science fiction, underworld grotesqueries, hypnotism, and murder by extravagant methods. The director of both is Katzman standby Robert F. "Bob" Hill, the silent-serials stalwart who had directed the original *Blake of Scotland Yard* (1927) for Universal Pictures.

Republic Pictures already had raised the stakes on production values in such yarns. The influence shows strikingly in *Kelly of the Secret Service*, with camerawork and lighting much improved over Victory's other entries. The motivating concept is extraordinary: the idea of a radio-controlled bomb, accurate within 200 miles, *was* science fiction in those days.

Kelly, from a story by Peter B. Kyne (of *A Face in the Fog*), tells of such an invention. The plans go missing after an attack upon the laboratory of one Dr. Marston (Forrest Taylor). Secret Service Operative Ted Kelly

(Lloyd Hughes) senses a Chinatown connection but finds himself distracted by an attraction to Sally Flint (Sheila Manors), Marston's evasive secretary. Marston, lurking in a hidden room, proves to have hypnotized an assistant, Walsh (John Elliott)—Sally's uncle and the bomb's true inventor—to commit murder in order to thwart one investigation.

Lloyd Hughes is a snappy Kelly despite an old-fashioned style of acting. Sheila Manners (a.k.a. Manors and Bromley) makes an efficient heroine, with an air of mystery. Low-comedy routines by Syd Saylor and Fuzzy Knight, as bumbling guards, contrast sharply with the prevailing menace. Gaunt, pale-eyed Forrest Taylor makes brash work of the villainy.

Katzman, a resourceful maverick, watched upstart Republic Pictures as it matured rapidly to a state hovering between Poverty Row independence and larger corporate pretensions. Like Katzman, Republic made both features and serials; the serials took precedence. Katzman determined to give Republic's cliffhanger machinery a rambunctious shot of competition with *Blake of Scotland Yard*, an energetic production though lacking in polish.

Katzman also established in Ralph Byrd a heroic prototype while amplifying the monstrous villainy of Mascot's serials: Byrd soon would land the title role in Republic's *Dick Tracy*. *Tracy*'s disfigured bad guy represents an elaboration upon the hunchbacked mastermind of *Blake*. This so-called Scorpion is fascinatingly monstrous—although such a vigorous figure would no doubt find the claw-wielding deformities more a liability than an asset.

Bob Hill's affiliation with Katzman yielded seven features and two serials. Hill also wrote under the name of Rock Hawkey, and he filled in as a bit player. His career in talking pictures unfolded for the most part at the smaller companies. His talent proved undiminished from the silent era, though slow to absorb modernized sound-film techniques.

Sir James Blake (Herbert Rawlinson), impatient with his retirement from Scotland Yard, finances a death ray invented by Jerry Sheehan (Byrd) and Blake's niece, Hope Mason (Joan Barclay). Count Basil

The silent-screen original version of Blake of Scotland Yard.

Zegaloff (William Farrell) enlists the mysterious Scorpion to nab the machinery. Forced to surrender the gizmo, Blake tracks the Scorpion to Paris—only to find himself captured. Back in London, the ostensibly helpful Dr. Marshall (Lloyd Hughes) is unmasked as the Scorpion and captured in an electrical field invented by Blake. (Lloyd Hughes was fresh from the heroic title role in *Kelly of the Secret Service*.) Blake entrusts the death ray to the League of Nations, the better to prevent a new war.

Hill's slight and politically naïve story, the source of *Blake*'s collaborative screenplay, comes ill equipped to sustain an extravagant length; a 73-minute feature-length condensation plays out more efficiently. Hill rescues the serial presentation, however, with a brisk pace and smart use of the studio-built representations of London and Paris. Stunt artist George de Normand delivers perilous thrills. The secret of the Scorpion's identity is hardly as well kept as that of the usual serial villain because there is a scarcity of suspects—and because Lloyd Hughes' Dr. Marshall seems entirely too helpful. Comedy relief includes a slapstick battle in a restaurant, with tableware as weaponry.

Ralph Byrd, Republic's Dick Tracy-in-waiting, is fine as *Blake*'s youthful hero, holding his own against the upstaging abilities of Herbert Rawlinson, an old-school serial champion. There is a good assortment of thugs, secret agents, streetwalkers, beggars, Cockneys, French Apaches—plus a giant homicidal idiot and a terrifying hag who blows her nose upon a shawl. The fog-filtered photography helps to mask the low budget while conveying a fitting mock-foreign aspect. Sound recording is tinny by comparison with the sonic clarity of Republic.

The economic pecking order of Poverty Row stands out in the unbilled appearance, in moustache and eye-patch, of Herman Brix—who was Katzman's biggest feature-film star at the time. Victory Pictures' studio was wiped out a few years later in a fire, but Katzman retrenched with production and distribution deals with Monogram Pictures and, eventually, Columbia. His films were anything but prestigious, but they were almost invariably profitable and remain robustly entertaining.

Prison Shadows

Mercury Pictures • Puritan Pictures • Victory Pictures • 1936

Another gem-in-the-rough from Sam Katzman, *Prison Shadows* is a companion-piece to *The Rogues' Tavern*. Katzman receives no formal credit, but the presence of director Robert F. "Bob" Hill and screenwriter Al Martin trumpets the Katzman identity.

Prizefighter Gene Harris (Eddie Nugent), sentenced to prison after an opponent had died in the ring, is paroled. Claire Thomas (Lucille

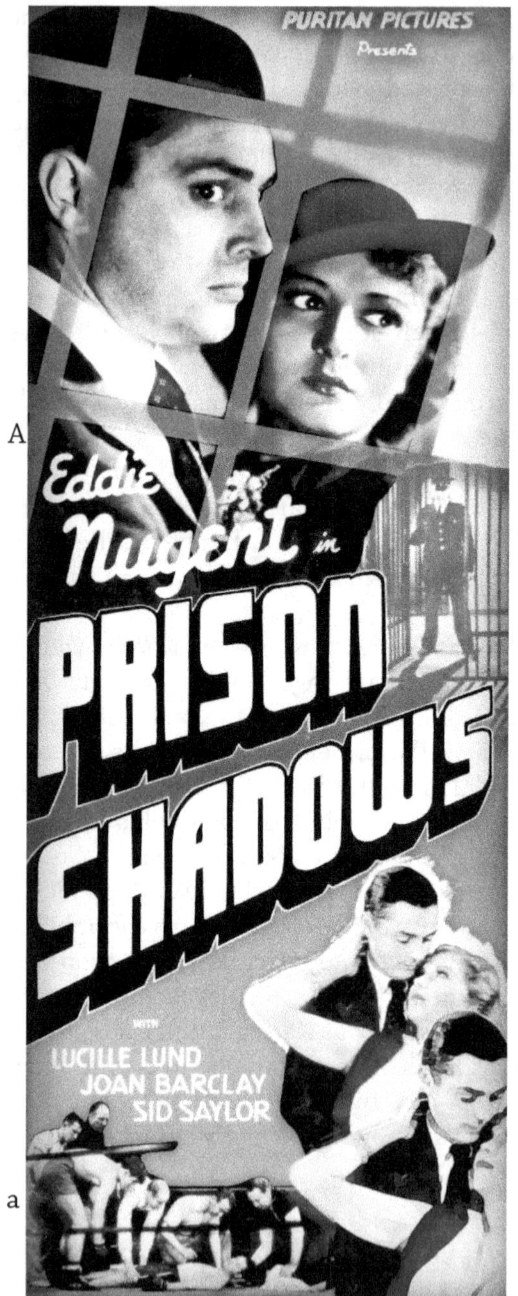

Lund), fiancée of Harris' manager (Forrest Taylor), feigns a fondness for Harris—who had been framed. Claire and gambler McNamee (Monte Blue) plot another fatal bout. McNamee subjects the rival to a subtle poisoning.

Harris convinces the police of his innocence. dog dies after taking hold of a tainted towel; a coroner recognizes the deadly substance. Harris agrees to play dead after another match. Upon hearing Claire and Blue gloating about the scam, Harris snaps to attention, reveals the conspiracy—and orders the killers arrested.

The mystery is not so much a case of whodunit as of whether the arrogant culprits will get away with another such killing. Eddie Nugent is fine as the wrongfully accused boxer who proposes a risky solution, and Joan Barclay makes patient romantic interest. The poisoning of the dog is a jarring touch that proves crucial. Comic relief specialist Syd Saylor gets in the last word, with an uncharacteristically philosophical monologue.

Beyond the Caribbean

a.k.a.: *Man Hunters of the Caribbean*
Inter-Continent Film • 1936–38

Anyone who has explored an obscure or dangerous region feels certain the adventure would make a swell movie. Few expeditioners have the know-how. For every exception—such as Merian C. Cooper & Ernest B. Schoedsack, Robert Flaherty, and Martin & Osa Johnson—there are many others whose jungle pictures resemble nothing so much as home movies with smug, amateurish dilettante pageantry.

Beyond the Caribbean falls into this trash-movie category, rendered all the worse by the occasional good idea, the random interesting scene,

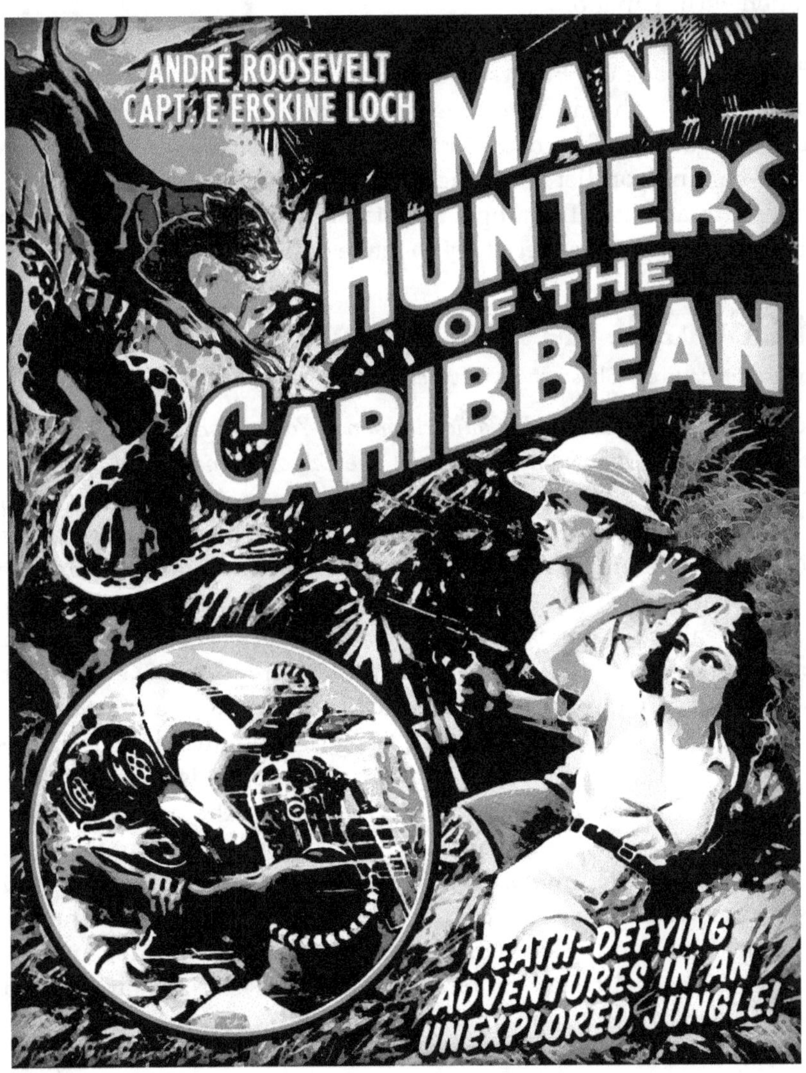

vitiated by inept acting, directing, and photography. The underwater scenes are so badly exposed as to represent a total loss. The vanity film's leading men, Capt. E. Erskine Loch and André Roosevelt, also are the directors-of-record.

In Panama, Capt. Benson (Loch) meets Rita de la Vega (Carol Jeffries), whose father had been killed while seeking a sunken treasure. Benson cables explorer Roosevelt (playing himself, more or less) to bring salvage equipment. (Roosevelt professed a kinship to Theodore Roosevelt.) Benson and Rita survive all manner of perils. They find the site guarded by murderous religious fanatics—an outpost of the Penitentes' torture-and-sanctimony cult. Caught spying upon the savages, the searchers fight their way to safety. Rita finds the treasure hidden within an idol.

Modest high points come amidst the rituals, complete with close-ups of the grotesque celebrants and a dreamlike long shot of a priestess, borne upon a high platform. These scenes are as arresting as the ceremonial footage in *The Lash of the Penitentes*. The clash of social imperatives is too big and conflicted a concern for so petty and ragged a film to pretend to address. The jungle zealots are patently a vicious lot—but who is invading whose territory to make off with whose valuables?

It Couldn't Have Happened (But It Did)

Invincible Pictures • Chesterfield Pictures • 1936

Not to be confused with *It Could Happen to You* or *It Happened Out West* or *It Happened One Night* or even *It! The Terror from Beyond Space*, this comedy-romance-thriller called *It Couldn't Have Happened (But It Did)* is a perplexing delight, complete with a seemingly impossible murder, a likably temperamental gangster with show-business aspirations, and enough backstage shenanigans to ground the fanciful plot in a recognizable reality. *It Couldn't Have Happened (But It Did)* is a Broadway counterpart to the 1932 Hollywood-studio murder yarn *The Death Kiss*, to the finer detail of a playwright who beats the law to a solution.

Dapper Reginald Denny plays Greg Stone, author of a murder mystery in production by New York impresarios Ellis Holden (Claude King) and Norman Carter (Bryant Washburn). The backer is Smiley Clark (career tough guy Jack La Rue), a glad-handling racketeer who turns threatening when the producers nix his idea of installing a none-too-promising actress (Diane Manners) among the cast. Leading lady Beverly Blake (Evelyn Brent) is producer Holden's wife—a shrew who orders the firing of actor Bob Bennett (J. Crauford Kent). Beverly also is involved in an illicit affair with Carter. A naïve leading man, Edward Forrest (John Marlowe), is infatuated with Beverly.

Reginald Denny.

For the staging of a murder scene, Smiley suggests a means of making homicide resemble suicide: He should know. Carter is shot to death; no bullet can be found. Holden, the likeliest suspect, turns up dead. Secretary Linda Sands (Inez Courtney), who is infatuated with Greg, interferes. Smiley has the right alibi: He was attending a Shirley, or Shoiley, Temple movie.

Following a hunch, Stone finds a published report of a remarkable suicide case. He thwarts an attempt upon his life and concludes he is on the right track. In a re-enactment of the Carter murder, Greg dramatizes his theory that the weapon was a gun loaded with compressed water—an untraceable missile. Greg identifies the killer as a man who had loved Beverly, and whom Beverly manipulated into committing murder. Beverly impulsively names Bennett as the brains behind the crime. Bennett, hiding in plain sight, is captured after a wild struggle. Smiley proposes to underwrite Greg's next show.

With its hair-raising qualities sturdily underpinned by droll wit, *It Couldn't Have Happened (But It Did)* benefits from the sharp contrast of Reginald Denny's polish with Jack La Rue's rock-jawed stolidity. La Rue serves as both Red Herring and comic relief. (Mike Price's cousin Vincent Price once defined the literary gimmick of a Red Herring as "the fish who's too guilty-looking to be caught red-handed.") Inez Courtney is just right as the impetuous secretary, and Crauford Kent takes an effectively jolting turn as the murderer. Director Phil Rosen juggles the contrasts gracefully, allowing for a fair deployment of clues.

I Cover Chinatown

Banner Pictures Corp. • Sack Amusements Enterprises • 1936

Norman Foster had settled in at Fox as an easygoing lead, only to find Henry Fonda landing the better such roles. Foster leapt at the chance to direct and star in *I Cover Chinatown*, for Fenn Kimball's new Banner label. (Producer Kimball had relieved an ailing Walter Futter on 1935's *Hong Kong Nights*.) The switch led Foster to some memorable *Charlie Chan* and *Mr. Moto* pictures at Fox; an affiliation with Orson Welles on

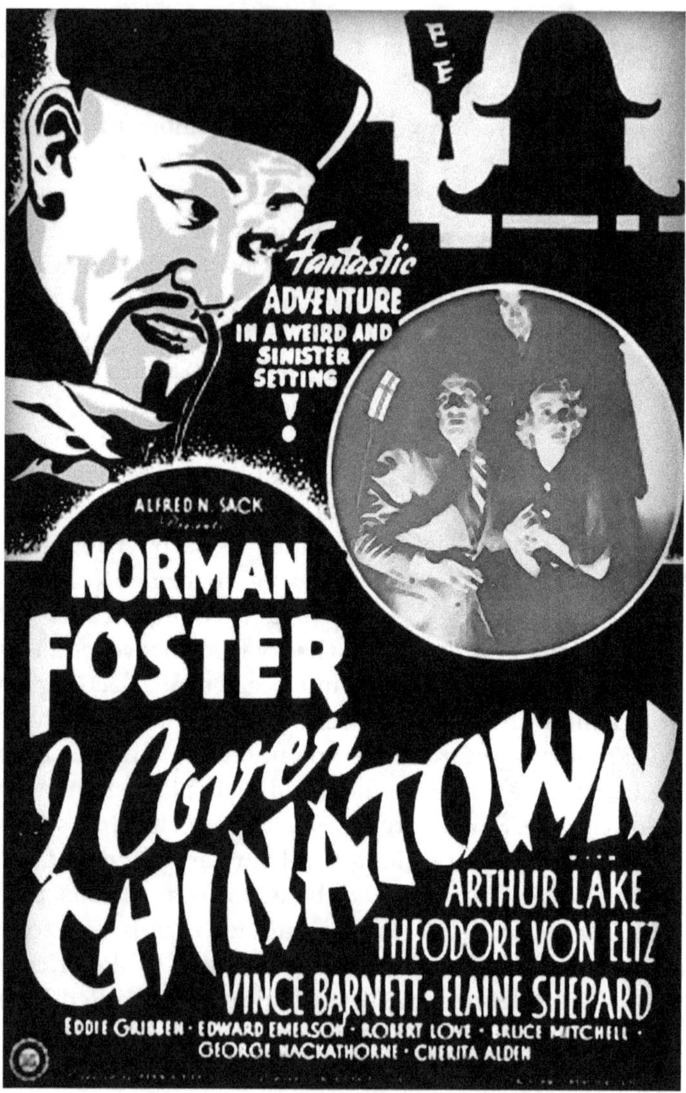

Journey into Fear (1943); such hard-boiled worthies as *Kiss the Blood Off My Hands* (1948) and *Woman on the Run* (1950); and many Disney projects. Foster's initial effort as a director, here, is strong on atmosphere.

Brothers Clark and Victor Duryea (Theodore von Eltz and Edward Emerson) are thieves posing as jewelers in San Francisco's Chinatown. Clark murders his wife, Myra (Polly Ann Young), and hides the body. The front attracts former policeman Eddie Barton (Foster). False counter-accusations follow, and a siege develops within a maze of hidden passageways. At last, the racketeers and the murderer are exposed.

The extremes of mood lie in a grim murder sequence and a wealth of comedy relief by Arthur Lake (the Dagwood Bumstead of the *Blondie* movies), Eddie Gribbon, and Vince Barnett. Foster and Theodore von Eltz are predominant as whimsical protagonist and weasly antagonist. The deft mixture of humor and chills foreshadows Foster's handling of the *Chan* and *Moto* pictures. The RKO-Pathé sets are impressive—so what else is new?

Ghost Patrol

Excelsior Pictures Corp. • Puritan Pictures Corp. • 1936

Though stranded on Poverty Row in a case of awkward timing (see: *Lightnin' Bill Carson*), Tim McCoy nonetheless gave full measure of stern heroic protagonism. Producers Sigmund Neufeld and Leslie Simmonds supplied McCoy with inventive scripts, though not all up to the grim standard of that first *Bill Carson* feature. *Ghost Patrol*, as written by serial specialists Wyndham Gittens and Joseph O' Donnell, applies elements of science fiction and mystery to an extent seldom encountered in the westerns as a class.

Lootings follow the inexplicable crashes of mail planes in an arid region. FBI Agent Tim McCoy infiltrates a criminal enclave nearby and determines that the planes have been brought down by a death ray invented by one Prof. Brent (Lloyd Igraham). Brent is a captive of ringleaders Dawson and Kincaid (Walter Miller and Wheeler Oakman).

Brent's daughter, Natalie (Claudia Dell), is held captive to keep the scientist enslaved.

McCoy survives a procession of perils while struggling to prevent another crash. He rescues Natalie and her father and brings about the collective demise of the killers with scarcely a second thought. Such wrathful decisiveness is a welcome anomaly in a time of evolution to more lighthearted attitudes for the Hollywood western.

The action is well staged in California desert settings. Minimal dialogue emphasizes the desperate situation. Kenneth Strickfaden's laboratory settings make patent the dangerous nature of the invention. Jim Burtis supplies comical touches. Walter Miller and Wheeler Oakman bring their familiar expertise to the brains-heavy roles. The menacing dog-heavies include Dick Curtis and Slim Whitaker, who lend a sharp degree of sadistic malice. (The archaic movie-business term, *brains-heavy*, translates to "smart bad guy." *Dog-heavy* refers to a subordinate mobster.)

Director Sam Newfield was in fact Shmuel Neufeld, the producer's brother—a prolific director of small-scale westerns and melodramas. Newfield also worked as Peter Stewart and Sherman Scott. Supervising editor Jack English became a leading director of serials at Republic.

Kliou (The Tiger)

a.k.a.: *Kliou / Kliou the Killer*
Bennett Pictures • DuWorld Pictures • 1936

After wrapping 1935's part-Technicolor *Legong*, Henri de la Falaise shot 30,000 feet of Technicolor stock in Southeast Asia. *Variety* reported that *Kliou*, the first full-Technicolor jungle-location feature, received support from the colonial government and local rulers. De la Falaise (whose wife at the time was the actress Constance Bennett) fell ill with a tropical virus and required hospitalization in Paris. He edited *Kliou* during 1934–1935 at General Service Studios in Los Angeles.

Kliou suffered in its day from a silent presentation, at odds with the prevailing talking-picture standard. The music-laden soundtrack and narrative insert cards seem quaintly charming today, but the film struck its original audiences as a primitive throwback.

An Indo-Chinese villager seems wanting in courage. A rogue tiger mauls an elder tribesman. The youth and a friend pursue the beast and return in triumph.

Release dates and distribution-company credentials vary. *Daily Variety*'s identification of RKO-Radio as the releasing company is patently a mistake. *The Motion Picture Herald* shows a 1937 release, but DuWorld had *Kliou* in circulation during 1936.

Shadow of Chinatown

Victory Pictures Corp. • 1936

We had briefly jumped the chronology to place the 1937 serial *Blake of Scotland Yard* in a more revealing context with *Kelly of the Secret Service*, given their Sam Katzman pedigree and their shared government-agent angle—Katzman's challenge to Republic Pictures' emerging mastery of the action-adventure picture. Katzman's 1936 breakthrough into serial-making, *Shadow of Chinatown*, is similarly competitive—distinguished by the biggest name Katzman's budgets would allow: Bela Lugosi. Katzman gave Lugosi a worthy nemesis in Victory Pictures' principal leading man, Herman Brix, in a heroic respite from a series of romantic sport-

ing features. *Shadow of Chinatown* allowed Lugosi the freedom to create a thoroughly evil character, distinguished by terroristic machinations.

Eurasian scientist Victor Poten (Lugosi) joins Eurasian Sonya Rokoff (Luana Walters) in an ethnic-cleansing bid to banish tourists from the West Coast's Chinatown districts. Poten launches a wave of destruction despite interference from novelist Martin Andrews (Brix). Sonya, who had envisioned no such lethal chaos, develops misgivings. In a strategic frame-up strategy, Poten has based the attacks upon incidents portrayed in Andrews' books—the better to deflect suspicion.

Poten mesmerizes Sonya after he has dodged an ambush by a former henchman (Charles King). Sonya recovers to join the resistance but winds up croaked. Poten, presumed dead, turns up as a waiter at a dinner celebrating his demise. Andrews attends to Poten's capture before the madman can serve a round of poisoned wine.

Mad rampages are a foregone conclusion. The suspense arises from the question of whether Lugosi will push his luck too far. Lugosi delivers a good performance of the never-say-die, lay-it-on-thick variety. The extraordinarily beautiful Luana Walters is terrific as a half-caste dragon lady whose change of heart comes jarringly early. Brix makes an energetic and indignant challenger, mingling brains and brawn. Joan Barclay, as a plucky reporter, also was a leading lady in many westerns. Prominent bad guy Charles King, also a favorite among western enthusiasts, leans surprisingly toward the side of heroism. Another horse-opera stalwart, Victor Adamson, plays a henchman.

Though lacking in mystery by comparison with the exaggerated secrecy of the Mascot serials, the plot derives intriguing complications from Lugosi's arsenal of treacheries. Fifteen chapters stretch the yarn beyond its potential; a 65-minute feature version serves the story more credibly. (That scissored edition implies Lugosi's death; in the serial, his character is captured.) Gimmicks aside, one misses the elaborate stunts and special effects of the better serials.

The scenario is the work of Isadore Bernstein, a principal developer of Universal City and co-founder of Hollywood's Temple Israel; serial-making pioneer Basil Dickey; and director Robert F. "Bob" Hill. Hill appears, with a bit of dialogue, during a wild rooftop struggle.

House of Secrets

Chesterfield Motion Pictures Corp. • 1936

Nearing economic collapse, Chesterfield remade its pioneering talkie, *The House of Secrets*. The new version benefits from improved sight-and-sound techniques and a solid ensemble cast. Substantial sets at Republic Studios, coupled with the soundtrack elements of howling dogs and maniacal shrieks, lend an unnerving atmosphere. Leslie Fenton and Sidney Blackmer, usually deployed as villains, make good offbeat heroes. Morgan Wallace and George Rosener add foreboding qualities. Principal villainy is in the capable hands of Noel Madison, Matty Fain, and a seriocomic Syd Saylor. Muriel Evans makes a winning heroine, though hardly as much a Britisher as the script would have it. The well-paced direction is the work of former film editor Roland D. Reed, a leader-to-be in the emergence of commercial television.

While crossing the English Channel, American Barry Wilding (Fenton) protects an Englishwoman (Evans) against a masher. Wilding learns he has inherited a grand but grim countryside estate, on

condition that he must never sell. Squatters drive him away. The woman from the shipboard encounter resurfaces as Julie Kenmore—a resident of the estate. She asks Wilding's permission to remain there with her father (Morgan Wallace) but warns Wilding to keep his distance. He replies that he will visit his estate whenever he bloody well pleases.

American gangsters attack Wilding within the grounds. He escapes but finds no assistance forthcoming from Scotland Yard or the Home Secretary (Holmes Herbert). Enlisting a detective (Blackmer), Wilding frees Julie and her father, a scientist in league with the government, from a criminal mob that seeks a hidden treasure. Wilding finds the loot and looks forward to a pleasant future with Julie.

Robinson Crusoe of Clipper Island

Republic Pictures Corp. • 1936

Ray Mala, often mistaken for a tropical sort, was Ray Wise, the Alaskan-born son of an American trader and an Eskimo tribeswoman. Mala lived as a hunter and fisherman under his tribal name, Chee-Ak, until a featured appearance in a 1932 expeditionary film, *Igloo*—a late-in-the-game silent, issued by Universal with imposed sound effects—encouraged his prospects in Hollywood. Mala's fourth film, *Robinson Crusoe on Clipper Island*, finds him handling the title role—a Polynesian agent with U.S. Intelligence—in an athletic and likable style, however awkward at handling dialogue. Neither the spirit nor the letter of Daniel Defoe's *Robinson Crusoe* figures here.

Mala's investigation of a dirigible crash leads him to Clipper Island, where his radio signals provoke a spy ring to trigger a volcanic eruption. The superstitious islanders blame Mala, who outwits the natives. He unites with tribal princess Melani (Mamo Clark) to put down a rebellion by a high priest (John Picorri)—all the while dodging the saboteurs' science-fictional traps. Porotu proclaims himself king. Mala trounces the spies and the disloyal islanders in (comparatively) short order.

Fourteen chapters is a peculiar measure for the serial form, whose installments usually run to 12 or 15. The length here allows too much padding for directors Mack V. Wright and Ray Taylor to honor the streamlined manner of Republic Pictures. The upstart studio had just begun to refine the style of its rough-and-ready ancestor, Mascot Pictures, with an approach distinct from other studios.

Mamo Clark is an effective secondary presence, prefiguring the *femme* leads whom Republic would later showcase. John Picorri, in a warm-up for his more flamboyant bad-guy part in *Dick Tracy*, makes a loathsome would-be dictator. Ray Mala continued as an action star and exotic supporting player until his death of a heart attack at age 46 in 1952.

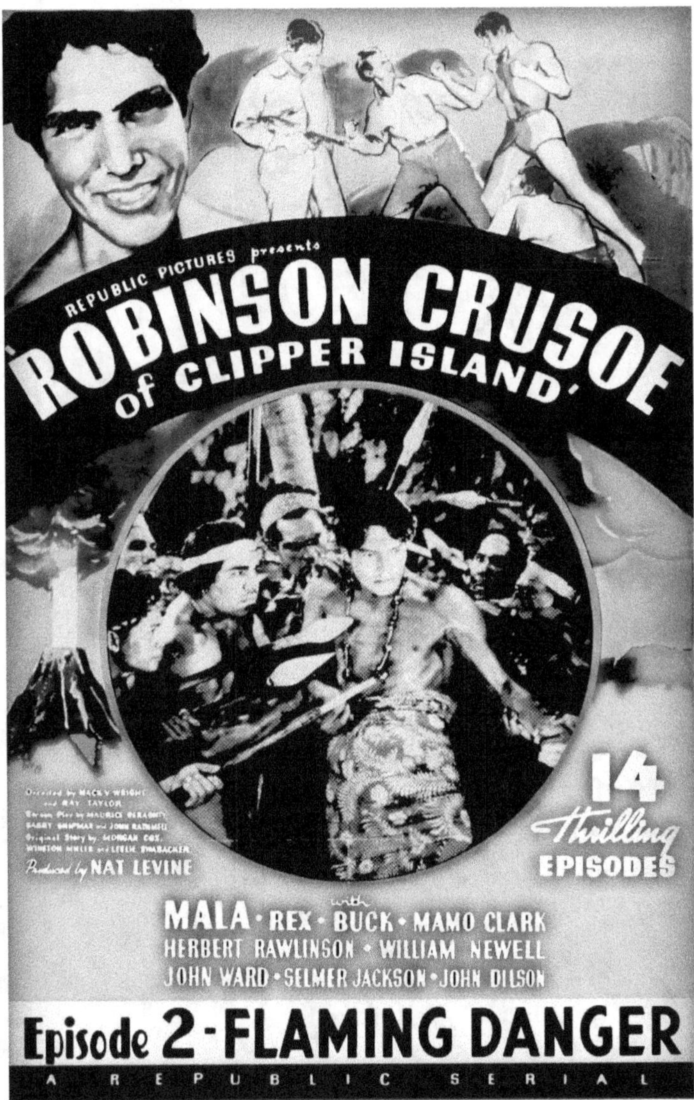

The Phantom of the Range

Victory Pictures Corp. • 1936

Sam Katzman hedged his bets for longevity with larger studios—yes, even the resurgent Monogram of the 1940s was large by Katzman's standards—by shaving costs and delivering moneymakers. A feature's schedule and budget seldom exceeded five days and $10,000. More than half the 30 Victory features are westerns starring Tom Tyler and Tim McCoy, who were too good for such modest circumstances. Both players radiate class, all the same. Tyler stars in *The Phantom*

of the Range, which like most of the Victory titles was shot on rocky scrubland on the Lazy A Ranch near Chatsworth, California. Interiors were staged at Katzman's small studio on Venice Boulevard near Culver City, within shouting distance of big-time Hollywood but a world apart. After the studio burned in 1940, Katzman established unit-production agreements with other companies.

Unlike most of the Victories, *The Phantom of the Range* obviously cost a bit more than usual. Location shooting at Lone Pine, utilizing the Alabama Hills, boosts the scenic values. Basil Dickey's scenario dusts off the shopworn haunted-ranch gimmick with a nod to Edgar Allan Poe—a hoard of gold that can be found only during a full moon.

Miser Hiram Moore, rumored to have hidden away a fortune, has died in debt. The locals fear a haunting, after sightings of a ghostly horseman. Jerry Lane (Tyler) outbids Moore's granddaughter, Jeanne (Beth Marion), for possession of the property but invites her to stay. Rival rancher Brandon (Forrest Taylor) plants a spy. A framed portrait believed to contain a map goes missing—stolen for safekeeping by Lane's valet (Sammy Cohen). The map is genuine. Brandon proves responsible for the apparition, and for a related murder—for which he frames Lane. A happy ending for all who deserve it includes the unearthing of the treasure.

Tom Tyler was ill with a stomach ulcer, but he displays the usual athletic skills and good humor. Beth Marion, a favorite with the Saturday-matinée crowd, and Yiddish comedian Sammy Cohen (playing a Cockney) are assets. Expert villainy comes from icy Forrest Taylor, hefty Charles King, and a sniveling John Elliott. Soledad Jimenez, the sinister housekeeper of the Spanish-language version of *The Cat Creeps* (1930), is similarly menacing here as a treacherous servant. Richard Cramer, usually seen as a snarling heavy, plays an honest lawman, and director Robert F. "Bob" Hill contributes an amusing cameo as an auctioneer.

The essential slugfests include a free-for-all at the ranchhouse and a terrific climactic fight between Tyler and King—business as usual for King, a favorite with the built-in audience. (King had been an operatic baritone before he joined the ranks of movie outlaws.)

The adequate photography betrays a harried pace. The audio is thin and grating—typical of Victory. Weird music accompanies the titles, and there is appropriate melodic scoring for the mysterious and comical business.

Death in the Air

a.k.a.: *Pilot X / Mysterious Bombardier*
Fanchon Royer Features • Puritan Distributing Co. • 1936

This furious tale of a skyborne serial killer made scarcely a ripple under any of three titles, although sporadic theatrical play continued into the 1940s. The film is an entertaining and provocative hair-raiser, combining melodramatic zeal with antiwar sentiments. Deranged menace is the clincher. *The Film Daily*'s review hailed the stunt flying and a certain social relevance—not so much in terms of combat shock or post-traumatic stress disorder (a valid psychological concern) as in light of "the prominent contemporary topic of airplane fatalities and [their] causes." Yes, and never mind that there were no Pilot X-type marauders prowling about the skies of the real world.

An outbreak of such disasters leads the Bureau of Aeronautics to investigate Henry Goering (Henry Hall), the manufacturer of several downed airplanes. A psychiatrist, Norris (John Elliott), advances a theory that some aviators of World War I "might go mad on the fixed idea of killing—in the air." A report of a maverick plane, marked with an *X*, lends credence. The agency assigns test pilot Jerry Blackwood (John Carroll) to assist Norris. The doctor arranges a meeting of five air-combat veterans, with electronic surveillance.

The guests are von Guttard (John S. Peters, of *Beast of Borneo*), of Germany; La Rue (Gaston Glass), of France; Saunders (Pat Somerset), a nervous Englishman; Blackwood's friend Thompson (Wheeler Oakman), of the Lafayette Escadrille; and the secretive Lt. Ives (Reed Howes). Carl Goering (Leon Ames), who manages his father's factory, seems to recognize Guttard, possibly from a prisoner-of-war encounter.

Pilot X does away with Guttard. Saunders breaks down and admits to a mania for killing. The mystery man, still at large, dupes Blackwood into gunning down Thompson. Norris turns up slain. A warrant is issued for Blackwood's arrest. Goering's ward, Helen Gage (Lona André), traces a clue to Saunders' plane. Saunders takes off with Helen in tow. Blackwood, aloft, finds himself under siege by Pilot X—and shoots down the marauding craft. Pilot X is unmasked as Carl Goering, who had falsified his war record to hide a desertion to the Kaiser's Air Force.

Elmer Clifton directs with an emphasis upon emotional tensions. The actors are not uniformly up to the challenge: Pat Somerset overplays the crack-up, and the various foreign accents

lack accuracy and conviction. The overriding impression is that of an attempt to understand the toll of war upon the minds of its participants. Lona André, a rare beauty with a heart-shaped face, makes much of an underwritten role.

John Carroll, a Republic star-to-be, carries the story as a fallible hero who finds himself manipulated to the killer's will. Henry Hall, as stern as ever, is excellent as the captain of industry who has self-serving reasons for wanting the case cracked. Kindly John Elliott pulls off a winning portrayal (despite the occasional patch of flubbed dialogue) as a visionary who advances the unpopular notion of war neurosis while deploying science-fictional devices as corroboration. Producer Fanchon Royer was a remarkable female-executive presence in a racket dominated by men.

The Mandarin Mystery

a.k.a.: *The Chinese Orange Mystery*
Republic Pictures Corp. • 1936

Having salvaged what it could of M.H. Hoffman's Liberty Pictures (see: *The Crime of Dr. Crespi*), Republic also picked up Hoffman's *Ellery Queen* option to carry on beyond *The Spanish Cape Mystery*. Eddie Quillan assumes here the role of crime novelist Queen, embroiled in the slaying of a counterfeiter (Anthony Merrill) and enamored with the woman (Charlotte Henry) who finds herself accused. The case hinges upon a rare Chinese postage stamp, which of course attracts thieves and murderers as well as unethical printers and engravers. If the title's suggestion of a Yellow Peril chiller seems a bait-and-switch, then the concentration of homicidal menace and treacherous intrigues compensates agreeably well.

Charlotte Henry.

Queen senses a frame-up against Jo Temple (Henry), in connection with an inheritance and an impatient heiress (Kay Hughes). The stolen stamp turns up attached to an ordinary letter, which promptly becomes lost in the labyrinth of the U.S. Postal Service. The heiress fears that her fiancé (George Walcott) may be the slayer—no particular stretch of the imagination, inasmuch as these two had stolen some purportedly valuable stamps, only to find them bogus. Queen solves the matter by reconstructing a vicious death trap that had claimed an unintended victim. And yes, the Chinese Mandarin stamp turns up in the mailbag of a friendly postman.

Border Phantom

Republic Pictures Corp. • 1936

After years of making Supreme-label westerns with Bob Steele and Johnny Mack Brown, A.W. Hackel signed in 1936 with Herbert J. Yates' new Republic brand. Before the end of 1938, Hackel had delivered eight Browns and 16 Steeles. S. Roy Luby's *Border Phantom*, a striking entry, plants Steele in a supposedly accursed hacienda amidst murder and madness with such distractions as a paranoid sheriff, a mail-order-wife racket, a crackpot hoodlum of a hog farmer, Chinese smugglers, a horndog cowhand who abducts the ingenue, and a fanatical scientist. Nary a lull in a packed six reels.

Prof. Hartwell (Frank Ball), an entomologist, is murdered at his laboratory near the Mexican border. His niece, Barbara (Harley Wood), fears wrangler Jim Barton (Perry Murdock) and rancher Obed Young (Karl Hackett). Young raves about an ancient curse. Drifters Larry O'Day (Steele) and Lucky Smith (Don Barclay) establish a campsite at the Hartwell hacienda. A shadowy figure attacks Smith. O'Day catches Dr. von Kurtz (John S. Peters) stealing lab specimens. A Chinese intruder stalks Young. The murder bullet is traced to Barbara's gun. Barbara is delivered to Barton.

Bob Steele.

Smith sees Chinese women emerging from barrels at Young's pig farm; they vanish into the hacienda. Chon Lee (Miki Morita) smuggles the women over the border as picture brides. Barton arranges for Barbara to join the shipment. O'Day rescues Smith and Barbara. He leads a posse to expose the racket, and Chon Lee is revealed as Hartwell's killer. The smuggler attempts suicide, but O'Day stops him.

Republic's largesse permits niceties that had been unavailable to the Supreme productions. A framing sequence in a big-city newsroom establishes the folly of a prominent scientist's decision to take his niece into a dangerous region. Close-ups, dramatic lighting, optical dissolves, and atmospheric music ennoble the story. Elaborate Chinese costuming underscores the disorientation of the lovely victims of a flesh-trafficking scam.

Jack Greenhalgh's cameras take scenic advantage of the exteriors and capture the Old Dark House qualities of the hacienda. Painted shadows reflect a Germanic Expressionistic influence. Steele's agonized crawl through a narrow, cobwebbed space will evoke claustrophobic unease in the most self-possessed viewer. *The Film Daily* hailed "much of the atmosphere one finds in a mystery play."

Steele is as comfortably intense with the dialogue as with the action, talking tough and fighting tougher. Don Barclay, a former cartoonist with the W.R. Hearst newspapers, vaudeville comedian, and veteran of *Ziegfeld's Follies*, handles the quips and pratfalls with baggy-pants grace.

The Japanese Miki Morita lends cold dignity to the Chinese villain. Lady-in-distress Harley Wood (later known as Jill Martin), heavies Perry Murdock and Karl Hackett, and mysterious German John S. Peters (of *Death in the Air*)—all fill the bill efficiently.

Forgotten Horrors of 1937

African Holiday

a.k.a.: *Jungle Adventure*
Harry C. Pearson • 1937

Gawking white interlopers blithely treat themselves to a pageant of Dark Continent horrors in this condescending vanity film, assembled from two years' worth of safari footage. Mr. and Mrs. Harry C. Pearson announce their travel plans, then load out for what they patently regard as a sideshow staged for their amusement.

Courageous Mrs. Pearson kills a rogue (term used advisedly) elephant, supplying steaks for a village and saving the legs to manufacture keepsakes for their wealthy friends back home. Apart from the spectacle of these dilettante mock-anthropologists, the most shocking incident is a ritual where tribesmen present themselves as willing victims of snakebite.

The Fighting Deputy

Spectrum Pictures Corp. • 1939

Veteran heavy Charles King dominates the tale as a scarred menace in this otherwise slight, part-musical horse opera from the classically inept producer Jed Buell. Sam Newfield, whose indiscriminate choices of assignment often neutralized his gifts as a director, directs *The Fighting Deputy* with the right Frontier Gothic attitude except when pandering to the emerging market for romantic westerns.

The law tips Scar Adams (King) to a payload in an attempt at entrapment. A holdup goes well for Adams, who leaves the sheriff (Frank LaRue) wounded. The sheriff's son, Deputy Tom Bentley (Fred Scott), takes up the chase but lapses when his fiancée (Phoebe Logan) demands that he resign. The sheriff pursues Adams, only to be gunned down. Adams' estranged father (Lafe McKee) draws on the homicidal prodigal but takes a bullet. Tom arrives and tackles Adams, who is slain by his dying father.

The perils—including the proto-*High Noon* element of a bridegroom lawman's marital quandary—are vitiated by some cringe-inducing drugstore-cowboy music. Phoebe Logan is a shrill nag. Fred Scott, an indifferent protagonist, rises at last to the occasion for violence. Comical sidekick Al "Fuzzy" St. John serves surprisingly as cannon fodder. King revels in the bad guy's viciousness: he not only kills the hero's father—but also sends the corpse to the chapel where Scott and Phoebe Logan intend to get hitched.

Riders of the Whistling Skull

Republic Pictures Corp. • 1937

A basis of Richard Connell's often-filmed tale of serial murder as sport, "The Most Dangerous Game" (1924), might lie in the same factual episode that inspired *Riders of the Whistling Skull*. The historical figure is John Eli Colter—first white man to explore Yellowstone Park, a region once known as Colter's Hell on account of its steaming eruptions. The Blackfoot Indians, ambushing Colter's expedition in 1809, took his clothing and weapons—then turned him out as quarry.

In 1817, John Bradbury chronicled the ordeal: "[Colter]...stopped, turned 'round, and spread out his arms. The [pursuing] Indian...fell whilst endeavoring to throw his spear, which stuck in the ground and broke in his hand. Colter instantly snatched up the pointed part, with which he pinned him to the earth." Colter dispatched another pursuer, circled back to reclaim clothing and firearms, and reached a fort in 11 days.

This episode is dramatized with liberties in Nat Levine's production of *Riders of the Whistling Skull*, part of a *Three Mesquiteers* series (so named in punning reference to Alexandre Dumas' *The Three Musketeers*). Other studios had adapted the novels of William Colt MacDonald before Levine delivered *The Three Mesquiteers* in 1936. Levine arranged for additional films—51 features resulted—utilizing MacDonald's frontiersmen.

Ray Corrigan, Robert "Bob" Livingston, and Syd Saylor had formed Republic's first Mesquiteers. Saylor's successor was the ventriloquist Max Terhune. Fourth of the series, Mack V. Wright's *Riders of the*

Whistling Skull, ranks among the finer horror-westerns, with a substantially original story (suggested by two MacDonald books and Colter's experiences) that also bespeaks the influence of RKO-Radio's *The Most Dangerous Game* (1932)—a film that had remained in chronic reissue.

Scientists Marsh and Flaxon (John Van Pelt and C. Montague Shaw) have vanished in Arizona during a hunt for a lost city. Outdoorsmen Stony, Tucson, and Lullaby (Livingston, Corrigan, and Terhune)—known as the Mesquiteers—find Flaxon half-crazed from torments suffered in captivity; he turns up murdered with an accursed dagger.

The searchers include Marsh's daughter (Mary Russell) and Otah (Yakima Canutt), a treacherous Indian guide. Cleary is slain with a consecrated arrow. Searcher Frone (George Godfrey) is tortured and branded. Warriors abduct Betty. Stony and Tucson rescue her. The party discovers the Whistling Skull, a towering rock. Marsh is there, gaunt but alive, amid mummies and skeletons. A re-animated mummy attacks, but Tucson disables it. Marsh reveals Rutledge (Roger Williams), a trader, as priest of the tribal cult.

Tucson reaches the valley, pursued by Otah and the warriors. One hurls a tomahawk, which Tucson returns with deadly accuracy. A rescue party arrives. Stony is saved from ritual sacrifice. Lullaby buries Rutledge and his fellow fanatics in a landslide.

In addition to robust leads, *Riders* offers a harrowing and imaginative story, high production values, beautiful scenery near St. George, Utah, stirring music, and Yakima Canutt's great stuntwork. Glass shots position the Whistling Skull atop natural pinnacles. The tribe is introduced by ominous drumming and distorted shadows. The story was remade in 1949 by Monogram as a Charlie Chan picture, *The Feathered Serpent*—with Mesquiteers alumnus Bob Livingston as the villain.

Larceny on the Air

Republic Pictures Corp. • 1937

A popular fascination with radium and radiation poisoning surfaces in such disparate films as Herb Jeffries' black-ensemble cowboy movies; William Wellman's antagonistic screwball comedy *Nothing Sacred*; and this quack-medicine thriller from producer Nat Levine and actor-turned-director Irving Pichel.

Bob Livingston, in a break from *Three Mesquiteers* duty, serves *Larceny on the Air* as Dr. Lawrence Baxter, who seeks to discredit a manufacturer of radium-based cure-alls.

Distinguished Pierre Watkin plays the bad-medicine man as more than a charlatan: as his customers turn up poisoned—including a

heart-rending portrayal by Byron Foulger—Watkin retrenches into extortion, kidnapping, and attempted murder, forcing Baxter to help develop a radioactive treatment for the common cold. Pichel paces the ordeal briskly. A safe-and-sound ending includes a promise of reform for one of Watkin's cohorts (Granville Bates).

The Devil Diamond

Conn Pictures Corp. • 1937

The curse that propels *The Devil Diamond* has more to do with greed than with supernatural perils, but the terrors stack up, in any event. The title refers to a gem that Detective Jerry Carter (Kane Richmond) means to protect against a plot to cut it into untraceable finished stones. Murders committed in the process are ascribed to a fabled malediction.

Kane Richmond is a dashingly old-fashioned hero. Frankie Darro earns laughs as a messenger who aspires to become a prizefighter. June Gale is a possessive love interest. The villainy is too generic for such high stakes. Production values test one's tolerance of the cheapskate studios.

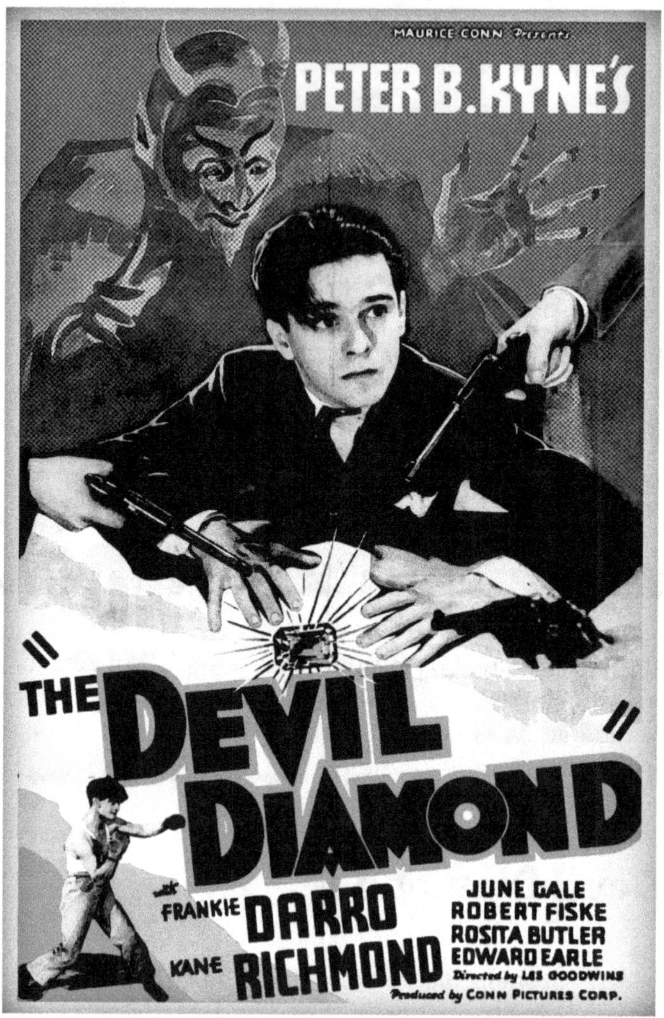

Dick Tracy

Republic Pictures Corp. • 1937

Universal Pictures' success with serial takeoffs upon comic strips—
Flash Gordon, in particular—prompted Republic to pay the Chicago
Tribune Syndicate $10,000 for the rights to adapt Chester Gould's cold-
blooded *Dick Tracy*. The transformation of Tracy from a big-city cop to
an FBI agent occurred in response to Sam Katzman's moneymaking
G-Man pictures. Republic chief Herbert J. Yates pitched the starring
role to Melvin Purvis, the famous real -world agent who had brought to
bay such Public Enemies as John Dillinger (himself an influence upon
Gould's array of comic-strip villains).

The screenwriters deleted Gould's supporting characters except for Junior Tracy, the detective's schoolboy ward. After the deal with Purvis fell through on the cusp of production, bit player Ralph Byrd—who had handled a star turn in Katzman's *Blake of Scotland Yard*—was selected to play the sharp-featured Tracy at $150 a week for 25 days. The casting proved ideal: Byrd starred in three additional Republic *Tracys*, two entries in an RKO feature series, and 39 television episodes, the latter batch shooting just before Byrd's death in 1952. As usual with the serial champions, Byrd's other feature-film turns proved unworthy of his talents.

Dick Tracy is one of the Epic serials—striving merely for generous entertainment value, but falling together as a genuinely great picture. The fundamental charm is a pervasive air of horror, a rancorous and unforgiving view of gangland that also figures in acknowledged classics from *The Public Enemy* (1931) to *GoodFellas* (1991).

Tracy investigates the murders of seven criminals, all renegades from a mob led by a mystery man known (by turns) as the Spider and the Lame One. Following the slaying of a philanthropist (John Dilson)—secretly, a Spider Gang turncoat—Tracy's lawyer brother, Gordon Tracy (Richard Beach), seeks a sealed envelope left by the victim. Gordon is abducted to the Spider's hideout. A crazed surgeon, Moloch (John Piccori), places Gordon under the knife. A transformed Gordon (played now by Carleton Young) is ordered to wreck a bridge. Tracy thwarts the plot, but the mobsters escape in a futuristic Flying Wing.

Dick Tracy falls captive but escapes via a threatening ruse. Tracy takes the place of an intended kidnap victim but is seized for outlaw surgery. Tracy overpowers Moloch and takes a stand—at last unmasking the Spider as a respected pillar of society (Edwin Stanley). The villain orders Gordon to drive him to safety. In an onrush of resurgent heroism, Gordon swerves to avoid striking Junior (Lee Van Atta) and Gwen Andrews (Kay Hughes), Tracy's secretary. The Spider is killed. Gordon, dying, tells his brother: "It's all like a terrible nightmare. ... I can't seem to remember anything. ... I think I'm going places."

High adventure is a foregone conclusion, but the opening sets a crepuscular tone: the shadow of the Spider appears to his mutinous subordinates. One, played by Byron Foulger, opens fire. The boss laughs. Later, along a darkened street, Foulger hears the Spider's footsteps. Foulger runs until, exhausted, he sees the shadow. A spidery beam of light crosses Foulger's forehead. The discovery of Foulger's body prompts Byrd's Tracy to escalate the manhunt.

Directors Ray Taylor and Alan James called a wrap on principal photography on Christmas Eve of 1936—recalling Chet Gould's comic-strip practice of closing a case in time for Tracy to mark the holiday—at a cost of $127,640. Unusual locations around Los Angeles and San Pedro, second-unit photography at San Francisco, spectacular miniature effects, and a huge cast lend a lavish appearance seldom seen in the serials. The accomplishment marked a farewell for Nat Levine, who soon sold his interest to Republic's chief executive, Herbert J. Yates. Levine worked briefly for MGM, then retired.

Tracy's master criminal is as grotesque as Gould's cartoon villains—face hidden throughout by shadows and camera angles, for a heightened perception of hideousness. A mad-scientist assistant is no less weird. Weirder yet is the transformation of mild-mannered Richard Beach into a villain hard of face and voice, played by Carleton Young with malice and a late softening of manner.

Construction favors a series of self-contained plots within a framing premise. The formula would bear repeating at Republic and often was emulated by Universal and Columbia. The defiance of logic is secondary to excitement. Fascinating trick effects include the Flying Wing, which predicts the real-world's Flying Wing—the Northrop B-35, a four-engine, 172-foot craft that came into development during 1942–46. The splendid musical scoring, a Republic hallmark, includes compositions by Alberto Colombo, augmented by refrains from Karl Hajos, Arthur Kay, Hugo Riesenfeld, William Frederick Peters, and Jean Beghon.

Hit the Saddle

Republic Pictures Corp. • 1937

William Colt MacDonald's *Three Mesquiteers* yarns (see: *Riders of the Whistling Skull*) turned promptly into a franchise for Republic, providing not only a model for rival teamings at Monogram and PRC Pictures but also a springboard for some impressive careers—including that of John Wayne.

Mack V. Wright's *Hit the Saddle* plants Bob Livingston, Ray Corrigan, and comical Max Terhune in the unnerving tale of a stallion that has been conditioned to kill upon command. The horse, Volcano, leads bad guy J.P. McGowan's herd on raids. The depredations endanger a campaign against the slaughter of wild horses. A friendly Pinto pony stands (falsely) accused.

Stony (Livingston) and Tucson (Corrigan) are at odds over a volatile combination of romance, money, and the horse-protection issue. Stony is about to be trampled when the Pinto attacks Volcano. As the Mesquiteers are reunited in a crisis, marauder Rance (McGowan) hightails it aboard Volcano, but Stony has learned the death command—and uses it to harrowing advantage.

The plot involves a troubled romantic entanglement for Livingston and 18-year-old Rita Hayworth, still working under her Spanish

ancestral name of Cansino but already oozing with star quality. It was in 1937 that she married tycoon Edward Judson, a generation her senior, and found herself transformed under his influence from a dark, exotic type to a redheaded figure of glamour, under contract to Columbia Pictures. Hayworth's breakthrough to leading roles came only gradually.

Hit the Saddle ends with an argument that the feral horses of the Plains must run free. Terhune administers the closing gag: the hog calls he has been practicing prove effective—at summoning a skunk.

Republic remade *Hit the Saddle* in 1944 as *Pride of the Plains*, an entry in the *John Paul Revere* series starring Bob Livingston and Lester "Smiley" Burnette. *Pride* is less ferocious than *Saddle*, but it gives Burnette the progressive role of a horse whisperer, a concept that would account for a hit movie of 1998 starring Robert Redford.

The Girl from Scotland Yard

Major Pictures Corp. • Paramount Pictures Corp. • 1937

Emmanuel Cohen's Major Pictures delivered an every-dollar-on-screen product and enjoyed a stepchild relationship with Paramount Pictures. In its last year, 1938, Major became a harbor for Bing Crosby and Mae West to develop their own starring pictures with autonomy—Crosby's *Dr. Rhythm* and West's *Every Day's a Holiday*, an inappropriately wholesome showcase, given her bawdier essence as an entertainer.

The Paramount brand sits awkwardly upon Robert Vignola's *The Girl from Scotland Yard*, a science-fictional trifle. Paramount had planned

in 1931 to base a picture called *Uncertain Woman* upon Edgar Wallace's novel, *The Girl from Scotland Yard*. That project was scuttled. As tempting as it is to read this *Girl from Scotland Yard* as a fresh attempt, the famous author has no bearing here.

The tale concerns the disappearance, rediscovery (in an ominous wax-museum setting), and murder of the husband of Mary Smith (Lynn Anders). Reporter Derrick Holt (Robert Baldwin) is accused. The victim had been connected with Linda Beech (Karen Morley), a Scotland Yard operative investigating explosions of military aircraft. Political exile Franz Jorg (Eduardo Cianelli) plans to deploy a death ray during the coronation of King George VI to destroy the Royal Air Force. Holt and Beech take to the air against Jorg, whose rampage escalates before he can be shot down.

Vivid character portrayals compensate for the lack of spectacle. Robert Baldwin excels as a bumbling hero with a fear of flying. A suspenseful and comical sequence finds Baldwin eluding the police by hiding within an orchestra during a party—only to betray himself with his inept musicianship. Eduardo Cianelli makes a suitably hateful enemy. Karen Morley is squarely in the no-nonsense assertive vein.

Co-screenwriter Dore Schary is remembered today as a big-leaguer, a producer for David O. Selznick and (later) chief of production for RKO and MGM, as well as a Tony-winning playwright-producer, outspoken opponent of Congress' anti-Communist scare tactics, and commissioner of cultural affairs for the city of New York. Before he cracked the major-league ranks with MGM's *Boys Town* in 1938, Schary was a struggling scenarist. *The Girl from Scotland Yard* is hardly a benchmark, but it displays the larger political concerns that would distinguish Schary's career among the high rollers.

Killers of the Sea

Grand National Films • Raymond Friedgen Productions • 1937

In which hack documentarian Raymond Friedgen glorifies the quest of Capt. Wallace Casewell of Florida to destroy what he calls "killers of the sea." Casewell had become vaguely famous by condemning oceanic predators as a threat to fishing. Yes, and never mind any balance of nature.

Casewell attacks a bottlenose whale, which escapes. A hammerhead shark is slaughtered. A black peg-legged crewman, assigned the demeaning name of Evolution Henderson, alerts Casewell to a tiger shark, which gets the knife. One diver finds a chest amid a shipwreck, seemingly guarded by a skeleton—a bit of staged hokum. A sea turtle cuts off the air supply, and an octopus attacks. Casewell kills the octopus. Sidelined by a sawfish, Casewell recovers to resume the bold crusade.

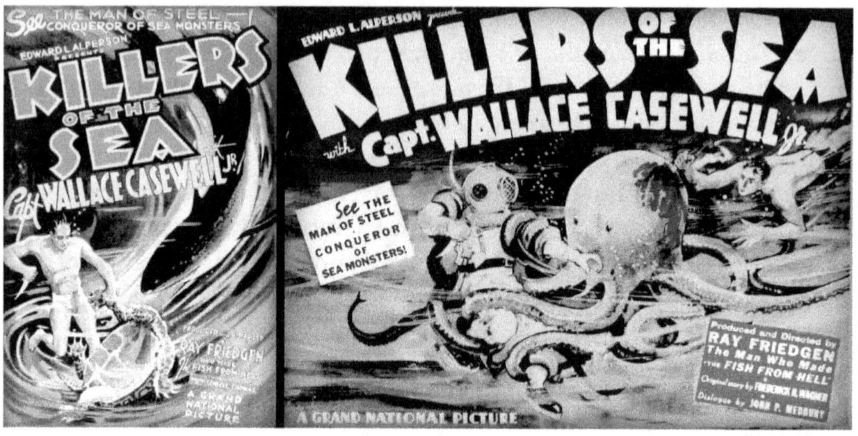

Lowell Thomas supplies the fatuous blowhard narration; the news commentator's condescending blathering also can be heard in such wealthy-dilettante films as *The Blonde Captive* and *Titans of the Deep*. Uneasy thrills abound, whether because of or despite the film's attitude. Friedgen's similarly conceived *Fish from Hell* finds Wilfred Lucas providing the motor-mouthed wisenheimer commentary—just as in *Angkor* (below).

Angkor

a.k.a.: *Forbidden Adventure (in Angkor)* / *Forbidden Adventure* / *Forbidden Adventure in Angkor* / *The Gorilla Woman* / *Jungle Gorillas* / *The Private Life of Ingagi*

Warner & Purdom Esper Roadshow Attractions & Mapel Attractions • Sonney Amusements • 1937

A trove of long-hidden motion-picture film yields a startling discovery: in 1912, two explorers had photographed their expedition to Southeast Asia. They had sought not only the ruined city of Angkor, but also the descendants of a ruling society of apes. The native bearers thus depicted are women, in a state of undress; the local men prefer to avoid the primates. The women seem unwholesomely attracted, and they threaten to mutiny if the chief ape should be harmed. A mad Buddhist priest menaces the safari. One explorer dreams (in a yellow-tinted sequence) of an ape-worship cult and a rebellion in ancient Angkor. No telling how a dream would figure in a muddle of purportedly authentic documentary footage.

So goes one of several versions of George M. Merrick's *Angkor*, or *Forbidden Adventure (in Angkor)*, to use the formally copyrighted title. A more coherent and presumably complete cut, rediscovered during the 1990s, frames the hokum in a vaguely sensible context: The pioneering filmmaker and actor Wilfred Lucas describes an expedition to trace the collapse of Angkor, 10 centuries past. Lucas explains that the expeditionary footage (bogus, but not to hear him tell it) has been augmented with dramatizations.

Thus couched as a documentary within a documentary within a documentary, *Angkor* suggests nothing so much as an ancestor of Peter Jackson's playful mock-history of cinema, *Forgotten Silver* (New Zealand, 1993)—but without Jackson's redeeming sense of the absurd.

Angkor made money for several distributors—no small accomplishment, given its origins as a knockoff of 1930's *Ingagi*. *Angkor* fared uneasily with the Production Code Administration, which at one point granted its elusive Purity Seal to distributor Dwain Esper, a seasoned hand at counter-harassing the agents of censorship.

Production Code enforcer Jerome Breen warned against "the idea of possible sexual intimacy between women and monkeys." If Breen could not tell a hair-suited stuntman from a monkey, then perhaps he also did not know his *os coccyx* from his *os calcis*. Of course, the film itself neglects to distinguish between the great apes and the lesser primates.

Esper agreed to Breen's suggested trimmings, and on March 17, 1937, the cherished Certificate of Wholesomeness was granted—only to be revoked a year later after a Code snitch had viewed a proxy-title print, *Forbidden Adventure*. Esper had scissored one version, but he took no chances at losing his primary audience of cheap-thrills oglers. Esper socked a bundle into promotion, providing such theatre-lobby standée-props as huge gorillas and snakes.

Breen registered no objection to *Angkor*'s conspicuous fakery, which is what a *Variety* critic noticed: "Phoney stuff is plentiful," declared the tradepaper, noting also: "[T]he colored [Asian, actually] girls wear a ragged towel around their waists and nothing else."

Angkor is among the last several films to feature Wilfred Lucas, who proceeded through such classier assignments as *Criminal Lawyer* (1937), *The Baroness and the Butler* (1938), *Zenobia* (1939), and *A Chump at Oxford, Brother Orchid*, and *The Sea Wolf* in 1940, the year of his death. Lucas had started with Biograph in 1907, becoming a favored leading man of D.W. Griffith and Mack Sennett while directing and writing as a sideline. Lucas' filmography includes the 1925 *Riders of the Purple Sage* and, within the present book, the likes of *I Cover the Waterfront* and *Strange People*. His distinguished career as a whole makes for an intriguing contrast with the shabby mockery that is *Angkor*.

The film, incidentally, often is confused with *Love Life of a Gorilla*, a later production of the same sort. Confusion also arises from two other *Forbidden Adventures*: one is a Paramount comedy from 1931, starring Mitzi Green and Edna May Oliver; the other is a Goona-Goona exploitationer, a.k.a. *Inyaah (Jungle Goddess)* among other aliases, whose copyright and sporadic showings date from 1934 but whose decisive release was withheld until 1938.

A curious sidelight comes from the literary agent and comic-book editor Julius Schwartz, who told us in 1993 that *Angkor* and *Ingagi* had inspired him and writer Gardner Fox to create the Gorilla City subplot in their *Flash* superhero comics of the 1960s. "We just took out the women-love-apes business," Schwartz said. "If the Comics Code Authority had known where we were coming from with that idea, we'd never have gotten away with it!" The Purity Seal mentality never dies.

Dr. Jekyll & Mr. Hyde

Pixilated Pictures • 1937

While Hollywood sweated out a foreign censors' ban against horror films, a few enterprising souls rolled their own. Most amateur films seldom go beyond the raw footage, but Glenn Alvey, Jr., entertained larger ambitions.

With several neighborhood pals in San Antonio, Texas, Alvey launched a production company while a junior high-school student, shooting in 16-millimeter semi-professional format. He made connections with Dallas-based Interstate Circuit Theatres. He delivered five featurettes—including a *Jekyll & Hyde* and, in 1940, a *Frankenstein*—that merited modest commercial play.

Robert Louis Stevenson's tale of an awakened evil fared impressively under Alvey, according to an account from Michael H. Price's theatre-operator uncle, Grady L. Wilson, an Interstate manager from the 1930s into the 1960s.

"Came off pretty good, for a bunch of kids," Wilson recalled around 1965. "Glenn followed the 1932 Paramount version fairly closely, patterned his makeup—he played the Jekyll-Hyde role—after [Frederic] March's appearance, and came up with a slick little job of work. The novelty, of course, was that it *was* kids, the oldest of 'em in their early-middle teens at the time. We [Interstate Circuit] had to make special arrangements to throw the 16-millimeter film and play its soundtrack discs in synch, 'cause our big houses were set up for 35mm sound-on-film. ... I suspect the pictures played better in the school auditoriums and recreation halls where Glenn mainly was showing 'em, in his hometown." A handmade poster (pictured) promotes a double-feature showing as a prelude to a schoolhouse dance.

"With the *Frankenstein*, now, Glenn was somewhat older and the production was more polished," Wilson added. "I mean, even though there was no question that this was *kid stuff*. That was mostly the charm of it, this kind of home-grown Orson Welles mystique. Glenn made personal appearances in a few of the cities where we played his pictures.

"There was some talk of blowing his *Jekyll & Hyde* and *Frankenstein* up to 35mm, but I don't believe anything ever came of that."

Glenn Alvey, Jr., and Babe Price in an improvised film-editing suite at the Price family's residence.

The productions caused a localized sensation and received national press in *American Cinematographer* magazine and the Bell & Howell camera company's house organ, *Filmo Topics*. Alvey seems not to have pursued a career in filmmaking.

The 13th Man

Monogram Pictures Corp. • 1937

Hollywood has dealt for generations with superstitions surrounding the number 13. Monogram was no exception, with *The Thirteenth Guest* and a remake, 1943's *The Mystery of the 13th Guest*. The eerie business of *The 13th Man* involves a murder-by-poison gimmick borrowed from Malaysian headhunters. The company is technically a New Monogram, re-organized following the absorption of the original Monogram by Republic Pictures Corp. The attitude is classic old-school Monogram.

DA Robert E. Sutherland (William Gould) has ramrodded a dozen gangland arrests as part of his campaign for re-election. He declares capture imminent for a 13th man while complaining that the local newspaper has compromised his investigation. Newsman Swifty Taylor (Weldon Heyburn) spots Sutherland and three likely suspects while attending a prizefight. Sutherland drops dead—a case of heart failure, according to a physician (Sidney D'Albrook) who is known to have harbored a grudge against Sutherland.

A fellow reporter, Jimmy Moran (Milburn Stone), learns that a poisoned dart had killed Sutherland. Taylor gathers the suspects at a radio station, intending to name the killer in a broadcast. The killer-kingpin proves to be the newspaper's publisher (Selmer Jackson)—who was *not* among the official suspects.

The 13th Man catches director William Nigh warming up for 1938's launch of a *Mr. Wong* detective series, which started out atmospherically well but deteriorated to mere competence. The *Wongs* could have used *The 13th Man*'s scenarist, John Krafft, who packs enough mayhem into a brisk 71 minutes to fill half again that length.

Weldon Heyburn and Milburn Stone make a relentless journalist-vigilante team. The villain hides behind the customary façade of good citizenship, and the suspects and accomplices are shady enough to keep the absorbed viewer guessing. It nurtures the suspense that the DA seems certain of only three suspects. Inez Courtney is just right as a helpful secretary, and Eadie Adams is a splendid *femme fatale*.

In Which Rod LaRocque Becomes the Shadow

(olony Pictures • Grand National Films • 1937–38

The Shadow, mystifying hero of the pulp magazines and radio, has long since proved too complex a character for any one movie to contain. Universal Pictures had attempted to do the Shadow justice in a string of short subjects dating from 1931's "A Burglar to the Rescue." Then, in 1937, Max Alexander and Arthur Alexander—nephews of ousted Universal president Carl Laemmle and themselves formerly on Universal's mollycoddling blood-kin payroll—announced four *Shadow* features for Colony Pictures, starring a lapsed silent-screen idol, Rod LaRocque. Only two were produced:

- *The Shadow Strikes* (1937). In his civilian identity of Lamont Cranston, the Shadow poses as a lawyer whose client, wealthy Caleb Delthern (John St. Polis), is slain after ordering a niece disinherited. The Shadow foils an estate-grabbing scam. LaRocque, who had become entrenched in character roles by this time, spends much of the picture impersonating other personages, to such an extent that the masked Shadow's appearances come as welcome surprises—though hardly as mysterious as the pulp-magazine enthusiasts might hope. Director Lynn Shores keeps the tone breezier than one would expect or desire. The revelation and dispatching of the murderer, prospective father-in-law of the rejected niece, seem slight in view of the

intrigues and their complications. The finale is almost a gag situation: the lawyer whom Cranston had impersonated seems grateful that the masquerade has cracked a case.

- *International Crime* (1938). Lamont Cranston becomes a newspaper columnist and radio personality, broadcasting as the Shadow—a risky proposition for one's secret identity. A financier's murder casts suspicion upon a gentlemanly safecracker (William Pawley), whom the Shadow believes innocent. Charles Lamont directs from a scenario based upon a pulp-*Shadow* yarn, "The Fox Hound." The Shadow is jailed and humiliated into apologizing to the police—indignities the pulps' Shadow would not tolerate. Like Gene Autry in *The Phantom Empire*, the Shadow closes the case just in time to stage a broadcast. Rod LaRocque bears up amiably, and it is difficult to dislike a picture where garrulous Lew Hearn plays a cabbie named Moe. LaRocque soon became a real estate broker. Monogram Pictures would tackle the franchise in 1946 with *The Shadow Returns*—a topic to be considered in a subsequent volume of *Forgotten Horrors*.

Paradise Isle

a.k.a.: *Siren of the South Seas*
Monogram Pictures Corp. • 1937

An earnest, over-emotional polemic with the myth of race distinguishes Arthur Greville Collins' *Paradise Isle*. The entertainment value lies in a tangle of homicidal greed and erotic tensions surrounding a supposedly accursed bed of pearls.

Blind painter Richard Kennedy (Warren Hull) becomes stranded while traveling to meet a surgeon. Ila (Movita Castañeda), an islander, shelters him. A trader (William Davidson) refuses to help unless

the artist can pay. The economy suffers from a superstitious fear of a haunting in pearl beds. Ila defies the taboo and siezes a huge pearl, which might pay for Kennedy's remedy. A love-struck native, Tono (George Piltz), assists her. The trader bribes a beach bum (John St. Polis) to pose as the doctor. The criminals kill one another.

Tono summons the surgeon, certain that Kennedy will find Ila's racial makeup repellent. The doctor (Pierre Watkin) operates on condition that Kennedy reject Ila. Once his sight has returned, Kennedy understands that he is too crazy about Ila to be bothered with any color-bar nonsense.

Dorothy (Mrs. Wallace) Reid—a recurring figure among Poverty Row talents—supervised location shooting in Samoa. A largely Polynesian backup cast lends authenticity; likewise for the ethnic music. Hull and the Mexican cinema's Movita Castañeda make an appealing match. And what better name than *Movita* for a movie star?

Shadows of the Orient / Outlaws of the Orient

Larry Darmour Productions • 1937

Shadows of the Orient and *Outlaws of the Orient* are a separated-at-birth combination. Both issue from one low-rent outfit, but *Outlaws* merited a Columbia release where *Shadows* stayed within the Poverty Row province as a Monogram title. Herewith:

- *Shadows of the Orient.* The Yellow Peril theme involves an immigrant-smuggling racket in league with aviator Flash Dawson (Eddie Featherstone). Dawson, at odds with slave-trade racketeer Chin Chu (James B. Leong), defies the gang—only to wind up slain. Rookie cop Baxter (Regis Toomey) is drawn to the mysterious Viola Avery (Esther Ralston). The mobsters abduct Viola, but she escapes by stealing a plane crammed with Chinese citizens, rendering herself a suspect. All ends romantically well for Baxter and Viola.

  Director Burt Lynwood finds little excitement in the

Jack Holt.

resolution: Regis Toomey appears content to have accumulated evidence for the appropriate arrests. James B. Leong is a properly menacing gang boss, and Sidney Blackmer is up to his usual sinister tricks as a white-guy crook. Old-timer J. Farrell MacDonald is a level-headed if befuddled investigator.

- *Outlaws of the Orient.* Ernest B. Schoedsack (of 1933's *King Kong*) directed *Outlaws* while slumming between a span at RKO-Radio and a resurgence with Paramount's *Dr. Cyclops* (1940). Schoedsack also handled Larry Darmour's production of *Trouble in Morocco* (1937), which was granted the Columbia brand, as well.

  Outlaws works the bigoted Yellow Peril angle for all its diminished relevance. Rugged Jack Holt stars as Chet Eaton, an oilman on assignment in China, who runs afoul of a treacherous warlord, Ho Fang (Harold Huber), with ambitions of conquest. A vindictive Mae Clarke (well past the better days of *Frankenstein* and *The Public Enemy*) complicates Eaton's attempt at a truce. Eaton bombards Ho Fang's forces from the air.

  An exciting finale aside, the film is not a patch on Schoedsack's major-league work. Harold Huber, if one discounts the caricatured mock-Chinese portrayal, makes an intimidating Ho Fang. Tough luck that the character's name has become unintentionally laughable on phonetic grounds alone.

  Producer Larry Darmour soon settled at Columbia to oversee the mystery franchises of *Ellery Queen*, *The Crime Doctor*, and *The Whistler*.

S-O-S Coast Guard

Republic Pictures Corp. • 1937

Bela Lugosi had been set to star in Republic's espionage thriller *The House of a Thousand Candles* but relinquished the spymaster role to Irving Pichel when sidelined by illness. Hard times followed in short order for Lugosi, what with the international horror ban calling for a strategic resourcefulness that the actor scarcely possessed. Although Lugosi had proved as adept at comedy and straightforward dramatic assignments as at grand-manner villainy, he yielded to typecasting. Lugosi had become by-and-large idled until Universal challenged and collapsed the embargo during 1938–39 with *Son of Frankenstein.* Lugosi's stop-gap film, Republic's epic-calibre *S-O-S Coast Guard*, is a horror picture in the true sense, but it proved subversive enough to get past the ban: the hellbent-for-censorship brain police considered serials to be harmless diversions for children.

And so perhaps they were. And yet, no other idiom faced a more discriminating, loyal, or adventurous audience. Beyond simplistic plotting, repetitive padding, and uneven acting, the episodic cliffhangers excelled at sustaining suspense beyond the reach of a feature film; schoolchildren had a week between showings to worry about what might happen next. The serials delivered stunt action more lifelike than that of many top-dollar productions. And the serials boasted special effects that, in their hand-wrought craftsmanship, remain impressive. The kids who made up the core audience might tolerate a cheating segué from one installment to the next, where certain doom turns to triumph or at least survival with the following chapter. But a faked stunt fall might cost a studio traffic over the long term.

The youth market also was the audience frustrated most by the embargo. When the Hollywood establishment called a formal halt to such movies in 1937, in response to the British and European censors' pusillanimous refusal to accept overtly hair-raising pictures, the effect was like that of Prohibition upon the tippling populace. But there were no horror-movie speakeasies, to speak of, and the resort of seeing so belovéd a bogeyman as Boris Karloff play the hero in the *Mr. Wong* detective pictures was but a matter of marking time until saner heads could prevail.

Karloff kept working, no matter what. Lugosi kept the faith with the chiller fans. His limited work during this period provided an oasis of horrors—if one looked to the serials—right under the censors' big blue noses.

S-O-S Coast Guard, team-directed by William Witney and Alan James, pits Agent Kent (Ralph Byrd) against Boroff (Lugosi), who offers a disintegrating gas to foreign powers. Boroff kills Kent's brother (future director Thomas Carr). Kent swears revenge.

Kent's sweetheart, journalist Jean Norman (Maxine Doyle), and Jean's photographer, McGee (Lee Ford), dodge an attack by Thorg (Richard Alexander), Boroff's monstrous slave. Kent demands the development of an antidote for the gas. Captured, Kent summons the Coast Guard. Boroff readies a barrage, but Jean arrives with the neutralizing gas. Boroff speeds away, only to find Thorg lurking. The giant has suffered enough abuse from Boroff. Boroff opens fire, but the servant kills the madman.

In his most unremittingly evil role short of *White Zombie*, Lugosi creates a turncoat who revels in sadomasochistic misconduct. Boroff— sounds suspiciously like an elision of *Boris* and *Karloff*—entrusts his barbering to the hulking servant even as he taunts the monster: "Thorg would like to cut my throat—*wouldn't* you, Thorg?" A henchman (*Bulldog Drummond*'s Lawrence Grant) kibitzes: "Why shouldn't he? He

has never forgiven you for mutilating his mind." As Thorg, Richard Alexander takes the cue to develop a nervous spasm. The effect recalls W.C. Fields' cringe-inducing razor-wielding act in "The Barbershop" (1933), but the stakes here run higher. Thorg would love to slit the boss' throat, if not for a simian dutifulness. Grant is unnerved: "I have never seen such fear and love—dumb loyalty and consuming hatred, in such violent opposition." Lugosi replies, worrying the syllables: "Thorg isn't *human*—but he *can* be *very useful*."

Elsewhere, Boroff plots to test the gas on a tethered dog. "Nice puppy," he says. "Don't be afraid." He changes his mind when reminded of a human captive, the dimwitted photographer McGee. As energetically played by Lee Ford, McGee lapses here from comic relief to honest terror. It is hardly giving away too much to note the timely arrival of Ralph Byrd—Republic's once-and-future Dick Tracy—and a scary internal climax in the (literal) melting of the laboratory set.

The combination of menaces makes heady stuff for a perceived children's entertainment, although the psychological torments are leavened by the bravura spirit that would characterize all Republic's serials. Ralph Byrd lends gravitas, too, as the hero whose patriotic duty runs a distant second to blood vengeance. The sense of justice cuts deeper than a vendetta, however, as the tensions between Lugosi and Alexander peak. Byrd makes an able nemesis, and Maxine Doyle renders the reporter more practical than decorative—but it is in the psychological realm, in seething hatreds between monsters, that *S-O-S Coast Guard* excels.

Excellence figures, too, in the special effects, which include a refinement of the melting-city spectacle from *The Phantom Empire*. The effects are the work of Ellis "Bud" Thackery, master photographer, and the sculptors and prop-builders Howard "Babe" Lydecker and Theodore Lydecker. As chief of effects cinematography, Thackery provided full-scale and miniature projections, matte and glass shots, and hundreds of superb miniature shots. The miniatures were made in collaboration with the Lydecker Bros., whose most striking contribution to *S-O-S Coast Guard* is a sequence where Lugosi's ship runs aground.

Although Thackery preferred to shoot the Lydeckers' detailed miniatures in natural light, the shipwreck required a night sky with lights beyond a distant horizon. The vessel crashes, then slides off a reef and is visited undersea by miniature divers. The illusion of reality is perfect.

Republic had hit its stride with *S-O-S Coast Guard*, whose stirring music, unflagging excitement, and wealth of visual delights could only overshadow Universal's Lugosi serial *The Phantom Creeps* (1939), with its stock music and stock footage (from 1936's *The Invisible Ray*, among others). Both serials are entertainments to cherish, however—especially *Coast Guard*, if only because it allowed Bela Lugosi the chance to strut some formidable stuff during those days when his greatest talent had become his worst professional liability.

Sky Racket

Victory Pictures Corp. • 1937

Sam Katzman had a gimmick for every occasion. With *Sky Racket*, he not only cashed in on a popular fascination with airborne piracy and fantastic gadgetry but also weighed in on the emerging screwball school of rambunctious romantic comedy. Katzman, an ultra-frugal, ultra-efficient moneymaking producer, also possessed a talent (rarely indulged) for broad-stroke directing. Here is such a rare indulgence.

In the screwball respect, *Sky Racket* is nothing to equal Frank Capra's *It Happened One Night* (1934) or William Wellman's *Nothing Sacred* (1937), but it anticipates William Keighley's *The Bride Came C.O.D.*

(1941) in its tale of aviational antagonisms leading to a sweetheart situation. Too, *Sky Racket*'s exaggerated comical tone compares favorably with such major-league titles. Herman Brix and Joan Barclay are no James Cagney/Bette Davis match, but the teaming was pure star power within its Poverty Row context. It bears noting that *Sky Racket* mixes its romantic shenanigans and hilarious indignities with a mail-robbery racket and a science-fictional method of tracking doomed planes.

Marion Bronson (Barclay), a high-society brat, balks at an arranged marriage and takes off at the moment of the wedding. Marion sneaks aboard an airplane whose pilot, Eric Lane (Brix), is a federal operative on the trail of bandits. The crooks disable the craft with a radio beam. Lane had sought to bait the robbers, but Marion's annoying presence requires him to tip his hand with a parachute leap. Before Lane can arrest her, they are captured and taken before the ringleader, Arnold (Monte Blue). Marion, thinking fast, claims that Lane had kidnapped her—prompting Arnold to consider Lane a prospective mobster. The masquerade does not work for long, but Lane sends up a decoy plane that smokes out the mob. Lane and Marion elope.

Sky Racket starts off as slapstick, with the members of a ruling-class household wallowing in pre-nuptial neuroses (a classic Jewish-wedding touch) and Hattie McDaniel—just two years away from *Gone with the Wind*—exaggerating every syllable and every gesture as Barclay's anxious maid. Katzman sustains the tone until Barclay and Brix find themselves airborne, just as Monte Blue's mob sets about its dirty work. The hostage situation is played for wisecracking wit and considerable suspense, and the romance that develops as a consequence is surprisingly convincing despite its abruptness. More abrupt romances have happened.

Special Agent K-7

a.k.a.: *Secret Agent K-7*
C.C. Burr Productions • 1937

Presumably based upon a popular broadcast serial (according to a credulous report in *Daily Variety*), this launch of an intended series proved to be the only one of its kind. Walter McGrail is an FBI man pushing a crackdown on the rackets as a prelude to retirement. Irving Pichel plays a spellbinding lawyer at the center of a serial-murder case.

After Pichel bungles the defense, Agent K-7 finds the incriminating fingerprints

Walter McGrail.

bogus. Pichel is unmasked as the killer—who has perfected the art of counterfeiting fingerprints. Pichel is better than the material, which is more than can be said for anyone else on duty here. Raymond K. Johnson is the style-deficient director-of-record.

Safari on Wheels

Esso, Inc. • 1937

The corporate name of Esso, Inc., is all but forgotten today; it is the ancestor of Exxon-Mobil and further merger-driven permutations. In its early years, Esso unwittingly contributed to the development of an important Afro-Caribbean musical form: Native artisans would transform discarded Esso petroleum barrels into melodic drums by hammering and twisting the steel vessels to register varying pitches—transforming industrial pollution into indigenous artistry. The craftsmen took care to purge the barrels of ferocious tropical bees, which found the empty vessels convenient for building hives. Hence the wise old tribal saying: "Watch out for those Esso bees!"

The Esso-produced oddity *Safari on Wheels* is a featurette designed for in-house and classroom use, the better to tout the company's products in an adventurous, semi-Goona-Goona context. The convoy of New York industrialist and art collector Lawrence Thaw tours the Atlas Mountains, explores French fortresses in the desert, and marks Christmas in the equatorial jungles with a festooned tropical plant. (Esso's previous self-glorifying films include the less exotic likes of *Wings over the Highway* and *The Magic of Oil*.)

No menace figures in this voyeuristically wholesome survey of *Ingagi* country. Grotesqueries include the Ubangi custom of slitting women's lips and stretching the flesh around wooden platters. Pygmy tribesmen stand alongside Esso tanks—product placement, in prototype—as a measure of height or lack thereof.

The 11,000-mile trek ends in an impeccable record of performance for Esso gasoline and oil. So what else is new?

Wallaby Jim of the Islands

Grand National Pictures • 1937

This seafaring adventure sought to launch a series that went no further. Four *Wallaby Jim* pictures were announced, all based upon Albert Richard Wetjen's yarns in *Collier's* magazine. The one that made it into production (under director Charles Lamont) went little seen in America but became a hit in Australia. Aussie actor Paul Hogan has acknowledged *Wallaby Jim* as an ancestor of his *Crocodile*

Dundee action-thriller comedies of the 1980s.

Roughhousing Wallaby Jim (George Houston) interrupts a pearling voyage when a stowaway, Allison (Ruth Coleman), proves to be the fiancée of Jim's partner, Norman (Douglas Walton). Allison is appalled by Jim's proclivity for violence. Rival pearl-harvester Rickert (William von Brincken) proves worse—a murderous sadist.

Norman has gambled away Jim's grubstake. Rickert covets Jim's pearl strike. Norman squares himself with Jim by taking a bullet from Rickert. Jim heads out for the next adventure—never to transpire. George Houston, chisel-jawed and personable, moved along to Sigmund Neufeld's *Lone Rider* series of frontier melodramas. Houston died at 46 in 1944.

Wallaby Jim's convincing South Seas setting was found at Lancaster Lake near Sunland, California, and at Catalina, where 20th Century-Fox had shot much of *Slave Ship* (1937). The purportedly native ranks were peopled with extras of Tahitian, Hawaiian, and Polynesian ancestry.

Love Life of a Gorilla

a.k.a.: *Kidnapping Gorillas* • *Life of a Gorilla*
Jewel Productions • 1937

A late boarder of the *Ingagi* bandwagon, *Love Life of a Gorilla* is a slop trough of mingled staged pageantry and expeditionary footage. A Col. Hubert Winstead, cited among players, may represent an inside-joke reference to the fraudulent chap associated with *Ingagi*'s brummagem. The *Forgotten Horrors* safari into the jungle of film history has grown annoyed, in any event, with the tangled mess of spurious ape rampage pictures, with their amateurism, fakery, and misleading proxy titles.

The pageant-style exposition includes native women, some authentically native and all authentically bare; an attack by lions; hunting excursions; and a fight between snakes. The tribes attract bigoted curiosity. The payoff—often subjected to censorship—involves the standard sacrifice of a purported tribal maiden to a gorilla-suited stuntman. The bold intruders dispatch the creature. A *Variety* critic noted: "Narrator becomes more excited than the audience, which hardly stirs at the inane series of events."

We have found four distinct cuts. Two, each labeled *Kidnapping Gorillas*, contain scraps from *Ingagi* and *Angkor*, probably inserted by unauthorized roadshow distributors. An entirely different picture, also called *Kidnapping Gorillas*, receives the Cine McNuggets treatment in our "In Media Res" section, in the chapter covering 1934.

Vu Iz Mayn Kind?

a.k.a.: *Where Is My Child?*
Menorah Productions • 1937

From *Forgotten Horrors* to *Forgotten Mothers* with scarcely a missed beat and no sacrifice of psychological terrorism: based upon a Yiddish play called *Forgotten Mothers*, producer-director Abraham Leff's *Where Is My Child?* is an agonized study of estrangement and inflicted mental illness. The dramatic pivot is Celia Adler's portrayal of a widow whose son is placed for adoption by the deceitful Dr. Adolf Reisner (Morris Strassberg).

Comprehending the treachery too late, Esther Leibmann (Adler) spends the next several years searching for an entrance to the child's new orbit. Reisner hovers perilously close, finally intervening when Esther is arrested for stalking the youngster, Victor Leibmann (Leo Schectman).

Promising assistance, Reisner conspires to imprison Esther in an asylum. The horrors she endures in this healing environment render her withdrawn, and a generation later—when Victor (played now by Mischa Stuchkof) begins working at the institution as a doctor— Esther cannot recognize her son. Victor takes an especial interest in Esther, vowing to punish whoever the rotter was who had stranded such a nice lady in this snake pit. Victor is engaged to marry Reisner's daughter (Ceril Arnon).

Reisner agrees to examine Esther, who struggles to remember his face. As Reisner, nervously denying recognition, declares Esther insane,

Celia Adler.

she transfixes him with a withering stare and demands: "Where is my child?" Victor's adoptive mother (Anna Lillian) comprehends who this woman is. Victor threatens Reisner with disgrace and prison. Esther regains her son and finds herself welcomed into Victor's adoptive family.

Powerfully moving in ways beyond the grasp of corporate hollywood, *Where Is My Child?* has remained largely unknown outside the realm of Jewish cultural scholarship. The picture seeks not to shock or thrill: its greater point amid the contrived ironies is a matter of piety and reconciliation, allowing a comeuppance for the bad doctor. Vincent Price told us in 1986 that his portrayal of a murderous psychiatrist in *Shock* (1946) had drawn upon the suave and manipulative arrogance of Morris Strassberg's Dr. Reisner. As such, Strassberg bears mentioning in the same breath with all those magnificent figures of abusive medical authority defined over the long haul by the likes of Price, Erich von Stroheim, Basil Rathbone, Lionel Atwill, Bela Lugosi, Boris Karloff, and George Zucco.

The beleaguered Esther Leibmann is Celia Adler's only screen role, barring sporadic television assignments from 1948 into the 1960s. Adler, a half-sister of the celebrated Adler dramatic clan, reserved her greater energies for the stage.

Telephone Operator

Monogram Pictures Corp. • 1937

Monogram is often accused of making disastrous movies, but the prolific studio made only one prototypical disaster movie. Scott Pembroke's *Telephone Operator* is, of course, a disastrous disaster movie if measured against the expansive likes of 1933's *Deluge* or 1935's *The Last Days of Pompeii*, but it works on a scale of boisterous horseplay, scandalous romantic intrigues, and two-fisted blue-collar heroic protagonism.

Telephone service must be connected to a dam site by linemen Red (Grant Withers, of *The Fighting Marines*) and Shorty (Warren Hymer, of *Hong Kong Nights*). The pals consult with switchboard operators Helen (Judith Allen) and Dottie (Alice White). Dottie and Shorty find an immediate attraction to one another. This is hardly the case with Helen and Red, despite his persistence.

During a worsening storm, Red agrees to convey Helen's friend, Sylvia Sommers (Greta Grandstedt), from an isolated cabin owned by Sylvia's adulterous sweetheart (Cornelius Keefe). Sylvia's possessive husband, Tom (Pat Flaherty), also is the supervi-

Grant Withers.

sor of the telephone operators. He arrives in search of Sylvia. Sylvia dodges her husband and leaves with Red. Helen remains. Tom gets the wrong idea and fires Helen. Red gets canned for slugging his gossip-mongering boss (William Haade).

The dam breaks. Helen commandeers the switchboard to transmit evacuation orders. Red, Shorty, and Dottie pitch in as the flood mounts. Helen and Red float away on a telephone pole. They decide to get married as soon as they can find a justice of the peace who can swim. The closing gag—forced, but workable in the context—is their choice of Niagara Falls as a honeymoon setting.

A rambunctious attitude on the part of scenarists Scott Darling and John Krafft renders the urgent situation lighthearted, even corny. The principals register a caliber of desperation that the limited cataclysmic scenes come ill prepared to support: one might even believe that Judith Allen's switchboard has become the nerve center of a life-saving campaign. The special-effects quotient is covered by heavy-weather stock footage, with adequate miniature work. *Telephone Operator* is more fun than most of the self-serious mock-epic flood-fire-earthquake-meteor mayhem that would proliferate during the 1970s and again since the 1990s.

Orphan of the Pecos

Victory Pictures Corp. • 1937

The British Board of Censors and its European counterparts may have accomplished more good than harm on behalf of the horror-film enthusiasts with their picayunish ban against the genre. To legislate morality is to provoke subversion. (Go figure how the most horrific English-speaking film of 1937, peak year of the ban, managed to get produced in Great Britain, well ahead of the ban: Rowland V. Lee's *Love from a Stranger* stars Basil Rathbone as a serial murderer.)

The infusion of weird, exotic, and fantastic elements into more conventionally conceived American pictures during 1936–37 helped to sustain the genre until a gradual resurgence during 1938–1940. (About which, more presently.) To find a morsel of strangeness outside the rigidly defined boundaries is as great a pleasure as to settle in for some unapologetic hair-raiser. Tough luck for those who prefer the arthritic reverence of categories.

We cannot determine what to make of the horror-busting fun police. Their constipated tribe professes to champion normalcy while denying the perfectly normal inclination to gaze into the abyss in the vain hope that it might not gaze back. And yet, no literary realm champions normalcy more so than classical horror, whether supernatural or naturalistic: the medium displays the pits of chaos at a safe distance, invites the absorbed reader or viewer to identify with the element of innocence threatened, and then vanquishes the menace with an implicit moral lesson against tampering with forbidden knowledge. This truism applies as readily to *The Vampire Bat* and *White Zombie* (yes, and even to Dwain Esper's scrofulous *Maniac*) as to such classier finery as *Frankenstein* and *Dracula* and *The Invisible Man*. The rule remained stable until the rise of the nihilistic shocker during the 1960s and 1970s—as epitomized by *Two Thousand Maniacs* and *The Texas Chain Saw Massacre*. (That upheaval is the concern of a companion volume by Michael H. Price and John Wooley, *Forgotten Horrors to the Nth Degree*.)

We exit calendar 1937, meanwhile, with a motion picture that illustrates well the horror-is-where-one-finds-it rule of H.P. Lovecraft. Sam Katzman scarcely could wait to get back to making such unabashed chillers as he had delivered with *The Rogues' Tavern* and *A Face in the Fog*. While marking time, Katzman sprinkled imaginative weirdness— from science fiction to derangement—through his comedies and tales of virile adventure. The devices in *Orphan of the Pecos* include an imaginary haunting and a show of rabid villainy from Forrest Taylor, a master at sneering intimidation.

The art of ventriloquism is supposed not to work outside the realm of in-person presentation, for the illusion is lost without the misdirection which results from deflected eye contact between an in-the-flesh performer and the audience. Try telling that to the movies and radio, which worked wonders for the careers of Edgar Bergen and Charlie McCarthy, and for Max Terhune and his dummy, Elmer, in the *Three Mesquiteers* and *Range Busters* shoot-em-ups. Ventriloquy applies to grimmer effect in *Orphan of the Pecos*, where Tom Tyler deploys a voice-throwing Theodore Lorch to pipe ghostly words into the air, the better to spook a confession from a murderer.

Ranch foreman Jess Brand (Taylor) kills his boss, Hank Gelbert (friendly duffer Lafe McKee), and escapes with a fortune, framing

Tom Rayburn (Tyler). Rayburn—whom Gelbert had summoned to straighten out the ranchlands' management—will tolerate none of this treachery. Lorch's ventriloquism act drives Brand to maddened distraction. The matter is settled with a slugfest, one of several that punctuate the picture.

The title suggests the presence of a child, but the orphan in question is portrayed by Tyler's wife, Jeanne Martel, as the slain rancher's embittered daughter—and a romantic interest for Tyler. Lorch, a busy player in the serials and low-budget thrillers, accounts for some lighter moments in addition to his role in cracking the case. The greater comical burden falls to sidekick Howard Bryant and to Marjorie Beebe, a google-eyed player with years of experience in the two-reeler comedies, as Martel's scared-silly pal.

Sam Katzman was a producer by choice and a director on occasion, "mostly by default," as he told us during the 1960s. "I kept a hand in as needed, but I'd rather be the guy who rides herd on the bank book." Katzman produced and directed *Orphan of the Pecos* back-to-back with *Lost Ranch* (1938), in which Tyler, Bryant, Martel, and Beebe must rescue Lafe McKee from kidnapper Taylor.

Katzman's eager return to unadulterated horror movies would have to wait until he could gain headway with the *Lightnin' Bill Carson* series of western thrillers, licensed from producer Sigmund Neufeld, and then retrench with an in-house but autonomous deal at Monogram Pictures following the burning in 1940 of Victory Pictures' studio. Katzman re-entered the realm of the chillers that same year with a spooky comedy for the East Side Kids' ensemble, *Boys of the City* (a.k.a. *The Ghost Creeps*), and with preparations for the launching in 1941 of a package of nine starring pictures for Bela Lugosi—a loose-knit series that would dovetail twice with the *East Side Kids* franchise. And yes, sometimes the horror and the humor would overlap. Stay tuned, and stay attuned, already.

Ah, To Be Young, Gifted, and Mantan Moreland

Michael H. Price and the late George E. Turner have taken film criticism into an altruistic realm which has come to be known as moving-picture archæology. They have cornered a truly forgotten outer landscape in film history, lending dignity to the potboilers of Poverty Row—which Price considers the true repository of the common man's cinema—not the elite domain of Hollywood or the national film studios of pre-war Europe. The years covered in this volume represent a time when Joe Palooka, America's common man, had better taste. At least, what was then considered junk has come to be art today.

Perhaps Price relates to the Poverty Row spookers as an analogy to his own career. He produces R&B albums, literary comic books, and theatrical productions (like *R. Crumb Comix*, the stage revue), all from down-home Fort Worth, Texas. Frighteningly prolific, he gets things done, doesn't wait for corporate sponsorship. Price, the 9-to-5 newspaper editor, published the most perceptive film criticism I've ever read, during 19 incorruptible years at the Fort Worth *Star-Telegram* (with New York Times News Service syndication). Price and Turner, as a team, literally dug into volatile nitrate film-stock canisters, risking life and limb, like bomb-squad detectives. They have helped to discover and restore silents and talkies not seen since the heyday of vaudeville. They were too modest to take credit.

Also tops on Mike Price's agenda is his breakthrough take on colored movies—as in forgotten Negro cinema. He points out the missing link between Spencer Williams and Somerset Maugham; is the first to give Pigmeat Markham his screenwriting due; and waxes poetic on the film acting of Mantan Moreland. (Price is Moreland's posthumous patron saint. No mere Negro comedian, Moreland was a deceptively brilliant comic who could have easily joined the Three Stooges, had Columbia Pictures offered him the gig instead of the Two Joes.)

Like a certain Viktor Frankenstein, Price & Turner breathe life into forgotten horror movies, reviving those precious, chilling artifacts of old American showbiz. They can thread my 16mm film projector any time.

—Josh Alan Friedman

Josh Alan Friedman is the author of such essential books as Black Cracker; Tell the Truth until They Bleed: Coming Clean in the Dirty World of Blues & Rock 'n' Roll; *and (with brother Drew Friedman)* Warts and All.

Interlocked Interlude
& Intermezzo

Scarcely anything to do but carry it on: George Turner's death in June of 1999 came only three days after he had received the first copies of our 20th-anniversary edition of *Forgotten Horrors* and declared himself ready to get cracking on an overdue sequel. The present section of this immediate and incumbent *Forgotten Horrors Omnibus*, that is— expanded and unified from two distinct editions.

We already had begun compiling materials for a sequel and planning additional volumes. The tasks played out consistently with our work together since 1968, when as a collegiate cub reporter I had imposed upon George's good graces to volunteer myself into the service of a book he was developing. That book would be *The Making of King Kong*. My assignment found me proofreading early drafts, filing research notes, and transcribing pertinent press notices from microfilm copies of Depression-era newspapers. Eyestrain City.

King Kong (1933) was George's favorite movie—run a close second and third by *Bride of Frankenstein* and *East of Java* (both from 1935)—and he was intent upon honoring *Kong* as no one else had done by relating its story from the vantage of every surviving participant. I became acquainted with the likes of Fay Wray, Bruce

Price and Turner, in a publicity shot for the first Forgotten Horrors.

Cabot, producers and co-directors Ernest B. Schoedsack and Merian C. Cooper, and Schoedsack's wife, the scenarist Ruth Rose, among many others. I spent days at a stretch in consultations with George and his co-author, the *Kong* effects artisan Orville Goldner.

In the process, George taught me to refine my raw movie-buff enthusiasm into a focused productivity. We pooled our respective collections of 16-millimeter feature films—consumer-video technology was almost a decade away from any practical reality—into the archive that would become a resource for *The American Film Institute Catalogue of Feature Films* and of course the basis of our own *Forgotten Horrors* project. The year was now 1975, shortly after *The Making of King Kong* had been published.

"Collaboration is really the ideal way to work," said George, "but legitimate collaboration is a hard thing to come by. Usually, one party does all the real work while the other contributes the *kibitzing* and *kvetching* and the Brilliant Ideas." He spoke from immediate experience, for even while his well-matched teaming with Orville Goldner was in progress, George had let himself be snookered into ghostwriting a paperback novel for a fellow journalist who insisted upon calling the effort a collaboration.

Shortly earlier, I had struck up a friendship with August W. Derleth, the Wisconsin-based author-poet-publisher, who described a partnership that he and Mark Schorer had sustained during the 1930s: The friends built an array of stories for *Weird Tales* magazine by batting their manuscripts back-and-forth until both pronounced this yarn or that fit for submission. George and I modified the Derleth-Schorer System and applied it to *Forgotten Horrors*, to a companion book called *Human Monsters*, and to any number of articles, essays, and comic-book stories. The tactic continues to serve, in the manuscripts and fragments that George had delivered as late as the week before his unexpected demise. I am reminded here of why I prefer dialogues over monologues.

An admission ticket for a midnight horror show from the 1940s.

George had resettled in Hollywood in 1978, at the behest of the master cinematographer Linwood G. Dunn. I have remained in Texas, George's and my native heath, for the longer stretch. It helps to have a colleague within strolling distance of the Motion Picture Academy's archives, but we both could only miss the in-person camaraderie of the newsroom. (In Los Angeles, George became a busy storyboard artist, effects artisan, and editor of *American Cinematographer* magazine. I became a syndicated film columnist and took every opportunity to travel to Hollywood on assignment, the better to prowl the museums and bookstores and institutional archives with George Turner.)

We had cut off the first *Forgotten Horrors* at the dawn of a ban on horror films, imposed by the British and European Boards of Censorship, remarking that, at length, "the genre rose from the grave for another go at it...a story for another day."

Got your other day, right here.

The ground rules remain consistent, calling for the coverage of weird mysteries and patent oddities, if not always outright chillers, from independent North American filmmaking companies and the occasional larger studio.

By this stage, the companies are fewer, the adventurous approach to subject matter and technique less prevalent, and the æsthetic values in flux. A name-brand company will figure now and again in the dealings of Poverty Row—witness Hal Roach's descent to the rank of a struggling independent in the long and unforgiving wake of a pre-WWII political indiscretion. Veteran indie-exploitation producer Walter Futter even crops at big-time Universal Pictures at one fleeting juncture, helping to launch a long-running *Crime Club* series with a comedy-spooker called *The Black Doll*.

Among the true Poverty Row (and beneath) studios that would forge on, obediently or subversively, through the horror ban or crop up in its wake, we find such developments as an amateur *Frankenstein* (1940), from a provincial schoolboy's communal hobby; the emergence of psychological horror on equal footing with the customary man-made monsters and supernatural predators; the explosion of surreal fershlugginer weirdness, in the lowbrow *Snuffy Smith* war-propaganda movies—of all places—as a foreshadowing of the Terry Southern-Stanley Kubrick *Dr. Strangelove* (1964); and the acceptance of the Third Reich as a metaphor for monstrousness in films both outlandish (*Black Dragons*, for example) and more nearly true to life (as in *Prisoner of Japan*).

Those principal bogeymen of Old Hollywood, Bela Lugosi and Boris Karloff, find themselves slumming more extensively along Poverty Row—Lugosi, as a consistent name-above-the-title menace at Monogram Pictures, and Karloff, as a sojourner at Monogram (in conventional mysteries), for the duration of the censors' embargo.

The great comedian Mantan Moreland asserts himself as a deft and commanding stealer of scenes, and with Moreland and Spencer Williams, Jr., as guiding lights, the black independent cinema as a class takes on a newfound assurance—adapting even horror and hellfire sanctimony to its concerns. (Of marginal note: Dewey "Pigmeat" Markham's starring featurette of 1940, *Mr. Smith Goes Ghost*, anticipates the comedian's more ambitious *Fight That Ghost* and *Pigmeat's Laugh Hepcats* [1946].)

Weird westerns, those phantoms of the horse opera, continue apace (as in the Depression years), even though their genre overall turns unnaturally cheery and tuneful. (But even Gene Autry and Roy Rogers made the occasional frontier chiller.)

Many such rediscoveries await: The point of George Turner's career was to render distant history both accessible and fascinating to as many souls as he could reach. Nice woik if you can get (away with) it.

—Michael H. Price
2019

Preface to
Forgotten Horrors of 1938–1942

Beyond the Horror Ban

Much as Universal Pictures' productions of *Dracula* and *Frankenstein* had laid a foundation for the modern horror film in 1931, so those pictures returned late in the decade to rescue the genre from a stretch of near-abandonment.

Because of a gradual embargo against horror movies by the British Board of Censors and its European counterparts, drastically fewer such films were made from 1936–37 until well along into 1939. The foreign market was sufficiently lucrative that it could influence what U.S. moviegoers were allowed to see. Careers suffered: Bela Lugosi was particularly hard-hit, and Boris Karloff enjoyed all he could tolerate of impersonating Mr. James Lee Wong, a low-rent riposte to 20th Century-Fox's *Charlie Chan* detective franchise. Despite the occasional subversive exception, impatience swelled among the paying customers.

Then, a turning point: Emil Umann, of the Regina Theatre (later known as the Fine Arts Theatre) in Beverly Hills, sensed a phenomenon that the mass-marketing geniuses of a later generation would characterize as pent-up demand. Umann acted, and decisively so.

The Regina was denied the use of first-run pictures because of the monopolistic dominance of studio-owned theatre chains, a recurring phenomenon in defiance of erratic federal antitrust regulations. Umann depended upon revival showings. He found long-neglected prints of *Dracula* and *Frankenstein* at a film-distribution warehouse; had trailers made up for purposes of ballyhoo; and opened what he called a "Mammoth Horror Show" double-feature on August 4, 1937— daring the locals to give it a try.

As the momentum crested, Umann hired Bela Lugosi for personal appearances. (Lugosi had been largely sidelined as a screen actor by the censors' dog-in-the-manger treacheries.) The Regina was packed for four weeks. In Seattle, the Blue Mouse Theatre picked up the bill, which broke the house record for paid attendance.

The international embargo persisted, but eventually Universal Pictures took note of the Regina's improvised master-stroke and ordered new prints for a full-scale reissue. The master negatives of both *Dracula* and *Frankenstein* had become battered from mishandling and careless storage. The films would sustain further damage when submitted anew to the Hays Office's Production Code Administration. The Code had grown severe and punitive since 1934, and the industry's chief censor, the sanctimonious and filthy-minded Joseph Breen, demanded several small but telling cuts. These included Colin Clive's line from *Frankenstein*, "Oh! In the name of God! Now I know what it feels like to be God!" along with the more violent action from the first fight with Boris Karloff's Monster; several close-ups from the sequence where Dwight Frye torments the Monster with a torch; and a close-up of Edward Van Sloan's Dr. Waldman jabbing the Monster with a hypodermic syringe. (The Monster's inadvertent drowning of a child had been removed in 1931, at the behest of Universal's president, Carl Laemmle. This instance of internal censorship had caused the deed to seem all the ghastlier via the power of suggestion.)

The new prints were made on Eastman's Aquagreen Colortone stock, in part because negative damage is less noticeable in a tinted print— but also because the green stock used on Universal's *Flash Gordon's Trip to Mars* (released on March 22, 1938) had caused a popular sensation. The suffusion of bluish-green proved equally right for the 1938 editions of *Dracula* and *Frankenstein*, which were issued on May 15.

The official resurrection echoed and amplified the success of the Regina Theatre: All seats were sold by 10 a.m. on opening day at the Victory Theatre in Salt Lake City, and police lines held back a mob of

Universal's formal announcement of the late-1930s reissue.

4,000 customers who had surrounded the place by noon. The crowd crushed the box office and caved in the doors. The manager hastily rented a vacant theatre across the street and had it filled within 20 minutes, keeping the program constant by bicycling the prints back-and-forth.

A 3,800-seat house in Waterbury, Connecticut, played to 6,500 paid admissions on opening day. The Warners Theatre in Fresno, California, did the biggest business in its history. Six policemen controlled the crowds at the Fox Uptown in Kansas City. The St. Louis (Missouri) Theatre did double the business of its nearest competitor for a week and held the program over for another week. On October 17, the double-feature opened on Broadway to huge crowds.

From this incremental progress came the realization that Hollywood did not need the foreign market to register big profits on a horror show. Universal announced *Son of Frankenstein*, whose production commenced on October 24, and sent out prints of additional 1930s chillers to fill the void. Other studios followed suit with reissues and new projects, and the horror ban found itself beaten. The foreign censors might have rationalized that there is no accounting for taste—so what else is new?—even though their repressive tribe had tried its damnedest to account for everyone else's tastes by dictatorial means.

Much of that renewed activity, of course, took place within the independent studios of Hollywood's Poverty Row. We had closed the first volume of *Forgotten Horrors* at 1936–37, with the emergence of the embargo, and now we resume at 1938 to demonstrate how the smaller studios fared through the ban and on into the earlier 1940s.

Conventional wisdom holds that no such films were made during that dry spell—a naïve and simplistic view, inasmuch as there can be

The independent double-billing that inspired Universal's official re-release.

The 1931 tradepaper announcement for Dracula.

no absolutes, neither in art nor in artifice. Other views acknowledge only a few such pictures, hewing to definitions more rigid than we care to employ. The fuller approach requires an inquiry beyond the conventional and convenient categories of genre.

Black independent films, ignored within the cultural mainstream, dealt with the bizarre as a means of documenting the conjoined folkways of religion and superstition. Crime melodramas are often

Universal's premature announcement for Frankenstein, *touting the intended casting of Bela Lugosi*

naturalistic horror pictures. And as to gallows comedies, we have seldom met one we did not admire.

We might once have used the term "black comedy" to describe an exercise in grim humor, but the same foolish compulsions of societal pigeonholing that once sidelined the horror pictures continue to compromise the popular culture. In our circle of working journalists during the 1990s, one well-intentioned but harebrained newspaper editor changed the phrase "black comedy" to read, instead, "African-American comedy," in an article about a Little Theatre production of *Arsenic and Old Lace.* The entirely Caucasian ensemble cast scarcely knew what to make of the published review.

Be that as it may. Here we have a picture-by-picture account of the independent chillers during a period when a real-world fear—the fear of offending a nebulous and ill-understood mass audience—had caused the American moviemaking establishment to shrink from the prospect of creating anything that might generate a welcome thrill of terror.

The basis of the counter-strike revival lay in the slow recognition of latent box-office potential in two watershed films that, as far as Universal Pictures was concerned, had served their purposes. The greater thrust belongs to one unassuming neighborhood theatre with the gumption to test the waters. The Poverty Row studios, in turn, kept a light burning against the day when unadulterated, unapologetic horror movies could come charging back with a vengeance.

—Michael H. Price and George E. Turner
Somewhere between the Vasquez Rocks and the Llano Estacado

Bela Lugosi.

Boris Karloff.

Forgotten Horrors of 1938

Wolves of the Sea

Guaranteed Pictures • J.D. Kendis • 1938

An heiress and a cargo of exotic animals survive a tropical shipwreck in this stock-footage seafaring jungle epic from the notoriously cheap J.D. Kendis. Jeanne Carmen, as the lovely castaway, has little more to occupy her time than to protect the gentler creatures from their natural predators until treasure hunters arrive. These opportunists are led by crusty old Hobart Bosworth as a captain driven mad by greed, with Warner Richmond lurking about as a snarling mutineer.

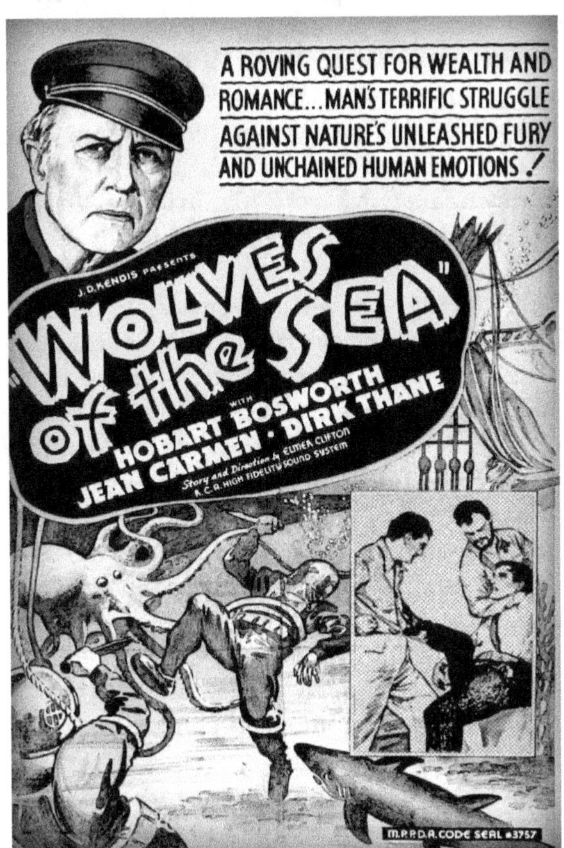

Carmen's acting is shrill enough to counteract her agreeable looks, but at least she is evenly matched with romantic lead Dirk Thane, a dreadful actor in his own right. Elmer Clifton's direction is of the traffic-cop school— momentum at the sacrifice of nuanced dramatic pacing.

To no one's surprise, the sunken diamonds (sought by Bosworth's Wolf Hansen) prove to belong to Carmen; she does not object to his claiming the jewels, presumably because she has more whence those came. True love prevails, even though Thane's William Rand puts up a remarkably thick-headed resistance to Carmen's aggressive Nadine Miller. The film is as short on thrills as it is on hour-and-change running time, and the clumsy editing and inept matching of patchwork footage are evident throughout.

The Black Doll

W.A. Futter • Crime Club • Universal Pictures • 1938

Poverty Row's sporadic infiltrations of the major leagues had seen a higher accomplishment in United Artists' release of the Halperin Bros.' *White Zombie* in 1932. The distinct sectors were constantly conversant with one another—witness, for example, the graduation of director Edwin L. Marin to big-time MGM from little Tiffany Studios. And the majors' lucrative B-picture units took many a cue from the independents.

Otis Garrett's *The Black Doll* represents another remarkable cross-over—a key series entry for the small-pictures unit of Universal Pictures (the term "B-picture" would come into general use during the 1940s), courtesy of the bare-bones producer Walter A. Futter.

Futter would not remain long in so regimented a corporate setting. He relinquished to higher overseers his involvement with Crime Club Productions, a Universal franchise tied to a series of novels. Futter found it better to concentrate on fare (such as 1940's lurid *The Leopard Men of Africa*) that would exert little bearing upon a big corporate outfit like Universal.

The Black Doll is enjoyably lurid, however conventional. The tale hangs upon C. Henry Gordon's seething portrayal of Nelson Rood, a grouch who berates his sister (Doris Lloyd), threatens a free-spending nephew (William Lundigan), drives private eye Nick Halstead (Donald Woods) from a campsite on the Rood estate, and torments his Mexican servants, Esteban and Rosita (Fred Malatesta and Inez Palange).

The appearance of *la Muñeca Negra*—the Black Doll, symbolic of a curse—prompts Rood to summon his former partners in a Mexican mining venture, Walling and Mallison (John Wray and Addison Richards), who determine that the effigy seems connected with a partner, Barrows, whom Rood had murdered.

Rood turns up, stabbed to death. His daughter, Marian (Nan Grey), summons Halstead, who tackles the case alongside an incompetent and indignant sheriff (Edgar Kennedy). Esteban and Mallison are slain. Halstead learns that Rood had prevented his sister from marrying one Dr. Giddings (Holmes Herbert), and had claimed Marian, Barrows' daughter, as his own. Giddings is revealed as the murderer.

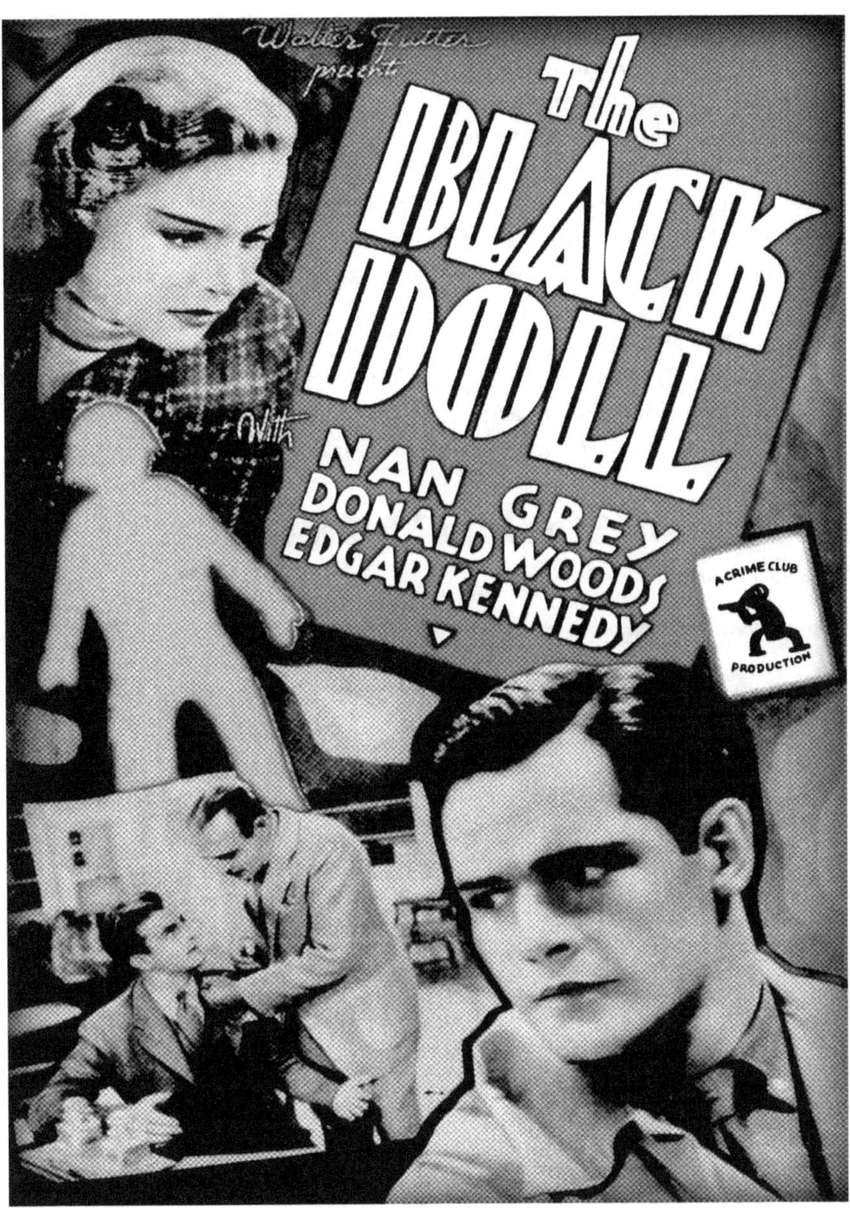

The accursed household yields a measure of shivers, all right, but veteran slow-burn comic Edgar Kennedy's performance as the hick constable propels the yarn on a crest of broad humor. Boyish Donald Woods upstages Kennedy in the detection department but plays backup throughout to Kennedy's grumpy vitality. Nan Grey, soon to become a dependable talent in such bigger Universal productions as *Tower of London* (1939) and *The Invisible Man Returns* (1941), offers an indifferent performance as the menaced daughter. C. Henry Gordon, for all the brevity of his performance, leaves a lasting impression of malice.

The Universal identity sits unsteadily upon *The Black Doll*, which—despite striking work by a fine cinematographer, Stanley Cortez—plays out more like a Monogram or a lesser Republic. The film seemed more rightly in its element during the late 1980s, when a company descended from Republic Pictures kept it in night-owl television rotation. The *Crime Club* series had commenced more auspiciously in 1937 with *The Westland Case* and would continue on bolder notes with such titles as *Danger on the Air*, *Gambling Ship*, *The Lady in the Morgue*, *The Last Express*, *The House of Fear*, *Inside Information*, *The Last Warning*, *Mystery of the White Room*, and *The Witness Vanishes*. The series anticipates Universal's *Inner Sanctum* pictures of the 1940s.

Hollywood Stadium Mystery

Republic Pictures Corp. • 1938

Suspense runs high despite a contrived script that "builds up suspicion against everybody but the [film's] producer," as *Variety* dismissed David Howard's *Hollywood Stadium Mystery*. For a picture made during an international ban on horror, this one indulges to a surprising extent in menace and madness.

Mystery writer Polly Ward (Evelyn Venable) intrudes upon the investigation of the slaying of a prizefighter—to the hindrance of DA Bill Devons (Neil Hamilton). All they accomplish as a team is to fall in love with one another. It is left to the killer, a flamboyant sportscaster (Jimmy Wallington), to crack up and confess.

Wallington's tightly wound performance makes

the character almost *too* likable until he inadvertently reveals his depraved nature. Howard keeps the action brisk as he inventories assorted red herrings—notably, weasly Lucien Littlefield and gaunt Reed Hadley—with insufficient explanation. The finale is well played despite its abruptness. Neil Hamilton makes a more convincing romancer than a figure of authority. (That sterner image would have to wait until the 1960s, when Hamilton became the *Batman* tele-series' Police Commissioner Gordon.) Either secondary *femme*, Barbara Pepper or Lynn Roberts, could have fared as well in Venable's part. Lester "Smiley" Burnette, better known as Gene Autry's Popeye-voiced sidekick, contributes such lowbrow humor as the mimicking of the noises of a hot-rod race.

Forbidden Adventure

a.k.a.: *Jungle Virgin / Inyaah the Jungle Goddess / Inyaah (Jungle Goddess) / The Virgin of Sarawak / Strange Adventures*

Ace Productions • Road Show Attractions • J.H. Hoffberg • Mapel Attractions Hollywood Producers & Distributors • Warner-Allender Roadshow Attractions • 1938

Again with the bogus safari pictures and the confusion attendant thereto which: the present stumbling-block is another *Forbidden Adventure*, but not the same *Forbidden Adventure* covered earlier in the present survey. This wilds-of-Borneo piece called *Forbidden Adventure* bears no kinship to the 1937 *Angkor*, which *Variety*, the show-business tradepaper, had cited as *Forbidden Adventure*, alias *Forbidden Adventure in Angkor*. (Sometimes with superfluous parentheses.) This selection predates that Southeast Asian women-love-apes picture by a few years. So what is it doing under the heading of 1938?

This particular *Forbidden Adventure* was produced in 1934 in Indonesia and then augmented with stock footage. The picture saw scattered showings during 1934–36, according to the American Film Institute. A Portuguese release, as *A Deusa da Floresta*, occurred in 1937. A formal announcement of issuance appears in *The Film Daily* in March of 1938. A print entitled *Jungle Virgin* bears a 1942 copyright but identifies no proprietor. The 1934 copyright registration records indicate the original title had been *Inyaah the Jungle Goddess*—a name that appears, with slight variations, on 16-millimeter television prints dating from the 1950s. There appears, meanwhile, to have been another *Inyaah*, from 1936, that remains a mystery, whether an alternate version or a different work altogether. Not that we're predisposed to go looking for one more stray piece of a puzzle that is scarcely all that fascinating in the first place. (A particularly helpful source on the Goona-Goona junkers, all due respect, can be found on the Web at the

Classic Horror Film Board. The posts associated with one Dr. Robert J. Kiss have proved both authoritative and involving.)

The film at hand involves the Dyak settlements of Borneo, where two explorers become intrigued with the legend of a white goddess—a plotting swipe from MGM's *Trader Horn* (1931). The searchers are captured by angry natives but released and welcomed upon a command from an unseen woman. Within the tribal grounds, they notice a young white woman who is venerated by the natives. She and one explorer, Tom, fall in love. The purported goddess, Ileana, tells of how she came to this place.

The daughter of planters from Russia, Ileana saw her happy existence shattered when a rival farmer kidnapped her and her mother and murdered her father. The killer raped Ileana's mother so savagely that "the spirits took her mind away." Stranded in the jungle with her daughter, the mother learned to control the animals. Her intentions naturally included revenge upon the planter and his thugs. The mother and daughter at length were given shelter in a tribal enclave. Tom and his pal, Sandy, plead with Ileana to leave the jungle, but she cannot take her deranged mother to civilization. A fire does away with the mother, and Ileana agrees to leave.

It all reads more rousingly than it plays. An inappropriate pipe-organ score drones throughout, underscoring an equally droning narration track and overemphasizing the silent-screen narrative style.

The more peculiar intrigues took place backstage. Dwain Esper, most notorious of the exploitation-film impresarios, had a hand in matters. The Motion Picture Association's Production Code Administration rejected *Forbidden Adventure* in August of 1938 on grounds of nudity and the ravishment that motivates the mayhem.

Esper was in charge of the film's affiliated Hollywood Producers & Distributors. He claimed a seal of approval upon agreeing to remove footage showing breasts and genitalia. Another distribution affiliate, Warner-Allender Roadshow Attractions, Inc., objected to Esper's receipt of the approval, on grounds that neither Esper nor director J.C. "Doc" Cook had authority to represent the film. Warner-Allender claimed further that Cook had stolen the negative. Records from this point onward seem no longer to exist, and the later theatrical prints bear not only proxy titles but also different distributor identities. If these 1940s prints are any indication, Esper's method of removing the offending footage consisted of masking black strips across those frames containing the bodily parts at issue.

It's All in Your Mind

a.k.a.: *Fools of Desire*
Bernard B. Ray • Continental Pictures • 1938

The adults-only crowd could not have known what to make of Bernard B. "B.B." Ray's *It's All in Your Mind* when the admitted sex picture began its tedious search for a mature audience in 1938. "To the vulgar," cautioned a press release, "it may have vulgar appeal. To the thoughtful observer, its appeal will be pathetic. To the psychologist, it is a representative case history of a man tortured by libidinous repressions."

At the risk of taking an anonymous publicity flack too seriously, we have grown to regard *It's All in Your Mind* as a groundbreaking work by any standard. The film proves at once lurid and tasteful, provocative by measures both intellectual and visceral, and as much a study in the cruel absurdity of lust as it is a portrait of a soul in torment. The movie also is as cheap and cheesy as its advertising campaign would suggest, and its method of revealing inner thoughts and the relentless voice of conscience is patently derivative of Eugene O'Neill's experimental play of 1927, *Strange Interlude* (filmed in 1932), and the Ben Hecht-Charles MacArthur picture *Crime Without Passion* (1934).

And yet in its reconciliation of mental anguish with physicality—often achieved with disturbingly surreal trick photography and Expressionistic audio collages—*It's All in Your Mind* bespeaks a bold *détente* between the cinema of ideas and the cinema of sensationalism. The picture bears mentioning in the same breath with any of the better-respected films that have confronted the erotic obsession over the long haul, from Erich von Stroheim's *Foolish Wives* (1922), to David Lynch's *Blue Velvet* (1986) and Stanley Kubrick's *Eyes Wide Shut* (1999).

The great streetlife photographer M.J. Jaffee captured this candid study in 1950 in Brooklyn. If the adults-only crowd knew not what to make of It's All in Your Mind *(alias* Fools of Desire*), then what of callow American youth?*

Byron Foulger.

Mousy Byron Foulger seems an embodiment of cartoonist H.V. Webster's Timid Soul, Caspar Milquetoast. Foulger plays Wilbur Crane, a bookkeeper whose wife (Betty Roadman) treats him only to insults and nagging. Crane's desire for feminine companionship is stoked by the idealized portraits of womanhood that are the stock-in-trade of the advertising agency where he works.

Emboldened by advice from a ladies'-man illustrator, Crane proves a flop at flirting, only to find willing companionship in a brash blonde named Dorothy (Constance Bergen). Unaware that she figures him for a chump, Crane wipes out his savings and resorts to theft, led on by Dorothy's promise of a passionate reward.

Crane finds his fulfillment undermined by a fear of arrest. Finally, Dorothy and her convict lover (Lynton Brent) ridicule him—driving Crane to an unaccustomed rage, which moves Dorothy to fork over the stolen money. Just as Crane is attempting to right his wrongdoing, the threat of detection drives him to a suicidal madness. Dorothy takes pity enough to rescue Crane and salvage his reputation. Crane begins to see his wife in a more sympathetic light.

The moral lesson scarcely could be blunter, or the resolution more simplistic, but writer-director Ray provides a study of gathering madness so complex as to obscure the rudimentary framework. Byron Foulger delivers a commanding performance that trades upon his familiar screen personality—more commonly applied for comical purposes—even as he reveals a self-loathing brute, lurking.

The naturalistic situation becomes engulfed with artifice as Foulger's Wilbur Crane finds himself driven headlong by the forbidden urges of satyrism but simultaneously pulled back toward a hated state of bourgeois normalcy. The voices that taunt and warn him may belong to his conscience, literalized, or they may be hallucinations provoked by guilt. As Crane's control slips, Ray wavers between subtlety and blatancy, augmenting the dense sound design with visual distortions that border on surrealism. These stylistic flourishes, coupled with Foulger's air of intensity, overshadow the supporting players. Constance Bergen seems quite the type to drive a horndog nerd to distraction, although her performance gets by merely on looks.

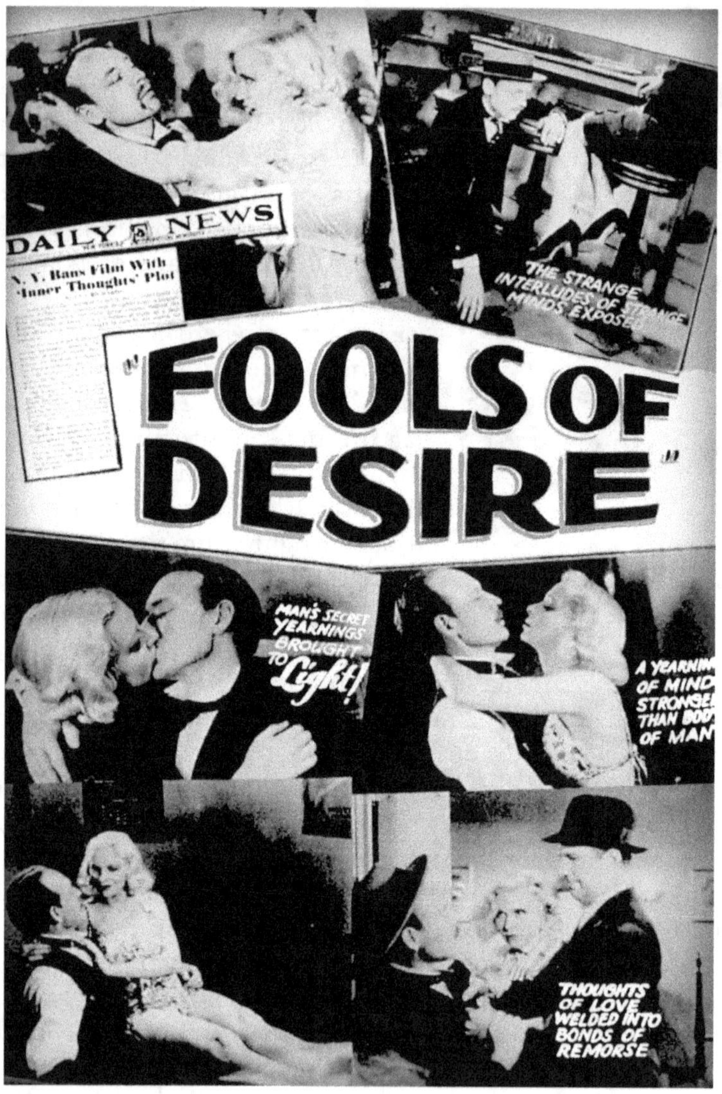

For a film that reeks of exploitation, *It's All in Your Mind* plays out with a surprising degree of restraint and puritanical tastefulness: there is a moral lesson amid the titillation. The flashes of nudity are as tantalizing to the viewer as they must be to Foulger's character. The unimaginative grindhouse audiences of the day can only have been infuriated by Ray's having left so much open to interpretation.

The censors' imaginations, conversely, kicked into overdrive: the Production Code Administration's Joseph I. Breen declared that he knew perfectly well the meaning of the *It* in the title: "The libidinous desires of a sex-hungry, middle-aged accountant." The PCA withheld its Purity Seal, on grounds of "improper treatment of illicit sex." Breen informed

Will H. Hays, president of the Motion Picture Association, that "the pretense of a psychological study...ought not to be taken seriously."

Whatever the connotations of *It*, the title proved of scant marquée value. The film was assigned a more titillating proxy title, *Fools of Desire*, for the adults-only circuit. It played as such well into the 1950s.

Byron Foulger had become a valued character man in 1937 via such films as *The Awful Truth*, *A Day at the Races*, and *The Prisoner of Zenda*. He became ever more popular for his portrayals of schemers, amusingly henpecked husbands, and under-assertive *nebbishes*. One can only wonder how Foulger might have regarded the rare star turn of *It's All in Your Mind* in the greater scheme of his career—what with the mixed blessing of dramatic challenge and sleazy promotion.

B.B. Ray had been a busy producer-director during the Depression years, with such titles as *The Mystic Hour* (1934), *Midnight Phantom* (1935), and Richard Talmadge's high-octane stunt opus, *The Live Wire* (1935). Ray's output lessened to a picture a year during the late 1930s. By the early 1940s, he had delivered two of PRC Pictures' more ambitious efforts, *Dangerous Lady* and *House of Errors*.

Its advertising come-on kept *It's All in Your Mind* out of the reach of those who might have taken it more seriously. The publicity strategy, self-defeating and awkwardly apologetic, cautioned mass-market theater operators: "Don't be afraid of the label 'sex picture.' ... This is a modern age, and hitherto subjects taboo...are openly discussed. ... Take advantage of the modern liberalism, and let your patrons know that...you have a new and novel piece of entertainment, possibly frank, but so finely handled they will have no cause to be embarrassed or ashamed. ... [A] picture that will linger long in one's memory, as a mere written description cannot describe [its] infinite beauty and daring entertainment."

And yes, right about here is where the hyperbole gets a tad thick. The dark fascination of this hidden gem is nonetheless undeniable. *It's All in Your Mind* is particularly noteworthy for its presaging of the quietly nightmarish style developed almost 50 years later by David Lynch. Lynch's *Blue Velvet* is a similarly puritanical, outwardly sensational, fable that also concerns itself with a perfectly respectable, straight-arrow Timid Soul who goes searching for forbidden kicks on the seamier side of existence.

Fury Below

J.E. Baum • Geo. Mercader • 1938

Jim Cole III (Russell Gleason) takes charge of a coal mine just in time to confront a mutiny. The nugget of horrific appeal is John Merton's impersonation of a driller driven mad by the dehumanizing nature of the work. The truer heroic protagonism belongs to veteran western champ Rex Lease, as the supervisor who routs the bullies. Mathew Betz is a thug bent upon making the takeover as violent as possible.

Harry Fraser directed the filming of *Fury Below* late in 1936 under the title *Hell Diggers*. The Production Code had demanded a rechristening: chief bluenose Joseph I. Breen informed producer George R. Mercader that the word *Hell* automatically disqualified the film for a Purity Seal. Censors have the dirtiest minds of all.

The Adventures of Chico

Woodard Productions • 1938

Though intended as an educational entry and a heartwarmer for the family trade, this unusual documentary piece also is an unnervingly naturalistic examination of a lonely and perilous existence: a central Mexican farmboy communes with the desert's many species of wildlife. The influence of Rudyard Kipling's "Rikki-Tikki-Tavi" is patent, with a terrifying set-piece in which a chaparral rooster and a rattlesnake re-enact Kipling's mongoose-vs.-cobra death match.

The story finds Chico (himself) sheltering a nest of orphaned roadrunner hatchlings. One of the flightless birds at length saves the boy from a snake. The attack and the rescue are captured with a confrontational intimacy; the sequence yielded some of the most frequently used stock footage in the history of filmmaking. Original context is best.

Filmmakers Stacy Woodard and Horace Woodard were Oscar winners (for 1933–34) in the Motion Picture Academy's short-subjects category. Stacy Woodard also had photographed Paré Lorentz' federally sponsored documentary feature *The River* (1937) about erosion in the Mississippi Basin. The now-sentimental, now-austere musical score that graces *The Adventures of Chico* is the work of the fine Hungarian composer Dr. Edward Kilenyi, mentor to George Gershwin, veteran of silent-screen scoring, and collaborator on the stirring orchestral refrains for the 1933 epic of nature amok, *Deluge*.

Zamboanga

Filippine Film Productions • Grand National Films • 1938

Tribal nudity, a near-constant in the broadly defined Goona-Goona subgenre, is conspicuously lacking in Eduardo de Castro's *Zamboanga*, an account of woman-hunting rivalries among the Moro Sea islanders of the western Philippines. The production outfit was mixed Filipino

and American, having been organized in Manila earlier in the decade by George F. Harris and Edward Tait. Musical scoring and the final cut were accomplished in Hollywood. The extensive use of Tagalog, the native language, called for English subtitling, which obscures many spoken nuances of meaning.

The story suggests a broad-stroke template for Hal Roach's 1939–1940 production of *One Million B.C.*, with the ruler of one island casting his sights upon a princess of another and conspiring to abduct her—and the rest of the ladies, as long as he's about it—while the men of her clan are away on a pearl-harvesting expedition. The native players seem to have absorbed some silent-screen acting techniques from director de Castro, with conspicuous mugging, Mary Pickford-style, from the leading lady and a melodramatically clownish show of villainy from the abductor. Dr. Edward Kilenyi's musical score foreshadows the Tiki Lounge melodic conceits of the mid-century jazz artists Martin Denny and Les Baxter.

Topa Topa

a.k.a.: *Killers of the Wild* / *Children of the Wild*
Pennant Pictures • Fine Arts Pictures • 1938

Not even the great Rin-Tin-Tin ever got to make such a wild wonder-dog thriller as *Topa Topa*, which stars the mighty—and mighty friendly—

Silver Wolf. The camera-savvy shepherd-wolf had a crucial supporting part as a furry red herring in the 1936 Old Dark House-styled shocker *The Rogues' Tavern*. In this more prominent role, the dog upstages all concerned as a half-wild creature wrongfully branded a menace.

Pete Taylor (LeRoy Mason) murders his trapping partner, Joe Morton (Trevor Bardette), and mutilates the corpse with the teeth from a wolf's carcass. Fangs (Silver Wolf), Morton's smarter-than-human pet, escapes into the woods with a bounty on his head. Taylor sets a fire to corner the animal. The fire spreads beyond control. Scientist Jim Turner (James Bush) finds the bloodied pelt.

The prevailing madness lapses from the chronic to the acute: Pete, heedless of the havoc he has caused, steals a nestful of eaglets, intending to train the birds as hunters. Morton's child, Jill (Jill L'Estrange, daughter of co-producer Dick L'Estrange), is at play nearby when the mother eagle attacks—carrying Jill away. Jim and Pete, rivals for the affections of Morton's niece, Margaret (Joan Valerie), unite to rescue the child. Fangs, lurking in the woods, forces Pete into a fatal fall. The dog locates the eagle's nest—drives away the mother bird—rescues the child—and then brings home his born-wild pups.

Some fun—and all in just over an hour. *Less* than an hour in other versions, which surfaced at intervals into the 1940s. The *Motion Picture Herald* cited the picture as a 1939 Grand National release called *Children of the Wild*, and later as a 1940 Grand National called *Killers of the Wild*. The confusion seems less confusing when it is considered that Fine Arts Pictures took charge of Grand National's troubled financial condition in 1938.

By whatever title, whenever and wherever it might have happened to play, *Topa Topa* is a raggedy winner that belongs on anybody's roster of great canine adventures—with the bonus of a co-director job (with Vin Moore) by a master of the silent serials, Charles "Hurricane Hutch" Hutchison. Source-author Charles Diltz doubled as editor; his cutting of the action sequences is dead-on-the-money exciting.

Wajan

a.k.a.: *Son of a Witch* / *Sins of Bali* / *Black Magic: A Story of Bali Island*
In Germany: *Die Insel der Dämonen*
Dalsheim Plessen Produktion • Tomfilms, Inc. • 1938

"Some mumbo-jumbo about a Balinese conjurer's curse motivates the limited mayhem and frenzied romance in this Goona-Goona travelogue, which feigns a cultural authenticity for the sake of a fair amount of Third World titillation." Or so we wrote during the late 1990s, adding: "From its lurid pun of a proxy title to its emphasis on a purportedly traditional shimmy dance, *Wajan* is purely cynical exploitation. There is a plot—*skit* is more like it—involving a forbidden romance, and rival Gods of Good and Evil put in token appearances. The greater point is ogling, plain and simple." So ran our perception of the conventional wisdom at the time. A more diligent inquiry by Dr. Robert J. Kiss and associates at the web-based Classic Horror Film Board yields a deeper view. And none too soon, granted *Forgotten Horrors*' impatience with the Goona-Goona pictures. Herewith, Dr. Kiss:

> As far as I know, *Wajan* isn't known to exist in the [documented] 70-minute edit, which was released in the U.S. during 1938–39.

However, the 78-minute, German-made movie from which all its footage was taken, *Die Insel der Dämonen* (*Island of Demons*; 1933), does exist, with a restored print having premiered at the Berlin Film Festival in 2003, and subsequently having been shown internationally. ... The British Film Institute also has a 62-minute edit under the title *Black Magic: A Story of Bali Island*, dating from its 1949–1950 British re-release. While the exploitation-minded *Wajan* edit obviously made certain changes to the original material, the basic story of [principal characters] Wajan and Sari and their encounters with the witch Léak remains at the core of all three edits. ... The U.S. lobby cards and poster likewise don't quite seem to trust the title *Wajan* alone to sell the movie, announcing the film as "*Wajan*— greater than *Goona-Goona.*"

Goona-Goona, a.k.a. *Kriss* (1932), is addressed in passing elsewhere in the present volume. *Goona-Goona* is hardly the first of its kind, but its title became a catch-all for the subgenre. Distributor Harry Thomas, who also handled the Latinate *She-Devil Island* (*Irma la Mala*), had been affiliated with First Division Pictures, whose titles included *Goona-Goona.*

Wajan purports to describe an expedition by Dr. Frederick Dalsheim and Victor Baron von Plessan, with authentication provided by Walter Spies of the Bali Museum (the film's director of record) and Gdeh Ray, governor general of Bali.

Dick Tracy Redactus:
In Appreciation of the Republic Serials

Republic Pictures cranked the momentum on May 28, 1938, with the release of *The Fighting Devil Dogs*, a Marine Corps buddy picture writ large, with Lee Powell and Herman Brix bent upon saving the world from a villain who brandishes manufactured thunderbolts. The prompt follow-through, *Dick Tracy Returns* (August 20, 1938), recaptures well the thrall of terror of the first *Tracy* (1937), with title player Ralph Byrd pitted against our often-invoked notion of the horror of the public enemy. *Dick Tracy's G-Men* (September 2, 1939) sets Byrd onto the trail of Irving Pichel, as a menace who outlasts a turn in the gas chamber to wreak 15 chapters' worth of bloody mayhem. Byrd returns in fine square-jawed form for *Dick Tracy vs. Crime, Inc.* (1941) to battle an invisibility-prone evildoer called the Ghost, whose arsenal includes a tidal wave (stock footage from 1933's *Deluge*) aimed at New York.

We lavished considerable attention on the Republic chapter plays in the 1936–37 stretch of *Forgotten Horrors*. We have considered the Republic cliffhanger scene more selectively since then, singling out such championship serialized horrors as *Adventures of Captain Marvel* and *Drums of Fu Manchu*, as well as the SF-laced rip-snorter *Spy Smasher*. The overriding tone of the serials by the late 1930s, however, had evolved to exploit the traditional element of weird menace more in the service of rampant heroic protagonism than as an unadulterated reason for being.

Then, too, the renewed availability since the 1990s of many Republic serials in primary-source video editions has rendered such stunt-action and special-effects epics significantly less *forgotten* than they had become during the 1970s, when we assembled the first collection in the *Forgotten Horrors* series.

In addition to those discussed in greater detail, we offer a historical context for the serial as a class—along with our short list of recommended favorites from the long haul of Republic, into 1955. Herewith:

If Erich von Stroheim had thought to mount his cumbersome masterwork, *Greed* (1923–25), as a serial, he might have saved himself abundant grief and even raised the grammar of the serial idiom to something nearer serious literature. The serials, of course, were never particularly concerned with the emotional depths or the psychosexual obsessions that had propelled Stroheim's artistry. (The reality of *Greed* is that Stroheim found the film whittled by corporate *fiat*, in painful stages, from a 42-reel, hours-at-a-sitting exercise to a 10-reel releasable product.)

By the 1920s, the serials had become an established crowd-pleasing form, having branched off France's continuing-adventure filmmaking style to reach the U.S. during the 1910s. A forerunner, Edison's *What Happened to Mary?* (1912), appeared simultaneously upon the screen and upon the printed page, as a moving picture in monthly episodes and as adapted chapters in *McClure's Ladies World* magazine. A truer serial format, with some incumbent peril closing each episode (hence the term "cliffhanger"), took shape with the Selig group's *The Adventures of Kathlyn* (1913–14). A more rigid standardization took shape with 1914's *The Perils of Pauline*, a 20-chapter hair-raiser that made a star of Pearl White. The record for chapter-play running time rests with *The Hazards of Helen*, whose 119 episodes (1,428 minutes) played during 1914–17.

France, well ahead of the idiom, invigorated the form with the serial-like *Fantômas* in 1913 and the prototypical miniseries *Les Vampires* (1915). Germany dabbled in serialized excitement. But America remained dominant, losing momentum when the talking-picture revolution of the late 1920s posed audio-control problems in outdoor shooting. The serials rebounded when the studios remembered the serials' action-over-talk imperative.

Universal's interplanetary gothic, *Flash Gordon* (1936; first in a series), approached epic-scale production values, with a three-times-average $350,000 production tab and the star-calibre presence of Buster Crabbe. Upstart Republic, however, delivered comparable polish on lesser budgets, and its serials are more vividly remembered today than those of Universal or RKO-Radio or Columbia, the major leagues' pre-eminent cliffhanger factories. When the industrywide serial machinery finally creaked its last in 1956, the swan-song entry from Columbia was assigned a title—*Blazing the Overland Trail*—that is bitterly evocative of the corporate slogan of a seminal serial studio, Mascot Pictures: "Blazing the Trail."

Formal history holds that the serials had their strongest appeal for the juvenile audience, but during the 1950s and 1960s we found many (then) old-timers who had reveled in the cliffhangers as young adults. In times of late, many (now) old-timers still cling to the serials as something more than cherished totems of childhood. The discerning viewer, of whatever generation, has always found more to admire about the serials than the standard simplistic plotting and superficial complications; the frequent cheating as to the identity of the principal villain; the hair's-breadth rescues and near-constant slugfests and chases; and the dime-a-dozen Machiavellian schemes to enslave the civilized and/or uncivilized world.

Much of the deeper charm rests with the technical advances that the serials—Republic, in particular—brought to the cinema at large. A great deal of the story has been researched by Jan Alan Henderson, for a book called *The Legendary Lydecker Brothers* (2011), a survey of the work of the effects wizards Howard and Theodore "Ted" Lydecker. (The book stems from a Henderson article for the December 1991 issue of *American Cinematographer* magazine. Scarcely a coincidence that George E. Turner, co-founder of *Forgotten Horrors*, served as editor of *American Cinematographer* from the 1980s into the 1990s.)

Late in 1935, after Republic was created through a strong-arm merger of Mascot, the original Monogram Pictures, and Majestic, Liberty and Herbert J. Yates' Consolidated Film Industries, Mascot artist Howard Lydecker summoned his brother from Idaho, where Ted was working as a cowboy. The final Mascot serial, *The Fighting Marines*, was issued via Republic; *Marines* features Howard's dynamic Flying Wing aircraft design, a convincing and prophetic miniature that would also figure in two Republic serials.

"In 1936, Republic produced the first of its 66 serials, *Darkest Africa*," writes Henderson. "This was a showcase for the Lydeckers' special-effects mastery. Miniature jungle cities, flying bat-men, volcanoes, and earthquakes, along with Clyde Beatty's [animal-training showmanship], made *Darkest Africa* most satisfying Saturday-matinée fare...[with] the Lydeckers' first flying dummies, both full-scale and miniature."

The closing of Republic in 1959 sent the Lydeckers on their separate ways. Howard worked on *Voyage to the Bottom of the Sea* (1961) and its

Emmy-winning television spinoff; and on *It's a Mad, Mad, Mad, Mad World* (1962) and the tele-series *Lost in Space*. Ted landed briefly at Disney, then at Universal, where he delivered miniatures for Alfred Hitchcock's *The Birds* (1963) and worked on *The Andromeda Strain* (1971). Ted complained that he found the new generation of stunt players less cooperative—and less attuned to collaboration—than their forerunners at Republic. Howard Lydecker died in 1969, Ted in 1991. As Henderson tells it: "Their pioneering, larger-than-miniature models, often photographed in natural light, provided the blueprint for the [George] Lucas & [Steven] Spielberg school of special effects." The Lydeckers do not consistently receive screen credit; they are nonetheless ever-present in the Republics.

Durango Valley Raiders

Supreme Pictures • Republic Pictures • 1938

Masked Marauder time again, back at the old corral. This relic called *Durango Valley Raiders*, old-fashioned even in its day, was cranked out by Sam Newfield for A.W. Hackel's Supreme Pictures, which sold the footage to product-hungry Republic. The yarn pivots upon a villain known as the Shadow, a brigand and serial killer.

Bob Steele plays wanderer Keene Cordner, whose father, Boone Cordner (Steve Clark), had been a *compadre* of rancher Mac McKay (Karl Hackett). McKay hires Keene as foreman. In a severe chain of developments, Keene is not only accused of being the Shadow—he also impersonates the Shadow, for the sake of ferreting out the real Shadow, who years ago had wrecked the partnership of Mac and Boone. The Shadow,

meanwhile, plots to massacre his own gang. Unmasked as the local sheriff (Forrest Taylor), the Shadow is killed by Lobo (Ted Adams), his second-in-command.

Crammed with action and played through clenched teeth by Steele and villains Ted Adams and Forrest Taylor, *Durango Valley Raiders* is a slight but welcome reminder of the earlier 1930s' more ferocious westerns, including *Under Texas Skies* and the Ken Maynard classic, *Tombstone Canyon.*

It Happened in Chicago

General Film Laboratory of Chicago • Chicago *Daily Times* • 1938

Director Clark Willis' borderline mad doctor yarn, *It Happened in Chicago*, is worth noting for its (unsensationalized) presaging of the role that Boris Karloff would play only two years later in Monogram's *The Ape.* The featurette is a home-grown semi-professional effort, featuring unknown talents in the tale of a banished physician (Charles Hughes) who retreats to the basement of his household to pursue a maverick quest to cure polio. (The notion was, of course, science fiction at the time.) The doctor's son (Lawrence Ulrich) becomes infected via a laboratory monkey, and the doctor is forced to call upon the medical establishment that had abandoned him. All turns out tolerably well. Local notices were charitable, and the film surprisingly attracted the Hollywood trade-papers' attention. *It Happened in Chicago* seems never to have played widely.

The Night Hawk

Republic Pictures Corp. • 1938

Tough-guy sentimentality mixes uneasily with a conspiracy to hijack an iron lung in this newspaperman-vs-gangsters yarn. There is an oasis of horrific impact, amid that long dry spell for out-and-out horror movies, in a sadistic attempt to kill the hero, Robert Livingston, with blasts of steam while he is trapped in a ship's cargo hold.

Livingston had been relieved from duty on the *Three Mesquiteers* western series by the arrival of John Wayne. He serves *The Night Hawk* as Slim Torrence, a reporter who leads an adventurous life outside the newsroom while romancing June Travis on the side.

Mobsters with a grudge against Charlie McCormick (Robert Armstrong), a tender-hearted underworld figure, steal a breathing tank destined for McCormick's dying brother (Billy Burrud). The crooks demand a hefty sum in exchange for a safe-and-sound return.

Livingston sneaks inside the lifesaving machine, steals the gang's

hauler in a hail of lead, incidentally cracks a confounding murder case and a booze-smuggling racket in the process, scoops the competing news-hacks, and gets himself trapped like a steamed lobster in the whiskey ship. The complications are a bit much for only an hour-and-change, but all turns out well for all who deserve it.

Livingston is as able a romancer as he is a battler, and Travis makes plenty of too little time on screen. Robert Armstrong, in a welcome return following a year's absence from the screen, does well by his character's conflicting traits of kindliness and criminality. Joseph Downing is the meanest of a vicious lot. Billy Burrud seems too chin-up plucky as the disabled youth. Dwight Frye, of *Dracula* and *Frankenstein*, and their follow-ups, has a surprisingly small role.

In Which Boris Karloff Rights Some Old Wongs

Monogram Pictures Corp. • 1938-1940

With his meat-and-potatoes genre, the unapologetic horror film, on official hiatus with the studios as a class, Boris Karloff retrenched to more generalized character roles, such as had been his lot as a working actor during the years before *Frankenstein*. Karloff told us in 1968:

> Any old port in the proverbial storm. The tactic was to keep one's name in the view of the public and the studios, even if it meant diminished circumstances. Now, Monogram was hardly as bad as all that—even though they *were not* Universal, of course—and I took Monogram's *Mr. Wong* series gratefully.

> *Mr. Wong* meant a holiday from bogeyman typecasting—and you should know, I've always been severely mixed about that typecasting, appreciative and yet rather painfully aware of its limita-

Portrait studies of Boris Karloff as James Lee Wong.

tions—but [the *Wong* series] also promised me a short-enough holding pattern until such time as the public's thwarted desire for some spanking-new, good old-fashioned scares would once again be honored. I rather enjoyed being Mr. Wong, but I was also glad to be reprieved, to be allowed to wrap up my little pact with Monogram with one of those good old-fashioned chillers.

A rundown on the Karloff *Wongs* follows. For the series' distinctive final entry, and for Karloff's welcome escape hatch from Monogram, see *Phantom of Chinatown* and *The Ape*.

Mr. Wong, Detective (1938). In an auspicious beginning for a modest and uneven series, the celebrated detective James Lee Wong (Karloff) is summoned too late to prevent the murder of San Francisco industrialist Simon Dayton (John Hamilton). The likeliest culprit is a surly inventor named Roemer (John St. Polis). Wong, unconvinced in view of reports that Roemer had threatened Dayton with a gun, finds shards from a glass vessel. An autopsy establishes that Dayton was killed by a poisonous gas. Suspects and slayings multiply, and finally Wong traps Roemer into betraying himself as a foreign agent by confronting him with one of the fragile spheres. (The murder-by-gas-laden-globe gimmick also figures in 1934's *Fifteen Wives*.)

Director William Nigh strikes an uncharacteristically suspenseful pace, and Karloff lends Mr. Wong the right measures of Asian patience,

Oxfordian demeanor, and relentless severity—far more inventive a presence than the imitation *Charlie Chan* franchise that Monogram had anticipated in securing the rights to Hugh Wiley's stories from *Collier's* magazine. Karloff had researched the role in greater detail than the studio could have asked; he based his appearance upon photographs of a westernized Chinese personage in the employ of one of Karloff's brothers, a diplomat with the British Foreign Service.

Grant Withers is memorable as a slow-on-the-uptake police officer, whose rank and name vary from film to film. Monogram eventually would pick up the *Charlie Chan* series from 20th Century-Fox, and indeed the 1947 *Docks of New Orleans*, starring Roland Winters as Chan, is a desultory remake of *Mr. Wong, Detective*.

The Mystery of Mr. Wong (1939). *Mr. Wong, Detective* had turned out so surprisingly well that expectations now ran unreasonably high. *The Mystery of Mr. Wong* turns upon the theft of an accursed jewel from China. The thief, an unscrupulous collector (Morgan Wallace), is first to die. Mr. Wong investigates, along with his San Francisco policeman colleague, Street (Withers). Wong suspects Stroganoff (Ivan Lebedeff), a sinister Russian, but other likely culprits and additional slayings abound.

The master sleuth clears all parties but one—the vengeful former brother-in-law (*The Black Doll*'s Holmes Herbert) of the first victim. The historic gem, whose purported curse has proved to be no such thing, is returned to its rightful place.

Director William Nigh holds down the fort but only just, leaving it to Karloff and Grant Withers—whose engaging cop-character varies throughout in rank—to carry the story through some unnecessarily vague detours and dead ends. Holmes Herbert makes a sympathetic wrongdoer, and Ivan Lebedeff is eminently suspect as a character calculated to distract the audience. The lovely Lotus Long weighs in as a recurring victim within the series, an accusing voice silenced by a poisoned cigarette.

Meanwhile, uptown at Universal Pictures, Karloff and Bela Lugosi had by now completed Universal's *Son of Frankenstein*, which went into release barely two months before this second *Wong* series entry. Still, a contract is a contract, and Karloff had a Wong way yet to go.

Mr. Wong in Chinatown (1939). Princess Lin Hwa (Lotus Long, again a victim) is murdered while visiting Wong's home during a mission to buy armaments for China. Her bank credit has been drained through forgery. The princess' attendants are slain, in turn, and Wong and banker Davidson (Huntly Gordon) are captured by two of the likelier suspects (Peter George Lynn and William Royle). Wong's police-force comrade, Inspector Street (Grant Withers), comes to the rescue. Wong exposes Davidson as both forger and slayer.

William Nigh is running short of creative steam here, and despite a generous deployment of culprits and crimes the picture for the most part just sits there waiting for Boris Karloff to turn up the next lead. Grant Withers helps, with a portrayal that is by turns indecisive and determined. Marjorie Reynolds' portrayal of a news reporter is energetic, and accurate to the profession.

The Fatal Hour (1940). The bigger mystery might involve how Grant Withers' Captain Sam Street of the opening picture had changed to Inspector, to Detective Sergeant, and now to Captain Bill Street. A Street by any other name or rank would be just as outraged to find a brother officer slain in the line of duty.

Street and Mr. Wong locate an Asian carving that can only represent a clue. They obtain help from Marjorie Reynolds' recurring character, reporter Bobbie Logan. Everything points to a crooked gambler (Frank Puglia), a smuggler (Craig Reynolds), and a scattering of murders—all committed with a single gun.

A perfectly respectable financier (Charles Trowbridge), with ties to all concerned, is unmasked as the menace when he takes aim at Mr. Wong. Bobbie rescues the "Chinese copper," and Street captures the murderer. A trifle except for the sake of completeness, this one does feature a measure of mysterious skulking and a rare show of impatience from Karloff, who seems ready to break character and walk at any moment. Impatient with the desultory plotting, perhaps.

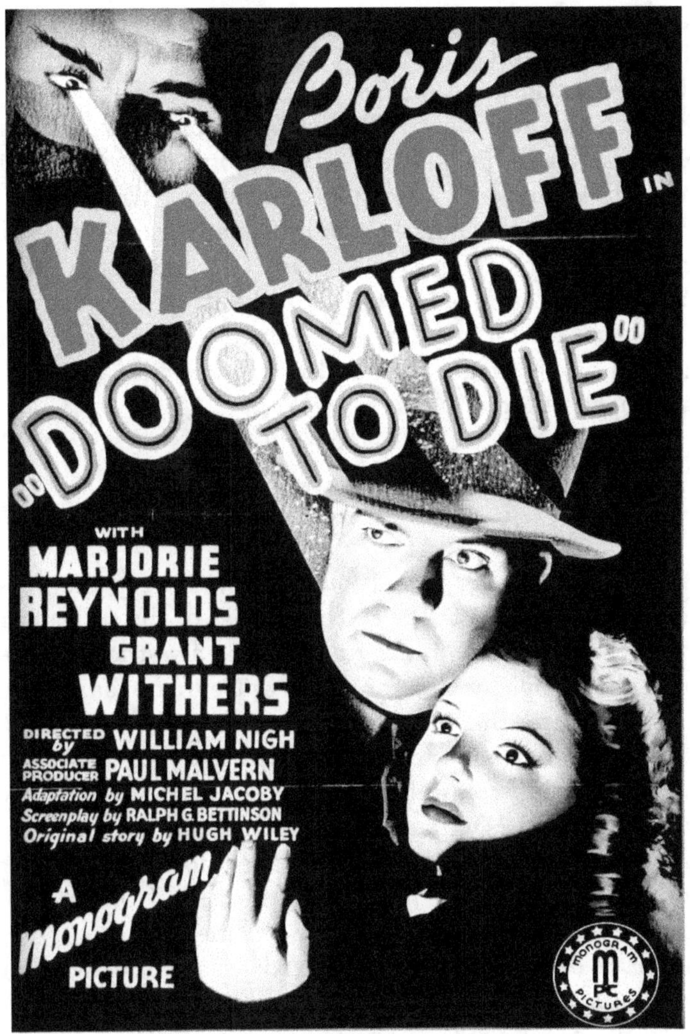

Doomed to Die. The adventures of James Lee Wong were nearing an end as a movie commodity when director William Nigh sent Boris Karloff puttering through this aimless effort. The time was nigh to put aside the sleuthing. With his Monogram contract yet to play out, however, Karloff found that some adjustments were in order—about which, more in our entries on *Phantom of Chinatown* (below) and *The Ape* (filed under 1940).

Doomed to Die is a nonetheless likable muddle about the slaying of a shipping tycoon and the theft of a fortune in bogus securities. Everyone is under suspicion, as usual, and only Karloff's Mr. Wong can sort things out. He must resort, of course, to clues that Ralph Bettison's ill-considered screenplay has scarcely bothered to show to the audience.

Magnate Cyrus Wentworth's flagship vessel been destroyed by fire. (The situation is depicted by stock footage of the headline-making *Morro Castle* conflagration of 1934.) Wentworth (Melvyn Lang) finds himself in a bitter argument with his chief competitor, Fleming (Guy Usher), over a plan to merge their sea-lane companies via marriage.

Wentworth's murder is a foregone conclusion. Wong and his stalwart if stolid colleague, Police Captain Street (Grant Withers) swing into action. Karloff's air of class is a joy to watch, even under such lesser circumstances. *Doomed to Die* is chiefly of interest as a fragment of a career strategy that had served its purpose. Withers is delightful in his recurring role, and Marjorie Reynolds is, as usual, a resourceful charmer.

Phantom of Chinatown

Monogram Pictures • 1940

A brief side-step further into 1940, merely to keep the *Mr. Wongs* together as a matched set: The sixth and last of the series is a breed apart: It is the one minus Boris Karloff. It is also the only *Mr. Wong* without William Nigh as director or Harry Neumann as cinematographer, and it is briefer than the others.

The series was in decline at the box office, and with one last entry to be filmed and Karloff committed to one picture more for Monogram, Vice President Scott R. Dunlap decided to place Karloff where he would attract the most money: in an old-fashioned horror picture. Karloff's last Monogram became the moderately successful *The Ape*, to which the usual *Mr. Wong* crew members were assigned.

Phantom of Chinatown was mounted as a throwaway, an easy exit from an awkward commitment to a fading franchise. The film has spark, nonetheless: Keye Luke lends a measure of pep with his younger, more romantically inclined Mr. Wong—now addressed as Jimmy, rather than James Lee—and lightens the character from Karloff's severely dignified reading.

The crucial subtext here is that Luke was still smarting from a crass bait-and-switch stunt that 20th Century-Fox had pulled on him two years earlier in connection with his extended supporting role in the *Charlie Chan* series. Luke was grateful to land the *Mr. Wong* assignment, which he regarded as "a kind of a circuitous consolation prize, you might say."

"You see, Fox had promised me a shot at the title role in the *Charlie Chan* series, should anything ever happen to Warner Oland," Luke told us in 1989. "I'd been playing No. 1 Son to Mr. Oland for a good while, there, and it seemed like a reasonable graduation for me, especially with

Mr. Oland's health failing as he couldn't seem to lay off the Tiger Tea—
his *martinis*, y'know. Well, the inevitable happened [Oland died in 1938],
and the Chans showed no sign of stopping as a series, so I reminded Fox
of their promise—and they told me to get lost. Just like that.

"So I landed back playing No. 1 Son, in that cameo in that *Mr. Moto*
picture [1938's *Mr. Moto's Gamble*], which Fox had originally intended
as a *Chan*. Sidney Toler wound up 'carrying on,' as it were, and he made
a perfectly okay Charlie Chan, himself, but it was a double heart-
breaker for me—first, to lose Mr. Oland, who for me remains the real
Charlie Chan, and then to lose a crack at succeeding Mr. Oland.

"But anyhow, yes, I was very grateful to drop some hints of what
I might have done as Chan for that little *Mr. Wong* picture." (In 1972,
Luke would supply the voice of a cheaply animated cartoon version of
Charlie Chan for Hanna-Barbera's *Amazing Chan and the Chan Clan*.)

With a fresh script by George Waggner (under the pseudonym of Joseph West), and Phil Rosen's snappier-than-Nigh direction, *Phantom of Chinatown* has more to offer than either *The Fatal Hour* or *Doomed to Die*. The indoor atmosphere is abundantly mysterious, and there is a fair measure of outdoor adventure involving an expedition into Mongolia, intercut via sophisticated flashback technique.

An invaluable scroll is discovered, along with the ancient tomb of a Chinese ruler, in an oil-rich desert region. A photographer (John H. Dilson), intent upon claiming the discovery, commits murder. The expedition's documentary footage figures in the unraveling. The new Mr. Wong investigates the poisoning of the chief archaeologist (Charles Miller). Suspicion falls upon practically everyone, even Jimmy Wong, until the detective has arrayed all the clues.

Grant Withers and Lee Tung Foo are back aboard. The Eurasian actress Lotus Long, who had served earlier *Mr. Wong* entries as a chronic victim, makes an attractive leading lady, but too little is made of what is patently a romantic attraction. Conspicuously missing is Marjorie Reynolds; a well-deserved breakthrough lay in store for her at Paramount.

Dark Rapture / Magié Africaine

Armand Denis Productions • Universal Pictures • 1938

Armand Denis and André Roosevelt had introduced to the cinematic consciousness the exciting concept of *Goona-Goona* (a Balinese term for aphrodisiac), which in turn became a descriptive catch-all for expeditionary pictures, scientifically attuned or bogus, from anywhere within the Third World. Their production of *Goona-Goona: An Authentic Melodrama of the Isle of Bali* (1932; also shown as *Kriss* and *Love Powder*) opened many doors, including a breakthrough for Denis at RKO-Radio Pictures, as director of *Wild Cargo* (1934), explorer Frank Buck's sequel to *Bring 'Em Back Alive* (1932).

For the independent production of *Dark Rapture*, an intimate travelogue through the Belgian Congo with the imperialist-oppressor blessings of the royal family of Belgium, Denis and his wife, Leila Roosevelt (daughter of André Roosevelt), secured U.S. distribution by big-time Universal Pictures. Denis persisted into the 1950s with this anthropologically based pursuit. The Americanized version of the Anglo-Belgian production inspired a song, "Dark Rapture" (composed in part by the bandleader Benny Goodman), which became a hit recording for Count Basie & His Orchestra.

The *New York Times* appraised the film in glowing terms:

If *Dark Rapture* … isn't the best film about Africa ever made, it is certainly the most beautiful and most richly documented production. … For here is a portfolio of anthropological facts more exciting and wonderful than the best of the fictions to which we have previously been exposed; here…is the very heart of darkness, immense, unknowable, and savage to the point of the unspeakable. … [I]t makes the Dark Continent seem as accessible as Bryce Canyon or Zion National Park.

But don't be misled; Africa is still…thousands of years removed in time. As soon as you meet the Long Heads, who got that way from having their skulls carefully bound in infancy, or witness the tribal ceremony of flagellation as a test of manhood…, your geographic perspective will be restored.

… The climax of beauty…is the joyous and abandoned dance of the strange people in the Valley of the Giants. The climax of humor is a matter of taste; perhaps it will be the building of a forest bridge by the pygmies, who send one of their little people across the stream with the first strand on a giant swing, or perhaps the training of an unwilling African elephant, which screams with temperamental rage.

The crossing of the volcanic region of Nyamlagira, the capture of an elephant in the Plains Country, and finally the cataclysmic grass fire before which the whole world flees are sequences any one of which might have established the reputation of a lesser film. ... Africa is so much more dramatic when it isn't dramatized.

Time magazine was similarly enthusiastic. *The Hollywood Reporter* chimed in with: "The pygmies of the forest have never been so graphically and clearly presented...not the savages that other African films have made them appear." And as to the gigantic Watusi: "[Their] dignity...will amaze those who think all African tribes are a low order of savages." The novelist and social critic Graham Greene weighed in with this: "It is impossible to exaggerate the beauty of this film."

For a more wide-ranging follow-up, *Dangerous Journey* (1944), Denis achieved distribution via 20th Century-Fox. Where he had dwelt in fascinating detail upon the vistas and folkways of *Dark Rapture*, Denis settled for tantalizing glimpses in *Dangerous Journey*, which touches upon the Congo, the Ganges, Ceylon, and Burma, and lifts intact the capture of the elephant from *Dark Rapture*.

Shadows over Shanghai

Fine Arts Pictures • Grand National Pictures • 1938

An exploitation of tensions between Japan and China, this Yellow Peril variant concerns a multimillion-dollar munitions deal. Too much of the tale is wasted on a soap-operatic marriage of convenience between an adventuress (Linda Gray) and a journalist (James Dunn), but there is an overriding suspense—and one shattering shock-value payoff. A Japanese agent (Paul Sutton) loads an incense burner with dynamite. A Russian spy (Robert Barrat) ignites the device and is impressively removed from the equation.

Camera chief Arthur Martinelli opens up the set-bound production with painted seascapes and airy compositions. He gives away the game, however, by dwelling on static backdrops where distant objects are supposed to be in motion. Pulp-fiction ace Richard Sale provided the source story. Charles Lamont handled the director and co-producer chores.

Paul Sutton, left, and James Dunn, Linda Gray, Ralph Moran, and Robert Barratt in Shadows over Shanghai.

Titans of the Deep

E.W. Hammons • Grand National • 1938

The *Jaws* of its day was *Titans of the Deep*, a naturally sensational featurette boasting authentic shark-attack footage and a rampaging barracuda. The film proved phenomenally popular despite the difficulties its awkward under-an-hour running time posed to conventional theatres. *Titans* found its truer market—and many years of mass-audience exposure—as a perennial rental for school-auditorium assemblies, admission a nickel-a-seat.

Dr. William Beebe and bathysphere developer Otis Barton plan an undersea expedition. All goes well on observational terms until one of the scientists finds himself cornered by a barracuda. Explorer Joan Igou must kill the marauding fish. In a harrowing encounter with a shark, Barton has no choice but to throw his camera rig into the monster's mouth. The crew members hoist the creature onto the deck and cut it open to retrieve the equipment.

Barton and Beebe, best known for their Bermuda expeditions, made numerous such moving-picture accounts, all expertly photographed and often edited into such concise entertainments as this one. Broadcaster Lowell Thomas' overwrought narration track is a debit.

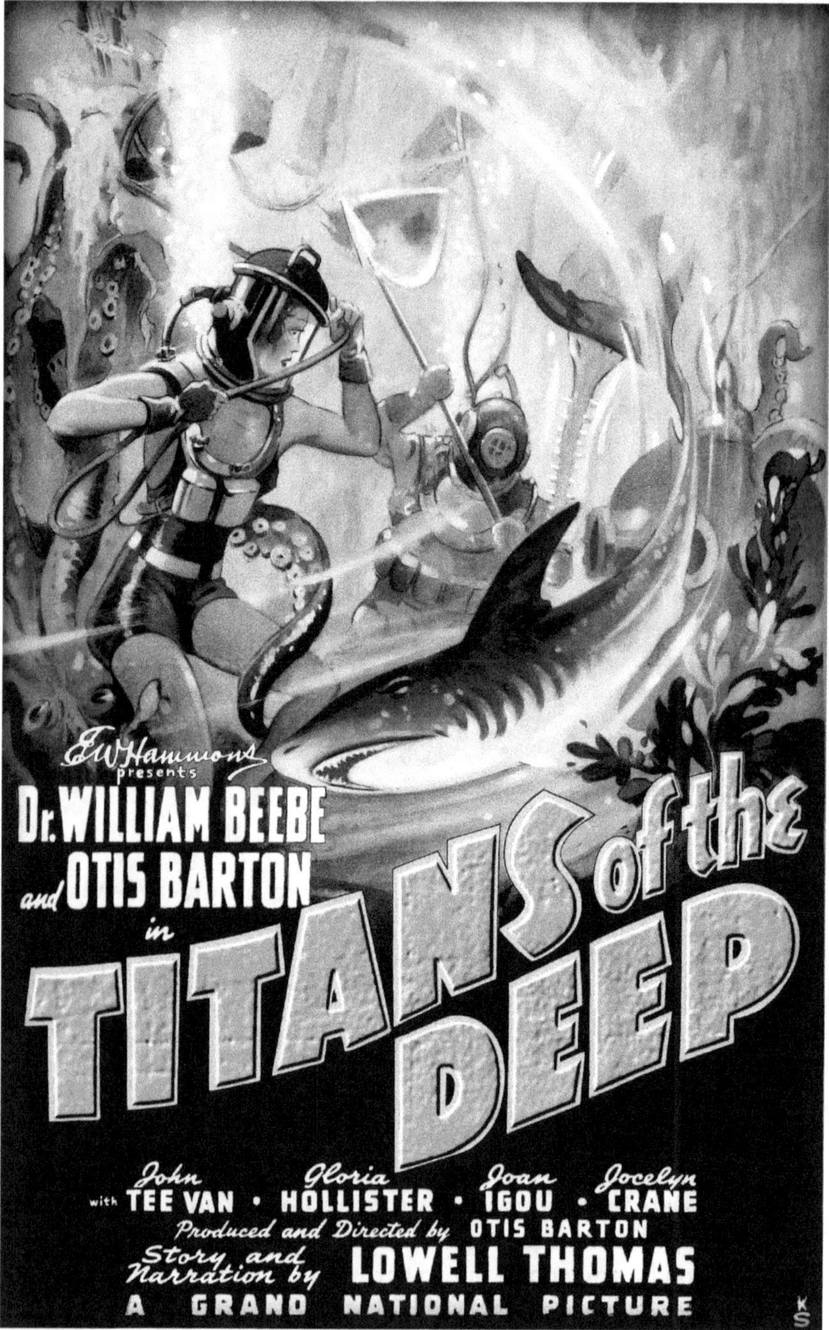

E.W. Hammons
presents
Dr. WILLIAM BEEBE
and OTIS BARTON
in
TITANS of the DEEP
with JOHN TEE VAN · Gloria HOLLISTER · Joan IGOU · Jocelyn CRANE
Produced and Directed by OTIS BARTON
Story and Narration by LOWELL THOMAS
A GRAND NATIONAL PICTURE

Gun Packer

Monogram Pictures Corp. • 1938

Addison "Jack" Randall, kid brother of the all-round matinée-western champ Bob Livingston, fared impressively well as a cowboy star in his own right, edging gracefully into villainous roles during the 1940s, until his sudden death-in-harness in 1945.

Wallace Fox's *Gun Packer* finds Randall investigating a fantastic scheme to smuggle gold without risk of detection. Special Deputy Jack Denton (Randall) finagles his way into gang membership and spots Prof. Angel (Barlowe Borland), a disappointed renegade genius who has perfected a process to transform the precious metal. The operative plot device amounts to speculative big science, passing for the ancient mysteries of alchemy.

Upon learning that Denton is an undercover agent, the professor defects to the side of the good, more or less, and he and Denton are forced into a showdown with ringleader Chance Moore (reliable heavy Charles King). Prof. Angel turns the tide by blowing up a mine—and himself with it. Denton and his sidekick, Pinky (the expressive black actor Ray Turner), escape, only to be pursued by Moore, whom Denton beats into senselessness. Leading lady Louise Stanley was Randall's fiancée; their short-lived marriage occurred after the film's completion. The extremely brief film is long on doom-laden attitude.

Marusia

Ukrafilm Corp. • 1938

Mikhail Staritsky's folkloric play, *Marusia*, dates from 1872. It served long and well as a staple of the Ukrainian theatre. This little-seen film version by Leo Bulgakov, the lone production of Ukrafilm Corp., is American but hardly Americanized, having been shot in a microcosm of ethnicity on quaint and forbidding natural locations in New York State, New Jersey, and Long Island. Surviving fragments bespeak a great care in the making—*The Hollywood Reporter* pegged the budget at a generous (for the circumstances) $45,000—but only hint at the dire epic of legend-come-alive that *Marusia* must have been when intact. The dialogue is Ukrainian, without English subtitling.

An innocent romance is threatened by Khoma (played with a snarling intensity by Peter Chorniuk), a wealthy and cruel hunchback who horns in on sweethearts Marusia (Stephania Melnik) and Hyrtz (Nicholas Stehnitzky). Khoma provokes Hyrtz into hostile confrontations with a friend, Potap (Mykola Novak), and with Marusia. Hyrtz quits the village in disgrace. Khoma places Marusia's parents in his debt and pursues the girl. Although she pines for Hyrtz, Marusia consents to marry Khoma. Hyrtz returns in time to reclaim his belovéd, whereupon Khoma attempts to poison the lovers. Exposed as a menace, Khoma flees the angry villagers. Potap captures Khoma and throws the madman to his death from a clifftop.

Forgotten Horrors of 1939

The Mysterious Miss X

Republic Pictures Corp. • 1939

Stranded stage actors find themselves roped into a law-officer impersonation in Gus Meins' *The Mysterious Miss X*, a comical mystery with the creepy finishing touch of a reluctant mystery woman who finds herself threatened as a consequence of the masquerade. "For the duals," as *Variety*'s assigned critic dismissed the picture—meaning fodder for double-bill engagements. "A cheapie that'll get back its production costs, plus some profit."

Their play about a heroic lawman has flopped and folded, leaving Keith Neville and Scooter Casey (Michael Whalen and Chick Chandler) hard-pressed to find a way back to New York. At a forced stopover en route, they take lodging but find their slumbers wrecked by a ruckus that ends with a gunshot from a neighboring room. Casey runs to summon the police. Neville, prowling about, gets locked in with the corpse of an important personage named Platt. A stage prop leads the local cops to assume that Neville must be one Inspector Desmond of Scotland Yard. The hick-town constabulary presses Neville and Casey into service.

Platt's widow, Alma (Dorothy Tree), hires the actors to recover a sum that her husband had carried. Julie Graham (Mary Hart), a new friend whose father has fallen under suspicion, asks Neville to represent her interests. Neville decides to smoke out the killer by having Julie, veiled and cloaked, lurk about the murder room. The killer turns the tables, however, by knocking out Julie and leaving her under suspicion. Alma's brother, Jack Webster (Regis Toomey), complicates matters by promising to reveal evidence under shady conditions. Webster turns up croaked, and suspicions multiply against Julie.

DA Ross (Frank M. Thomas) determines that Neville is an actor. Ross declines to reveal the mistaken assumption lest he look foolish. He orders Neville and Casey to leave town. At the hotel, Casey and landlady Annie Botts (Mabel Todd) find the missing loot. Alma is wounded just as she is about to reveal the killer's name. Neville reaches Julie in time to rescue her from Platt's lawyer, Fredericks (Don

Douglas). Fredericks proves to have had perfectly okay reasons for killing two bad rascals; his wounding of Alma was a matter of panic. No such excuse will matter to the police. The case generates sufficient notoriety to spur a reopening of Neville and Casey's play.

Mystery Plane

Monogram Pictures Corp. • 1939

The Hal Forrest-Glenn Chaffin comic strip, *Tailspin Tommy*, had inspired two serials at Universal Pictures during 1934–35—*Tailspin Tommy* and *Tailspin Tommy in the Great Air Mystery*—starring Maurice Murphy and Clark Williams, respectively, as the title aviator and featuring Noah Beery, Jr., as a sidekick. Quite a comedown, then, that the property should lapse from Universal's bravura chapter-play style to a small batch of hour-long adventures at Monogram. These entries are briskly done for the most part, however, under George Waggner's direction.

The heroic protagonism is often played out with currents of science fiction and mad treachery in addition to the airborne hair-raisers.

Mystery Plane finds John Trent and Milburn Stone portraying flyboys Tommy and Skeeter. Their invention—a bombing device designed for accuracy from extreme altitudes—attracts a spy (slimy Lucien Littlefield). The bombing scenes pack excitement; likewise for a brisk battle in which Tommy's childhood hero, a disgraced WWI ace (Peter George Lynn), saves the day in tragic fashion.

The film sequelized itself with *Stunt Pilot* (1939), which follows through bitterly upon *Mystery Plane*'s curtain-closing proposal of imminent Hollywood stardom for Tailspin Tommy Tomkins. In a development borrowed from 1932's murder-in-movieland thriller *The Death Kiss*, Tommy finds himself framed for the slaying of a vain stunt pilot (George Meeker); a prop gun proves loaded. The culprit is a vengeful movie director (Pat O'Malley), who carelessly had allowed himself to be photographed while tampering with Tommy's artillery. The 1930 *Hell's Angels* is a source of much stock footage.

The short-order third *Tommy*, 1939's *Sky Patrol*, puts the Tailspinner in charge of a pilots' academy, where greenhorn Jackie Coogan manifests a paralyzing fear of guns and Bryant Washburn harbors a smuggling racket. The coda, *Danger Flight* (also from 1939), scuttles the high-adventure angle, settling instead for a children's entertainment about good citizenship through model-aircraft building.

Religious Racketeers

a.k.a.: *The Mystic Circle Murder*

Fanchon Royer • Continental Pictures • Merit Pictures • 1939

Fanchon Royer, one of the most independent of independent producers—and a woman at large in a male-dominated racket—raised and spent some $35,000 to make *Religious Racketeers*, or *The Mystic Circle Murder* (the title depending upon when and where the picture was playing). This sum was a bundle for a company whose previous pictures, including *Death in the Air*, a.k.a. *Pilot X* and *Mysterious Bombardier*, had been brought in for around $25,000 each, tops.

Royer's incentive here was a show of interest from Bess Houdini, widow of the mystifying entertainer Harry Houdini (*né* Erich Weiss). Mme. Houdini, as she styled herself, had long vowed to take up her husband's campaign against the spook-summoning trade but also had garnered publicity from a 10-year span of conspicuous silence on the topic.

Apart from his crowd-pleasing displays of magic and impossible escapes, the Great Houdini had pursued a sideline of debunking spiritualists who professed to commune with departed souls. Hence the film's original title, *Religious Racketeers*. Bess Houdini would have preferred to call the film *Mme. Houdini Speaks*. Her partner in this venture was Edward Saint, a publicist and all-round scamboozling huckster.

In 1937, having persuaded Paramount Pictures to begin planning a Houdini life-story picture, Saint and Mrs. Houdini looked to Hollywood's Poverty Row district to develop a starring film for Bess Houdini herself. Despite a theatrical background, she had no marquée name other than that of her late husband. Fanchon Royer's studio entertained artistic pretensions but lacked polish, capital, and commercial appeal—many flights below even Monogram Pictures or Grand National along the vertiginous staircase of corporate Hollywood.

Edward Saint announced a "sensational picture...ghostly dynamite that will blast the fakes, frauds, and humbugging religious racketeers hiding behind the cloak of spiritualistic superstition. Mme. Houdini will play the part of herself..., and her long experience in tracking down the miracle-mongers will

Mme. Houdini.

be vividly portrayed." Saint hailed Royer as "one of Hollywood's out-standing independent women producers." The assigned director, Frank O'Connor, was a prolific bit-parts actor and scenario hack. O'Connor had begun writing a script on speculation of sale for the proposed Houdini biography at Paramount.

Religious Racketeers saw principal photography during March of 1938 at Grand National Studios, a shabbier neighbor to United Artists along Santa Monica Boulevard. Bess Houdini appeared in no dramatized sequences but rather shot a prologue and an epilogue. She pronounces communication with the dead impossible and refers to the spiritualists as leeches, according to one published review based upon the un-scissored picture. The closing sequence is missing from the known surviving print.

A promotional piece for Houdini his ownself.

Here we have an embarrassingly earnest social-reformer film with mock-exotic touches, calculated to convince the viewer that spiritualism is a load of baloney—a self-evident truth, in the first place, without coaching from Mme. Houdini. The introductory cameo by Mrs. Houdini hammers the interest in exposing crystal gawkers, spook walkers, hoodoo hawkers, and spirit talkers as charlatans.

One advertisement warned: "Watch Out! For the Medium Who Will Tell Your Fortune and SLIT YOUR THROAT!" The point has less to do with murder than with a pageant of aimless globetrotting accomplished by faded silent star Betty Compson (of *The Great Gabbo*), as a subordinate sucker-baiter, and Helen LeBerthon, as a willing sucker, in the service of fake fakir Robert Fiske. Arthur Gardner plays an impatient newspaperman who seeks to put paid to Fiske's crooked game. All concerned appear ill at ease with the stilted dialogue, and O'Connor's direction lacks tension.

Royer tried to lend spectacle with scenic footage of the Egyptian pyramids—evocative imagery long associated with Houdini's stage career and pulp-literary endeavors. (H.P. Lovecraft had served as Houdini's ghost-writer on a trifle called "Imprisoned with the Pharaohs.") The film's stock-footage sequences are poorly matched with the studio material. We have not seen the original hour-and-a-half cut—but given the overall qualities of forced performances and flaccid pacing in the surviving version, that preview edition must have been a mess.

Religious Racketeers had an invitational showing for working magicians on April 12, 1938—a matter of preaching to the converted. Richard Frohmann wrote thusly in a trade journal, *Goldston's Magical Quarterly*: "Although *Religious Racketeer* [sic] makes no pretense at being a million-dollar production, it tells a good story in an arresting and memorable manner. Mrs. Houdini plays an outstanding part. ... The film is undoubtedly good-class entertainment for discriminating filmgoers, and never once borders on bathos or unreality." So there, already.

A predictable backlash from the tribe of spiritualists included a communal booing-and-hissing at a theatre in Buffalo, New York. *The Psychic Observer* published a letter, purportedly from Mrs. Houdini, describing a beyond-the-grave communiqué from Houdini himself. A tremendous fuss over not much of a movie, in other words.

Frank O'Connor concentrated hereafter (pardon the expression) upon small-roles acting assignments. His intended Houdini biopic never made it into production, although Paramount finally mounted a lavish and colorful *Houdini* in 1953, with Tony Curtis in the title role, Janet Leigh as Bess, and Frank O'Connor nowhere within shouting distance. By which time, Mrs. Houdini had died, in 1943.

Exile Express

United Players • Grand National Pictures • 1939

Dr. Eugen Frenke forged through two decades of a hit-and-miss, catch-as-can moviemaking career, missing more often than he hit but registering the occasional accomplished job. In late 1938, undaunted after the Pyrrhic victory of finagling his soap-operatic riff upon *Frankenstein, Life Returns,* away from Universal Pictures, Frenke produced *Exile Express,* an unusual merger of espionage and science fiction. The project afforded a Hollywood comeback after four years' exile for the luminous beauty Anna Sten, who had taken Dr. Frenke as her second husband. (Since 1935, Sten had graced only *A Woman Alone,* in England.) Sten's energetic screwball-comedy heroic protagonism works ideally in the service of an audacious thriller about a campaign to steal a powerful chemical weapon.

Nadine Nikolas (Sten), soon to be granted American citizenship, is an assistant to Dr. Hite (Harry Davenport), who has perfected a formula to wither the crops of enemy nations. An agent wants Nadine to steal the process for her former homeland. Hite is murdered before he can secure his papers. Nadine is arrested; though exonerated, she finds herself forced onto a deportées' train. A supposed friend (Jerome Cowan) encourages her to disembark illegally; this weasel is secretly responsible for the slaying of Dr. Hite.

A strange ploy to force Nadine to marry an American (George Chandler) is foiled when reporter Steve Reynolds (Alan Marshal) barges in on the ceremony and, scaring away the impromptu bridegroom with a threat of publicity, takes his place. After a wild chase involving the customary ill-placed trusts and crass betrayals, bogus news reports, a harrowing automobile crash, and a pursuit through the woods, the spy chief is exposed. Nadine finally gets herself naturalized—as Mrs. Steve Reynolds.

Director Otis Garrett keeps the complications on track. An extended running time—10 minutes more than Poverty Row's hour-and-change norm—accommodates satisfactory exposition. Sten is defiant and determined, and "splendidly photographed by John Mescall," as *The Film Daily* noted. Alan Marshal makes a smart-mouthed and opportunistic hero. Jerome Cowan is persuasively treacherous, and Leonid Kinsky plays a henchman as a bungler too faithful to warrant a sacking. Spencer Charters contributes a humorous cameo as a local-yokel judge.

The journalistic backdrop accounts for much comedy, with Jed Prouty as a hard-nosed editor and Walter Catlett (less grumpy than usual) as a nervous photographer. Feodor Chaliapin stands out as a double-talking Bolshevik orator, and rock-jawed Stanley Fields is a deportée too tough for Alcatraz. Irving Pichel is a suave enemy of the state. Vince Barnett contributes his specialty, an inept authority figure.

Russian-born Anna Sten gave better to Hollywood than she received. Samuel Goldwyn had brought her to America from Germany amid a barrage of hyperbole, but stateside audiences did not take fondly to her, and after several features Goldwyn cancelled her contract. Though more interested in painting, Sten persisted with the occasional acting assignment on into the 1960s.

The reviews were largely enthusiastic: The *Los Angeles Times* called Sten's absence from the screen "long and regrettable," and *The Film Bulletin* held the picture to be "swiftly paced...with conviction." *Daily Variety* found Exile Express "a decided credit to Eugen Frenke's careful preparation and showmanship," where *Weekly Variety* griped that "it won't satisfy even the most indulgent meller [melodrama] fans." No accounting for taste.

Across the Plains

Monogram Pictures Corp. • 1939

Yes, and where have we heard *this* one before? Brothers Jimmy and Jack lose track of one another following a murderous raid upon their family's Conestoga wagon. Sounds a great deal like *The Rawhide Terror* and *Branded a Coward*, those long-obscured frontier gothics that we had unearthed for a 20th-anniversary edition of *Forgotten Horrors* in 1999. Spencer Gordon Bennet's *Across the Plains*, an economical star vehicle for Jack Randall—kid brother of the *Three Mesquiteers* films' Bob Livingston—flogs that dead horse of a plotting device to a fare-thee-well but still justifies the modest investment of film stock and talent.

Jack grows up to become a gunslinging hero known as Cherokee (Randall), so named in light of his rescue and raising by a band of Indians. Jimmy, who had been kidnapped by his parents' killers, becomes the black-hearted Kansas Kid (Dennis Moore).

Cherokee and wagonmaster Buckskin (Hal Price) have teamed to avenge the long-ago victims. The Kansas Kid, meanwhile, leads a wagon train into an ambush. Cherokee thwarts the plot, but Buckskin is abducted; he overhears the outlaws reminiscing fondly about the time they did away with the Kansas Kid's parents.

The Kid, bound for a showdown with his unsuspected brother, undergoes a transformation when Buckskin reveals to him the truth; seems the Kid had believed his folks slain by Indians. The brothers set aside their differences to wipe out the gang. The Kid, mortally wounded, accepts his situation philosophically.

The antagonistic leading portrayals make *Across the Plains* a grim and uncompromising confrontation throughout. Randall invests enough anger into his model-citizen character to keep the heroism credible, and Dennis Moore registers a realistically bewildered anguish upon learning of a sudden that everything he knows is wrong. Director Bennet orchestrates a harrowing shoot-out for the climax. Moore's death scene seems an episode of the very sort that moved the cowboy singers of the 19th century to compose all those heart-wrenching death-on-the-prairie ballads.

Another wagon-train massacre yarn, incidentally, occurs in Sam Newfield's *Valley of Vengeance* (1944), a *Billy Carson* series entry starring Buster Crabbe and Fuzzy St. John. The *Billy Carson* series, incidentally, represents a tangent from the *Lightnin' Bill Carson* series.

S.O.S.—Tidal Wave

Republic Pictures Corp. • 1939

"Wells and Welles," sniped the *Variety* review, sarcastically pegging John Auer's *S.O.S.—Tidal Wave* as a composite swipe from H.G. and Orson. The title disaster is, of course, a hoax, perpetrated by a corrupt political machine to distract the populace from a contested election. The writers can only have been laboring under the influence of Orson Welles' October 31, 1938, radio adaptation of H.G. Wells' *The War of the Worlds*, whose real-time straight-faced documentary-like presentation had struck an excitable mass audience as a genuine news broadcast.

Where *Variety* trashed *S.O.S.—Tidal Wave* despite kind words for Ralph Byrd's heroic portrayal, *The Hollywood Reporter* likened the picture favorably to Welles' Halloween broadcast and raved about the

scenes of catastrophe: "Process work, picturing the waterfront, then the entire city of New York, collapsing under...a surging tidal wave, is amazingly vital drama."

Some collective memory: the "amazingly vital drama" of *S.O.S.*'s effects work belongs to a too-soon-forgotten 1933 epic called *Deluge*. Republic had purchased the elaborate displays of devastation, which are too distinctive to have been put to such trivial use as stock footage. The sequences also were employed in the serials *Dick Tracy vs. Crime, Inc.* (another starrer for Ralph Byrd, from 1941) and *King of the Rocket Men* (1949).

The larger story of *S.O.S.* is a great deal smaller than the *Deluge* excerpts that help to drive the plot: Byrd plays a television newsman —in those days when television was still popularly regarded as science fiction—who helps an upstanding mayoral candidate to prevail against a crooked politico. When Byrd discovers an incriminating piece of film, the kingmaker (Marc Lawrence) counters by broadcasting the tidal-wave footage in the guise of breaking news. Panic results, and the badman winds up killed by a truck whose driver is fleeing the make-believe disaster. Karmic justice, Republic-style.

Death Goes North

Central Films • Columbia Pictures • Warwick Pictures • 1939

An impersonation-and-murder yarn of considerable viciousness, the Canadian production of *Death Goes North* stars those Hollywood-based Poverty Row dependables, Rin-Tin-Tin, Jr., and Sheila Bromley (alias Sheila Manners and Sheila Manors), as canine sleuth and lady in distress. Rinty the Younger, for once, shows some of the fire of his old man, upstaging human heroes Edgar Edwards and Michael Heppell at every turn.

There is a wealth of villainy and suspicious lurking-about, too, from Walter Byron and Arthur Kerr as wicked brothers who are Bromley's competitors in the lumber-mill industry; Reginald Hincks, as a deranged vagrant; and Dorothy Bradshaw and Jameson Thomas, as an English couple who may or may not be Bromley's devoted kinfolks. The film was shot chiefly (and rather murkily) on interior sets—unaccountably neglecting to take fuller advantage of the North Woods setting.

After cabling her uncle, whom she has never met, to take charge of a troubled business, Elsie Barlow (Bromley) learns that a dead man has been found in possession of her message. The worst is feared, until the purported Uncle Herbert and Aunt Martha (Thomas

and Bradshaw) identify the corpse as their emissary, Robert Druid. Borrowing Elsie's dog, King (Rinty, Jr.), to track the killer, Mountie Dan MacKenzie (Heppell) reaches a desolate barn, where he is slain by a hammer-wielding assailant. Bad lumberman Albert Norton (Byron) is arrested, but his brother, Bart (Kerr), engineers a jailbreak. The hoodlums sneak into the Barlow residence just as Elsie finds herself attacked by a would-be strangler. Mountie Ken Strange (Edwards) reveals the fake uncle as Robert Druid. When called upon to point out Elsie's assailant, King pounces on Druid. The bogus aunt almost pulls off a getaway—emphasis on that *almost*.

Daughter of the Tong

Metropolitan Pictures Corp. • 1939

Evelyn Brent, a silent-screen star, had made a semi-graceful segué into the talkers. Her menacing lead in Raymond K. Johnson's *Daughter of the Tong* is a sad echo of her roles for Josef von Sternberg in *Underworld* (1927) and *The Last Command* (1928). The portrayal is nonetheless consistent with her image as a seductive fringe-dweller.

Brent, Dave O'Brien, Grant Withers, Richard Loo, *et al.*, are finer than the fabric of *Daughter of the Tong*, which suffers from simplistic writing and clunky stunt-action, as well as dialogue demeaning to the Asian populace. The photography is dim and lacking in tonal range. *Variety* ascribed this muddiness to inferior film stock, but the pictorial compositions and visual storytelling are lousy, too.

Evelyn Brent and Dave O'Brien.

Brent plays the Illustrious One, a gangleader who hides behind the name of Carney, quarry of an FBI dragnet. Withers is a federal infiltrator. He was soon to début as a producer at Monogram Pictures, with *Irish Luck* (coming right up).

O'Brien stands out as a former (legitimate) business partner who turns hostile after learning the truer nature of the Illustrious One. Dorothy Short, as O'Brien's sister and a vengeful former captive of the gang, helps to lead the inevitable crackdown.

Irish Luck

Monogram Pictures Corp. • 1939

Howard Bretherton's *Irish Luck* introduces Frankie Darro and Mantan Moreland as teammates in a loosely connected comedy-thriller series that not only would mature strikingly over the course of an all-too-brief run, but also would cement a lifelong friendship. No one among the published critics seems to have remarked upon the ground-breaking ploy of a white-guy/black-guy comedy team. Perhaps this is because the stories placed Darro and Moreland on an equal social standing, usually portraying servants of various types, aspiring to become detectives. Or perhaps it is because Monogram neglected to pitch the team *as a team*. A simple ampersand connecting Moreland & Darro, Frankie & Mantan, or whatever, would have worked wonders at announcing a distinctive identity.

Darro is Buzzy O'Brien, a hotel bellhop and amateur sleuth whose nose for clues leads him into trouble. Mantan plays baggageman Jefferson, who plays along (despite eloquent misgivings) with O'Brien's dangerous escapades. Kitty Monohan (Sheila Darcy), a guest, is incriminated by a telegram warning the mysterious Thad Porter to watch out for a woman with the initials K.M. Upon finding Porter slain, O'Brien helps Kitty elude the law. She had sought Porter in the belief that he might help find her missing brother, Jim Monohan. The brother stands accused in a heist at Porter's bank.

O'Brien suspects that a guest registered as a Mr. Elliott (Dennis Moore) must be Jim Monohan. Knocked unconscious while snooping, O'Brien wakes to find another corpse, along with a dazed Elliott, survivor of an attempted drowning in a bathtub. Elliott admits he is Kitty's brother. The hotel detective, Fluger (James Flavin), steals in just as O'Brien and Jefferson discover a cache of stolen securities. Jefferson, in hiding, hears Fluger's threat and raises a ruckus that draws the police.

Irish Luck suffers from Monogram's customary deficiencies in production values, narrative sense, inventiveness in camerawork, and overall polish. Such failings are alleviated by the sense of community that informs most of the studio's pictures, which though often desultory in technical matters and literary structure still convey the fun that the assignments must have been for the participants. (Darro's fond reminiscences have borne out this observation.) Director Bretherton moves *Irish Luck* along briskly but dwells rewardingly upon such bursts of surprise as Darro's discoveries of the murder scenes and his abrupt confrontation with the killer.

Darro and Moreland are equally matched in the google-eyes department when it comes to scared-silly reactions. Darro

concentrates upon the boyish impulsiveness that generates the close shaves. Moreland is more the wise and resourceful party who has a philosophical quip for every occasion and an outlandish solution for the final desperate encounter. How much of Moreland's banter is scripted, and how much improvised, is a matter for conjecture, for he was a master at making every utterance sound spontaneous. His long-term contract with Monogram was an actor-writer deal: the writing function involved no original screenplays, but rather an ability to make his characters deliver statements that nobody but Moreland would have the gumption to utter. His recurring character name, Jefferson, is a sly, subversive reference to the open secret of founding father and slaveholder Thomas Jefferson's having sired black offspring. (Also of interest: Moreland's scene-stealing butler in 1938's *Frontier Scout*.)

Despite the sterner heroic presence of Dick Purcell and the vulnerably innocent beauty of Sheila Darcy, *Irish Luck* belongs thoroughly to Moreland and Darro, whose next such picture would be 1940's *Chasing Trouble*. *Irish Luck* marks actor Grant Withers' arrival as a producer.

The Fighting Renegade

Victory Pictures Corp. • 1939

Tim McCoy never found his way back to major-studio stardom after an impulsive leap onto Poverty Row during the mid-1930s. The community of smaller production companies treated him well, however, in the rapid-fire terms of one assignment after another. An upshot of this backfired strategy was that McCoy got to make one of his best pictures, Sigmund Neufeld and Leslie Simmonds' production of *Lightnin' Bill Carson*, a dire meditation upon mortality and fate in a cruel frontier.

The *Carson* concept was picked up as a series in 1938 by Sam Katzman's Victory Pictures and continued down a long, dark trail under the original director, Sam Newfield. Although it would be misleading to profess an outright horrific impact for these quickies—indeed, there is more mayhem than outright weirdness, and McCoy's undercover disguises are often laughable—still the series honors the foreboding atmosphere of the original. These entries also foreshadow the brooding severity of producer Katzman's more emphatic thrillers of the 1940s—and of the emerging *noir* style as a class. (And no, *film noir* does not require trenchcoats or fedoras as preconditions.)

The best and most representative of the sequels, *The Fighting Renegade*, revels in offbeat viciousness: El Puma, supposedly a Mexican Robin Hood, is actually Lightnin' Bill Carson—not that the masquerade is evident to the archaeologists who hire El Puma to shepherd them through hostile territory.

Carson is alleged to have murdered a prior expeditioner. Using the slain Prof. Willis' diary as their guide to a lost treasure, the scientists run into trouble before the first reel has passed through the projector. Carson knows that Benson (Ted Adams), the party's foreman, is the killer—but before Bill can act, a hired hand known as Old Dobie (Budd Buster) disposes of the professor-in-charge (Forrest Taylor) and frames Carson anew. Benson plots to kidnap Willis' daughter, Marian (Joyce Bryant), because she can decipher a crucial map, but Carson abducts her for safekeeping. As good guys and bad converge upon the stark mesa where the treasure lies hidden, Lightnin' Bill gets the drop on Benson. Old Dobie confesses all.

The additional companion titles are *Lightning Carson Rides Again* and *Six-Gun Trail* (both from 1938); *Code of the Cactus* (1939), which boasts a high-technology cattle-rustling racket; *Outlaw's Paradise* (1939), with McCoy playing both Carson and a notorious criminal; *Texas Wildcats* and *Trigger Fingers* (1939); and *Straight Shooter* (1940). Sig Neufeld and Sam Newfield (the artists were brothers) liked the Carson identity well enough that they later retooled Producers Releasing Corp.'s *Billy the Kid* series as a *Billy Carson* series for Buster Crabbe; 1944's *Wild Horse Phantom* is a splendid example, and a centerpiece of a forthcoming volume of *Forgotten Horrors*.

Adventures of the Masked Phantom

B.F. Ziedman Productions • Equity Pictures • 1939

Director Charles Abbott's peppy vehicle for the undeservedly obscure one-shot western star Monte "Alamo" Rawlins pivots on a feisty grandmother's folk tales about a Masked Phantom who once conquered the agents of evil with a terroristic dose of their own medicine. Evil abounds in the film's here-and-now, what with a string of killings plaguing a gold-mining operation run by Stan Barton (Matty Kemp) and his Grandma Mary (Dot Karroll). Foreman Murdock (George Douglas) is the hidden ringleader, smelting hijacked gold for sale to the federal government.

Wandering horseman Alamo (Rawlins) and his dog, Boots, find Barton cornered in a Murdock ambush. At Grandma's ranch, Alamo listens in fascination to the old lady's tales of the Phantom, who brandished a death's-head knife and put paid to all manner of lawlessness.

Alamo, cobbling together a Masked Phantom identity, terrorizes Stan's captors. Regaining their composure sufficiently to ride in pursuit, Murdock and his men are captured with no little help from Grandma and her ranch hands.

Nothing further came of *The Masked Phantom*, which had been intended as the launcher of a series. Rawlins is a boisterous hero, and Dot Karroll—in her only feature-film appearance—is delightful as the plain-spoken Grandma Mary.

Torture Ship

Producers Distributing Corp. • 1939

"They sneered at the hangman, but a doctor's needle sent them screaming to their doom!" declares the promotional campaign for Victor Halperin's *Torture Ship*. The doctor in question is Irving Pichel, who as an emerging director had collaborated with Ernest B. Schoedsack (against Schoedsack's preferences) on the helming of *The Most Dangerous Game* (1932) and with Lansing C. Holden on *She* (1935). Pichel solo-directed the fine mystery *Before Dawn* (1933). He portrayed a memorable criminal mastermind in the 1933 *Oliver Twist* and an intense Josef Stalin in *British Agent* (1934), turned in an impressive pinch-hit job of villainy for an ailing Bela Lugosi in *The House of a Thousand Candles*, and lent *Dracula's Daughter* (1937) its creepiest presence. By 1939, despite acceptance as a versatile character actor, Pichel had determined to concentrate more intently on directing—at which he would prove consistently prolific and proficient until his death in 1954. He continued to act, however, as the occasion suited, showing an abiding preference for offbeat roles including a top-shelf job of villainy in *Dick Tracy's G-Men* (1939) and the elegaic off-camera narration that courses through John Ford's Welsh pocket-epic *How Green Was My Valley* (1941).

Little known even in its day, *Torture Ship* boasts a typically fine Pichel performance as Dr. Herbert Stander, a renegade surgeon who intends to prove that glandular tampering can eradicate the criminal instinct. Adapted from one of Jack London's crueler short stories, "A Thousand Deaths," the film finds Stander frustrated within the hell-bent-for-status-quo medical establishment. He outfits a yacht with

a laboratory and hospital, promises asylum to several fugitives from justice, and puts out to sea. His subjects include Poison Mary Slavish (Sheila Bromley), chief of a murder-for-insurance racket; Joan Martel (Jacqueline Wells), indicted as an accomplice to Mary; a modern-day Bluebeard named Ezra (Leander de Cordova); assassin Jesse (Skelton Knaggs); the sadistic Ritter (Wheeler Oakman); and Harry-the-Carver (Russell Hopton), who has claimed six victims. Lyle Talbot plays Stander's nephew, Navy Lt. Bob Bennett. Stalwart but apprehensive, Bennett cannot develop a sympathy with the cause; he falls in love with Martel with only a passing concern as to her guilt or innocence.

The ironies at play are emphasized in grim fashion by director Halperin, of *White Zombie* and *Supernatural*, in addition to other films outside that narrow realm. It develops that Stander is no crackpot—but that his subjects are becoming just as dangerously rebellious as if he *were* a quack. Amid uprisings that result in the doctor's slaying, Stander manages not only to vindicate his theory (by putting tough dame Mary Slavish under the knife and rehabilitating her in the process) but also to establish Joan Martel's innocence—to Bennett's relief. The film finds its dramatic center in Stander's dawning realization that he must experiment upon a normal person; he chooses Bennett. Talbot fares well with the character's desperation at this point, feigning helplessness following an injection and then freeing the killers.

Second-billed Pichel dominates a strong cast, conveying a Lionel Atwill calibre of self-assured intensity but stopping short of thoroughgoing ruthlessness in his quest to alter the species. Anthony Averill, as Pichel's assistant, seems more keenly attuned to the outlawry implicit in the radical quest. As the essentially respectable doctor, Pichel is chagrined to have been driven to such desperate measures, but his belief in a potential social boon is enough to settle any misgivings. Even so, Pichel displays sufficient megalomania to seem disturbingly akin to the vividly defined individual bad guys among his grotesque recruits. Their shared resentment comes across more as a seething, impersonal social force, and they manage a nice job of herd-instinct ensemble acting when, finally, panic drives them into Talbot's custody.

The romantic element is occasionally obtrusive, but Talbot and Jacqueline Wells make a convincing match. Sheila Bromley is properly brassy, but at length she submits to sentimentality, as her nature proves altered, and delivers a dreadful speech asking forgiveness. "She'll live—to prove my theory is right," declares the dying surgeon. "I feel as though I've been born again!" gushes Bromley.

Halperin had by now—too late to do his faltering career much good—overcome the silent-screen style that had plagued his work as late as 1936's *Revolt of the Zombies*. He took on *Torture Ship* in the stead of the originally announced director, Rex Hale. Halperin's deployment of the uprisings is calculated to unsettle the viewer with a sense of dangerously random misfortune. The foreboding look of *Torture Ship* is surprisingly well textured and suitably dressed, despite the small budget that was business as usual for the conjoined Producers Pictures Corp. and Producers Distributing Corp. (soon to become Producers Releasing Corp., or PRC). Jack Greenhalgh's cameras capture a suitably dungeon-like atmosphere.

David Chudnow's brooding musical score descends from Abe Meyer's Synchronization Service, long a source of inexpensive pre-recorded cues—favored by the smaller studios. Chudnow at length would develop the MUTEL (or Music for Television) Library, a boon to the independent film-and-TV sector, but a chronic annoyance to the U.S.-based International Federation of Musicians on account of its use of foreign orchestras to compile prefabricated scoring cues.

Hitler—Beast of Berlin

a.k.a.: *Beasts of Berlin* • *Goose Step* • *Beast of Berlin* • *Hell's Devils*
Producers Distributing Corp. • 1939

"It isn't the brutality of the Nazis that is their real evil," declared *Variety* on the occasion of the troubled release of Sam Newfield's *Hitler—Beast of Berlin.* "It's what's behind that brutality, the reason for it, that makes compassionate people shudder."

If the horror-ban zealots had worked as hard at eliminating real-world horrors as they did at suppressing horror movies, the culture might have had no need for such films as *Hitler—Beast of Berlin*, or of 1934's *Dealers in Death* and *Hitler's Reign of Terror*, 1936's *I Was a Captive of Nazi Germany*, and 1938's *Inside Nazi Germany*, to name a few of the American cinema's long-unheeded documentary cries for intervention. With the film they had intended to distribute as *Hitler—Beast of Berlin*, Ben Judell, Sigmund Neufeld, and Samuel Newfield ran promptly afoul of attempts at repression.

The Motion Picture Association's Production Code Administration, fearful of offending anyone—even the Nazi-sympathizer contingent—lest the German export market be compromised, approved the title *Goose Step.* The just-forming Producers (a.k.a. PRC) group placed its advertisements, however, as *Hitler—Beast of Berlin.* The Code objected on grounds that the title was inflammatory (precisely the intent, of course) and in defiance of the industry's pusillanimous rules and regulations as to the respectful portrayal of other nationalities. (Though essentially and predominantly Jewish in cultural bearings and membership, the Motion Picture Association also had allowed itself to be infiltrated by the anti-Semitic Legion of Decency of the Roman Catholic Church, a parasitic influence.)

Provincial censorship boards in New York and Massachusetts guardedly approved the title *Beasts of Berlin*, which the Production Code also rejected. A Purity Seal finally came through for *Goose Step*, with a warning that no other title could be used. The sanctimonious, Nazi-appeasing Catholic censors looked beyond the title, too, to compromise the impact of a lengthy barroom scene: carousing Nazis were one thing, but carousing Nazis lusting after feminine drinking companions—nope. Too inflammatory.

The short-memoried watchdogs, of course, failed to comprehend the irony: Neufeld and Judell had meant the original title as a specific evocation of Rupert Julian's *The Kaiser, the Beast of Berlin* (1918), a wishful-thinking melodrama that ends with Kaiser Wilhelm's imprisonment at the hands of a vengeful Belgian citizen.

In *Hitler—Beast of Berlin*, Roland Drew plays Hans Manling, who leads an underground resistance. The inner circle includes Hans' brother-in-law, Karl (Alan Ladd, in a tentative breakthrough role); Gustav Schulz (John Ellis); Father Pommer (Frederick Giermann); and Albert (Hans H. von Twardowski), whose assignment is to infiltrate the Nazi ranks. Manling's pregnant wife (Steffi Duna) wants to flee to America. Manling is arrested after a seemingly sympathetic tavern owner, Lustig (Vernon Dent), betrays him under torture. Albert loses his composure during a drinking bout with the Nazis and gives away the other undergrounders.

Everyone is imprisoned under Col. Hess (Walter O. Stahl), who had been Hans Manling's commander in the prior war. Hess might be forgiving, if only Manling would switch loyalties, but Manling is adamant—and suffers as a consequence. A guard, Braun (Hans von Morhart), is unexpectedly moved by Manling's plight. After Karl is slain in an escape attempt, Manling bides his time until he sees a way out. Braun pretends not to notice as Manling leaps into a farmer's wagon. Manling is reunited with his wife and their infant son in Switzerland; he swears to carry on with the cause.

Hitler—Beast of Berlin suffers from simplistic situational plotting and a tendency to concentrate more upon the Nazis' overt thuggishness and less upon attempted insights into the society's embrace of cruelty. The film is nonetheless a brilliantly delivered piece of received wisdom, more intuitive than intellectualized, from the Yiddish heart of the U.S. motion-picture industry. Now that the Nazis had begun to impose their own self-glorifying movies, such as *Sieg im Westen* (*Victory in the West*), with impunity onto U.S. screens in that day of bigoted America First isolationism, somebody in Hollywood sooner or later was bound to mount a dramatic exercise in opposition. As usual, the responsibility fell to the risk-prone independent sector: Big-time MGM's purported breakthrough picture of a kindred nature, *Escape*, would not come until the autumn of the following year.

Director Sam Newfield handled *Hitler—Beast of Berlin* under his pseudonym of Sherman Scott; this was hardly a bid for anonymity. Everybody who was anybody in Hollywood knew that Newfield and Sigmund Neufeld were brothers, and that Sam (*né* Shmuel Neufeld) used the aliases of Scott and Peter Stewart to make less obvious his habit of accepting any and all low-rent assignments. If the Scott identity was meant to mask anything here, it probably sought a distraction from Newfield's association with actionful escapism. Newfield's style for this film is under-obvious and often symbolic, making much of the smoky underworld of the secret resistance and finding pleasing subtleties in characters (such as the oddly sympathetic Nazi guard) who would more easily have been rendered monolithic hoodlums. Roland Drew is affecting as the determined freedom fighter, and young Alan Ladd conveys the star quality that mainstream Hollywood had yet to discover; a reissue would impose star billing for Ladd. Hans H. von Twardosky accounts well for the center of gravity of the crucial drunk scene, where he turns fink amid a bout of Nazi revelry.

Buried Alive

Producers Pictures Corp. • 1939

A crime melodrama of essential conventionality, Victor Halperin's *Buried Alive* turns toward the bizarre in the elements of a career executioner driven to drink by the dehumanizing nature of his profession, an ill-balanced jailbird who cracks up after one indignity too many, and a hard-luck hero whose inflicted misfortunes make for a striking prefiguration of the soon-to-flourish *noir* school of narrative cinema.

Prison trusty Johnny Martin (Robert Wilcox) is caught up in a barroom brawl while trying to assist executioner Ernie Mathews (George Pembroke). Manning (Wheeler Oakman), a mean-spirited newspaperman who had started the fight, blames Martin and thereby scandalizes the governor's office. Prison nurse Joan Wright (Beverly Roberts) attempts to cushion Martin from the letdown of a stalled parole; they fall in love. Martin's deranged cellmate (Don Rowan) kills an abusive guard during an attempted breakout. Martin is wounded, accused in the slaying, and condemned on false testimony from a resentful inmate, Gus Barth (Peter George Lynn).

Mathews, readying the execution chamber, has conspired instead with the powers-that-be to stage a bogus death. Barth, believing Martin defunct, reveals his own lies. Martin gets an overdue crack at freedom.

Hackneyed on the one hand and yet progressive on the other, *Buried Alive* is a seethingly well-enacted picture in need of recognition as a seminal *film noir*. Its very raggedness matches the suffocating desperation that courses through Robert Wilcox's figurative title portrayal, a pulp-fiction archetype sprung to life. Beverly Roberts is equally good as the nurse who represents Wilcox's every motivation to rejoin polite society. George Pembroke delivers a tough-but-sensitive impersonation of the executioner who never forgets a kindness; Pembroke's acuity at interpreting tormented souls receives a workout on the side of mad villainy in the following year's *The Last Alarm*.

The Devil's Daughter

a.k.a.: *Pocomania*
Lenwal Productions • Sack Amusement Enterprises • 1939

Pocomania is a Jamaicanized English slang term describing the frenzied thrall of voodoo enchantment. This might have been the state of mind that gripped veteran filmmaker George W. Terwilliger—one of those names W.C. Fields would have loved—when he recalled his perilous misadventures in shooting the dark-magic melodrama *Ouanga* (1936) on location in the West Indies. Nothing went right with *Ouanga*, not even the finished product. And even though Terwilliger must have enjoyed all he could tolerate of the ooga-booga business, still he could not resist retooling his script as the basis of Arthur Leonard's *The Devil's Daughter*.

The Devil's Daughter, filmed on location around Kingston, Jamaica, takes a lighter approach than *Ouanga*, narrowing the class-and-color conflicts to a clash between sisters—one, an educated New Yorker; the other, a superstition-maddened islander—and emphasizing funnyman James Carl "Hamtree" Harrington's portrayal of a dice-rattling Harlem cone artist who tips his hand too quickly to the savvy Jamaicans.

New arrival Sylvia Walton (Ida James) is the cultured half-sister of banana farmer Isabelle Walton (Nina Mae McKinney). Isabelle has run the family's plantation in the long absence of Sylvia, the true heiress. Isabelle plots to terrorize Sylvia into leaving. Isabelle's complications include a tense romantic triangle involving foreman Phil Ramsay (Jack Carter) and persistent suitor John Lowden (Emmett Wallace). Elvira (Willa MacLane), Sylvia's maidservant, falls for Percy Jackson (Harrington) and subjects him to a love-charm hoodoo from Isabelle, who informs Percy that his soul has been transmigrated into a hog.

Phil proposes marriage to Sylvia. Sylvia proposes equal owner-ship of the estate to Isabelle. Isabelle proposes to subject Sylvia to a bloodthirsty ritual. Phil proposes to scam Sylvia out of her fortune. John beats the truth out of Phil, who reveals Isabelle's treacheries. John breaks in upon the ritual, and the sisters find themselves reconciled. Percy and Elvira are aghast to learn that the Soul Pig has been slaugh-tered for dinner. Isabel tells Percy she was just woofing him about the soul-swapping business. Everybody chows down on barbecued pork.

Setting aside the crippling flaws of *Ouanga*, one might argue that the 1936 original at least possesses a relentless severity that *The Devil's Daughter* could have used as dramatic ballast. The character portrayals are quite good—especially those of Harrington and McKinney—and the pace cracks right along. The make-nice finale is as close to an ultimate cheat as a film can get, however, short of resorting to the old standby just-a-dream denouement. Speaking of which, see our accompanying chapters on *Mr. Washington Goes to Town* and *Professor Creeps* and, on the Caucasian side of the equation, *Man with Two Lives*.

Forgotten Horrors of 1940

Hidden Enemy

Monogram Pictures Corp. • 1940

Lighter than aluminum and tougher than steel, an experimental metal developed by scientist John MacGregor (George Cleveland) stands to revolutionize warfare. No mention is made here of any specifically foreign enemies, but villains William von Brinken and William Castello play things with Germanic and Italianate overtones. Howard Bretherton's *Hidden Enemy* plays out with an overriding ignorance of how the world really works.

The naïve plotting (by C.B. Williams and Marion Orth) expects the viewer to believe that MacGregor is working in a vacuum, aware of the potential but never suspecting that his breakthrough might draw spies. Warren Hull is better than the material as the inventor's son, a newspaper reporter who finds himself pressed into a heroic stance. Kay Linaker accounts for most of the twists and turns, as an out-of-town journalist who shows a decidedly un-journalistic interest and at one point steals the formula. Hull's approach to journalism is more of the conflict-of-interest variety: Fired for missing a big development, he regains his job by helping Linaker dispose of von Brinken, then by rushing into print with the lowdown on their role in protecting his father's discovery. Such irresponsible mock-journalism used to be the exception to the rule.

Chasing Trouble

Monogram Pictures Corp. • 1940

For their second run at a series that was shaping up as an anticipation of Universal Pictures' soon-to-erupt Abbott & Costello comedies, Frankie Darro and Mantan Moreland tackled a novel but ill-developed twist on the old-standby espionage formula. Howard Bretherton's *Chasing Trouble* is a lesser Darro and Moreland entry, but the star players are never less than right for the circumstances.

Darro is Cupid O'Brien, a floral-shop flunky and matchmaking fool who undertakes to find the proper sweetheart for a pal named Susie (Marjorie Reynolds). O'Brien and his colleague, Jefferson (Moreland), find themselves fooled into working for agents who use floral arrangements to transmit forbidden information.

The narrative gimmick is a running gag about the pseudo-science of handwriting analysis, which was in fashion during the early 1940s. O'Brien, a novice at determining character via penmanship, at first

mistakes the head spy, Morgan (Alex Callam), for a G-Man because of the crook's impressive signature. He rethinks the appraisal along sinister lines, with practical results.

O'Brien connects with a reporter, Callahan (Milburn Stone), who not only proves to be an ideal beau for Susie—but also helps to rescue her from Morgan's gang of traitors.

Marjorie Reynolds' character has little more than a decorative function, leading one to wonder why the bad guys would want her put out of the way, except perhaps for knowing too much. Moreland, too, has altogether too little to do in this one—a lapse corrected in subsequent teamings. Next up for Darro and Moreland: *On the Spot* and *Laughing at Danger*.

The Invisible Killer

Producers Distributing Corp. • 1940

The title, though honest, is still a come-on that can only have disappointed the fantasy-film enthusiasts. The title menace of Sam Newfield's *The Invisible Killer* is no transparent miscreant, but rather a poisonous substance hidden in a telephone receiver. Which is weird enough—but hardly so ferocious as the marquee billing would suggest.

Other problems include ill-at-ease supporting performances and a cheapness of presentation. The sense of danger is everpresent, however; not even Joseph O'Donnell's stilted dialogue can defeat the tension.

Murder stalks the members of a gambling syndicate. Reporter Sue Walker (Grace Bradley) and homicide cop Jerry Brown (Roland Drew) must break the case before a mob war can erupt.

Too late. The situation turns so ugly, so rapidly, that the law must shut down the betting houses. Racketeer Lefty Ross (Sydney Grayler) is dispatched by an unseen force just as he is about to turn fink. A self-important reformer (Boyd Irwin) is next to die—and this time, Sue confiscates a telephone receiver as evidence. The diabolical mechanism is discovered. Finally, a trusted staff member (Harry Worth) is revealed as a snitch between police and underworld, and the gangsters' lawyer (Alex Callam) proves to be the big cheese himself.

Grace Bradley is efficiently relentless as the impulsive free-agent sleuth, and Jeanne Kelly has a nice turn as the endangered daughter of a key victim. Roland Drew, the leading man of director Newfield's breakthrough PRC picture, *Hitler—Beast of Berlin*, is less impressive here as Bradley's homicide-squad fiancé. Bradley makes a fairly convincing gal reporter (once the customary term for a woman in the newsroom) until one of her published stories comes to light—an

extraordinarily awful job of attempted journalism that no self-respecting newspaper would inflict upon its readership. As with *Hitler—Beast of Berlin*, Newfield travels under his alter-ego of Sherman Scott.

Though no great shakes by any standard, *The Invisible Killer* is all the same a crucial title in the early development of the rough-edged studio remembered today as Producers Releasing Corp. Ben Judell had launched the company in 1938 under the Progressive Pictures banner, renaming it Producers Distributing Corp. in 1939 and then ceding control to Sigmund Neufeld. Neufeld changed the name in 1940 to Sigmund Neufeld Productions. The switch to Producers Releasing Corp., a branch of Pathé Laboratories, Inc., also came about in 1940. The PRC identity would remain in place until 1946–47, when the company became Eagle-Lion Films in a bid for greater respectability. (Eagle-Lion's open-secret underwriting by Mafia money gave the company a steadier footing—but *respectability*? Forget it.)

Two Frankensteins from Texas

Pixilated Pictures • George E. Turner • 1940–49

We have not experienced the luxury of viewing 1940's *Frankenstein*, a labor-of-love production from San Antonio, Texas—but then, neither have we had the good fortune of seeing George E. Turner's own, somewhat later, amateur production of *Frankenstein* in any reasonably coherent form.

At least we know what became of the Turner *Frankenstein*, which was shot in 16-millimeter color in Amarillo, Texas, during the postwar 1940s and early 1950s: one of Turner's offspring inadvertently destroyed the long-dormant footage around 1970 while attempting to project it without appropriate supervision. *Vita longa, ars brevis.*

It was during the 1970s, too, that Turner came up with the idea of a genre-study book called *Forgotten Horrors: Early Talkie Chillers from Poverty Row*, to invoke the 1979 edition's mouthful of a title. George scarcely sensed that his own filmmaking efforts would one day figure in a *Forgotten Horrors* series.

We can describe the Turner *Frankenstein*, in George's words, as "more [H.P.] Lovecraft, really, than Mrs. Shelley. … I was coming directly off ol' Lovecraft's serialized novel, *Herbert West: Reanimator*, rather than trying to adapt *Frankenstein* or do any kind of takeoff on the Universal [Pictures] movies. The Monster, as I played 'im, was closer to what Chris Lee wound up doing in the first Hammer *Frankenstein*—except

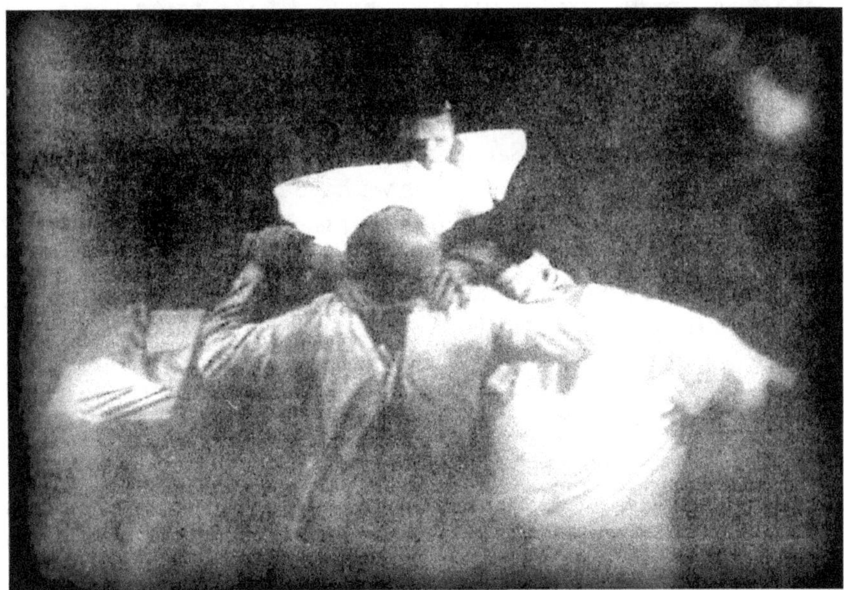

Forgotten Horrors originator George E. Turner plays the Monster in his late-1940s abortive filming of a takeoff on *Frankenstein*

for my being somewhat chubbier than ol' Chris ever was—than to any of the three Karloff interpretations." Turner also managed the occasional moment of homage to the 1931 *Frankenstein*, as evidenced by a surviving frame enlargement (pictured above).

Yes, and so much for one of the mysteries of the missing *Frankensteins*. The other remains a misplaced film, and—the proverbial six degrees of separation notwithstanding—attempts to trace its crafters, or any surviving footage, have proved frustrating. But we know that this film and four other 16-millimeter featurettes (see also: *Dr. Jekyll and Mr. Hyde*, under 1937) were completed and shown provincially, along with short subjects. And we know that the popular sensation these films caused in San Antonio led to some generous publicity on a national scale. We have turned up such artifacts as a production contract and several soundtrack platters, rendered unplayable by the passage of time and groove deterioration in the Victor Talking Machine Co. home-recording disks.

"Amateur moviemaking is generally admitted to be a young man's game—but down in Texas there's a group of moviemaking amateurs for whose activities some new and super-youthful adjectives ought to be coined," wrote Wilton Scott in the April 1941 issue of *American Cinematographer* magazine. "Officially they call themselves Pixilated Pictures..., [and] for five years these youngsters have operated a thriving 16mm production company." The journal of the American Society of Cinematographers was running over a year behind the activities in question, for Pixilated's *Frankenstein* had premiered in February of 1940 and had become, in turn, a sufficiently well-received attraction to merit showing in a few of Texas' Interstate Circuit Theatres. (See also: *Dr. Jekyll & Mr. Hyde*, under 1937.)

In 1937, at the home of San Antonio's E. Humphrey Price family— no kin to Michael H. Price, as far as we have determined—daughter Babe Price and several neighborhood chums staged a music-and-comedy pageant. Babe's mother, a home-movie enthusiast, shot portions of the show with a Bell & Howell Filmo rig and then encouraged the youngsters to make a picture of their own. Mrs. Price supplied the camera and film stock and recommended that the children—who ranged in age from 10 to 13—organize a company and sell shares.

Glenn Alvey, Jr., one of the older members, modeled a shooting script after the 1931–1932 Paramount version of *Dr. Jekyll and Mr. Hyde*. Completed in June of 1937, the production paid for itself and then some, enabling Pixilated Pictures to declare a dividend of 100 per cent and mount a new issue at 20 cents a share—double the original price. Subsequent productions were "It's Laughter We're After" (December 1937), "Hollywood Ho!" (1938), "Snazzy Sixteen" (1939), and the 1939–1940 production of *Frankenstein*. The company also made newsreels and landed a commission from a dance studio for a five-minute promotional film.

Alvey derived his script for *Frankenstein* from the 1931 Universal version, embellished by his familiarity with the 1935 *Bride of Frankenstein* and the then-new *Son of Frankenstein*, whose striking wardrobe design for Boris Karloff was reflected in the shaggy pelt worn by Alvey's conception of the Monster, played by Henry Dielmann, Jr. Where surviving photographs show little in the way of makeup or elaborate costuming on Alvey (as Henry Frankenstein) or leading lady Edith Jarrell, considerable extravagance is obvious in the appearances of both the Monster and Dr. Frankenstein's helper, Fritz, played by Paul Meador.

"As the youthful actor [playing the Monster] didn't particularly resemble Karloff, the foundation of the makeup had to be a mask," reported *American Cinematographer*. "Yet…it must move naturally…and let the expressions show through."

After failed experiments with *papier-maché* and paste, Alvey and a local taxidermist cast Dielmann's head in plaster, from which they built a mask of rubber, modeled after photographs of Karloff. A wig was fashioned from the hair of a black goat.

More elaborate yet were sets representing a laboratory: one was built outdoors in human scale, the better to take advantage of natural light and spare Dielmann the discomfort of wearing the mask under a Photoflood barrage. The other was an intricate miniature, complete with figurines of Dielmann, Alvey, and Meaders and a pulley apparatus that would allow the raising of the operating table through the

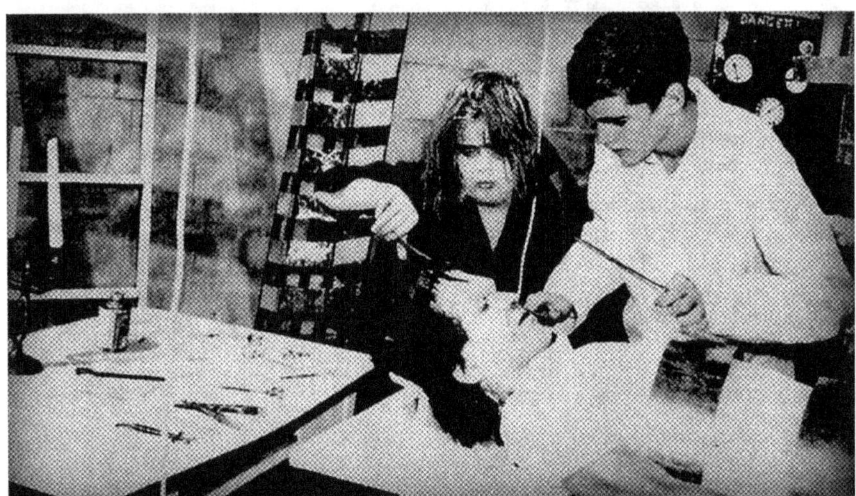

Paul Meador and Glenn Alvey, Jr., in the San Antonio version of Frankenstein.

ceiling. "The [sets] matched up surprisingly well," said *Cinematographer*. Another miniature was built of the windmill where the climactic confrontation and fire take place. Mrs. Price's Model 121 magazine-loading B&H Filmo was used for most of the shooting, but camera operator Jack Locke rented a Model 70D-A Filmo to accommodate the higher speed necessary to make the miniatures appear more convincing. Dialogue and sound effects were captured on home-recording discs, with musical scoring selected from commercial phonograph records. The production tab was reported at $100.

Alvey, Locke, and Babe Price edited the film and shot titles in the attic of the Price residence. Alvey, Russell Bertsch, and Tish Walker designed posters. *Frankenstein* had its premiere in the ballroom of San

PIXILATED PICTURES

CONTRACT

THIS CERTIFIES THAT ... Paul Meaders ....

has received the part of ... Fritz, the hunchback .... in Pixilated

Pictures film production of ... "FRANKENSTEIN" ....,

which will start on ... September 1, ... 19 39 ... and will probably

be finished by ... February 1, ... 19 40 ...

At the beginning of this motion picture the signer must deposit in the treasury $ 1 . 50 , to insure the safe participation of the signer in the above mentioned production. If the signer is duly notified as to the location of the shooting of the picture but fails to appear $ 0 . 25 will be deducted from the original sum, or if he is not prompt $ 0 . 10 will be taken from the money deposited. When the motion picture is completed, the remainder of the money will be returned.

The signer must also agree to sell two adult's and two Children's tickets to both the premier and one subordinate showing of the said production.

In compensation for the above, Pixilated Pictures will pay the signer a salary of $ 1 . 00 at the end of the production.

This contract expires as soon as all retakes are finished and it cannot be broken while the said motion picture is in production.

This contract is valid only if it is completely signed below.

SIGNED: *Paul Meaders*

SIGNER'S PARENT: *Mrs. Meaders*

APPROVED BY:

PRODUCTION MANAGER: *Glenn Alvey Jr.*

DIRECTOR: *Joe McMordie*

PRESIDENT: *Howard Hudson*

A formal casting contract for Alvey's Frankenstein.

Antonio's St. Anthony Hotel before an audience of 400 people. The presentation required as much real-time performance as it did mechanical projection, with staffers manning multiple phonographs to keep the music and dialogue and sound effects—at 78 r.p.m., with only two to five minutes' playing time per side of a disc—in organic synchronization with the picture. The San Antonio newspapers contributed promotional space. Interstate Circuit Theatres not only supplied production resources but also played *Frankenstein* and a re-edited *Jekyll & Hyde*, garnished with sound effects, on a limited basis.

Son of Ingagi

Hollywood Productions • Richard C. Kahn • Sack Amusement Enterprises • 1940

The connection appears tenuous between *Ingagi* (1930) and Richard C. Kahn's *Son of Ingagi*—films separated by a decade, by unrelated corporate pedigrees, and by the one's being a jungle adventure and the other, a domestic mad-doctor-and-apeman picture jazzed up with slapstick comedy and romantic intrigues. The linkage runs deep, nonetheless.

And why the lapse of time between *Ingagi* (1930) and its professed sequel of 1940? Because 10 years pass like no time at all when a source-film possesses staying power.

Pop-cultural phenomena lasted longer in the day of Nat Spitzer's *Ingagi*, a notoriously bogus documentary-styled production that caused a mass-market sensation by pretending to display forbidden rituals and the off-limits vistas of an African jungle. Never mind that the customs were fictional and the fauna phony, and that the jungle consisted primarily of a Hollywood sound-stage, imaginatively dressed, and locations scouted out in Darkest Southern California. The impression remained vital. *Ingagi* references and one-liners remained commonplace

Original promotional banner for the 1930 Ingagi.

well into the 1940s; even Hal Roach's *Our Gang* series and Columbia Pictures' *Three Stooges* franchise devoted throwaway gags to *Ingagi*.

Ingagi augmented its mock-Africa with authentic African-safari footage pirated from a vanity film of 1914, Lady Grace Mackenzie's *Heart of Africa*. That film represented a peculiar and demeaning genre, the white-man's-burden mock-epic—calculated to argue on behalf of the imagined imperial supremacy of wealthy white interlopers over the indigenous tribes. Spitzer's fabricated filming, when combined with the lifts from *Heart of Africa*, presented an Africa unknown to *National Geographic* (itself a bastion of white-supremacist egghead blather-ing), where plant-and-animal life of the tropical Americas flourished alongside species exclusive to the African continent. One presumably venomous creature was a concoction of the properties department: a leopard tortoise, decked out with the armor of a scaly anteater.

Ingagi means gorilla—in this instance, a 600-pound specimen whose society of apes purportedly practiced the abduction of tribal women for the sake of interbreeding. Semi-human offspring, cryptids before the term had gained currency, were a foregone conclusion in the film's ogler-bait mythology. The star player, Ingagi himself, was a stuntman and makeup master named Charles Gemora, whose persuasive gorilla costumes graced many a motion picture of Old Hollywood. A sequence involving Gemora's abduction of a tribal maiden triggered much of the sensation that made *Ingagi* a box-office roadshow draw (often bootlegged) for many years. The response was altogether different at an exhibi-tors' preview screening in 1930 in Los Angeles, where members of the show-business audience recognized the captive woman as a familiar face at Central Casting. *Ingagi* also provoked a lawsuit, charging plagiarism, by the family of Lady Mackenzie, in addition to widespread regional censor-ship and indignant condemnations from various scientific institutions.

Spitzer might have been smart to mount a prompt sequel to *Ingagi*, but that phenomenon played long enough and well enough to fulfill its purpose—and *Ingagi* inspired various imitations, most notably George M. Merrick's *Angkor* (a.k.a. *Forbidden Adventure [in Angkor]*), from 1937, which transplanted the horndog-gorilla angle to Southeast Asia.

We can skip over a great deal of the rest to cut to *Son of Ingagi*, which the film historian George E. Turner and I had dismissed as "a sequel in name only" in the original edition of *Forgotten Horrors: Early Talkie Chillers from Poverty Row* (1979–1980). The appraisal is technically correct, for *Son of Ingagi* originated not with Spitzer's Congo Pictures, Ltd., but rather with a scrappy, more prolific, company based in Texas, Alfred Sack's Sack Amusements Enterprises.

Al Sack, a niche-savvy Jewish entrepreneur, had prospered in the gemstones trade in Dallas, catering to the city's oil-and-cattle ruling

class. He also aligned himself with the Poverty Row stepchild-studios of Hollywood. Sack sensed a little-tapped profitable market in the southern black population, whose citizens seldom received a welcome from the dominant culture's mass-market downtown movie theatres. Nor did the black citizenry often see its reflection upon the screen, except in caricatured token roles. (The general policy among theatre operators was one of blacks-to-the-balcony, whether in cities or in towns, augmented by a weekly "coloreds-only" night.)

Spencer Williams, Jr., right, with Amos 'n' Andy's Alvin Childress, left, and Tim "Kingfish" Moore.

Sack's strategy was to provide black-neighborhood theatres with black-ensemble motion pictures; though hardly the first small-time producer to develop black-player attractions, Sack proved more consistent and prolific. *Son of Ingagi*, following his involvement as an investor-distributor in a series of black-ensemble westerns starring the jazz singer Herb Jeffries, was Sack's first such effort as key producer in a surge that would persist into 1947. All he lacked was a writer and all-round filmmaker of color to validate the credential.

Sack found that versatile artist in Spencer Williams, Jr., a heavyset actor who had handled villainous roles and contributed additional dialogue for William J. "Jed" Buell's late-1930s productions of such Jeffries pictures as *Harlem on the Prairie, Two-Gun Man from Harlem, The Bronze Buckaroo,* and *Harlem Rides the Range.* Sack was a distributor for Buell's Los Angeles-based production company. While visiting the *Harlem* series' location shoots in rural Texas and Oklahoma, Sack had developed a friendship with Williams, whose silent-screen writing accomplishments proved especially impressive. Hence their agreement to develop *Son of Ingagi*, with Williams as writer and leading player. Sack touted the film as the first "all-colored" horror movie, but it was hardly that: Gus Smith's *Drums o' Voodoo* had arrived in 1934, along with the predominantly black voodoo melodramas *Chloe (Love Is Calling You)* and *Ouanga* during 1934–36.

Williams had envisioned a semi-sequel, or spinoff, for *Ingagi*. (The title had remained familiar, as a consequence of long-term showings.) Sack bought Williams' script for *Son of Ingagi* and hired him to play a bumbling but ultimately helpful police detective. Sack was so pleased with the result that he enlisted Williams as a one-man producer-director-writer-star combination. In Al Sack, Williams found a *laissez-faire* backer who afforded him prominence in a limited orbit; money to spare, given Williams' dollar-stretching abilities; and the freedom to develop his own stories. The result is a legacy of nine splendidly rough-hewn motion pictures (10, if one counts *Son of Ingagi*, which Williams did not direct), all filmed on budgets of between $10,000 and $15,000 each. The titles seem to represent a variety of genres (one horror fantasy, two comedies, three spiritual exercises, and four melodramas), but in fact each is *sui generis*, each a worthy example of what a Hollywood outsider can achieve when he reconciles his own ideas with a knowledge of what his fixed audience wants. (And more about Spencer Williams and Al Sack in our discussion of *The Blood of Jesus*, under 1941.)

Son of Ingagi is no more a conventional mad-doctor yarn than it is a formal sequel to *Ingagi*. Laura Bowman, a stage actress and alumna of *Drums o' Voodoo*, plays *Son*'s renegade physician as a surly schemer, plotting to lure a virginal young woman into a forbidden tryst with a captive apeman named N'Gena (Zack Williams). There are hints, of course, that the creature hails from Africa, so he might very well be some unclaimed offspring of Ingagi. Bowman's character seems careless to the point of harboring a death-wish, for she allows the monster the run of the house and finally dies at its hands before her plans can be fulfilled. The kinship with *Ingagi*'s interbreeding angle is implicit.

Williams' screenplay concerns itself more with a lifelike domestic state between the romantic leads, Daisy Bufford and Alfred Grant, and with Williams' comical portrayal of a self-important cop who seems incapable of detecting the monster at close range. In a comically timed sequence, Williams putters about a kitchen while the apeman hovers out of sight. No sooner has Williams built a sandwich and turned away, than the beast darts in and devours the

Spencer Williams, Jr.

delicacy. Williams finds himself more concerned with the Case of the Missing Sandwich than with tracking down the cause of the mayhem.

The story has as much to do with a hidden fortune in African gold, which is sought by the scientist's crooked brother (Arthur Ray) with homicidal results. Finally, N'Gena abducts Miss Bufford but accidentally torches the house before he can get on about his business with her. Williams and Grant save the day—and Williams saves the gold, in a twist ending.

Williams' deft comic presence accounts for much of the charm here, and so does Bowman's formidable but too-brief portrayal of the grouchy renegade doctor. Williams' script is rich in the finer points of citified black folklife, dwelling on the hospitable details of a wedding reception, reveling in a love of music, and establishing early on that the doctor has deep reasons—some friendly, some sinister—for wanting to see the young lady inherit the mysterious old house and its ominous laboratory. Miss Bufford and Grant make convincingly devoted newlyweds, to the finer point of a bickering outbreak. Lanky Zack Williams, a versatile player and alumnus of MGM's *Gone with the Wind*, lends a ferocious, expressive vigor to the title character.

Spencer Williams followed through with such Sack Amusements productions as *The Blood of Jesus*, *Dirty Gertie from Harlem, U.S.A.*, and *Juke Joint*. He cracked network television in 1950 with the CBS series *Amos 'n' Andy*, which proved as controversial as it was popular and faced cancellation by 1953. Williams had flourished in the cheapskate domain of Al Sack, but Sack had discontinued the black-ensemble pictures, sensing a gradual desegregation in moviegoing. Williams' career collapsed from neglect in mainstream Hollywood, leaving *Son of Ingagi* and its follow-through titles as tiny monuments to a cause too progressive for the industry-at-large.

Incidentally: The lead photographer on *Son of Ingagi* is Roland C. Price, the self-styled vagabond cameraman responsible for that cruel southwestern film, *Lash of the Penitentes*—and a distant relative of *Forgotten Horrors*' Michael H. Price. A comic-strip version of *Son of Ingagi* appears in our companion volume, *Forgotten Horrors Comics & Stories* (2011).

Phantom Rancher

Colony Pictures, Inc. • 1940

Indiana-born but claiming native-Texan status in a smart publicity ploy, Ken Maynard (1895–1973) was the roughest, toughest, straight-shootin'est, picture-makin'est *hombre* who ever laid siege to Old Hollywood. Unnervingly proud and plain-spoken, Maynard had come to the screen in 1924 as a veteran of the rodeo and Wild West Exposition circuits, winning a devoted following even as he estranged himself from one studio after another with his intimidating martinet tactics and his insistence upon creative autonomy.

Harry Fraser's *Phantom Rancher*, with its impoverished production values and spotty release via the sub-distributor states'-rights system, is a sobering example of how far Maynard had fallen since the mid-1930s, when he alienated Mascot Pictures' Nat Levine while setting attendance records for the company with *Mystery Mountain*. Levine had salvaged Maynard from a sacking at Universal, aware of the star's volatile combination of marquée

value and irascibility. Levine found Maynard insufficiently grateful and replaced him on hot-headed impulse with a then-obscure Gene Autry in a manic science-fictional musical western serial, 1935's *The Phantom Empire*. That wild production could have put Maynard at the top of the game for years to come. At any rate, *Empire* certainly had that effect upon Autry.

And while Autry coursed to mass acclaim—thanks, in great measure, to a parallel recording and radio-broadcasting career that

Maynard scarcely could have matched—the mighty Ken turned anew to the rodeo arena. He certainly wasn't "out of films" by this time, as Ephraim Katz's *The Film Encyclopedia* declares: The Maynard rèsumé includes a 1935–1944 stretch of 24 features. But Maynard's big-screen fortunes had diminished. (The 1938 *Phantom Ranger* that Katz lists as a Maynard picture is in fact a Tim McCoy starrer, dealing with a counterfeiting racket.)

Easy to misread *Phantom Ranger* as *Phantom Rancher*. But *Rancher* proves to be an out-and-out weird one, in which Ken Mitchell (Maynard) inherits both the ranch and the bad reputation of an uncle who had been suspected of provoking an outbreak of stampedes. The distrustful ranchers will have none of Ken's help, and so he insinuates his way into a murderous outlaw gang, learns that a big-shot cattleman named Collins (Ted Adams) is the genuine menace, and poses as the Phantom Rancher—thwarting Collins' takeover plans by helping the locals to meet their mortgages.

The masquerade is more Robin Hood than Phantom of the Horse Opera, but Maynard's very anger and indignation render this Phantom a figure of menace, at least to those who deserve menacing. Maynard may have lapsed beyond recovery of his stardom and backstage clout, but his attitude is still that of the rambunctious, hard-riding westerner. And his magnificent charger, Tarzan, is still the smartest horse in the movies, Roy Rogers' Trigger notwithstanding.

This long, final exile on Poverty Row finds undiminished Maynard's appetite for slugfests—and for berating his opponents, like Popeye the Sailor, while thrashing them. Another 1940 Colony entry featuring Maynard, *Death Rides the Range*, boasts a garnish of eeriness in the person of a homicidal land-grabber named Baron Starkoff (Sven Hugo Borg). Colony Pictures executives Max and Arthur Alexander were, like Maynard, exiles from Universal Pictures.

The Alexander brothers were cousins of Universal's former production chief, Carl Laemmle, Jr., who had been ousted with the lot of his family in a corporate takeover of the waning 1930s. It was Junior Laemmle who in 1934 had clashed bitterly with Maynard over the perceived debacle of the offbeat western *Smoking Guns*—and fired Maynard in retaliation.

A long span of reclusiveness, coupled with a taste for strong drink, had left Maynard a bloated shadow of his larger-than-life self by the time he cropped up in a 1970 exploitation picture called *Bigfoot*. Maynard died of malnutrition at age 77 in 1973.

Marginal Ground: Additional Titles

These incidental selections lend context and perspective to the overall lineup:

- *Midnight Limited* (Sherwill Productions and Monogram Pictures, 1940). This impossible-getaway mystery involves a chain of train robberies between Montreal and Albany. John King stars as sleuth Valentine Lennon, who loses an assistant to a skulking killer before determining that the culprit, in cahoots with baggageman Monte Collins, has been sneaking onto and off the train in caskets. A marginal entry, all right—but even the margins can contain some interesting scribbles.

- *Beyond Tomorrow*, a.k.a. *Beyond Christmas* (Academy Productions and RKO-Radio., 1940). A benevolent haunting. Old-timers Harry Carey, C. Aubrey Smith, and Charles Winninger portray ghosts who return to help struggling singer Richard Carlson. Things turn grim after lethal lady Helen Vinson seduces Carlson into a threatening situation. Jean Parker provides the good-girl romantic interest, and Maria Ouspenskaya plays a servant psychically attuned to sense the guardian spirits. Edward Sutherland directs.

Drums of Fu Manchu

Republic Pictures Corp. • 1940

From the Prologue: "...the most sinister figure of all time—Fu Manchu. Schooled in the ancient mysteries of the Orient, he is as modern as tomorrow! Ruthless, ageless, holding himself above human law, he embarks upon his most stupendous crime—the conquest of Asia! And with him comes the thunder of his summons to death...the Drums of Fu Manchu!"

For its 17th serial and its first splash of 1940, Republic Pictures turned to Sax Rohmer as a heavy-duty pop-literary source: the world-beating Fu Manchu, ageless mandarin and master of tortures and treacheries, had held in thrall a mass audience since his début in *Story Teller* magazine in 1912—wicked protagonist of novels and short stories, motion pictures, a comic strip, and a radio program. Dr. Fu had outlived the Yellow Peril subgenre to become by 1940 as recognizable a figure as Popeye the Sailor, Mickey Mouse, or Superman. Republic sought to restore the big-screen presence of a character whose exploits had made Rohmer (Arthur Sarsfield Ward, in civilian life) a millionaire many times over. Team-directors William Witney and John English proved ideally attuned to both the prevailing darkness and the spirit of desperate adventure.

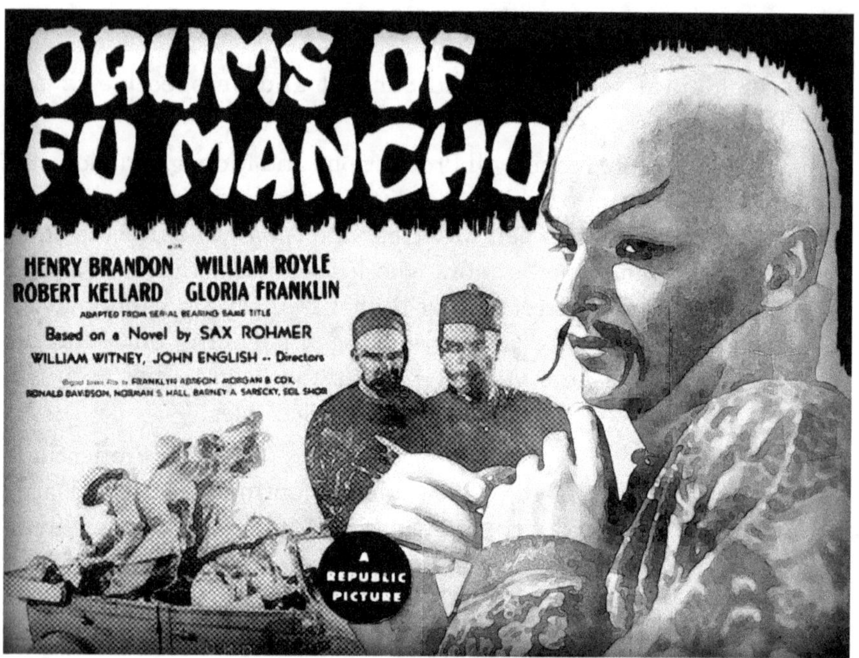

Six screenwriters wove elements from Rohmer's yarns into one of the more nearly perfect chapter-play structures. The adaptation boasts as much striking originality as Republic had shown during 1936–37 in transforming the title character of Dick Tracy from a plainclothes cop into an FBI agent. Fu Manchu (Henry Brandon) and his poisonous daughter, Fah Lo Suee (Gloria Franklin), are sufficiently loyal to the source. Fu's Nemesis from Scotland Yard, Sir Denis Nayland Smith (William Royle), and Sir Denis' chronicler Dr. Petrie (Olaf Hytten), yield to an original-for-the-screen hero named Allan Parker (Robert Kellard). The action is surprisingly subdued for a Republic picture, yielding to favor plot development and characterization. *Drums of Fu Manchu* is unique among Republic's serials, playing out more like an extraordinarily long feature film with chapter breaks—which is the way most enthusiasts today watch the serials, as sustained blocks of time on video—than a typically episodic pageant of cliffhangers.

Republic may have intended a cosmetic adjustment in making Fu's elite guard of blindly obedient hoodlums—known as Dacoits—something more or less than human in appearance. The massed impact of the servants is more substantial, underscoring the film with a visceral, unreasoning horror in counterpoint to Fu's thoroughly rational malice. These Dacoits, as fashioned from a corps of stuntmen and character actors by makeup artist Bob Mark, are nightmare-inducing creatures, each bearing a ghastly arrow-point scar to signify brain surgery

performed by Dr. Fu. The lead Dacoit, Loki (John Merton), is distinguished further by a fanged grimace.

As Fu Manchu, veteran movie villain Henry Brandon, who had been discovered on the Los Angeles stage by Hal Roach, is a study in restraint—a quality all the more impressive in light of his flamboyant Chinese-Deco wardrobe—and displays a mingling of menace and droll humor that is consistent with the defining portrayals of times past by Boris Karloff, Warner Oland, and Harry Agar Lyons. Gloria Franklin is delectably creepy as Fah Lo Suee.

The story finds Fu searching for the sceptre of Genghis Kahn, which the superstitious Himalayans will accept as his credential as a conqueror. Nayland Smith of the British Foreign Office sets out to put the kibosh on his chronic enemy. Joining Sir Denis are Allan Parker, son of an early victim, and Mary Randolph (Luana Walters), whose father has lost a priceless artifact to Fu. After any number of desperate encounters, Parker places the sceptre in safe hands, proving to the Himalayans that Fu does not bear following. Fu Manchu begins plotting anew.

Republic promptly announced a sequel. Upon the onslaught of World War II, a twist was added: Fu Manchu would shelve the conquering urge and place himself—however grudgingly—at the service of the Allies. National sensitivities intruded, however, and on July 19, 1942, the *New York Times* carried the following report:

Phooey, Dr. Fu

International protocol has disturbed Republic Pictures Corp. a good deal this week. *Fu Manchu Strikes Again*, a photoplay in which Sax Rohmer's indestructible Chinese villain was to have switched over to the side of the angels and harried the Japanese, had to be shelved "out of deference to the Chinese people." Dr. Fu has long been a source of displeasure to the Chinese government, Republic learned, and he is not even wanted as an ally.

The *Times'* account, derived from *The Hollywood Reporter*, was followed with a late-July *Reporter* announcement that Republic would proceed, after all, with *Fu Manchu Strikes Again*, emphasizing the Axis-buster stance. Nothing came of the project, after all, but Republic did issue a feature-length condensation of *Drums of Fu Manchu* in 1943. The studio hardly did so with impunity, however, for that fall the U.S. government denied a clearance for export on grounds of *Drums'* "derogatory picturization of our Chinese allies." Capricious martial law beats constitutional freedoms any day.

And so where Nayland Smith and all the might of the British Empire had succeeded only in frustrating Fu Manchu's ambitions, the forces of censorship idled the villain's movie career for the duration. Only after the Axis had fallen and the ensuing Cold War had resurrected the Yellow Peril as a fashionable component of a larger Red Menace, could Fu regain traction as a screen character.

Mr. Washington Goes to Town

Dixie National Pictures • Consolidated National Film • 1940

Moreland & Miller, one of the finer comedy teams of black vaudeville, stuck together in pictures as well, even though Mantan Moreland's fortunes as a solo act in Hollywood proved greater. Flournoy E. Miller preferred to work behind the scenes as a writer and casting director. Their co-starring movies, including the Harlem-out-west adventures of Herb Jeffries, were aimed at black audiences. These films contain a curiously larger measure of black caricature than the mainstream pictures that Moreland graced without Miller.

Three Moreland & Miller movies in particular capture the artists' teamwork much as it must have appeared in the black-neighborhood nightspots where they perfected their precise senses of timing and absurd wordplay. These are *Mr. Washington Goes to Town* and 1942's back-to-back *Lucky Ghost* and *Professor Creeps*, all from the white-guy exploitation producer Jed Buell. Buell's *Up Jumped the Devil* is an interim effort, minus Miller.

Buell, as much a huckster as a picturemaker, publicized *Mr. Washington* to the black newspapers as "the first all-Negro comedy feature ever made." Of course, most of the talents behind the cameras were white—and black artists had been appearing in comedy films since the silent era, both among themselves and with integrated casts.

Neither Buell's extravagant baloney nor his amateurish filmmaking skills can diminish the fun of *Mr. Washington Goes to Town*. A jailbird named Schenectady (Moreland) learns that he has inherited a hotel. Next thing he knows, Schenectady has arrived at the Hotel Ethiopia, where he takes charge of the elevators and hires cell-mate Wallingford (Miller).

A gorilla (Clarence Morehouse) shows up, accompanied by a man in formal attire (Clarence Hargarve). Headless men (John Lester

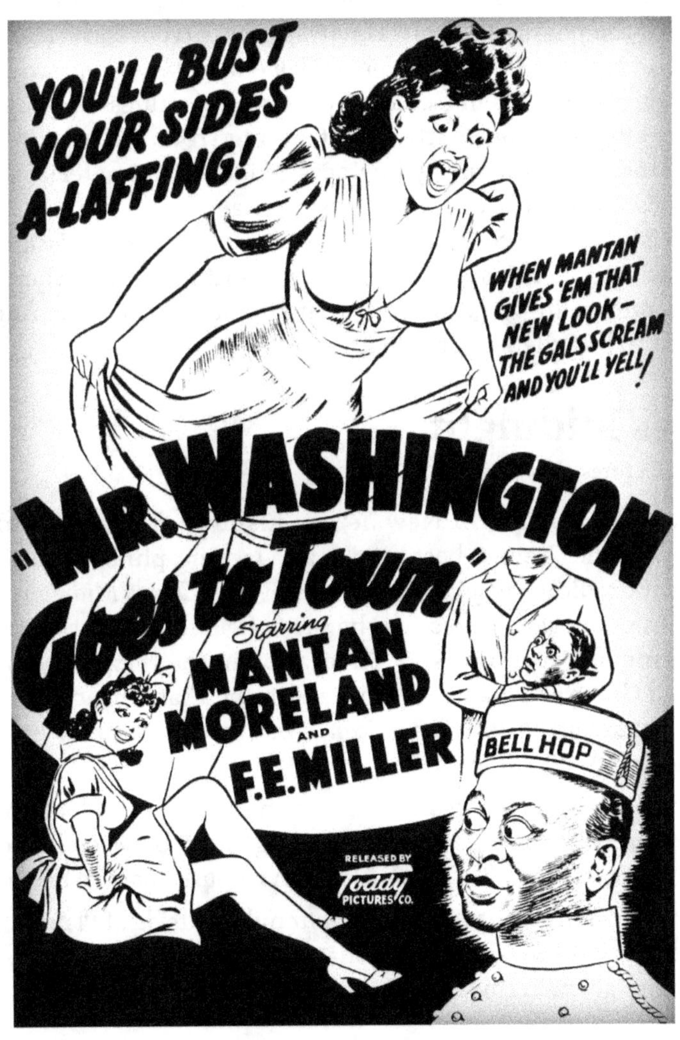

Johnson and DeForrest Coven) prowl about. A knife thrower (Monte Hawley), an invisible man (Vernon McCalla), and a magician (Arthur Ray) harass Schenectady and Wallingford. A roughhouser (Maceo B. Sheffield) begins dismantling the hotel in search of a hidden treasure. Schenectady snaps awake from a nightmare.

Wallingford wants to visit the hotel once the pals have served their time, but Schenectady nixes the idea: he has already been there, he says, and he finds the place none to his liking.

There is no other narrative exit quite as infuriating as the just-a-dream resolution, but at least the ending of *Mr. Washington Goes to Town* is a foregone conclusion. Too many such finales—including those of two otherwise superior *noirs*, *The Strange Affair of Uncle Harry* (1945) and *Fear* (1946)—have come about as hasty afterthoughts to placate the censors. *Mr. Washington*'s dream setting is more nearly on a par with the phantasmagorical newspaper cartoons and silent films of Winsor McCay (including *Little Nemo in Slumberland* and *Dream of a Rarebit Fiend*). Buell's shabby production values emphasize the otherworldly ambiance without detracting from the work of Miller & Moreland. The pals' funny business renders it immaterial whether there is a story to be found amid the wreckage.

There is no reference, incidentally, to anybody named *Washington* in Dixie National Pictures' publicity kit or in either of the rather choppy prints screened in preparation for this book. Maybe Washington is supposed to be Schenectady's last name.

Comes Midnight

Sepia-Art Pictures • 1940

A legendary haunting in New Jersey inspired the stage-and-radio comedian Eddie Green—best known as a laconic, philosophical waiter on network radio's *Duffy's Tavern*—to develop *Comes Midnight* as part of a series of short features for the black neighborhood theatres. The film, presumably lost, was shot on location in the very house that had prompted Green's scenario. That is, assuming that one accepts a credulous report from *The Afro-American*, a Baltimore-based newspaper, as published on April 13, 1940:

> The Sepia-Art Pictures Co., now in the midst of production on the featurette *Comes Midnight,* is shooting scenes between Eddie Green and the ghost of "Old Man Mose" in a house…said to be haunted.
>
> This old house is situated…just four miles outside of Plainfield [New Jersey]. Old residents…say that night after night, many strange things go on in this house where no one has lived for 50 years.

Various persons are said to have heard weird groans and moans, and some say that on stormy nights the pale face and flowing hair of a beautiful young woman may be seen pressed against the window when the lightning flashes. On clear nights, around midnight, the heavy tread of Jonas Bedford, original owner of the house, can be heard as he walks from room to room.

Sidney Easton, well-known comedian who contracted originally to play in the picture, refused to enter the house. He was replaced by Honey Boy Thompson [*sic*; obviously an erroneous citation].

Some sources nonetheless include Sidney Easton, the high-spirited leading man-by-default of the jinxed voodoo thriller *Ouanga* (1936), among the players of *Comes Midnight*. The account of Easton's refusal to enter a purportedly haunted house catches an Afro-centric newspaper playing surprisingly to a cultural stereotype in a day of gathering resistance to such images.

The reference to one Honey Boy Thompson can only be a gaffe: Green's ensemble cast includes Honey Boy *Johnson* as a dancer, but no *Thompson*, Honey Boy or otherwise. The only name of broader cinematic prominence is James Baskett, Mantan Moreland's tormentor in 1943's *Revenge of the Zombies*. Baskett would become famous as Uncle Remus in Disney's *Song of the South* (1946), with a Special Accomplishment Oscar to show for his work.

Sepia-Art's other pictures include *Dress Rehearsal* and *What Goes Up* (both from 1939) and, a decade later, *Mr. Adam's Bomb*. Eddie Green died in 1950; he was succeeded in the *Duffy's Tavern* role by Mantan Moreland.

Sky Bandits

Criterion Pictures • Monogram Pictures Corp. • 1940

Grand National, one of the last old-school Poverty Row studios of the late Depression years, scored in 1937 with Laurie York Erskine's popular character, Sgt. Renfrew of the Royal Canadian Mounted Police. The series lapsed to a production-distribution deal between Criterion and Monogram, sustaining consistency under various creative talents. As generously sprinkled with heroic ballads as the singing-cowboy westerns, the *Renfrew* pictures also boast an appetite for bizarre menaces.

George E. Turner, who cared little for cowboy-crooner movies and even less for baritone-Mountie movies, once suggested that there should have been a *Renfrew* picture called *Yukon Have It*. George granted there was plenty to like about the *Renfrews*, "if you can get around all that pseudo-operatic caterwauling."

Ralph Straub's *Sky Bandits*, from a screenplay by *White Zombie*'s Edward Halperin, pays off generously for the science-fantasy fans: Renfrew (radio singer James Newill) and Constable Kelly (Dave O'Brien) connect an outbreak of plane wrecks to a gang of smugglers. Renfrew's pal, Buzz Murphy (Eddie Featherstone), takes to the skies with a payload of gold. A radio announcer has wiretapped the mining company, the better to sneak encrypted information into his broadcasts. A devoted listener is master smuggler Morgan (William Pawley), who zaps Murphy's plane. Renfrew watches in horror as his friend crashes.

The inventor of the deadly beam, Prof. Lewis (Joseph Stefani), fancies himself to be working on a defense weapon for some patriotic cause. When he learns otherwise and complains accordingly, Morgan turns threatening. Something might be said here about Samuel Johnson's definition of patriotism as "the last refuge of a scoundrel."

Renfrew finds the machinery but has not the time to collect evidence. When he returns with backup, the lab has been dismantled.

Refrew's colleagues begin to question his state of mind. Obsessed with vengeance, Renfrew goes airborne—with the professor's daughter (Louise Stanley) as a stowaway.

Morgan takes aim at Renfrew, but Lewis trains the death ray upon Morgan. Constable Kelly and the professor make short work of the surviving hoodlums.

The *Renfrews* found little critical respect in their day, but some first-generation fans have recalled a pang of sadness upon learning that the rip-snorting *Sky Bandits* would be the final adventure. Alert viewers among any generation of genre enthusiasts will enjoy spotting *Dracula*'s Dwight Frye among *Sky Bandits*' players.

The other installments are *Renfrew of the Royal Mounted* (1937), a counterfeiter thriller with a (literally) chilling set piece in a slaughterhouse locker; *Renfrew on the Great White Trail* (1938), with Richard Alexander as a likably drunken physician harboring a grim secret; *Fighting Mad* (1939), with Sally Blane as a kidnap victim-turned-suspect and Milburn Stone as a gang boss; *Crashing Thru* (1939), in which Stone plays a mining executive leading a murderous secret life; *Danger Ahead* (1940), scripted by Edward Halperin, with Renfrew taking charge of an armored-truck fleet to find a vanished driver and his payload; *Yukon Flight* (1940), from another Halperin script, with James Newill's Renfrew baiting bad-guy mail-service boss William Pawley into a skybound confrontation; and *Murder on the Yukon* (1940), in which James Newill and Dave O'Brien, en route to a peaceable retreat from crimebusting, find instead the corpse of a newly wealthy miner.

On the Spot

Monogram Pictures Corp. • 1940

Soda-fountain jerk and hotel porter are the respective stations in life of Frankie Darro and Mantan Moreland in this continuation of their progressive comedy-team series. There is nothing particularly comical about the story itself, whose serial-murder case provokes the pals into rising good-humoredly above their second-class citizenship to outperform the local police as crimebusters. The film is an effortless (if inadvertent) illustration of Mark Twain's definition of humor as a necessary response to the essential wretchedness of the human condition.

Even the shared impulsive interest in amateur sleuthery is an adventurous rebellion against the drudgery of wage slavery: better to risk mortal peril than to succumb to the unfeeling nothingness. Such tacit existentialism, perhaps more so than the trailblazing integrationalism, distinguishes the Darro-Moreland pictures from even the more finely developed work of Laurel & Hardy and Abbott & Costello. Where Stan Laurel and Oliver Hardy exist on screen in a state of grace however downtrodden ("the *shabby* gentlemen," as a character regards them in one early talking picture), and where Bud Abbott and Lou Costello are patently stage-and-screen stars playing at fringe-dweller buffoonery, Darro and Moreland seem documentary representations of the serving class, bent upon benevolent subversion. *On the Spot* is emphatic in this regard, what with the victims being mobsters preferred dead and the criminal ringleader posing as a pillar of society.

Amateur Detective was the work-in-progress title of Howard Bretherton's *On the Spot*, and as such the phrase captures the tone of almost the entire series. Whatever their character identities from picture to picture, Darro and Moreland are throughout simply Darro & Moreland (emphasis on the connective ampersand), a fast-talking, quick-thinking buddy act. When the pictures are unearthed today with deep-perspective hindsight, Darro seems a genetic template for Michael J. Fox, the preeminent juvenile comic player of the late 20th century. Moreland remains incomparable, despite the best funny

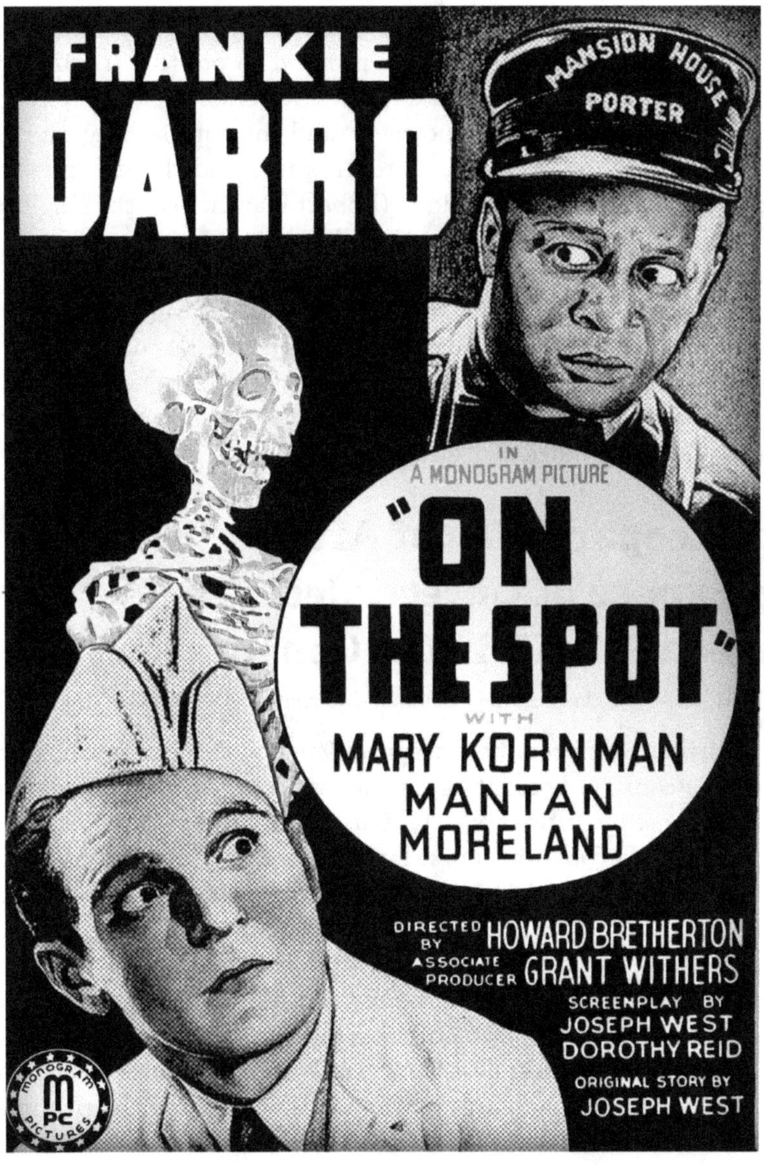

business of such (likewise, late 20th century) breakout talents as Robin Harris, Eddie Murphy, Jamie Foxx, and Martin Lawrence. Darro and Moreland's work retains an insurgent freshness as a mixed-color elaboration upon Moreland's work elsewhere with Flournoy E. Miller.

Frankie (Darro) is minding the soda-fountain counter at a small-town pharmacy when a big-city mobster lurches in, dying from gunshot wounds. Frankie and his chum, Jefferson (Moreland), are quickly assumed to have become the men who know too much: both the police and the underworld—not to mention the press—believe that the victim must have told the pals about a hidden fortune from a bank robbery. Another gangster turns up dead. Frankie decides to flush out the killer, convincing Jefferson to pretend to possess crucial information while Frankie lurks in ambush. Jefferson nervously topples a pallet of shipping cartons, however, and the approaching murderer escapes. Among the shattered crates, Frankie finds hidden clues that betray local banker Cyrus Haddon (Robert Warwick) as the ringleader.

The sense of menace is palpable, and Robert Warwick—a key figure in the transition from silents to talking pictures—is just right as the stuffed-shirt mastermind. Darro and Moreland seem particularly pleased with themselves at having found triumph amid a disastrous bungle. Far more than just a rediscovered oddity from the Depression-into-wartime years, this series sheds light upon Hollywood's comedy-thriller tradition as a class.

The Leopard Men of Africa: An Exposé of Unrecorded Savage Rituals in the Congo

Paul L. Hoefler • Walter A. Futter • Zeidman International • 1940

"It's a thriller," declared the newspaper *Variety*, whose severe box-office bias more commonly led its assigned critics to denounce the *Goona-Goona*-style exploitationers as tedious fakes. Dr. Paul L. Hoefler's *The Leopard Men of Africa* is of course largely a fake in its own right. At least the film has the gumption to announce up front that its ticket-selling cannibal rituals were enacted for the camera. There is a helpful basis in authenticity, and the natural and staged sequences dovetail impressively, all thanks to an assured continuity by Allyn Butterfield, a respected editor of big-screen newsreels.

The larger mouthful of a title appears on screen but is not part of the copyright record. George E. Turner, who relished the pastime of parodying movie titles with extravagant wordplay, often referred

Hoefler's better-respected precursor of Leopard Men.

to this picture as *The Léotard Men of Africa: An Exposé of Unrecorded Sausage Rituals.* The pun probably was inspired by a typographical error in a newspaper's television listings. (The publication's gaffe cited Val Lewton's *The Leopard Man* as *The Léotard Man.* But we digress. As usual.)

A generous 65 minutes of Green Hell horrors, *The Leopard Men of Africa* starts with a quest by Hoefler to rout a society of cannibalistic Leopard Men. These fiends dress in cat skins and wear gloves rigged with steel blades that Robert Englund's Freddie Krueger might envy. Recruits must suffer a branding in silence, lest their outcries mean instant death.

The film, incidentally, is consistent in manner and attitude with Hoefler's acknowledged classic of the subgenre, *Africa Speaks* (1930), which had attained major-studio distribution. *Leopard Men,* however, takes the palm for outlandish terrors.

The British colonial government wants the Leopard Men put out of commission. Hoefler treks toward a confrontation. Ali, Hoefler's scout, witnesses a prelude to a ritual disemboweling, then hurries to summon help. Hoefler and his guardsmen charge to the rescue, but the Leopard Men charge right back at them, driving away the would-be protectors. The Leopard Men proceed. Hoefler vows better results next time and denounces (rather ineffectually) the entrenched savagery.

Where some Saturday-matinée version of such a story would have assured a safe-and-sound finale, Hoefler's dire account dares to inform the audience that his heroic forces are no match for this band of killers. The attitude only amplifies the ring of authenticity, which benefits from a documentary-like travelogue framework, highlighted by a destructive siege from swarming locusts.

A screen credit indicates color photography. The two prints we have turned up since the 1970s are entirely in black-and-white. The Production Code

Paul Hoefler.

Administration demanded scissorings of some of the more explicit depictions of cannibalism and nudity, but our viewings reveal abundant harrowing detail, and abundant toplessness.

It becomes evident that the production company had placated the Code with a sacrificial print—and then distributed the undiluted film for general exposure, you should pardon the expression. The Poverty Row studios had a great deal less to lose than the majors in their dealings with the industry's institutionalized censorship machine, and subterfuge was necessary to survival in a cinematic demimonde whose customers preferred their shock value unadulterated.

The Last Alarm

Sherwill Productions • Monogram Pictures Corp. • 1940

Movies about pyromaniacs are a fairly common staple for the action market, but William West's *The Last Alarm* is the only one we have found whose firebug worships Vulcan and fancies the conflagrations to be sacrifices to that ancient Roman god of flame. (Other worthy titles of similar concern—though altogether conventional by crime-melodrama standards—are Burt Lynwood's *The Fire Trap* and Joe Kane's *Arson Gang Busters*, from 1937–38.)

George Pembroke, an Irish-American actor known for his portrayals of disordered mentality for the smaller studios, keeps a statuette of Vulcan and laughs with mordant glee as he peers through google-eyed spectacles at each new atrocity. Pembroke adds a chilling dimension to an old-fashioned family yarn about a veteran fireman forced into retirement.

George Pembroke.

Ted Williams, heading a subsidiary company for Monogram, made this one for the lower tier of the double-feature market. *The Last Alarm* stands on its own, even so—staged straightforwardly to alternate the homelier sequences with the weird machinations. Footage of genuine fires matches persuasively with the staged action.

After 40 years as a firefighter, Jim Hadley (J. Farrell MacDonald) proves restless in retirement, especially now that a pyromaniac seems intent upon razing the city. Jim's daughter, Joan (Polly Ann Young), tries to persuade him to join her fiancé, Frank Rogers (Warren Hull), an insurance investigator, in an effort to put down the menace. When Jim's best friend, Burt Stanford (Joel Friedkin), is killed in one of the fires, Jim takes up the chase. The audience learns early on that the firebug is a dealer in antiques named Wendell (Pembroke), who believes himself a disciple of Vulcan. While watching one blaze, Wendell drops the effigy, which Hadley finds. Wendell retrieves the evidence. When Hadley describes the clue to Frank and Joan, they remember having seen such a figure at the antiques store. Hadley searches the shop and finds sawdust that matches the wood used in setting the fires. Wendell plants a firebomb in the basement of the Hadleys' home. Hadley and Rogers find the culprit holding Joan and Mrs. Hadley (Mary Gordon) prisoner in the burning house. They rescue the women, and Wendell is trapped and left to roast. The city fathers appoint Hadley as honorary fire chief.

J. Farrell MacDonald should have obtained a patent on his role as the heroic old-timer, which he also played as policeman, railroad engineer, tramp, frontier sheriff, cavalryman, factory boss, and sea captain. Here he is as expert as ever. Polly Ann Young and Mary Gordon (soon to become the definitive Mrs. Hudson to Basil Rathbone's Sherlock Holmes) offer good support as MacDonald's family. Warren Hull, who portrayed the Spider, Mandrake the Magician, and the Green Hornet most ably for the serial fans, is overqualified for his part here as the juvenile lead. Pembroke lays it on thick—precisely what the part wants.

Boys of the City

a.k.a.: *The Ghost Creeps*

Four Bells Pictures • Monogram Pictures Corp. • 1940

Monogram's *East Side Kids* series began in 1940, carrying on with an ensemble-comedy pattern that had begun under more grimly earnest dramatic circumstances: Sidney Kingsley's Broadway play *Dead End* (filmed in 1937) had cast a reformer's eye on the big-city slum conditions that could transform children into criminals.

The stage and screen versions went over so well with the mass audience that the original players—including Huntz Hall, Bernard Punsley, Leo Gorcey, Billy Halop, Gabriel Dell, Hally Chester, and Bobby Jordan—became the Dead End Kids, stars of half a dozen social-problem sequels including *They Made Me a Criminal* and *Angels with Dirty Faces.*

A loose-knit batch of *Dead End Kids* and *Little Tough Guys* features and serials followed at Universal, becoming ever more adventurous and comical and less concerned with blaming society-at-large for juvenile delinquency; it was society-at-large, after all, that was buying all those movie tickets to watch the kids act like delinquents. By the time Gorcey, Jordan, and Chester joined producer Sam Katzman at Monogram, the template had been struck for a slapstick franchise that would last well into the 1950s, finally evolving into the *Bowery Boys* films. Hall would remain with the *Little Tough Guys* long enough for the rival series to overlap confusingly, but he soon joined the *East Siders* for the longer stretch.

Joseph H. Lewis's *Boys of the City*, second of the *East Side Kids* pictures, harks back to the original *Dead End* with an unexpectedly serious opening note—the pals face a hitch in detention—but soon hits a more adventurous and comical stride. It also delivers "more than the usual serving of suspense," as *Exhibitor*, the tradepaper, noted.

The East Side Kids play along with a court order to visit a philanthropist's camp. Meanwhile, the notoriously crooked Judge Parker (Forrest Taylor) is bound for the same region—intent upon hiding out from both the law and the underworld.

Parker's car is bombed by a mob bent upon his destruction. The East Siders offer Parker and his ward, Louise (Inna Gest), a lift. The kids' station wagon breaks down near Parker's gloomy estate. A creepy servant, Agnes (played by Minerva Urecal), harbors an old grudge against Parker and seems to be in touch with the spirit of the judge's late wife. Louise is abducted through a hidden panel. Judge Parker is found strangled.

Giles (Dennis Moore) and Simp (Vince Barnett), Parker's bodyguards, accuse Knuckles (Dave O'Brien), a grown-up East Sider who once had been wrongfully convicted in Parker's court. The kids help Knuckles get away and begin a search for the culprit. In a hidden passageway, they find Louise and encounter Harrison (Alden Chase), a detective who has been trailing Parker.

The murderer clubs Knuckles and pursues Louise. The kids and Harrison give chase and capture the slayer, revealing him as Simp—least likely of the suspects, a mobster who had infiltrated the judge's circle.

The dangers seem convincingly real, and Forrest Taylor is just right as the disgraced big shot. The Old Dark House setting is genuine—a castle-like residence above Sunset Boulevard near Beverly Hills. The mixed studio and location interiors vary from opulent to jury-rigged, but the nighttime exteriors are top-notch, especially a finely detailed graveyard setting.

Taylor's death scene is a jewel of shocker in the *Cat and the Canary* tradition, photographed in silhouette. The discovery of an incidental victim behind a doorway also stems from the Mystery Farce tradition that the silent screen and early talkers had appropriated from Broadway. Minerva Urecal is every bit the classic-manner sinister housekeeper until she changes her tone for a blackout gag at the finale.

Dave O'Brien is right in his element as a heroic sort who has not forgotten his origins as a tenement ruffian. The all-'round stunt artist, westerner, city slicker, and slapstick comedian—and dope-addled maniac of 1936's *Reefer Madness*—toiled steadfastly on Poverty Row until a fortunate connection with MGM landed him the recurring role of put-upon everyman in the *Pete Smith Specialties* series of short comedies. O'Brien moved from there into prominence as a comedy writer in network television, notably with *The Red Skelton Show*.

Boys of the City finds Leo Gorcey approaching the brash dominance he would come to show as the series progressed. The inclusion of Sunshine Sammy Morrison is an inspired touch; the expressive black player had been a mainstay of Hal Roach's *Our Gang* comedies during the silent years, and Morrison fits in amiably despite the film's tendency to temper a tacit argument for integration with an overabundance of color gags. Similarly broad comedy relief comes from Vince Barnett, as a squirmy lunkhead who proves to be the phantom killer. Leading lady Inna Gest, whom Katzman had noticed while she was working on a Tex Ritter western, shows a fair amount of gumption as the judge's defiant ward, although the screenplay gives her little more to do than be menaced and rescued.

Haunted House

Monogram Pictures Corp. • 1940

All of a sudden, Monogram Pictures begins looking intolerably shabby, on the flimsy evidence of one annoying picture. Robert McGowan's *Haunted House*, however, is more significant as a missing link in the tangled history of Hal Roach's *Our Gang* kid-comedy franchise (originally known as *Roach's Rascals*). The *Our Gang* concept stretches from the silent-screen age—through the earliest talking pictures and Roach's ill-advised sale of the trademark in 1938 to MGM—to Roach's misfired attempt at a revival with two *Curley & His Gang* features during the post-WWII years.

The connection with *Haunted House* lies not in Roach—who maintained an autonomous studio and remained a major-league independent until the outbreak of war (see: *The Devil with Hitler*)—but rather with director McGowan, a pivotal figure with the *Our Gang* series, and with screenwriter Dorothy Davenport (Mrs. Wallace) Reid. The celebrity widow, who had exploited her movie-star husband's scandalous death since the 1920s, had retreated by now from social-problem melodramas into attempted comedy. She at length would join Hal Roach's organization, cribbing from the earlier and better *Our Gang* scripts as writer of those dreadful *Curley* pictures. McGowan would serve the *Curleys* as producer. Their teaming on *Haunted House* is a bridging assignment, essential to the history of kid-stuff humor but hardly a marker of pleasurable distinction.

Our acceptance of subpar production values and incoherent storytelling ordinarily has a forgiving threshold, on condition that the film under scrutiny convey an Attitude with a capital *A*. It might be

an attitude of solemnity or disorientation (as in Monogram's *Invisible Ghost*), of defiant hilarity or adventurous desperation (both bases covered throughout the *Range Busters* pictures), or of sheer cockamamie fershlugginer lunacy (see, at peril of equilibrium, the *Snuffy Smith* features). Monogram earns considerable slack because so many of its pictures pack an emotional resonance, a certain set of the jaw and conspiratorial glint that bespeak a communion with the absorbed viewer.

It matters not what the attitude is, just so long as it figures in one's art, one's work, one's being. In cinema, the artist who cannot announce an attitude before the first reel has elapsed is foredoomed to failure.

Stultifyingly overlong and blandly irritating, *Haunted House* lacks any semblance of attitude. Give it the opportunity to show compassion, and it waits for the occasion to pass. Present a crisis, and the passive protagonists fritter away the time until the urgency has evaporated. The line of least resistance is pursued throughout. It is a wonder that the leads even venture inside the purportedly possessed house of the title—not that they accomplish much while on the premises.

The collapse of Marcia Mae Jones' once-promising career can be traced to such pictures as this one and the following year's *The Gang's All Here*. And if Jackie Moran's career had not already collapsed, his work alongside Jones in these same two films would have sunk him straightaway. Moran continued in small parts while pursuing a parallel career in music, and Jones kept puttering about in film into the 1950s. Neither ever regained the plateaus both had known—such as Jones' terror-stricken presence in *These Three* (1936) and Moran's spirited Huckleberry Finn in *The Adventures of Tom Sawyer* (1938).

Haunted House finds Moran clinging embarrassingly to a lapsed air of adventurous boyishness as a small-town newspaper reporter named Jimmie Atkins. A laborer (Christian Rub) is charged with robbery and murder. Atkins rushes to the defense with an ill-advised article. His insipid arrogance is compounded when Mildred (Jones), niece of the publisher, arrives. These irksome little snots have nothing better to occupy their interests than to pretend to investigate; their meddling gets Atkins fired. As the kids' misgivings focus on lawyer Cy Burton (Henry Hall), they find themselves drawn to the victim's abandoned farmhouse, where cryptic messages are found that lead to the lawyer's office, to another reprimand for the youngsters, and back to the farmhouse.

Burton gives himself away as the culprit, and Atkins performs a bit of mild heroism before the authorities can close the case. Mildred is so pleased that she throws a party in Atkins' honor. Atkins gets back his job. Which only reminds us of the passive-aggressive, invasive state of journalism in the present day—but no, we have more interesting ground to cover just now.

Billy the Kid Outlawed

Sigmund Neufeld Productions • Producers Releasing Corp. • 1940

"Nobody knows for certain...what ratio of evil distorted the good that was in him," wrote George E. Turner in *Secrets of Billy the Kid* (1974). "He has been depicted as...an outlaw only because the law was corrupt. An opposing faction...brands him a sadistic monster. A third view is that he was...deserving of no more attention than is accorded any other such creature. One thing only is beyond disputing: Billy the Kid has become the most popular and fascinating legend in American folklore."

We had wanted a representative selection from Bob Steele's *Billy the Kid* series for the present volume, and this dark fable of the great southwestern plains fills the bill. It is easy to become engrossed with a search for the grislier elements in Hollywood's low-budget horse operas—especially when the authors happen to be born-and-bred Texans who share a fondness for the cowboy life—and so we have reined ourselves in, you should pardon the expression, to keep the western selections from predominating.

Billy the Kid Outlawed is the first of 18 *Billy the Kid* features that Sigmund Neufeld produced during 1940–43. The first half-dozen feature Bob Steele, that emotive horseback Hamlet whose outlandish starring picture *Big Calibre* (1935) is a linchpin of the *Forgotten Horrors* canon. Buster Crabbe assumed the role for the remainder of the *Kid* series, then continued it, more or less, in Neufeld's *Billy Carson* series of 1943–46 (itself a tangent from Neufeld's Depression-era *Lightnin' Bill Carson* series). Neither incarnation boasts a factual communion with the Billy the Kid who ranged the frontier late in the 19th century, but Steele captures the tormented, distrustful nature that has come to light in research of times more recent.

Outlawed ascribes a prevailing lawlessness around Lincoln City, New Mexico, to storekeepers Pete Morgan and Sam Daly (Joe McGuinn

and Ted Adams). Daly seeks election as sheriff. Billy the Kid stops to visit two ranchers while passing through—only to learn that his friends have been murdered by a gang led by the brutal Lije Ellis (John Merton), a shadowy enforcer of the Morgan & Daly interests. After a gun battle with Ellis' hirelings, Billy encounters Judge John Fitzgerald (Walter McGrail), arriving on orders to clean up the territory. Daly and Morgan order Fitzgerald slain. Daly's new role as sheriff enables him to brand Billy and his pals Jeff Travis and Fuzzy Q. Jones (Carleton Young and Al St. John) as outlaws. Hence the title.

Billy becomes so devoted a terrorist against the entrenched racket that the crooked partners turn to the defunct judge's daughter (Louise Curry) and law partner (Ken Duncan) to engineer a pardon. An ambush against Billy backfires. His trust in law and order damaged beyond repair, Billy rejects clemency and rides away.

The *Billy the Kid* westerns, like the kindred *Lone Rider* series, proved a welcome hard-bitten alternative to the cowboy-crooner pictures that had become prevalent since Gene Autry's ascent to stardom during the mid–1930s. At 34, Steele may have been a bit long in the tooth to be impersonating a legendary owlhoot who lived only to the age of 21, but the actor's angry-young-man attitude is precisely right. This picture set a pace that seldom flagged as long as Steele occupied the role, rendering the cheap hastiness of production irrelevant to the dire storytelling.

Director Sam Newfield (Sigmund Neufeld's brother, working here under the *nom de guerre* of Peter Stewart) fixes the darkening mood and confronts Steele with enough menacing characters—from out-and-out outlaws to human monsters cloaked in respectability—to drive any self-respecting cowpoke to a righteous rage. Joe McGuinn and Ted Adams are suitably loathsome as the kingmakers, and John Merton makes a terrifying principal thug. Incidental good guy Ken Duncan is better known as Kenne Duncan, of Edward D. Wood, Jr.'s stock company of the 1950s. Carleton Young and Al St. John lend leavening as Steele's sidekicks, and Louise Currie (a.k.a. Curry) shows gumption as a determined survivor. A more merciful story would have permitted some romantic mush, but the film would have proved less honest as a consequence.

Steele's other *Billy the Kid* entries for 1940–41 include *Billy the Kid in Texas*, *Billy the Kid's Gun Justice*, *Billy the Kid in Santa Fe*, *Billy the Kid's Fighting Pals*, and *Billy the Kid's Range War*.

The Ranger and the Lady

Republic Pictures Corp. • 1940

Roy Rogers may have nurtured a clean-cut and wholesome image as Republic Pictures' King of the Cowboys, but he enjoyed a good scare as much as the next guy. He told us as much in 1970 during a stage-show engagement in the Texas Panhandle:

> I enjoy a good scare as much as the next guy. And there's no rule that says you can't have your harmonies and your yodeling and your smooching on your leading lady in the same picture where

there's a monster on the loose. I reckon there must have been plenty of monsters on the loose, back in the frontier days. Most of 'em were thieves and murderers who, really, must have seemed about as normal as the guy next door—but there must have been some subhuman brutes around, too.

'Course, now, Republic wanted me to deliver a certain quota of pictures that'd play things mostly light and adventurous, with lots of singin' and smoochin' and comedy relief, along with the shootin' and the fistfightin'. But once in a while, they'd let me make something *really dark*. I remember those exceptions very fondly: there was one I did in the late '40s called *Eyes of Texas*, which had this mean ol' crooked lawyer-woman with a pack of trained-killer dogs.

And in 1940, we did a kind of a *Most Dangerous Game* type of thing. It was called *The Ranger and the Lady*, except I reckon maybe we should have called it *The Ranger and the Lady and the Monster*. Because we even had Noble Johnson in it, playing the kind of brute he had played in the real *Most Dangerous Game*— only scarier, I like to think.

We reckon that Rogers' reminiscent rambles were as great a delight as his movies. This interview began backstage one afternoon at the Tri-State Fairgrounds in Amarillo, Texas, and continued into the evening, resuming the next morning over a round of golf with Rogers, Dale Evans, and fellow entertainer Pat Brady—and it covered more ground than we can accommodate here.

We cut to the chase that is Joseph Kane's *The Ranger and the Lady*: Henry Brandon is a study in abusive authority as Gen. LaRue, corrupt chief of the Texas Rangers, who in 1836 declares the wide-open Santa Fe Trail a toll road. Jacqueline Wells, an A-list star among B-movie leading ladies, is Jane Tabor, an indignant trader who resists the scam with a detour. Rogers is Capt. Colt, who chafes at LaRue's orders. After Jane aligns her interests with LaRue to develop a monopoly, Colt and Sgt. Gabby Whittaker (George Hayes) resign in disgust and conspire to unseat LaRue. Jane is revealed to have a plot of her own. With Colt's help, she takes vengeance upon LaRue—the man who had killed her father.

Heightening the tensions throughout—though in a role that eventually fell prey to the editing shears—is Noble Johnson, playing a monstrous thug named El Lobo: the distinguished mulatto actor, whose sullen viciousness indeed recalls his *Most Dangerous Game* performance, is a fine stealer of scenes in what prints his performance was left intact. A censored television cut from the 1950s so marginalizes El Lobo that the horrific essence is lost. Just take our word, and Roy Rogers' word: *The Ranger and the Lady* is as terrifying as they come, if seen in the 1940 cut.

Laughing at Danger

Monogram Pictures Corp. • 1940

A devil-made-flesh with the heavenly name of Celeste makes life a hell-on-earth for Frankie Darro and Mantan Moreland in the pals' fourth comedy-thriller. Monogram was drawing such support for anything featuring Moreland that the studio moved his billing higher and made his expressive mug more prominent in the advertising.

At Celeste's Beauty Shop, a laundry chute yields a corpse—Florence (Maxine Leslie), one of the operators. Mary Baker (Joy Hodges), last to have visited with the victim, stands accused. Pageboy Frankie Kelly (Darro) and his pal, Jefferson (Moreland), set out to prove Mary's innocence. They learn that Florence had intended to give information on a blackmail racket to a detective (George Houston).

The body of Florence's fiancé is discovered in a dumbwaiter. One of Mary's clients (Kay Sutton) turns up croaked. A phono-recording contains a blackmail message between a victim and someone at the parlor. Frankie determines that the boss, Celeste (Veda Ann Borg), has been recording her customers' more embarrassing moments and using the Dictaphone documents to coerce hush-money. Celeste and her lawyer (Guy Usher) imprison Frankie and Jeff, but the friends stall long enough for the cops to barge in.

The danger here is nothing at which to laugh, of course—which is the quality that makes the Darro and Moreland pictures so funny and so hair-raising. Veda Ann Borg is fine as a schemer-turned-killer, and her final show of malice (at first, merely intending to skip town, then deciding upon blood vengeance) makes for a delectably cold twist.

Mantan Moreland.

Frankie Darro.

The Range Busters

Phoenix Productions • Monogram Pictures Corp. • 1940

In Louis Weiss' 1932 production of *The Night Rider*, Harry Carey hits the trail in search of the cause of a ghostly reign of terror. Gunfire, seemingly from nowhere, figures as a favorite element of the folkloric tradition from which many western movies had sprung. The element would persist in such striking examples of the cowboy gothic cinema as *The Star Packer* (1934) and *Desert Phantom* (1936).

Some sources cite *Desert Phantom*, starring the easygoing Johnny Mack Brown in a grim avenging role, as a remake of *The Night Rider*. It is at least an echo, though altogether more severe than the essentially comical Weiss production. Certainly, however, *The Range Busters* is an unattributed remake of *Desert Phantom*: the credits ignore the 1936 film's writers, E.B. Mann and Earle Snell. Director S. Roy Luby handled both *Desert Phantom* and *The Range Busters*. The chief alteration is to have three heroic protagonists instead of one. The influence of Republic Pictures' *Three Mesquiteers* series is patent.

Serial murder plagues a ranch whose owner (Horace Murphy) is the latest victim. The heroic Plainsmen known as the Range Busters (Ray "Crash" Corrigan, John "Dusty" King, and Max "Alibi" Terhune) rescue the surviving daughter, Carol (Luana Walters), from a rival rancher named Torrence (LeRoy Mason). Carol rewards the Range

The Range Busters: Terhune, left, Corrigan, and King.

Busters with employment. Friendly Doc Stengle (Frank LaRue) tells Crash about a legendary Phantom. Crash and Dusty dodge a barrage supposedly fired by this Phantom.

The partners find a mineshaft where Torrence has stashed contraband weapons. Crash evades an ambush and helps Dusty to get away from Torrence's thugs. Alibi becomes curious about the purported blindness of Carol's crochety Uncle Rolf (Earle Hodgins). After several tense encounters, Torrence is captured and seems ready to reveal the truth about the haunting—but he is felled by a shot from Rolf's room.

Dusty and Alibi find a tunnel leading into Rolf's quarters. Doc Stengle, who has held the uncle captive, opens fire. Subdued, the once-lovable physician proves to have found a hidden vein of gold; he had exploited the Phantom myth to gain control of the ranch.

This first of 22 *Range Busters* pictures is a winner whose ties to *Desert Phantom* run even deeper than director Luby and the appropriated storyline: Karl Hackett, who had played the disabled rancher in the 1936 picture, serves here as the sheriff.

Marked Men

Sigmund Neufeld • PRC • 1940

The brotherly partnership of Sigmund Neufeld and Sam Newfield exercised an undeniable taste for terroristic mayhem, even in the rip-snorting outdoor melodramas. The chilling element of *Marked Men*—an otherwise conventional revenge yarn about a convict's quest for vindication—takes place in the withering heat of the Arizona wilderness. A splendidly trained dog, Gray Shadow, moves the plot, with the antagonistic support of a marauding, strategically little-seen pack of wolves.

Framed into prison by rackets boss Joe Mallon (Paul Bryar), Bill Carver (Warren Hull) is carried along with a jailbreak engineered by Mallon. Carver alone reaches freedom. He is rejoined by his dog, Wolf. Carver settles in with newfound friends—Dr. Harkness (John Dilson) and his daughter, Linda Harkness (Isabel Jewell).

Recaptured, Mallon breaks free and implicates Carver in a new crime. Carver takes up the trail. The enemies meet in the desert. Mallon comprehends that he and his henchmen cannot reach the border without Carver's guidance. Starving wolves attack. Mallon kills his accomplices (Art Miles, Ted Erwin, and Eddie Featherstone) as the struggle drives the lot of them to madness. Mallon agrees to sign a confession, but he turns murderous once again when Dr. Harkness and Linda approach. The courageous dog attacks none too soon.

Warren Hull's performance seems indifferent until his intensity deepens during the desperate trek. Isabel Jewell never quite registers

the suggested depth of affection toward Hull. Paul Bryar approaches the intensity of a Humphrey Bogart as the unhinged mobster. Gray Shadow is smart and ferocious. Sam Newfield rides the ragged edge of an identity crisis here as Sherman Scott, although advertising materials list the director as Peter Stewart—another Newfield pseudonym.

Up in the Air

Monogram Pictures Corp.

Mantan Moreland and Frankie Darro served their comedy-team thrillers as working stiffs who aspire to more ennobling circumstances. The running irony is that these ill-respected citizens are perfectly capable of meeting any desperate occasion, however unconventionally so. In the shining instance of *Up in the Air*, the guys' reality is to labor as a porter and a messenger at a Hollywood broadcasting studio, where they seek to become performers.

Frankie (Darro) and Jeff (Moreland) land in trouble for helping another toiler, Anne Mason (Marjorie Reynolds), to seek an audition as a singer. The chums find themselves pressed into a more heroic state after an ill-tempered vocalist, Rita Wilson (Lorna Gray), is murdered during a rehearsal. The killer proves elusive, and so what else is new?

The likeliest suspect, Tex Barton (Gordon James), fancies himself a glamorous cowboy singer but conceals a darker nature. Producer Farrell (Tristam Coffin) asks Frankie to keep mum about an argument between Farrell and Wilson; Frankie has Farrell promise to give Anne a shot at stardom. The murder gun is traced to Barton, and furthermore to an earlier slaying. Barton turns up dead.

Acting upon evidence found among Barton's effects, the police arrest Anne, believing her tied to the cold case. It develops that a pivotal mystery woman was in fact Rita—who had cuckolded her husband,

Frankie Darro and Mantan Moreland.

Tex Barton, for a broadcasting honcho. An unobtrusive character, radio announcer Van Martin (Alex Callam), confesses to the murders while holding the assembled station brass at gunpoint. Jeff clumsily throws open a door and topples Martin, who is captured as a consequence.

Darro and Moreland handle the bumbling heroic business in high style, with Darro as the impulsive meddler and Moreland as the hesitant voice of reason who cannot resist becoming involved. While scouring a crime scene, Darro teases Moreland about being afraid of ghosts—a bold and curious confrontation of stereotype. "It ain't the *ghost*," Moreland replies, worrying the syllables like a blues singer. "It's the person that *made her a ghost—that*'s what's botherin' *me*!" The actors also are allowed the occasional showcase of comedy for comedy's sake, involving their efforts to prove what a hit they could be on radio if allowed half a chance.

Darro's brief appearance in blackface plays out objectionably in the enlightened here-and-now, but in 1940 the *shtick* was still a norm of the waning vaudeville tradition: like Al Jolson, Emmett Miller, and Bing Crosby before him, Darro is not ridiculing black sensibilities, but rather trying (too hard) to *become* black, while playfully acknowledging the cultural debts that white America owes to black America. As the friends prepare for a rehearsal, Moreland asks, indignantly: "You don't expect me to speak in no *dialect*, do you?" When Darro's rapid-fire delivery proves too rapid for Moreland, Mantan halts the routine to tell his overeager partner to slacken the pace. Like the white-boy rock 'n' roll acts, from early-day Fleetwood Mac to Eric Clapton, that would attempt almost to become the deep blues artists they admired, Darro is forcing the process. (Yes, and Muddy Waters found it necessary to rein in Paul Butterfield, too, when their paths crossed during the 1960s.)

When station boss Tristram Coffin angrily swipes at the greasepaint on Darro's face and then glances at Moreland, Mantan snaps: "Don't touch *me*! *I* don't rub *off*!" In such subtextual insights into a cross-cultural shadowland, perhaps more so than in its conscious humor, the Darro and Moreland combination is a marvel of quick-wittedness and spontaneous patter. What makes it work is the sense of unconditional friendship, of disregarding class-and-color barriers.

The plotting of *Up in the Air* is a muddle of coincidence and contradiction—standard fare for Monogram, where productive haste took precedence over literary finesse—that keeps crucial clues well out of the audience's reach. If the unmasking of the killer comes off as less than a satisfactory resolution, then Moreland's inadvertent capture of the culprit compensates.

The Ape

Monogram Pictures Corp. • 1940

It was during 1936–39 that Boris Karloff, Bela Lugosi, and Peter Lorre—the original triumvirate of talkie horror-movie stars—found their careers compromised by the British and European embargo on films of the very sort that had defined the actors' popular appeal. Karloff retrenched by signing with Monogram for a series of mysteries based on Hugh Wiley's tales of an Oxford-educated sleuth named James Lee Wong. These *Mr. Wong* pictures (no kin to Monogram's *The Mysterious Mr. Wong*, a 1934 starrer for Lugosi) were designed to compete with Fox's *Charlie Chan* series. Lorre took refuge in the *Mr. Moto* detective pictures at Fox. Lugosi, less well attuned to strategy, found himself sidelined during this long dry spell—although he managed subversively to make one serial in 1937, Republic's *S-O-S Coast Guard*, which is as much a horror thriller as an action-adventure piece.

Karloff held forth in five *Wongs*. By 1940, horror had come back into fashion with the studios, and Karloff fulfilled his six-film contract at Monogram by starring in *The Ape*. Keye Luke, who had graced Fox's *Charlie Chans* as No. 1 Son to Warner Oland's Chan, replaced Karloff in the final Wong entry, *Phantom of Chinatown*. William Nigh, who had directed the Karloff *Wongs*, took charge of *The Ape*.

Although *The Ape* is a lesser entry for Karloff, it is a cut above most of his others at Monogram. (*Mr. Wong, Detective*, that series' opener, is a jewel.) But of course, Monogram seldom made remarkably fine pictures; it was a true Poverty Row company, having neither the money nor the talent pool of the majors except when a name-brand actor might go slumming at a bargain rate.

Karloff serves *The Ape* as the kindly Dr. Bernard Adrian, who in his obsession with finding a cure

From Monogram's first Depression-days announcement of a film to be called The Ape, *from playwright Adam Hull Shirk. That effort was completed as 1934's* The House of Mystery.

for infantile paralysis has resettled in a small town, far from the medical establishment that had rejected his theories. His neighbors shun Adrian. An uncommonly friendly local, Frances Clifford (Maris Wrixon), is confined to a wheelchair; she makes a trusting if hesitant subject for Adrian's sudden breakthrough.

A circus gorilla escapes after fatally mauling a sadistic trainer (I. Stanford Jolley). Adrian takes the opportunity to extract a vial of spinal fluid. He prepares a serum and administers it to Frances, with promising results. When the gorilla breaks into Adrian's laboratory, drawn by the scent of its tormentor, the doctor kills the beast.

And yet an ape remains on the prowl, attacking the town's most despised citizens. Frances' treatments continue. An intended victim stabs the ape, which staggers toward Adrian's house. The sheriff fires on the ape—then finds the dying creature to be a disguised Adrian. The doctor lives long enough to see Frances rise and walk toward him.

Ray Corrigan, in full hair-suit regalia, joins The Ape's *camera crew in a backstage gag-shot. At left is cinematographer Harry Neumann, with assistant cameraman Roy Ivey and camera operator Fleet Southcott.*

Exteriors were filmed at the old western town set at Newhall. The gloomy interiors were shot at Monogram's studio in East Hollywood. A surprisingly big name is that of screenwriter Curtis (a.k.a. Kurt and Curt) Siodmak, the German-born author whose novel *Donovan's Brain* would yield a variety of adaptations and knockoffs, and whose many stories and screenplays for Universal include the first two *Wolf Man* films. The basis of *The Ape* is an unspecified play by Adam Hull Shirk—possibly the same work that Monogram had adapted as *The House of Mystery* in 1934. *The Ape* resembles *The House of Mystery* only in its menacing use of a gorilla. Shirk also had written continuity for the notorious gorilla-hunt thriller of 1930, *Ingagi.*

The Ape boasts one of Karloff's more driven portrayals, a gentlemanly monster who confines his killing rage to rascals, rotters, and nincompoops whose passing can only improve the species. The first victim is a malicious carnival hand, played by that

grand-manner bad-guy actor I. Stanford Jolley. Later on, Karloff's counterfeit ape does away with a wife-beating loan shark, done to a repulsive turn by Philo McCullough. Karloff's patient, Maris Wrixon, tells him, "You're so intense, you frighten me sometimes."

The story neglects to explain why the townspeople should harbor such a fearful hatred of Karloff's Dr. Adrian. He seems a sad, genial sort who rides about on a bicycle, heals an injured dog, and treats the skinned knee of a local brat who has vandalized Adrian's house. (That boy, incidentally, is Buddy Swan, who portrays Charles Foster Kane as a child in *Citizen Kane.*)

It defies reason that the elderly physician could mangle his victims with such ferocity, and that he might fashion the carcass so handily into a suit. (The implied butchery of the gorilla lends a subliminal chill.) But whatever its failings, *The Ape* anticipated a staggering medical breakthrough by more than a decade. The film's generalized prediction of the Salk vaccine against polio is as striking as the prophecies of cryogenics and artificial-organ technology in which Karloff participated during the same period as the star player in a series of mad-doctor pictures at Columbia.

The title creature is played by Ray "Crash" Corrigan, who also worked as a western star within the independent sector. His other contracts allowed Corrigan to carry on with the lucrative gorilla-suit sideline, on condition that it must not conflict with his heroic portrayals. In gorilla guise, Corrigan did not receive billing. Corrigan's several ape outfits are far from realistic, but they are abundantly scary.

Maris Wrixon contributes a pleasant and touching portrayal as Karloff's apprehensive patient, who might represent to the doctor a daughter he had lost to polio. The slender blonde had registered impressively at Warner Bros., but she seems not to have minded her sojourn on Poverty Row. Wrixon spoke with us in 1984 about *The Ape*: "It wasn't so much a horror picture, as it was a tragic drama about a man obsessed with the desire to benefit mankind. Boris Karloff was wonderful to work with."

Philo McCullough has a rousing prelude to his demise, in a cruel scene with his abused wife, touchingly played by Mary Field. Gertrude W. Hoffman, in her youth a pioneer in modern dance, is most effective as Karloff's housekeeper, whose silent comings and goings are punctuated strikingly by one whispered line. Gene O'Donnell is a stock small-town juvenile lead, serving chiefly to embody the locals' passive intolerance. The atmospheric cinematography is by Harry Neumann, who usually shot westerns. Edward Kay's elaborate musical score ranges from blaring circus-march cues to sentimental melodies to the requisite swells and stings of incumbent menace.

Midnight Shadow

George Randol Productions • Sack Amusement Enterprises • 1940

"Here, in certain communities, the life of which is found nowhere else in all the world, these people of darker hue have demonstrated their abilities in self-government by the orderly processes of law of which they are capable when unhampered by outside influences."

So declares the "Say *what?!*" prologue to George Randol's *Midnight Shadow*, a manifesto of black separatism disguised as a crime thriller disguised as a slapstick comedy disguised as a domestic romance. The black independent cinema often demonstrates such orderly processes of dream logic of which it is capable when unhampered by outside influences.

Today, the eerie malice of George Randol's *Midnight Shadow* would fall under the fashionable heading of black-on-black crime, subject to vigilante action to the near-exclusion of law and order. In 1940, in a picture whose cultural isolation was at once a blessing and a curse, the story emerged as a portrait that could never have been realized—not even visualized—by any conventional dominant-culture Hollywood studio. The rescue of the only surviving print, abandoned by its own culture as a relic of segregationalism, was accomplished two generations later by an institutional film-archive team.

An itinerant showman, Prince Alihabad (John Criner), takes lodging with the Wilson family—and takes a romantic interest in daughter Margaret (Frances Redd). Dan Wilson (Clinton Rosemond), the father, seems impressed. Mama Emma Wilson (Ollie Ann Robinson) harbors doubts. Margaret's beau, Buster Barnett (Edward Brandon), is nonplussed. Mrs. Wilson advises Buster to stand his ground.

Dan displays an oilfield deed intended as Margaret's dowry. Alihabad presses Margaret to accompany him on an ocean voyage. A

Richard Bates and Buck Woods play detective.

shadowy figure breaks in, overwhelms Emma and Dan with poisonous fumes, and nabs the deed. Margaret finds her father slain.

Margaret consults the wealthy Langleys (Napoleon Simpson and Ruby Dandridge), whose mama's-boy adult son, Junior (Richard Bates), is an aspiring detective. Buster is jailed as a suspect. Junior and his helper, Lightfoot (Buck Woods), find the paw-prints of a pet housecat. "Could've been one of them *were-cats*!" deduces Junior.

A stranger approaches a businessman (Pete Webster) who had tried to purchase the Wilson deed: "The man I stole [it] from is dead, and one more murder won't make much difference." A local investigator nabs the killer. Buster is freed. Alihabad, whose presence had provoked the slaying, is revealed as a fraud.

The preservation of *Midnight Shadow* began in August of 1983, spearheaded by a preservation team including Dr. G. William Jones, of Dallas' Southwest Film & Video Archive at Southern Methodist University; Philip Wuntch of the Dallas *Morning News*; and Michael H. Price, then based at the Fort Worth *Star-Telegram*. *Midnight Shadow*, along with more than 100 other titles, was found in an abandoned warehouse in the east Texas town of Tyler.

"Roughly a third...were perhaps the last—or the best—remaining prints of a little-known but important group of films made from the 1920s through the early 1950s, strictly for black audiences," as Jones explained in his 1991 book, *Black Cinema Treasures: Lost and Found*.

Midnight Shadow borrows from a broader tradition of melodrama— the skulking killer, the bumbling amateur sleuths, the red-herring char- latan—but applies such instinctive shadings as to seem fresh. The un- attributed screenplay (likely improvisational) hardly plays fair with the element of mystery, but it submits an unusual conspiracy to capture the killer. Richard Bates and Buck Woods are delightful as the would-be Holmes-and-Watson team, and John Criner makes an oily Prince Ali- habad. Ruby Dandridge, who plays the proud mother of the aspiring Sher- lock, was the mother of the major-league star-to-be Dorothy Dandridge.

Who Killed Aunt Maggie?

Republic Pictures Corp. • 1940

Atlanta, Georgia, had gone world-premiere crazy in 1939 with the first official showing of MGM's epic-scale white-supremacist soap opera, *Gone with the Wind*. The opportunity to land another such ruling-class event in rapid order proved appealing to the city fathers—especially so, if the picture bore the glorifying title *Belle of Atlanta*.

Belle of Atlanta was the working title of this solidly crafted but less than remarkable multiple-murder yarn from director Arthur Lubin.

Medora Field's source-novel.

A lurid rechristening as *Who Killed Aunt Maggie?*—title of the popular source-novel—occurred after the premiere agreement had been reached.

Republic Pictures, as far removed from MGM Pictures as the servants' quarters from the plantation house, sent in members of the cast, with studio brass. *The Hollywood Reporter* described a festive scene in which "excited thousands thronged the streets." Anything to lure the rubes. Premieres have more to do with the ritual of seeing and being seen than with earnestly absorbed filmgoing, and so it is scarcely a matter of record what those "excited thousands" thought of *Who Killed Aunt Maggie?*

The tradepaper *Variety*, which screened the film privately in New York a week after the premiere, found it "a sufficiently tight entertainment" that was nonetheless "for the duals"—an extinct bit of exhibitor lingo for double-feature engagements.

New Yorker Kirk Pierce (John Hubbard) and his fiancée, Sally Ambler (Wendy Barrie), are at odds over his contempt for a play she has written—a tale of a forbidden room in a creepy mansion. Summoned to Atlanta by her Aunt Maggie (Elizabeth Patterson), Sally finds herself in such a situation as she has been fictionalizing. Another mysterious summons, from meddling Dr. George Benedict (Walter Abel), brings Pierce.

The body of a newly croaked great-uncle has disappeared. Maggie, the lone heir, insists that a secret room contains a treasure. Sally is next in line to inherit. A storm strands everyone. A stranger (Milton Parsons) presents himself as a gravestone salesman.

Maggie turns up strangled. Her cousin, Eve (Mona Barrie), seeks out the hidden room but is soon found slain. Maggie's corpse vanishes. Eve's husband, Dr. Benedict, reveals himself as the killer. The stranger proves to be a detective in pursuit of Benedict, who is captured just in time to allow room for a forcibly cute denouement. Back in New York, Sally and Kirk turn their misadventure into a radio program.

A frenzy of action keeps things clicking along, but *Who Killed Aunt Maggie?* adds little to the Old Dark House tradition. Director Lubin—teamed here with script doctor and producer Albert J. Cohen—had been handling pictures competently but often unremarkably since 1934. Lubin's splendid *Black Friday*, with Boris Karloff and Bela Lugosi, dates from the same year as *Who Killed Aunt Maggie?* The following year, Lubin would prove one of the better directors of the Abbott & Costello comedies, and in 1943 he would deliver his masterpiece of a long and uneven career: *The Phantom of the Opera*, with Claude Rains.

The performances in *Who Killed Aunt Maggie?* are energetic, though stock-fiction portrayals more so than sharply defined

Maggie Barrie.

personalities. The bickering-sweethearts device forces a precious finale. The most winning performance belongs not to a participant in the terrors, but to a talkative observer—a terrified butler, played by the fine black comedian Willie Best. Granted that the role is an indefensible stereotype, Best gives it full measure of trepidatious hilarity.

The Devil Bat

a.k.a.: *Killer Bats*
Producers Releasing Corp. • 1940

We have caught Jean Yarbrough's *The Devil Bat* on screens large and small over the long stretch, under pristine first-run conditions; in late-show corruptions during the 1960s, complete with lopsided framing and commercial interruptions every quarter-hour for salvage-carpet warehouses and miracle-diet scams; in big-screen revivals of the 1980s, invariably tainted by the reactionary *badfilm* craze that substitutes crass ridicule for responsible criticism; and finally in ever-improving digital restorations that recapture the ragged beauty of the piece.

Here is a film that wears its age increasingly well, proving to have intended itself all along as a dark comedy. In its day, just slightly outside Bela Lugosi's professional heyday, it provided the actor with his most sardonic role apart from all those triumphant portrayals of the 1930s. If his nine similarly conceived films for Monogram Pictures (see: the "Monogram Nine" chapter under 1941) represent Lugosi's principal body of work of the 1940s—his big-studio assignments had deteriorated largely to desultory tokenism—then *The Devil Bat* makes an emphatic prologue. Monogram and PRC were kindred studios, for that matter, and both treated Lugosi as Hollywood royalty, however impoverished the conditions.

In a more appreciative modern-day climate for the maverick filmmaking imperative, *The Devil Bat*'s mocking contempt for corporate America is sufficient to transcend technical and literary failings: when Lugosi's Dr. Paul Carruthers rails against the company that has treated him with dismissive condescension, it might as well be Lugosi himself, brooding over the halt-and-go progress he had known at the hands of opportunistic Universal Pictures.

Lugosi is Dr. Paul Carruthers, a respected small-town physician, whose cosmetic formulas have made a fortune for a company owned by the local Heath and Morton families. Not that Carruthers has reaped the benefits: he had sold out, rather than accept a partnership.

Maddened by a festering resentment, Carruthers has developed a remarkable fragrance—designed to attract a bloodthirsty mutated bat. (The film's prediction of pheromone research is remarkable, as well.) The slaying of Roy Heath (John Ellis) attracts a big-city newspaperman, Johnny Layton (Dave O'Brien), and his mouthy photographer, One-Shot Maguire (Donald Kerr).

As the victims accumulate, Layton perceives a connection between the wounds and a pungent scent. Carruthers gives Layton a bottle of the stuff, which Maguire tries. Layton kills the bat when it swoops toward Maguire. The doctor has another such creature at the ready.

Before Carruthers can dispose of Mary Heath (Suzanne Kaaren), Layton steals into the laboratory. Dousing Carruthers with the potion, Layton holds the doctor at gunpoint and awaits an attack. Carruthers bolts, and the bat makes short work of him. The bat is killed as it bears down upon Mary.

Lugosi's ability to convey a conflicted personality, torn between benevolence and resentful malice, had been put nicely to the test in the British-made *Dark Eyes of London* (a.k.a. *The Human Monster*; 1939). This gift, forged further in *The Devil Bat*, would figure in his lengthy span of restored star appeal at Monogram Pictures, even as the bigger studios persisted in putting the artist to lesser use while exploiting his name.

But it is *The Devil Bat*—a morbid delight, warts and all—that grants Lugosi the greatest latitude in using his friendlier nature to secure the trust of the very people he means to harm. He frets and fumes with profound indignation when alone but seems the soul of affability when presenting his chosen victims with a sample of the deadly cologne, beaming as he recommends a splash onto "the *tender* part of your neck."

Yes, and what other actor could make the simple expression, "*Good*bye," sound so much like a death sentence? Lugosi, of course, is on a par with Mantan Moreland as a master at italicizing the spoken word for dramatic effect.

The Devil Bat provided a striking showcase for director Jean Yarbrough, who proceeded through a long career of (mostly) more of the same—budget-bound spookers, slapstick comedies, and action yarns—with the occasional remarkable highs and remarkable lows. Yarbrough would hit his stride more confidently in 1941's *King of the Zombies*, which had started out as an intended starrer for Lugosi.

Going way beyond the essential emphasis upon

Lugosi, Yarbrough renders *The Devil Bat* a fairly involved ensemble piece. The victims are an engaging, well-intentioned lot of self-absorbed fat cats, especially Guy Usher as perfume tycoon Henry Morton and boyish Gene O'Donnell (also prominent in *The Ape*) as a doomed offspring. In later years, O'Donnell developed the habit of autographing photos of himself under attack with: "Hey! Watch out for that [*expletive*] bat!"

Suzanne Kaaren is precisely the type to make the men in the audience want to rescue her from Lugosi's Devil Bat, and Dave O'Brien makes the heroic newspaperman an identifiably regular guy. As a counterpoint to Lugosi's droll wit, Donald Kerr overplays the comedy relief.

Arthur Q. Bryan, who also supplied the voice of the Warner cartoons' Elmer Fudd, has a nice bit as a gwouchy newswoom boss—though without the diawect. Bryan stayed busier in radio than in live-action movies, establishing signature broadcasting presences with *Fibber McGee & Molly* and *The Grouch Club*. He referred to this institition, of course, as "*The Gwouch Cwub*" and addressed the master of ceremonies, Jack Lescoulie, as "Mr. Wescouwie." Nice work if you can get (away with) it.

An official but over-inventive sequel, 1946's *Devil Bat's Daughter*, neutralizes the gleeful animosity of the now-absent Lugosi character, characterizing the late Dr. Carruthers as merely a misunderstood genius. *The Devil Bat* was remade, too, in 1946, as *The Flying Serpent*, starring George Zucco. The original film's gigantic bat, preserved as a warehouse property, took an encore in 1944—swooping down to menace Fuzzy St. John in PRC's *Wild Horse Phantom*.

Aside from Michael H. Price:

> In the earlier years of a long association with George E. Turner, I frequented a barbershop operated by George's father, George A. Turner, a lanky former cowboy who hardly seemed the type to make with the jokes. One afternoon, the elder George offered me a splash of after-shave lotion for "the tender part of your neck"—never cracked a smile.
>
> Later on, I mentioned the line to George E., who chuckled: "Yeah, Pop's a big fan of *The Devil Bat*—been using that routine on his customers for years. Most of 'em don't get it, of course." Later on, I caught George's dad adapting a bit from Tod Slaughter's *The Demon Barber of Fleet Street* (England, 1936): after administering the shave-and-a-haircut treatment, he'd say: "Now—let me polish you off!" (George A. Turner had practiced the tonsorial arts in Hollywood during the 1930s, with a clientele including such movie-biz people as Oliver Hardy and Bela Lugosi.)

Forgotten Horrors of 1941

The Blood of Jesus

Amegro Films • Sack Amusement Enterprises • 1941

Spencer Williams, Jr., leapt from a screenwriter-actor job on *Son of Ingagi* to a directing assignment (also writing and acting) on *The Blood of Jesus*. These oddly matched films triggered a long collaboration between Williams, an ambitious black artist, and Alfred Sack, a Dallas-based Yiddish entrepreneur who sought the well-hidden but lucrative market of black neighborhood theaters. The change in subject matter, from horror to sanctimony, seems more drastic than the heightened responsibility—Williams had long since learned how to run a shoot—but in fact *The Blood of Jesus* is far and away a weirder and creepier piece than *Son of Ingagi*, whose mad-doctor malfeasance and comic-relief slapstick routines themselves defy convention.

Few conventions of narrative cinema intrude upon *The Blood of Jesus*, which plays out like a cross between one of Georges Méliès' pioneering special-effects fantasies (footage from Méliès' "Going to Heaven" [1916] is inserted at one point) and a rough-sketch prototype for Steven Spielberg's *The Color Purple* (1985). Williams' simplistic,

ardent view of southern black spiritual life is distinguished by a sense of struggle between piety and profanity.

Backsliding poacher Ras Jackson (Williams), makes himself conspicuously absent from the riverside baptism of his bride, Martha (Cathryn Caviness). When Martha returns home, one of the more self-righteous churchwomen confronts Jackson. Jackson's gun falls—discharging and wounding Martha. The air of naturalism lapses to supernatural fantasy as Martha's disembodied soul traverses a crossroads between heaven and hell. Satan (James B. Jones), lurking in ambush, sends a suave rascal (Frank H. McClennan) to tempt Martha. After some harrowing detours, she reaches a symbolic crossroads—only to run blindly into the fork toward Hades. She drags herself to the base of a cross, where she is anointed in blood. Whereupon Martha wakes to find her husband in mourning. She assures him that she will recover. The superstitious neighbors revel in the seeming resurrection.

Williams' artistry is as raw and rudimentary as the rough-hewn production values. The saving grace—pardon the expression—lies in the unabashed frankness of Williams' pious pandering and a dream-like narrative sense. The dime-store Halloween costume that identifies Satan is so lacking in artifice that it becomes its own artifice, a defiance of the limitations that would defeat a less determined filmmaker. When Dr. G. William Jones, who headed the restoration campaign for this and other long-mislaid black-ensemble films, titled his book about the project *Black Cinema Treasures: Lost and Found* (University of North Texas Press; 1991), he was thinking primarily of *The Blood of Jesus*, a centerpiece of the Tyler, Texas, Black Film Collection at Southern Methodist University in Dallas.

The Lone Rider Rides On

Sigmund Neufeld Productions • Producers Releasing Corp. • 1941

Sigmund Neufeld's *Lone Rider* series took shape with this picture as a *Lone Ranger* knockoff, trusting in a sound-alike name and a mysterious maverick hero to siphon popular interest from the more polished genuine article—which Republic Pictures had treated definitively as a serial in 1939. The *Lone Rider* concept quickly developed a distinctively darker attitude, however, where the *Lone Ranger* pictures veered away from the shadows and into a sun-drenched wholesomeness.

George Houston (late of the failed *Wallaby Jim* adventure series) weighs in as Tom Cameron, who in 1901 has become known as the Lone Rider—a determined cuss, haunted by memories of a childhood episode involving a massacre at his family's campsite. (A recurring motif in the gothic westerns, that.) Upon encountering a new murder under similar

conditions, the Rider finds the deed to a ranch among the effects of the victim, one Richard Brown. Cameron decides to look into the matter.

The ranch is in foreclosure. Crooked Frank Mitchell (Frank Hagney) and an accomplice, Curly (Lee Powell), propose to evict Brown's sister, Sue (Hillary Brooke). Mitchell frames Cameron for Brown's slaying. A merchant, Fuzzy Q. Jones (Al St. John), proves helpful to Cameron. While on trial, Cameron recognizes the presiding judge (Karl Hackett) as the thug responsible for the attack upon Cameron's family.

Cameron is sentenced to hang. Fuzzy orchestrates a jailbreak. Amid the mayhem, Tom finally recognizes the brutal Curly as his lost brother. Curly softens, revealing that Mitchell had adopted him and told him that his family had been killed by Indians.

In an attack by a Mitchell henchman, Curly stops a bullet meant for Cameron, who proceeds to clean up the territory. The gang routed, Fuzzy pitches Cameron as a candidate for judge. Tom declines and rides on—hence the title—in search of new wrongs to set right.

As the series progressed the Lone Rider would take on Al St. John's Fuzzy Q. Jones as a recurring sidekick—PRC's answer to Republic's Gabby Hayes. After 11 PRC assignments, George Houston relinquished the Lone Rider role to former Republic star Bob Livingston, but St. John remained a constant. Houston died in 1944.

The screenplay of this opening adventure relies upon such stock-in-trade elements as the campsite massacre, the murderers' assumption of positions of respectable authority, and the recognition of the lost brother by a birthmark. One likely template is 1935's *Branded a Coward*. *The Lone Rider Rides On* marks, withal, a promising launch for a franchise that helped keep the western film true to its essential Germanic fatalism.

You're Out of Luck

Monogram Pictures Corp. • 1940

The lowly elevator man has seldom been recognized as a driving force in metropolitan life. Before automation made *everybody* an elevator operator, these dedicated professionals—economically speaking, just a step or two up from Skid Row—took a tribal pride in seeing that each passenger reached the appropriate floor in due course.

Few real-world elevator men can have harbored an ambition to play detective. This quirk makes a delight of the Frankie Darro-Mantan Moreland team in Howard Bretherton's *You're Out of Luck*. These guys know their way around the inner chambers of a ritzy hotel; thus do the actors ground their extravagant deeds in practical reality.

If Mantan Moreland is an unacknowledged great comedian of Old Hollywood (see also: *King of the Zombies*), then Moreland & Darro want consideration as one of the better comedy teams, ill recognized. Their imperiled partnership holds up as a poor man's Abbott & Costello—whose big-screen teaming Moreland & Darro foreshadowed. The combination of Darro's overzealous boyishness and Moreland's wisecracking deep-southern wisdom is a wonder to behold. That they sustained an integrated comedy-adventure act long before Robert Culp and Bill Cosby (network television's *I Spy*) or Danny Glover and Mel Gibson (the *Lethal Weapon* pictures), makes these films all the more ripe for rediscovery.

Darro was born Frank Johnson in 1917 in Chicago, son of circus aerialists. Compact and agile, he started early in adventurous roles; a sustained example occurs in 1935's *The Phantom Empire*.

Darro serves *You're Out of Luck* as elevator operator Frankie O'Reilly. O'Reilly and Jeff (Moreland), a mechanic, witness a mob hit. A crime wave has found Frankie's brother, police detective Tom O'Reilly (Richard Bond), hard-pressed for a solution. Tom and Frankie trace Dick Whitney (Tristram Coffin), a playboy resident of the hotel, to criminal elements.

Whitney shakes down gangster Johnny Burke (Willie Costello) and passes an envelope of money to Frankie, for delivery to the murder victim's sister. Whitney arranges for Tom's humiliation in the press. Frankie has hidden the envelope within the hotel.

When ordered to repair a lift, Jeff and Frankie find Whitney's body atop the elevator car. It develops that Burke is responsible for the slayings, which were provoked by gambling-racket intrigues. Burke's hoodlums capture Jeff and Frankie and Sonya (Vicki Lester), a *femme fatale* involved with Burke and Whitney. Burke herds the captives into a freight elevator, the better to stave off a police siege. Jeff and Frankie freeze the elevator via emergency controls.

The complications run needlessly thick, what with Vicki Lester walking a fine line between helping the cops and bum-steering them as she tries to lay her mitts on a small fortune in illicit loot, while still seeming a dutiful gang moll; Moreland pursuing a romance with the moll's housekeeper; detective Richard Bond tackling the underworld while fending off an abusive press corps; and a cash-laden envelope defying all attempts to nab it. Moreland & Darro keep the messy scenario under control with brisk wordplay and whiplash slapstick timing—and ultimately, with a heroism born of their unique knowledge of the inner workings of an elevator.

The Great Train Robbery

Republic Pictures Corp. • 1940

Although only its title betokens a kinship with a watershed Edison film of 1903, Joseph Kane's *The Great Train Robbery* is nonetheless an old-fashioned rip-snorter. *Old-fashioned* in this case denotes more of a welcome throwback to the early 1930s—that age of grimmer, less tunefully romanticized westerns. Republic's production values are many notches above those of Bob Steele's shoot-em-ups of the Depression years, but there is a tremendous fidelity here to the style and attitude of the independent studios' early-talkie efforts.

Steele plays Tom Logan, a hard-bitten, short-fused railroad detective, who must guard a million-dollar shipment of gold. Although Logan is a fair-and-square straight-shooting sort, his family's wicked reputation catches up with him at an awkward crucial moment. Another investigator, Pierce (Hal Taliaferro, a.k.a. Wally Wales), develops suspicions that Logan's train-robbing father might have passed along his criminal nature. It helps matters none at all that Logan's brother, Duke (Milburn Stone), is the operator of a gambling den and brothel. Tom

shows up almost too late for duty, looking dishevelled. One of Duke's floozies, Kay Stevens (Claire Carleton), follows Tom aboard.

Signaling to have Kay removed at the next stop, the superintendent (Monte Blue) learns that the passengers have been robbed and dropped off. A search for the train turns up only a phantom whistling noise, even though the line has but one track.

A flashback reveals that Duke had ordered his men to waylay and beat Tom, who had escaped in time to make the run. Kay, who loves Tom in spite of Duke's possessive affections, had followed out of legitimate concern. Duke's gang had laid siege to the train, taking advantage of Tom's hesitation to open fire upon his brother. Steering the train onto an abandoned mining spur and covering their path with a landslide, the mobsters played a recording of a whistle to make it appear the cargo had gone through.

Tom and Kay escape. Amid a wild running battle, Tom crashes the train through the landslide. Pierce arrives and mows down Duke, whose dying confession clears Tom.

Director Kane's sharp deployment of mystery and near-spectacle makes this particular *Great Train Robbery* a delight, with a pleasing hint of supernatural interference and a chilling current of deadly tensions between brothers. Steele deploys his familiar air of righteous indignation, becoming more handsome and heroic with every frown. Future television western favorite Milburn Stone, who alternated gracefully between sympathetic and villainous parts as a B-movie dependable, matches Steele for intensity as the despicable brother. Saucy Claire Carleton completes the triangle with an added touch of romantic heroism. Old-timer Si Jenks is delightful as an eccentric prospector who arrives at the right moment. Helen MacKellar has a telling small role as the mother of the warring Logan boys.

The success of *The Great Train Robbery* prompted Republic to plan a series of "melodramas in the old-time style," as *The Hollywood Reporter* noted. The idea progressed only as far as Joe Kane's *Rags to Riches* (1941), an underworld adventure with musical interludes.

The Forgotten Village

Pan-American Films • Mayer-Burstyn, Inc. • 1940

A study in backwater superstition in dramatized documentary form, *The Forgotten Village* is of interest beyond the genre as a little-known original work by John Steinbeck whose epic novel *The Grapes of Wrath* and a kindred novella, *Of Mice and Men*, had recently been adapted to film. The acclaim that greeted those pictures encouraged Steinbeck to write a piece directly for the screen. He sought to heighten popular awareness of the enforced ignorance that gripped (and still grips) rural Mexico in poverty, superstition, and vulnerability to disease.

Steinbeck wanted Max Wagner, a friend who was struggling in Hollywood, to narrate. Producer-director Herbert Kline wanted a box-office name. Spencer Tracy, who admired Steinbeck and later became his friend, was interested, but MGM nixed Tracy's participation—unless the actor would consent to tackle an MGM project he did not care to do, *Dr. Jekyll and Mr. Hyde*. Tracy agreed, and MGM gave him permission to narrate *The Forgotten Village*.

Just as Tracy had begun preparations for *The Forgotten Village* and launched himself into *Jekyll & Hyde*, MGM reneged—figuring correctly that Tracy would not shut down a big film that was already in production. Steinbeck was furious, especially now that he had found it necessary to un-invite Max Wagner. Steinbeck scarcely could bring himself to ask Wagner again after so conspicuous a dismissal. Whereupon the author enlisted Burgess Meredith, co-star of Lewis Milestone's 1939 filming of Steinbeck's *Of Mice and Men*.

Steinbeck vowed to disparage MGM's adaptation of his *Tortilla Flat*. Of course, the author did not follow through upon the threat. (The insights on this ordeal come from Steinbeck biographers Jackson L. Benson and Jay Parini and *Forgotten Horrors* affiliate John Wooley.)

Principal photography for *The Forgotten Village* was completed over a period of 10 months on location in a mountainous region of Mexico. The players are native villagers. In the town of Santiago, a conjurer

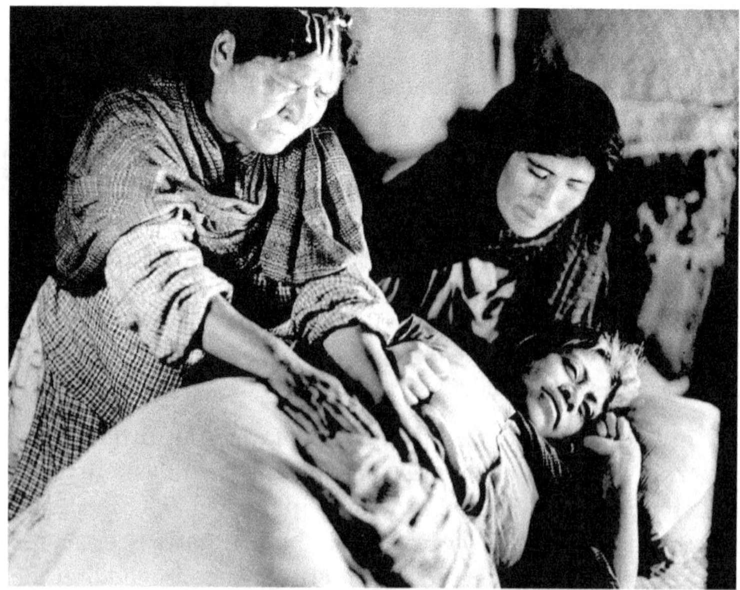

The agonies of The Forgotten Village.

Burgess Meredith.

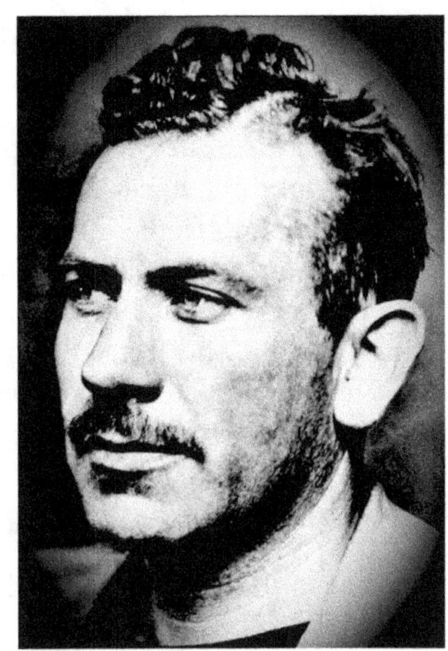

John Steinbeck.

named Trini foretells a long and distinguished life for a child yet unborn. A boy, Paco, falls ill, and Trini casts a spell that she believes will drive the disease into a clutch of eggs. A schoolteacher more reasonably ascribes the malady to contaminated water, but Paco's mother maintains that Trini alone can work a cure.

Paco dies, and an outbreak broadens. The villagers pray in vain for protection. The teacher and Paco's surviving brother, Juan Diego, risk banishment to bring in a doctor from civilization. The physician purifies a dank well. Trini accuses him of poisoning the water. Juan Diego, rejected by his family, decides he must journey to the world outside to study medicine.

Steinbeck and Kline found themselves frustrated by the very conditions they sought to expose and correct. The *New York Herald Tribune* reported that the film company had arranged to pay its actors more than they were earning as field-hands; and that the local farm owners, finding such largesse a threat to their predatory feudal dominion, vowed to disrupt the shoot. Only after the wealthiest of the region's *padrónes* endorsed the project could the artists proceed unmolested, according to the newspaper's account. The picture works better as a documentary account than as a (melo)drama, but the conjure woman is suitably intimidating and the portrayal of Juan Diego is pleasingly natural.

The New York censors banned *The Forgotten Village* in view of depictions of childbirth and breast-feeding. An appeal cleared the film by December of 1941 for showings in New York State. *The Forgotten Village* also appeared as a book, illustrated with photographs from the movie.

Mr. District Attorney

Republic Pictures Corp. • 1940

Peter Lorre was hardly the type to play Dr. Jekyll, but he did get to play a memorably wicked Mr. Hyde in William Morgan's *Mr. District Attorney*, an ambitious but flawed attempt at launching a series.

Mr. District Attorney, like *Gangbusters* one of the more successful radio productions of Phillips H. Lord (see also: *Obeah!*), had begun airing in 1939 and long remained a Wednesday-night staple of the NBC Network, eventually spawning a television series and a run of comic books. Republic tackled this big-screen spinoff during 1940–41,

starting out modestly but yielding such promising early results that studio boss Herbert J. Yates boosted it to the Republic Special class. The radio writers favored offbeat, *noir*-flavored themes. Scenarists Karl Brown and Malcolm Stuart Boylan followed suit, pitting greenhorn prosecutor Dennis O'Keefe against a corrupt politician named Mr. Hyde—an allusion, nothing more, to Robert Louis Stevenson—with a troublesome Mrs. Hyde as a climactic garnish.

Leading man Dennis O'Keefe has too ineffectual a role—and too laughable a character name—to pose much of a threat to Lorre's murderous scheming. As novice prosecutor P. Cadwallader Jones, the only edge O'Keefe can muster is with the help of a muddled script, whose convenient coincidences and over-obvious plot developments leave much to be desired. Pre-production censorship plagued the project, too—to such an extent that an obviously prostitutional character is dismissed as merely a crusty dame.

Lorre's fugitive Mr. Hyde represents a hopeless case to DA Winton (Stanley Ridges). When Jones, fresh from Harvard, fumbles a trial in a gangland case, he finds himself ordered to track down Mr. Hyde, who had vanished four years ago with a fortune in misappropriated tax revenues. Jones stumbles onto marked currency connected with Hyde. Winton interferes, hoping to tie the loot to a political enemy named Barrett (Minor Watson).

A seemingly unrelated case involves tough Betty Paradise (Joan Blair) and a crooked bank clerk, Herman Winkle (Charles Arnt). Hyde makes a furtive appearance, apparently as Winkle's benefactor—but then kills the clerk, who has been lifting cash from one of Hyde's false-identity depositories. Hyde does away with Betty.

Barrett fails in an attempt to have Jones killed but persuades Hyde's abandoned wife (Helen Brown) to murder Hyde. Helen Brown's abrupt confrontation with Lorre is a jewel, but she lays things on a bit thickly with an overwrought confession. Jones and meddling reporter Terry Parker (Florence Rice), humiliated by their own clumsiness, set matters right by catching Barrett as he ransacks Hyde's safe-deposit box. Better the yarn should have concentrated more on Peter Lorre's suave and soft-spoken brand of evil-doing and less on Minor Watson's conventional show of villainy.

Despite an awkward beginning, the series would continue more impressively with *Mr. District Attorney in the Carter Case* and with *Secrets of the Underground*. *Secrets of the Underground* was conceived and filmed as a *Mr. District Attorney* entry, but not released as such. Columbia Pictures would attempt a revival in 1947, but a successful long-term picturization of *Mr. District Attorney* would have to wait until NBC's television version of 1951–54.

Middle Ground:
Some Incidental Discoveries

Marginal entries, for context:

- *Emergency Landing*, a.k.a. *Robot Pilot* (PRC, 1941). Test pilot Forrest Tucker tackles the development of a remote-controlled aeroplane. I. Stanford Jolley is a hostage-taking German spy. Spooky desert-by-night business is leavened by screwball romance, with Carol Hughes as the headstrong daughter of an aviation executive.

- *Tumbledown Ranch in Arizona* (Range Busters, Inc./Geo. W. Weeks/Monogram, 1941). The *Range Busters* series takes a time-warp to the year 1900: Ray "Crash" Corrigan, dazed in a rodeo accident (hence the name *Crash*), finds himself caught up in a land-grabbing murder mystery. It all seems to have been a dream until an eerie *déjà vu* coda kicks in: Corrigan's nurse proves to be a descendant of a woman in his fevered flashback.

- *Law of the Wolf* (Arthur Ziehm, Inc., 1941). Further experimental-aviation shenanigans, pitting dog star Rin-Tin-Tin, III, against badman George Chesebro. Dennis Moore is an escaped jailbird determined to achieve vindication.

- *Borrowed Hero* (Monogram, 1941). Alan Baxter is an inept lawyer at odds with a murderous graft cult. The money shot comes when the killers massacre two of their own by mistake.

- *The Deadly Game* (Monogram, 1941). Marginal science fiction figures in the tale of an invention designed to forecast nighttime air raids. Charles Farrell stars as an FBI agent on the trail of spy chief John Miljan.

City of Missing Girls

Select Attractions • Merrick-Alexander Productions • 1941

White slavery and serial murder hold a promise of thrills largely unfulfilled in Elmer Clifton's *City of Missing Girls*, a tale of feigned respectability, journalistic persistence, and hamstrung law enforcement.

Astrid Allwyn (a.k.a. Allyn) is Nora Page, a hellbent-for-bylines reporter who has no inkling that her father (Boyd Irwin), a theatrical agent, is tight with a racket involving a nightclub and a purported school of fine arts—whose students, shanghaied into the prostitutional service of procurer King Peterson (Philip Van Zandt), appear likely as not to land in the county morgue. A tough cop (H.B. Warner) connects the underworld with the academic realm. Nora charges into

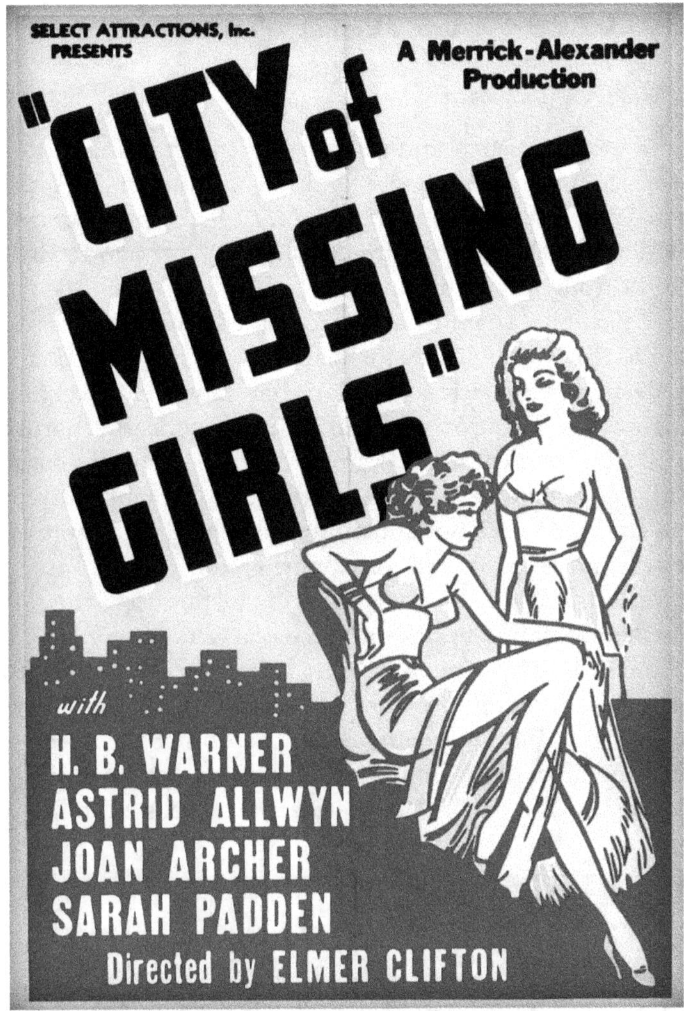

a maverick investigation—intent upon beating an assistant district attorney (John Archer) to a solution.

John Archer and Allwyn spend too much time in pursuit of an antagonistic romantic attraction to allow a concentration upon the underlying horrors. The motivating tragedies seem incidental to an inconvenient frame-up for one slaying and Allwyn's risky ploy of enlisting in the bogus school.

Director Clifton, late of the D.W. Griffith company and amply well represented in the long run of *Forgotten Horrors*, allows a lax pace that finally snaps taut when one crooked agent experiences a change of heart—only to fall prey to Philip Van Zandt.

H.B. Warner is the soul of determination as the gruff but benevolent detective. Future television star Gale Storm occupies a small role.

Adventures of Captain Marvel

a.k.a.: *Return of Captain Marvel*
Republic Pictures Corp. • 1941

Among the more polished and relentlessly entertaining of Republic's serials, though hardly in a class with Universal's splendid *Flash Gordon* chapter plays, is *Adventures of Captain Marvel*. The project was undertaken by default when an attempt to adapt *Superman* to live-action cinema fell through in preproduction.

Republic's switch can only have exacerbated a war of nerves between the characters' rival publishers, whose lawyers sniped at one another for years over the simplistic accusation that Captain Marvel (magically endowed) was an imitation of Superman (a cosmically charged space alien). The *Superman* camp finally prevailed to no one's advantage—driving the *Captain Marvel* comic books out of print while gaining control of the trademark but allowing it to lie fallow for many years.

Of course, *all* the comic-book superheroes, from whatever publishers, were imitations of one character or another; the *Superman* franchise merely claimed pride-of-place as a takeoff on heroic legends dating from antiquity and the heroic prose fiction of the 19th and 20th centuries. The *Captain Marvel* stories' larger originality lies in a playful sense of humor—courtesy of cartoonist C.C. Beck—where Superman and most of his dour kind represented self-serious juvenile power fantasies. The distinction between Marvel's childlike wit and

Superman's temperamental bluster went sailing over the heads of the litigation-crazed copyright wranglers.

An aftertaste of Republic's abortive *Superman* found its way into *Adventures of Captain Marvel*. Western-movies veteran Tom Tyler looks quite the image of a funnybook superhero, but only in the generic sense. Lacking the beefy and bumpkin-like aspect of Beck's character (modeled after Fred MacMurray), Tyler proves a leaner, sterner— more Superman-like—Captain Marvel than the comics' readers had known. This Marvel's ruthlessness in dealing with criminals is often scary, and Tyler's clipped delivery is calculated to intimidate. A more accurate job of casting would have placed Granville Owen, a more easygoing type, in the role.

The comics' Captain Marvel has about him an air suggestive of Al Capp's satirical hillbilly-as-hero comic strip *Li'l Abner*—whose title character Owen had portrayed in a like-titled Poverty Row film of 1940. That picture's director, Albert Rogell, also is responsible for a seminal *Forgotten Horrors* selection, the jungle thriller *Mamba* (1930). Our study of Rogell's *Li'l Abner*, a film sufficiently grotesque to bear mentioning in the present context, can be found in the Kitchen Sink Press anthology *Li'l Abner Dailies Vol. 6: 1940* (1988).

As directed by William Witney and John English, *Adventures of Captain Marvel* retells the familiar fantasy about an urchin named Billy Batson (Frank Coghlan, Jr.), who is granted the ability to transform himself into the world's mightiest mortal, Captain Marvel, upon uttering the name of an ancient wizard, Shazam. In the film's closest

resemblance to the comic-book yarns, Nigel de Brulier seems to have stepped from one of C.C. Beck's drawings of Shazam.

An expedition approaches a burial ground along the Burmese border. Lying in wait are a simmering volcano, a curse involving the secrets of alchemy, and the mixed blessing of Shazam's sorcerous gifts. An other-worldly menace finds its focus in a cloaked badman called the Scorpion. Billy Batson's chums land in near-constant peril, and Billy-become-Marvel faces explosions, falling blades, floods of lava, electrocution, bombs, and machine-gun barrages, among other annoyances.

Any pretense of plot is beside the point: *Adventures of Captain Marvel* finds its reason for being in a splendid pageant of visual effects, stirring musical cues that lend dramatic momentum where there is no drama, to speak of, and the headlong pacing that kept the kids of 1941—and of 1953, when a reissue took place—coming back, week after week. The Scorpion only looks hokey; his sepulchral voice (by Gerald Mohr) resonates with malice, and his murderous devices bring out the best in Republic's crackerjack special-effects team. Bud Thackery's process photography is typically convincing. The special props by the Lydecker Bros., Howard and Theodore, include an astonishingly realistic larger-than-life mannequin, which represents Captain Marvel in flight. Dave Sharpe's stunting as Marvel includes numerous bone-rattling drops and leaps, with a particularly impressive display of acrobatics in Chapter No. 1.

Later on in 1941, Superman fared impressively well in a series of animated cartoons, reconceived along more playful lines and launched by the Fleischer Bros.' studios for Paramount Pictures. A 1948 *Superman* serial and its 1950 sequel, *Atom Man vs. Superman*, produced by Sam Katzman for Columbia, proved largely disappointing despite smart casting and the sense of cheapskate generosity that issues from practically any Katzman project.

Federal Fugitives

Producers Releasing Corp. • 1941

An officially deceased madman posing as a distinguished financier makes a worthy quarry for a dyspeptic undercover agent in this crisp thriller from director William Beaudine and producer John T. Coyle. Silent-era star Neil Hamilton serves *Federal Fugitives* as Capt. James Madison, in pursuit of Capitol Hill lobbyist Bruce Lane (Charles Wilson) on suspicion of international malfeasance. At a restaurant, with a supply of antacid tablets at the ready, Madison spots a ringer for a master criminal, Otto Lieberman, long believed dead. It becomes evident that Lieberman had staged a false demise—the better to reinvent himself as Dr. Frederic Haskell (Victor Varconi), a Lane crony. Haskell and

Neil Hamilton.

Lane conspire to buy the rights to an experimental aircraft from inventor Henry Gregory (George Carleton). Madison persuades Gregory to take part in an entrapment.

Madison is distracted by Lane's seductive cohort, Rita Bennett (a since-forgotten actress with the unforgettable name of Doris Day). Haskell determines the G-Man's identity and slips poison into his reflux remedy. Rita switches loyalties when she learns of the plot to kill Madison, but she is sidelined by an automobile accident. She regains her bearings, steals away from a hospital, and finds Madison captive. Haskell has lost patience with the game of medicinal Russian roulette—and is about to force the agent to swallow the tainted pill. While Madison's helpers (Lyle Latell and Frank Moran) battle Haskell's thugs, Madison chases after Haskell, who takes a fatal plunge. All ends romantically well for Madison and a reformed Rita.

The charm of *Federal Fugitives* lies in a canny balance between menace and lunkheaded comedy. The latter is supplied by Lyle Latell and Frank Moran, as the brawn-over-brains types who enable Hamilton to concentrate on taking out the chief heavy. Hamilton, seen here at age 41, still radiates the star power he had commanded as Paramount's biggest box-office name of the late 1920s. More than a generation later, Hamilton would find an entirely new mass audience as Commissioner Gordon on the tele-series *Batman*.

The chemistry between Hamilton and this particular Doris Day is bittersweet, but their final encounter rings true. (The other Doris Day was several years away from her own movie breakthrough, but was just then on the verge of becoming a popular vocalist.) Victor Varconi, whose career ran a less prominent parallel to that of fellow Hungarian Bela Lugosi, plays the mob boss with suave Continental malice.

Producer Coyle had been a busy talent on Poverty Row during the Depression years; this project marked an impressive arrival at PRC. The material must have inspired Beaudine, as well, for the old-timer generates an unaccustomed wealth of suspense. Pre-production press notices, by the way, identify the director as William X. Crowley—a Beaudine alias—but the screen credits use the artist's genuine name.

India Speaks / Bride of Buddha

Record Pictures • WAFilms • RKO-Radio • Film Classics • 1941

A *Variety* critic was treated on April 14, 1941, to a double-bill program at New York's Central Theatre: *Kidnapping Gorillas*—a rechristened *Love Life of a Gorilla*, still cluttering the film exchanges from its late-1930s release—along with the somewhat more distinguished *Bride of Buddha*, another resurrection, similarly obscure.

Both published reviews missed the larger point, neglecting to tie either film to an earlier incarnation and thus confusing matters for generations of Movieland spelunkers down the line. The anonymous reviewer (*Variety* long practiced the use of single-name aliases) bluffed

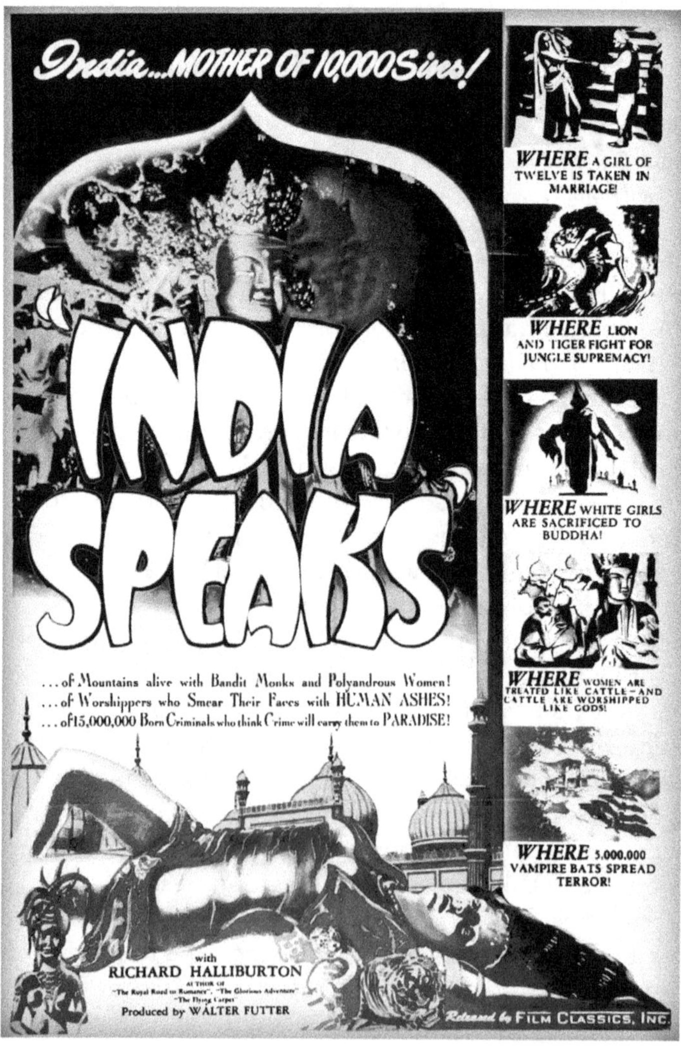

and faked it through the *Bride* review as "apparently...a compilation of material from a Walter Futter trek through India." The notice fails to recognize the film as a Futter Corp. production of 1933, originally issued by major-league RKO-Radio Pictures as *India Speaks*. (The title was a riposte, or an imitative homonymous gesture, to Columbia's moneymaking acquisition, *Africa Speaks*.)

Bride of Buddha, a Poverty Row distillation of *India Speaks*, scraps a quarter-hour of exposition but retains the more harrowing elements: director and narrator Richard Halliburton appears as an explorer fascinated with legends of a White Goddess of a remote Himalayan outpost. Halliburton remarks with revulsion upon a ceremony in homage to the bloodthirsty deity Kali, rituals of self-torture, and encounters with snakes and vampire bats, which are presumed to harbor wicked souls.

Following a peaceful interlude in the Shalimar Gardens of Srinigar, the adventurer forges into taboo territory, beholding such phoney soul-cleansing ceremonies as cremations, a lion-vs-tiger fight, and a ritual in which Halliburton finds himself exposed as an outsider. Pursued by a murderous horde of Third World holy-rollers, he reaches a forbidden valley. Despite his conditional acceptance as an emissary to the White Goddess, he proves incapable of rescuing her from a lethal rite. An earthquake interrupts the ceremony. Halliburton and a sympathetic priest escape. The goddess submits to sacrifice as a bride of Buddah.

"Too gruesome for the screen," complained *Variety*, granting nonetheless that much of this version was found entertaining.

Although Halliburton was a *bona fide* globetrotter, he had acknowledged during the 1933 New York premiere of *India Speaks* that he did not accompany the filming crew to India. The RKO cut of *India Speaks* features a prologue explaining that fictionalized Hollywood sound-stage footage is intercut with the documentary scenes; this acknowledgment of fakery is missing from the print we have seen of *Bride of Buddha*. By the time Walter Futter premiered this diminished version, Halliburton had died at sea, during a voyage from Hong Kong to San Francisco in 1939.

Invisible Ghost and the Launching of Bela Lugosi's Monogram Nine

Monogram Pictures Corp. • 1941–44

Indecision plagued the christening of *Invisible Ghost*, Bela Lugosi's first of nine starring assignments for a new incarnation of Monogram Pictures. (Monogram had re-organized during the late 1930s, following the absorption of the seminal Monogram into Republic Pictures.)

Announced variously as *The Maniac*, *Murder by the Stars*, and *Phantom Monster* but then launched into production in March of 1941 as *Phantom Killer*, the film was completed in April and issued as *Invisible Ghost*, a title that at least captures the haunting dream-state incoherence of the story, ghost or no ghost. (A more descriptive title might have been *Mad Love*—the pivot is a deranged passion—but MGM already had used that one.) *Phantom Killer*, in turn, became the name of a 1942 remake of Monogram's *The Sphinx* [1933]; about which, more presently.)

As meandering and defiant of logic as a fever-fugue, *Invisible Ghost* trades upon the assumption that a cuckolded and bereaved husband could be driven to a killing rage when reminded of an irremediable loss. Lugosi is Charles Kessler, a genial country squire living in denial of his departed wife's disloyalty.

Long presumed dead, Mrs. Kessler (Betty Compson) lives on in hiding—a passive nutcase, sheltered in a nearby cellar by Kessler's

secretive gardener, Jules Mason (Ernie Adams, in fine weasly form). Mrs. Kessler roams by night; her fleeting appearances have so unsettled her husband that he has committed murder while entranced.

A chauffeur had been first to die, followed by the household's new cook, Cecile (Terry Walker). Ralph Dickson (John McGuire), sweetheart of Kessler's daughter, Virginia (Polly Ann Young), is learned to have quarreled with Cecile over a bygone affair. Dickson finds himself railroaded into a death sentence on circumstantial evidence.

Director Joseph H. Lewis barges onward with an assurance at odds with the rampant implausibilities. Kessler cites sentimental reasons in his refusal to vacate the accurséd mansion, even as the gardener hopes against hope that he may reunite the mad Mrs. Kessler with her husband.

The wrongfully convicted Ralph Dickson proves to have a look-alike brother, Paul (McGuire, again), whose sudden arrival tests the film's confidence in its own grim attitude. Sombreness prevails, however, via a tiny, gemlike transitional scene between Ernie Adams and the fine black actor Clarence Muse, who plays the butler with a stern authority: the twin shows up unannounced, unnerving all concerned. Muse approaches Adams and asks, "Do I look *pale*?" A lesser film would have used the line as a setup for a dismissive color gag, but here Adams merely appears caught off his guard, at a loss for a reply. Muse finishes with a solemn declaration: "I *feel* pale."

The killings continue with an attack on Jules Mason, whose sudden revival and expiration on a coroner's slab reinforces the sense of helplessness. (This scene is incomplete in some editions; the missing footage appears intact in a surviving reissue trailer from Astor Pictures.) Finally, as suspicion is trained upon the butler, Mrs. Kessler is found and brought before her husband, who unwittingly cracks the case by losing control in view of witnesses. Mrs. Kessler collapses in death. At this moment, her husband regains his senses—only to learn too late of his secret life as the strangler.

Such chain-reactions render the story beyond belief. Lewis subdues the extravagant conceits with an even greater extravagance of style. This tactic, coupled with crisp character definition and headlong pacing, was Lewis' trademark from 1937 until the late 1950s, when he entered television. He became a leading figure in the *film noir* movement. (Lewis would revisit the notion of the slayer unknown to himself in 1946's *So Dark the Night*, for Columbia Pictures.)

Massive, quivering shadows loom forebodingly in *Invisible Ghost*. The more intimate exchanges are framed by flames, seen from within a fireplace. Lugosi's transformations are accomplished with subtle facial expressions, emphasized by sophisticated camera angles and ominous lighting, as he gazes in disbelief from within the house while a haggard Betty Compson prowls about outside.

Compson, a lapsed star of the silent era (see: *The Great Gabbo*), plays the figurative ghost with a generous avoidance of vanity. She establishes her character's lunacy with a trembling voice and a wild stare and exhibits the courage to stand alongside a large portrait of herself in better days—a prominent prop. All concerned, especially Muse, Adams, and Polly Ann Young, match the sincerity with which Lugosi distinguishes the picture.

Monogram's Lugosi starrers had been prefaced by PRC's *The Devil Bat*. A constant is the friendship between producers—Sigmund Neufeld at PRC, Sam Katzman at Monogram. As a whole, the films convey a wild unevenness, from calculated black comedy to existential gloom to slapstick absurdity to unintentional humor. All allow Lugosi the prominence that the major studios had begun denying him, except in the exploitation of his ticket-selling name.

Entries on the additional Lugosi Monograms (into 1944) follow. Two variants from England bear mentioning, as well: Distributor E.J. Fancey compiled parts of the more straightforward chillers into *Lock Up Your Daughters* in 1959. Then, in 1961, Fancey excerpted *Spooks Run Wild* (with portions of *Boys of the City*, a.k.a. *The Ghost Creeps*) to cobble together an eight-chapter serial called *Spooky House Kids*.

Spooks Run Wild (1941). Often confused with *Ghosts on the Loose* (below) in view of shared star billing for Bela Lugosi and the *East Side Kids* ensemble, Phil Rosen's *Spooks Run Wild* is a distinctive picture. It allows Lugosi the mixed-nuts opportunity to act scary, act scared, and finally turn out to be—but no, don't let's give everything away all at once.

The picture raises the ante on slapstick by pitting Leo Gorcey, Huntz Hall *et al.*, against a prowling murderer who means business. Somebody could get slaughtered here, any minute now, and therein lies the quality that sustains the essential humor: remember Mark Twain's belief in hilarity as the only plausible response to misery.

Bound for summer camp, the East Siders—Muggs, Danny, Glimpy, Scruno, Skinny, and Peewee—hear a news broadcast about a monster at large. A cloaked stranger, Nardo (Lugosi), and his dwarf helper, Luigi (Angelo Rossitto), stop at a gasoline station to ask the way to an abandoned mansion, site of a long-ago murder. There arrives a car bearing a popular mystery writer, Dr. von Grosch (Dennis Moore). The local constable (Guy Wilkerson) pegs Nardo as a suspect.

Nardo and Luigi, prowling about a cemetery, draw gunfire from a gravedigger. The East Siders wander into the boneyard. Peewee (David Gorcey) is wounded, and the pals take him to the house. Nardo

treats the boy's injury and invites the kids to stay. Peewee goes sleep-walking. The stock complications—hidden passageways, convenient and inconvenient disappearances—lead the authorities to conclude that the East Side Kids have fallen prey to the monster. The boys frighten Nardo with a ghostly impersonation. Nurse Linda Mason (Dorothy Short) arrives with von Grosch, who turns menacing. Muggs (Leo Gorcey), drawn by Linda's screams, tackles von Grosch, the killer. Nardo, who has proved to be a stage magician, entertains the gang; a trick disappearance caps the film with a blackout gag.

Shot during the late summer of 1941 as *Ghosts in the Night*, this smooth and brisk trifle is pure formula for the East Side Kids and little more than a lurk-through for a clearly delighted Lugosi. Everyone on hand seems to enjoy the pageantry. Dennis Moore makes a properly troublesome celebrity author, who seems—like Michael Gough in 1959's *Horrors of the Black Museum*—the sort who commits murder as a means of keeping his muse stimulated.

The *East Side Kids* entries for 1941 also include *Pride of the Bowery*, *Flying Wild*, and *Bowery Blitzkreig*.

Black Dragons (1942). Attempts to exploit prevailing social conditions for the sake of entertainment have seldom been so pronounced as during World War II, when the Axis menace proved a persistently embittered muse. No odder such result exists than William Nigh's *Black Dragons*, which is as fascinating for its suggestion of infiltration and sabotage via plastic surgery as it is for Bela Lugosi's darkly comic starring presence.

Lugosi prowls and ponders with philosophical good humor through this one while staging a murderous war of nerves. The story concerns a larger menace for whose creation Lugosi stands responsible. At a gathering of captains of industry, commerce, and politics, the festive mood darkens with the disclosure that six of these big shots are face-lift ringers—Japanese agents of the Black Dragon Society, transformed courtesy of the Third Reich to resemble slain Americans. Thus strategically placed, the cultists range at large to undermine the Allied campaign.

The arrival of Monsieur Colomb (Lugosi) in the household of the bogus Dr. Saunders (George Pembroke) touches off a hostage situation: Colomb settles in as a vaguely honored guest while his host becomes a forced recluse. The fake Kerney (Max Hoffman, Jr.) is first to die, ambushed in a taxicab and dumped upon the steps of the barricaded Japanese Embassy, a ceremonial dagger clutched in one hand.

Saunders' niece—or *is* she?—Alice (Joan Barclay) chooses an awkward time to visit. Her purported uncle refuses to see her, and Alice finds herself strangely attracted to Colomb. Novice plainclothes cop Dick Martin (Clayton Moore) traces Kerney's path back to the Saunders residence, only to wait in vain to see the hidden master of the household. Martin finds himself not so strangely attracted to Alice.

Colomb disables the ersatz Wallace (Edward Piel, Sr.) and uses him as bait for additional impostors before killing him. He taunts the false Ryder (Bob Fiske) by sending an advertisement for a plastic surgeon, then lures Ryder and the substitute Van Dyke (Irving Mitchell) into a trap. Colomb vanishes. Martin gets wise, belatedly, and catches a plane to meet the supposed banker Amos Hanlin (Robert Frazer), persuading him to come to Washington for protection.

Colomb, too, has backtracked. The benighted Saunders household falls into turmoil as Alice is revealed to be a government agent, sent to investigate on behalf of the genuine niece. Saunders comes out of hiding, keeping his head blanketed. Colomb kills Hanlin and is wounded in return. Finally, Saunders offers an explanation.

For his help in altering Japanese saboteurs to resemble the slain Americans, the Nazi surgeon Dr. Melcher—Colomb, that is—was rewarded with imprisonment. Trading places with a look-alike captive, Colomb had gained an exit and trailed the agents to America. As he finishes his confession, the counterfeit Saunders reveals his face: Colomb has infected him with a disfiguring glandular disease. Colomb gets in the last word—"And *you* must go on *living!*"—before collapsing in death.

Nazi conspirator though his character be, Lugosi comes across as a wholly sympathetic predator—a man betrayed, on a mission of vengeance, with a droll sense of humor about the ease with which he terrifies and manipulates his ungrateful clients. Romance figures in strange ways: Lugosi engages in ominously flirtatious banter with Joan Barclay, who plays another surrogate personage with nervy authority. Serial favorite and former aerialist Clayton Moore, the Lone Ranger-to-be, makes a boyishly arrogant cop, astonished that Barclay should find Lugosi alluring. Lugosi has the advantage of suave confidence, even though he stands aloof from romantic complications. The hint of rivalry could have become a tensely balanced triangle with extra care and a heftier running time.

After Lugosi has throttled one of the false Americans within the Saunders house, Barclay hastens to report she had heard a gurgling sound. Lugosi has a ready explanation: "Oh! I was *humming*. Is my voice as bad as *that*?" While fleeing an intruder, Barclay dashes into a collision with Lugosi. He tells her, "When a young woman's nerves commence to give way, it is time she sought refuge in a *strong* man's arms." She replies, "I just ran into yours." He misses not a beat: "*Mine* might be *dangerous*." When he sets out for parts unknown to mislead the authorities, she asks, "Will we see you again?" Lugosi: "Who *knows*, in this crazy world?" The killer's choice of an alias is a smart touch of wartime irony: *Colomb* suggests the French term for *dove*.

The complications of identity are a bit overmuch for *Black Dragons'* scant 61 minutes, and director Nigh is hardly a master of suspenseful pacing. There is one fine surprise, when an airliner, bound for a meeting with the last intended victim, proves to be carrying Moore and not Lugosi. The change-of-pace role seems to delight Lugosi, and the five ghastly murders plus a shock-value finale make for a generously gradual payoff. Of course, any picture in which that championship bad-guy player, I. Stanford Jolley, impersonates a Japanese warlord is okay in our book.

The Corpse Vanishes (1942). Beyond the overstated advertising claim of being "unequalled for sheer horror," Wallace Fox's *The Corpse Vanishes* proves to be the most coherent and suspenseful of the Lugosi Monograms. The film pivots on a plausible unfolding, so long as one accepts the implausible situation. It places Monogram's signature cold grey weirdness at the service of a determined newspaperwoman's campaign to sort out the complications. And it gives Bela Lugosi a role that is persuasively torn between sympathetic devotion and sadistic malevolence.

One bride after another collapses at the altar. Each is pronounced dead, and each supposed corpse is stolen within moments. Each is duly delivered to the isolated mansion of Dr. Lorenz (Lugosi), who requires the young women for an extravagant experiment to restore beauty to his grotesquely agéd wife (Elizabeth Russell). Lorenz' household includes a hag of a servant, Fagah (Minerva Urecal), and her sons, the dwarf Toby (Angelo Rossitto) and the half-witted Angel (Frank Moran). Lorenz relies upon Toby's loyalty, and he and Toby take delight in bullyragging Angel, who is obsessed with the comatose brides whom Lorenz has collected. (The part of Angel anticipates Tor Johnson's recurring role as Lobo—a name suggestive of *lobotomized*—in such films of the 1950s as *Bride of the Monster*, with Lugosi, and *The Unearthly*, with John Carradine.)

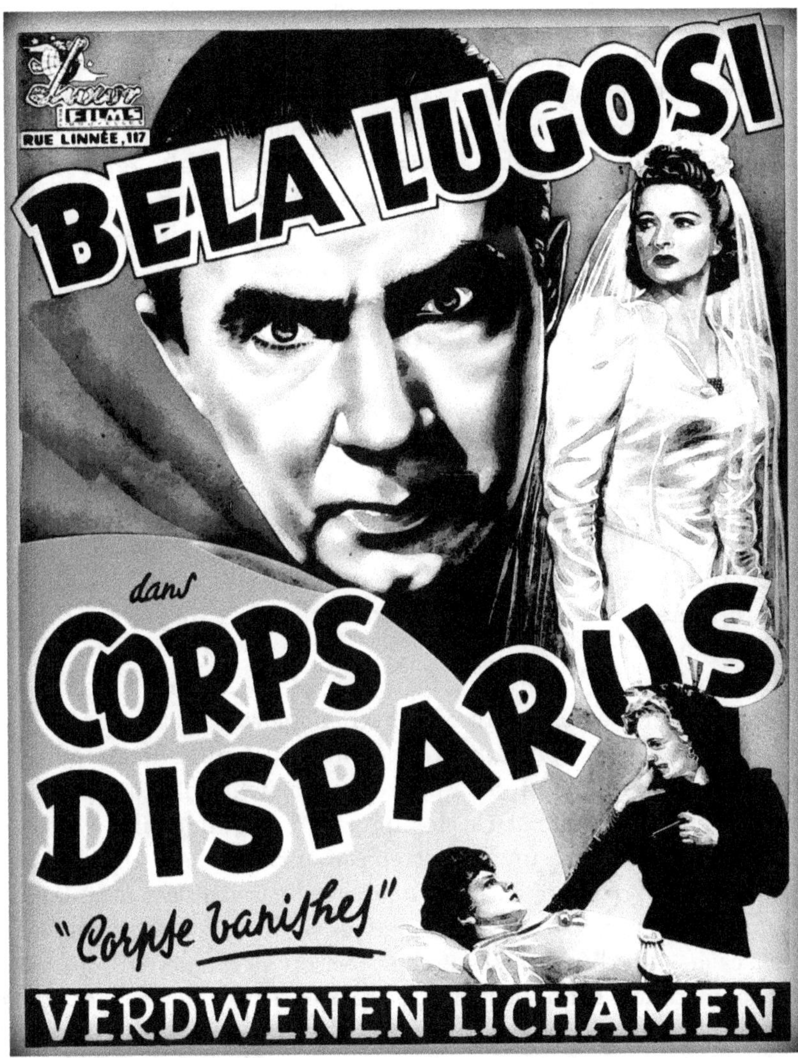

Patricia Hunter (Luana Walters), a journalist with ambitions bigger than the coverage of weddings, finds that each of the vanished brides had received a hybrid orchid from some unknown person. She traces the exotic bloom to Lorenz, a horticulturalist, and visits him under the pretense of seeking an interview. Another visitor is Dr. Foster (Tristram Coffin), a physician who works with Lorenz but knows nothing of the secretive experiments. Lorenz' wife rebuffs Patricia, but then becomes unnervingly friendly after a storm forces the reporter to stay the night. Terrified by the appearance of Angel, Patricia roams the house and finds grim evidence. Half-convinced that she has dreamed the experience, she is as anxious to leave as she is eager to establish a connection with the crimes. Lorenz loses patience with Angel and kills him.

Patricia arranges a spurious wedding. One of Lorenz' orchids—source of a trance-inducing vapor—is delivered and confiscated. The case seems all but solved when Lorenz appears, accompanied by Toby, and kidnaps Patricia. Toby is felled by a policeman's gunfire. Lorenz rushes back to the lab with Patricia. Mrs. Lorenz awaits rejuvenation. Fagah, angered at the loss of her sons, stabs Lorenz. He retaliates before collapsing in death. Mrs. Lorenz attacks Patricia—only to be done in by the dying Fagah.

Director Fox keeps the telling reasonably straightforward for a Monogram spooker, but the eerie qualities predominate. Elizabeth Russell's introduction as the vain and malicious Mrs. Lorenz is particularly unsettling; she gives forth with the most mournful cries of agony this side of *Island of Lost Souls* (1932). Dwarf actor Angelo Rossitto revels in a show of passive sadism.

"I loved working with Bela Lugosi," Rossitto told us in 1990. "He was a very kind and humorous man, and those *el cheapo* pictures we did together [also including 1941's *Spooks Run Wild* and 1947's *Scared to Death*] were so much fun that we didn't really care whether they'd win us any awards."

Minerva Urecal's spirited performance as the hovering, antagonistic housekeeper is a far cry from her rather disoriented turn as Lugosi's sister in 1943's *The Ape Man* (forthcoming). Minimal comedy relief belongs to Vince Barnett, as a photographer who intrudes upon the happy ending for a slapstick closing gag. Tristram Coffin struggles valiantly with a blandly underwritten romantic sub-leading role; more could have been made of whether he might be in cahoots with Lugosi.

Luana Walters is persuasive as the journalist who risks her life to crack a case—anything to escape the newsroom's Women's Page ghetto. Her circumstances echo the genuine experiences of a newspaperwoman named Joan Lowell, whose infiltration of several criminal rackets informed a fine memoir called *Gal Reporter*, published in 1933. Lugosi is his familiar suave-and-sinister self, with an air of weary paternalism giving way to a show of desperate vigor in the climactic kidnap scene.

Producer Sam Katzman, an *eminènce grisé* of Poverty Row, was still working on the quick-and-cheap when we encountered him during the 1950s and 1960s on his frequent visits to West Texas. The occasions had less to do with show business than with long-standing friendships: these Katzman croneys included Michael H. Price's theatre-manager uncle, Grady L. Wilson, for whom George Turner had worked; and the retail clothiers Ben Solnick, Ben and Buck Altman, and Ben Cohen, for whom Price worked as a fashion buyer and display designer. Katzman was ever at the ready to spin a movie-biz story; he became especially animated when speaking of Lugosi:

Ol' Bela—what a *mensch*! He was a *handsome* dog, and the picture of class with a capital *K*, I should tell you! Still had the matinée-idol magnetism, even at that advanced age [Lugosi was 59, and Katzman 41, at the time of *The Corpse Vanishes*], and even though he was suffering with a chronic case of sciatica, so he told me, and had got saddled taking some kind of dope that some quack doctor had given him..., he was still smooth as you please, and full of pep as far as anybody could tell.

Always ready for anything a picture called for—just give him a two-dollar cigar and let him know he's appreciated, and he's beaming. He sprained his back—threw it out of joint, y'know, which had to be extraordinarily painful, in his condition—carrying Luana Walters off in the kidnap scene of *Corpse Vanishes*, but—like I said, a *mensch*. Never griped, and there's always been plenty to gripe about with *my* pictures. I wish Hollywood, its big-timers, had treated him better, 'cause there was no way Monogram could've given him what he deserved.

Corpse makes efficient use of the roadways (ostensibly rural) of Los Angeles' Griffith Park. The unusually nuançed musical score includes a funereal rendition of Schubert's "Ave, Maria" and the ironic subtlety of a minor-mode wedding-ceremony recessional. The spare-parts soul-parasite surgical angle would prove influential over the long term upon such disparate titles as *Voodoo Man* and *Revenge of the Zombies* (below), *The Black Sleep* (1956), *Eyes Without a Face* (France, 1960), *Atom Age Vampire* (Italy, 1960), and *The Brain That Wouldn't Die* (1962).

Bowery at Midnight (1942). Bela Lugosi delivers a chilling variant upon his work in the more accomplished *Dark Eyes of London* (a.k.a. *The Human Monster*, 1939), a British adaptation of a novel by Edgar Wallace. *Bowery*'s director, Wallace Fox, contrasts Lugosi's academic respectability, as an opinionated professor of criminal psychology, with a guarded secret life as a Skid Row missionary. There is a third existence, as well: Lugosi's Prof. Brenner uses his haven as a front for crime, conscripting tramps as expendable slave-labor thieves. Lugosi juggles the personalities effectively, establishing that, while his slum missionary, Karl Wagner, is patently a masquerade, there is a conflict raging between Brenner the questing intellectual and Brenner the murderous gangster.

Lugosi relinquishes the signature mad-doctor business to Lew Kelly, who plays a drug-addicted physician in the service of the mob. Taking charge of the bodies of slain hirelings, Kelly's Doc Brooks sets out to prove himself a genius and begins reviving the corpses. Never mind how: Gerald Schnitzer's fever-dream screenplay requires an imaginative response from the absorbed viewer.

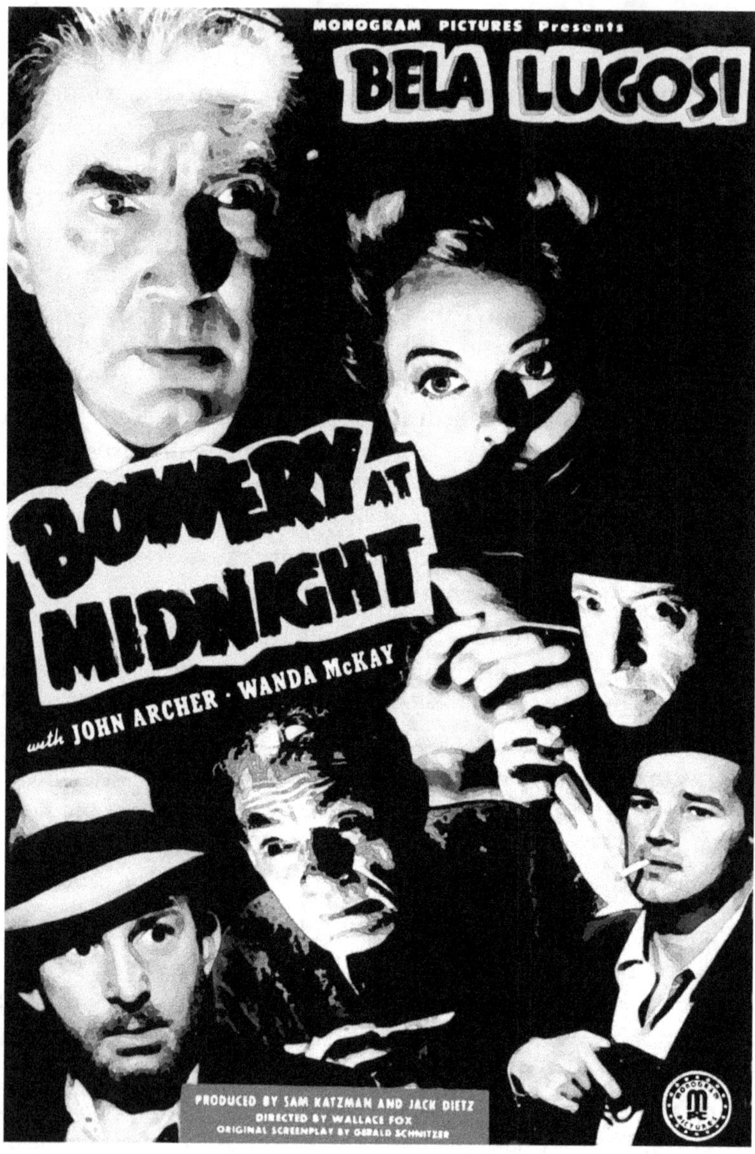

These morbid complications form the backdrop for what seems at first a bright and adventurous conflict between sweethearts. Judy Malvern (Wanda McKay) is an innocent helper at the mission, and Richard Dennison (John Archer) is an upper-crust collegian who discourages Malvern's charitable endeavors.

For his class under Prof. Brenner, Dennison proposes a study of the psychology of derelicts. Disguising himself as a bum, Dennison is astonished to spot his teacher posing as Wagner. Brenner feigns acceptance of the infiltration—and then orders the boy's murder.

Dennison's disappearance jolts the law into action. At the Brenner home, Officer Pete Crawford (Dave O'Brien) recognizes a resemblance to the missionary. The professor's wife (Anna Hope), finally comprehending a reason for his neglectful behavior, is slain by Brenner before she can accompany the cops downtown. Judy, snooping about the shelter with Doc, is interrupted by Brenner, who demands her execution. Trigger-man Mills (Tom Neal) is too much the gentleman to croak a dame. Mills is slain in a police raid. Doc, leading Brenner to a hidden passageway, turns him over to the mercies of the walking corpses. Dennison proves to have been merely wounded.

Dark by design and darker by attitude, this ostensible throwaway is yet another striking example of Lugosi's prevailing air of grace-under-pressure. Tragic complications commence early and build through the climax; even an outwardly happy ending seems tainted. Had John Archer's character been written as more of an impulsively determined, modern-dress Beowulf and less as a bored buttinsky, the role would seem more an ancestor of Kyle MacLachlan's performance in David Lynch's masterful *Blue Velvet* (1986), a picture that owes its soul to the B-movie thrillers of the 1940s. Lugosi establishes the professor's confused depravity with lethal efficiency, ordering the slaying of one trusting henchman after another, but underscores the performance with self-doubt. Here is a performance to relish in a film to relish—a film of modest technical accomplishments but considerable emotional depth. The fashionable sneers that *Bowery at Midnight* continues to inspire reveal more about its critics than about the picture.

The Ape Man (1943). In an bluffing attempt at critical insight beyond its basic function of gauging box-office prospects, *Variety* commented in 1943 on the star player of *The Ape Man*: "[Bela] Lugosi seems somewhat bewildered and bemused by his role and acts accordingly." The influential tradepaper cannot have been ignorant of the circumstances that had landed Lugosi in the minor leagues, but the critique neglects to recognize Lugosi's struggle to invest his Monogram roles with an intensity that cannot have occurred to his writers or directors.

Lugosi lavishes a greater care upon William Beaudine's *The Ape Man* than the film merits. The clash between his artistry and the prevailing shabbiness generates a tension greater than could be expected of any of Poverty Row's man-into-beast fantasies. If Boris Karloff had been merely treading turbulent waters in Monogram's *The Ape*, then Lugosi was hanging on for dear life at the little studio—responding with dignity to the indignities Monogram inflicted. One suspects Monogram knew no better, although producer Sam Katzman often voiced regret that "we didn't have the budgets—or the moxie—to give ol' Bela as good as he deserved. He seemed grateful enough just to keep working steady."

Dr. James Brewster (Lugosi) has transformed himself into an apelike creature. Brewster requires human spinal fluid; he must resort to murder. Prying journalists Jeff Carter and Billie Mason (Wallace Ford and Louise Currie) wind up at the mercy of Brewster and his gorilla accomplice (Emil Van Horn); they are saved by the arrival of the police. A goofy-looking stranger (played by Ralph Littlefield in baggy-pants comic fashion), having cropped up throughout to make

wisecracks and prod the action, reveals himself as the author responsible for this load of banana oil.

The *actual* author of the source-story, "They Creep in the Dark," is Karl Brown, a capable enough hand at mad-doctor yarns, especially in a series that Columbia Pictures had tailored to Boris Karloff. The screenwriter, associate producer Barney A. Sarecky, muddled things considerably, torn between tragedy and absurdity. Ralph Littlefield's intrusive Greek chorus burlesque act foreshadows the fatuous babblings of Cassandra "Elvira" Peterson and the insufferable cheap-shot heckling of the *Mystery Science Theatre 3000* vandals. The script's facile self-mockery is more unintentional sub-realism than conscious surrealism.

Lugosi allowed his work to speak for him all through an irreversible decline, sending out encrypted signals. Still bankable though stranded in the low-budget sector, he dealt in embittered, pitiable villains—a contrast with the flamboyant and authoritative renegades of his Depression-era glory days. A Lugosi signature is the resentful, regretful soliloquy in which a character fumes over wrongs done him and muses hopefully upon vengeance if not vindication. In the PRC production of *The Devil Bat*, Lugosi seems philosophical enough about typecast entrapment to read the role as a defiantly morbid joke. In *The Ape Man* for Monogram—a slightly more pretentious but less adventurous studio than PRC—Lugosi appears less pleased to be on board and crystallizes the situation in this line: "What a *mess* I made of things!"

Lugosi also propels the simplistic dialogue beyond the laughable context, creating a self-portrait of nobility under siege. Just as Sam Katzman recalled it, Lugosi was grateful to be working steadily, even in lessened circumstances; he shaded his portrayals with the disappointments he had known as a lapsed major-leaguer. The tone and bearing of this performance bespeak a personal tragedy more harrowing than the character's outlandish predicament.

Lugosi had resigned himself to such conditions, of course. It is fascinating to watch the artist flout the slovenly writing and careless handling that would have overwhelmed a lesser talent. Though at the mercy of exploitation and unimaginative casting, Lugosi never let the system grind him down to an indifferent performance.

He is in mixed company in *The Ape Man*, with Wallace Ford as a lippy newspaperman—not unlike his part opposite Lugosi in 1935's *The Mysterious Mr. Wong*—and a more genuinely bemused job of acting from Minerva Urecal, who plays the scientist's worried sister in an over-reactive silent-screen style. Louise Currie is a bantering delight as Ford's cohort. Henry Hall lends antagonism as Lugosi's treacherous colleague. Emil Van Horn's impersonation of a gorilla is as unwittingly absurd as his gorilla routine is deliberately preposterous in W.C. Fields' monumental comedy, *Never Give a Sucker an Even Break* (1941).

Director William Beaudine (1892–1970) was practically a founding father of the movies, but apart from some masterful silent pictures (notably, 1926's *Sparrows*) and the occasional inspired talker he seldom excelled. *The Ape Man* is a low-water mark even for Beaudine, who seems to have been more concerned with grinding out a salable product than with committing artistry. The film suffers from Beaudine's characteristic inattention to nuançes or even plain consistency, but Lugosi provides a fascinating subtext.

Ghosts on the Loose (1943). The Broadway smash *Dead End* moved to Hollywood in 1937, provoking a comparable sensation on film and establishing a youth-ensemble act that would stick together on screen well into the 1950s—retaining its members' smart-aleck childlike qualities for an unnaturally long time. From the earnest social-problem histrionics of *Dead End* and its immediate sequel-like follow-throughs, there was scarcely any direction to take beyond low comedy.

The Dead End Kids identity de-evolved into a tribe of personable near-delinquents, then forked off into the *Little Tough Guys* franchise at Universal Pictures and the *East Side Kids* series at Monogram. The overlap persisted as late as 1943. The ensemble would wind up under the *Bowery Boys* brand as Monogram gradually transformed itself into Allied Artists, which at first was a classier outfit. The team changed scarcely at all, save for the process of growing to goofball adulthood.

The transitional year of 1943 saw the act lapse decisively from Universal to Monogram, there to begin a consolidated agenda of misadventures. One of the better entries, William Beaudine's *Ghosts on the Loose*, is an old-fashioned Mystery Farce, in broad strokes. It is embellished by what amounts to little more than a walk-through from Bela Lugosi—and it is graced by an early display of surprisingly mature presence from Ava Gardner, appearing on loan from MGM for what amounts to a screen test, underwritten by Monogram. The big guys always enjoy letting the little guys pick up the tab.

A creepy old mansion harbors Nazi spies. East-Sider Glimpy (Huntz Hall) has a brother (Richard "Rick" Vallin, a.k.a. Rik and Ricki) who is about to get married; Gardner plays the bride. The couple has some crackpot notion about spending the honeymoon in a haunted house. The East Side Kids wind up occupying the place, and after the usual hokum with the usual hidden passages and camouflaged doorways, the kids almost unwittingly thwart Lugosi's Axis-infiltration plans.

The films of the East Side Kids are an acquired taste, of course, but there is no denying their generosity with the low-brow wit and

malaprop-ridden wordplay. *Ghosts on the Loose* is the Kids' show all the way, with emerging ringleader Leo Gorcey mangling the language and mugging the cameras as few others could. Huntz Hall plays the genial stooge, sometimes indignant—a sad-eyed goofball equivalent of the Three Stooges' Shemp Howard. Sammy Morrison, the former Sunshine Sammy of Hal Roach's *Our Gang* comedies, lends a welcome sense of integration based on friendship—though still accounting for the occasional dismissive color gag. Billy Benedict and Bobby Jordan are prominent, too, although Gorcey and Hall are the anchoring presences.

Director Beaudine captures the antics nicely; this is a film that requires little formal direction, accommodating Beaudine's cynical definition of the director as a traffic cop. Lugosi has scarcely more to do than appear by turns irritable and menacing. Gardner, bound of course for bigger things, is a knockout in a part that demands far less than her stunning presence.

Voodoo Man (1944). Running *The Ape Man* a close second as the silliest of Bela Lugosi's Monograms is *Voodoo Man*, which nonetheless is a great deal more likable. Co-star John Carradine characterized the picture as "the worst thing *I* ever did, even though Lugosi and [George] Zucco were tremendous fun to work with." Marvel Comics honcho Stan Lee, no slouch at appropriating the artistry of his betters, once credited the crockheaded self-consciousness of *Voodoo Man* as an inspiration for a well-worn gimmick at early-day Marvel: the comic-book story about a comic-book writer whose outlandish yarns somehow spring to life.

Here, the awareness *of* the work, *by* the work, is such that a main character is presented as a screenwriter who is ordered to look into a crime wave for the sake of hacking out a scenario. Ralph Dawson (Michael Ames) cares but little for the assignment, being too distracted by the approach of his marriage. It seems that young women have disappeared near a certain rural crossroads. Dawson heads for that place to meet his fiancée, Betty (Wanda McKay). His car conks out, and he catches a lift with Betty's cousin, Stella (Louise Currie). Her car misfires. Dawson goes to summon help.

Halfwit servants (Carradine and Pat McKee) of one Dr. Marlowe (Lugosi) nab Stella. Marlowe places her in a trance, seeking to transmigrate her life-force into the body of his wife

(Ellen Hall). A cohort, Nicholas (Zucco), professes to be in communion with the powers of voodoo.

Dawson calls at the Marlowe house in search of an auto boost. Ordered to scram, Dawson hoofs it back to the roadside, finds Stella strayed, reaches Betty's house, and learns that Stella has gone missing altogether.

The soul-swapping ritual fails. Marlowe calls for another abduction. The sheriff (western-movie stalwart Henry Hall) arrives, with questions. Marlowe is evasive. Stella wanders outside, where she is found and taken to her sister. Marlowe calls upon the women—then lures Stella back. Betty is kidnapped. Dawson barges in on a voodoo ceremony. The sheriff shoots Marlowe, whose death breaks the spells all round. Dawson records his adventure in a movie script and suggests Bela Lugosi for the starring role.

"We were really scraping the bottom of the barrel with *Voodoo Man*," producer Sam Katzman told us. "Not that we were ever whatcha might call ashamed of scraping bottom, but—now, there's a picture that makes the rest of what we were doing at the time look pretty slick. By comparison, I mean to say." Only Lugosi gets much of a chance to shine, reveling in a tone of sarcastic irony. Carradine and Zucco are stranded in marginal roles that hardly play to their strengths of confident bombast.

In 1945, Katzman had intended to feature Acquanetta Davenport (of Universal Pictures' *Captive Wild Woman*) in a similarly conceived picture called *Voodoo Queen*. The project failed to materialize, owing to Acquanetta's displeasure with her prospects at Monogram Pictures.

Return of the Ape Man (1944). The kinship to *The Ape Man* (above) lies only in the presence of Bela Lugosi, and in Sam Katzman's Banner-Monogram *imprimatur*. Lugosi's Hollywood stardom effectively ends with *Return of the Ape Man*, although there would be later attempts at resurgence—including a sly return to the role of Count Dracula in 1948's *Bud Abbott & Lou Costello Meet Frankenstein*—before the artistically disastrous connections that Lugosi would make during the 1950s.

Life eternal is the quest. Prof. Dexter (Lugosi) is the seeker, barely anchored by a comparatively more level-headed colleague, John Gilmore (John Carradine). The partners thaw back to life a derelict (Ernie Adams), whom they have kept frozen.

Dexter mounts an expedition to the Arctic in search of the remains of a prehistoric subhuman. The hunt yields results, but the researchers are disappointed to find that the revived creature (Frank Moran) seems incapable of absorbing civilized ways. Dexter proposes to transplant the reasoning portion of a human brain into the apeman.

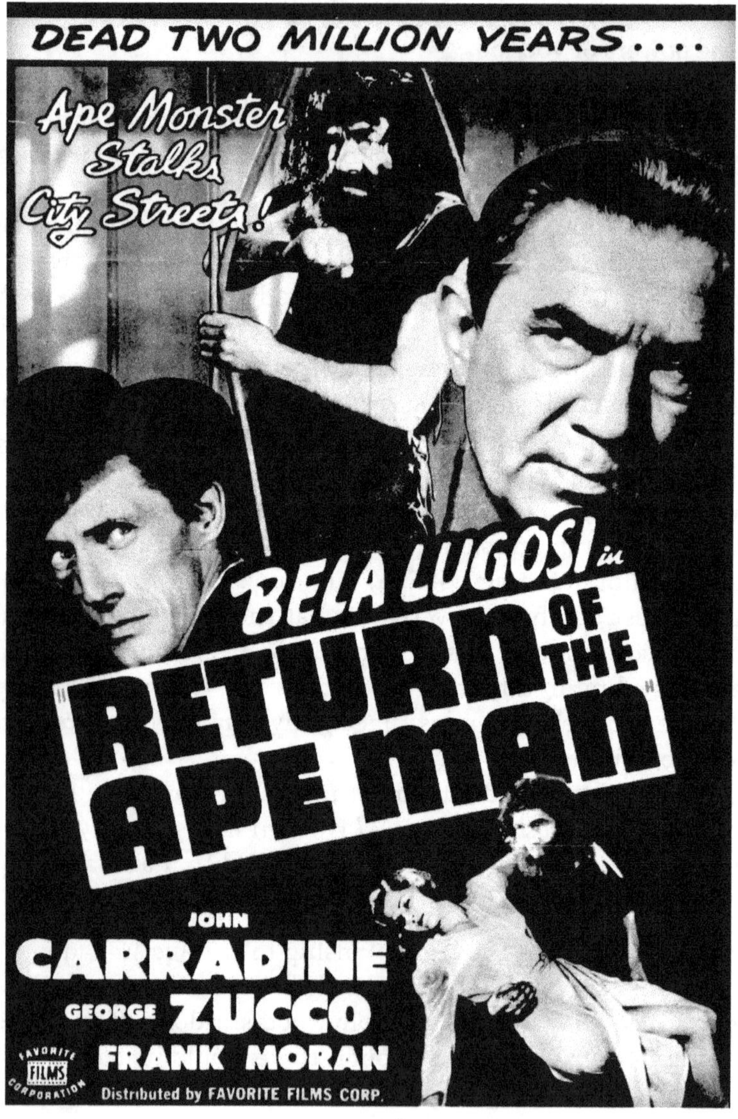

Rallying from the passive-aggressive, resentful attitude that had characterized even his better wartime work along Poverty Row, Lugosi summons a measure of his Depression-era ferocity, becoming a reflection of his characters in *Murders in the Rue Morgue* and *The Raven*. Dexter casts an eye on the fiancé (Michael Ames) of Gilmore's niece, Anne (Judith Gibson). Gilmore catches Dexter inviting the youth home, intending a brain extraction. The caged apeman glowers—as menacingly as an apeman can glower, that is, when the makeup department has made him look more like a bum in need of a shave and a hangover remedy.

The apeman escapes and kills a policeman before Dexter can recapture it. Dexter begs Gilmore's help to destroy the monster, but of course Gilmore is taken captive as a brain donor. The loss of Carradine at this point is crippling—not only because he and Lugosi play so well off one another, but also because Frank Moran's title creature is such a ridiculous presence.

Hollywood's notion of the sub-hominid as a fear-inducing presence had deteriorated terribly in the years since Bull Montana had played such nightmarish creatures in *Go and Get It* (1920) and *The Lost World* (1925). By the 1940s, even a bigger picture such as *One Million B.C.* was content to saddle an actor with pelts and a scruffy hairpiece and call him a caveman—the imaginative imperative, sidelined.

Return of the Ape Man takes the line of lesser resistance to an absurd extreme, entrusting the title role to sleepy-eyed, slump-shouldered Frank Moran and allowing him to amble through the ostensibly predatory moments while grumbling as if dyspeptic. Moran's droll tough-guy intelligence, as seen in *Sullivan's Travels* (1941), goes untapped.

The more problematical walk-through here is committed by director Phil Rosen, who seems to have put his characteristically emphatic command of pace and performance on holiday. Carradine and Lugosi scarcely need stern direction, for those fine actors know their proverbial motivations better, probably, than the people who had hired them. It is as well that George Zucco, who shares co-billing with Moran as the apeman, seems not to have suffered the indignity of actually playing the role. Only Moran appears on screen—and so do his underpants, guaranteeing a horse-laugh from the audience at precisely the moment when the suspense should be mounting.

Another outbreak of guffaws is inevitable when the apeman, now in possession of a modern intellect, steals into Carradine's house and begins playing a mournful fragment from Beethoven upon a piano. Here is a scene of sobering depth, meant to show the homing instincts of Carradine's slain character, that benefits from dimmed lighting and a more nuanced reading than any moment that has come before. It occurs too cruelly late, however, to overcome the unintentional hilarity with which Rosen has suffused the picture, and not even a new fatality can salvage the sequence.

Phil Rosen was a trailblazing camera artist—first president (1918–1921) of the American Society of Cinematographers—whose work as a talking-picture director was largely confined to the smaller studios. Rosen had a sure eye for the proper photographic treatment, with a naturalistic approach. This style serves well the more genuinely fine Rosen pictures, notably 1933's *The Sphinx*, where the grim doings take place in workaday settings. Rosen also knew when to apply artistic touches for the occasional costume melodrama, such as Universal's *The Mystery of Marie Rogét* (1942), that ill-acknowledged companion-piece to Robert Florey's *Murders in the Rue Morgue* (1932).

For *Return of the Ape Man*, Rosen takes his customarily unaffected tack, but for once it does not work. Even Lugosi gets done away with prematurely. There follow the abduction of Judith Gibson, a tedious backstage chase at a theatre, a nick-of-time rescue, and a conflagration started by the apeman himself. None too soon.

King of the Zombies

Monogram Pictures Corp. • 1941

Originally announced in early 1941 as a starring picture for Bela Lugosi, this wild fantasia on a Nazi-buster propaganda theme wound up instead as the most elaborate showcase Mantan Moreland ever found during his short but emphatic movie career. Henry Victor assumed the intended Lugosi role, as a scientist bent upon raising the dead for war-mongering purposes, and he brought to it a perfectly serviceable competence that has none of the good-humored subtleties or mournful intensity one would have expected from Lugosi. Meanwhile, Lugosi lavished his gifts upon *Invisible Ghost*.

Moreland had come to Hollywood in 1936 from the southern Chitlin' Circuit of black-neighborhood nightclubs and vaudeville theatres. Given improvisational freedom on *King of the Zombies*, Moreland brought to bear a distinctive wit and energy to spare. The result is his transformation of an incidental comic-relief assignment to the heart and soul of the picture. *King of the Zombies* ranks with W.C. Fields' *The Bank Dick* and the Marx Bros.' *Duck Soup* as a signature comedy film, given Moreland's transformation of a desultory horror script into a personalized showcase. Some ineffable quality other than the stock scenario inspired director Jean Yarbrough to make the film better than its raw materials. In any case, the picture validated Moreland's credential early on as a uniquely dependable supporting player and led to consistent employment if not bigger opportunities.

Moreland plays Jefferson Jackson, valet to Naval Intelligence Agent Bill Summers (John Archer). They are airborne with pilot James McCarthy (Dick Purcell) over the Caribbean in search of a vanished plane when forced to land. The men regain their bearings and proceed to a castle occupied by Dr. Miklos Sangre (Victor). Sangre seems hospitable enough—although he insists that Jeff be lodged with the servants lest they become resentful, and he seems amused that Jeff finds the butler, Momba (Leigh Whipper), an unnerving presence. Jeff, who has a wisecrack for even the most desperate occasion, pretends to

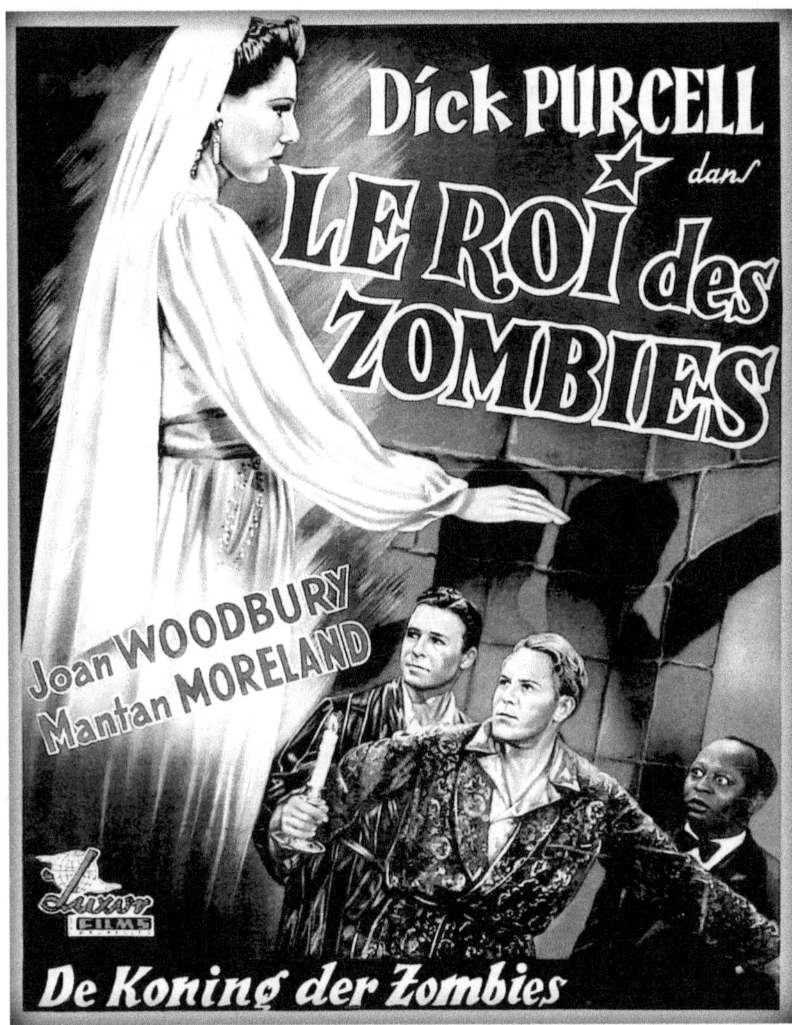

mistake Momba for a fellow lodge member and then mutters, "Harlem never was like *this*!"

Jeff flirts with a servant, Samantha (Marguerite Whitten). Nearby lurks Tahama (Madame Sul-Te-Wan, *né* Nellie Conley), a cadaverous-looking cook. "I know a *museum* that would give a *fortune* just to have *her* under *glass*!" Jeff observes. Samantha tells of the zombies that stalk the grounds; Jeff is disinclined to believe her until Samantha summons the living-dead creatures. Jeff hightails it. He cannot get Bill or Mack to believe his account. Sangre holds Jeff up to ridicule.

Sangre is cultivating zombies for the Third Reich. The idea derives from an earnest interest among some of the more superstitious Nazis to learn whether the dead might be reanimated as a *todenkorps* of unquestioning cannon fodder. But of course the Nazis could never have imagined an Allied secret weapon like Mantan Moreland.

Suffice that the screenplay contains such trappings as come with the turf for pulp-magazine horrors and budget-bound Hollywood spookers—the captive military official, the wraithlike wife of the renegade scientist, the voodoo ritual, the inevitable loss of control of the massed zombies—and let it be known that Moreland overwhelms the clichés and subverts all manner of black-comedian stereotypes at every turn. The Louisiana-born actor uses a richly southern voice to render his subversions all the more disarming. He owns up to dread and runs for cover when discretion dictates, but instead of a scared-silly act, Moreland laughs in the face of danger, demands that the menace be confronted, and gives the white guys abundant jovial back-talk in protesting his second-class citizenship.

Moreland also indulges to an unusual extent in flirtatious banter with Marguerite Whitten, bringing his characterization nearer the romantically robust, fully rounded performances that the great Paul Robeson had delivered in Dudley Murphy's *The Emperor Jones* and James Whale's *Show Boat* (1936), while moving away from the buffoonish and figuratively impotent portrayals that were the stock-in-trade of Lincoln "Stepin Fetchit" Perry and Willie "Sleep'n' Eat" Best.

Upon learning of romantic competition, Moreland seems relieved to learn his presumed rival is dead. Whitten explains that her sweetheart had been killed in an accident involving "a revolving crane." Moreland absorbs this revelation and then comments: "Mmmm—*mmm*! Y'all *sho'* have some *fierce birds* around this country!" He is less pleased to learn that the deceased has been revived as a zombie.

Later on, Henry Victor's Dr. Sangre decides that Moreland belongs among the zombies. Pretending to yield to Victor's hypnotic influence, Moreland joins the ranks of the living dead with, "Move *over*, boys—I'm one of the *gang*, now." Later, when Whitten challenges his zombiehood on grounds that "zombies can't talk," Moreland replies, "Can *I* help it 'cause I'm lo*qua*cious?"

As tempting as it is to characterize *King of the Zombies* as Moreland's movie, plain and simple, even a cursory viewing will point up the brisk pacing, the conversational flow of dialogue, and the keen stylistic technique of director Yarbrough. A fine visual invention (similar to Robert N. Bradbury's variations on the swish-pan transitional device in the *Lone Star Westerns*) illustrates the speed with which Moreland reacts to his first encounter with the zombies: the camera exaggerates the comedian's takeoff, then dashes around and ahead of him, seemingly through the very foundations of the castle, and catches him arriving to report the threat.

Edward Kay's original music, too, is broadly distinctive, built upon tribal-chant rhythms and incorporating a breezy, jazz-tinged leitmotif for Moreland in contrast to the low-brass martial cues for the zombies. In a watershed year for acknowledged great movies, the Kay score gave Monogram a rare crack at an Academy Award: it made the cut of 20 nominees (the field was broader then), in competition with works by Alfred Newman (*How Green Was My Valley* and *Ball of Fire*), Bernard Herrmann (*All That Money Can Buy* and *Citizen Kane*), Miklos Rosza (*Lydia* and *Sundown*), Edward Ward (*Cheers for Miss Bishop* and *Tanks a Million*), Franz Waxman (*Dr. Jekyll and Mr. Hyde* and *Suspicion*), Frank Skinner (*Back Street*), Morris Stoloff and Ernest Toch (*Ladies in Retirement*), Meredith Willson (*The Little Foxes*), Cy Feuer & Walter Scharf (Republic Pictures' *Mercy Island*); Louis Gruenberg (*So Ends Our Night*), Victor Young (*Hold Back the Dawn*), Werner Heymann (*That Uncertain Feeling*), Richard Hageman (*That Woman Is Mine*), and Max Steiner (*Sergeant York*). Herrmann won the Oscar, for *All That Money Can Buy*.

Yarbrough had weighed in modestly, with a string of broad comedies (including 1934's *Kentucky Kernels* and 1936's *Silly Billies*) to his credit. He joined the formative PRC with 1938's *Rebellious Daughters*, but found his truer niche with PRC's blackly humorous Lugosi-starrer *The Devil Bat* and by 1941 had established himself as a stylish director of low-budget comedies. Yarbrough spent the 1940s and 1950s alternating between humor and horror, building a rèsumé distinguished by the two starring pictures of the tragic Rondo Hatton (*House of Horrors* and *The Brute Man*, both from 1946) and two of the better entries of

Bud Abbott & Lou Costello (*Here Come the Co-Eds* and *The Naughty Nineties*, both from 1945). Yarbrough also handled two of the least effective Abbott & Costellos, *Jack and the Beanstalk* and *Lost in Alaska* (both from 1952) and bowed out at age 67 in 1967 with a dreadful hybrid of horror spoof and country-music extravaganza, *Hillbillys in a Haunted House* (1967).

Henry Victor had been a silent-era leading man in England but delivered his most noted portrayal in early-talkie Hollywood, as a treacherous circus star named Hercules in Tod Browning's *Freaks* (1932). Dick Purcell is largely sidelined in *King of the Zombies*. Purcell proceeded through such assignments as *Phantom Killer* and *Mystery of the 13th Guest* (1943); he died of a heart attack in 1944 at age 36 after

completing Republic's *Captain America* serial. John Archer, who plays Moreland's boss, seems more the heroic type, although conventional heroism, or even a protagonist's stance, is beside the point here. Joan Woodbury has too little to occupy her time as a reluctant inmate of Victor's benighted household. Leigh Whipper and Madame Sul-Te-Wan, as glowering servants, and Patricia Stacey, as Victor's entranced wife, lend appropriately macabre touches.

By 1939, Mantan Moreland had asserted a mastery of screen acting, particularly in the black-ensemble feature *One Dark Night*—which, the title notwithstanding, is not a chiller but a domestic comedy with faint undertones of crime melodrama and science fiction. Moreland had handled more than 30 scene-stealing bit parts and featured appearances by the time he landed in *King of the Zombies*. He became a favorite with the critics at *Variety*, whose various notices raved that "he works with remarkable ease and at all times is natural" and "never fails to garner a laugh, no matter how feeble the line." Among Moreland's many assignments to come, at studios large and small, was a similarly conceived role in Monogram's *Revenge of the Zombies* (1943), which is more an elaboration than a sequel or a remake.

Moreland sustained a relentless pace through Monogram's *Charlie Chan* series but reached a *cul-de-sac* during 1949–1950: he became a moving target for the NAACP's campaign to eliminate purportedly demeaning stereotypes from the movies. A more subdued Moreland appeared in a handful of pictures during the mid-1950s, again in the 1960s (including a brief turn in Jack Hill's *Spider Baby*), and again from 1970 until 1973, the year of his death. (See our companion volume, *Mantan the Funnyman: The Life & Times of Mantan Moreland*.)

Melvin Van Peebles, who cast Moreland strikingly in the color-bar satire *Watermelon Man* (1970), has called it "a tragedy...that Mantan was left out in the cold in his prime, that the studios let themselves be bullied into thinking his image fostered some sort of racism." Frankie Darro, who spent the early 1940s on a series of comedy-team pictures with Moreland, recalled the comedian fondly as "anything but a stereotype. Mantan was unique among humanity, and as great a pal as he was an actor."

The Shark Woman

B.F. Ziedman Productions • World Pictures Corp. • 1941

A little beauty of a natural drama, Ward Wing's *The Shark Woman* captures thrills aplenty in its struggles between Malaysian pearl divers and various beasts of the wild, both on land and in the sea. A romantic subplot plays out with a disarming naturalism, but the greater substance is the crystalline photography—especially in a battle between a shark and an octopus. The underwater footage is the work of Stacy Woodard, who with his brother Horace Woodard had made the 1938 documentary *The Adventures of Chico*.

The Gang's All Here

Sterling Productions • Monogram Pictures • 1941

This entry in the Frankie Darro-Mantan Moreland series finds the pals saving the day through dumb luck and courage. The film represents a lapse, but the stars are on the money as usual, and director Jean Yarbrough dawdles in search of a steady pace.

Pop Wallace (Robert Homans) finds his freight company threatened by sabotage and murder. His friends Frankie (Darro) and Jeff (Moreland) are hardly professional drivers, but Pop's situation moves them to apply. Patsy Wallace (Marcia Mae Jones), the boss's opportunistic daughter, intends to use Frankie to provoke to jealousy her timid sweetheart, a grease-monkey named Chick (Jackie Moran).

Wallace is secretly involved: he and an insurance agent, Saunders (Irving Mitchell), have been splitting the payoffs from the wrecks. Appalled that the incidents have turned deadly, Wallace pleads with Saunders to call off the wreckers. Frankie and Jeff encounter the

saboteurs but are saved inadvertently when nabbed by a traffic cop. The shipment comes through.

Nosy trucker George Lee (Keye Luke) reveals himself as an undercover investigator after Frankie and Jeff are kidnapped and imprisoned by trucking boss Norton (Ed Cassidy) and his brutal mechanic, Ham Shanks (Laurence Criner). Pop threatens Saunders with exposure unless Frankie and Jeff are freed, but the buddies escape—only to find Pop beaten nearly to death. Frankie comprehends that Pop had been strong-armed into playing along. After a last-minute hostage situation involving Jeff, Frankie, Patsy, Chick, and the crooked insurance agent, the good guys are saved by another speeding citation.

The least of the Darro & Moreland thrillers, *The Gang's All Here* detours into sentimentality with the plight of Robert Homans' character, and it allows the irritating Marcia Mae Jones a prominent role that she comes but ill equipped to justify. Jackie Moran, as in their shared star vehicle *Haunted House*, serves chiefly to prompt Jones to a nagging frenzy. Keye Luke wavers between needless comedy relief and real heroism; the nature of his mission is given away too abruptly. Yarbrough's direction meanders by comparison with his purposeful handling of *King of the Zombies*, and Mack Stengler's photography is hastily composed. Darro & Moreland are delightful, especially in a scene where Frankie tries to teach his reluctant chum the finer points of wrangling a truck.

Darro & Moreland would wrap the teaming with *Let's Go Collegiate* (1941)—a decidedly un-murderous situation comedy.

Murder by Invitation

Monogram Pictures Corp. • 1941

This throwback to the *Cat and the Canary* school of Mystery Farce makes up in generosity what it lacks in subtlety. The *Variety* reviewer complained of "sliding panels, hidden passageways, and secret doors in such corny proportions that it will have to struggle holding onto the lower rung of a dualer." (A dualer is a double-feature of the type once programmed by most urban theatres, in a day when 70 minutes was a lengthy clock-in time for a B-picture.)

The point that *Variety* missed is that Phil Rosen's *Murder by Invitation* revels in its hokum, confronting and embracing one Jazz Age and Depression-era cliché after another, then filtering the accumulation through the altered sensibilities of wartime. The film closes with a blistering clinch between Wallace Ford and Marian Marsh—in defiance of the forces of institutionalized censorship that had taken hold of Will Hays' Motion Picture Association in 1934—only to upstage

Wallace Ford and Marian Marsh.

the smooch with a wisecrack from backup player Herbert Vigran: "The Hays Office ain't gonna *like* that long kiss!"

Dowager Cassandra Denham (Sarah Padden) defies all attempts to have her declared incapable; a fortune seems at stake. Her grasping nephew, lawyer Garson Denham (Gavin Gordon), is among relatives invited to Cassandra's mountainside estate. All are informed that Cassie intends to weed out the undeserving souls. Garson, who had coveted the inheritance, is first to die.

Newspaperman Bob White (Ford) and his girlfriend, Nora O'Brien (Marsh), visit with a photographer, Eddie (Vigran). Despite the presence of a sheriff (George Guhl), another relative is soon croaked. The corpses vanish and reappear. After a chance encounter in a revolving bookcase, Cassie promises Eddie a reward for protecting a strongbox. Another relative dies.

Cassie reveals her plan to torch the house—figuring that the killer will rush inside to nab the loot. As fire consumes the place, Cassie's niece and resident helper, Mary Denham (Hazel Keener), reveals herself and her secret husband—Cassie's chauffeur, Michael (Dave O'Brien)—as the plotters. Michael attempts to escape through a hidden tunnel, but White heads him off. Cassie springs another surprise when she proposes marriage to neighbor Trowbridge Montrose (J. Arthur Young), an admirer who had seemed a red herring, or likely suspect. Eddie collects his reward—a worthless Confederate bank note. It develops that all Cassie's money is Confederate, but Montrose seems more interested in Cassie than in any supposéd fortune.

Wallace Ford had been playing the impatient smart-aleck hero since the Depression years; he seems not to have outgrown the image. He pairs appealingly with Marian Marsh—a discovery of John Barrymore, as his victimized leading lady in the 1931 *Svengali*. Marsh's career was winding down, with only *Gentleman from Dixie* (1941) and *House of Errors* (1942) yet to go.

Sarah Padden seems by turns deranged and sweet-natured as the dotty aunt, and although she is too easy a suspect—still, one can't help wondering. The Old Dark House setting is one of Monogram's better-designed collections of properties and furnishings, tricked out with sinister gadgets, shadowy nooks, and hidden tunnels, and its inmates react appropriately. Stuntman-actor Dave O'Brien has a nice bit as a cowardly menace, hidden in plain sight, and Hazel Keener shows a suitably self-justifying indignation when revealed as the agent of murder.

Criminals Within

a.k.a.: *Army Mystery*
Producers Releasing Corp. • 1941

A veneer of top-secret science-fictional mumbo-jumbo and a frenzy of harrowing events scarcely can camouflage the ordinariness of this spy melodrama from George R. Batcheller's unit at PRC. The standout elements lie in extraordinary casting, with I. Stanford Jolley in top form as an outwardly meek Fifth Column menace, Constance Worth as a seductive spy, and Eric Linden as a heroic army man on a mission combining duty with vengeance. Ann Doran, ostensibly cast as a love interest for Linden, becomes a strong heroic presence in short order.

Corporal Greg Carroll (Linden) is imprisoned for having read a forbidden document. A recreation-hall hostess named Alma Barton (Worth) hides a coded message in a pair of shoes to be delivered to a cobbler named Carl Flegler (Jolley). Greg, who has palmed a key to his cell, ditches the guardhouse and attempts to telephone his brother, a scientist—who proves to have been murdered.

Greg's commander, Bryant (Robert Frazer), is found dead after an attempt to interrogate Alma. Greg, accused, escapes after memorizing a roster of scientists' names. Haphazard complications involve a reporter-turned-sergeant (Weldon Heyburn), a newspaperwoman (Doran), a determined lieutenant (Don Curtis), and another sergeant (Ben Alexander). The murder of the hostess comes about too early. The unmasking of Ben Alexander's friendly top-kick as a fiend is too small a revelation.

Ann Doran is terrific as the spirited journalist. Eric Linden, too boyish but nonetheless game, rises above the outlandish developments with a show of desperate heroic protagonism. The tension reaches critical mass when

Eric Linden.

Linden is captured by Jolley's agents and Alexander locks Doran inside a suffocating chamber. The turning of the tables is too simply handled, but for a moment there, director Joseph H. Lewis generates a powerful sense of dread.

Peer Gynt

David Bradley • Willow Corp. • 1941

Charlton Heston told us in 1996:

> I was just 18 when I made my first picture, an amateur concoction, based on Ibsen's *Peer Gynt*, which a classmate of mine named David Bradley, there at Northwestern University, put together as an experimental thing. David used [Edvard] Grieg's [*Peer Gynt*] suite for the musical scoring, pacing the drama to [the rhythm of] the compositions. He shot it mostly by himself in 16-millimeter, on various locations in Illinois and Wisconsin, including this incredibly accurate Norwegian-type little village he had found. Turned out pretty well, but not what you'd call Hollywood calibre.
>
> David and I made another one, later, a *Julius Caesar* in 1949, after I'd already graduated to Broadway and to live television. David's *Caesar*—where I played Marc Antony—actually got some kind of limited theatrical release. *Peer Gynt*, now, it had to wait quite a long time before it got formally finished. David was hurrying so as to get on with going into the army. He tampered with it some more during the 1960s and got it shown in some of the art theatres.

Indeed, few films have known such a long gestation between the making and the definitive showing as David Bradley's *Peer Gynt*. The weird Norwegian legend, as dramatized by Henrik Ibsen in 1867's *Peer Gynt: A Dramatic Poem*, had accounted for one of the early-day cinema's more important productions: a 1915 version by the Oliver Morosco Photoplay Co. appears to be the first film for which a musical score was expressly assembled.

The play withstands even the 21-year-old Bradley's amateurish limitations. Heston is Peer Gynt, a lout who, when spurned by a lovely newcomer (Katherine Elfstrom), abducts and ravishes his former sweetheart (Betty Barton) just before she is to marry another man (Alan Eckhart). Gynt finds himself imprisoned by a troll and confronted by a hag and a deformed child that may be his own offspring—only to be transformed into a wealthy man of influence. His evils catch up with him, however, and after witnessing a vision of his funeral, Peer Gynt is allowed one last chance to justify his existence.

Heston moved along to become an Oscar contender, a political eminence whose platforms varied from left-of-center to rightward, and a master at portyraying "larger-than-life characters from Moses to Michelangelo," as the historian Ephraim Katz once put it.

David Bradley took a more peculiar path. He weighed in as a credentialed director with MGM's *noir* programmer *Talk about a Stranger* (1952). His sparse rèsumé also includes *Dragstrip Riot* (1958) and *Twelve to the Moon* (1960). The greater center-piece of Bradley's body of work

Charlton Heston.

must be a freakish patchwork hodgepodge called *Madmen of Mandoras* (1963), better known in a variant cut as *They Saved Hitler's Brain*.

In 1965, Bradley re-edited *Peer Gynt*. Venerable Francis X. Bushman added the voice of the troll. Bradley retained the tinting process that had washed the black-and-white image in greens, blues, and reds during the supernaturally conceived sequences. The Willow Corp. mounted a limited theatrical release.

Up Jumped the Devil

Dixie National • Toddy Pictures • Consolidated National • 1941

Impressions from our long-ago and incomplete screening of this elusive black-ensemble comedy, coupled with sparse documentation by the American Film Institute and the Southwest Film & Video Archive, must suffice until the genuine article turns up intact. Mantan Moreland and songwriter-comedian Shelton Brooks play bickering pals who land jobs with a wealthy matron, only to learn that one of the positions is for a maidservant—which means that Moreland spends much of the picture in drag. Director William Beaudine allows the yarn to unravel as if on autopilot.

The villain of the piece is a phony mystic (Maceo B. Sheffield), who intends to infiltrate the household for the sake of thievery. There is nothing particularly horrific about the film, but the title and the soothsayer angle render it of interest in the present context. Moreland gets back into manly attire by shooting dice with the luckless gents attending a ritzy party. And so much for the notion that black stereotypes belong entirely to the Hollywood mainstream.

Saddle Mountain Roundup

Range Busters, Inc. • George W. Weeks • Monogram Pictures • 1941

In the Depression-era sweep of *Forgotten Horrors*, we had rediscovered *Big Boy Rides Again*, in which Guinn "Big Boy" Williams crosses paths with a masked prowler and a skulking Chinese villain while attempting to take charge of a ranch. *Saddle Mountain Roundup* is the remake, splitting the leading role among the Range Busters—Monogram's answer to Republic Pictures' popular Three Mesquiteers team.

Saddle Mountain Roundup is directed for abundant suspense and suspicion by S. Roy Luby. The picture showcases two-fisted Ray "Crash" Corrigan, balladeer John "Dusty" King, and the comical voice-thrower Max "Alibi" Terhune for full measure of robust heroic protagonism and incidental humor. The adventurous frontiersmen are stirring up trail dust on behalf of grouchy rancher Magpie Harper (John Elliott) when summoned back to his ranch. Alibi is left to herd Harper's cattle while Crash and Dusty return to headquarters—only to find the boss slain under creepy circumstances. Blackie (George Chesebro), the foreman, is a ready suspect, for he had objected to Harper's plan to have the Range Busters supervise the trail drive.

Harper had left a note revealing the location of a cache of money. The ranch's cook, Fang Way (Willie Fung), hides the note. Blackie attempts to incriminate Henderson (Steve Clark), a neighboring rancher who had formed an uneasy partnership with Harper. Alibi is ambushed and imprisoned. Dusty and Blackie go missing. Dusty, lost in a tunnel beneath the ranchhouse, spooks Alibi's captors by pretending to be Harper's ghost. A mysterious intruder—the killer—proves to be Harper's trusted lawyer, Dan Freeman (Jack Mulhall).

The rambunctious spirit of *Big Boy Rides Again* is smartly recaptured, with helpful amplifications. Screenwriters John Vlahos and Earle Snell improve upon William Nolte's original continuity by making the foreman more than a red herring and rendering the Chinese nuisance's behavior more explicable if no less furtive. Jack Mulhall is as formidable here as he had been in his star-player years, almost a decade earlier, and the Range Busters cover the bases from action to music to whimsy. Feisty Lita Conway is saddled with a merely decorative role, as the neighbor's daughter. Radio comedian Cousin Herald Goodman takes an extended cameo of the overbearing-rube variety, and Max Terhune's ventriloquism is strategically deployed. Ray Corrigan played host to the shooting at Corriganville, his movie-location ranch at Chatsworth, California.

The *Range Busters* series entries for 1941 also include *Trail of the Silver Spurs*, *The Kid's Last Ride*, *Tumbledown Ranch in Arizona* (which see), *Wrangler's Roost*, *Fugitive Valley*, and *Tonto Basin Outlaws*.

Mercy Island

Republic Pictures Corp. • 1941

We had remembered this unusual Oscar-bait Republic as a merciless study of gathering madness amid desperate adventure. The rediscovery proves *Mercy Island* even crueler than memory had allowed, wallowing in the embittered irony of its title.

A big-game fishing party sets out from Key West. Aboard are a respected prosecuting attorney, Warren Ramsey (Ray Middleton); his wife, Leslie (Gloria Dickson); his friend Clay Foster (Don Douglas); the skipper, Lowe (Forrester Harvey); and a dockhand and guide known as the Kid (Terry Kilburn).

Bent upon pursuing one extraordinary fish, Ramsey causes the party to become stranded, with a damaged boat and no provisions. The island's lone inhabitant, Sanderson (Otto Kruger), proves helpful. Sanderson is a physician who had fled a mercy-killing conviction. Ramsey recognizes Sanderson, whom he had prosecuted, and proves so appreciative that he promises to clear the doctor's name.

Ramsey's erratic behavior reasserts itself. He becomes equally determined to see Sanderson executed, and to put the Kid in prison for harboring the fugitive. Clay slaps Ramsey. "You shouldn't have hit him," Leslie says. "Yes, I know—particularly with my open hand," Clay snarls.

Sanderson finally tells Leslie, "Who's to say where sanity ends and insanity begins? The borderline is as imaginary as the equator."

An alligator depletes the lagoon's supply of fish. The party saves itself from starvation by catching a huge grouper. Hoping to spare Sanderson, the others refuse to help Ramsey signal an airplane. Ramsey knocks Leslie down and tears away her dress, then attempts to stab Clay. The alligator kills Ramsey, and none too soon.

The dominance of Ramsey is played in grand style by Juilliard graduate and Chicago Opera baritone Ray Middleton. The deterioration of a brilliant mind makes for a confrontational experience seldom associated with the B-movie thrillers. It is an unusual touch of casting, in that Middleton cuts the tallest, most handsome, and most charismatic figure. He handles Ramsey's snarling dialogue and despicable scheming with thorough conviction. Ramsey seems affable at first, but he lets slip subtle signs of megalomania: he has an imperious manner of dealing with the local fishermen, and he develops an obsession with landing that one certain fish, to the exclusion of reason or concern for the common good.

After he suffers a head wound and his wife stitches it, Ramsey says, sardonically, "Well, there's a dutiful wife for you—in sickness and in health." Sizing up the situation, he notes, "Only 20 miles from civilization, and we might as well be struggling in the mud of the Eocene." He declares: "I'm going to be the greatest criminal attorney since Clarence Darrow." When Ramsey announces, "I can't afford to have it known I have an unfaithful wife," Leslie protests, "I have not been unfaithful to you in any way." He retorts: "Then let's say you've been merely disloyal." Ramsey's descent to the brute is accentuated by a repulsive scene in which he wolfs down the fat from a fish's carcass. After several years as a leading man in the more expensive dramas and musicals at Republic, Middleton moved along to stardom on Broadway.

The supporting players are suitably befuddled and horrified. Gloria Dickson delivers an outstanding show of patience and defiance. Otto Kruger anchors the situation in heroic decency as the homesick hermit. Forrester Harvey and Terry Kilburn provide helpful touches of coastal southern folksiness, emphasizing the near-exotic setting. Director William Morgan uses the semitropical background to solid dramatic effect, emphasizing the characters' ineptitude at dealing with nature.

The secondary menace is an unusually large and photogenic alligator, which solves the castaways' biggest problem in the most gruesome comeuppance the Production Code would permit: The gator charges after Ramsey, who is holding the hideous, dripping head of a fish, and after a splendid musical buildup and some horrendous screaming the saurian is seen feasting upon what remains of the madman.

Camera chief Reggie Lanning, regarded by Republic chief Herbert J. Yates as the studio's finest resident artisan, brings the location to life with ultra-sharp images in which a judicious use of filters sharpens the tones and textures of sand, sea, sky, and faces. The gorgeous underwater sequences were filmed at Silver Springs, Florida—the same location where the celebrated swimming scenes of MGM's *Tarzan Finds a Son!* had been shot in 1938. Some process-projection shots were made at Studio

City, but the visual soul lies in the natural scenic values and the glimpses of wildlife—the gigantic black grouper, birds, alligators, and sea snakes—whose appearances are intercut with Ramsey's crazed actions.

Republic's musical director, Cy Feuer, and fellow composer Walter Scharf put some of their best efforts into *Mercy Island*, extending to the use of a stirring choral refrain for the finale. The score received an Academy Award nomination.

Jungle Man

Producers Releasing Corp. • 1941

Clarence "Buster" Crabbe was a robust and athletic 34 when he played *Jungle Man*'s intellectualized variant upon Tarzan—a distinguished physician attempting to defeat a plague among the tribes of Africa. In addition to developing a serum, Crabbe finds himself obliged to rescue a spoiled-brat heiress (Sheila Darcy) from lions, trek from village to village on a grueling errand of mercy, and dive into a roiling mass of sharks in order to retrieve a cargo of medicine from a shipwreck. The ordeal is as tedious for Crabbe's Dr. Hammond as it is for the viewer who attempts to stick with it.

The going is sluggish if not more so, what with stock-footage padding accounting for easily half the running time and a severe lack of narrative tension and shock value from director Harry Fraser. Championship villain Charles Middleton, slumming for the sake of a payday, has an odd role as a priest whose pet tiger proves not entirely domesticated. Crabbe is better than the picture deserves, but at least he manages to steal Darcy away from her photographer fiancé (Weldon Heyburn). One can only hope that her various ordeals have made her a less self-centered and more honorable human being.

The Devil Pays Off

Republic Pictures Corp. • 1941

Forgotten tough guy William Wright plays a disgraced navy man who finds a backhanded shot at redemption in this convoluted tale of a ship-hijacker's hijinks, augmented with adulterous treacheries and dope traffic. *The Devil Pays Off* catches director John Auer at a peak of accomplishment though stranded in the Cheapskate Studio Zone.

Chris Waring (Wright) feels insulted to learn that the navy wants him on duty for his reputation as a playboy. A shady shipping magnate, Arnold DeBrock (J. Edward Bromberg), has a wife of loose morals, Valerie (Osa Massen), who might prove vulnerable to an undercover sting.

Waring invites a strange woman to his shipboard cabin—only to find Joan Millard (Margaret Tallichet), secretary to the admiral in charge, waiting there and pretending to be Mrs. Waring. The mystery woman identifies herself as Valerie DeBrock and leaves in a huff.

A rescued castaway proves to be Captain Jonathan Hunt (Charles D. Brown), who had rebelled against DeBrock. A menacing Captain Brigham (Ivan Miller) and his shipboard doctor (Ronald Varno) attempt to drug Hunt into talking; Hunt is ordered slain. Brigham consigns a coffin to the depths—but Waring has secretly rescued Hunt.

The betrayals, beatings, befuddlements, and beratings pile up with lifelike randomness, peaking when DeBrock is confronted by

Hunt—whom he mistakes for a ghost. DeBrock at length maneuvers himself into a fatal fall, closing the case now that the misappropriated seagoing vessels have been accounted for. Along the meandering way, Waring and Joan have fallen in love.

Transgressions are well deployed among a sadistic J. Edward Bromberg, snarling thug Ivan Miller, and eager-to-please henchmen Martin Kosleck and Roland Varno.

Osa Massen is alluring and enigmatic, and Margaret Tallichet is quite good as Wright's stalwart romantic interest. Wright's heroism is convincingly reluctant, but once he rises to the occasion he stays for the duration. Abner Biberman takes a strong turn as a secondary hero, a Cuban military intelligence agent in disguise as a deckhand.

I Killed That Man

K-B Productions • Monogram Pictures Corp. • 1941

Phil Rosen's *Devil's Mate* is one of the jewels of the Depression-era stretch of *Forgotten Horrors*, a work of such cold ferocity as to defy improvement. Rosen gave it another go, all the same, with this worthy formal remake.

Screenwriter Henry Bancroft efficiently reworks the original script by Leonard Fields and David Silverstein. Structure and exposition are retained intact—from the murder by poisoned dart of a condemned killer (Ralf Harolde) within the execution chamber through the unmasking of the culprit (George Pembroke, of *The Last Alarm*) as a candidate for responsible office. The creepy benchmark developments, too, remain, such as the discovery of a cigarette holder that might have been used as a blowgun, and the planting of a contaminated spike in an automobile's horn.

The revelation of George Pembroke as the perpetrator comes as less of a surprise than that of squeamish Hobart Cavanaugh in *Devil's Mate*—or maybe that goes only for those familiar with the source-film. Cavanaugh, of course, was by now identified with ill-balanced characterizations. Many critics at large in 1941 hailed *I Killed That Man* as a thriller without precedent.

Ricardo Cortez steps ably into Preston Foster's role of a determined investigator. Joan Woodbury seems better prepared than *Devil's Mate*'s Peggy Shannon at taking care of herself during the desperate finale. The reworking is helped along in the exposition department by a generous running time of 71 minutes, but this one is hardly a match for its model in terms of meanness. Producers Maurice and Franklin King deploy higher-than-usual production values, which promised greater things ahead for Monogram as their King Bros. partnership settled into a steady berth at the studio.

Four Shall Die

a.k.a.: *Condemned Men*
Million Dollar Productions • Toddy Pictures • 1941

Dorothy Dandridge was poised for major-league stardom—which proved long in arriving—when she graced this eerie comedy about restless spirits and omens of doom. Encouraged by her mother, the stage-and-screen actress Ruby Dandridge, Dorothy had been performing since early childhood, first in a song-and-dance act with her sister, Vivian Dandridge. Dorothy cracked Hollywood at 24 with a notable bit part in the Marx Bros.' hit *A Day at the Races* (1937). Her busiest year over the long haul was 1941, which brought modest parts in *Lady from Louisiana* at Republic, *Sun Valley Serenade* at Fox, *Bahama Passage* at Paramount, and a showy romantic lead in *Four Shall Die*.

Four Shall Die is a black-ensemble piece from a studio of predominantly black ownership. The picture finds Dandridge in the role of an heiress, Helen Fielding, whose crooked former sweetheart (Jack Carr) plots to regain her affections and her fortune. A spiritualistic medium (Vernon McCalla) summons a disembodied voice foretelling doom.

Upon the apparent fulfillment of the prophecy, Helen's suitor (Johnny Thomas) falls under suspicion. No sooner have detective Pierre Toussaint (Pete Webster) and his boisterous helper, Beefus (Mantan Moreland), arrived, however, than another slaying is reported. One beneficiary prepares to leave the country on the medium's advice, but Toussaint establishes that the purported victims are alive—and awaiting the outcome of a scam to terrorize the heirs.

Its sheer scarcity is reason enough to take an interest in *Four Shall Die*, but the film is neither particularly well made nor original in concept. The credits show an overabundance of producers, suggesting a too-many-chiefs situation. Only Dandridge and Mantan Moreland would prove to possess that elusive element of star quality over the long haul. Moreland had already begun proving his worth at the larger, nearer-the-mainstream, studios. Dandridge's big breakthroughs, despite steady work all along, would have to wait until *Carmen Jones* in 1954 and *Porgy and Bess* in 1959. By 1960, she was among the world's most popular film personalities but died by her own hand after losing a fortune in an oil-investment scam.

Mr. District Attorney in the Carter Case

a.k.a.: *The Carter Case*
Republic Pictures Corp. • 1941

More a matter of selfishly motivated amateur sleuthery than formal investigation, this second entry in a radio-derived series (see: *Mr. District Attorney*) is noteworthy for its outlandish means of extracting clues from what Smiley Burnette, a busy sidekick and comedian in an entirely different class of Republic productions, would have called "one of them ol' dead corpses." The film also pitches a convincing argument that Franklin Pangborn—the movies' finest prissy meddler and a favorite foil of W.C. Fields—was possessed of a range broader than persnickety comedy.

Assistant DA P. Cadwallader Jones (James Ellison, picking up where Dennis O'Keefe had left off) tackles the murder of Elliott Carter (Bradley Page), a celebrity-gossip publisher, by railroading the likeliest suspect, Andrew Belmont (John Eldredge), into a death sentence. The evidence establishes that Carter had seduced Belmont's wife, actress Joyce Belmont (Lynne Carver), and that Carter's associate, Charley Towne (Pangborn), had seen Belmont confront the victim shortly before the slaying.

Jones' fiancée, reporter Terry Parker (Virginia Gilmore, taking the place of Florence Rice), is demoted for filing a premature report of acquittal.

Otto Strucker (John Bleifer), whose company prints Carter's *Society Spotlight* magazine, telephones Terry with a promise of new evidence. She finds Strucker murdered, lying against a press containing metallic fragments of a typeset article involving Carter and Mrs. Belmont. Terry learns that Carter had withdrawn a hefty sum from his business account without Towne's authorization. Jones agrees to reopen the case, demanding that Terry stop her meddling. She promises but reneges by calling on Joyce Belmont—who winds up croaked.

Vincent Mackay (Douglas Fowley), one of Joyce's more persistent admirers, comes out of hiding to explain his situation to Terry. He had known that Strucker was printing an article that could have been

used to blackmail the actress; the anonymous blackmailer must be the killer. Because Strucker had fallen against the type form, the text may have been pressed into his flesh. Mackay and Terry visit the morgue and find the account imprinted upon the corpse—along with the name of Charlie Towne. No sooner has Terry passed this information along to Jones, than Towne traps her and Mackay, glibly admitting to the murders and herding them out to be killed. Jones and a police squadron arrive in time to perform a rescue and nab Towne.

Pangborn gives a splendidly cold-blooded reading of the vengeful businessman. His snarling arrogance when exposed comes as a revelation—not merely to the plot, but also to all those who picture the actor chiefly in light of his many portrayals of flustered bureaucrats, floorwalkers, hotel managers, and general-purpose fussbudgets over a 30-year career. Even the studio's press materials made a fuss of this change-of-pace for Pangborn, but like ZaSu Pitts, another capable dramatic player who became too good at the fidgety mannerisms, Pangborn was typecast for the long haul.

James Ellison and Lynne Carver make an appealingly combative pair. Carver—fresh from a well-received appearance in the southern gothic *Swamp Water*—nudges the investigation along with an impetuous manner and a willingness to venture into dark places that Ellison's snooty Ivy League prosecutor would likelier shun. Douglas Fowley serves an admirably heroic function, as a star-struck type who helps to seize upon the grisly clue in the morgue. The movies have used autopsies, séances, and re-animation as a means of making the dead relinquish their secrets, but this may be the only time that a printer's block of cold type, pressed into a cadaver, has yielded a solution.

Essential grisliness aside, however, *Mr. District Attorney in the Carter Case* packs a wealth of breezy comedy, thanks to Eddie Acuff's portrayal of a brash photographer, and to crisp dialogue throughout. Old-timer Paul Harvey, whose career in film dated from the nickelodeon days, is impressive as the senior district attorney. Director Bernard Vorhaus, a German who had worked extensively in England, was as adept with comedy and sentimental fare (including the forcibly wholesome *Dr. Christian* series) as at suspense; his Hollywood career ended in 1951, when the House Committee on UnAmerican Activities branded him a Communist.

And herewith, the most ephemeral and compelling scrap of Hollywood trivia ever to cross our desks: *Mr. District Attorney in The Carter Case* accounts for the 145th appearance of a life-sized dummy named Oscar—sturdiest and most versatile of the many effigies that Republic used to represent corpses. Oscar was a creation of Howard and Theodore Lydecker, who ran Republic's first-rate workshop for hand-wrought special-effects properties.

Forgotten Horrors of 1942

The Strange Holiday of
This Precious Freedom

(General Motors • Sound Masters • Elite Pictures • Mike J. Levinson • Producers Releasing Corp. • 1942)

Present-day viewers of this bold patchwork curiosity, *Strange Holiday*, have noted a resemblance to some *Twilight Zone* television episode, what with its Kafkaesque attitude of disorientation and persecution and its air of humanistic righteousness. Rod Serling would have approved, for *The Twilight Zone*'s mastermind owed much to radio pioneer Arch Oboler. Oboler's NBC-Radio series, *Lights Out*, proved a decisive influence upon Serling—and more so upon Serling's much later *Night Gallery*—and *Strange Holiday* derives from an Oboler broadcast called *This Precious Freedom*. The tale concerns a returning vacationer's discovery that America has been taken over by a foreign oppressor.

The history of *Strange Holiday* is as unusual as the film itself: The 1940 airing of *This Precious Freedom*, starring Raymond Massey, had caught the attention of a General Motors executive, Paul Garrett. Garrett arranged to finance a movie version, which at one point was to have been called *Terror on Main Street*. Like most manufacturers, the automotive company made films for showing to its employees, but these were by-and-large training and motivational items. *This Precious Freedom* would be different: Garrett intended a morale-booster entertainment for GM's home-front workforce.

Oboler was enlisted to write, produce, and direct, and a nontheatrical studio-laboratory, Sound Masters, Inc., of New York, handled the processing. Garrett appointed himself supervisor. The casting tapped marquée names—unusual among the institutional-industrial movie-making sector—including Claude Rains, Gloria Holden, Milton Kibbee, and perennial villain Martin Kosleck. Accounts vary as to whether the featurette clocked in at 20 minutes or 40 minutes; we viewed a 20-minute version during the 1960s. *International Photographer* magazine reported that "thousands of General Motors war workers and their families" were treated to screenings. Sensing a broader popular appeal, MGM acquired the film but then allowed it to languish.

Bigger developments, and bigger disappointments, lay in store: In a slow-moving process of strategy, Oboler and Rains struck an arrangement with the low-budget producer A.W. Hackel (a steady source of matinée westerns, and a *Forgotten Horrors* mainstay) and his partners, Max King and Edward Finney. Together, they formed Elite Pictures Corp. as an *ad hoc* studio that would take *This Precious Freedom* off MGM's neglectful hands and expand the film. (Oboler had an inside track, having co-written MGM's anti-Nazi epic of 1940, *Escape*, and having directed the psychological thriller *Bewitched* at MGM during 1944.)

The embellished version of *This Precious Freedom* (rechristened *Strange Holiday*, in a bid for broader popular appeal) is a mess, and so was the attempt at theatrical distribution.

John Stevenson (Rains), a victim of torture, recalls a carefree existence. A flashback establishes Stevenson as a devoted family man, fed up with the turmoil of wartime. John and a friend, Sam Morgan (Kibbee), take a vacation in an unpopulated area. Morgan becomes homesick after three weeks, but Stevenson insists upon staying—then agrees to return after he remembers his wedding anniversary. Stranded after their aeroplane develops mechanical problems, the men approach a farmer, who seems afraid to talk to them.

Stevenson pays an apprehensive trucker for a ride into town. The locale seems all but abandoned. The residents he encounters will speak only of "the way things are," without explanation. Stevenson's family has vanished. Attacked by hoodlums and rendered unconscious, Stevenson awakes in a cell and complains of the violation of his rights. His cellmate, a philosophical black man (Thaddeus Jones), explains vaguely that some intruding force has eliminated constitutional liberties.

Stevenson is given the third-degree treatment by a figure of harsh authority (Kosleck), who demands in a German-accented snarl that Stevenson must explain himself. Stevenson protests that he has nothing to do with any resistance movement. Beyond a brief reunion with Stevenson's wife (Holden), the examiner allows no quarter. Stevenson is informed that general complacency had allowed a new order to take charge. Stevenson vows to become a freedom fighter—at which point, he wakes at the campsite and tells Morgan that they must return home.

The Hollywood Reporter announced in early 1944 that new scenes were being filmed to reflect what the trade paper called "recent events." The new shooting, re-editing, and rechristening were completed within a year, and in March of 1945 *Daily Variety* announced that Elite was on the hunt for "a major distributor" for *Strange Holiday*. No such luck: the minor-league distributor Mike J. Levinson took possession of the film and opened it only sporadically after showings in New York and Los Angeles during October of 1945. A year later, *The Hollywood Reporter* ran a notice that Producers Releasing Corp.—now in need of product "to fill in for the lapse in production plans brought on by the organization of Eagle-Lion [Films]"—had agreed to distribute *Strange Holiday*.

The troubled little picture deserved smarter handling. But then, Oboler's story also had deserved a more painstaking transformation. The avoidance of explicit references to Nazi Germany may have been merely disingenuous in the 1942 filming, but that omission becomes a case of intellectual dishonesty in the footage created during 1944–45. Oboler's Jewish birthright should have asserted itself. Even Columbia Pictures' overtly humorous Three Stooges—Yiddish intellectuals first and no-holds-barred slapstick artists second—had made a point of razzing Nazi Germany. Continuity problems are damaging, as well: *Strange Holiday*'s dialogue refers to a state of war here, a postwar setting there.

Claude Rains' anguished performance is as fine as anything the great actor ever did. Martin Kosleck matches Rains for intensity as a mannered sadist. Gloria Holden is an impassioned wonder as Rains' wife, her presence varying from devotion to careworn brokenness.

Thaddeus Jones, in a movie debut that should have led somewhere better, is effective as Rains' cellmate; the casting of a black player is unusually progressive, typical of Oboler. Jones followed through with small appearances in Oboler's *The Arnelo Affair* and Robert Z. Leonard's political drama *B.F.'s Daughter* (1947–48) before quitting the profession.

Oboler's greater fortunes lay in radio, but he reserved the right to take on the occasional movie project, favoring offbeat subject matter and novelty gimmicks. He contemplated the collapse of civilization in *Five* (1951), helped to advance the use of three-dimensional cinematography with *Bwana Devil* (1952), and satirized the dehumanizing threat of television in *The Twonky* (1953). For an early-1960s record album called *Drop Dead! An Exercise in Horror!*, Oboler retooled several of his radio scripts in a beautifully designed wide-stereo mix. Oboler died in 1987.

Private Snuffy Smith's Hillbilly Blitzkrieg

Capitol Productions • Monogram Pictures Corp. • 1942

If it should seem weird that two slapstickers based upon a big-nose/big-foot comic strip should surface on a *Forgotten Horrors* playbill, then consider: *Forgotten Horrors* is about weird choices, foremost. The process is hardly any simple matter of belaboring the obvious.

Weirdness comes no weirder than the matched set of *Private Snuffy Smith* and *Hillbilly Blitzkrieg*. *Private Snuffy*'s semblance of a plot contains the science-fictional notion of an invisibility potion. *Blitzkrieg* takes the peculiarities to *Suicide Squad* lengths.

Yes, and *Blitzkrieg*'s rocket-borne finale foreshadows explicitly the deranged hilarity of Slim Pickens' missile-straddling climax in *Dr. Strangelove or: How I Learned To Stop Worrying and Love the Bomb* (1964), the last word in Cold War satire. The influence is patent, whether or not Stanley Kubrick might ever have acknowledged such a lowbrow muse. *Strangelove*'s author, Terry Southern, of course, made no bones about his overriding fondness for the seamier side of the popular culture. It bears mentioning, too, that Lou Costello, the Three Stooges, and Lum & Abner also mounted the occasional misguided missile. (The image came full circle in 1986 when set designer Cary White installed a skeletal Slim Pickens, bareback on a doomsday bomb, among the background scenery of Tobe Hooper and Kit Carson's *The Texas Chainsaw Massacre Part 2*.)

The *Snuffy* films, not to say *snuff* films, are enumerated herewith:

Private Snuffy Smith. Smith (played by Bud Duncan) is a backwoods moonshiner who originated as a supporting character in the newspaper cartoon *Barney Google*, created in 1919 by Billy DeBeck and long carried on (into the 21st century), though ultimately without DeBeck's epic sense of philosophical absurdity. The character of Barney Google, a hard-luck high roller, has long since been overshadowed by the upstart supporting player Snuffy Smith.

Snuffy and his boisterous wife, Lowizie (a.k.a. Loweezy), were ripe for the movies by 1942, for backwoods comedies had become quite the rage. *Grand Ole Opry* stalwart Roy Acuff pursued a movie career, the music-and-comedy trio of the Weaver Bros. & Elviry had a popular series at Republic, and Chester Lauck and Norris Goff had parlayed their hick-town radio program, *Lum & Abner*, into a string of sentimental chucklers distributed by RKO-Radio Pictures.

Edward Cline's *Private Snuffy Smith* opens as Snuffy, weary of a constant struggle with a revenue agent named Cooper (Edgar Kennedy), develops a hankering to join the army. Disqualified for being too short, and appalled to learn that Cooper is now a sergeant, Snuffy nonetheless becomes the camp's yardbird, or janitor. He is accompanied by an invisible dog, rendered thus by a liquid concocted by Lowizie.

Had more been made of the invisibility angle, and less of a routine sabotage plot, *Private Snuffy Smith* would be a more rewarding picture. There are treats to be had, nonetheless, in the jovial antagonism between bulb-nosed Bud Duncan and grouchy Edgar Kennedy and in a boondocks war-games exercise that turns comparatively serious. Lowizie (an ebullient Sarah Padden) captures a gang of Axis troublemakers after all else has failed. *Private Snuffy Smith* was intended as a comeback vehicle for the diminutive Duncan, who had been absent from the screen since the *Ham 'n' Bud* comedy-team pictures of the prior decade. The series-in-miniature of *Snuffy* and *Hillbilly Blitzkreig*

led only to a lasting obscurity for Duncan; the pictures, acquired by Monogram from a production company even smaller, were given the sparsest of provincial distribution.

Hillbilly Blitzkrieg, a.k.a. *Enemy Round-Up*. Snuffy Smith (Bud Duncan) develops a rivalry with his blowhard sergeant (Edgar Kennedy), who in civilian life had demolished many of Snuffy's moonshine stills. Snuffy's cousin, Barney Google (Cliff Nazarro), shows up as an investor in a radio-controlled rocket system. A Nazi spy (Nicolle Andre) poses as a potential romantic interest for Snuffy or the sergeant, whomever succumbs first to her wiles. A rocket scientist (Lucien Littlefield) gets plastered on Snuffy's thousand-proof whiskey and designs an improved distillery. The Nazis mistake the drawings for the rocket's blueprints. The misadventure peaks—twice—with a bareback missile ride for Snuffy Smith, and then an encore with the sergeant. Slim Pickens has nothing on these uniformed yokels. Roy Mack directs for full measure of rambunctious absurdity.

Law of the Jungle

Monogram Pictures Corp. • 1942

Mantan Moreland raises this Third Reich-vs-Third World adventure well above the ordinary. Arline Judge is no slouch, either, as an entertainer who has been manipulated into helping the Axis. The story, too, sends an African tribe to the rescue in an inversion of stereotype.

Nona Brooks (Judge), whose treacherous boss, Simmons (Arthur O'Connell), has implicated her in the slaying of a British agent, has become lost in the bush country. She encounters explorers Larry Mason (John King) and Jefferson Jones (Moreland). Simmons has begun spreading rumors about Nona; Mason shelters her on condition that she must make herself scarce the following morning.

Stashed in Nona's clothing are papers from the slain Englishman. Nazi agents (Victor Kendall and Feodor Chaliapin) kill Simmons and pursue Nona. Mason begins to comprehend her plight, but his bearers are slain by tribesmen in the employ of the Germans. Mason, Jeff, and Nona take refuge in a cave littered with human remains; they hide the documents in a skull. The warlike tribe captures them, but Jeff saves the day, taking advantage of the kindnesses of a native woman who has developed a crush on him. Jeff and the chief discover that they are lodge brothers. Larry and the chief capture the Nazis.

Jean Yarbrough brings an almost impatient sense of timing to *Law of the Jungle*, dwelling primarily on Moreland's showcase scenes. The director and the show-stopping comedian had worked together to

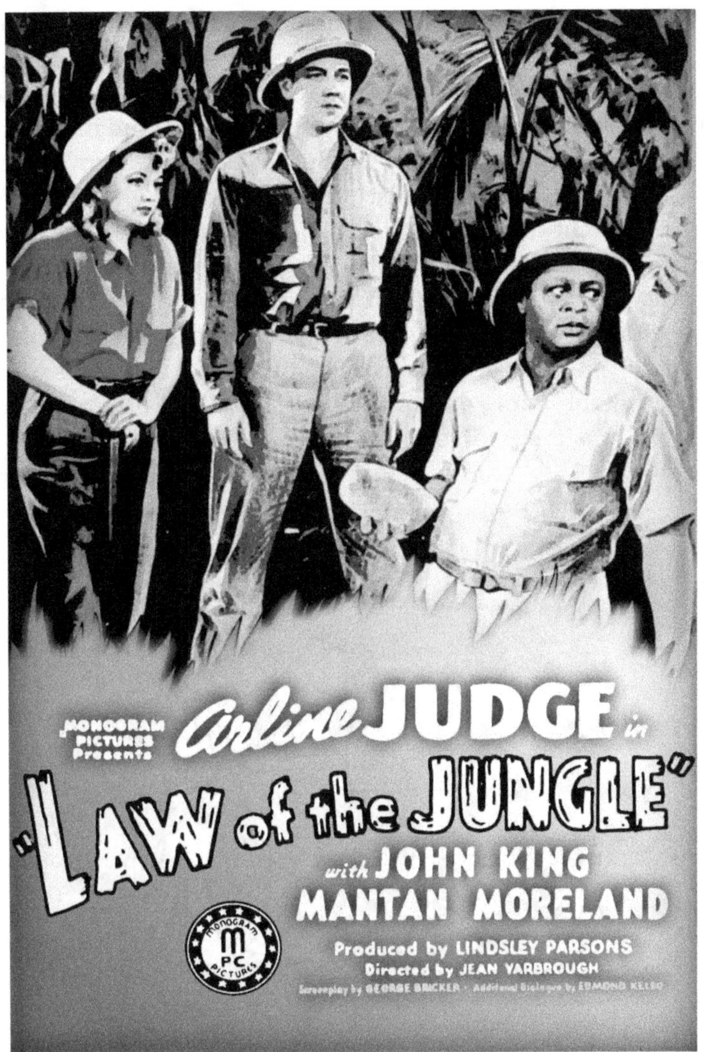

sharper advantage in *King of the Zombies*, but this one makes a nice incidental companion-piece to that essential picture. The cave-of-bones sequence is suitably eerie.

Lucky Ghost

(Dixie National • Consolidated National Film • Toddy Pictures • 1942)

The team of Moreland & Miller followed through on *Mr. Washington Goes to Town* with this more literally supernatural entry. Producer Jed Buell planned seven such titles, but got only as far as *Professor Creeps* (coming right up). Mantan Moreland's solo career took prior claim, and he wound up as both a long-term contract player for Monogram Pictures and a busy character man at most of the major studios.

Moreland and Flournoy E. Miller are in their Negro vaudeville element as career loafers Jones and Jefferson, who land in a posh sanitarium run as a gambling den by Dr. Brutus Blake (Maceo B. Sheffield) and his partner, Blackstone (Arthur Ray). Blake's ghostly ancestors convene to lament their having left so grand a place to such a wastrel. The spirit of Uncle Ezra (Henry Hastings) proposes to throw a scare into Blake. Ezra arrives just after Washington and Jefferson have won the establishment in a game of dice; the pals run the place just as crookedly, and the ghosts lay siege while Blake and Blackstone plot to regain control. Ezra confronts Blake while the other spirits send Washington and Jefferson packing.

The slight story benefits from a brisk telling—three prints viewed range from 50 to 68 minutes—and from the wisecracking joviality of Moreland & Miller. Henry Hastings makes a severe lead ghost, and burly Maceo Sheffield is fine as the badman in charge. The primitive special effects lend a stage-play sensibility; a piano-playing skeleton accounts for the closing gag. *Lucky Ghost* has been acknowledged by Sherman Hemsley as an inspiration for the oddball comedy *Ghost Fever* (1984–87), which features Luis Avalos and Hemsley as cops who encounter an absurd haunting.

Professor Creeps

Hollywood-Dixie National • Consolidated National • Toddy Pictures • 1942

"Our modern generation knows very little of the old minstrel show..., but we must give it credit for being the father of America's stage comedy and the element which promoted vaudeville," wrote producer Jed Buell in the press materials for this Moreland & Miller gem. "The natural wit and fun of the Negro [were] personified in these minstrel shows, as the Negro is a natural-born comedian and entertainer. ... For more than a century..., the humor of the Negro...was recognized as the essence of show business. ... We are trying to recapture...the true value of the old minstrel show and to put it into modern dress."

Its honky-fied condescension notwithstanding, Buell's appeal to the critics bespeaks a heartfelt sympathy with the very style he was exploiting in such pictures as *Mr. Washington Goes to Town*, *Lucky Ghost*, and *Professor Creeps*. Although Buell insisted that *Professor Creeps* "was not...designed for Negro [theatres] alone," still it was black America that gave the picture a persistent resilience in reissues into the 1950s.

"Yes, it's a genuine cure for the wartime blues," wrote *The Pittsburgh Courier*'s Herman Hill, a pioneering civil-rights journalist who had taken to task many black-ensemble pictures for what he called "age-old *Amos 'n' Andy* business" and "dialected dialogue." Reporting from the southcentral Los Angeles premiere for a mixed black-and-white audience, Hill raved: "Previewed in typical Hollywood fashion Thursday night at Sepia Town's leading theatre..., Jed Buell's latest opus starring gawky F.E. Miller and button-eyed, ground-hoggish Mantan Moreland, [the] Mutt & Jeff of the cinema, all but convulsed the crowd with laughter."

Yes, well, and of course, the "age-old *Amos 'n' Andy* business" is nonetheless abundant in *Professor Creeps*—and such humor was an established black style before the white-guy talents behind *Amos 'n' Andy* appropriated the *shtick*—but the film's good-natured generosity with the scares and chuckles is undeniable.

Private eyes Washington (Moreland) and Jefferson (Miller) spend most of their time dodging the landlord (Maceo B. Sheffield). The workload at their agency—where a sign proclaims: "Carrier & Stool Pigeons Furnished"—allows time for snoozing. Washington dreams of a big case: Socialite Daffodil Dixon (Florence O'Brien) reports her boyfriend, Alexander (Clarence Hargrave), missing. Alexander is hardly the first to have vanished.

At the home of Daffodil's uncle, the mysterious Prof. Whackingham Creeps (Arthur Ray), the sleuths re-enact the circumstances. Prof.

Creeps can suspend gravity and change people to beasts. A disembodied voice—belonging to Alexander—announces that several of Daffodil's suitors have been transformed, along with a Japanese visitor whom the professor had imprisoned on wartime principle. Jefferson becomes a gorilla. The professor becomes a duck. An escaped circus gorilla joins the fray, and its handlers capture Jefferson by mistake. Washington wakes, having enjoyed all he can tolerate of the absurd dream.

Such unapologetic silliness earned high marks from *Box Office* and *Motion Picture Daily*, which characterized Moreland & Miller as "a sepia Abbott & Costello." Even the *New York Times* weighed in on a favorable note, likening title player Arthur Ray to "a dark-skinned Bela Lugosi" and noting of the L.A. premiere, "No Academy Award-winning production has ever received more enthusiasm." *The Hollywood Reporter* wrote: "It is a revelation to observe how Moreland, long regarded among the big three Negro comics in the industry, goes over with his own race." (The pre-eminent black comedians of the day also included Eddie "Rochester" Anderson and Willie Best.) *The Motion Picture Herald* likened *Professor Creeps* to *Hold That Ghost*, Universal Pictures' Abbott & Costello hit of 1941, and as though that weren't enough of a stretch, added: "Veteran William Beaudine's direction makes every foot of film count."

Such overzealous notices miss the finer point—which is merely that an able cast is having a good deal of fun with a silly story—but still it's nice to find a kind word written about William Beaudine, whose finer accomplishments of the silent-picture era had long since given way to amiable hackwork. The only nay-sayer on record was a humorless official of the Motion Picture Association's Production Code Administration, who challenged the film's original title.

Professor Creeps had been shot as *Goodbye, Mr. Creeps*. MGM had made the uplifting heartstrings-puller *Goodbye, Mr. Chips* in England in 1939. The Production Code's Carl E. Milliken warned that spoofs of important titles must be submitted for the approval of the iportant producers involved, and the First Amendment be damned. Another Code personage, Geoffrey Shurlock, replied that *Creeps'* standing as "an all-Negro picture" posed no threat to the eminence of *Goodbye, Mr. Chips*. Even so, Buell rechristened the film as *Professor Creeps*. To this day, many people know not whether to take the word *Creeps* as a noun or a verb, and some sources have recorded the title as *The Professor Creeps*. So is the professor a creep, or does the professor creep? Go figure.

Man with Two Lives

Monogram Pictures Corp. • 1942

The *Frankenstein* myth colors this cheap sham from A.W. Hackel's Monogram unit in fascinating but ultimately false ways. Still and all, *The Man with Two Lives* deserves better than *Variety*'s cavalier dismissal: "What a nightmare!"

The engagement party of Philip Bennett (Edward Norris) and Louise Hammond (Eleanor Lawson) turns grim with an argument between Dr. Clark (Edward Keane) and Prof. Toller (Hugh Sothern). Clark boasts of his attempts to resurrect the dead.

Psychologist Toller is but ill impressed. Much talk concerns the approaching execution of Al Panino, a notorious criminal. An automobile wreck proves fatal to Bennett, whose father (Frederick Burton) implores Clark to bring the youth back to life. The attempt takes place just at the moment of Panino's last gasp in the death chamber of a distant prison. (An influence is patent upon 1987's *Retribution*, a latecomer in the since-extinct grindhouse-horror genre.)

Bennett is revived, but his mind seems a blank. He grows increasingly antisocial and begins visiting Panino's old haunts—eventually taking over the Panino mob. At last, Clark is forced to take Bennett's restored life. Bennett suddenly wakes from the dream-state fugue that has gripped him since the automobile accident.

So much malice comes to flower that it is difficult to dislike *The Man with Two Lives*. Edward Norris establishes his genial socialite character

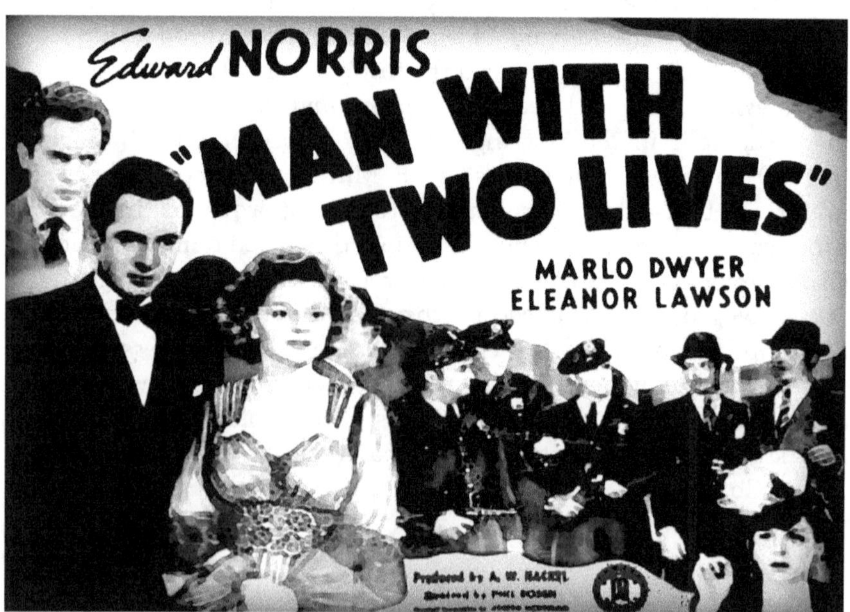

so efficiently that his resurrection and transformation make for some harrowing moments. Norris is equally effective as the criminal personality, especially in a deadly confrontation with the defunct mobster's former sweetheart (Marlo Dwyer) and in an ambush at a desolate warehouse. Director Phil Rosen makes much of Norris' underworld activities and his family's inability to comprehend what has happened. The abrupt ending is more than a cheat—it is a cold and reprehensible denial of a pleasurably dark fantasy.

Spy Smasher

Republic Pictures Corp. • 1942

The comics hero Spy Smasher, from the *Captain Marvel* funny-books' Fawcett Publications, had fostered a strong popular dislike for the congealing Axis powers by the time a movie incarnation began taking shape in November of 1941. Republic had nailed a shooting script days before the Japanese invasion of Pearl Harbor, and it was with a newfound sense of propagandistic ferocity that the serial went into production on December 22.

The movie takes smart liberties, providing Alan Armstrong, alias Spy Smasher, with a civilian twin—obliging Kane Richmond to handle three roles. A recurring villain, the Mask, is *un*-masked for the screen, allowing Hans Schumm a richer opportunity for characterization.

The story commences in bravura fashion: Spy Smasher finds himself captured in occupied France while uncovering a Nazi plot to undermine the American economy. Over the dozen chapters, Spy Smasher faces certain doom from a gasoline explosion, machine-gun and torpedo volleys, a flood, the crash of a futuristic flying machine, a descending elevator car, an industrial brick-cutting blade, a blast of steam, a collapsing tower, a comparatively mundane automobile crash, a factory's blast-furnace, and a headlong fall from a rooftop amid a hail of bullets. The costumed protagonist survives to receive an official big-deal medal for valor—although the story takes on a tragic resonance in the unexpected death of the brother.

Richmond makes not only an impressive costumed crimebuster, but a winning pair of guys in street clothes, as well. A sophisticated combination of split-screen shots and body-double casting leaves the impression that there are two Kane Richmonds on the scene. A strong romantic interest is Marguerite Chapman, a striking beauty who usually graced the B-unit productions of Columbia Pictures. Sam Flint makes a classy officer of naval intelligence.

Director William Witney departs here from serial-shooting tradition, handling the assignment solo rather than following the customary co-directors arrangement. Seventeen prior chapter plays had found Witney teamed with John English. The tactic of attaching two directors to one serial had become standard operating procedure in 1932 at Mascot Pictures (a forerunner of Republic), enabling one director to prepare for the next day's shooting while his colleague was on the set. Witney wrapped *Spy Smasher* in 38 days.

Typical of Republic is the magnificent variety of found industrial locations and natural scenery, including an imposing brick-making factory in Temecula Canyon—where Spy Smasher comes within an ace of being sliced into pieces. Set designers Russell Kimball and John McCarthy provided magnificent interiors that would have been right at home in some top-of-the-line picture from MGM. The Lydecker Bros., Howard and Theodore, delivered their usual astonishingly realistic miniatures and life-size properties, including a fantastic flying machine that figures in one of the more dazzling escape stunts.

House of Errors

Beaumont Productions • PRC • 1942

It is the unfortunate fashion to regard the pacesetting comedian Harry Langdon as a deserving casualty of both his own egocentric excesses and the talkie revolution, a has-been by 1928 who had estranged himself from an industry he had helped to invent. But Langdon also bestowed upon the early-talkie years a wealth of short subjects and feature-film assignments that the film snob elite has long ignored. The rediscovery of Langdon's late-in-life pictures—including this gem-in-the-rough called *House of Errors*—proves the artist to have kept himself prepared for a resurgence that should have happened.

Langdon was hardly just going through the motions. Bernard B. Ray's *House of Errors*, from Langdon's collaborative original scenario, is a brush with science fiction and hair-raising adventure that finds the childlike star player at 57 as generously amusing as ever, gifted with a piping, cartoonish voice that he uses to splendid effect. If Langdon's age tells—well, then, whose age does *not* tell?

Langdon and Charles Rogers play newspaper messengers who aspire to become reporters. Their opportunity comes via an eccentric inventor (Richard Kipling) who despises journalists. The chums find themselves in possession of a fantastic new species of machine gun, which must be kept out of the hands of munitions racketeers. No such caveat about keeping the weapon out of the hands of nincompoops, and of course Langdon winds up causing a disaster.

There is some welcome scary business during a storm. The lovely but fading Marian Marsh makes an appealing leading lady whose affections might even be reserved for Langdon—no fair giving away too much—and John Holland and Ray Walker score as villain and hero, respectively. The teaming with Charles Rogers is gratuitous; this one is Langdon's show, all the way.

Marian Marsh.

Langdon died of a cerebral hemorrhage three days before Christmas of 1944, having fallen ill while on assignment at Columbia Pictures.

The Panther's Claw

Motion Picture Associates • Producers Releasing Corp. • 1942

Fulton Oursler, longtime editor of *Liberty* magazine and popular novelist, had established the potential for a movie series in his tales of a stubborn police commissioner named Thatcher Colt, published under the pseudonym of Anthony Abbot. Columbia Pictures mounted two such pictures during 1932–33, *The Night Club Lady* and *The Circus Queen Murder*, starring Adolphe Menjou.

The first Columbia finds Colt thwarting an attack by gunfire, only to find his quarry slain by an eight-legged concealed weapon—a scorpion. The second pits Colt against a crazed aerialist (Dwight Frye) who fakes his demise in order to plot a leisurely revenge against his former wife (Greta Nissen). The climactic mad scene, in which Frye delivers a thrilling performance before taking a deliberately fatal fall, is a stunner. An intended third Columbia *Colt* never materialized.

Thatcher Colt's return to the screen at PRC Pictures—played now with grim efficiency by Sidney Blackmer—likewise sought a sequel but proved merely a self-contained coda, ill acknowledged, to the Columbias. From a creepy opening in a cemetery to the unmasking of a money-maddened criminal, William Beaudine's *The Panther's Claw* unspools as an engrossing murder-and-blackmail thriller.

Everett P. Digberry (timid Byron Foulger) is a show-business wig-maker—hardly the type to be arrested on charges of lurking about a graveyard after hours, but such is his lot. Colt and his resident Watson, Anthony Abbot (impersonated in the author's stead by Ricki Vallin), listen to Digberry's account of how he had been ordered to leave $1,000 among the tombstones under threat of blackmail by a character known as the Black Panther.

Other members of an operatic company, Digberry's employer, have received similar demands. A likely suspect is temperamental tenor Enrico Lombardi (Joaquin Edwards). The police catch Digberry in a lie. Digberry's pet cat had supplied a paw-print used on the blackmail notes. As Digberry hastens to explain himself, word comes that one of his neighbors has been murdered. The victim proves to be a disguised singer, Nina Politza (Gerta Rozan). Digberry is quick to remember threats made against her by both her former husband and Lombardi. A rival wigmaker (Frank Darien) turns up dead before he can shed any light, and yet Colt keeps an open mind as to Digberry's innocence or complicity.

The commissioner finds Nina's manager, Walters (Barry Bernard), responsible for the murders and a frame-up job against Digberry.

Digberry's involvement with Nina can only mean trouble when his vacationing wife returns. The *nebbish* takes solace, nonetheless, in a reward that Walters had posted as a smokescreen.

Unusually lengthy (at 72 minutes) for a PRC title, *The Panther's Claw* boasts a tangle of fascinating misdirection—not quite forcing judgment upon Byron Foulger while piling complications upon complications upon further complications. The revelation of Foulger as the mock-blackmailer is almost enough to seal his doom, and the unveiling of self-important Barry Bernard as the perpetrator comes at a breathtakingly late stage of the ordeal.

Why a series failed to materialize is nobody's choice and anybody's guess. Could be because of the absence of marquée names. Sidney Blackmer makes a fittingly stern Thatcher Colt. Foulger is surprisingly sympathetic as the squirmy liar whose deceptions mask his essential innocence. (The portrayal is remarkably similar to Foulger's satyristic Milquetoast in *It's All in Your Mind*.) Joaquin Edwards makes a menacing brute of a red herring.

The Anthony Abbot byline remained a moneymaker for Oursler. A much later Abbot anthology, *These Are Strange Tales* (1948), has become an acknowledged classic of crime journalism and offbeat raconteurism. Michael H. Price and Mark Evan Walker's prose-fiction adaptation of one of Abbot's nonfiction yarns, "Vengeance Rents a House," appears in the crime-and-horror anthology *Dark Borderlands* (2019). Oursler also had a hand in *The President's Mystery*, a multiple-author serialized novel for *Liberty* magazine, based upon an idea that Oursler attributed to Franklin D. Roosevelt. Republic Pictures filmed *The President's Mystery* in 1936.

Home in Wyomin'

Republic Pictures Corp. • 1942

Gene Autry had found a shortcut to Hollywood stardom in 1935 with a bit part in a frontier gothic, Ken Maynard's star vehicle *Mystery Mountain*, and an almost premature leading role in a science-fictional musical western, *The Phantom Empire*. No point in belaboring what we have covered about those films in previous chapters: the greater point is that, despite his increasing popular acceptance in lighthearted cowboy-crooner fare, Autry still occasionally indulged a taste for grimmer material of the sort that his martyred counterpart-turned-rival, Maynard, had preferred.

Such a dark delight is William Morgan's *Home in Wyomin'*, an ostensibly nostalgic piece of tuneful rustic Americana that pivots on a finely etched portrayal of paranoid malice by low-billed Olin Howlin.

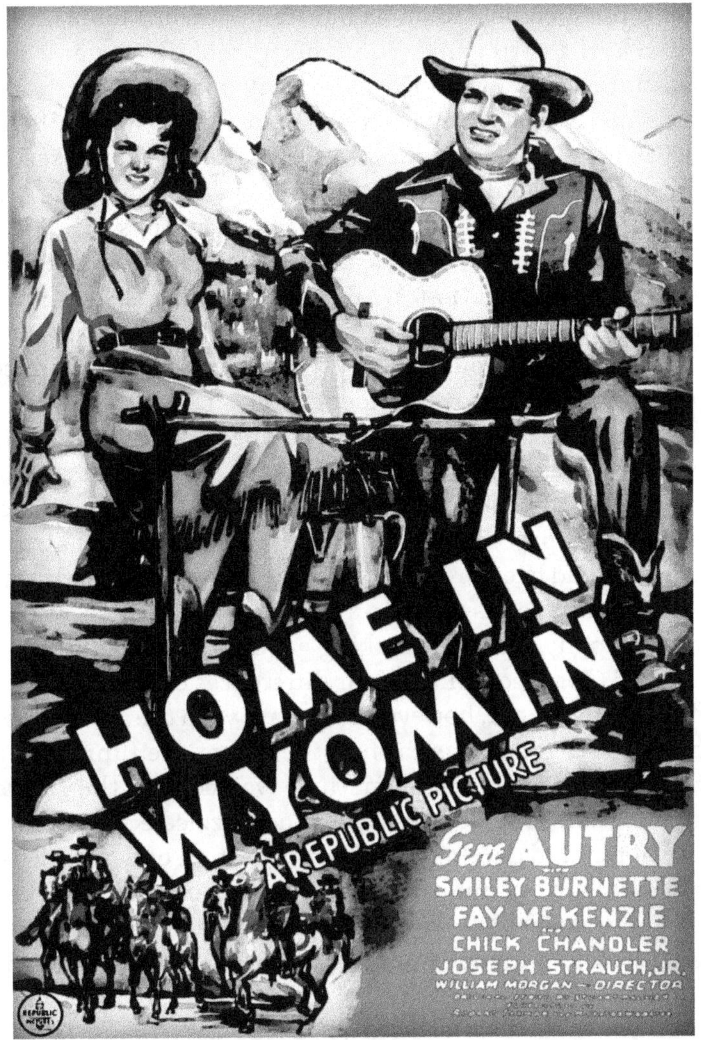

A breezy beginning befits Autry's image. The tale soon takes on a grimmer subtext: news photographer Clementine "Clem" Benson (Fay McKenzie) and reporter Hack Hackett (Chick Chandler) stalk the famous singing cowboy Gene Autry. Gene despises journalists, for their tribe has made a practice of giving him the razz in print. Gene is more concerned with the troubled fortunes of Pop Harrison (Forrest Taylor), a Wild West Exposition promoter who—according to the fiction of the script—had given Gene a break in show business. Pop's disreputable son, Tex Harrison (James Seay), is wrecking the troupe with his appetite for booze and gambling.

Clem and Hack bait Tex into a fight. Tex takes a beating and promises he will shape up. Hack follows three shadowy figures.

A crusty prospector known as Sunrise (Howlin) loses a pouch of gold to Hack in a card game. The other gamblers, Tex and the men Hack had trailed, seem troubled when Hack boasts that he is aware of the guests' questionable reputations. Their leader, who calls himself Crowley (George Douglas), is incognito mobster Luigi Scalese. Crowley orders his cohorts to kill Hack, who survives an ambush.

Hack is shot to death the following day during Tex's marksmanship show. Tex had been firing blanks, but someone had replaced the cartridges with live ammunition. While Gene and his pal, Frog Millhouse (Lester "Smiley" Burnette), attempt to clear Tex, Clem advises Gene of Hack's suspicions about Crowley. Pop is wounded upon receiving a telegram concerning Crowley's identity.

Sunrise leads Clem on a tour of the abandoned mining tunnels underlying the ranch. His eccentric manner becomes threatening by degrees, and finally Clem learns that Sunrise had killed Hack and opened fire on Pop because he feared they knew he had struck gold where the vein had been presumed barren. Gene arrives in time to save Clem. Sunrise falls to his death in a mineshaft.

All ends happily, with Tex making good on his promise to reform and Gene and Clem reconciling their differences on romantic terms. It is Howlin's performance, however, that stays with the absorbed viewer. The crazed miner might pass at first for one of the funny-old-geezer sidekicks who graced so many matinée westerns of the Depression and wartime years, but Howlin shades the grizzled eccentricities with subtle facial tics and darting eyes. The suggestion of dementia is casually dismissed at first, but director Morgan finds the character more haggard, more desperate, with each reappearance. Howlin suggests a redneck variant of Claude Rains—a Phantom of the Horse Opera.

The final confrontation, in a labyrinth as claustrophobically nightmarish as any stretch of the Paris Opera's catacombs, is a chiller. Camera chief Ernest Miller contrasts well Autry's lighthearted musical sequences and increasingly capable horsemanship with the foreboding gloom of a benighted rodeo where a killer ranges at large.

Autry and sidekick Smiley Burnette are as spirited as ever, although a brooding darkness colors Autry's portrayal of himself as a celebrity figure hounded by star-gawking gossip journalists—one of whom is killed off while the other becomes a love interest. Two varieties, no doubt, of wish-fulfillment fantasy: restrain the annoyances by any and all means.

Chick Chandler is in his element as the man who knows too much. Fay McKenzie shows gumption as the aggressive photographer. The question of whether George Douglas' incognito mobster will be railroaded is left dangling in the prints we have screened.

Well-paced musical sequences advance the story, but Autry's pre-recorded singing is not always in sync with his mouth. Irving Berlin's war-booster jingle, "Any Bonds Today?" (also used in a *Bugs Bunny* cartoon) débuts as a pitch for U.S. Defense Bonds. Donnell Clyde "Spade" Cooley, stuntman and fiddle-playing western-swing bandleader, appears among the musicians. Autry sings three standards-to-be—his own "Be Honest with Me" and "Tweedle-O-Twill," and the Carter Family's "I'm Thinking Tonight of My Blue Eyes"—and Smiley Burnette contributes a satirical novelty called "Modern Design." In a shortened version that Autry supervised for early-day mass-market television, several tunes were eliminated—leaving *Home in Wyomin'* looking altogether more forbidding than when it had graced the big screen.

The Mad Monster

Producers Releasing Corp. • 1942

"Producers turning out pictures for Producers Releasing Corp. do so on very low budgets," noted *Variety* in March of 1942, emphasizing that PRC's "rentals are proportionately less than for films from the majors." A cheaply acquired PRC production, though handicapped in terms of production values if not necessarily artistry, could ring the cash registers as surely as some prefabricated hit from the larger studios—if given sufficient general-audience ballyhoo along with the right push in the direction of its genre-attuned likelier customers.

A ticket to see something from PRC cost the same as a ticket to see the latest star-power extravaganza from MGM or Universal. The little studio's product required extra promotion as a consequence. Where the major-league releases required a hefty guaranteed percentage of box-office receipts, even the newest pictures from PRC could be had for a flat rental of $20 to $25 a day from Oklahoma City-based Adams Film Exchange, which represented many of the Poverty Row studios.

Such a PRC is Sigmund Neufeld's production of *The Mad Monster*, directed by Neufeld's brother, Sam Newfield, and boasting sufficient appeal in George Zucco to draw the very crowd that would turn out to see Zucco—or Bela Lugosi, or Lionel Atwill, or Boris Karloff, or Lon Chaney, Jr.—in practically anything, irrespective of studio pedigree. Today, the tactic of identifying a core group of enthusiasts and catering to them is known as niche marketing, but the practice thrived for generations before it received that highfalutin' name. Culturally and historically speaking, the approach is akin to the evangelistic charlatans' ploy of preaching to the choir in order to generate a frenzy that might lure curious outsiders. The pioneering film historian and lecturer William K. Everson was not joshing when he said, often and solemnly, "The cinema is my only religion," and he backed up that assertion with a missionary zeal.

For as any capable niche marketer (or tent-revival huckster, for that matter) will affirm, the practice is ultimately limiting unless coupled with an attempt to broaden that niche. No doubt some members of *The Mad Monster*'s built-in audience initiated friends into the pleasures of PRC's modest chillers—but it is just as certain that most of the theatres showing the film neglected to heed *Variety*'s advice about courting a more generalized trade.

Theatre managers are a peculiar breed, existing apart from normal humankind, and we mean that in the nicest way possible. The view from here is sympathetic as well as jaundiced: George Turner and Michael H. Price have a combined experience in the picture-show business that stretches from the 1930s into the 21st century, and they have observed movie exhibition at its best and its worst in the theatre-men of four generations. As a rule, the operators neglect to accept the self-evident truth that film is film, and they so compartmentalize their audiences that they lose sight of the fact that they have *only one audience*, a prospective audience that comprises everybody within shouting distance. Exhibitors have a contempt toward genre pictures—the very pictures that will draw the most loyal paying customers—and most movie-house operators from way-back-when to the here-and-now become as irritated with finding it needful to play a horror picture (or a western, or a space opera, or a black-exploitation melodrama) as they are delighted to watch the fans queue up and shell out.

This dichotomy reached a zenith in the summer of 1999, when thousands of managers cringed at the prospect of massed gatherings of fans, days in advance, for the opening of *Star Wars Episode I—The Phantom Menace*, even as they counted the inevitable hundreds of millions of dollars in paid admissions. George Lucas' intergalactic cash cow is an extreme example of niche marketing writ large, a phenomenon that can be traced all the way back to *Variety*'s good advice to push the enthusiasts' anticipation of a film beyond its likeliest customers. (Big openings are less meaningful in the present day, when one summer's blockbuster attraction is certain to become a stocking-stuffer DVD by Christmastime.)

Michael H. Price's uncle, the Texas theatre operator Grady L. Wilson, was among the few of the breed who looked forward to the next low-budget horror movie and took pains to court a general trade for such specialized fare. From the Depression years until his death in 1968, Grady ran his Interstate Circuit showplaces like the interim getaway resorts they were meant to be, and he especially relished the challenge of pitching a genre-bound movie to a wider range of customers.

After Wilson and his nephew had watched that very film on television one afternoon around 1960, he told young Michael:

> Y'know how we hooked 'em in for *The Mad Monster* down at the ol' Rialto? You can't depend on the advertisements to do more than just announce each new title as it comes along, and the critics are useless, more interested in showin' how snide they can be than in givin' their readers some usable information, except

George Zucco.

when they're suckin' up to some big-deal picture that they know they're *supposed* to get all gushy over.

Anyhow, what we did with *The Mad Monster* was this: we traded on the bigger audience's fond memories of a somewhat earlier picture called *Of Mice and Men*, and we announced it right there in the lobby and the auditorium that we had this picture coming up soon called *The Mad Monster*, and that it featured this dead-solid impersonation [by Glenn Strange] of Lon Chaney, Jr.'s performance in *Of Mice and Men*, plus a takeoff on Chaney's *Wolf Man* in the bargain. This is why theater managers should attend *all* the trade-show previews—not to decide whether they want to run the picture, but to understand what-all's coming out so they can deal with it. You've got no business selling a product if you haven't formed your own opinion of it.

Now, you may hear people say how they *hate* horror movies, but what they're really saying is that they *don't know how to watch* a horror movie—that they can't be bothered with givin' in to the scary business in the way that they'll give in to the exhila-ration of a romantic comedy or the excitement of a war picture. What it's *our* job to do, is to show people how every film they'll ever see ties in with every *other* film they'll ever see, and that whether or not they *like* this particular movie, it's gonna give them a stronger background for appreciating the films they *do* 'specially like. Now, *Mice and Men* and *The Wolf Man* are far and away the classier pictures, but this li'l ol' *Mad Monster* thing just shows you how lasting an impression Lon Chaney had made.

See, back in the 1940s, once a movie in the theatre had run its course, the odds were that you'd never get a chance to *see* it again. No television, and very few official reissues. So for the people who had enjoyed *Of Mice and Men* and expected never to see it again, well, a little throwaway like this *Mad Monster*, it gave 'em a chance to see this other actor do his takeoff on ol' Chaney. Chances are they didn't even like *The Mad Monster* on its own, but we pulled a better box office on it by appealing to that more generalized audience than we would have if we'd just plastered up the posters and run the ad in the newspapers.

Sam Newfield and his ensemble cast patently knew what they were doing in making *The Mad Monster* as a composite takeoff on Lewis Milestone's *Of Mice and Men* (1939) and George Waggner's *The Wolf Man* (1941), with a riff upon *Frankenstein* thrown in for good measure. PRC's publicists failed to pitch any exploitable connection, however, and the critics of the day were more concerned with their usual gratuitous bashing of horror movies than with noticing the cunning subtext of this superficially crude and over-obvious shocker.

Glenn Strange has scarcely the formidable dramatic presence of Lon Chaney, Jr., but Strange mimics the Chaney mannerisms well enough in portraying George Zucco's handyman as a slow-witted, compliant sort, with a ferocious scowl as needed. Where the tragedies of Lenny Small in *Of Mice and Men* and Larry Talbot in *The Wolf Man*, both soulfully portrayed by Chaney, capture a sense of existential doom, their curious amalgamation in *The Mad Monster* amounts to hardly more than an expendable plot device. Strange brings more to the role than is written, all the same: the burly Irish-Cherokee actor registers a persuasive anguish upon comprehending his place in Zucco's vicious scheme. It helps to remember that Strange and Chaney were great pals—and that, for years to come, Chaney would rib Strange about his Chaney-channeling *shtick* of *The Mad Monster.*

Zucco, second-billed after bland leading man Johnny Downs, is of course the crucial player. As a disgraced physician, banished from the academic realm for radical experimentation, Zucco troops through the outlandish revenge yarn with conviction, his luminous eyes and resonant baritone voice conveying both the depths of madness and an earnest indignation. The objective is to wake the beast in civilized humankind, and Zucco's means of doing so is a regimen of wolf-blood injections. Proof of his theories is no longer enough: having once proposed to present the War Department with an army of wolf-man soldiers, Zucco now will settle for doing away with the scientists who had forced his ouster.

After a trial run in which a transformed Strange kills a backwoods child, Zucco takes his servant along to confront the erstwhile colleagues. The campaign of vengeance proceeds agreeably until Zucco's rebellious daughter (Anne Nagel) nearly falls prey. Her news-reporter sweetheart (Downs) stalls Strange long enough for them to get away. The wolfman strangles Zucco while a fire sweeps through the scientist's rural southern mansion.

Plain production values serve *The Mad Monster* well, with an oppressive atmosphere in the imposing house, a fogbound and moss-draped swampland exterior, and an austere and eerily dressed laboratory. Zucco's impassioned emoting would be just as effective on a bare stage. Strange's transformations are elementary time-lapse dissolves, but effective enough in their static way. More impressive, and just as simply accomplished, is a long sequence where Zucco fancies himself embroiled in an argument with his former associates, who appear as ghostly figments of his imagination via deliberately transparent double-exposure photography.

Between the Acts: Incidentals

A few incidental discoveries to deepen the perspective:

- *Lure of the Islands* (Monogram, 1942). Robert Lowery and Guinn "Big Boy" Williams tackle Japanese infiltrators in Tahiti. Lowery uses a radio-beam device to cause an enemy aircraft to mistake a forested region for a landing strip, with cracking good crack-up results.

- *Scattergood Survives a Murder*, a.k.a. *Cat's Claw Murder Mystery* (Pyramid Pictures and RKO-Radio, 1942). The *Scattergood Baines* series stars lovable Guy Kibbee as a storekeeper in down-home New England. The pictures, based upon stories dating from 1920 in *American Magazine*, span 1941–43—a northerner counterpart to the deep southern *Lum & Abner* films. A *Scattergood* radio series, with Jess Pugh and Wendell Holmes (by turns) handling the title role, had originated in 1938 over the CBS Network.

  This fifth *Scattergood* film boasts a tale of ghastly savagery, involving a killer who does away with two elderly recluses (Margaret McWade and Margaret Seddon) in quest of an inheritance. The weapon of choice is the severed paw of a lynx, steeped in poison. (Cornell Woolrich's similarly concerned novel, *Black Alibi*, also arrived in 1942 and was adapted to film as Val Lewton's *The Leopard Man* the following year.)

  The perpetrator proves to be dependable Wallace Ford, playing both with and against the grain, by turns, of his familiar lovable wisenheimer image. Ford is rendered helpless by a faceful of dipping snuff, that favorite controlled substance of many a folksy down-easterner. The working title, *Cat's Claw Murder Mystery*, was restored for a reissue by Favorite Films. RKO's campaign emphasized the genial dignity of Guy Kibbee; the encore promotion touted a horrific essence.

  Another entry, 1941's *Scattergood Pulls the Strings*, pivots on a bygone murder case that has repercussions in the present day.

- *Jacaré*, a.k.a. *Jacaré, Killer of the Amazon* (Mayfair Productions & United Artists, 1942). The *jacaré*, a gigantic alligator-like caiman, menaces an expedition along the Amazon. Explorer Frank Buck entrusts the greater measure of the adventure to James Dannaldson and Miguel Roginsky.

Prisoner of Japan

Atlantis Pictures • Producers Releasing Corp. • 1942

Arthur Ripley weighed in as a director with this dire tale of cold-blooded agonies within a microcosm of World War II. As a vicious trifle, *Prisoner of Japan* serves admirably. As a foreshadowing of the doom-laden themes that Ripley would explore in detail in the Holocaust drama *Voice in the Wind* (1944), *Prisoner of Japan* is a revelation.

The islanders of Nukuloa know David Bowman (Alan Baxter) as a busy merchant and the husband of a Eurasian entertainer named Loti (Corinna Mura). In fact, Bowman is a prisoner in his own home under the secretive domination of a Japanese spy named Matsuru (Ernest Dorian), whom Loti serves as both consort and agent. Naval Ensign Bailey (Tommy Seidel), visiting on furlough, blabs the nature of his crew's mission to Loti, but she assures him that the information will go no further.

Toni Chase (Gertrude Michael), an American who runs a café on the island, seeks help to return to the United States, but Bowman seems aloof—even when informed of a threat to the American fleet off-shore. Matsuru gives himself away when he prevents Toni from transmitting a warning. Bailey's ship is destroyed. The ensign survives, but Matsuru orders his execution. Maui (Billy

Boya), a child who has given Bowman information about an escape route, is found murdered. David, finally moved to vengeful action, overpowers Matsuru with the help of Loti, whose loyalties have shifted.

While Bowman commandeers a hidden radio, Matsuru disposes of Loti. Raising no response from the cautious American convoy, David and Toni comprehend that they must order the U.S. ships to blast the island. Before Matsuru can break into the radio room, a bomb lands upon the compound—killing all concerned.

Bleakness seldom comes bleaker. Here can be seen the dire narrative influence of source-author Edgar G. Ulmer, himself a director of note and one of the more emphatic voices in *film noir*. The exception is often more interesting than the rule it tests, and this exception is exceptional. Every character of consequence meets with foul play. The clean-up scarcely matters: there is nothing left to clean up.

Ripley offers more than nihilism, however. Ernest Dorian, in his first assignment of a brief career, makes a grandly loathsome villain, cunning as well as ferocious. Alan Baxter, in the late-blooming heroic role, seems to have lost interest in whether he regains freedom—only to become an avenging force too late except in the matter of disposing of the saboteur. Though necessarily hurried, the wrap-up accommodates a gathering tenderness between Baxter and Gertrude Michael, just enough to render bittersweet their martyrdom.

Jungle Siren

Producers Releasing Corp. • 1942

Credit the Axis menace with an excuse, if not properly an inspiration, for the making of any number of indignant wartime films, such as Sam Newfield's *Jungle Siren*. Any excuse for two resolutely Yiddish brothers, Newfield and producer Sigmund Neufeld, to rout the Nazis, if but figuratively. High adventure makes for good Axis-buster propaganda.

Ann Corio also was an excuse to make *Jungle Siren*. Neufeld knew the former burlesque dancer would be a draw, even if cast in a routine underbrush actioner, and the prospect of seeing Corio cavorting in the wild was a sure-fire ticket-seller.

Such motivation can only have led to disappointment for the would-be oglers. *The Hollywood Reporter* lamented that "a handful of long shots...show the strip-tease queen swimming, but otherwise her display of epidermis is even less than one is accustomed to observing at the seaside." So *hmph*, already.

Not much excitement in the action department, either. Clarence "Buster" Crabbe, the embodiment of heroic protagonists from Flash Gordon and Tarzan to Sigmund Neufeld's version of Billy the Kid, is

a military officer tracking Nazis and tribal Fifth Columnists in Africa. Corio is a female Tarzan who has lost her parents to a renegade chieftain (Jess Brooks). Crabbe and Corio find romance almost in lieu of the desultory mayhem. The handsome leads are well cast for mush and mayhem, but too much of the former and too little of the latter make for a picture that drags when it should be getting on with a slight story.

A helpful subplot involves a German woman (Evelyn Wahl) who becomes fed up with the treacheries of her *sieg-heiler* husband (Arno Frey) and suffers as a consequence. A touch of bogus zombiism issues from bad tribesman Jess Brooks, who claims that he can return the dead to life; the purported croakers are in fact victims of poisoning, stirred by an antidote. The cornball finale finds Crabbe issuing a summons for armed personnel—and a chaplain, by the way, so that he and Corio can get hitched on the spot.

Tomorrow We Live

Atlantis Pictures • Producers Releasing Corp. • 1942

Ricardo Cortez, the movies' original Sam Spade and all-round suave leading man of the early talkies, had developed a lived-in face and an attitude of weary defiance by the time he tackled the role of a hellacious menace in Edgar G. Ulmer's *Tomorrow We Live*. Cortez' aspect foreshadows the mid-century aging of Humphrey Bogart (the movies' third Sam Spade) to suit the role of a similarly world-weary menace in *In a Lonely Place*, the tale of a prospective murderer on the verge of succumbing to the killing urge.

Tomorrow We Live is one rousingly warped gangster thriller. Persuasive to almost a supernatural extent and self-centered to the point of megalomania, Cortez' severe combination of villain and romantic lead seems so vastly larger than life that no conventional civilian identity would suit him: his character is known as the Ghost, so called within his isolated underworld domain because he has defied all attempts to destroy him. And who better to call such a bluff than an ordinary figure of grace and gumption?

The audacious extended confrontation between sophisticated evil and self-possessed common sense is as offbeat a piece as Ulmer ever delivered—in a career top-heavy with offbeat assignments. The film is, as fine a showcase for self-possessed arrogance as Cortez ever found.

Julie Bronson (Jean Parker) suspects dealings between her father, Pop Bronson (Emmett Lynn), and the Ghost. Pop's patch of the Arizona desert is a storage depot for the Ghost's hijacking raids. Julie visits the Ghost—and finds herself enchanted. He reveals himself as the owner of Pop's café and proposes a romantic arrangement to her financial advantage. Julie nixes the offer but remains attracted.

A waitress (Roseanne Stevens) warns Julie's former fiancé, Lt. Bob Lord (William Marshall), of the intrigues. Lord and Julie restore their engagement. The Ghost prevails against a rival mob. Julie snubs him. The Ghost threatens to reveal Pop's murderous past. An intrusion by two thugs (Rex Lease and Jack Ingram) forces Pop and the Ghost to join forces. To placate the Ghost, Jean rejects Lord.

Rivals torch the Ghost's nightclub and beat the Ghost nearly to death. The Ghost accuses Pop, and the men exchange gunfire. Pop is killed outright. The Ghost lives on long enough to hear Julie berate him. Julie decides to try another go at it with Lord.

The critical brethren as a class despised *Tomorrow We Live*. Among the more articulate hostilities were *Daily Variety*'s appraisal as "confusing to average minds" and *The Hollywood Reporter*'s assertion that the yarn "confuses itself beyond...analysis." The only confused souls here were the critics, their own self-important dimwit selves. No such bourgeois jackal intolerance, of course, has any business playing critic in the first place. Which is why journalism—especially that which professes to wield cultural authority—should be a licensed profession. Not bloody likely, of course.

Phantom Killer

Monogram Pictures Corp. • 1942

What few critics paid earnest attention to this small gem of a remake in its day, missed the point entirely by mentioning a purported uniqueness of plotting. *Phantom Killer* is, all the same, about as unique as a close copy can get, given its origins in one of the better independent shockers of the Depression years, Phil Rosen's *The Sphinx* (1933). William Beaudine directs the remake with brusque efficiency.

Not that the hidden-twin motif is all that groundbreaking an idea, to begin with, but the yarn is a treat in either version, an audacious

variation upon a timeworn theme. Where the story-and-screenplay credit goes to Albert DeMond on *The Sphinx*, Karl Brown is given as author and scenarist on *Phantom Killer*. What with Monogram's corporate ownership of the yarn, one can only suppose the studio could afford to have a short memory as to work-for-hire authorship.

The remake's finest touch is the casting of Mantan Moreland, Old Hollywood's most dependable and most underappreciated comedian, as a witness to the motivating crime. Luis Alberni had served the original in the equivalent role, but Moreland transforms an unnerving encounter into a concise showcase of artistry. Here lies the truer uniqueness of *Phantom Killer*: only his African ancestry kept Moreland from finding acclaim in his day on a par with that of W.C. Fields and the Marx Bros. A test of that truism is to see how sorely Moreland is missed after *Phantom Killer* has dismissed his character.

Prominent citizen John G. Harrison (John Hamilton, later to become Perry White on television's *The Adventures of Superman*) is on trial for murder. Harrison is deaf and mute, but his accuser (Moreland) swears that the killer asked him for a light and the time of day. The resulting humiliation drives ambitious prosecutor Edward Clark (Dick Purcell) to quit his job.

Moreland's seemingly effortless theft of the show comes in three stages. He reacts to the shock of finding a corpse by downing a quart bottle of booze in a guzzle. While studying mug shots at headquarters, he renders a desultory scene at once hilarious and poignant: "Well, *looka there*—High Pockets Johnson! I *wondered* what happened to him! Ol' High Pockets. He wasn't a *bad boy*, at that. He was *awful* good to his *mother*." In the courtroom, Moreland works the witness stand like a nightclub stage, trading in particular upon an almost musical ability to worry the syllables:

"Do you ever drink anything?" Moreland is asked under oath.

"Sho'. *Anything*."

"How much whiskey did you drink that night?"

"Not a *drop*."

"Now, think: That was six weeks ago. How can you be so sure?"

"Sure that I didn't drink any *whiskey*?"

"Yes."

"Well, *that* night, I was only drinkin' *gin*!"

No sooner is the case against Harrison dismissed, however, than such killings resume. The impaired big shot serves to establish an alibi while his speaking-and-hearing twin goes about a secretive family trade of murdering for money and vengeance. John Hamilton is scarcely a match for the scowling intensity of Lionel Atwill, his dual-role counterpart in *The Sphinx*, but Hamilton pulls off the masquerade with a somber dignity and accounts grimly for the disclosure of the brothers' secret. The sudden appearance of Hamilton-times-two, each with murder in mind, conveys the terror of the moment without recourse to tricky camera angles or extravagant lighting effects; the matter-of-fact presentation is enough.

Dick Purcell is fine as the determined prosecutor, and the delicious and assertive Joan Woodbury provides both a romantic function and a crucial narrative pivot as a newspaper reporter who endangers herself by taking a hand in the unraveling.

Warren Hymer is right in his element of tough-talking comedy as a hard-boiled detective who is also a henpecked husband, and old-timer Kenneth Harlan stands out as a ranking plainclothesman.

Beaudine juggles gracefully the desperate urgency, the broad comedy, and the bantering sweetheart business, moving things along briskly enough to sidestep the patent implausibility of the brothers' malicious scam.

The Devil with Hitler /
That Nazty Nuisance

Hal Roach Studos • United Artists • Favorite Films • 1942

Hal Roach, the popularly belovéd big-time producer who outlived most of his star players—even including many of the *Our Gang* young-sters—by many years, found himself reduced to a level nearer Poverty Row during the early 1940s. He had sold out some crucial trademarks (including the lucrative *Our Gang* franchise) to MGM, the big studio with which he had enjoyed a prestigious releasing deal. Much of Hollywood believed Roach had sold out to the very devil in 1937, in an ill-advised filmmaking pact with Benito Mussolini.

"Mussolini wasn't getting a *thing* out of it," Roach told us shortly after his 100th birthday in 1992. "That is, nothing but a fulfillment of his wish to see some Hollywood-calibre pictures made in Italy." Roach threw a party in Hollywood for the dictator. The movie capital's influential Jewish population objected to an extent that Roach found alarming.

"I mean, Mussolini wasn't particularly an anti-Semite, and I told him, going in, that I wouldn't have anything to do with him if he *was*," said Irishman Roach. "Because he *was* a Fascist, y'know. But I mean, it's like, Italy didn't even *have* anti-Jewish sanctions until Hitler imposed his Jewish problem on Italy. But I backed out on the deal as it became so plain that our simple artistic and commercial arrangement was creating an international stinkeroo."

Roach persisted with such big pictures as *Of Mice and Men* (1939) and *One Million B.C.* (1940), but his resources and his reputation had been so diminished that Roach became a low-budget operator merely to stay in the game. His *Streamlined Comedies* featurettes issue from this period—distinguished by a distribution deal with United Artists (and later with MGM), but afflicted with lesser production values and even briefer running times than those of the Poverty Row stalwarts PRC and Monogram.

Although the government commandeered many production facilities as World War II intensified, the Army Air Corps' occupation of Roach Studios was accepted as "a penance, I suppose you might say," by the boss. It was during this period, while two sound stages were crammed with immense relief maps of Japan and mechanisms for detailed photography, that Roach mounted a more creative penance in war-effort slapstick comedy: he called the centerpiece project *The Devil with Hitler*. A sequel, *That Nazty Nuisance*, arrived in 1943. We jump the customary chronology herewith to place the pictures in a sharper context:

The Devil with Hitler, a.k.a. *The Furious Phoney*. Roach's erstwhile colleague, Mussolini, comes in for a razzing alongside Hitler and Hirohito. The Board of Directors of Hades votes to oust Satan (Alan Mowbray) and replace him with Adolf Hitler (Bobby Watson, who made a career-in-miniature of the impersonation). Satan, determined to prove himself fit to rule, is allowed a deadline to catch Hitler in an act of kindness. Insinuating

himself into *der Fuehrer*'s circle, Satan provokes the madman to a frenzy of mass murder. In a sublimely absurd digression involving insurance policies upon the lives of Hitler, Mussolini (lump-jawed Joe Devlin) and a Hirohito surrogate named Suki Yaki (George E. Stone), the Axis power trio spends an inordinately hilarious span attempting to slaughter one another. Finally, Hitler is manipulated into a deed of near-clemency, and Satan is restored to power. A bombing leaves Hitler a well-tormented resident of hell.

This slight effort affords a clear if warped window into the mass American psyche during the war. The slapstick hilarity never undercuts the essential bitterness; the piece plays out like some newspaper's editorial cartoon come to life. The Axis villains are well cast, and Alan Mowbray makes a peculiarly sympathetic Mr. Scratch. Douglas Fowley and Marjorie Woodworth supply a faint romantic relief, as prisoners of Hitler. The film provided more than yocks in its day, however: it vindicated the politically naïve Roach in the eyes of those who still might have fancied him in sympathy with an enemy of the people.

"I remember those little pictures fondly," Roach said, "but none of the *Streamlined Comedies* turned out, really, to suit me. Probably because my studio wasn't really quite my own, all during the war, there—but we did the best we could under reduced circumstances. And United Artists never really had what it took to sell such a radical concept in short feature-making." (Movies of less than an hour created schedule-wrangling problems for the theatres, which preferred double-feature bills of two hours to 140 minutes, plus short subjects.) To his last days, however, Roach maintained that "most features, and especially most comedies, don't really need to be longer than 20, 30 minutes in lengh, 50 minutes at tops."

The first *Streamlined*, the likewise topical *Tanks a Million*, dates from 1941. *That Natzy Nuisance* (below) was cut later into an expanded edition of *The Devil with Hitler*. The spoof found itself echoed in 1999—doubtless unwittingly so, given the tribal amnesia that afflicts the culture—when the animated satire *South Park: Bigger, Longer & Uncut*, portrayed Saddam Hussein as a strange bedfellow for a sissified Satan.

That Nazty Nuisance. The Devil with Hitler had succeeded beyond a vindication of Roach's American loyalties. The film spawned a prompt sequel—*coda* is more like it—in *That Nazty Nuisance*. This one plays better if taken in context with the original. The abrupt finale is like the squealing of air brakes—a Roach signature since the short-subject years.

Adolf Hitler (Bobby Watson) has survived a straight-to-hell bombing and resumed his shenanigans. In a plot to betray Mussolini (Joe Devlin) and Suki Yaki (Johnny Arthur, a Roach stock-company mainstay),

Hitler heads for the Island of Norom (*moron*, reversed) and a meeting
with a dignitary named Paj Mub (Ian Keith; and *you* can take up the
bass-ackwards spelling from here). Mussolini and Suki Yaki horn in. A
ceremonial banquet features a magician, who is replaced by an American
sailor (Frank Faylen). Suki Yaki vanishes—to be replaced with an ape.
The Axis leaders wind up imprisoned aboard a submarine, subjected to
a bogus flooding scare, and catapulted like torpedoes onto a beach.

The humiliating silliness is intact, but *Nuisance* lacks the murderous
ferocity of *The Devil with Hitler*. Roach told us: "Well, perhaps I felt
I had less to prove, this time 'round. And Bobby Watson *had* to come
back..., because an Axis spoof without Hitler would be like a—well,
like, why even *bother*?"

Although the *Streamlined Comedies* series represented a comedown for Roach, he philosophically heralded these entries as a progressive experiment. The U.S. Copyright record for *That Nazty Nuisance*, incidentally, documents the title only as *Nazty Nuisance*.

Criminal Investigator

Monogram Pictures Corp. • 1942

Jean Yarbrough's *Criminal Investigator* is an intense remake, with bloodthirsty variations, of C.C. Burr's *The Midnight Patrol*, with Lawrence Creighton snarling through the deaf-mute killer role that had been originated by Mischa Auer.

Hired as a news reporter only because of his father's connections, Bob Martin (Robert Lowery) boasts that he can snag an exclusive interview with a jailed killer named Black (Creighton), who is notorious for rebuffing the press.

Martin's editor (John Maxwell) takes the dare, certain that Martin will bungle the job. Martin learns that Black is deaf and mute; the greenhorn resorts to sign language with scarcely a missed beat. Black is so impressed with this display of resourcefulness that he provides an encrypted message. Martin's banner story leads to Black's release.

Martin is assigned to interview a crooked beauty named Joyce Greeley (Vivian Wilcox). The circle begins drawing shut when Joyce is murdered by Drake (Jan Wiley) and Soapy (Charles Hall), hoodlums in the employ of Edward Judson (John Miljan)—Black's lawyer.

Coincidences begin looking less coincidental when Martin rescues Joyce's sister, Ellen (Edith Fellows), from a kidnapping attempt. Martin does not comprehend the kinship because Ellen refers to her sister by her christened name, Joan; Ellen is unaware of Joyce's slaying.

Complications involve the missing keys to a depository vault. Judson seems ready to confess to an intricate scam when he is killed by a thrown knife. Black proves to be the hidden slayer—and the murderer of Joyce. The strongbox discloses Ellen's inheritance of Joyce Greeley's estate, which Judson had coveted.

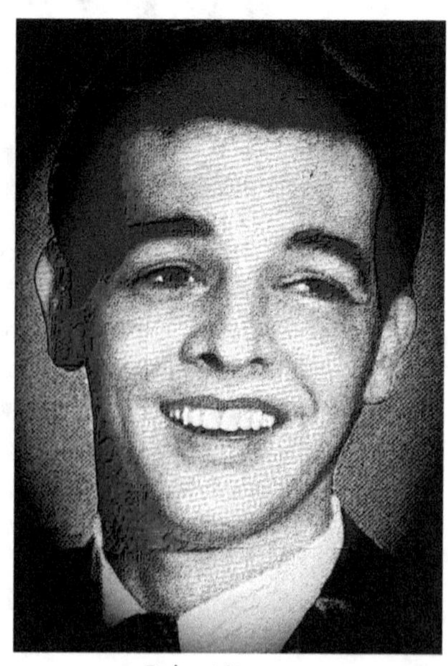

Robert Lowery.

The female of the species would emerge soon as a pivotal element of psychological horror—a cultural phenomenon covered in our companion volume, *Human Monsters*—but in 1942 the trend was just dawning. The murderous dame here is a feral Jan Wiley. Robert Lowery's determined protagonist stumbles into one bad patch after another but improvises impressively well. Edith Fellows is memorable as an innocent who cannot imagine why she has become a gangland target.

Outlaws of Boulder Pass

Producers Releasing Corp. • 1942

Sigmund Neufeld's lean-and-angry *Lone Rider* series takes a striking detour into backwater superstition with *Outlaws of Boulder Pass*, which hangs on Dennis "Smoky" Moore's impersonation of a ghost—the better to flush out the *hombres* who have tried to kill him, and who long ago had slain his father. The vigilante Lone Rider (George Houston) and his geezery rascal of a sidekick, Fuzzy Q. Jones (Al St. John), are along for the ride, with the Rider doing more observing than interfering. (If he is the Lone Rider, then why the sidekick?) Moore and Marjorie Manners, as an endangered rancher harboring a mystery of her own, hold the plot in place. I. Stanford Jolley and Karl Hackett account for the villainy. The finale registers an eerie resonance.

Hitler—Dead or Alive

Charles House Productions • 1942

Geoffrey Household's novel *Rogue Male* (1939) takes a cue from Richard Connell's "The Most Dangerous Game" (1924) in setting a big-game hunter upon the trail of a reclusive dictator patterned after Adolf Hitler. (Connell's yarn was first filmed in 1932, by RKO-Radio Pictures.)

Household's virile tale of blood vengeance and daring political motives, perennially relevant in the face of perennial fascism, became a stirring movie at 20th Century-Fox, *Man Hunt*, starring Walter Pidgeon and directed by Fritz Lang, a self-exile from Nazi Germany. *Man*

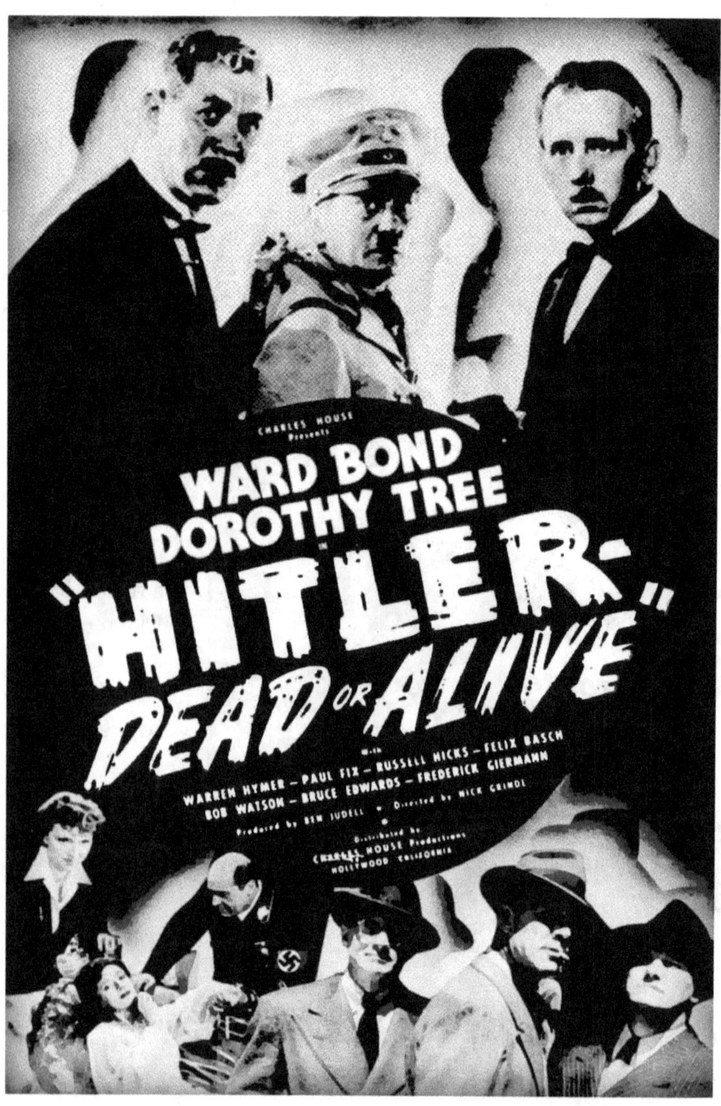

Hunt renders explicit the reference to Hitler in defiance of the Motion Picture Association's tacit caveat against Reich-baiting pictures, lest the German market be offended. Fox opened *Man Hunt* six months before the Japanese invasion of Pearl Harbor put an end to the dead-end U.S. policy of fair-play America First isolationism—after which, Nazi-buster propaganda films became standard issue in Hollywood, from high drama to slapstick comedy to westerns, science-fictioners, and chillers.

A shabbier companion piece to *Man Hunt*, Harry A. "Nick" Grinde's *Hitler—Dead or Alive*, owes less to Geoffrey Household or Fritz Lang than to a newspaper advertisement posted in May of 1940: in the *New York Times*, Dr. Samuel H. Church, president of the Carnegie Institute of Pittsburgh, offered a million-dollar reward "to the person or persons who will deliver Adolf Hitler alive, unwounded, and unharmed into the custody of the League of Nations." There were no takers, of course, although Dr. Church reported many responses requesting expenses in advance.

Nobody said anything about a dead-or-alive bounty; that is an easy conceit of Sam Neuman's source-story. Threadbare production values prevent the tale from achieving its potential, but dependable Ward Bond is in fine boisterous form as the leader of a trio of lunkheaded daredevils—a Dirty Dozen prototype, quartered, and an ancestor of Quentin Tarantino's Hitler-killing gem of 2009, *Inglourious Basterds*. Director Grinde proves as able at boisterous satire as he had long been at crime melodramas and westerns. Producer Ben Judell had been responsible for *Hitler—Beast of Berlin*.

Dark undercurrents are ever-present, even though *Hitler—Dead or Alive* patently intends a provocative amusement. A self-serious coda, an unfortunate afterthought in the picture's troubled progress toward release, spoils much of the attitude of freewheeling pleasure.

Ruffians Steve Maschik (Bond), Dutch Havermann (Warren Hymer), and Joe "the Book" Conway (Paul Fix), newly sprung from prison, take up the challenge: They hijack a Canadian Air Force craft and head for a crash landing in Germany, where they infiltrate Adolf Hitler's inner circle by posing, variously, as entertainers and Nazi loyalists.

The mayhem establishes the evils of the Reich beyond dispute, but the element of ridicule is broad to the point of knockabout. The forced irony of the finale involves the shaving of Hitler's paintbrush moustache: the dictator becomes a target for his own corpsmen, who do not recognize *der Feuhrer* mitoudt der lip-fungus. Hitler is acknowledged to have been but a tin god, and the heroes come to understand that the good fight is far from finished.

Ward Bond, Warren Hymer, and Paul Fix weather the absurdities well—a mixed lot of rowdiness, stolid determination, and weasly connivance. Bob Watson makes a convincing and loathsome Hitler, delighted with the suffering that follows his every move. He plays the role more straightforwardly than his caricatured Schickelgrüber of *The Devil with Hitler* and *That Nazty Nuisance*. Watson's transformation from arrogant world-beater to sniveling coward is delightful. No red-blooded American of the day can have resisted the spectacle of seeing even a wish-dream Hitler facing humiliation and violent death.

Not that all that many Americans, red-blooded or otherwise, were treated to a showing. An opening in Chicago, late in 1942, was followed by a long silence. The film was not registered for copyright until a year later, when it secured a New York engagement. The commercial failure, complicated by critical notices that neglected to buy into the embittered joke but seized upon every technical failing, must have been daunting to Nick Grinde. Grinde had excelled during the waning 1930s as a member of Columbia's B-picture unit, where he collaborated with *Dead or Alive*'s co-scenarist, Karl Brown, on elements of Boris Karloff's popular mad-doctor series. He made two more features— as screenwriter on 1943's *We've Never Been Licked* and as director on 1945's *Road to Alcatraz*—and then became involved with the making of television programs and commercials.

Valley of Hunted Men

Republic Pictures Corp. • 1942

A rampage by fugitive Nazis propels this entry in the *Three Mesquiteers* series. Ringleader Roland Varno upstages the heroic protagonists— Bob Steele, Tom Tyler, and Jimmie Dodd—at every turn barring his inevitable comeuppance. The venerable Edward Van Sloan, the voice of reason of Universal's horror-movie machinery of the 1930s, stands out as a benevolent German scientist who runs afoul of bigotry.

John English's *Valley of Hunted Men* finds Capt. Carl Baum (Varno) engineering a breakout from a Canadian war-prison camp. Baum and two fellow goose-steppers cross into Wyoming and begin a killing spree. Rancher Clem Parker (Hal Price) senses that local Americanized Germans are assisting the war criminals; suspicion falls on the refugée Dr. Steiner (Van Sloan) and his daughter, Laura (Anna Marie Stewart). The Steiners are in fact attempting to aid the Allied cause with their research.

The Nazis' ranks dwindle to Baum alone, who kills and impersonates Steiner's visiting nephew. The complications run thick, what with Baum's abduction by a band of Nazi sympathizers, the disastrous contamination of one of Steiner's experimental formulas, and a near-lynching for the doctor. The Mesquiteers find themselves

relegated almost to a supporting status in their own show. Varno is so effective as the predatory Krautknocker that his mere capture and confession seem too lenient a resolution.

The Living Ghost

a.k.a.: *A Walking Nightmare*
Monogram Pictures Corp. • 1942

William Beaudine's *The Living Ghost*, an uneven fusion of horror and wisecracking wit in the Mystery Farce tradition, is one of those films that threaten the very institution of film criticism simply by grace of a graceless existence. A predictably petty backlash against *The Living Ghost* persists, from avoid-at-all-costs tirades from the critical brethren in 1942 to snide dismissals in the bourgeois movies-on-video guides of the present day.

Probably the scariest thing about *The Living Ghost*—representative of its under-capitalized upstart kind—is that it comes prepared to jolt the tribe of self-professed film critics to a state of inarticulate ridicule. Incapable of couching their dislikes in thoughtful or informative commentary, these ivory-tower snipers concoct snarky gibberish—the BOMB rating is a favorite—to convey a contempt they cannot bother to render eloquent. Which is what one might expect from a narcissistic dilettantes' profession that has corrupted a meaningful industrial

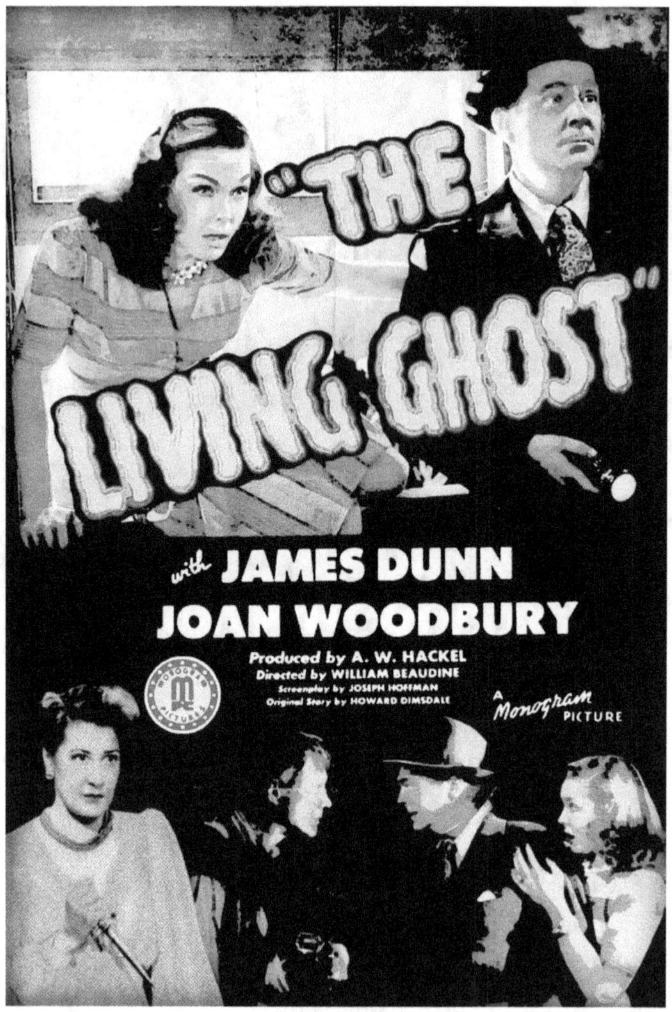

term, "B-movie," from its truer *B*-as-in-budget context to suggest some performance-review grading system.

The letter *B* also stands for Briskin, by no coincidence. Samuel Briskin, a tactful manager for the tactless studio tyrant Harry Cohn, proved crucial to Columbia Pictures' climb from the fringes of Poverty Row to a major-studio ranking. The original name, Cohn-Brandt-Cohn, or CBC, often was spoofed within the trade as Corned Beef & Cabbage Studios, in view of its working-class appeal. Cohn placed Briskin in charge of Columbia's fixed-budget division early in the 1940s. The formally designated Briskin Unit became the B-Unit in the shorthand of office memoranda. Hence the term, B-picture.

And there but for fortune, of course, might Columbia Pictures have gone the way of Monogram Pictures, a blue-collar outfit from the

Depression into the 1950s despite sporadic rallyings of higher ambition. Scarcely a coincidence that Monogram standby Sam Katzman spent much of the 1940s dividing his energies between Monogram and Columbia before settling during the postwar years at the larger studio.

Monogram's *The Living Ghost* is not a Katzman production, but rather a project of his crony, A.W. Hackel, a specialist in grim westerns and a recurring figure on the *Forgotten Horrors* scene. We come neither to bury nor to praise *The Living Ghost*, but merely to acknowledge that the film still has less going in its favor than even a tolerant viewer might desire. The picture's chief charm today is its survival as a relic of a time when horror and hokum could co-exist without corrupting one another. The attempted balance here lacks finesse, and so what else is new?

James Dunn is by turns annoying and annoyed as Nick Trayne, an unconventional detective. Trayne has retrenched as a bogus swami, enduring his miserable clients' litanies of self-pity in exchange for cash. Trayne balks at an invitation to investigate the disappearance of banker Walter Craig (Gus Glassmire), but a challenge to his abilities proves persuasive. Trayne finds the Craig household to be a snake-pit of grasping relatives and hangers-on. Craig reappears—a zombie-fied shade of himself. A physician (*Bulldog Drummond*'s Lawrence Grant) determines that someone has afflicted Craig with brain damage.

Craig's brother-in-law (J. Arthur Young) turns up slain. Craig attacks Trayne, who traces a brain-paralyzing apparatus to a mysterious figure who has leased a shunned house nearby. Craig's former partner (George Eldridge) and Craig's second wife (Edna Johnson)

attempt to kill Trayne as he nears a solution. He turns the tables on the crooks and betrays their scheme: the lapsed colleague had posed as a doctor and administered the debilitating treatment, certain that the wife could keep the estate out of the hands of Craig's daughter (Jan Wiley) as long as Craig remained alive but incapacitated.

The picture would have fared better without Dunn's forcibly eccentric portrayal, which nevertheless does little to compromise the severity of the investigation. A pure-comedy introductory sequence features a splendid bit of double-talk *shtick* from the Yiddish vaudeville artist Danny Beck. Hatchet-faced Minerva Urecal, as a superstitious sort, plays nicely off Dunn during the main body of the story.

Dunn's romance with the spirited secretary (Joan Woodbury) of the transformed banker exists for the sake of a happy ending—happy for the detective, if for no one else. The members of the troubled household may be beyond happy endings. More assuredly doomed is an incidental subject of the mind-destroying process, discovered in the deserted house in one of the more jarring moments.

Director William Beaudine handles things with his usual steamroller efficiency, heedless of the ironies of Dunn's laughing-to-keep-from-screaming performance and more concerned with getting on to the next project than with nurturing such a strange yarn to any higher levels of weirdness or emotional resonance. *The Living Ghost* fails simply on grounds of its being an assembly-line production of a story whose twists deserve a more painstaking development. All the same, enough heavy-duty crepuscularity seeps through the tidy contrivances to bear a look.

Secrets of the Underground

Republic Pictures Corp. • 1942

Completing Republic's *Mr. District Attorney* trilogy—although Republic removed the *Mr. D.A.* identity—is William Morgan's *Secrets of the Underground*, a tale of trunk murderers and human shop-window dummies, entangled with Fifth Column intrigues. The picture stands without the connection to a formal series, but it remains a mystery why the studio jettisoned the tie-in with a popular radio program. Of course, 1941's *Mr. District Attorney* and *Mr. District Attorney in the Carter Case* had hardly provoked any stampedes to the box office.

The pictures already had suffered from inconsistencies of casting, starting with Dennis O'Keefe in the lead and then lapsing to James Ellison. Now comes John Hubbard. Perhaps no self-respecting B-movie leading man cared to be identified over the long term with a character named P. Cadwallader Jones.

The film is a crackerjack murder mystery, long on chills with the right comic-relief grace notes. Hubbard's Jones finds himself embroiled in a Nazi scam to flood the market with counterfeit War Tax stamps. Paul Panois (Miles Mander), a French artist, has been forced to create the fakes lest the Third Reich kill his daughter, Marianne (Robin Raymond). Father and daughter escape, but then Panois turns up croaked inside a trunk that had been reserved for his fraudulent engravings.

Jones is promoted to district attorney. His news-reporter sweetheart, Terry Parker (Virginia Grey), undermines his work because Jones had neglected to clue her in on the murder. She also resents Jones' interest in Marianne Panois. Terry's snooping causes the death of a depot attendant who could have identified one racketeer. (This victim is played by Olin Howlin, the homicidal prospector of *Home in Wyomin'*.)

The reporter's reckless manipulations endanger Marianne. Dressmaker Maurice Vaughan (Lloyd Corrigan), secretly in charge of the gang, hogties Marianne and places her on view like a mannequin in a display window. (This element recalls a creepier such sequence, in one of the great horror-is-where-you-find-it films from Universal Pictures: 1934's *Cross Country Cruise*.)

Terry finally imperils herself, for a change. Vaughan and his cohorts make ready to suffocate Marianne and Terry in a granary's silo. Jones comes to the rescue, then reconciles with Terry.

Lloyd Corrigan gives a splendid show of villainy as the Axis' hidden agent—always a pleasure to watch a pudgy fussbudget turn menacing. Marla Shelton arouses suspicions as an excessively patriotic chief of the Women's Defense Corps. John Hubbard and Virginia Grey make much of the antagonistic sweetheart roles.

Secrets of the Underground was shot during the autumn of 1942 under varying work-in-progress titles, including *Mr. District Attorney* and *Mr. District Attorney Does His Bit*. A later intended title was *The Corpse Came C.O.D.*, without reference to the *Mr. D.A.* franchise. Title-card billing originally contained an acknowledgment of Phillips H. Lord's famous radio series, but the credit was withdrawn without explanation. (Lord, a lasting success in radio as both personality and producer, experienced consistently bad luck when crossing over to the movies. An account of his jinxed pictures *Way Back Home* and *Obeah!* can be found elsewhere in the present collection.)

The *Mr. D.A.* series' next screen version came about in 1947 with a one-shot Columbia production called *Mr. District Attorney*. Dennis O'Keefe returned to play the title character—wisely rechristened as Steve Bennett. ZIV-Television's versions of the early-to-mid-1950s feature Jay Jostyn and David Bryan in the role of a district attorney named Paul Garrett.

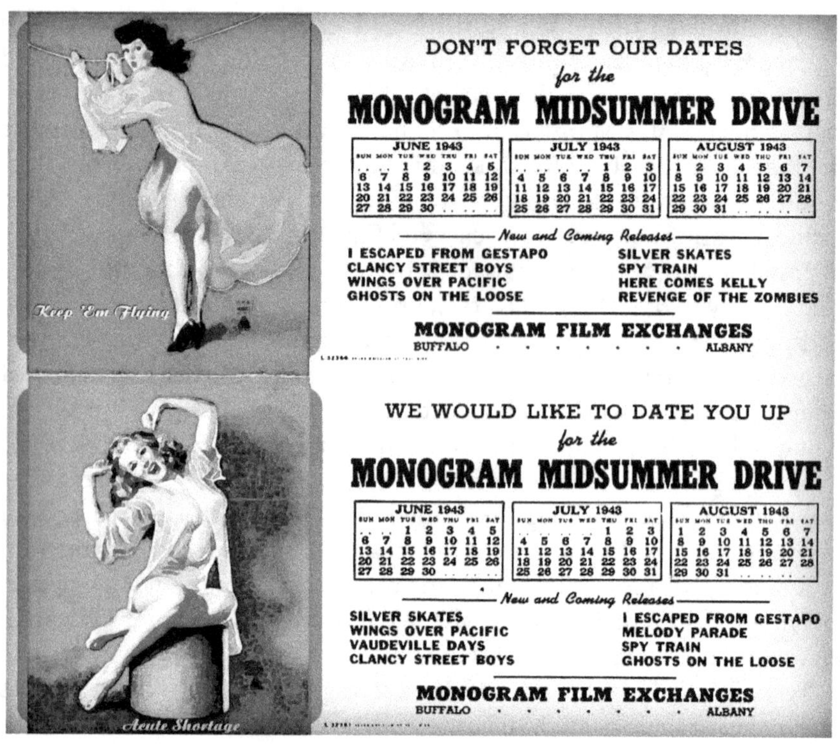

And looking forward to 1943 and a further volume of the Forgotten Horrors Omnibus, *Monogram Pictures proposes a lineup of features for the coming year.*

www.ingramcontent.com/pod-product-compliance
Lightning Source LLC
Chambersburg PA
CBHW051011060726
47593CB00016B/8